ENGENDERING APHRODITE

WOMEN AND SOCIETY IN ANCIENT CYPRUS

ASOR Archaeological Reports

Gloria London, series editor

Volume 07
ENGENDERING APHRODITE
WOMEN AND SOCIETY IN ANCIENT CYPRUS

ENGENDERING APHRODITE

WOMEN AND SOCIETY IN ANCIENT CYPRUS

Edited by

DIANE BOLGER AND NANCY SERWINT

CAARI Monographs volume 3

American Schools of Oriental Research • Boston, MA

ENGENDERING APHRODITE
WOMEN AND SOCIETY IN ANCIENT CYPRUS

edited by

Diane Bolger and Nancy Serwint

Billie Jean Collins
ASOR Director of Publications

Library of Congress Cataloging-in-Publication Data

Engendering Aphrodite : women and society in ancient Cyprus / edited by
Diane Bolger and Nancy Serwint.
      p. cm. -- (American Schools of Oriental Research archaeological
reports ; 7) (American schools of oriental research archaeological
reports ; 7)
Includes bibliographical references and index.
  ISBN 0-89757-059-6 (alk. paper)
  1. Women--Cyprus--History--To 500. 2. Cyprus--Civilization. 3.
Cyprus--Antiquities. 4. Antiquities, Prehistoric--Cyprus. I. Bolger,
Diane R. II. Serwint, Nancy J. III. Series. IV. Series: American schools
of oriental research archaeological reports ; 7
  HQ1137.C93 E54 2002
  305.4'0939'37--dc21

                      2002011976

TABLE OF CONTENTS

v

LIST OF FIGURES

2. GENDER AND SOCIAL ORGANIZATION (NEOLITHIC-MIDDLE BRONZE AGE)

3. Gender and Social Organization (Late Bronze Age-Medieval)

4. GENDER, IDENTITY AND ETHNICITY

5. GENDER, TECHNOLOGY AND MATERIAL CULTURE

6. GENDER AND THE GODDESS

Budin

Serwint

7. Gender and Cypriot Archaeology: Critical Views

PREFACE

In Cyprus there is an old custom practiced in many villages of the Paphos district in which the birth of a baby girl is announced to the family and friends by calling her "halloumi," the salty white cheese for which our island is so well-known. By proclaiming that he has "halloumi" rather than an infant girl, the infant's father is carrying out a centuries-old tradition that symbolically celebrates the birth of a girl and the gift of life. The origins of this tradition are as obscure as they are interesting, and similar customs were practiced in some festivals in antiquity. Even further back in time, in prehistory, it is possible that women may not have been very different from their modern counterparts.

The conference *Engendering Aphrodite: Women and Society in Ancient Cyprus*, held in Nicosia from 19–23 March 1998, provided the opportunity for a wide community of international scholars to explore the changing traditions and definitions of gender in Cypriot society from Neolithic times to the present day. During the three-day conference, specialists from Cyprus and from a variety of foreign countries presented papers on various aspects of gender in ancient Cypriot society; this was done in a spirit of collaborative effort and healthy debate and without preconceived ideas of gender norms. While the current volume represents the final, permanent record of the conference, it certainly cannot convey the enthusiasm and excitement of the speakers and especially the audience, who were aware that they were attending a unique and unprecedented event: the explication of women's contributions to art, religion, economy, and society on the island over the course of many thousands of years. Planning and organizing the conference were labors of love, and Nancy Serwint, Diane Bolger, and the staff of the Cyprus American Archaeological Research Institute insured its quality and created a cordial ambiance of academic exchange.

The richness and depth of Cypriot culture have made the island a focal point for archaeological and historical research over the last several centuries. The results of those studies can serve as a substantial database containing invaluable material which can be used to investigate the roles of women in ancient Cypriot society throughout its various prehistoric and historical phases. Although much has been written about the cultures of the Cypriot past, about the island's important role in the development of complex societies of the ancient Mediterranean world, and about its strategic economic position as a link between east and west, it has usually been assumed that major socio-historical developments were accomplished primarily by men and that women played only negligible roles. It is my profound hope that *Engendering Aphrodite* will begin to change the traditional, male-oriented view of the Cypriot past by documenting some of the important contributions made by women in antiquity and by inspiring others to carry out further research in this important field of scholarship. This is only fitting on the island that gave birth to the Olympian goddess known to Homer as "the Cyprian."

Maria A. Kyriacou
Registrar of Companies and Official Receiver
The Republic of Cyprus

ACKNOWLEDGMENTS

The success of *Engendering Aphrodite* was due to the unstinting effort of many people, and words cannot fully express our deep gratitude for their support. First and foremost, we would like to convey our heartfelt thanks to Maria Kyriacou, Registrar of Companies of the Republic of Cyprus and CAARI Trustee. Maria galvanized the support in Cyprus that was essential for the financial organization of the conference; in addition, she offered generous hospitality to conference participants and graced the conference sessions and social events with her passion for archaeology. That the conference evolved in the way it did was due largely to her efforts, and without her involvement it may never have come to fruition.

In addition, we would like to express our appreciation for the generous support of the following corporate Conference Sponsors: the American Center, the Cleopatra Hotel, the Cyprus Tourism Organization, the Fulbright Commission, the Hellenic Bank Ltd., Keo Ltd., Lanitis Development Ltd., the Ministry of Foreign Affairs of the Republic of Cyprus, the Ministry of Justice and Public Order of the Republic of Cyprus, the Press and Information Office of the Republic of Cyprus, and the West Semitic Research Project (The Ahmanson Foundation Grant) of the University of Southern California. The generosity of the following individual Sponsors is also gratefully acknowledged: Diane Bolger, Linda Clougherty, Hugh and Shirley Harcourt, Maria Kyriacou, Marilyn Lundberg, Barbara Lyssarides, Nancy Serwint, Charles Sohn, Karl Tate, Gerald Vincent, Paul Wallace, and Bruce Zuckerman.

Special thanks are due to the Department of Antiquities of Cyprus and especially to Dr. Pavlos Flourentzos and Dr. Maria Hadjicosti, who facilitated the photographic exhibit "Images of Women in Ancient Cyprus," which was held at CAARI in tandem with the conference. We are also grateful to Demetrios Michaelides and Edgar Peltenburg, who generously served as guides and provided invaluable commentary during excursions to the mosaics at Nea Paphos and the Sanctuary of Aphrodite at Palaepaphos. Ambassador and Mrs. Kenneth Brill honored the conference participants with a reception at The Embassy of the United States of America in Nicosia, and the Archaeological Research Unit of the Department of History and Archaeology of the University of Cyprus graciously hosted a reception for participants on the closing night of the conference; to them we offer our deep appreciation for their hospitality.

The CAARI staff participated in countless ways and, as always, were generous with their time and talents. Warmest thanks go to Diana Constantinides, Vathoulla Moustoukki, Maria Stavrou, Fotoulla Christodoulou, Georgia Nicolaou, and Roy Smith.

The complicated process of turning conference papers into a published volume has been greatly expedited by Billie Jean Collins, Gloria London and Charles Sohn. Their efforts and editorial skills are most appreciated. The perceptive comments and observations of anonymous peer reviewers have been most valuable in the evolution of this publication.

And finally, the success of the conference ultimately rested on the participants who offered scholarly papers and panel presentations that stimulated an audience eager for information on gender issues. Commentary on individual papers was lively, discussion was extensive, and the embracing of new ideas about gender roles was challenging. All participants deserve credit for their thought-provoking contributions which made the conference groundbreaking in its scope. A comment frequently heard throughout the five days of the conference was that there was a dynamism and enthusiasm among all involved, audience as well as participants. We believe this was more than a feeling; it was palpable and real, like an electrical current that positively charged the atmosphere, and it reinforced the belief in many of us that we were engaged in a dialogue truly critical for Cypriot studies. To all those who created that current and continue to sustain it, we offer you our most ardent thanks and we hope that this book might serve as a springboard for further investigations of gender in the years to come.

D. Bolger
N. Serwint
March 2001

PART ONE

INTRODUCTION

INTRODUCTION: APPROACHING GENDER
IN CYPRIOT ARCHAEOLOGY

The study of gender is a risky business since it forces us to consider who we are and why. Closely held beliefs that have consciously or unconsciously filtered our "lenses of gender" must be confronted, reconsidered, and realigned within social, historical, and ideological frameworks (Bem 1993). In particular, we need to confront and revise the widespread view that women's roles are static and unchanging since they are shaped by biological "facts" that are thought to govern "eternal" or "essential" female activities such as procreation, nurturing, and motherhood. Sex-linked activities or attributes and the differential values attached to them often stem from unmediated assumptions that the process of engendering helps to make explicit. A fundamental aspect of engendering the past, therefore, is learning to come to terms with our subjective selves.

Among the social sciences, archaeology, on account of its long-term perspective, has the potential to expose and undermine misconceptions about gender since the discipline can examine changes in gender constructs over long stretches of time and space. In theory, archaeological investigation should enable us to perceive of gender not as a reified entity but as a dynamic process shaped by changing social circumstances. It should also allow us to see where we stand within that process and, thus, can serve to link us personally to societies of the remote past, groups that we have often professed to be studying "objectively." By examining archaeological remains from the perspective of gender, we can begin to formulate approaches to the study of past cultures more deliberately and intimately—"*because* we are searching for ways to think about ourselves" (Rosaldo and Lamphere 1974: 1; emphasis ours).

The last three decades have witnessed the introduction of gendered approaches to the social sciences in general and archaeology in particular, developing initially within the rubric of "women's studies" by American feminist and other politically-minded academics who formed part of the Women's Movement of the early 1970s. Within the social sciences, gender studies can be traced back to the landmark publication in 1974 of *Women, Culture and Society* (Rosaldo and Lamphere), which represents the first comprehensive effort at correlating economic, social, and political factors with gender ideologies. Ortner's essay in that volume ("Is Female to Male as Nature is to Culture?") had a particularly strong impact in the field of women's studies and generated a critical discussion of the biological basis of social behavior, a debate that continues in the social and biological sciences today.

It was not until ten years later, in 1984, that the first major publication on gender and archaeology appeared: Conkey and Spector's article "The Archaeology of Gender." This was the first "high profile" contribution on the archaeology of gender, and as it appeared in a prominent theoretical series (Schiffer 1984), it could not be disregarded. Its main focal point was the issue of the persistent failure of archaeology to address issues of androcentric bias within the field and to bring gender and related issues into the mainstream of archaeological theory and method. The article also served as a catalyst for the first large-scale works on gender and archaeology, in particular Gero and Conkey's important edited volume *Engendering Archaeology: Women and Prehistory* (1991), a wide-ranging, multi-authored publication of the first academic conference devoted specifically to considerations of gender in the prehistoric cultures of the Old and New worlds.

Many of the issues and themes addressed in "The Archaeology of Gender" and *Engendering Archaeology* are still relevant today, especially to archaeologists working in Cyprus where gender studies remain in their infancy. These include the rejection or revision of biologically-based, essentialist approaches to the past, the overcoming of androcentric and "presentist" biases, the opportunity to apply a generation of feminist theory to archaeological data, a critical evaluation of the limitations of positivistic, systemic approaches associated with processual archaeology, and a recognition of the greater latitude of cultural perspectives afforded by post-processual archaeology. Post-processual archaeology has furnished opportunities for new ways of looking at the past, both on account of its greater degree of relativism and self-criticism and through its legitimization of topics such as gender and ethnicity that had previously been regarded as too "subjective" or "invisible" for scholarly consideration. As a result, the archaeology of gender has become one of the fastest growing disciplines within the field.

GENDER AND PREHISTORY

To date, the bulk of the research conducted on gender and archaeology has been carried out by prehistorians. This is especially true of Old World prehistory in which a considerable number of books and articles have appeared during the last decade that address issues as diverse as the study of gender in the development of human evolution, the growth of social complexity and its relationship to the rise of state society, the role of women as agents in the invention of agriculture and other technological advances, and changing images of the gendered body through analysis of early anthropomorphic representations. Particular attention has been paid to the ways in which women's contributions to the past have been ignored or undervalued, often as the result of androcentric bias.

Critical readings of earlier, male-dominated research have served as starting points for engendering the prehistoric past. In their place, investigations have been undertaken that demonstrate the positive roles played by women in early societies, and new theoretical approaches have been developed that are beginning to revise previous male-dominated views of the past. Central to many of these new approaches has been the theoretical separation of sex and gender, the former being biologically based and the latter culturally determined. The notion of gender as a cultural construct has now become commonplace and serves as a starting point for the formulation of a wide range of methodological approaches that aim to overcome static, essentialist assumptions concerning male and female roles. Less frequently addressed, but equally important for overcoming gender bias, is the awareness that sex, like gender, is a cultural construct and that just as there were multiple genders in past societies, so may there have been more than just two sexes (Butler 1990). The use of binary models such as male/ female and man/woman to analyze and interpret gender constructs, whether for contemporary societies or for those in the past, is another tacit assumption that has recently undergone revision, and increasing emphasis is being placed on gender ambiguity among the cultures of the ancient world.

The last decade has witnessed a marked increase in publications on gender in prehistoric and protohistoric archaeology. These include far-ranging surveys by single authors (Ehrenberg 1989; Nelson 1997), collected essays and conference volumes (Hager 1997; Wright ed. 1996; Hays-Gilpin and Whitley 1998; Claassen and Joyce 1997), geographical area treatments (Tyldesley 1994 and Robins 1993 for Egypt; Pollock 1991, Lerner 1986, and Wright 1996 for Mesopotamia; Ehrenberg 1989, Hitchcock 1997; Olsen 1998 for the Aegean; Brumfiel 1991, 1996; Watson and Kennedy 1991; and papers in Claassen and Joyce 1997 for the Americas), economic or technological studies (Claassen 1991; Gero 1991; Hastorf 1991; Spector 1991; Wright 1991, 1996), and gendered representations of the body (Pollock 1991; all contributions in Montserrat 1997; Wilfong and Jones 1998; Wyke 1998). And these are just a few. Taken as a whole, the corpus of research on gender to date encompasses a range of theoretical and methodological approaches rather than a unified school of thought. The plurality of research agendas has been addressed recently in a book edited by Wright, who very aptly refers in her introduction to archaeologies, rather than an archaeology of gender. Gender, she believes, is gradually being integrated into all facets of the field and should no longer be regarded as a separate discipline (Wright ed. 1996: 3).

Still, we must caution against overestimating the successes that have been gained during the last ten years. In most archaeological reports and in many university curricula, issues of gender continue to be ignored or marginalized. Even within the domain of post-processual archaeology, gender is often conspicuously absent from discussions of social complexity in which the emergence of complex societies appears to coincide with the coming to power of sexless, genderless, or implicitly male "elites." Other, more traditional archaeologists avoid discussions of gender, presumably on account of a vague fear that it is either politically charged or "unscientific." To the criticism by Binford and others that gender in prehistoric archaeology is "unobjective posturing," Wylie (1998: 79) has responded with the thought-provoking reply that "politically engaged science is often much more rigorous, self-critiÀal and responsive to the facts than allegedly neutral science, for which nothing much is at stake." The continuation of engaged approaches in the decades to come will help to further refine our understanding of the importance played by gender in the prehistoric past and to the formulation of new research agendas that place gender at their core.

GENDER, ANCIENT HISTORY AND CLASSICAL ARCHAEOLOGY

Within the discipline of classical studies, gender has remained a focal point for several decades. Certainly part of the motivation to evaluate the role of women in antiquity was spawned by the force of the contemporary feminist movement of the 1970s, although there had been earlier scholarly treatments attempting to establish the feminine position in ancient life and some of those treatments were badly in need of revision (Blok 1987 and Goodwater 1975). The publication of the groundbreaking "*Arethusa* Papers," emanating from the 1973 conference "Women in Antiquity" (esp. Peradotto and Sullivan 1984), as well as the critical *Goddesses, Whores, Wives, and Slaves* (Pomeroy 1975), served as important catalysts for subsequent research and laid the foundation for a breadth of inquiry that continues to quicken. The initial impetus behind posing questions related to gender clearly was the desire to acknowledge and document the presence of females in the societies of ancient Greece and Rome. The jarring realization that the female presence had been obscured to a degree not attested for males—even to the point that in some standard reference works treating the social history of the ancient world women received no mention at all—has forced scholars to reevaluate the evidence at hand. Since that evidence was primarily literary and historical, the consequence was a reassessment of literary texts (Lefkowitz 1986 and Foley 1981, among others) and a reexamination of the historical record (Just 1975 and 1989; Redfield 1977/78; Gould 1980; Cartledge 1981; Mossé 1983; and Pomeroy 1991 are but a few).

Because of the nature of the literary and historical evidence, much of the research on questions of gender focusing on the Greek and Roman world has been conducted by scholars whose expertise lay outside the field of classical archaeology, and one of the most telling features of many of the published compendia focusing on questions of gender is that the authors tend to be classicists and ancient historians (Foley 1981; Cameron and Kuhrt 1983; Peradotto and Sullivan 1984; Blok and Mason 1987; Pomeroy 1991; Archer, Fischler, and Wyke 1994; and McAuslan and Walcot 1996). The preponderance of written source material has led to an investigation of the past that was based primarily on textual criticism, and one of the key questions that was asked early on was how reliable or unbiased the textual sources were. Critical assessment of the sources led to other questions: Do purely literary texts (drama, epic, lyric) adequately depict the position of real women? Do the historical documents (legal tracts, decrees, historical narratives) reflect crucial class distinctions in their treatment of women? Do the philosophical and medical treatises indicate a negative bias towards women?

Already in the early scholarship of the 19th century on women in antiquity, there had been a tendency to treat women as though the female was an entity unto herself, isolated from the larger society around her (Blok 1987: 6). So, too, there had been a propensity to consider women from the position of one of two spheres, the public or the private, as though ancient women could not (or did not) negotiate between the two. The limitations of this narrow perspective had a tremendous impact on the discussion of gendered roles that women assumed, and, thus, that discussion remained mute until the 1970s. Since that time, there has been a consistent focus on examining ancient women as what they were—social beings—who interacted within households among husbands, children, and slaves; outside the household among friends and clan or tribal affiliates; and in a wider and more anonymous social sphere. The literature on ancient women now consistently embraces studies, both diachronic and synchronic, of the varied and critical roles women played within societal structures (Cameron and Kuhrt 1983; Fantham et al. 1994; Blundell 1995; McAuslan and Walcot 1996; Blundell and Williamson 1998).

Several decades of scholarship also reflect varied methodologies and theoretical approaches that have expanded the interpretation of the ancient evidence. Feminist theory has been key to those interpretations (Rabinowitz and Richlin 1993) as has been psychoanalytic theory (duBois 1988). In addition, anthropological perspectives, Marxist approaches, and literary criticism have all been employed to great value (Pomeroy 1984; Zweig 1993; Rose 1993). Increasingly, consideration of ancient women has been widened in edited volumes to encompass discussions of gender roles outside of the Greek and Roman world, with inclusion of Etruscan and Jewish women as well as women of the Early Christian and Byzantine periods (Archer 1983; Harvey 1983; Pomeroy 1984; Cohen 1991; Archer 1994; Bonfante 1994; Cameron 1994 are but a few examples).

The participation of classical archaeologists in the discussion of women and antiquity has emerged rather late in the progression of research (Brown 1993). While there have been several studies of immense value that have made use of art historical or archaeological data, advancing the understanding of the roles and status of women in antiquity (Walker 1983; Williams 1983; Keuls 1985; Ridgway 1987; Fantham et al. 1994; Reeder 1995; Kampen 1996; Koloski-Ostrow and Lyons 1997; Stewart 1997), classical archaeology as a tool for investigating gendered roles has generally been a late-comer. The complexity of factors contributing to classical archaeology's untimely arrival in the field of gender studies has been ably summarized in an important analysis by Shelby Brown (1993). Most important among those factors has been a relative unawareness among classical archaeologists of the bibliography of feminist literature from other allied disciplines (classics and anthropology) and the widespread belief that feminist theory is the purview of special interest groups. The strong current of conservatism within the discipline has even led to disagreement as to what the goals of classical archaeology should be (Brown 1993: 238–41, 248; also see Dyson 1998).

Within classical archaeology there has been a longstanding proclivity for research and scholarship focusing on established classes of objects—architecture, sculpture, vase painting, numismatics. As a result, classical archaeology has, at times, participated in a pervasive tendency within art history to apply value judgments to types of objects, thereby establishing faulty criteria for what art is "good" and worthy of study (Brown 1993: 244–48). Assessing ancient art from the perspective of monolithic, hierarchical categories that carry a positive approbation can result in the exclusion of women from the picture, quite simply because females did not assume active roles in construction, manufacture, and production of certain types of objects. Happily, though, different questions are now being asked of the same material and here the female is strongly felt as patron, dedicant, user, and even advisor (Keuls 1985; Ridgway 1987; Reeder 1995; Kampen 1996; Koloski-Ostrow and Lyons 1997; Stewart 1997).

The discovery of physical evidence—architecture and an abundance and diversity of artifacts—presents possibilities for immediate contact with antiquity in a way that texts and historical records do not necessarily offer. However, in order to develop theories and methods that can shed light on gender roles of the past, archaeologists must approach the material in ways that allow for productively extracting evidence of gender. For example, large-scale archaeological projects that focus on the examination of public spaces might well miss the presence of women (or certain classes of women) whose lives were centered within less public environments; equally so, archaeological investigation of technological processes has often considered and given priority to those activities characteristically involving males while sidelining female involvement in manufacturing strategies that have been regarded as having little consequence to society. The reality of everyday existence in antiquity is most penetrating when artifacts used on a frequent basis are considered, and it is here that archaeology and archaeologists can be of most service in providing information about how females and males negotiated their daily lives. Ironically, the materials that can offer a great deal of information about gender roles (such as how households were set up and by whom, how various activities were conducted by different family members within the confines of the home, and how people interacted with and utilized objects requisite for a properly functioning household) are often overlooked in deference to artifacts with a greater artistic cachet. Sensitivity to and awareness of the value of even mundane objects are critical in assessing gendered activities, even though the evidence may not be easy to employ. A sound approach to the interpretation of gender in the archaeological record is offered by Shelby Brown (1993: 250), who argues that "while it is often true that gender relations and activities cannot be securely identified in the physical record of the past, that is no reason to ignore them." Gendered approaches in archaeology, like other socially based interpretations seeking to go beyond the purely descriptive approaches of earlier eras of scholarly research, are, thus, important for understanding, explaining and reconstructing social networks of past societies.

Archaeological interpretation has always been subject to a multiplicity of influences, not least of which are contemporary gender prejudices (Trigger 1989: 380, Brown 1993: 240; Gero 1994; Nixon 1994; Webb and Frankel 1995; and the panel discussion "Gender Equity Issues in Archaeology Today" in this volume). Those biases can range from personal ideologies to stereotyped assumptions about gender roles and the belief that those roles remain fixed over time as well as to the presumed priority and greater importance of the role of males in society today. Certainly these biases, and others besides, interfere with the interpretation of archaeological data. Nevertheless, what is encouraging within the discipline of classical archaeology is its potential to contribute to a gendered view of the ancient world that cannot be attained by analysis of written records alone (Brown 1993: 261). In tandem with written evidence and the historical record, classical archaeology and the material resources it recovers can reconstruct and substantiate the contributions made by women and men to ancient society.

GENDER AND CYPRIOT ARCHAEOLOGY

"The role of women in Cyprus in ancient times is a vast and fairly unexplored field of research." So begins a brief report by Åström (1992) in which he outlined various topics and approaches that might be undertaken with regard to gender, drawing upon the richness of Cypriot artifactual and non-artifactual materials: figurines and terracotta models, burials, textual evidence, human skeletal remains, nose-rings and other jewelry. Nearly a decade later, only a handful of publications exist (Bolger 1992, 1993, 1994, and 1996; Frankel 1993; Hamilton 1994, 1996, and 2000), and *Engendering Aphrodite* is the first large-scale and wide-ranging attempt to apply analyses of gender to the Cypriot past. We certainly hope that it will not be the last effort and that the collection of papers presented here might serve as a point of departure for future research in all periods of Cypriot archaeology.

The conference *Engendering Aphrodite: Women and Society in Ancient Cyprus*, which was held in Nicosia from 19–23 March 1998, brought together scholars specializing in a broad range of disciplines and chronological periods within the Cypriot field. Participation in the conference was not arranged by select invitation but came about as the result of a widely circulated Call for Papers that included announcement on the internet. Most of those who responded had worked in Cyprus for a number of years and were well versed in their particular fields. Few had done prior work on gender, however, and in most cases this conference provided their first opportunity to do so. Participants were challenged to rethink their material from very different perspectives than they had previously done. Several participants, on the other hand, were coming to Cyprus or Cypriot material for the first time; we welcomed these new faces and were appreciative of the fresh perspectives and ideas they offered. We hope they will continue to work on Cypriot material in the years to come. The healthy response we received from the Call for Papers and the range of periods and themes presented in the contributions in this volume are, we trust, indicative of a genuine widespread interest in the topic of gender and support our strong conviction that gender as a concept in Cypriot archaeology is a legitimate research topic whose time is long overdue.

But why another book on gender? There are a number of reasons why we believe a book on gender in Cypriot archaeology might make a significant contribution to the existing literature on the subject. In the first place, the position of Cyprus located at the eastern end of the Mediterranean basin makes the island unique within the cultures of the ancient Near East. For much of its prehistoric past, Cyprus was isolated from the surrounding mainland and, thus, provides us with an opportunity to chart the interfaces between gender, the development of social complexity, and the emergence of the pristine state unadulterated by the "background noise" of foreign influence. By the same token, the involvement of Cyprus in a larger geographical and economic sphere during the Late Bronze Age allows us to observe changes in gender roles resulting from new ideologies imported from abroad and from the introduction through trade networks of unprecedented wealth that radically transformed traditional political and economic structures.

For later periods on the island there is a variety of evidence of all kinds—archaeological, artistic, literary, and epigraphic—that promises the reward of new interpretations and conclusions if questions are asked by researchers sensitive to the issues of gender. For example, during the Iron Age, when Cyprus became a principal center of worship of the goddess Aphrodite, cult activities and religious ritual had a profound significance for the inhabitants of the island. The massive numbers of votive offerings found in sanctuaries associated with the goddess can, with some scrutiny, be used to examine gender roles assumed by women and men in the service of her cult and in the development of religious ideologies that transformed the goddess into a powerful and complex deity manifest in various guises. Epigraphic documentation for the Iron Age and later periods allows for assessments of the position of select classes of women in relation to societal constructs. The advent of Christianity on the island and the subsequent rise of the Byzantine imperial court allowed for the ascent of influential women in Cyprus, a trend that continued throughout the Frankish period, as historical and literary sources demonstrate. And within the modern period, a wide range of information can be utilized to demonstrate the complexity and diversity of gender roles assumed by men, women, and children throughout the island.

Another reason why a book on gender roles in Cyprus should be written is the fact that the island's importance to the world of the eastern Mediterranean has always been fundamental. The appraisal of the Cypriot contribution to the history of the region surely rests on factors such as geology, geography, economics, trade and mercantile exchanges, technological developments, and politics. But all those factors are fueled by women and men and the roles they assumed and performed to accomplish social, cultural, political and economic agendas, whether it be in the highly visible political arena, in the critical industrial sector where new techniques and manufacturing methods invariably remained strategic, in the academic and cultural spheres of education, research, art, and literature, or in the more private sphere of the household, which always served as an essential unit of social organization. If the social interactions among Cypriot societies of the past are more expressly understood, we stand a far greater chance of appreciating and coming to terms with the social reality of Cyprus today.

ENGENDERING APHRODITE

The papers in this volume focus primarily on issues of gender and society in ancient Cyprus (Neolithic to Roman periods). In addition, two papers discuss gender constructs in Cyprus during the Medieval and modern periods (Christoforaki and Given, respectively). The invitation to publish conference papers was extended to all participants, and manuscripts submitted were subject to a rigorous peer review assessment. The contributions selected for publication reflect additional thought and an elaboration of research and scope beyond the conference presentation, and each contributes something fresh to the understanding of gender roles in ancient Cyprus.

The arrangement of the papers closely parallels the structure that was created for the conference presentations. Rather than presenting the papers within a purely chronological framework, a thematic approach has been adopted that allows for focus on particular gender-related topics: Gender and Social Organization (Parts 2–3); Gender, Identity and Ethnicity (Part 4); Gender, Technology and Material Culture (Part 5); Gender and the Goddess (Part 6); and Engendering the Cypriot Past: Critical Views (Part 7). Although papers are presented chronologically within each of those broad gender-based categories, allowing the reader to observe changes in gender constructs over long periods of time, the basic thematic approach makes visible many of the close correspondences between papers that focus on different chronological periods. Some of the continuous thematic strands that emerge from a non-synchronic reading of these papers include the critical assessment of previous, androcentric approaches to the material culture of ancient Cyprus; the need to overcome and transcend essentialist positions regarding gender roles in the past; the pressing need for archaeologists in Cyprus to consider more extensively models of social interaction, including gender-based approaches that have been adopted widely in other social sciences during the last decades; and the need for more rigorous excavations and detailed recording of excavated material that will provide a healthier database of material and contextual evidence for future investigations. An awareness of these and other cross-over themes not only enables us to appreciate how far we have advanced in our understanding of past societies during the last decades but also exposes some of the theoretical and methodological weaknesses of past research in Cypriot archaeology that will help us to record and interpret more successfully the evidence needed to further the pursuit of gender and archaeology in the years to come.

The papers that form the second and third parts of the book (Gender and Social Organization 1, 2) consider various classes of material evidence—domestic architecture, funerary remains, figurines, sculpture, and ceramics—in order to shed light on the complex interactions between gender and social organization from the 7th millennium to the 3rd century B.C. The first paper in Part 2 (Le Brun) looks at the question of differential status of females and males at the Aceramic Neolithic site of Khirokitia by focusing on evidence for spatial arrangements of domestic units, treatment of individuals in funerary contexts, and gendered images of anthropomorphic figurines. Le Brun stresses the importance of both "horizontal" (synchronic) and "vertical" (diachronic) readings of the excavated remains and notes considerable contradictions within Neolithic society with regard to the position and status of women. While funerary evidence suggests a relative equality between male and female groups, figurative evidence can be interpreted as "phallocentric" and appears to exclude females. The theme of variation and contradiction is continued in the paper by Papaconstantinou, which deals exclusively with domestic architecture of the Neolithic period. Using a contextual approach that makes use of microscale analysis, she draws attention to the lack of uniformity in the architectural remains at the Neolithic site of Ayios Epiktitos-*Vrysi*, a phenomenon that she attributes to an underlying diversity in social organization. The absence of uniform and standardized modes of behavior that might otherwise foster increasingly rigid and structured gender roles echoes Le Brun's conclusions about the "contradictions" in the material evidence at Khirokitia and suggests that gender roles at this early stage of sedentary life in Cyprus were not yet sharply defined.

The next two papers in this section (Bolger, Peltenburg) consider changes in gender constructs during the Chalcolithic period (4th–3rd millennia B.C.). Peltenburg's paper focuses on the interaction between gender and the reorganization of settlement in Cyprus ca. 3000 B.C. by examining the evidence of architecture, burial practices, and anthropomorphic figurines from the major Chalcolithic site of Kissonerga-*Mosphilia*. Using theoretical models developed by Meillassoux and others that emphasize the power of elders in sedentary societies to maintain control of human reproduction, Peltenburg proposes that similar political changes in Cyprus during the Middle Chalcolithic period may have brought about fundamental changes in gender constructs, leading to a decline in female status. Similarly, Bolger's paper points to fundamental shifts in gender relations during the Chalcolithic period as evidenced by changes in mortuary ritual during the third millennium B.C. The replacement of individual pit burials during the Late Chalcolithic period by larger mortuary structures that accommodated group burials is argued by Bolger to adumbrate changes in kinship structures that, in turn, would have altered the relationships between men, women and children. These changes are seen to occur within a village-based economy that is still relatively egalitarian, pre-dating the advent of state-level polities by more than a millennium.

The final paper in Part 2 (Webb) carries the theme of gender and social organization into the Bronze Age by examining evidence for the relationship between gender and the built environment at the ECIII/MCI settlement of *Marki-Alonia*. While emphasizing the difficulties of reconstructing behavioral systems from archaeological evidence of households, Webb believes that domestic structures potentially offer some of the most relevant evidence for gendered approaches since they represent the physical conditions in which gender relations were constructed, performed and negotiated. In contrast to most of the previous papers in this section, Webb argues for the necessity of dissociating changes in gender constructs from the developments of social complexity and believes that patterns of gendered behavior must be demonstrated independently and specifically rather than being automatically linked to generalized trajectories of socio-economic change.

Part 3 begins with two papers (Steel, Sørensen) that examine the gender constructs among elite groups of the Late Bronze and Early Iron Ages by assessing the degree to which male and female members could gain access to and manipulate valuable artifacts. Steel investigates the relationships between gender and social complexity during the Late Bronze and Early Iron Ages by examining evidence for the ritual consumption of alcohol by emergent elites. Elaborately decorated drinking vessels, many imported from abroad, furnish the principal evidence for this activity, and their association in tombs with elite individuals indicates that conspicuous consumption of alcohol was a high-status endeavor. According to Steel, there is good evidence to suggest that the ritual consumption of alcohol during the Late Bronze Age was not gender specific and that women as well as men were involved. During the Early Iron Age, however, perhaps as a result of Mycenaean influence and social upheavals during the 12th and 11th centuries B.C., this behavioral pattern changed and drinking ritual became exclusively associated with males. In the paper by Sørensen, evidence from the Archaic period in Cyprus is used to explore the ways in which male and female identities were constructed through the ritual display of large-scale figurative sculptures. These statues, which were dedicated in sanctuaries by elites within the local kingdoms of Iron Age Cyprus, served as an important means by which privileged members of society displayed publicly the gendered characteristics that society deemed "ideal." Gendered identities are characterized by Sørensen as a mosaic of traits, some of which belonged exclusively to one or the other sex, but others of which were transferred from males to females over time as gender identities were redefined and reconstructed.

The next two papers in this section (Hadjicosti, Vandervondelen) consider issues of gender and social organization during the later Iron Age. Hadjicosti's paper examines remains from an unlooted tomb of the mid-7th century B.C. in the Larnaca district in which an adult male, adult female, and young child were buried. Contextual analysis of these remains and their associated grave goods leads her to conclude that differential status was accorded to the male and female: while the male appears to have been a warrior or high ranking officer in the army and was accompanied by rich and elaborate funerary offerings, the female was not buried with prestige items; given her close proximity to the child in the tomb, it seems likely that her social importance and identity were linked primarily to her role as mother.

The role of women as mothers is also a central theme in the paper by Vandervondelen, who uses textual and figurative evidence to investigate the social organization of childbirth from the 6th to 3rd centuries B.C. She concludes that childbirth was predominantly "women's business" during the late Iron Age but that men may have been involved to some degree through participation in rituals of couvade. The dedication of numerous statues and terracotta figurines depicting childbirth scenes demonstrates the importance—and dangers—of childbirth to the entire community and reflects the high social value placed on women's reproductive roles at this time.

The final paper in this section (Christoforaki) critically analyzes the images of several prominent women during the Medieval period in Cyprus. Starting with the premise that women in the Middle Ages were regarded either as "good" or "evil" depending on their degree of conformity to gender constructs established by dominant males, Christoforaki applies this binary construct to the treatment in historical and biographical sources of three prominent women: Saint Helen, the mother of Constantine I, judged as "good" on account of her religious piety and asexuality; Elenora of Aragon, wife of Peter I, considered "evil" on account of her overt sexuality; and Helena Palaiologina, wife of John I, regarded as "treacherous" for her attempts to appropriate political power, a behavior deemed inappropriate for women of that day. These "case studies" demonstrate the ways in which male perceptions shaped female identity and underscore the dearth of evidence for female self-expression during the Medieval period.

Part 4 addresses issues of gender, identity and ethnicity over a wide chronological range, covering topics from the Chalcolithic to the Roman periods. The first paper (Frankel) argues, as does Webb's, for the need to dissociate gender from broad evolutionary models of social development. In order to evaluate the exegetical importance of other factors like ethnicity, Frankel asserts that archaeologists should focus on "historically contingent events" rather than broad trajectories of social change. Frankel then looks in detail at the evidence for ethnic diversity in Cyprus during the transition from the Chalolithic to the Bronze Age when archaeological data from Marki-*Alonia* and other contemporary sites around the island furnish compelling proof for immigration to the island from southwestern Anatolia during the latter part of the third millennium B.C. Changes in gender constructs during the Bronze Age may, thus, have been brought about through processes of ethnic interaction rather than through immanent processes of advancing socio-economic complexity.

The next two papers in Part 4 (Talalay/Cullen and Ribeiro) draw upon archaeological evidence from EC III–MC I contexts on the island to challenge traditional gender assumptions regarding the nature and significance of female figurines. The contribution by Talalay and Cullen offers a critical view of past studies of a major group of coroplastic images, the so-called "plank figurines," by questioning the assumption that they can uniformly be categorized as "female." They offer instead an interpretative model that moves beyond simple binary categories of sex and gender. Talalay and Cullen argue that the lack of clear and unambiguous sexual attributes on these figurines may have been deliberately intended, allowing these objects to serve as fluid, flexible symbols of group identity. Contextual evidence from settlements and cemeteries at this time supports this interpretation. Likewise, Ribeiro's paper cautions against the adoption of simple binary oppositions in the interpretation of figurative art. In a discussion of the well-known "scenic compositions" of EC III–MC I date, Ribeiro argues that the absence of sexual characteristics on many of the anthropomorphic figures in these scenes was not accidental but deliberate. Human figures lacking sexual traits, she maintains, should not be assumed to belong to binary categories of "male" or "female." Citing ethnographic parallels from traditional pre-state societies, Ribeiro proposes that these "sexless" figures may have been deliberately modeled to portray physically immature, pre-pubescent children who, thus, constitute a "third sex and separate gender grouping."

Issues of gender and immigration are taken up again in the joint paper by Bunimovitz and Yasur-Landau, which looks at the role of women in the large-scale migrations of the second millennium B.C.

Women, they argue, have been excluded in previous discussions of these events, the assumption being that only men were involved. Questions of the geographical and ethnic origins of women who may have taken part in these movements of people across the Mediterranean during the 12th and 11th centuries B.C. are investigated through an assessment of relevant archaeological evidence from Ashdod in Israel and Maa-*Paleokastro* in Cyprus.

The final paper in Part 4 (Gilby) investigates issues of ethnicity and ethnocentrism in ancient Cypriot society through an examination of works of art depicting black African women. Only a small number of objects exist, dating from the Middle Bronze Age to Roman periods. Whether these artifacts were manufactured on the island or imported from abroad, they convey a particular "ethnogynic" view of African women based on stereotypical features. Gilby argues that the appearance of such ethnocentric stereotypes present in Cypriot society early on is indicative of the long tradition within the ancient Mediterranean in which black women were grouped together as "other" and individual identities of African women were obscured.

Part 5 comprises four papers addressing the theme of gender, technology and material culture in prehistoric proto-historic periods on Cyprus. In the first paper, McCartney uses typological and contextual analyses of chipped stone assemblages from the Neolithic period to test models of tool use and task differentiation. Previous scholars, most notably Stekelis in his work at Sotira, have attempted to link certain tool types with women and other, more technologically complex, types with men. McCartney challenges these assumptions by revealing weaknesses in methodology, both in the means by which tools are assigned to taxonomic categories and by the misuse of ethnographic parallels. Furthermore, she argues that the social organization of the chipped stone industry in Cyprus during the Neolithic period, rather than being segregated along gender lines, involved the participation of men as well as women.

The next two papers in this section (Clarke, London) consider women's roles in ceramic production among the pre-state societies of Cyprus. Clarke's paper challenges two widespread assumptions developed by Deetz, Longacre and others in the 1970s, which are still widely employed in archaeological models today: that women are the primary producers of pottery in pre-state societies and that stylistic variation on pottery vessels is due to exogamic social structures in which females "married out" of their villages of birth. Using as a case study a number of sites of the Sotira culture (i.e., Ceramic Neolithic period) in Cyprus, Clarke demonstrates that the first assumption lacks foundation and that the second assumption is more satisfactorily accounted for by factors other than marriage and residence patterns, such as settlement fissioning. London's paper examines the role of women in early phases of ceramic production and investigates changes that may have taken place in the social organization of the pottery industry as society became more complex. She suggests that female participation in pottery production extends back to its earliest phases and was linked to women's long-term involvement in food gathering and the domestication of plants. London then considers changes in gender roles that are likely to have ensued as production on a domestic scale was replaced gradually by new technologies such as the fast wheel and the emergence of separate work spaces outside of the home.

The last paper in this section (Smith) explores changes in the social organization of labor during the Late Bronze Age through a detailed analysis of the textile industry. As textiles rarely survive in the archaeological record, evidence of their production must be gleaned from materials and equipment found at a number of Bronze Age sites on the island, in particular from Enkomi. Using archaeological, textual and ethnographic evidence, Smith reconstructs the various stages of textile production and analyzes it from the perspective of task allocation. She argues for an increasing diversification within the work force during the 13th – 11th centuries B.C. and that the advent of permanent textile workshops, which replaced household production during this period, as well as the larger scale of textile manufacture, would have necessitated changes in social organization within the industry. Smith concludes that although women were probably the primary producers during earlier phases of the Late Bronze Age, a more integrated structure involving male participation is likely to have developed during the later phases of the period.

The papers in Part 6 address gendered aspects of the goddess Aphrodite/Venus in various historical, literary, artistic and geographical contexts. The paper by Budin emphasizes the role of sexuality in the construction of the goddess in Cyprus, an attribute that, in her opinion, has been neglected and avoided by confusing it with fertility. Iconographic evidence of the goddess in Cyprus, in tandem with mythological evidence and artistic and literary parallels from the ancient Near East are used to establish Aphrodite as a goddess of sex and eroticism rather than simply one of fertility, a perspective that she deems essential to an appreciation of the power and importance of the goddess in the ancient world. Serwint continues the theme of Aphrodite's role in ancient Cyprus by focusing on her Near Eastern pedigree. Textual and literary evidence together link the origins of Aphrodite to "sister" deities such as Inanna, Ishtar, Astarte and Ashera, whose attributes were syncretized with local traditions to create the Cypriot goddess. Rather than being merely the product of western, Greek ideals, Serwint argues that Aphrodite can be shown to incorporate a complexity of attributes including sexuality, fertility and military prowess, that were introduced to Cyprus from the Near East well before her emergence in the pantheon of classical Greece. Many of the androgynous elements in the iconography of Aphrodite in Cyprus stem from those eastern roots, and, thus, Aphrodite belongs to a long-standing tradition of "female" deities whose power was great and whose gender was ambiguous.

The theme of Aphrodite's ambiguity and bisexuality is explored further in the papers by MacLachlan and Michaelides. After reviewing some of the figurative evidence in Cyprus for dual-sexed images in earlier phases of prehistory (Neolithic–Chalcolithic) and proto-history (Bronze–Iron Ages), MacLachlan considers archaeological and textual evidence for gender ambiguity in the construction of Aphrodite. The frequent depiction of the goddess with a beard, male genitalia, and weapons, textual references employing the male grammatical ending -os (*Aphroditos*), and literary references to her bisexuality furnish compelling evidence for the goddess's dual nature and show that ambiguity and duality were central features of her cult. Michaelides, likewise, argues for androgyny as a strong element in the cult of Aphrodite/Venus as evidenced by a decorated mirror of the Roman period found in 1983 in Paphos that portrays Venus bearing arms and surrounded by Cupids. The muting of sexuality on the figure of Venus, the emphasis instead on warlike attributes, and the close proximity of other "male" elements, such as an ithyphallic herm and a phallus, emphasize the duality of the goddess in Roman society. Moreover, Michaelides concludes that the existence of similar features on other contemporary works of art in Cyprus indicates that androgyny was a central feature in the local iconography of the goddess.

The three papers in Part 7 (Hamilton, Bazemore, Given) furnish critical examinations of various aspects (archaeological, epigraphical, historical) of gender in the Cypriot past. Hamilton's paper has a threefold aim to document and critique the influence of androcentric bias in the interpretation of Cypriot prehistoric remains, to assess the degree to which recent gender-based studies in Cypriot archaeology have succeeded in addressing and overcoming those biases, and to chart a course for future directions in the field of Cypriot archaeology that explicitly address gender issues. Hamilton concludes that while a certain degree of progress has been made (primarily in the study of burial evidence, anthropomorphic figurines, scenic compositions, and goddesses), gender is still marginal within the field, even in recent studies that focus on social complexity and the transformation of egalitarian society during the Bronze Age. If gender is to become central to the study of archaeology in Cyprus, Hamilton argues, we must closely scrutinize traditional methods and approaches to the material remains and begin to develop broad-based social theories that give gendered perspectives a central exegetical role.

The paper by Bazemore reveals some of the gendered assumptions used by past scholars to interpret textual evidence in Cyprus by critically examining previous translations of the Cypriot syllabic inscriptions. The Cypriot syllabary, a rectilinear script comprising approximately sixty signs, was the main system of writing in use on the island during the first millennium B.C. As the primary textual sources for ancient Cyprus, the syllabic inscriptions can potentially shed valuable light on the role of men and women in society over the course of a thousand years. Previous scholarship in the translations of these texts, however, as well as reliance on unproven assumptions concerning gender roles in the past, have obscured the evidence for Cypriot women in the ancient world.

The final paper in this section (Given) critically reviews the ethnocentric accounts of European travelers, archaeologists, colonial officials, missionaries, and writers who visited or worked in Cyprus during the late 19th century. Stereotypical views of Oriental sexuality, as manifested in portrayals of Eastern women, in general, and the goddess Aphrodite, in particular, reflect contradicting attitudes of fear, fascination, attraction and repulsion by colonists toward the indigenous population of the island. By appropriating and "corrupting" Aphrodite and reconstructing her in their image, Given argues, colonials were able to conquer their fears of the "other" and ideologically legitimize their political and economic control.

As our summary of the papers amply attests, the conference presentations were varied and wide ranging, and we would like once again to offer our warmest appreciation to all those who participated in the conference, and, in particular, to the contributors of this volume, whose papers constitute the permanent written record of the conference proceedings. In addition, we would also like to express our deep appreciation for the lively and provocative input of panelists Clarke, Cullen, Igoumenidou, Pilides, Sørensen and Webb, who took part in the panel discussion "Gender Equity Issues in Archaeology Today." Their published talks are introduced separately at the beginning of Part 8. To all participants at the conference, to the audience who attended the conference sessions, and to the readers of this volume, we offer the sincere hope that this book does not represent the "final word" on gender in Cypriot archaeology. The overwhelming response to themes addressed at the conference as well as the broad range of topics and diversity of ideas presented by the contributors to this volume are positive indicators that gendered approaches are finally beginning to emerge as legitimate areas of scholarly endeavor within the fields of Cypriot history and archaeology. We also trust that the introduction of gender as a focal point in archaeological research will continue to advance our discipline in the decades to come by contributing vital new approaches to the social interactions of the island's rich and dynamic past.

Diane Bolger
Nancy Serwint
March 2001

REFERENCES

Archer, L. J.
1983   The Role of Jewish Women in the Religion, Ritual and Cult of Graeco-Roman Palestine. Pp. 273–87 in *Images of Women in Antiquity*, eds. A. Cameron and A. Kuhrt. London and Canberra: Croom Helm.
1994   Notions of Community and the Exclusion of the Female in Jewish History and Historiography. Pp. 53–69 in *Women in Ancient Societies. An Illusion of the Night*, eds. L. J. Archer, S. Fischler, and M. Wyke. New York: Routledge.
Archer, L. J.; Fischler, S.; and Wyke, M., eds.
1994   *Women in Ancient Societies. An Illusion of the Night.* New York: Routledge.
Åström, P.
1992   Approaches to the Study of Women in Ancient Cyprus. Pp. 5–8 in *Acta Cypria: Acts of an International Congress on Cypriote Archaeology Held in Göteborg on 22–24 August 1991*, Part 2, ed. P. Åström. Studies in Mediterranean Archaeology Pocketbook 117. Jonsered: Åströms.
Bem, S. L.
1993   *The Lenses of Gender: Transforming the Debate on Sexual Inequality.* New Haven: Yale University.
Blok, J.
1987   Sexual Asymmetry. A Historiographical Essay. Pp. 1–57 in *Sexual Asymmetry. Studies in Ancient Society*, eds. J. Blok and P. Mason. Amsterdam: J. C. Gieben.
Blok, J., and Mason, P., eds.
1987   *Sexual Asymmetry. Studies in Ancient Society.* Amsterdam: J. C. Gieben.
Blundell, S.
1995   *Women in Ancient Greece.* Cambridge, MA: Harvard University.
Blundell, S., and Williamson, M., eds.
1998   *The Sacred and the Feminine in Ancient Greece.* New York: Routledge.
Bolger, D.
1992   The Archaeology of Fertility and Birth: A Ritual Deposit from Chalcolithic Cyprus. *Journal of Anthropological Research* 48, 2: 145–64.
1993   The Feminine Mystique: Gender and Society in Prehistoric Cypriot Studies. *Report of the Department of Antiquities of Cyprus*: 29–41.
1994   Engendering Cypriot Archaeology: Women's Roles and Statuses before the Bronze Age. *Opuscula Atheniensia* 20: 9–17.
1996   Figurines, Fertility and the Emergence of Complex Society in Prehistoric Cyprus. *Current Anthropology* 37: 365–73.
Bonfante, L.
1994   Excursus, Etruscan Women. Pp. 243–59 in *Women in the Classical World. Image and Text*, eds. E. Fantham, H. P. Foley, N. B. Kampen, S. B. Pomeroy, and H. A. Shapiro. New York: Oxford University.
Brown, S.
1993   Feminist Research in Archaeology: What Does It Mean? Why is It Taking So Long? Pp. 238–71 in *Feminist Theory and the Classics,* eds. N. S. Rabinowitz and A. Richlin. New York: Routledge.
Brumfiel, E.
1991   Weaving and Cooking: Women's Production in Aztec Mexico. Pp. 224–51 in *Engendering Archaeology: Women and Prehistory*, eds. J. M. Gero and M. W. Conkey. Oxford: Blackwell.
1996   Figurines and the Aztec State: Testing the Effectiveness of Ideological Domination. Pp. 143–66 in *Gender and Archaeology*, ed. R. P. Wright. Philadelphia: University of Pennsylvania.
Butler, J.
1990   *Gender Trouble: Feminism and the Subversion of Identity.* New York: Routledge.
Cameron, A.
1994   Early Christianity and the Discourse of Female Desire. Pp. 152–68 in *Women in Ancient Societies. An Illusion of the Night*, eds. L. J. Archer, S. Fischler, and M. Wyke. New York: Routledge.

Cameron, A., and Kuhrt, A., eds.
   1983   *Images of Women in Antiquity*. London and Canberra: Croom Helm.
Cartledge, P.
   1981   Spartan Wives: Liberation or Licence? *Classical Quarterly* 31: 84–105.
Claassen, C. P.
   1991   Gender, Shellfishing, and the Shell Mound Archaic. Pp. 276–300 in *Engendering Archaeology: Women and Prehistory*, eds. J. M. Gero and M. W. Conkey. Oxford: Blackwell.
Claassen, C., and Joyce, R. A., eds.
   1997   *Women in Prehistory: North America and Mesoamerica*. Philadelphia: University of Pennsylvania.
Cohen, S. J. D.
   1991   Menstruants and the Sacred in Judaism and Christianity. Pp. 273–99 in *Women's History and Ancient History*, ed. S. Pomeroy. Chapel Hill, NC: University of North Carolina.
Conkey, M. W. and Spector, J.D.
   1984   Archaeology and the Study of Gender. Pp. 1–38 in *Advances in Archaeological Method and Theory* 7, ed. M. B. Schiffer. Orlando: Academic.
duBois, P.
   1988   *Sowing the Body. Psychoanalysis and Ancient Representations of Women*. Chicago: University of Chicago.
Dyson, S.
   1998   *Ancient Marbles to American Shores: Classical Archaeology in the United States*. Philadelphia: University of Pennsylvania.
Ehrenberg, M.
   1989   *Women in Prehistory*. London: British Museum Publications.
Fantham, E.; Foley, H. P.; Kampen, N. B.; Pomeroy, S. B.; and Shapiro, H. A.
   1994   *Women in the Classical World. Image and Text*. New York: Oxford University.
Foley, H. P., ed.
   1981   *Reflections of Women in Antiquity*. New York: Gordon and Breach Science.
Frankel, D.
   1993   Is This a Trivial Observation? Gender in Prehistoric Bronze Age Cyprus. Pp. 138–42 in *Women in Archaeology: A Feminist Critique*, eds. H. du Cros and L. Smith. Department of Prehistory, Australian National University, Occasional Paper 23. Canberra: Australian National University.
Gero, J. M.
   1991   Genderlithics: Women's Roles in Stone Tool Production. Pp. 163–93 in *Engendering Archaeology: Women and Prehistory*, eds. J. M. Gero and M. W. Conkey. Oxford: Blackwell.
   1994   Excavation Bias and the Woman-at-Home Ideology. Pp. 37–42 in *Equity Issues for Women in Archeology*, eds. M. C. Nelson, S. M. Nelson and A. Wylie. Archeological Papers of the American Anthropological Association Number 5. Arlington, VA: American Anthropological Association.
Gero, J. M., and Conkey, M. W.
   1991   *Engendering Archaeology: Women and Prehistory*, eds. J. M.Gero and M. W. Conkey. Oxford: Blackwell.
 Goodwater, L.
   1975   *Women in Antiquity: An Annotated Bibliography*. Metuchen, NJ: Scarecrow.
Gould, J.
   1980   Law Custom and Myth: Aspects of the Social Position of Women in Classical Athens. *Journal of Hellenic Studies* 100: 38–59.
Hager, L., ed.
   1997   *Women in Human Evolution*. New York: Routledge.
Hamilton, N.
   1994   A Fresh Look at the "Seated Gentleman" in the Pierides Foundation Museum, Republic of Cyprus. *Cambridge Archaeological Journal* 4: 302–12.
   1996   The Personal is Political. [In Viewpoint: Can We Interpret Figurines? Hamilton et al.] *Cambridge Archaeological Journal* 6,2: 282–85.
   2000   Ungendering Archaeology: Concepts of Sex and Gender in Figurine Studies in Prehistory. Pp. 17–30 in *Representations of Gender from Prehistory to the Present*. Proceedings of the Conference on

Gender and Material Culture Held at *Exeter University, July 1994*, eds. M. Donald and L. Hurcombe. Studies in Gender and Material Culture Series. London: Macmillan.

Harvey, S. A.
1983   Women in Early Syrian Christianity. Pp. 288–98 in *Images of Women in Antiquity,* eds. A. Cameron and A. Kuhrt. London and Canberra: Croom Helm.

Hastorf, C. A.
1991   Gender, Space and Food in Prehistory. Pp. 132–59 in *Engendering Archaeology: Women and Prehistory*, eds. J. M. Gero and M. W. Conkey. Oxford: Blackwell.

Hays-Gilpin, K., and Whitley, D. S., eds.
1998   *Reader in Gender Archaeology*. New York: Routledge.

Hitchcock, L.
1997   Engendering Domination: A Structural and Contextual Analysis of Minoan Neopalatial Bronze Figurines. Pp. 113–40 in *Invisible People and Processes: Writing Gender and Childhood into European Archaeology*, eds. J. Moore and E. Scott. London: Leicester University.

Just, R.
1975   Conceptions of Women in Classical Athens. *Journal of the Anthropological Society of Oxford* 6: 153–70.
1989   *Women in Athenian Law and Life*. London: Routledge.

Kampen, N.B., ed.
1996   *Sexuality in Ancient Art*. New York: Cambridge University.

Keuls, E. C.
1985   *The Reign of the Phallus*. Berkeley and Los Angeles: University of California.

Koloski-Ostrow, A. O., and Lyons, C. L., eds.
1997   *Naked Truths: Women, Sexuality, and Gender in Classical Art and Archaeology*. London: Routledge.

Lefkowitz, M. R.
1986   *Women in Greek Myth*. Baltimore: The Johns Hopkins University.

Lerner, G.
1986   *The Creation of Patriarchy*. New York: Oxford University.

McAuslan, I., and Walcot, P., eds.
1996   *Women in Antiquity*. Greece and Rome Studies 3. Oxford: Oxford University.

Montserrat, D., ed.
1997   *Changing Bodies, Changing Meanings: Studies of the Human Body in Antiquity*. London: Routledge.

Mossé, C.
1983   *La femme dans la Grèce antique*. Paris: A. Michel.

Nelson, S. M.
1997   *Gender in Archaeology: Analyzing Power and Prestige*. Walnut Creek, CA: Altamira.

Nixon, L.
1994   Gender Bias in Archaeology. Pp. 1–23 in *Women in Ancient Societies. An Illusion of the Night*, eds. L. J. Archer, S. Fischler, and M. Wyke. New York: Routledge.

Olsen, B. A.
1988   Women, Children and the Family in the Late Aegean Bronze Age: Differences in Minoan and Mycenaean Constructions of Gender. *World Archaeology* 29, 3: 380–92.

Ortner, S.
1974   Is Female to Male as Nature is to Culture? Pp. 67–88 in *Woman, Culture and Society*, eds. M. Rosaldo and L. Lamphere. Stanford: Stanford University.

Peradotto, J., and Sullivan, J. P., eds.
1984   *Women in the Ancient World. The Arethusa Papers*. Albany: State University of New York.

Pollock, S.
1991   Women in a Men's World: Images of Sumerian Women. Pp. 366–87 in *Engendering Archaeology: Women and Prehistory*, eds. J. M. Gero and M. W. Conkey. Oxford: Blackwell.

Pomeroy, S.
1975   *Goddesses, Whores, Wives, and Slaves. Women in Classical Antiquity*. New York: Schocken Books.

1984   Selected Bibliography on Women in Classical Antiquity. Pp. 315–72 in *Women in the Ancient World. The Arethusa Papers*, eds. J. Peradotto and J. P. Sullivan. Albany: State University of New York.

Pomeroy, S., ed.
1991   *Women's History and Ancient History*. Chapel Hill, NC: University of North Carolina.

Rabinowitz, N. S., and Richlin, A., eds.
1993   *Feminist Theory and the Classics*. New York: Routledge.

Redfield, J.
1977/78   The Women of Sparta. *Classical Journal* 73: 146–61.

Reeder, E. D.
1995   *Pandora. Women in Classical Athens*. Baltimore: Walters Art Gallery (in association with Princeton University Press).

Ridgway, B. S.
1987   Ancient Greek Women and Art: The Material Evidence. *American Journal of Archaeology* 91, 3: 399–409.

Robins, G.
1993   *Women in Ancient Egypt*. London: British Museum.

Rosaldo, M. Z., and Lamphere, L., eds.
1974   *Woman, Culture and Society*. Stanford: Stanford University.

Rose, P. W.
1993   The Case for Not Ignoring Marx in the Study of Women in Antiquity. Pp. 211–37 in *Feminist Theory and the Classics*, eds. N. S. Rabinowitz and A. Richlin. New York: Routledge.

Schiffer, M., ed.
1984   *Advances in Archaeological Method and Theory*, Vol. 7. Orlando: Academic.

Spector, J.
1991   What this Awl Means: Towards a Feminist Archaeology. Pp. 388–406 in *Engendering Archaeology: Women and Prehistory*, eds. J. M. Gero and M. W. Conkey. Oxford: Blackwell.

Stewart, A.
1997   *Art, Desire, and the Body in Ancient Greece*. New York: Cambridge University.

Trigger, B. G.
1989   *A History of Archaeological Thought*. New York: Cambridge University.

Tyldesley, J.
1994   *Daughters of Isis*. London: Penguin Books.

Walker, S.
1983   Women and Housing in Classical Greece: The Archaeological Evidence. Pp. 81–91 in *Images of Women in Antiquity*, eds. A. Cameron and A. Kuhrt. London and Canberra: Croom Helm.

Watson, P. J., and Kennedy, M. C.
1991   The Development of Horticulture in the Eastern Woodlands of North America: Women's Role. Pp. 255–75 in *Engendering Archaeology: Women and Prehistory*, eds. J. M. Gero and M. W. Conkey. Oxford: Blackwell.

Webb, J., and Frankel, D.
1995   "This Fair Paper, This Most Goodly Book." Gender and International Scholarship in Cypriot Archaeology, 1920–1991. Pp. 34–42 in *Gendered Archaeology. Proceedings of the Second Australian Women in Archaeology Conference*, eds. J. Balme and W. Beck. Research Papers in Archaeology and Natural History 26. Canberra: ANH Publications, Research School of Pacific and Asian Studies, Australian National University.

Wilfong, T. G., and Jones, C. E., eds.
1998   *The Human Body in the Ancient Near East*. Groeningen: Styx.

Williams, D.
1983   Women on Athenian Vases: Problems of Interpretation. Pp. 92–106 in *Images of Women in Antiquity*, eds. A. Cameron and A. Kuhrt. London and Canberra: Croom Helm.

Wright, R. P.
1991   Women's Labor and Pottery Production in Prehistory. Pp. 194–223 in *Engendering Archaeology: Women and Prehistory*, eds. J. M. Gero and M. W. Conkey. Oxford: Blackwell.

1996   Technology, Gender and Class: Worlds of Difference in Ur III Mesopotamia. Pp. 79–110 in *Gender and Archaeology*, ed. R. P. Wright. Philadelphia: University of Pennsylvania.

Wright, R .P., ed.
1996   *Gender and Archaeology*. Philadelphia: University of Pennsylvania.

Wyke, M., ed.
1998   *Gender and the Body in the Ancient Mediterranean*. Oxford: Blackwell.

Wylie, A.
1998   The Interplay of Evidential Constraints and Political Interests: Recent Archaeological Research on Gender. Pp. 57–84 in *Reader in Gender Archaeology*, eds. K. Hays-Gilpin and D. S. Whitley. New York: Routledge.

Zweig, B.
1993   The Primal Mind: Using Native American Models for the Study of Women in Ancient Greece. Pp. 145–80 in *Feminist Theory and the Classics*, eds. N. S. Rabinowitz and A. Richlin. New York: Routledge.

PART TWO

GENDER AND SOCIAL ORGANIZATION (NEOLITHIC–MIDDLE BRONZE AGE)

NEOLITHIC SOCIETY IN CYPRUS:
A TENTATIVE ANALYSIS

ALAIN LE BRUN

CNRS, UMR7041 Maison René Ginouvès
Nanterre, France
lebrun.daune@wanadoo.fr

That a community such as Khirokitia at many times during the course of its history con-
ceived of, and was capable of carrying out, works of large-scale collective interest and was
capable of ensuring their preservation, testifies to its cohesion and the strength of its social
structure. But if the reality of social organization is thus visible and tangible, who among those
inhabiting this space animated it? Where in this tangled web is it possible to ascertain the
relationships between men and women? Did they have the same visibility? Is that visibility at
all readable, and are we capable of reading it? Furthermore, does the evidence we use permit
us to undertake such an endeavor? At the very least, it permits us to pursue several different
courses, the results of which can then be interpreted and compared. Despite the reservations
that this investigation raises for those who might wish to obscure the role of women at the
expense of that of men, or the reverse, to over-value it, a course of investigation is suggested by
the spatial distribution of the material remains of everyday life. Death, or rather the image of
death and the related customs that a society needs to provide when it is confronted with death
offers a second line of investigation. A third proposed course of inquiry is to discern whether
and how human relations find their expression in the body, in the physical and figurative
images in which Neolithic people were rendered.

In the realm of fancy in literature, islands have taken on different appearances. One of the most fascinating is the utopic island where the author expresses his or her conception of social order and social organization. I, too, may succumb to this temptation by making a tentative analysis of the nature of the Aceramic Neolithic society, in particular by trying to evaluate the place of women in the society as it appears or, rather, as we can perceive it from the documents provided by the excavation of a village community—that of Khirokitia (Dikaios 1953; Le Brun 1984, 1989a, 1994a).

This Neolithic village, which was occupied during the 7th millennium (calibrated), represents the outcome of an evolution, the beginning of which dates back to the first half of the 8th millennium or even to the last centuries of the 9th millennium, according to the data recently provided by the site of Parekklisia-*Shillourokambos* (Guilaine et al. 1996). This is a date more or less contemporary with the Middle PPNB (Pre-Pottery Neolithic B) of the Levant. Thus, the society of Khirokitia has a long and eventful history behind it, for it must not be forgotten that the island was settled initially by people from the neighboring mainland.

Even if we cannot measure the role of social factors in the initiation and achievement of this undertaking, the fact remains that social structures not only allowed for the fissioning off of part of society and its settling somewhere else far away in a new environment, they also allowed for the success of the new settlement. This fact alone is an inducement to take a close look at social structures

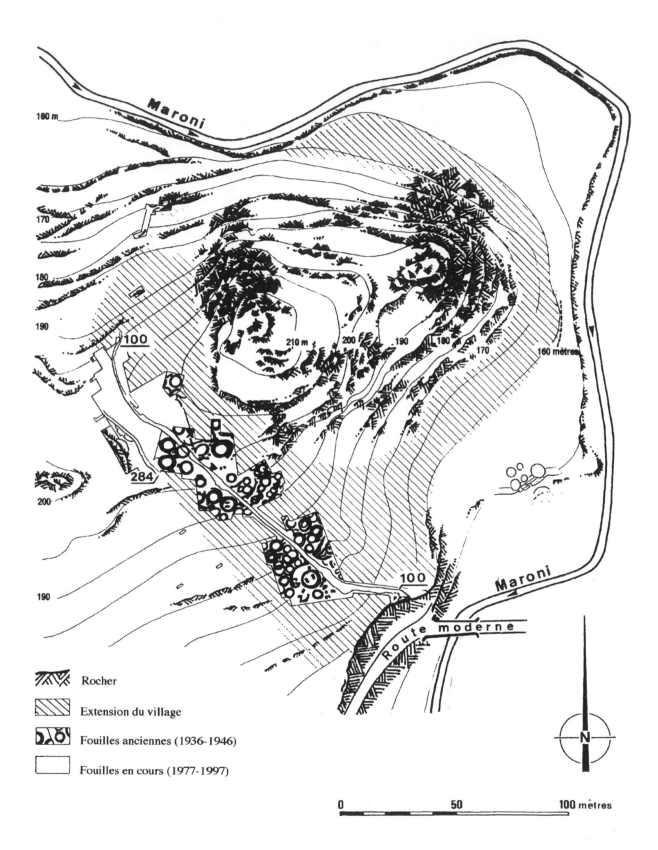

Figure 1. *General plan of the Aceramic Neolithic settlement of Khirokitia.*

at Khirokitia during the Aceramic Neolithic period. Indeed, social structures come immediately to mind after a quick glance at the general plan of the village (fig. 1) and at its constructions.

What strikes us first is that the village, stretching more than 180 m on the slope of the hill, is enclosed by a wall that was built at the same time as the habitation units. We are therefore dealing with a project that was thought out well in advance. The realization of this project suggests the existence of a society sufficiently structured, and capable of assembling the necessary labor, to bring about its plan.

But the enclosure of the village has other implications. The community within the village communicated with the outside world by arranged access points. Only one has been found, but the extent of the village suggests the existence of several such structures, placed at intervals along the slope, each one serving a distinctly defined area. These structures created drainage basins which, even if intended merely as circulation facilities, appear to demarcate territorial subdivisions. The latter may articulate divisions within society itself, such as segments or membership groups which, in turn, may have defined a framework for the functioning of society, especially with regard to the marriage system. But this, of course, remains to be demonstrated.

The spatial arrangement of houses at Khirokitia raises another question that concerns the type of family that may have been sheltered there. The ideal form of the house, as far as can be reconstructed from the excavations, may be defined as a compound of several circular units around an unroofed space, a sort of small inner courtyard, equipped with an installation for grinding grains. Each of these units, or almost each of them, shares characteristics with the others: the size—usually small, which was accordingly unable to shelter many people; and the equipment—internal partitions and, above all, hearths of the same type. In terms of function, these units do not seem to differ much from one structure to another. The settlement, thus, consisted of multiple small domestic spaces of the same kind, each one capable of accomodating a nuclear family, parents and children. In other words, the composition of the house, characterized by the fragmentation of domestic space, might reflect the association of several nuclear families into a wider and more complex aggregate, such as an extended family or even polygamous family as suggested by ethnographic parallels (Rapoport 1969; Seignobos 1982). There are, of course, very few arguments to support this hypothesis. But I would like to point out that polygamy, which is usually used in order to increase the reproductive capacity of a group, is a rather plausible strategy for settlers who, more than other human groups, had to face the crucial problem of survival in a distant land, knowing that they would not receive any help from the mainland.

The space defined by each unit of a house is fragmented by partition walls, platforms and domestic equipment such as fireplaces, basins or pits. Unfortunately, the habit of Neolithic people to empty the floor of a dwelling before deserting it deprives us of almost all evidence of the activities that may have been carried out there. Nevertheless, the presence of fireplaces and grinding installations suggests that food preparation was among the activities taking place within the house. Ethnographic evidence (e.g., Hastorf 1991: 134) suggests that food preparation is often the responsibility of women. But what should be pointed out is not so much the feminine character attributable to this domestic space but the central location within the house of the grinding installation, the use of which has just been characterized as feminine.

Until now we have been engaged in the reading of plans, that is, a horizontal reading. If we move from this type of reading to a vertical one, through time, it appears that as a result of the constant remodelling that took place within the village network, the different units composing the house had different life expectancies. Such is also the case in a continuously occupied modern village. Some structures at Khirokitia had very short life spans while others remained occupied for longer periods—some of the latter constituting "hard cores" or pivots, which furnish excellent evidence for the continuous occupation of the unit.

This is of particular significance when one knows that the dead are buried inside the buildings because to the continuity of the occupation by the living corresponds the continuity of the occupation by the dead. Some sequences are available that are consistent in terms of space and chronological succession and, thus, may constitute "lineages" or "genealogies" whose composition remains to be investigated.

The entire population is represented in the funerary evidence, including new-borns, children and adults. The percentage of children over one year old is unusually low (Le Mort 1995: 116). Among the adults, men and women appear, and the sequences of new-born infants, children, men and women, which illustrate this uniform treatment are not rare. But other configurations also exist for which the criteria of age and sex seem to work in a more selective way. Some sequences include members of a particular age-set: adults only, as in *tholoi* XIX, XX, XXV, XXXVI, XLV(I) or in structure 90; new-borns only, as in *tholoi* XVI, XXXIX or in structure 85 or 89; or new-borns and children, as in structures 91, 96 and 127. In other cases the selectivity occurs according to sex. In this case the series include, besides new-born or children, men only, as in *tholoi* V, VIII or in structures 125, 126, or women only, as in *tholos* XV(II) or in structures 117, 122, 123 or 124. It is as if the unit had kept, during its occupation, the same sexual marking. Thus, in addition to mixed units, there appear to be masculine units and feminine units, and if women seem to be excluded from certain units, men are excluded from others.

Does this equal treatment of men and women as concerns the location of the burials extend to all funerary practices? And if, despite a series of criticisms (Byrd and Monahan 1995: 253), we accept the assertion that there is a direct relationship between funerary practices, the status of an individual in the living community, and the general organization of society, what conclusions is it possible to draw from the analysis of Khirokitia burial data concerning the structure of the Aceramic Neolithic society? In our attempt to answer this question, we have a sample consisting of only 60 adults whose sex could be determined; men and women are represented almost equally in this sample, with 33 women and 27 men.

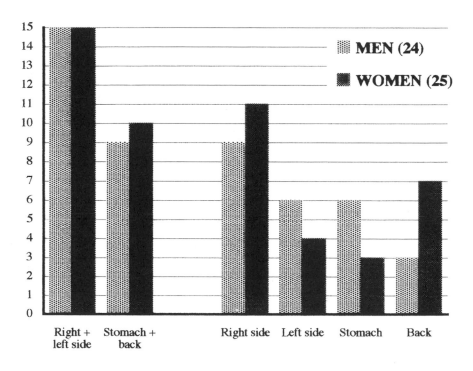

Figure 2. *The position of the body in the masculine and feminine burials at Khirokitia.*

The burials at Khirokitia are individual, primary inhumations in pits. Two types may be distinguished according to the time and energy expended in preparing the burial: a simple type where the dead are laid in an unmodified pit without any additional grave elaboration, occurring in 88 percent of the burials; and a more elaborate type with rim lined with pisé and pebbles, occuring in 12 percent of the burials.

Small though they are, these arrangements nevertheless suggest that some people were treated differently from others and that they might have a different status—achieved or ascribed. Consequently, it is important to consider which individuals received the stamp of a particular status. But first we must point out the constancy of this particular treatment during the occupation of Khirokitia as evidenced by examples found both in the eastern and western sectors; the western sector is known to have been occupied after the eastern sector (Le Brun and Daune-Le Brun 1989).

There is no restriction as to the age or the sex of the dead. The eldest individuals were not the only ones to receive this treatment. With regard to gender, the most elaborate burials have almost the same proportions of men and women. In addition, there does not seem to be any correlation between burial type and richnes of grave goods. Among the seven elaborate burials at Khirokitia, only four contained grave goods, i.e., artifacts that lie adjacent or against the skeleton and clearly represent an intentional deposit. And with regard to the practice of providing objects in the burials, stones covered the body and/or other objects frequently, i.e., in more than 50 percent of our sample, with both men and women equally represented. This percentage may have be higher because the absence of plant offerings as indicated by pollen analysis (Renault-Miskovsky 1994: 212) does not necessarily signify the absence of other perishable grave goods.

The burials provided with grave goods are distributed almost evenly between the different units, each unit including at least one. Conversely, not all the burials located in the same unit are provided with material. Therefore, if one hypothesizes that individuals buried in the same unit are related by kinship ties, then it would seem that social inequality was not hereditary and that status was achieved individually. While the presence of grave goods in some new-born or child burials might be used as evidence against such an hypothesis, we must remember that in small-scale societies the burial of children with grave goods is not necessarily indicative of ascribed status. A number of other social and demographic variables are often more significant to the interpretation of children's burials (Brown 1981: 29).

The lack of correlation between pit elaboration and grave goods, the high proportion of burials with grave goods, and their equal distribution in the structures suggest that we are dealing with an egalitarian society where each individual has an achieved status, and that status was achieved by men as well as women. However, women were not treated in exactly the same way as men. This difference in treatment was visible during their lifetimes, as evidenced by the artificial flattening of the skull twice as frequently on women as on men (Angel 1953: 416). Differences were also visible after their death, as differences in both the position and the orientation of the body as well as the types of grave goods indicate.

The differences concerning the position and the orientation of the body have been discussed elsewhere (Le Brun 1989b) and have been confirmed by recent excavations. In most cases, bodies of men and women are found lying on their sides, more frequently on the right side (fig. 2). However, sometimes they are found lying on the stomach, a position normally reserved for men, or on the back, a position normally reserved for women. With regard to the orientation of the skull, let us consider the northeast/southwest axis (fig. 3), which includes almost one third of the burials of both sexes. Here, male skeletons face northeast only, whereas females face both northeast and southwest. This difference is significant, since it means that only male burials (not female ones) are orientated in a particular direction.

With regard to grave goods, we have already stated above that it is not so much their presence or absence that marks the difference between masculine and feminine burials but rather their type and variety (fig. 4). The types of goods differ depending on whether the burial is feminine or masculine:

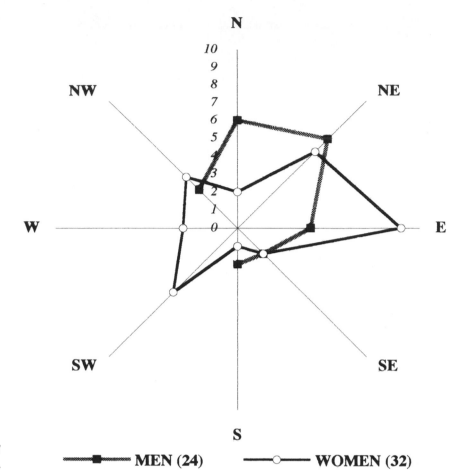

Figure 3. The orientation of
the body in the masculine and
feminine burials at Khirokitia.

━■━ **MEN (24)**   ━○━ **WOMEN (32)**

- stones, querns are preferably found in masculine burials
- diabase vessels are preferably found in feminine burials
- personal adornment occurs only with women

In addition, although bone tools can be found equally in masculine as well as in feminine burials, they appear in batches only in burials of males. For example, the male buried in grave XLV/7 held in his right hand a group of ten bone tools, and a tubular case containing a hoard of eight needles was found among the bones in grave XLVII/25 (Dikaios 1953: 169–70, 179). Female burials contain more objects of different types than masculine burials, the maximum being seven for a woman: a stone vessel, flint implements, a bone tool, a stone chisel, a piece of obsidian, a dentalium shell necklace with bone beads, and a fragment of red pigment, as in grave X(II)/5 (Dikaios 1953: 81); for men, the maximum is just three items: a quern, a stone vessel, and pigment.

These objects also have a cost of raw material acquisition and/or production, which is higher than the objects found in masculine burials. I refer to the spouted stone vessel as well as to adornments made of exotic materials such as picrolite (Peltenburg 1991), carnelian, which is not indigenous to Cyprus, and dentalium shells (Demetropoulos 1984: 181). Thus, the burials that appear to be the most prestigious are feminime burials. This eminent position persists throughout the occupation of the settlement, that is, throughout the final phase of the Aceramic Neolithic, despite changes of all kinds, including the extension of the village beyond its primitive limit, changes in building techniques and in the division of domestic space, and changes in the ecomony.

WOMEN

Item	754	664	601	580	558	XLV/1	XIX/6	XIX/7	XVIII/1	XV(II)/2	XV(II)/3	XV(II)/16	X(II)/5	III/6	IA/6	IA/7
Quern / Stone		M	Mo	M	M	Mo					M			M M		
Stone vessel	3 1	3						2	3			1	1			
Stone tool													1			
Bone tool							5	1		3			1	1		
Flint tool							2	3?					12	5		
Obsidian tool													1			
Pigment													3			
Engraved pebble																
"Dress pin"																
Ornament								N	N			N (Necklace)	N			
picrolite								◆	◆							
cornelian								◆	◆							3
stone									2							
bone													◆			
dentalium								◆	◆				◆			

MEN

Item	641	638	XLVII/5	XLVII/25	XLV/2	XLV/7	XXVII/1	XX/3	XX/4	XIIA/6	VIII/2	V/1	V/6	V/7	III/3
Quern / Stone	P M			P	P	P	M P	M	Mo	M	M				M 1 1?
Stone vessel			1							1?					
Stone tool															
Bone tool				2+8		10			2?					1	
Flint tool													1		
Obsidian tool															1
Pigment															
Engraved pebble														2	
"Dress pin"													1		
Ornament															
picrolite															
cornelian															
stone															
bone															
dentalium															

Figure 4. Nature and distribution of the grave goods at Khirokitia.

Changes in the division of domestic space tend, on the one hand, towards simplification. For example, the platform supporting the fireplace loses its independence and joins with a another, larger platform (Le Brun 1994a: 491). On the other hand, domestic space tends towards increasing fragmentation by a more frequent use of partition walls (Le Brun 1984: 51). I do not know how to interpret these contradictory tendencies, but it should be noted that this evolution takes place in tandem with another type of evolution, the faunal (Davis 1994).

Over the course of time at Khirokitia, the percentage of sheep/goat increases gradually relative to the percentage of both pigs and fallow deer. Whether this reflects a degradation of the environment or a decrease of hunting activities and an increase of animal husbandry, it nevertheless follows that the sphere of everyone's activity, the sphere of men as well as that of women, must have been remodeled, although without any apparent modification of the social status; at least no sign of it has been noticed in the funerary practices.

In contrast, representations of the human body at Khirokitia convey a completely different image, the image of a world in which woman is practically absent, a world apparently ambiguous with regard to the indication of sex. However, this circumspection may just be an appearance, for a fair number of figurines do have an unmistakably phallic character. The violence of these largely vertical representations of the human body may lie in their mixture of restraint and unstated liberty, and in their refusal of the explicit for the implicit. By asserting the body in its phallic violence, they exclude the representation of the female body (Le Brun 1994b).

If that is the case, Neolithic society in Cyprus appears to be marked by a deep contradiction of two opposing worlds. On the one hand, it was a world that was apparently "harmonious," as reflected in the funerary practices, where everyone was rewarded according to his or her personal merits, and where women were the object of a preferential treatment. On the other hand, it was a world, as represented by the figurines, where masculine preeminence asserted itself and where mental structures appeared that obscured or blotted out the image of woman. This contradiction is also revealed by funerary practices, beyond their "harmonious" appearance, for the richness and the variety of grave goods in feminine burials should not mask the fact that only masculine burials are oriented in a particular direction.

It is difficult to conclude without asking the question: Why this contradiction? Why such care and effort for a posthumous harmony when a fair number of the figurines display an incontestable masculine pre-eminence?

REFERENCES

Angel, J. L.
  1953   The Human Remains from Khirokitia. Pp. 416–30 in *Khirokitia*, by P. Dikaios. Oxford: Oxford Univer-
            sity.
Brown, J. A.
  1981   The Search for Rank in Prehistoric Burials. Pp. 25–38 in *The Archaeology of Death*, eds. R. Chapman,
            I. Kinnes and K. Randsborg. Cambridge: Cambridge University.
Byrd, F. B., and Monahan, Chr. M.
  1995   Death, Mortuary Ritual, and Natufian Social Structure. *Journal of Anthropological Archaeology*
            14: 251–87.
Davis, S. J. M.
  1994   Even More Bones from Khirokitia: the 1988–1991 Excavations. Pp. 305–33 in *Fouilles récentes à
            Khirokitia (Chypre), 1988–1991,* by A. Le Brun. Paris: Editions Recherche sur les Civilisations.
Demetropoulos, A.
  1984   Marine Molluscs, Land Snails, etc. Pp. 169–82 in *Fouilles récentes à Khirokitia (Chypre), 1977–
            1981*, by A. Le Brun. Paris: Editions Recherche sur les Civilisations.
Dikaios, P.
  1953   *Khirokitia*. Oxford: Oxford University.
Guilaine, J.; Briois, Fr.; Coularou, J.; Vigne, J.-D.; and Carrère, I.
  1996   Shillourokambos et les débuts du Néolithique à Chypre. *Espacio, Tiempo y Forma*, *Revista de la
            Facultad de Geografia e Historia*. Serie I, Prehistoria y Arqueologia 9: 159–71.
Hastorf, C. A.
  1991   Gender, Space and Food. Pp. 132–59 in *Engendering Archaeology*, eds. J. M. Gero and M. W. Conkey.
            Oxford: Blackwell.
Le Brun, A.
  1984   *Fouilles récentes à Khirokitia (Chypre), 1977–1981*. Paris: Editions Recherche sur les Civilisations.
  1989a   *Fouilles récentes à Khirokitia (Chypre), 1983–1986*. Paris: Editions Recherche sur les Civilisations.
  1989b   Le traitement des morts et les représentations des vivants à Khirokitia. Pp. 71–81 in *Early Society in
            Cyprus*, ed. E. J. Peltenburg. Edinburgh: University of Edinburgh.
  1994a   *Fouilles récentes à Khirokitia (Chypre), 1988–1991*. Paris: Edition Recherche sur les Civilisations.
  1994b   Les figurines anthropomorphes du Néolithique précéramique chypriote. Pp. 15–21 in *Cypriote Stone
            Sculpture. Proceedings of the Second International Conference of Cypriote Studies, Brussels-Liège,
            17–19 May, 1993,* eds. F. Vandenabeele and R. Laffineur. Brussels-Liège: A. G. Leventis Founda-
            tion, Vrije Universiteit Brussel, Université de Liège.
Le Brun, A., and Daune-Le Brun, O.
  1989   Stratigraphie. Pp. 11–16 in *Fouilles récentes à Khirokitia (Chypre), 1983–1986*, A. Le Brun. Paris:
            Editions Recherche sur les Civilisations.
Le Mort, Fr.
  1995   Le peuplement de Chypre: apport des données anthropologiques. *Paléorient* 21, 2: 111–21.
Peltenburg, E. J.
  1991   Local Exchange in Prehistoric Cyprus: An Initial Assessment of Picrolite. *Bulletin of the American
            Schools of Oriental Research* 282/283: 107–26.
Rapoport, A.
  1969   *House Form and Culture*. Englewood Cliffs: Prentice Hall.
Renault-Miskovsky, J.
  1994   Palynologie des sépultures. Pp. 209–12 in *Fouilles récentes à Khirokitia (Chypre), 1988–1991*, A.
            Le Brun. Paris: Editions Recherche sur les Civilisations.
Seignobos, Chr.
  1982   *Montagnes et hautes terres du Nord-Cameroun*. Roquevaire: Editions Parenthèses.

LIFE CYCLES AND THE DYNAMICS OF DOMESTIC ARCHITECTURE: HOUSEHOLDS IN NEOLITHIC CYPRUS

DEMETRA PAPACONSTANTINOU

22A S. Merkouri St.
116 34 Pangrati
Athens, Greece
papacon@hol.gr

One of the main contributions of gender to current archaeological research is the reconceptualization of what writing prehistory is about and the plurality of ways in which one can use and "read" the archaeological record. With regard to architectural remains, emphasis in recent years has been placed on the importance of microscale analysis and the examination of archaeological evidence from a contextual perspective.

The present paper investigates social and gender relations as reflected in the architecture of Neolithic Cyprus and argues against the traditionally "static" portrayal of everyday life in past societies. Its aim is to demonstrate the potential of contextual approaches to archaeology and to stress the need to re-evaluate current archaeological practices and interpretations.

The study of social organization constitutes one of the most fundamental fields of inquiry for archaeology. Discussions about the ways in which past societies were organized, including issues of social complexity and the institutionalization of power, are part of almost every current analysis and reconstruction of the past. Research on these issues, however, has been focussed primarily on later prehistory or historical times where differentiation is more or less evident in the archaeological record, either in the form of public structures, such as temples and palaces, or in the form of differential burials.

The study of gender has become equally popular in the last decades. Having already a long history in social anthropology, sociology and other related fields, gender issues are at the center of many recent archaeological debates. Here also, the relevant studies are based on specific fields, such as ethnoarchaeology and historic archaeology, or have treated specific types of evidence, such as figurines and skeletal remains, regarded as having a more obvious connection to women and their role in society.

In theory, prehistory should have a lot to offer to both domains. Social organization on a small-scale (so-called egalitarian societies) displays complexity in the making and reflects social relations in their most direct form before they are channelled and masked by institutions and hierarchies (Upham 1990). Gender relations are equally important, as there is acceptance among researchers that "differentiation by sex and age is fairly widespread and fundamental in human societies" and one can, therefore, expect that these will be "the first axes along which differentiation will emerge" (Conkey 1991: 67). In practice, however, the study of these issues in relation to prehistory and especially to the Neolithic period seems to be rather marginalized. The lack of specialization and architectural differentiation, which often characterize early prehistory, are considered to point to a homogenous and static pattern in which social organization seems rather "simple" and gender relations merely invisible (Bender 1990; Kent 1997).

The present paper investigates the potential of the prehistoric record to provide useful insights into social and gender relations in past societies. The analysis concentrates on the architectural remains of Neolithic Cyprus and indicates that part of the difficulty we face in dealing with these issues derives from the way we approach the archaeological record, rather than the nature of the record itself.

As archaeologists, we tend to discuss and describe the past in representative and general terms: we take a diachronic process—life in a settlement, for example—and divide it into analytical, synchronic units called periods. We then identify the most characteristic cultural forms and events in each of these periods and, by comparing them, attempt a complete reconstruction of what happened in a particular area at a particular time. But what if some processes operate on a different temporal scale than the one we have initially set? What if differentiation in Neolithic societies is invisible, not because of a real homogenous and static pattern, but because of the way we choose to approach the archaeological record? What about the changes that take place within each period and within each structure?

Although traditional chronological schemes and emphasis on general cultural characteristics are certainly necessary as a first step to understanding a settlement and a culture, they cannot possibly cover every research objective nor can they always do justice to the wealth of material we have available. Change and time are what archaeology is about, and the suggested analysis highlights the existence of the multiple temporal scales in which people and societies operate. Based on the study of individual houses rather than settlements in general, and focusing on contextual information and the study of microscale changes within settlements, I will investigate the dynamics of domestic architecture in archaeology and will consider some of the new directions such an approach has to offer in the study of social organization and gender relations in early societies.

MICROSCALE ANALYSIS AND GENDER STUDIES: THE RE-INTRODUCTION OF THE CONCEPT OF HOUSEHOLDS IN ARCHAEOLOGY

Since the time when settlement studies were introduced to archaeology as a special field, from the 1950s onwards (Willey 1953, 1974; Trigger 1968; Chang 1968; Tringham 1972), analysis has moved in various directions, with settlement patterns (macroscale analysis) attracting most of the archaeological interest (Knapp 1997: 1–18). The study of individual structures (microscale analysis) and the association of structures within a settlement (semi-microscale analysis) were also recognized as important fields of inquiry but drew less attention and were often considered problematic due to the fragmented nature of the archaeological record and the methodological problems this involved (Hodder and Orton 1976; Clarke 1977; Hietala 1984).

In recent decades, the archaeology of gender in particular and post-processualism in general, have reintroduced microscale analysis, emphasizing the need to go beyond general, cross-cultural patterns and discuss social relations initially on a "domestic scale" (Conkey and Spector 1984; Conkey and Gero 1991; Tringham 1991; Hodder 1986, 1990, 1992).

The involvement of gender studies with the "domestic scale" of social relations goes back to the early history of anthropology and the time when categories like "women/men," "domestic/public," "marriage," "family" and "household" were first constructed. The concept of the "household" as the "basic unit of society involved in production, reproduction, consumption and socialization" (Moore 1988: 55) provided anthropology with what seemed to be a universal model for the understanding of kinship and economy and was, therefore, regarded as a valuable analytical tool. On the basis of that model, however, women were associated with certain social functions (e.g., rearing of children) and were confined to the domestic domain.

Inevitably, the "anthropology of women" in the early 1970s saw in the above categories a "universal model for the explanation of women's subordination" (Moore 1988: 21) and attempted to deconstruct them. This process of deconstruction demonstrated the difficulty of defining the "amorphous concepts and entities" that overlapped and interacted in many complex ways (Moore 1988: 54). Despite the definitional difficulties, however, "households" remained important for feminist analysis since their composition and organization were considered to have "a direct impact on women's ability to gain access to resources, to labour and to income" (Moore 1988: 55).

Although archaeology joined the feminist critique concerning the social role of women much later, the anthropological concept of "households" had been used at an interpretative level since the 1970s (Flannery and Winter 1976; Wilk and Rathje 1982; Wilk and Ashmore 1988). Archaeologists, however, do not excavate "households" but the material remains of dwellings (Bender 1967; David 1971; Yanagisako 1979; Smith 1992). As a result, in order to "crack the architectural code" of a site, they have to overcome at least two levels of inferences: one referring to the spatial arrangements and function of the excavated structures, and a second one explaining how this information could actually be translated in social terms.

In order to overcome some of these problems, the American archaeologists who initially introduced the term "household" to the discipline emphasized the main functional activities performed in a household (production, distribution, transition and reproduction) and sought to understand not what a household's social form *is*, but what a household *does* (Wilk and Rathje 1982: 620–31; Reid and Whittlesey 1982: 690–93).

This functionalistic approach, which was in complete accordance with the spirit of New Archaeology (Clarke 1968; 1973), led to the study of artifact distributions and activity areas within structures, a development that soon equated microscale analysis with the use of statistics (Hodder and Orton 1976; Hietala 1984). Those studies were usually based on evidence from well-preserved archaeological sites where many of the types of the artifacts recovered were still in use by contemporary communities, and the identification of their function was, therefore, readily apparent (Ciolek-Torrello 1984; Wilk and Rathje 1982; Hill and Evans 1972).

These two aspects, statistics and ethnographic analogy, were probably what kept the study of households out of mainstream archaeology, since they revealed the limited potential of "regular," less well preserved, archaeological sites to deal with similar issues. In view of these limitations, most archaeologists emphasized the study of settlements rather than individual structures and, when referring to households, preferred to make general statements based on the layout of the sites (Kemp 1978; Stanley-Price 1979; Akkermans et al. 1981; Peltenburg 1985; Le Brun 1985; 1993; Byrd 1994). As a result, household studies were confined to ethnographic or historic material (Aurenche 1995, 1996; Blanton 1993; Daviau 1993; Kent 1984, 1990, 1991, 1995; Kramer 1982; Moore 1986; Netting et al. 1984; Watson 1978).

Thus, at a time when microscale analysis in archaeology seemed to have reached a deadlock, gender studies re-opened the issue and maintained that the study of residential architecture and household organization and production is an "essential prerequisite for an engendering prehistory" and for the understanding of social relations on a larger scale (Tringham 1991: 125). Gender archaeology criticized the rather limited way in which household analysis had been used previously and encouraged researchers to draw their attention to facets of sites that have previously been neglected and to focus on different levels of detail and organize their material in novel ways (Nelson 1997: 111). The "faceless" and "genderless" reconstructions of the past that had been produced beforehand (Tringham 1991: 101), and the attempts to put forward universal models that had no bearing on either anthropology or archaeology, emphasized the need to re-evaluate the archaeological record, to work in complementary ways with anthropology, and to redefine the objectives and the methods of both disciplines.

The contrast between the multiple temporal rhythms represented in the archaeological record and the "fundamentally synchronic mode" of anthropology has been the subject of long debates already from the 1970s (Ascher 1968; Gould and Watson 1982; Binford 1982, 1983b; Schiffer 1972, 1975, 1985, 1987; Schiffer and House 1977; Sabloff et al. 1987; Smith 1992: 24; Wylie 1982), and it is probably one of the main reasons for the methodological deadlocks archaeologists come up against whenever they attempt to apply anthropological models to their field (Kent 1987a). It is quite ironic that New Archaeology, which was the first to open this discussion and emphasize the need to study formation and abandonment processes in the archaeological record (Binford 1980, 1981, 1983a; Schiffer 1976, 1983, 1987; Nash and Petraglia 1987), actually took an anthropological course and concentrated on creating its own universal models and cross-cultural comparisons, neglecting the dynamics of the archaeological record at the microscale level (Binford 1964, 1965, 1972, 1978a, 1978b; Flannery 1967; Schiffer 1975, 1976; Hodder 1986; Tringham 1991). As a result, archaeology has thus far been used mainly to show what it lacks in comparison to ethnography rather than what it can reveal in relation to the many dynamic processes that operate in a community.

At this point, it is important to keep in mind that the archaeological record consists of abandoned and/or destroyed sites and presents the way life *ended* in a community. Archaeology, therefore, lies at the opposite end of the spectrum from anthropology, and in that respect, it can sometimes lead to very different patterns.

Architecture is probably the most characteristic example for the understanding of these different perspectives. From an archaeological point of view, architectural remains go through a whole life cycle of construction, utilization, maintenance, abandonment, destruction or replacement, which a horizontal/synchronic approach can only examine partly. In this respect, with regard to households, an alternative archaeological concept, that of the "household series" or "household cycles," has been suggested, which refers to "the sequence of households that successively inhabit a given structure," and attempts to identify a unit of analysis that would be closer to the nature of the archaeological record (Smith 1992: 30; Tringham 1991).

Furthermore, anthropological research has recently recognized that it has been treating dwellings "as 'cases' of symbolism or cosmology rather than a subject in their own right" (Humphrey 1988: 16), and it now seeks to develop an "alternative language of the house" that will move beyond issues of kinship and economy and examine them "in the round" (Carsten and Hugh-Jones 1995: 2). Developments in both disciplines, therefore, are promising for the construction of a beneficial dialogue that would rely on their common interests but at the same time acknowledge the different nature of their records.

NEOLITHIC HOUSEHOLDS IN CYPRUS

The prehistoric record in Cyprus is exceptionally rich and well preserved. Research has revealed a considerable number of Neolithic sites, many of which have been extensively excavated and published, providing in this way a unique sample for both synthetic and detailed analysis.

The main characteristic of the Neolithic settlements on the island is their variety in construction, layout and spatial arrangement. There are sites with monumental architecture and spacious, well-defined structures (Khirokitia-*Vounoi*, Sotira-*Teppes*), others with simple huts made of flimsy material (Cape Andreas-*Kastros*, Parekklisia-*Shillourokambos*), and still others, such as Ayios Epiktitos-*Vrysi*, which are subterranean (fig. 1).

Despite the existence of works of collective interest, as, for example, the surrounding walls in most of the sites or even some indications of central structures (Kalavasos-*Tenta*) and differentiation in material wealth (Ayios Epiktitos-*Vrysi*), there seems to be no clear social differentiation and the communities are usually characterized as "egalitarian" (Le Brun 1981, 1994; Peltenburg 1985, 1993; Todd 1987). Excavations have revealed densely occupied settlements with adjacent or free-standing structures of similar characteristics. The lack of considerable differentiation among architectural remains, as well as the size of the samples available for analysis, has given ground to several interpretations about the social organization and the structure of households in these communities. It has been suggested, for

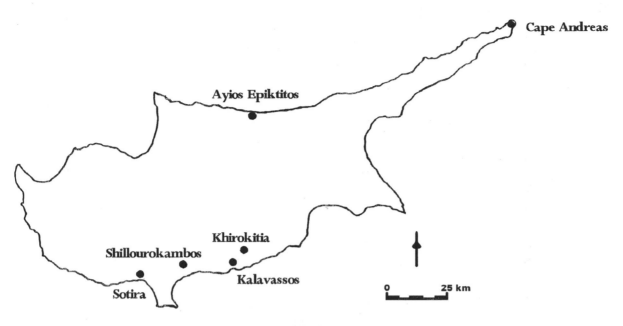

Figure 1. Neolithic sites in Cyprus. After Todd (1987).

example, that at Khirokitia-*Vounoi* (Le Brun 1984, 1985, 1989, 1994) and Sotira-*Teppes* (Dikaios 1961; Stanley-Price 1979), households consisted of families or larger kin groups that occupied complexes of structures, while at Kalavasos-*Tenta* (Todd 1987) and Ayios Epiktitos-*Vrysi* (Peltenburg 1978, 1983, 1985, 1993) there was a more uniform pattern of one nuclear family per structure.[1]

The distinction between the two patterns was based on the distribution of features and the size and spatial arrangements of the structures. It is worth noting, however, that in most of these analyses the number of the associated features and finds does not refer to specific floors but to structures, in general (Peltenburg 1983; 1985; Stanley-Price 1979). As a result, detailed analysis based on floor assemblages has not been possible, and the study of the variability of social action at the microscale level has been considerably restricted.

Given the quality of the material available, Neolithic Cyprus is an excellent case study for testing the potential of the archaeological record to present a more dynamic, heterogeneous and probably realistic picture of past societies. Although microscale analysis has been possible for three Neolithic sites—Khirokitia-*Vounoi* from the Aceramic Neolithic period; Sotira-*Teppes* and Ayios Epiktitos-*Vrysi* from the Ceramic Neolithic (Papaconstantinou 1997)—here I will concentrate on only one of them, that of Ayios Epiktitos-*Vrysi*.

THE SITE OF AYIOS EPIKTITOS-*VRYSI*

Ayios Epiktitos-*Vrysi* is located on the north coast of the island of Cyprus. The excavation has revealed a settlement that was subterranean, constructed inside hollows and separated by a ridge, thus forming two sectors, the north and the south (fig. 2). The structures were of irregular shape, built by stones and developed on a vertical axis, providing in this way a remarkably deep stratigraphy. Chronologically, the site is divided into three phases, early, middle and late. Occupation started in the northern sector and later, during the middle phase, expanded to the south (Peltenburg 1983). The present analysis will attempt to shed more light on two patterns that have been identified already at the site: 1) the imbalance in material "wealth" between the two sectors, north and south (Peltenburg 1985; 1993: 11), and 2) the character of the structures, which seem to be "uniform, general-purpose habitation units, probably for nuclear families" (Peltenburg 1993: 10).

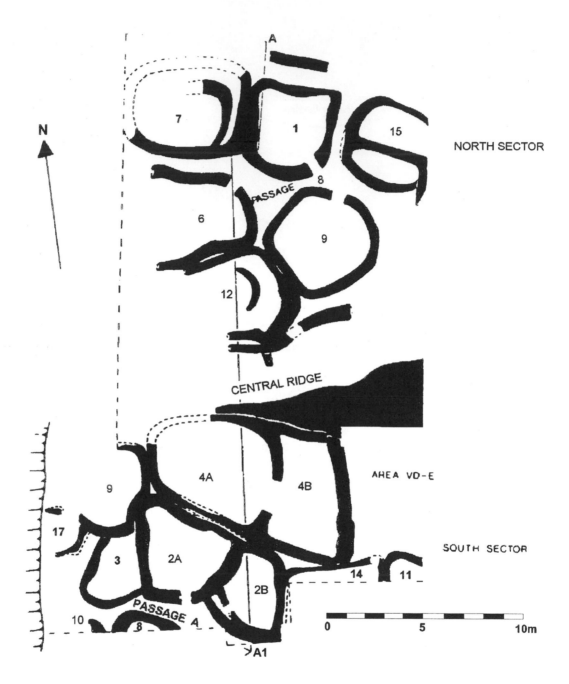

Figure 2. *Plan of Ayios Epiktitos-*Vrysi. *After Peltenburg (1983).*

Variability Between Sectors

Imbalance in material wealth is often perceived in archaeology as an indicator of "asymmetric social relations," and the distribution of finds is a common route that archaeological practice takes in its attempt to identify similar patterns (Peltenburg 1993: 11). Research, however, rarely has the advantage of testing this hypothesis on a sample large enough to provide good-quality contextual information. The record at Ayios Epiktitos-*Vrysi*, rich in material culture and well-preserved, offers the opportunity for such an attempt, while the publication of the site (Peltenburg 1983), provides the rel-

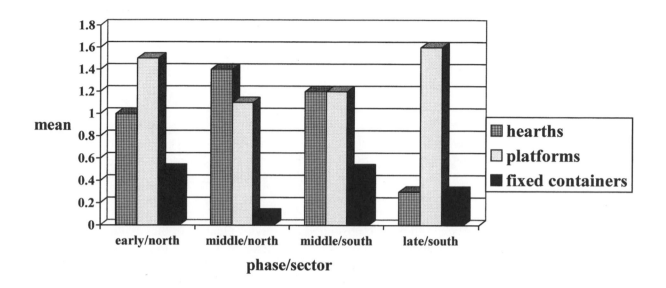

Figure 3. Average number of features (hearths, platforms, fixed containers) per floor in each phase and sector.

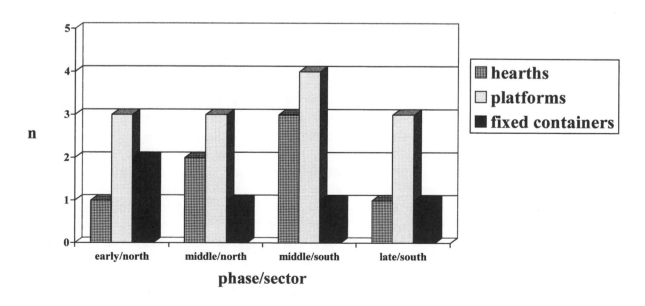

Figure 4. Number of types of features (hearths, platforms, fixed containers) per phase and sector.

evant stratigraphic information for the association of finds on each floor, and allows their study from a contextual perspective.

As already mentioned, the analysis conducted so far on the site (Peltenburg 1985: 56; 1993: 10) emphasized the distribution of features and finds per structure rather than per floor, thus "compressing" variability. The following discussion approaches the material in a more detailed way and examines two sets of data: 1) the average number of features and finds per floor in each phase and sector (figs. 3, 5), and 2) the number of the types of features and finds in each phase and sector (figs. 4, 6). For the purpose of the analysis, features and finds were divided into three main functional categories each: "hearths," "platforms," and "fixed containers" for features, and "implements," "miscellaneous," and "vessels" for small finds. The sample concerning the finds is smaller because it refers only to material derived from undisturbed units (Papaconstantinou 1997: 72–78; Peltenburg 1983).

The evidence regarding features indicates no real difference between the two sectors, and life in the south seems to have been as "active" as that in the north (figs. 3–4). The distribution of finds, however, is different. Although in quantitative terms (the average number of finds), the north sector seems, indeed, much richer in comparison to the south, in qualitative terms (the types of finds), the picture changes and differences are eliminated (figs. 5–6).

Despite the difference in material wealth, therefore, both sectors had the same access to all types of artefacts. The distinction between these two attributes is rarely as clear as in the above example and points to new and more refined questions about social relations: is it *access* to the material, for example, that constitutes "asymmetric social relations" or possession of *quantities* of material?

The above pattern could be explained in several ways. It could be attributed to differences in "disposal habits" between the two sectors (see also Peltenburg 1983: 105), to a more intense use and reuse of objects in the south sector in contrast to what was happening to the north, or to a young hard-working generation in the south versus an older sedentary generation who merely accumulated goods in the north.

This last hypothesis is intriguing when compared to anthropological models. Anthropology has shown that, in a living community, one might expect the young and "active" generation to possess and use more material than the elderly (Longacre 1985). In the case of Ayios Epiktitos-*Vrysi* there is evidence for exactly the opposite pattern since the bulk of the material derives from the older (north) sector; this might be an indication of the different time scales the two disciplines (anthropology and archaeology) represent. It would seem quite reasonable for archaeology, which depicts the way life has ended in a settlement, to present a pattern according to which the less wealthy deposits are the deposits where occupants had a greater dependence on material culture and the will to remove the necessary artefacts when abandoning a site or resurfacing a floor.

Regardless of how far one is prepared to go with a hypothesis, it is clear that these patterns can be used as stepping-stones for further research. Analysis could concentrate, for example, on each floor separately and examine, with the help of specialists, the nature of the objects by applying use-wear, abrasion, or re-fitting techniques (Villa 1982; Schild 1984; Gamble 1991; Stark 1993). Furthermore, research could focus on the study of different types of evidence, such as fauna, flora or even the distribution of sherds for the identification of discard patterns.

Ethnoarchaeology has drawn attention to the variability and use-life of ceramics in settlements as well as the role that different abandonment processes can play in spatial patterning (Yellen 1977; Cameron and Tomka 1993; Goldberg et al. 1993; Gould 1978, 1980; Hayden and Cannon 1983; Hodder 1982, 1987; Kent 1981; Longacre 1991; Moore 1982; Nelson 1997), and it is now clear that even an *in situ* agglomeration, which is traditionally considered the safest sample for analysis, could be the result of several contrasting activities, e.g., use, discard or storage (see also Nelson 1997: 62–64). In light of this evidence, it is obvious that there are still many assumptions to be re-examined in household archaeology, and microscale analysis seems to be the only way to gain the relevant information.

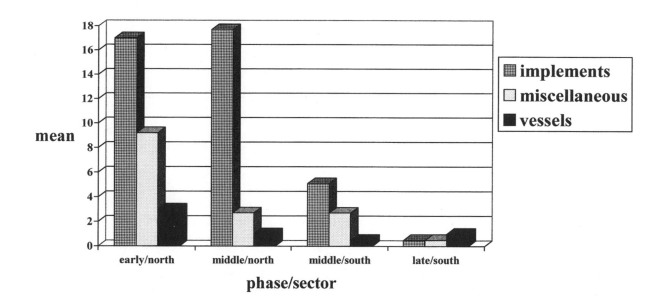

Figure 5. Average number of finds (implements, miscellaneous, vessels) per floor in each phase and sector.

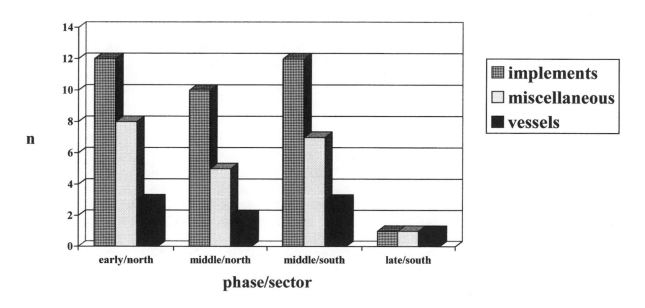

Figure 6. Number of types of finds (implements, miscellaneous, vessels) per phase and sector.

Variability at a Microscale

The second pattern refers to the structures in Ayios Epiktitos-*Vrysi*, which, as already noted, appear to be "uniform, general-purpose habitation units, probably for nuclear families" (Peltenburg 1993: 10). The nature of the habitation units in a settlement is directly related to the social organization of the society that operates in it. So far, the studies concerning this issue in Ayios Epiktitos-*Vrysi* were based on a phase-by-phase analysis of the material (Peltenburg 1978; 1983; 1985), which emphasized the comparison between structures and highlighted the existence of similar types of features throughout the settlement. The deep stratigraphy of the site, however, as well as the quality of its material, call for a more refined level of analysis that would allow for the examination of differences within structures and highlight even more the dynamic nature of architectural remains.

Fig. 7 presents the internal partitions and the features found on the floors of four of the better-preserved buildings on the site. Building 1, in the north sector, was occupied both in the early and middle phases, while buildings 2A, 2B and 3, in the south sector, were built later, in the middle phase. The evidence indicates that while all structures seem to have accommodated similar features through their use life (Peltenburg 1993: 10), when examined in detail, on a floor-to-floor basis, there are very few similarities in the type and number of features they accommodated. It is, therefore, clear that despite the general uniformity among architectural remains, there was actually considerable variety regarding the way habitation units were used on the site.

The detailed recording of stratigraphic information in the publication of the site takes the evidence one step further, making possible the identification of abandonment episodes during the occupation. Based on the nature and thickness of the deposits that covered the floors and marked the end of occupation, one can tentatively reconstruct the domestic cycles of structures and discern phases of abandonment and discontinuity in their use life (fig. 7).

Habitation, therefore, goes through cycles and has peaks, even within the same phase: periods in which structures are intensively occupied and others in which their use is restricted. According to the number and type of features in each floor, one can distinguish structures that have similar features for most of their lives (building 1), others that change character over time by adopting a more restricted (building 2B) or intensive use (building 2A), and still others that throughout their life cycle seem to have restricted use and features that change constantly from floor to floor (building 3).

Similar observations can be made with regard to continuity and discontinuity in the archaeological record. While there are structures which retain the same type of features, even when habitation is interrupted for a while (building 1), there are others in which features change, despite continuous occupation (as, for example, building 3).

The interpretations and questions these patterns raise are indeed numerous:

1) Could "changing" and "unchanging" structures indicate differences between "powerful" and "less powerful" households? Hierarchical relations among houses are a common pattern in anthropology (Carsten and Hugh-Jones 1995). The recent work of McKinnon on the Tanimbarese society in Indonesia shows that houses are characterized by hierarchical relations based on "contrastive forms of marriage, affiliation and residence" and can be divided into "permanent, named houses and impermanent, unnamed ones" (McKinnon 1995: 29). The different life cycles of buildings in a community have been neglected by archaeology and were brought to light by gender studies (Bailey 1990; Thomas 1995; Tringham 1991; Watkins 1990). Ayios Epiktitos-*Vrysi* is a characteristic example of the contribution archaeology can make to the subject (see Le Brun, this volume).

2) Changes in use also indicate changes in domestic needs and probably also in the number, gender and age of occupants. What can one say, for example, about building 2B, which initially seemed to have all the features of a general habitation unit but whose later use was

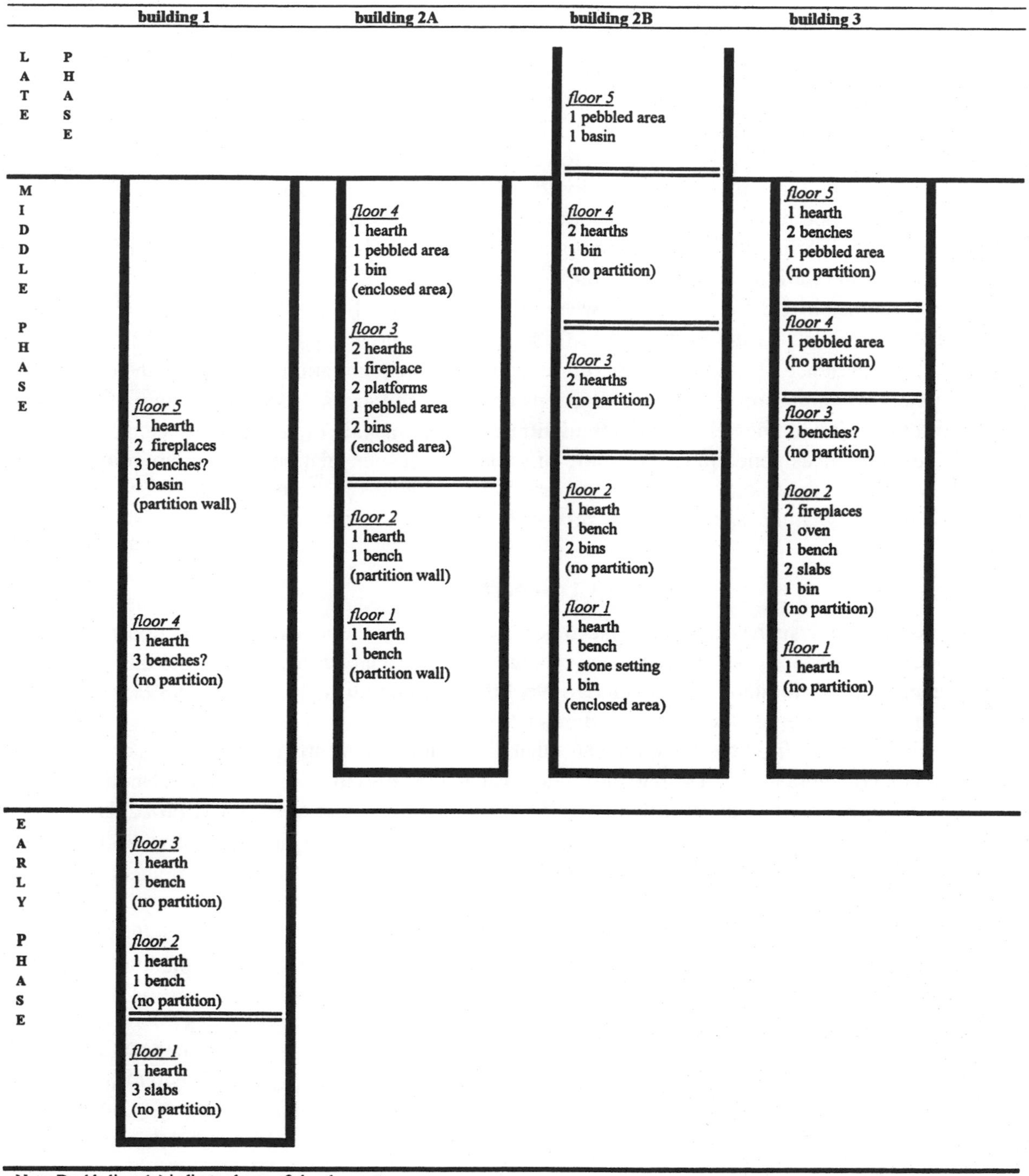

	building 1	building 2A	building 2B	building 3
LATE PHASE			*floor 5* 1 pebbled area 1 basin	
MIDDLE PHASE	*floor 5* 1 hearth 2 fireplaces 3 benches? 1 basin (partition wall) *floor 4* 1 hearth 3 benches? (no partition)	*floor 4* 1 hearth 1 pebbled area 1 bin (enclosed area) *floor 3* 2 hearths 1 fireplace 2 platforms 1 pebbled area 2 bins (enclosed area) *floor 2* 1 hearth 1 bench (partition wall) *floor 1* 1 hearth 1 bench (partition wall)	*floor 4* 2 hearths 1 bin (no partition) *floor 3* 2 hearths (no partition) *floor 2* 1 hearth 1 bench 2 bins (no partition) *floor 1* 1 hearth 1 bench 1 stone setting 1 bin (enclosed area)	*floor 5* 1 hearth 2 benches 1 pebbled area (no partition) *floor 4* 1 pebbled area (no partition) *floor 3* 2 benches? (no partition) *floor 2* 2 fireplaces 1 oven 1 bench 2 slabs 1 bin (no partition) *floor 1* 1 hearth (no partition)
EARLY PHASE	*floor 3* 1 hearth 1 bench (no partition) *floor 2* 1 hearth 1 bench (no partition) *floor 1* 1 hearth 3 slabs (no partition)			

Note: Double lines (=) indicate phases of abandonment

Figure 7. *The furnishing of four buildings in Ayios Epiktitos-*Vrysi.

more restricted? Does this indicate simply a change in use or does it also signify a different number, gender or age of occupants?

3) What does the evidence for structures with a secondary or a more specific use mean? How do we interpret structures that only have one type of feature, e.g., a hearth (building 2B: floor 3; building 3: floor 1) or a bench/paving (building 3: floors 3, 4) (fig. 7)? And what does the creation of specific enclosed areas within structures indicate? Was there an attempt to separate certain activities from others? And, if so, what was the nature of these activities? Who made the decision to separate them, and who performed them?

Building 1 is representative of the north sector (Peltenburg 1983) and, at least for the early phase, indicates structures with fewer features and fewer changes. In the south sector, however, space changes character constantly through the use of enclosed areas and the variety of features from floor to floor. If the division of space reflects a more elaborate division of household activities and tasks (Tringham 1991: 109; Kent 1987b, 1990, 1991), then one might ask what bearing these labor divisions had on gender and social relations in the community.

The difference in the use of space between the two sectors indicates that, regardless of the gender roles of the occupants in the north sector, these roles were probably renegotiated and transformed through the experience of living and working together. This renegotiation is reflected and crystallized in the variety of habitational units and divisions one finds in the south sector. In view of the above reconstructions, it becomes clear that although microscale analysis in archaeology cannot reconcile the various inferences concerning the nature of social and gender relations in a community, it can at least move beyond the traditionally static picture of a horizontal/synchronic approach and can help to reveal the more dynamic aspects of these relations.

CONCLUSIONS

Microscale analysis has been introduced here not as a panacea but as a refinement of our knowledge about domestic architecture and social organization. The analysis has shown that the "incoherent homogeneity" often thought to characterize Neolithic communities (Rowlands 1989) is neither so incoherent, nor so homogenous after all (Bender 1990).

The site of Ayios Epiktitos-*Vrysi* indicates that differentiation in early prehistory lies on a different scale than that of later periods. Despite the common characteristics in material culture, Neolithic settlements in Cyprus are characterized by a great variety of forms, and one should probably expect a similar diversity in the way these communities organized themselves and related to each other. A closer look at the material, therefore, and an emphasis on the rhythms of each settlement separately would undoubtedly be rewarding.

The lack of uniformity in the way space was used is common in the Neolithic period and indicates that social relations and structures were not yet institutionalized enough to be conspicuously reflected in standardized architectural forms. As a result, the renegotiation of gender authority was still expressed through the renegotiation of architectural conditions (see also Barrett 1988).

Gender studies in anthropology have gone through several phases, from the "study of women" to the "study of gender," and the study of "differences between women" (Moore 1988). Gender is perceived as a socially and culturally constructed relationship, and archaeology's role in this discourse, therefore, is not to "secure" women's visibility in its record but to gain evidence of differential control in the way social actions were performed in the past (Hastorf 1991: 134).

The discussion of how women are represented in anthropological and archaeological writings would inevitably touch upon disciplinary practices and the way data is "constructed" and "manipulated" by researchers. By presenting a rather disadvantaged and fragmented record, prehistory is the period which, more than any other, has a role to play in this debate as it brings archaeologists face to face with the shortcomings of their practices. The example of Cyprus has made clear that the identification of patterns depends not only on a well-preserved record but also on the questions we ask, the size of the samples we have available, our recordings in the process of excavation and the quality of our publications.

In order to see differentiation in prehistory, we have to create the space and time for it, and in our reconstructions and interpretations we usually compress time. By compressing time, however, we compress life. We compress the very human beings whose lives we are supposed to be examining, and this inevitably limits our ability to talk about the past.

ACKNOWLEDGMENTS

I wish to acknowledge the support of the State Scholarship Foundation (IKY) in Greece for funding my research in the years 1999–2000. I am also indebted to J. Barash, R. Barber, E. Baxevani, M. Boyd and N. Menti who took time to read this paper and made helpful comments.

NOTE

1. As already mentioned, the terms "household" and "family" are used in archaeological texts in a rather conventional way and are based on cross-cultural models constructed by social anthropologists (Goody 1958, 1972; Nelson 1997). Social units are usually inferred from the layout of a settlement with the assumption being, at least for the Neolithic period, that "nuclear families" (i.e., a man, a woman and their children) are represented by monocellular structures, while extended or polygamous families are represented by complexes of structures (see, e.g., Ember 1973).

REFERENCES

Akkermans, P.A., et al.
1981   Bouqras Revisited: Preliminary Report on a Project in Eastern Syria. *Proceedings of the Prehistoric Society* 49: 335-72.

Ascher, R.
1968   Time's arrow and the archaeology of a contemporary community. Pp. 43-52 in *Settlement Archaeology*, ed. K. C. Chang. Palo Alto: National Press Books.

Aurenche, O.
1995   Pour éthnoarchéologie des cycles d'évolution dans l'habitat du Proche-Orient. *Studies in the History and Archaeology of Jordan* 5: 307–19.

1996   Famille, fortune, pouvoir et architecture domestique dans les villages du Proche Orient. Pp. 1–16 in *Houses and Households in Ancient Mesopotamia*, ed. K. R. Veenhof. Istanbul: Nederlands Historisch-Archaeologisch Institut.

Bailey, D.
1990   The Living House: Signifying Continuity. Pp. 19–48 in *The Social Archaeology of Houses*, ed. R. Samson. Edinburgh: Edinburgh University.

Barrett, J. C.
1988   Fields of Discourse: Reconstituting a Social Archaeology. *Critique of Anthropology* 7, 3: 5–16.

Bender, B.
1990   The Dynamics of Nonhierarchical Societies. Pp. 247–63 in *The Evolution of Political Systems: Sociopolitics in Small-Scale Sedentary Societies*, ed. S. Upham. Cambridge: Cambridge University.

Bender, D.
1967   A Refinement of the Concept of Household: Families, Co-residence, and Domestic Functions. *American Anthropologist* 69: 493–504.

Binford, L. R.
1964   A Consideration of Archaeological Research Design. *American Antiquity* 29: 425–41.

1965   Archaeological Systemics and the Study of Culture Process. *American Antiquity* 31: 203–210.

1972   Some Comments on Historical versus Processual Archaeology. Pp. 114–21 in *An Archaeological Perspective*, ed. L. Binford. London: Seminar.

1978a   Dimensional Analysis of Behavior and Site Structure: Learning from an Eskimo Hunting Stand. *American Antiquity* 43: 330–61.

1978b   *Nunamiut Ethnoarchaeology*. New York: Academic.

1980   Willow Smoke and Dogs' Tails: Hunter-gatherer Settlement Systems and Archaeological Site Formation. *American Antiquity* 45: 4–20.

1981   *Bones, Ancient Men, and Modern Myths*. New York: Academic.

1982   The Archaeology of Place. *Journal of Anthropological Archaeology* 1: 5–31.

1983a   Behavioral Archaeology and the "Pompeii Premise." Pp. 229–41 in *Working at Archaeology*, ed. L. Binford. London: Academic.

Binford, L. R., ed.
1983b   *Working at Archaeology*. London: Academic.

Blanton, R. E.
1993   *Houses and Households: A Comparative Study*. New York: Plenum.

Byrd, B. F.
1994   Public and Private, Domestic and Corporate: The Emergence of the Southwest Asian Village. *American Antiquity* 59, 4: 639–66.

Cameron, C. M., and Tomka, S. A., eds.
1993   *Abandonment of Settlements and Regions: Ethnoarchaeological and Archaeological Approaches*. Cambridge: Cambridge University.

Carsten, J., and Hugh-Jones, S.
1995   Introduction. Pp. 1–46 in *About the House: Lévi-Strauss and Beyond*, eds. J. Carsten and S. Hugh-Jones. Cambridge: Cambridge University.

Carsten, J., and Hugh-Jones, S., eds.
1995   *About the House: Lévi-Strauss and Beyond*. Cambridge: Cambridge University.
Chang, K. C., ed.
1968   *Settlement Archaeology*. Palo Alto, CA: National.
Ciolek- Torrello, R.
1984   An Alternative Model of Room Function from Grasshopper Pueblo, Arizona. Pp. 127–53 in *Intrasite Spatial Analysis in Archaeology*, ed. H. Hietala. Cambridge: Cambridge University.
Clarke, D.
1968   *Analytical Archaeology*. London: Methuen.
1973   Archaeology: The Loss of Innocence. *Antiquity* 47: 6–18.
Clarke, D., ed.
1977   *Spatial Archaeology*. London, New York, San Francisco: Academic.
Conkey, M. W.
1991   Contexts of Action, Contexts for Power: Material Culture and Gender in the Magdalenian. Pp. 57–92 in *Engendering Archaeology: Women and Prehistory*, eds. J. Gero and M. W. Conkey. Oxford: Blackwell.
Conkey, M. W., and Gero, J.
1991   Tensions, Pluralities, and Engendering Archaeology: An Introduction to Women and Prehistory. Pp. 3–30 in *Engendering Archaeology: Women and Prehistory*, eds. J. Gero and M. W. Conkey. Oxford: Blackwell.
Conkey, M., and Spector, J.
1984   Archaeology and the Study of Gender. Pp. 1–38 in *Advances in Archaeological Method and Theory* 7, ed. M. Schiffer. New York: Academic.
Daviau, P. M.
1993   *Houses and their Furnishings in Bronze Age Palestine*. Sheffield: Sheffield Academic.
David, N.
1971   The Fulani Compound and the Archaeologist. *World Archaeology* 3: 111–31.
Dikaios, P.
1961   *Sotira*. Philadelphia: University of Pennsylvania.
Ember, M.
1973   An Archaeological Indicator of Matrilocal versus Patrilocal Residence. *American Antiquity* 38: 177–82.
Flannery, K.
1967   Culture History v. Culture Process: A Debate in American Archaeology. *Scientific American* 217: 119–22.
Flannery, K., and Winter, M.
1976   Analyzing Household Activities. Pp. 34–47 in *The Early Mesoamerican Village*, ed. K. V. Flannery. New York: Academic.
Gamble, C.
1991   An Introduction to the Living Spaces of Mobile Peoples. Pp. 1–23 in *Ethnoarchaeological Approaches to Mobile Campsites. Hunter-Gatherer and Pastoralist Case Studies*, eds. C. Gamble and W. A. Boismier. International Monographs in Prehistory. Ethnoarchaeological Series 1. Ann Arbor: University of Michigan.
Goldberg, P.; Nash, D. T.; and Petraglia, M. D., eds.
1993   *Formation Processes in Archaeological Context*. Monographs in World Archaeology 17. Madison, WI: Prehistory.
Goody, J.
1958   *The Developmental Cycle in Domestic Groups*. Cambridge: Cambridge University.
1972   The Evolution of the Family. Pp. 103–24 in *Household and Family in Past Time*, eds. P. Laslett and R. Wall. Cambridge: Cambridge University.
Gould, R.
1978   The Anthropology of Human Residues. *American Anthropologist* 80, 4: 815–35.
1980   *Living Archaeology*. Cambridge: Cambridge University.

Gould, R., and Watson, P. J.
1982   A Dialogue on the Meaning and Use of Analogy in Ethnoarchaeological Reasoning. *Journal of Anthropological Archaeology* 1: 355–81.

Hastorf, C. A.
1991   Gender, Space and Food in Prehistory. Pp. 132–59 in *Engendering Archaeology: Women and Prehistory*, eds. J. Gero and M. W. Conkey. Oxford: Blackwell.

Hayden, H., and Cannon, A.
1983   Where the Garbage Goes: Refuse Disposal in the Maya Highlands. *Journal of Anthropological Archaeology* 2(2): 117–63.

Hietala, H., ed.
1984   *Intrasite Spatial Analysis in Archaeology*. Cambridge: Cambridge University.

Hill, J. N., and Evans, R. K.
1972   A Model for Classification and Typology. Pp. 231–73 in *Models in Archaeology*, ed. D. L. Clarke. London: Methuen.

Hodder, I.
1982   *Symbols in Action*. Cambridge: Cambridge University.
1986   *Reading the Past*. Cambridge: Cambridge University.
1987   The Meaning of Discard: Ash and Domestic Space in Baringo. Pp. 424–48 in *Method and Theory for Activity Area Research: An Ethnoarchaeological Approach*, ed. S. Kent. New York: Columbia University.
1990   *The Domestication of Europe: Structure and Contingency in Neolithic Societies*. Oxford: Blackwell.
1992   *Theory and Practice in Archaeology*. London: Routledge.

Hodder, I., and Orton, C.
1976   *Spatial Analysis in Archaeology*. Cambridge: Cambridge University.

Humphrey, C.
1988   No Place like Home in Anthropology: The Neglect of Architecture. *Anthropology Today* 4, 1: 16–18.

Kemp, B.
1978   The City of El-Amarna as a Source for the Study of Urban Society in Ancient Egypt. *World Archaeology* 9, 2: 123–39.

Kent, S.
1981   The Dog: An Archaeologist's Best Friend or Worst Enemy? The Spatial Distribution of Faunal Remains. *Journal of Field Archaeology* 8: 367–72.
1984   *Analyzing Activity Areas: An Ethnoarchaeological Study of the Use of Space*. Albuquerque: University of New Mexico.
1987a   Parts as Wholes—A Critique of Theory in Archaeology. Pp. 513–46 in *Method and Theory for Activity Area Research: An Ethnoarchaeological Approach*, ed. S. Kent. New York: Columbia University.
1987b   Understanding the Use of Space—An Ethnoarchaeological Perspective. Pp. 1–60 in *Method and Theory for Activity Area Research: An Ethnoarchaeological Approach*, ed. S. Kent. New York: Columbia University.
1990   A Cross-cultural Study of Segmentation Architecture and the Use of Space. Pp. 127–52 in *Domestic Architecture and the Use of Space*, ed. S. Kent. Cambridge: Cambridge University.
1991   Partitioning Space: Cross-Cultural Factors Influencing Domestic Spatial Segmentation. *Environment and Behavior* 23, 4: 438–73.
1995   Unstable Households in a Stable Kalahari Community in Botswana. *American Anthropologist* 97, 2: 297–312.

Kent, S., ed.
1997   *Gender in African Archaeology*. Walnut Creek, CA: Altamira.

Knapp, A. B.
1997   *The Archaeology of Late Bronze Age Cypriot Society: The Study of Settlement, Survey and Landscape*. Glasgow: University of Glasgow.

Kramer, C.
1982   Ethnographic Households and Archaeological Interpretation. *American Behavioral Scientist* 25, 6: 663–76.

Le Brun, A.
1981   *Un site Néolithique précéramiqueen Chypre: Cap Andreas-Kastros*. Paris: Éditions Recherche sur les Civilisations, ADPF.

1984   *Fouilles récentes à Khirokitia (Chypre): 1977–1981*. Paris: Éditions Recherche sur les Civilisations, ADPF.

1985   Espace collectif et espace domestique à Khirokitia. Pp. 33–45 in *Chypre: La Vie Quotidienne de l'Antiquite a Nos Jours*, ed. Y. de Sike. Paris: Actes du Colloque, Musée de l' Homme.

1989   *Fouilles récentes à Khirokitia (Chypre): 1983–1986*. Paris: Éditions Recherche sur les Civilisations, ADPF.

1993   Research on Pre-Pottery Neolithic Period of Cyprus. Pp. 55–80 in *Kinyras. French Archaeology in Cyprus*, ed. M. Yon. Symposium held in Lyons, 5th–6th November 1991. Lyons: Maison de l'Orient; Paris: Diffusion de Boccard.

1994   *Fouilles récentes à Khirokitia (Chypre): 1988–1993*. Paris: Éditions Recherche sur les Civilisations, ADPF.

Longacre, W. A.
1985   Pottery Use-life among the Kalinga, Northern Luzon, the Philippines. Pp. 334–46 in *Decoding Prehistoric Ceramics*, ed. B. Nelson. Carbondale: Southern Illinois University.

Longacre, W. A., ed.
1991   *Ceramic Ethnoarchaeology*. Tucson: University of Arizona.

McKinnon, S.
1995   Houses and Hierarchy: The View from a South Moluccan Society. Pp. 170–88 in *About the House: Lévi-Strauss and Beyond*, eds. J. Carsten and S. Hugh-Jones. Cambridge: Cambridge University.

Moore, H. L.
1982   The Interpretation of Spatial Patterning in Settlement Residues. Pp. 74–79 in *Symbolic and Structural Archaeology*, ed. I. Hodder. Cambridge: Cambridge University.

1986   *Space, Text, and Gender*. Cambridge: Cambridge University.

1988   *Feminism and Anthropology*. Cambridge: Polity.

Nash, D. T., and Petraglia, M. D., eds.
1987   *Natural Formation Processes and the Archaeological Record*. BAR International Series 352. Oxford: British Archaeological Reports.

Nelson, S. M.
1997   *Gender in Archaeology: Analyzing Power and Prestige*. Walnut Creek, CA: Altamira.

Netting, R. McC.; Wilk, R. R.; and Arnould, E. J.
1984   *Households: Comparative and Historical Studies of the Domestic Group*. Berkeley: University of California.

Papaconstantinou, D.
1997   Identifying Domestic Space in Neolithic Eastern Mediterranean: Method and Theory in Spatial Studies. Unpublished Ph.D. Dissertation, Edinburgh University.

Peltenburg, E.
1978   The Sotira Culture: Regional Diversity and Cultural Unity in Late Neolithic Cyprus. *Levant* 10: 55–74.

1983   *Vrysi: A Subterranean Settlement in Cyprus*. Warminster: Aris and Phillips.

1985   Pattern and Purpose in the Prehistoric Cypriot Village of Ayios Epiktitos-*Vrysi*. Pp. 46–64 in *Chypre: La Vie Quotidienne de l'Antiquite a Nos Jours*, ed. Y. de Sike. Paris: Actes du Colloque, MusJe de l' Homme.

1993   Settlement Discontinuity and Resistance to Complexity in Cyprus, ca. 4500–2500 B.C.E. *Bulletin of the American Schools of Oriental Research* 292: 9–23.

Reid, J. J., and Whittlesey, S. M.
1982   Households at Grasshopper Pueblo. *American Behavioral Scientist* 25, 6: 687–703.

Rowlands, M. J.
1989   A Question of Complexity. Pp. 29–40 in *Domination and Resistance*, eds. D. Miller, M. Rowlands, and C. Tilley. London: Hyman Unwin.

Sabloff, J. A.; Binford, L. R.; and McAnany, P. F.
1987   Understanding the Archaeological Record. *Antiquity* 61: 203–9.
Schiffer, M.
1972   Archaeological Context and Systemic Context. *American Antiquity* 37: 156–65.
1975   Archaeology as Behavioral Science. *American Anthropologist* 77: 836–48.
1976   *Behavioral Archaeology*. New York: Academic.
1983   Towards the Identification of Formation Processes. *American Antiquity* 48: 675–706.
1985   Is there a "Pompeii premise" in Archaeology? *Journal of Anthropological Archaeology* 41: 18–41.
1987   *Formation Processes of the Archaeological Record*. Albuquerque: University of New Mexico.
Schiffer, M., and House, J. H.
1977   An Approach to Assessing Scientific Significance. Pp. 249–57 in *Conservation Archaeology: A Guide for Cultural Resource Management Studies*, eds. M. B. Schiffer and G. J. Gummerman. New York: Academic.
Schild, R.
1984   Terminal Palaeolithic of the North European Plain: A Review of Lost Chances, Potential, and Hopes. *Advances in World Archaeology* 3: 193–274.
Smith, M. E.
1992   Braudel's Temporal Rhythms and Chronology Theory in Archaeology. Pp. 23–34 in *Archaeology, Annales, and Ethnohistory*, ed. A. B. Knapp. Cambridge: Cambridge University.
Stanley Price, N. P.
1979   The Structure of Settlement at Sotira in Cyprus. *Levant* 11: 46–83.
Stark, M.
1993   Re-fitting the "Cracked and Broken Façade": The Case for Empiricism in Post-processual Ethnoarchaeology. Pp. 93–104 in *Archaeological Theory: Who Sets the Agenda?*, eds. N. Yoffee and A. Sherratt. Cambridge: Cambridge University.
Thomas, G.
1995   *Prehistoric Cypriot Mud Buildings and their Impact on the Formation of Archaeological Sites*. Unpublished Ph.D. Dissertation, Edinburgh University.
Todd, I.
1987   *Vasilikos Valley Project 6: Excavations at Kalavassos–Tenta 1*. Studies in Mediterranean Archaeology 71.6. Göteborg: Åströms.
Trigger, B.
1968   The Determinants of Settlement Patterns. Pp. 53–78 in *Settlement Archaeology*, ed. K. C. Chang. Palo Alto, CA: National.
Tringham, R.
1972   Introduction: Settlement Patterns and Urbanization. Pp. xx–xxviii in *Man, Settlement and Urbanism*, eds. P. J. Ucko, R. Tringham, and G. W. Dimbleby. London: Duckworth.
1991   Households with Faces: The Challenge of Gender in Prehistoric Architectural Remains. Pp. 93–131 in *Engendering Archaeology: Women and Prehistory*, eds. J. Gero and M. W. Conkey. Oxford: Blackwell.
Upham, S., ed.
1990   *The Evolution of Political Systems: Sociopolitics in Small-Scale Sedentary Societies*. Cambridge: Cambridge University.
Villa, P.
1982   Conjoinable Pieces and Site Formation Processes. *American Antiquity* 47: 276–90.
Watkins, T.
1990   The Origins of House and Home? *World Archaeology* 21: 336–47.
Watson, P. J.
1978   Architectural Differentiation in Some Near Eastern Communities, Prehistoric and Contemporary. Pp. 131–58 in *Social Archaeology. Beyond Subsistence and Dating*, eds. C. Redman et al. New York: Academic.
Wilk, R. R., and Ashmore, W., eds.
1988   *Household and Community in the Mesoamerican Past*. Albuquerque: University of New Mexico.

Wilk, R. R., and Rathje, W.
  1982   Household Archaeology. *American Behavioral Scientist* 25: 617–39.
Willey, G. R.
  1953   *Prehistoric Settlement Patterns in the Viru Valley, Peru.* Bureau of American Ethnology, Bulletin
              155. Washington, D.C.: Smithsonian Institution.
  1974   The Viru Valley Settlement Pattern Study. Pp. 147–79 in *Archaeological Researches in Retrospect*,
              ed. G. R. Willey. Cambridge, MA: Winthrop.
Wylie, A.
  1982   An Analogy by Any Other Name Is Just as Analogical: A Commentary on the Gould-Watson Dia-
              logue. *Journal of Anthropological Archaeology* 1: 382–401.
Yanagisako, S.
  1979   Family and Household: The Analysis of Domestic Groups. *Annual Reviews of Anthropology* 8:
              161–205.
Yellen, J. E.
  1977   *Archaeological Approaches to the Present: Models for Reconstructing the Past.* New York: Academic.

GENDER AND SOCIAL STRUCTURE
IN PREHISTORIC CYPRUS:
A CASE STUDY FROM KISSONERGA

EDGAR PELTENBURG

Department of Archaeology
University of Edinburgh
Old High School
Edinburgh EH1 1LT, Scotland
e.peltenburg@ed.ac.uk

*Based on recently published results of extensive excavations of 3rd–4th millennia B.C. levels
at Kissonerga in western Cyprus, this study attempts to determine if gender tensions of the
Chalcolithic period played a part in significant settlement reorganization at the turn of the
millennium. Female images, burial customs, hierarchical settlement planning and object distributions are deployed in a contextual analysis informed by Meillassoux's theories of the roles
of elders in pre-traction agricultural societies and by ethnographic analogies.*

Throughout antiquity, Cypriot communities produced distinctive anthropomorphic images. They
have been the subject of many investigations, although one suspects that their omission from
Ucko's influential analysis of prehistoric figurines from the eastern Mediterranean hindered
progress in their study (Ucko 1968). There is a discernible trend in these evaluations, from attempts to
consider them as divinities (e.g., J. Karageorghis 1977) or other manifestations (e.g., Merrillees 1980)
to assessments of their roles in society and the insights that they may provide into the organization of
society (e.g., Hamilton 1994). Of course, there have been many other types of studies, such as their
value for an appreciation of foreign influence (e.g., Begg 1991; Hulin 1989). Of these varied approaches, attribute analysis (a Campo 1994) and wear analysis to indicate how the figurines may have
been used (Goring 1992, following Marschak's [1991] approaches) seem to hold much promise. More
recently, as several contributions to this volume demonstrate, they have been examined to infer gender
relations, probably because their often explicit sexual attributes might be thought to provide more
direct correlates for human behavior. However, Hodder's *The Domestication of Europe* provides a
useful caution against simplistic correlates. He describes how his survey started out as an in-depth
discussion of gender relations, but in the conclusion he admits,

> I came to realize that it was possible to read representations of women as either representing "real"
> power held by women, or as expressions of the lack of power held by women ... I came to see that I
> would have to extend the same principles to male representations. In the end I realized that I was not
> writing a book about gender relations, but a book about the way in which representations of gender
> relations were manipulated within more general structures (Hodder 1990: 308).

In prehistoric Europe, as in prehistoric Cyprus, female images predominate. Of this pre-eminence, Hodder states that "the elaboration and symbolic centrality of the female might imply either abject domination of women or a relative degree of independent power" (Hodder 1990: 233). In using analogous Cypriot evidence, therefore, it is necessary to contextualize figurines within the evolution of broader behavioral patterns (cf. Hodder's "more general structures") and, where possible, to weigh the evidence in association with pertinent data like sex-based nutrition and mortuary practices (cf. Gibbs 1987) in order to provide a meaningful analytical framework.

The first period in which Cypriots produced numerous anthropomorphic images in a variety of media is the Chalcolithic ca. 3800–2400 B.C. (Karageorghis 1991). Prior to that time, figurines are sexually ambiguous, but during the Chalcolithic there is a pronounced emphasis on "womanhood" (Rice 1981) and, more particularly, birth (Peltenburg 1982 and 1992), perhaps reflecting the greater centrality of females in society. Small-scale society at that time consisted of sedentary communities mostly living in villages or hamlets and engaged in hoe agriculture, animal husbandry and deer management. There was little contact with the outside world, and so, in the absence of evidence for cattle after the Cypro-Pre-Pottery Neolithic B period, it lacked ploughs that were common in adjacent Levantine regions. In spite of this technological and symbolic lag (for symbolism, see Cauvin 1994: 44–52), cultural evolutionary re-assessments of primitive and early sedentary societies have indicated the prevalence of economic intensification and low-level socio-political inequalities, regardless of the existence of plough agriculture (e.g., Price and Feinman 1995). This important re-conceptualization of inequalities in foraging and especially early agricultural societies has recently received strong support from the appearance of special, large buildings or sanctuaries in 7th millennium B.C. western Asia. Cauvin, however, highlights the problem of correlating these precocious structures and their sculptures with inequalities in society by preferring to interpret them as corporate expressions, though without elaborating (Cauvin 1994: 155–60). But even within corporate, group-oriented societies, as distinct from communities that privileged network, individualizing strategies, leaders are likely to have been present (Feinman 1995; Renfrew 1974). Many implications for the organization of pre-state Cyprus flow from this revision. Paramount amongst them is the admission of the presence, to a greater or lesser degree, of leaders who may have been individuals or subgroups such as lineages. Meillassoux has considered the roles of such leaders in domestic agricultural economies, and his cross-cultural studies are particularly relevant to this attempt to provide a framework for analysis since a central tenet of his work is that leaders have control over the means of human reproduction. Gender relations, therefore, are a key element of his models.

In a number of influential works, Meillassoux (1972, 1978, 1981) argues that in pre-traction agricultural communities there are strong reasons to believe that elders typically exist with power over people as well as produce. He writes of norms, and while we need to be cautious about programmatic generalizations, especially using ethnographic analogies in cases where there is no demonstrable long-term cultural continuity (Gould and Watson 1982), his conclusions are of heuristic value in developing models for the Cypriot Chalcolithic.

According to this view, significant differences exist between those societies in which cereals are supplemented by extractive methods (hunting and gathering) and those where cereal production dominates since in the latter, storage and management become more important. In this system older workers gradually assume enhanced roles,

> The changing composition of the producing team is reflected in the evaluating hierarchy which dominates agricultural communities, and which divides those "who come first" from those "who come after." This hierarchy relies on positions of *anteriority*. The "first ones," the elders, are those to whom the seed and subsistence goods are owed; the oldest among them in the productive cycle owes nothing to any living person, only to the ancestors, while he concentrates on himself all that junior people owe to the community, which he therefore comes to embody.

Because of his position at the apex of the community, the elder is logically appointed to store and centralize its produce. He is also in a good position to manage it. So the need for management to ensure reproduction of the productive cycle creates a function. (Meillassoux 1981: 42).

Thus, elders are generally responsible for the circulation of subsistence goods in pre-state agricultural societies. Other characteristic features provide them with opportunities to exercise additional power.

Exogamy is an indispensable condition of such small groups and it is these gerontocrats who tend to have the authority and contacts to organize alliances and matrimonial relations between communities (Bender 1978: 212). To negotiate effectively with allied communities, elders need to maintain control over the fate of pubescent females within their group. In this way, "the elder's power tends to shift from control over subsistence to control over women—from the management of material goods to political control over people" (Meillassoux 1981: 45). Meillassoux thus situates gender relations firmly within the organization of economy and society.

In her treatment of the prehistoric Cypriot evidence, Bolger (1992, 1993, 1994, 1996 and in this volume) has sought to contextualize the issue of gender relations in terms of pottery production, circulation of figurative works, reproductive rituals, mortuary patterns and the growth of social complexity, especially state formation. One of her main conclusions is that a major transformation in the status of women occurred in the later 3rd millennium B.C. with the appearance of cattle, plough agriculture, weaponry and the depiction of women as mothers (Bolger 1996; see also Peltenburg 1994; contra Frankel 1997). Negotiations of status, however, were not static before then (see Bolger 1992). Using insights provided by the significant rethinking of egalitarian societies and by Meillassoux's reconstructions, I shall assess the possibility that gender played an equally important role in the re-structuring of social relations in the late 4th millennium B.C. To do so, I will mainly use enhanced information recently provided by the large-scale exposure of Kissonerga-*Mosphilia*, a multi-period site in the west of the island (Peltenburg et al. 1998). This requires a brief description of a sequence of developments that led to the desecration and deposition of figurines in the well-known Kissonerga ceremonial deposit in the Middle Chalcolithic (Peltenburg et al. 1991). These developments are summarized in fig. 1.

KISSONERGA 2, 3A AND 3B[1]

Kissonerga was the location for an unprecedented sequence of occupations from the Aceramic Neolithic to the Early Bronze Age (Peltenburg et al. 1998). The earliest surviving upstanding buildings belong to the Middle Chalcolithic, a period in which we were able to identify two consecutive phases, 3A and 3B. Earlier signs of habitation mainly consisted of pits and timber structures. Immediately

Period	Storage	Settlement Organization	Representative Art	Burials
3	communal	grouped timber huts	few examples	–
3A	household	grouped stone-based buildings	female	beside houses
3B	?centralized	hierarchical sectors	female	differential
Hiatus				
4a	?centralized	?	none survive	beside houses
4b	household	discrete zones	none survive	beside house

Figure 1. Selected developments at Kissonerga during the 4th and 3rd millennia B.C.

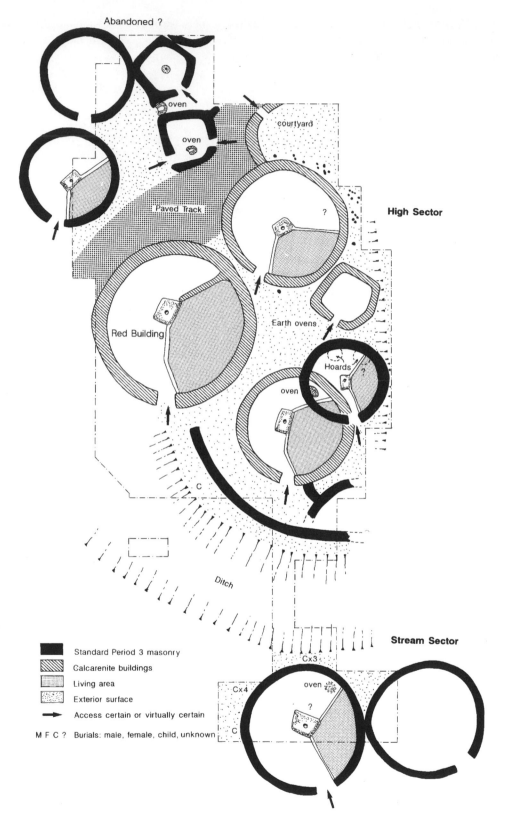

Figure 2. *Schematic plan of Kissonerga 3B. The location of the figurine deposit is indicated by "hoards" below the late building, which intruded into the area of calcarenite structures in the upper sector.*

preceding Period 3A, deep Period 2 pits of a type consistent with grain storage occurred amongst out-of-door work areas and a group of timber buildings. Large bottle-shaped pits of this kind are rare in prehistoric Cyprus, but earlier instances of functionally equivalent features may include smaller storage pits and the more elaborate underground galleries at Philia-*Drakos* A (Watkins 1969: 34–35) and Kalavasos-*Ayios* (Todd 1985: 86–87). These are capacious features that very likely contained bulk quantities of grain far in excess of the requirements of nuclear families. Thus, they probably served as communal storage for settlements.

These pits disappear in Kissonerga 3A when, in one locale, stone-founded Building 1547 was placed directly over an open store zone, absorbing that public storage space within the boundary of the structure. Communal, extra-mural storage was thus privatized with the introduction of stone-based buildings. Consumables were kept inside houses and storage became a prerogative of individual households. The problem of how to store without digging large pits inside small buildings was overcome by the manufacture of storage pots, the first in Cyprus. During Periods 2 and 3A, therefore, there is a discernible trend away from a communal sharing network in the economy to the control of agricultural produce by more individual productive cells based on permanent structures with central hearths.

According to stratigraphic, ceramic and C[14] evidence, the next period, 3B, followed directly after 3A. Its inception was apparently the result of a conscious policy by at least some inhabitants to move to a previously unoccupied part of the site, to inaugurate a new settlement organization and to elaborate many aspects of material culture. The act of founding a new settlement, in other words, by shifting a group of people simultaneously to a new locale within the area of the same site was but one element in a package of initiatives designed to announce, legitimate and consolidate a beginning, a new social order. Many characteristics of these innovations are most clearly characterized in the Main Area of excavations at Kissonerga (fig. 2). There, the community was divided into two physically separate sectors, a high sector of variable-sized structures, the most imposing arranged around an open space, which is referred to as the Ceremonial Area, and less substantial structures in a slightly lower locality, the stream sector. The conspicuous high sector structures, including the largest building so far recovered in prehistoric Cyprus, were built after several centuries of continuous development on the island and they serve as a symbol of new forms of integration in an enlarged community aggregation (cf. Adler and Wilshusen 1990: 140–41). As we shall see, this episode was associated with unprecedented rituals, perhaps to legitimate the new order. Since differences between the sectors are of scale and elaboration rather than of kind, they are likely to denote the existence of weakly articulated corporate groups, but the effort made to distinguish one of these groups remains impressive. Some of the salient features suggest that we may be dealing with engendered space, and, hence, they merit our attention here.

Boundedness

The locality of the high sector buildings was defined by diverse features that separated it from the rest of the community. The clearest markers today are a broad, shallow ditch to the south and west, and a paved track to the north. No buildings intruded on the ditch in the south which, given the general density of structures, means that it was deliberately regarded as a distancing measure. To the west, ancient erosion or a terrace interfered with the ditch which could, therefore, have continued beyond the limit of excavation. Traces of linear walls on its inner lip may be the remains of an early enclosure wall(s) that further helped to define the space. A wide, paved track to the north similarly was kept free of encroachments. On its far side stood insubstantial buildings, one of which may have served as a cooking place. To the east, the sector was bounded by slightly rising ground that lacked all traces of structures in the small soundings placed in that area. Thus, the high sector was physically separated from the south and west by a wall(?) and ditch, from the east by open space and from the north by a formal approach.

Architectural Distinctiveness

Size, building materials, internal rooms and special floors distinguished high sector buildings. The largest of these, Red Building 206, was painted red and enclosed 133 m^2. Their foundations were of calcarenite stone, which was quarried and transported by hand to the sector, probably from coastal exposures, ca. 500 m to the west. Outside the sector, fieldstones sufficed for building purposes. Calcarenites have no structural advantages over the latter nor were they used subsequently. Only the structures grouped around the Ceremonial Area, Building 2, 4, 206 and 1000, were built in this way; hence, a specific group's status was made conspicuous by the imposing size, special materials and outstanding quality of its calcarenite buildings.

Differences are also evident inside these structures. They have cement-plaster floors lacking in other buildings, and partition walls rather than radial floor dividers. Internal walls, of course, created rooms, that is the first enclosed spaces within Cypriot structures, designed to separate and exclude storage and work activities from the living/sleeping room. This is a further example of the elaboration of existing spatial patterns to establish new social relations. It seems that ascendant sub-groups were in the vanguard of attempts to create a new architectural vocabulary that set themselves apart from others.

Feasting

Comparison of intact pottery assemblages in two destroyed buildings, one from each sector, reveals important functional differences. The stream sector building contained some deep mixing bowls, flasks and especially small upright bowls or cups. The Red Building in the high sector had an ostentatious assemblage of display pottery, especially large serving bowls with a homogenous, vivacious style of painted decoration. Some are decorated with finely executed torsional compositions, the most adventurous designs produced at Kissonerga. So many of these large bowls were recovered from this context that it is likely they were used as display objects in serving larger numbers of people than lived in the structure.

This evidence needs to be treated in association with contiguous cooking installations. Cut into the area between the calcarenite buildings is an unparalleled density of earth ovens or roasting pits; hence, cooking was a major activity here. Taken together, the bowls and ovens suggest that feasting also distinguished this sub-group. By hosting feasts, the inhabitants of these imposing structures were in a position to generate bonds and debts (Bender 1978, Friedman and Rowlands 1982, and Hayden 1995: 38–42). Feasts-givers, moreover, required the production of surpluses, so these associations imply that parts of the community were prepared to surrender some of the products of their labor to this group or, as Meillassoux (1978) argues, labor and services. These signs of emerging inequalities could well have led to gender tensions which may underpin the public ritual discussed next.

Public Ritual

In the open Ceremonial Area between the calcarenite buildings we found a deliberate deposit of some 50 mutilated objects, including a building model and ca. 20 pottery and stone figurines, mostly with female characteristics. The deposit has been described in detail elsewhere (Peltenburg et al. 1991), but it is worthwhile pointing out here that, in spite of a growing number of exposures of Chalcolithic settlements and cemeteries, this remains an utterly exceptional deposit. It is probably a very special social statement, therefore, and those responsible for the deposition had or accrued special status. Consciously selected, time-factored images (Marschak 1991) were deliberately broken, decoration was concealed and the assemblage was placed in the ground where it was carefully oriented inside the pit, so a series of rites accompanied this extra-mural and, hence, public ritual. The deposit is chronologically and spatially linked with a segregated part of the community, new grandiose buildings, roasting pits and surplus production, associations that point to the existence of an ascendant social minority (cf. Hayden 1995: 56–57).

If taken in isolation, a seemingly endless variety of reasons may be subjectively adduced for the deliberate disfigurement of so many female images placed inside the house model. One way to narrow the possibilities is to consider this event contextually in terms of evolving practices and synchronous actions. To some extent we have dealt with the latter. It was an unusual public statement enacted upon or soon after the foundation of a new settlement type. Other Chalcolithic stone and pottery figurines were normally discarded in general settlement accumulation. The contemporary, soft picrolite cruciform pendants fulfilled different functions since they were excluded from the deposit and are frequently found in graves. Since they were personal ornaments, they help to distinguish the female representations in this cache as public in some sense. Viewed in terms of figurine use and development, the deposit also marks the beginning of the end of the production of these types of images. Thus, in the ensuing Late Chalcolithic there is a complete absence of birthing symbols in primary deposits. Not one of the 55 individuals buried in 48 Late Chalcolithic funerary facilities at Kissonerga possessed a birth pendant. The disappearance of pervasive symbols that explicitly conveyed the importance of birth, so emphasizing the roles of females in society, may well denote a restructuring of gender roles.

The dramatic disjunction in settlement type and figurine usage/destruction at the beginning of Kissonerga 3B suggests that there existed an underlying set of tensions which, given the mutilation and deliberate burial of so many female figurines, could be connected with the balance of male-female relations. Economic roles may be pertinent to an understanding of these tensions. Kissonerga has yielded a relatively lengthy sequence of occupations, from the Aceramic Neolithic to the Early Bronze Age, one that allows us to monitor long term economic trends. In the course of those occupations, the vicinity of the site was increasingly exploited for natural resources such as stone and timber. The expansion of settlement population throughout the Chalcolithic resulted in ever more extensive ground clearance. The impact of this intensification on the fallow deer, which were such a staple of the known diet, was to drive them further away to more congenial habitats. This reconstruction is supported by Croft (1998: 212–13) who points out that there is an unambiguous evolution of economic animals in the history of Kissonerga away from deer management towards the more labor intensive control of pig. The decline of herding contrasts with an increase in the size, number and variety of food preparation implements and the expanded use of storage pots.[2] These relationships suggest that agricultural production became more important to the enlarged community at least by the 3rd millennium B.C. Tools for the preparation of cultivars, especially cereals, are concentrated inside houses and, as suggested by the figurines inside the model and burial evidence (below), females are also closely connected to Kissonerga buildings. If, indeed, these correlations reflect real lifestyles, females may have been closely identified with agriculture, males with hunting and herd management. Although such economic identities have almost assumed the status of universal constants, identifications at Kissonerga are based on independent, if limited, empirical evidence. Thus, with the growing importance of agriculture in the economy, coupled with the decline of herding, there may have come a perceived need for females, as economic producers, to negotiate for social position and for males to redefine their strategic roles. The public ritual in the high sector and subsequent decline in female figurine production may have been one episode in the adjustments of gender relations brought about by economic trends. Following Meillassoux, the emerging dominance of cereal production provides a context for the rise of male elders and their control of the destiny of young females.

DISCUSSION

To summarize developments at Kissonerga, in Period 3A, we have seen that the growth of the settlement was accompanied by a lessening of the consensual, community network in the use and

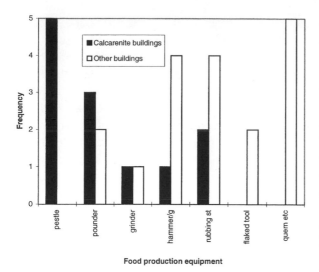

Figure 3. *Occurrence of food producing equipment in calcarenite and other buildings of Kissonerga 3B.*

distribution of cereal supplies. In 3B, an ascendant segment of society was able to obtain surplus foodstuffs for feasting and other purposes. It exercized controls over the procurement and distribution of agricultural produce. We have seen that, according to the models described above, this evidence is consistent with the existence of leaders, but to consider gender more explicitly, it may be useful to explore ethnographic examples of spatial divisions in settlements. Common to many of these pre-traction agricultural societies are integrative facilities like dance houses, sudatories, clan houses, plazas and men's houses (Adler and Wilshusen 1990: 133). Of these, men's houses conform most closely to the 3B evidence since they are usually grander expressions of ordinary houses. They are the products of social relations in which, generally, men are oriented towards the public sphere and women to the house and other, less public spaces (Rosaldo 1974). Sexual segregation, of course, is not complete, but the structuring principles of these types of societies mean that men spend much time away from the house and in ceremonial houses characterized by large size and valued group display (Duncan 1981 and Rapoport 1969: 64–65). We have already mentioned the conspicuous architecture and display pottery of this sector of the Kissonerga settlement. Two other features merit more detailed assessment to determine if the Kissonerga sectors represent gender specific spaces: non-domestic characteristics and special funerary customs.

I noted above that feasting is implied by some of the evidence from the high sector, a feature that is consistent with the many ceremonies associated with ethnographically attested men's houses (Foster 1995). The type of food consumed may be distinct in this area since nowhere else is there such a concentration of earth ovens. They may have been used as roasting pits for meat, for example, since Kissonerga 3B faunal remains increase in line with excavated volume of soil, whereas palaeobotanical remains decrease (Peltenburg et al. 1998: 244). If the calcarenite buildings simply functioned as larger versions of other houses, we may expect an equivalent density of domestic items, but in this, too, they are different. In terms of food producing equipment, for example, the complete absence of rubbers, querns and mortars from high sector buildings is noticeable when one compares their frequency in other contemporary buildings (fig. 3: see "quern etc"). The opposite pattern obtains for pestles, but at Kissonerga these were also used for red ochre working (Peltenburg et al. 1998: 185, Table 7.3), a function wholly appropriate to the needs of Building 206, the Red Building. The distribution of needles and pot discs (whorls?) also reveals a disparity in which these ostensibly domestic items are frequent in subsidiary structures, virtually absent from the calcarenite buildings (fig. 4). Since we are dealing with a number of abandoned and destroyed structures in both sectors, the dataset may be regarded as more than usually representative and, hence, greater confidence can be placed on these patterned distributions. The contrasts between the contents of the curvilinear calcarenite buildings and their anomalous, small rectilinear neighbors to the north, at least one of which was dedicated to oven cooking, are particularly marked. In other words, the high sector is composed of fine calcarenite buildings with little evidence for domestic activities and, on the other side of the paved approach, a suite of what might be termed ancillary service structures. Above, we argued for the existence of gendered, subsistence-related objects; hence, this patterning supports the notion of a more male-oriented high sector.

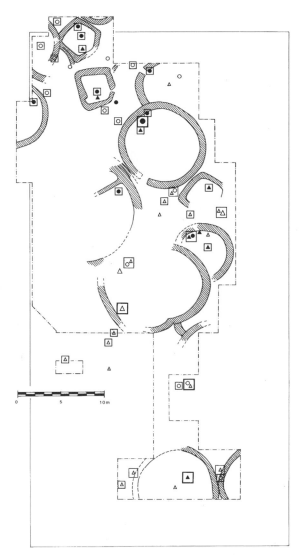

Figure 4. *Distribution of pottery discs and bone needles in Kissonerga 3B. Circles are discs, triangles needles. Note that black symbols post-date the structures.*

Funerary practices lend further support to the distinct nature of the high sector. Settlement space at Kissonerga is normally crowded with burials, preferentially located beside or cut into the outer wall that defined the living/sleeping area of houses (fig. 5). In contrast to this normal pattern, graves are conspicuous by their rarity in the high sector. Only one of the children recovered from Period 3B occurred there, and it was not placed as usual beside or in a house but outside a possible enclosure wall, on the berm between it and the surrounding ditch (Gr. 560). The remaining two or three graves were deliberately emptied, another contrast with traditional burial practices. Where associations between burials and houses are clear in Kissonerga 3A-4, females and children consistently predominate, and males are scarce (fig. 6). Gender relations, therefore, seem to structure settlement organization. This highlights the special status of the high sector. While we cannot be certain if males, females or both were interred in the high sector, structuring principles suggest that they may have been males.

The absence of empirical evidence for storage of foodstuffs in the high sector is interesting since, according to Meillassoux, elders stored, centralized and circulated subsistence goods (above). On the face of it, this would seem to distinguish the functions of the high sector from essential roles played by elders. However, evidence from contemporary Lemba-*Lakkous* 2 shows that central storage did exist at this time. There, located in a yard bounded on at least one side by a stone wall that separates it from all buildings, was a concentration of pits that originally contained storage pots (Peltenburg et al. 1985: 316–17, 325, pl. 25.4–6). At least 11 pot pits were recovered, but more lie beyond the limit of excavation. This evidence suggests that specially designated compounds near, but not inside zones reserved for buildings, were set aside for storage. Clearly, ample space was required for this bulk storage system and equally clearly such space was unavailable in the built-up settlement environment. In other words, Middle Chalcolithic settlements had discrete zones for bulk storage, a circumstance that could well correspond with the dictates of Meillassoux's model.

CONCLUSIONS

Regulation of female reproductive roles has often been linked to the rise of the state (cf. Bolger 1996: 371). According to Meillassoux, this regulation occurred much earlier as part of elders' manipulation of power in pre-state agricultural societies. At Middle Chalcolithic Kissonerga, we have inferred

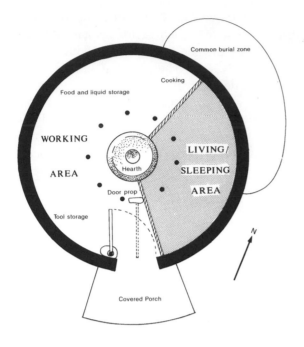

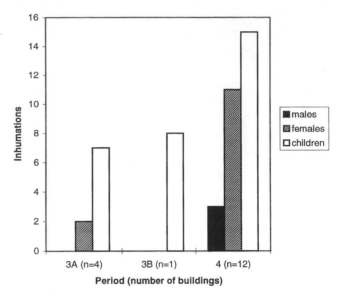

Figure 5. *Standardized Chalcolithic house plan showing close relationship of interments with buildings.*

Figure 6. *Occurrence of interred males, females and children with houses in the 4th and 3rd millennia B.C. at Kissonerga. Note that with the exception of anomalous Period 3B, females occur regularly in association with houses.*

sociopolitical restructuring from a sequence of interlocked changes, some of which suggest that this may have involved a shift in gender relations. These should be seen against a general trend of intensification of agricultural production and greater control over stored yields. They include the inception of a new ideology in Period 3B, the public destruction and burial of many birth figures inside a house model at that time, followed by a marked decline in production of female images and evidence for the existence of gendered space. We have also argued that the upper sector where the images were buried shows signs of male dominance, but to construe this as the introduction of a masculinist ideology would require more evidence than is currently at our disposal. Clearly, significant changes occurred at the beginning of Kissonerga 3B, but it must be admitted that many of our inferences about gender relations remain speculative. Pertinent evidence is available in other aspects of the archaeological record of the prehistoric Cyprus, and this should now form the subject of a broader investigation in a structured rather than simply formal manner (cf. Moore 1982).

ACKNOWLEDGMENTS

I am grateful to the organizers for inviting me to join the conference and for providing ample discussion time for participants. Excavations at Kissonerga were conducted within the framework of the Lemba Archaeological Project research program. The project was generously funded, in part, by the British Academy, Council for British Research in the Levant and the National Museums of Scotland.

NOTES

1. Kissonerga refers to the site of Kissonerga-*Mosphilia*. There are many sites in the village boundary of Kissonerga, but as Kissonerga-*Mosphilia* is spatially so dominant, it is abbreviated here to Kissonerga (see Peltenburg et al. 1998).

2. See Peltenburg et al. 1998, Tables 19.10–26. Tools such as pestles, querns and rubbers from Periods 3B/4 and 4 are far more numerous than in preceding periods, even when one factors in the disparities of excavated amount of soil.

REFERENCES

a Campo, A.
 1994   *Anthropomorphic Representations in Prehistoric Cyprus, A Formal and Symbolic Analysis of Figu-
          rines, c. 3000–1800 B.C.* Studies in Mediterranean Archaeology Pocket-book 109. Jonsered: Åströms.

Adler, M., and Wilshusen R.
 1990   Large-scale Integrative Facilities in Tribal Societies, Cross-Cultural and Southwestern US Examples.
          World Archaeology 22: 133–44.

Begg, P.
 1991   *Late Cypriot Terracotta Figurines, A Study in Context.* Studies in Mediterranean Archaeology Pocket-
          book 101. Jonsered: Åströms.

Bender, B.
 1978   Gatherer-hunter to Farmer, A Social Perspective. *World Archaeology* 10: 204–22.

Bolger D.
 1992   The Archaeology of Fertility and Birth, A Ritual Deposit from Chalcolithic Cyprus. *Journal of An-
          thropological Research* 48: 145–54.
 1993   The Feminine Mystique, Gender and Society in Prehistoric Cypriot Studies. *Report of the Depart-
          ment of Antiquities of Cyprus*: 29–41.
 1994   Engendering Cypriot Archaeology: Women's Roles and Statuses before the Bronze Age. *Opuscula
          Atheniensia* 20: 9–17.
 1996   Figurines, Fertility, and the Emergence of Complex Society in Prehistoric Cyprus. *Current Anthro-
          pology* 37: 265–72.

Cauvin, J.
 1994   *Naissance des divinités Naissance de l'agriculture. La Révolution des symboles Néolithique.* Paris:
          CNRS Éditions.

Croft, P.
 1998   Animal Remains, Synopsis. Pp. 207–14 in *Lemba Archaeological Project* II.1A. *Excavations at
          Kissonerga-Mosphilia, 1979–1992,* by E. Peltenburg et al. Studies in Mediterranean Archaeology
          70:2. Jonsered: Åströms.

Duncan, J.
 1981   From Container of Women to Status Symbol, the Impact of Social Structure on the Meaning of the
          House, Pp. 36–59 in *Housing and Identity, Cross-cultural Perspectives,* ed. J. Duncan. London:
          Croom Helm.

Feinman, G.
 1995   The Emergence of Inequality, A Focus on Strategies and Processes. Pp. 255–79 in *Foundations of
          Social Inequality,* ed. T. Price and G. Feinman. New York: Plenum.

Foster, R.
 1995   *Social Reproduction and History in Melanesia.* Cambridge: Cambridge University.

Frankel, D.
 1997   On Cypriot Figurines and the Origins of Patriarchy. *Current Anthropology* 38: 84–86.

Friedman, J., and Rowlands, M.
 1982   Notes Towards an Epigenetic Model of the Evolution of "Civilisation." Pp. 201–76 in *The Evolution
          of Social Systems,* 2nd ed., eds. J. Friedman and M. Rowlands. London: Duckworth.

Gibbs, L.
 1987   Identifying Gender Representation in the Archaeological Record, A Contextual Study. Pp. 79–89 in
          The Archaeology of Contextual Meanings, ed. I. Hodder. Cambridge: Cambridge University.

Goring, E.
 1992   Secondary Treatment of Prehistoric Figurines, An Example from Chalcolithic Cyprus. Pp. 37–40 in
          Studies in Honour of Vassos Karageorghis, ed. G. Ioannides. Nicosia: Society of Cypriot Studies.

Gould, R., and Watson, P.
 1982   A Dialogue on the Meaning and Use of Analogy in Ethnoarchaeological Reasoning. *Journal of An-
          thropological Archaeology* 4: 355–81.

Hamilton. N.
1994   A Fresh Look at the "Seated Gentleman" in the Pierides Foundation Museum, Republic of Cyprus. *Cambridge Archaeological Journal* 4: 302–12.

Hayden, B.
1995   Pathways to Power, Principles for Creating Socioeconomic Inequalities. Pp.15–103 in T. Price and G. Feinman, *Foundations of Social Inequality*. New York: Plenum.

Hodder, I.
1990   *The Domestication of Europe*. Oxford: Blackwell.

Hulin, L.
1989   The Identification of Cypriot Cult Figures Through Cross-Cultural Comparison, Some Problems. Pp. 127– 79 in *Early Society in Cyprus*, ed. E. Peltenburg. Edinburgh: Edinburgh University.

Karageorghis, J.
1977   *La grande déesse de Chypre et son culte*. Lyons: Maison de l'Orient Méditerranéen.

Karageorghis, V.
1991   *The Coroplastic Art of Ancient Cyprus*. Vol. I: *Chalcolithic-Late Cypriote I*. Nicosia: A. G. Leventis Foundation.

Marschak, A.
1991   The Female Image, a "Time-Factored" Symbol. A Study in Style and Aspects of Image Use in the Upper Palaeolithic. *Proceedings of the Prehistoric Society* 57: 17–31.

Meillassoux, C.
1972   From Production to Reproduction. *Economy and Society* 1: 93–105.
1978   "The Economy" in Agricultural Self-Sustaining Societies, A Preliminary Analysis. Pp. 127–57 in *Relations of Production, Marxist Approaches to Economic Anthropology*, ed. D. Seddon. London: Cass.
1981   *Maidens, Meal and Money. Capitalism and the Domestic Community*. Cambridge: Cambridge University.

Merrillees, R.
1980   Representation of the Human Form in Prehistoric Cyprus. *Opuscula Atheniensia* 13: 171–84.

Moore, H.
1982   The Interpretation of Spatial Patterning in Settlement Residues. Pp. 74–79 in *Symbolic and Structural Archaeology*, ed. I. Hodder. Cambridge: Cambridge University.

Peltenburg, E.
1982   The Evolution of the Cypriot Cruciform Figurine. *Report of the Department of Antiquities of Cyprus*: 12–14.
1992   Birth Pendants in Life and Death, Evidence from Kissonerga Grave 563. Pp. 25–36 in *Studies in Honour of Vassos Karageorghis*, ed. G. Ioannides. Nicosia: Society of Cypriot Studies.
1994   Constructing Authority, the Vounous Enclosure Model. *Opuscula Atheniensia* 20: 157–62.

Peltenburg, E., et al.
1985   *Lemba Archaeological Project I, Excavations at Lemba-Lakkous 1976–83*. Studies in Mediterranean Archaeology 70:1. Göteborg: Åströms.
1991   *Lemba Archaeological Project II.2. A Ceremonial Area at Kissonerga*. Studies in Mediterranean Archaeology 70:3. Göteborg: Åströms.
1998   *Lemba Archaeological Project II.1A. Excavations at Kissonerga-Mosphilia, 1979–1992*. Studies in Mediterranean Archaeology 70:2. Jonsered: Åströms.

Price, T., and G. Feinman
1995   *Foundations of Social Inequality*. New York: Plenum.

Rapoport, A.
1969   *House Form and Culture*. Englewood Cliffs: Prentice-Hall.

Renfrew, C.
1974   Beyond a Subsistence Economy, The Evolution of Social Organization in Prehistoric Europe. Pp. 69–85 in *Reconstructing Complex Societies. BASOR Supplements,* 20, ed. C. Moore. Cambridge, MA: American Schools of Oriental Research.

Rice, P.
1981   Prehistoric Venuses, Symbols of Motherhood or Womanhood? *Journal of Anthropological Research*
37: 402–14.

Rosaldo, M.
1974   Women and Society, a Theoretical Overview. In *Woman, Culture and Society*, eds. M. Rosaldo and L.
Lamphere. Stanford: Stanford University.

Todd, I.
1985   Excavations in the Vasilikos Valley. Pp. 81–95 in *Archaeology in Cyprus 1960–1985*, ed. V.
Karageorghis. Nicosia: A. G. Leventis Foundation.

Ucko, P.
1968   Anthropomorphic Figurines of Predynastic Egypt and Neolithic Crete with Comparative Material
from the Prehistoric Near East and Mainland Greece. *Royal Anthropological Institute. Occasional
Papers,* No. 24. London: A. Szmidla.

Watkins, T.
1969   The First Village Settlements. *Archaeologia Viva* 2, 3: 29–38.

GENDER AND MORTUARY RITUAL IN CHALCOLITHIC CYPRUS

DIANE BOLGER

Department of Archaeology
University of Edinburgh
Edinburgh EH1 1LT, Scotland
dbolger@arcl.ed.ac.uk

The adoption of new mortuary practices in Cyprus during the Late Chalcolithic period in Cyprus furnishes important evidence for changes in social relations during the course of the 3rd millennium B.C. In particular, the introduction of chamber tombs and the advent of group burials signal the emergence of new kinship structures that brought about fundamental changes in the relationships between men, women and children. These developments, which continued into the Bronze Age, took place against a backdrop of advancing social complexity that included the intensification of agriculture, the growth of trade and metallurgy, and the introduction of new technologies from the Anatolian mainland. In this paper I will consider the means by which new social definitions of gender were visibly underscored through transformations in the symbolic system associated with life-cycle rituals of birth and death, as well as the degree to which the social construction of gender during the Late Chalcolithic period, as perceived through the evidence of mortuary ritual, formed the basis for new gender constructs during the Early Bronze Age.

To judge from the evidence of prehistoric sites on the island, early sedentary society in Cyprus comprised relatively small, egalitarian groups of village-based subsistence-level cultivators. During the Chalcolithic period (ca. 3900–2500/2300 B.C.), however, social and economic factors such as population growth, surplus storage, intensive exploitation of copper resources, and the acquisition of foreign prestige items began to contribute to higher levels of social inequality. By the middle of the third millennium and continuing into the Bronze Age, Cyprus had begun to take part in a larger geographical and economic sphere, a development that can be inferred from new patterns of settlement, accelerated rates of craft specialization, trade in prestige items, and technological advances inspired and very likely introduced from abroad (Frankel, Webb and Eslick 1996). The latter include the introduction of plow agriculture, bronze working, and weaving. Increased production and greater levels of sedentism, developments that accompanied the intensification of agriculture, changed society in profound ways by fostering social divisions and creating a need for alliances. This, in turn, promoted the rise of interest groups and social hierarchies intent on exercising authority and maintaining control (Knapp 1993; Manning 1993). Although these attempts were not always successful (Peltenburg 1993), the overall long-term trend during the late 3rd and 2nd millennia was a shift from egalitarianism to hierarchy resulting ultimately in the rise of rich and powerful bureaucratic centers such as Kition and Enkomi.

It is against this backdrop of socio-economic change that I wish to investigate the evolution of funerary practices during the late 4th and 3rd millennia B.C. Grave goods of the Middle Chalcolithic, which include dentalium shell necklaces, cruciform pendants, figurines and painted pottery vessels, were replaced during the Late Chalcolithic by monochorome vessels of new morphological types, annular shell earrings, and beaded necklaces of faience and stone (Peltenburg 1991); and alongside the traditional Chalcolithic pit grave there appeared new mortuary structures, most notably the rock-cut chamber tomb, a type that continued on a larger, more elaborate scale during the Bronze Age. Such major changes in infrastructural and superstructural elements as have been outlined above must reflect equally significant changes in social relations and can be identified by patterns of mortuary differentiation (O'Shea 1984: 21).

Three Chalcolithic sites will be considered in detail: the settlement of Lemba-*Lakkous*, 4 km north of Paphos, which was occupied during the Middle and Late phases of the period, from roughly the mid-4th to mid-3rd millennium B.C.; the settlement of Kissonerga-*Mosphilia*, approximately 2 km north of Lemba, with a chronological range of nearly two millennia (from the Late Neolithic to the Philia phase of the Early Bronze Age); and the cemetery of Souskiou-*Vathyrkakas* near Palaepaphos (Kouklia), which falls entirely within the Middle Chalcolithic period (ca. 3500–3000 B.C.). The earliest phase of the Chalcolithic (ca. 3900–3500 B.C.), represented in the west of Cyprus at Kissonerga-*Mylouthkia*, Kissonerga-*Mosphilia* and Maa-*Paleokastro*, and at other sites around the island (e.g., Kalavasos-*Ayious*) will not be considered here due to the restricted nature of the early 4th millennium mortuary record. References to "Kissonerga" will henceforth refer only to Kissonerga-*Mosphilia*.

MORTUARY EVIDENCE AT LEMBA

With the exception of Souskiou (Christou 1989), graves excavated at Chalcolithic sites in Cyprus occur within the built environment and have not been found in separate cemeteries. Within the settlements, very few burials are to be found inside buildings (as was often the case during the Neolithic period), but the association between interments and buildings remains strong since interments are placed adjacent to exterior walls (fig. 1). This was certainly the case at Lemba-*Lakkous*, where 59 graves of Middle to Late Chalcolithic date were excavated during the 1970s and early 1980s by the Lemba Project under the direction of Edgar Peltenburg (Peltenburg and Project Members 1985). All graves uncovered at Lemba were pit graves, and the overwhelming majority comprised single inhumations of infants and children (fig. 2). Multiple inhumations are rare at Lemba, accounting for only three (roughly five percent) of the total graves excavated at the site (Table 1). Moreover, they occur only in certain combinations: either a single adult (male or female) is buried with a child or infant; or children are buried with other children. Adults, it seems, were never buried together and men, women and children were not interred in what might be interpreted as "family" groups.

Patterned behavior is also discernible in the construction techniques of some of the Lemba graves. In a recent reappraisal of the Lemba burials, Niklasson (1991) isolated "special features" in a small proportion of these graves (Table 2). Due to poor stratigraphical evidence and the lack of sufficient pottery, not all graves could be assigned to sub-periods within the Chalcolithic; those that could were attributable to Period 1 (Middle Chalcolithic, early phase) or to Period 3 (Late Chalcolithic). Special features include the construction of ridges in havara and pise around the rims of the pit graves (Graves 31, 32, 34); rings of stones around pit rims (Graves 29, 50); double pits (Graves 4, 5); a circular extension for a skull (Grave 45); linked networks of pit graves (Graves 12–15, 20); tubular apertures within graves, interpreted as possible libation holes (Graves 12, 13, 15); and capstones (Graves 48, 50). The pattern that emerges from the distribution of these unorthodox features is their exclusive association with infants and children during the Middle Chalcolithic period and their association with adults during the Late Chalcolithic.

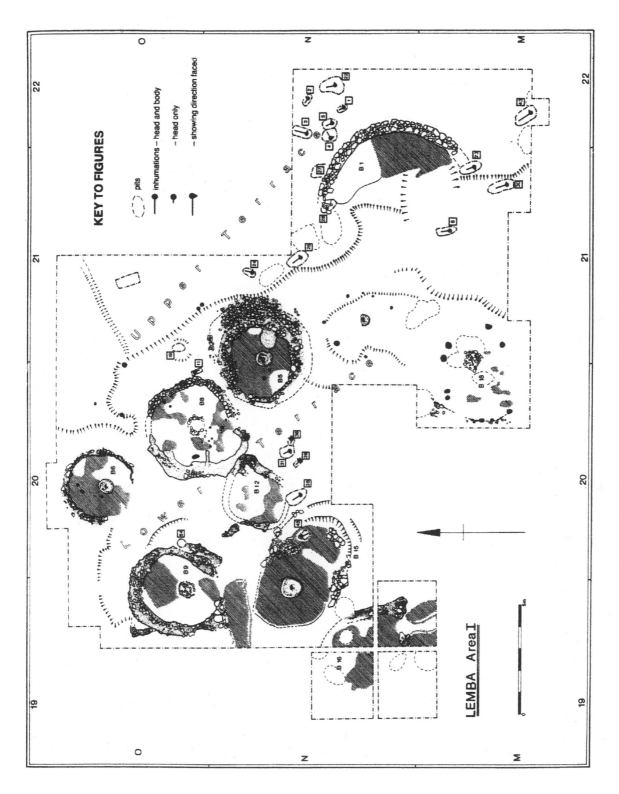

Figure 1. Plan of Lemba Area I showing buildings and adjacent graves.

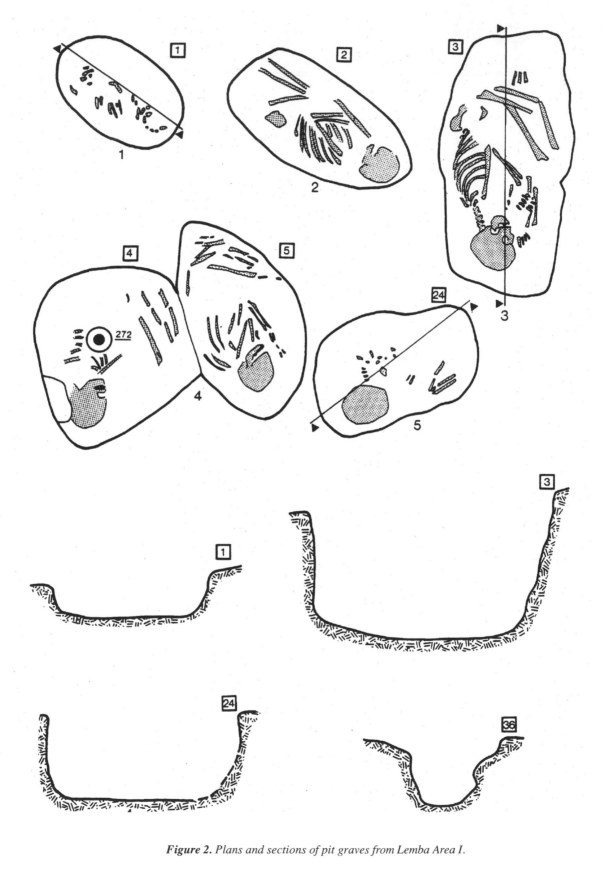

Figure 2. Plans and sections of pit graves from Lemba Area I.

Table 1. Mortuary Data from Lemba and Kissonerga.

BURIAL RECORD	LEMBA	KISSONERGA
Total Graves & Tombs	59	73
Total with Human Bone Analyzed	48	60
Total Graves with Single Inhumations	55	51
Total with Human Bone Analyzed	45	51
A) Single Adult	19	19
B) Single Child	26	32
Total Graves with Multiple Inhumations	3	9
Total with Human Bone Analyzed	3	9
A) Adult Males	--	1
B) Adult Females	--	2
C) Mutiple Childern	1	2
D) Adult Male + Adult Female	--	--
E) Adult Male + Infant/Child	1	--
F) Adult Female + Infant/Child	1	2
G)Adult Male + Adult Female + Infant/Child	--	2
Total Chamber Tombs		13
Chamber Tombs with Multiple Inhumations		7

Table 2. Special Features of Lemba Graves.

Period	Grave No.	Special Feature(s)	Interment(s)
1	31	havara ridge	infant
1	32	havara/pise ridge	child
1?	34	havara ridge/capstone	infant
1	45	niche for skull	child
1–2	4 & 5	double pit	infant, child
1–early3	12	aperture to upper pit	child
1–early3	13	aperture to upper pit	child
1–early3	14	joined upper pit	child
1–early3	15	aperture to upper pit	child
1–early3	20	joined upper pit	child
3	29	stones around pit rim	adult
3	48	capstones	adolescent
3	50	stones / capstones	adult

Table 3. Grave Goods from Lemba Burials.

Grave No.	Grave Goods	Probable Date	Interment
18	quern	?	adolescent
41	quern	?	child
38	RMP bowl	Middle Chalcolithic	infant
47	dentalium necklace	Middle Chalcolithic	infant
21	picrolite pendant	Middle Chalcolithic	child
44	picrolite pendant	Middle Chalcolithic	child
46	picrolite pendant	Middle Chalcolithic	child
20	picrolite figurine	M Chal/early L Chal	none

Grave goods, though limited in number, occur in similar patterns to those just mentioned. Infants and children were sometimes accompanied by querns, pottery, necklaces and pendants (Table 3). Querns were discovered in adolescent Grave 18 and over the head of a child in Grave 41. A pottery vessel was found in infant Grave 38. A dentalium shell necklace was found in Grave 47, which contained an infant burial. Picrolite pendants were unearthed in Graves 21, 44, and 46, all of which were child burials. In addition, one grave at Lemba contained a picrolite figurine. This was a cruciform figure from Grave 20, a rectangular pit cut into bedrock (similar in design but much smaller than the large shaft burials at Souskiou) and part of the children's burial complex under Building 2 (pictured in Peltenburg and Project Members 1985: fig. 41).

Although the dating of these graves with grave goods is not certain (Table 3 includes possible dates), the monochrome bowl in Grave 38 is a Middle Chalcolithic type, and Grave 20 (part of the burial complex under Building 2), according to stratigraphic evidence, cannot be later than the early part of the Late Chalcolithic. Moreover, at Kissonerga, where relative dating is clearer, dentalium shell necklaces and cruciform pendants occur in graves of Middle Chalcolithic, rather than Late Chalcolithic, date. In sum, mortuary evidence at Lemba strongly suggests that only children were buried with grave goods, and that those burials fall early on within the Chalcolithic sequence. Deceased adults do not appear to have been furnished with grave goods during either phase of the period.

FROM PIT GRAVE TO CHAMBER TOMB: MORTUARY EVIDENCE AT KISSONERGA

Seventy-three graves and tombs have been recorded at Kissonerga; these date to the Middle and Late Chalcolithic periods and collectively span more than half a millennium. Although most burials were incorporated into simple pit graves like those at Lemba, there is a greater variety of structural types (see chapter 4 in Peltenburg and Project Members 1998 for a full discussion of the types). Chief among them is the chamber tomb, which makes its initial appearance at Kissonerga during Period 4 (Late Chalcolithic period). There are a total of 13 chamber tombs, of which seven contained multiple inhumations. Two of the tombs (Tombs 505 and 515) comprised group burials consisting of an adult male, an adult female and one or more children. From their closely intertwined positions (e.g., Tomb 505, fig. 4) it would appear that the deceased were buried at the same time and do not represent separate, successive interments. The burial of adults and children together in a single tomb represents a marked departure from customs of the Middle Chalcolithic period.

Differential treatment of adults and children, witnessed at Lemba, occurs at Kissonerga as well, although it manifests itself in a somewhat different manner. According to Peltenburg, the low proportion of adult burials at the site constitutes one of the most remarkable features of the Kissonerga mor-

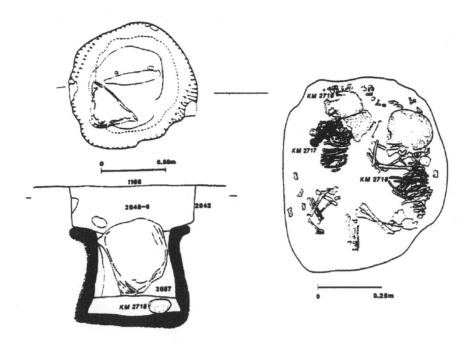

Figure 3. Plan and section of Kissonerga-Mosphilia *Grave 563.*

tuary population (see fig. 4.5 in Peltenburg and Project Members 1998). He further proposes that adults were buried extramurally in remote cemeteries such as Souskiou-*Vathyrkakas*. By the Late Chalcolithic, however, this trend had reversed itself, and mortuary data signal the return to a complete age structure in the burial population (chapter 4 in Peltenburg and Project Members 1998). Peltenburg regards this change as a "major ideological shift" between Middle and late Chalcolithic Kissonerga. The inclusion of adult burials within the built environment at Late Chalcolithic Kissonerga is in keeping with the evidence at Lemba Period 3 (Late Chalcolithic) where special structural features previously reserved for children were transferred to adults. These and other related phenomena adumbrate a fundamental shift in attitudes toward adults and children within society as a whole.

RITUALS OF BIRTH AND DEATH : THE CEMETERY AT SOUSKIOU

The cemetery of Souskiou-*Vathyrkakas* near Kouklia village is situated on the edge of a plateau overlooking the Dhiarrizos River and is comprised of deep rectangular shafts cut into the bedrock. Due to the richness of their associated burial goods, the Souskiou tombs have been targets of repeated illicit digging, but excavations by Iliffe and Mitford in 1951, Maier in 1972, and the Department of Antiquities (directed by Demos Christou) in 1972 and from 1991–97 (fig. 5), have yielded a great deal of information on this important cemetery site of the Middle Chalcolithic period (for a preliminary report, see Christou 1989). Multiple burials of adults in deep shaft-like tombs represent a significant departure from funerary traditions elsewhere on the island. Moreover, the unusually rich and unorthodox character of grave goods in a distinct and remote cemetery distinguishes the site as something extraordinary. A particularly spectacular example from the most recent campaign by the Department of Antiquities was the discovery of an anthropomorphic pottery vessel in the form of a pregnant female, now on display in Room 1 of the Cyprus Museum in Nicosia. It was found in a multiple burial of an adult together with three small children and a possible adolescent (unfortunately, the sex of the adult could not be determined due to its poorly preserved state). The final report of the Department of Antiquities

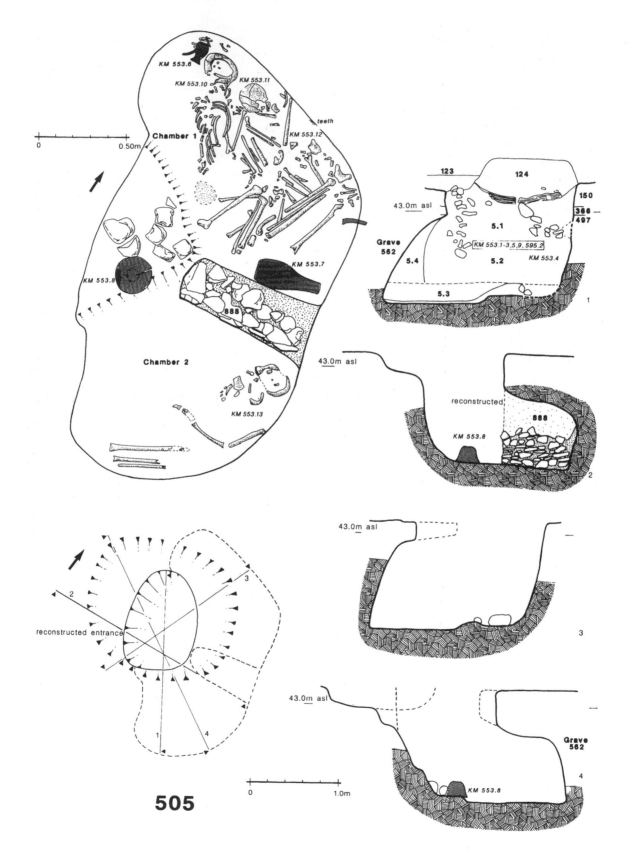

Figure 4. *Plan and section of Kissonerga-*Mosphilia *Tomb 505.*

excavations at Souskiou is currently in preparation, and not all of the human skeletal material has been fully analyzed, but preliminary examination suggests much higher proportions of adult inhumations than we have seen at Lemba and Kissonerga. Many of these appear to be adult females, with or without accompanying children.

BIRTHING RITUALS AT KISSONERGA AND LEMBA

Figurines of similar design to the Souskiou anthropomorphic vessel are known from other contemporary sites in Cyprus, but they have usually been recovered in disturbed contexts or as the unprovenanced spoils of illicit digging. The exception to this rule is the site of Kissonerga, where 19 figurines of stone and pottery were found in a ceremonial pit together with pottery vessels, stone tools, a triton shell and a ceramic building model (Peltenburg and Project Members 1991). One of the most important finds, a Red-on-White ware pottery figurine seated on a stool in the act of labor, clearly demonstrates that these objects were connected to birthing rituals (fig. 6, KM 1451; the child, painted in red, emerges between her legs). A second figurine in Red-on-White ware was hollow and may actually have been an anthropomorphic vessel like the one from Souskiou (fig. 6, KM 1475). Variations in attributes of form and wear suggest that the stone figurines were held or clutched in the hand, while the ceramic examples were free-standing and had restricted areas of wear indicating their possible use as didactic models in puberty rituals (chapter 4 in Peltenburg and Project Members 1991).

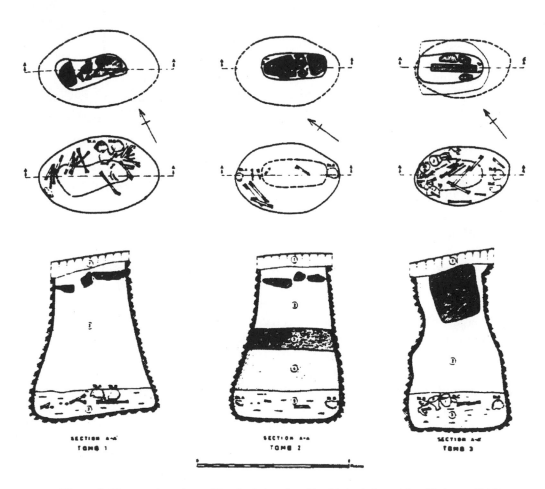

Figure 5. Plans and sections of Tombs 1–3 at Souskiou-Vathyrkakas. After Christou (1989).

Birthing symbols may also be represented in the picrolite anthropomorphic pendants that occasionally formed part of dentalium shell necklaces in Middle Chalcolithic graves (Peltenburg 1992). These necklaces are associated with women, as indicated around the neck of the Kisonerga birthing figurine (fig. 6, KM1451) and children, as in Grave 563 at Kissonerga (fig. 3). From the relative scarcity of these ornaments in graves, we can infer that they were regarded as luxury items. Of the 73 graves excavated at Kissonerga, for example, only a handful contained picrolites. Similar ratios have been recorded at other sites as well: Lemba yielded picrolites in only five of its 59 graves, and at Souskiou only one of the five tombs excavated by the Department of Antiquities in the 1970s contained picrolites (that ratio has not increased significantly as the result of the most recent excavations at the site). The tomb in question, Tomb 3 (fig. 5), yielded 20 picrolite pendants, 16 of which were the anthropomorphic cruciform variety; they were found in association with the burials of three adult females and an eight year old child. Similar patterns recur at Kissonerga and Lemba. To date, no picrolite pendant has been found in the burial of an adult male, and the repeated association of picrolites with certain women and children suggests restricted, differential access to the procurement of raw picrolite and the possession of picrolite ornaments among the Middle Chalcolithic populations of Cyprus. Moreover, it suggests that women at this time were centrally involved in their production and exchange and thus played important economic roles.

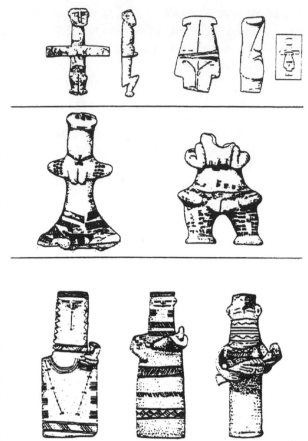

Figure 6. Anthropomorphic figurines from Chalcolithic and Bronze Age Cyprus. Top row: picrolite (LL 300, left; LL 152, right). Center row: Red-on-White figurines (KM 1451, left; KM 1475, right). Bottom row: Early Bronze Age Figurines (Lapithos, left; unprovenanced, center and right). After Morris (1985).

The deliberate breakage of several of the Kissonerga figurines and the careful placement of all the objects into a ceremonial pit together with burnt debris are ritual acts that signify the end of a long tradition of birthing ritual. Anthropomorphic figurines are not found in Late Chalcolithic contexts at Lemba or Kissonerga, nor are the birth pendants and cruciform picrolite figurines with bent knees that Peltenburg has argued constitute a continuation of the same symbol set and should likewise be regarded as seated birthing figures (Peltenburg 1992). The end of birthing symbolism, as we have seen, coincides with changes in mortuary ritual that involved a reduction of grave goods and special architectural features in child and infant burials, and with a shift from single inhumations to group burials of men, women and children. Prior to the Chalcolithic period, such as the well-known intra-mural burials at the Aceramic Neolithic site of Khirokitia, the deceased were normally buried under the floors of buildings. As only a single burial was usually allocated to each structure, it appears unlikely that burials took place during the Neolithic according to family groups (Niklasson 1991: 167). As we have already seen, the change to group burials appears to have taken place much later, i.e., sometime around the middle of the 3rd millennium B.C.

In attempting to sum up what we have seen so far regarding the development of mortuary ritual during the Middle Chalcolithic period, the following patterns emerge: the high proportions of children and infants in intra-settlment burials; the segregation of children from adults in intra-site burials; the predominance of single inhumations in pit graves; and the possibility of separate, remote cemeteries for adults; the segregation of male and female adults; the linking of "special" architectural features and grave goods with children; and the association of women and children with fertility and birthing symbolism, in general, and picrolite figurines and pendants, in particular. These practices changed dramatically during the Late Chalcolithic with the introduction of chamber tombs, the increased incidence of multiple inhumation, the decline of birthing symbols, and the first recorded instances of group burials comprising women, men and children. The joint burial of adults and children during the Late Chalcolithic signifies a dramatic ideological shift that can be understood only within the larger perspective of changing socio-economic conditions.

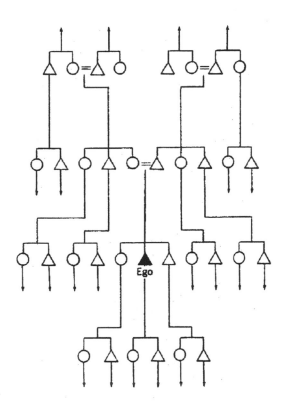

△ MALE

○ FEMALE

⚌ IS MARRIED TO

│ IS DESCENDED FROM

⌐ IS THE SIBLING OF

● FEMALE EGO WHOSE KINSMEN ARE BEING SHOWN

▲ MALE EGO WHOSE KINSMEN ARE BEING SHOWN

Figure 7. Diagram of Kinship Reckoned by Bilateral Descent. After Harris (1971).

PATTERNS OF KINSHIP AND DESCENT

Perhaps the most significant social development suggested by the changes in funerary practices outlined above is the emergence of new kinship structures, since kinship, in addition to organizing the relations of production, constitutes the basis for ideologies and other elements of superstructure (Peletz 1995: 353). In ethnographic accounts of pre-industrial societies, a major distinction is drawn between kindreds and lineages, with the former characteristic of nomadic or semi-nomadic hunter-gatherers and horticulturalists and the latter ascribed to infrastructural changes associated with increasing sedentism, agricultural intensification, and social complexity.

The principal structural feature of kindreds is the unrestricted span and depth of bilateral reckoning in which there is no uniform principle for limiting the extension of the kinship circle (fig. 7). Similarly, there is no possibility for large scale social segmentation, as only ego's siblings have the same relationship to kindred as ego. This kinship structure is normally found in societies that are not agriculturally based and where corporate ownership of or rights to land are not central to economic production. Egalitarian societies, in which there is little social hierarchy and minimal ownership of property or wealth, fall into this category. Divisions within the social structure of egalitarian groups normally occur along lines of age and/or gender such as age sets and the sexual division of labor. Also characteristic of kindreds are communal rites of passage such as those that

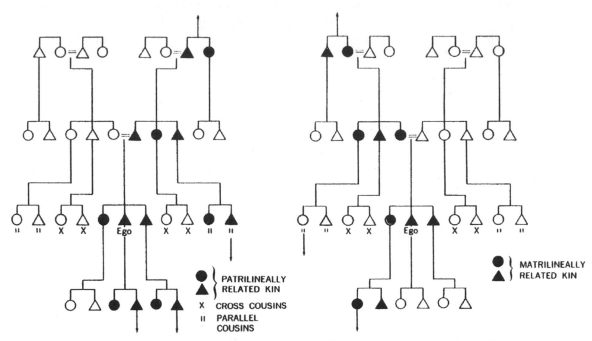

Figure 8. Diagram of Kinship Reckoned by Unilineal Descent. After Harris (1971).

accompany birth, marriage, and death—rituals that help to promote and maintain group identity and cohesion.

Lineages, in contrast, are groups related vertically by descent from a common ancestor. In patrilineages and matrilineages, membership in a kinship group is reckoned along a single line of descent, either paternal or maternal (fig. 8). Here, the cultural restrictions used to define "kin" lead to group segmentation (lineages and sub-lineages), which may pose threats to group integrity. Potential divisions within society are to some degree resolved by affinities, or marriage links, which are important for creating economic and social bonds and for maintaining group cohesion. Marriage thus takes on new functional importance as the far-ranging network of social relations characteristic of kindreds is replaced as an organizing principle by smaller, domestically differentiated groups or "families" consisting of husbands, wives and children.

The emergence of lineages in Cyprus is strongly suggested by the evolution of mortuary practices during the 3rd millennium: the gradual phasing out of single inhumations and burials according to age sets (e.g., multiple child burials), the appearance of chamber tombs, the advent of communal burials of mixed ages and sexes, the declining attention paid to children in mortuary rituals, and the transformations of birthing symbolism within life-cycle rituals (Bolger 1996). Further evidence of close vertical links in kinship structures is suggested by unprecedented mortuary features such as the tube-like apertures in the Late Chalcolithic children's burial complex below Building 2 at Lemba, which were apparently used to maintain contact between the living and the dead. Specifically, it has been proposed that these tubular shafts may have been used as libation holes as part of recurring funerary rituals (Niklasson in Peltenburg and Project Members 1985: 244). The reinforcement of social bonds between adults and children suggested by these acts, as well as by the joint burial of adults and children elsewhere during the Late Chalcolithic, strongly suggests that children as well as adults were affected by advances in social complexity and that changes in treatment and status of children were bound up with changing gender constructs that exercised an equally marked impact upon the relationships between women and men.

GENDER AND SOCIETY IN PREHISTORIC CYPRUS

Engendering the prehistoric past allows us to explore the dynamics of social relations and to chart some of the pathways to social complexity at the microscale level, rather than at a broader, systemic level. Analyses of complex society which address developments at the systemic level alone (whether emphasis be given to indigenous models such as Knapp 1993, Manning 1993, or to the transfer of technologies from abroad, as in Frankel, Webb and Eslick 1996) often fail to consider the importance of gender constructs, domestic organization and personal relations in proposed trajectories of social change. By correlating changes in mortuary practices and kinship structures to advances in socio-economic complexity, we are able to consider some of the ways in which the roles of men, women and children may have been fundamentally transformed.

If we consider the evidence discussed in the preceding pages, there would appear to be at least four ways in which the emergence of lineages and the intensification of agriculture during the 3rd millennium may have altered gender constructs and parent-child relations by redefining the relations of production and reproduction:

1) Changes in modes of economic production would have had an impact upon gender-based divisions of labor by increasing women's input within the domestic environment. Ethnographic studies on present-day agricultural societies (e.g., Boserup 1970; Sanday 1973; Ember 1983) demonstrate a decline in women's contribution to primary economic production in societies where intensive agriculture is practiced. Ember (1983), citing time allocation data gathered by Minge-Klevana (1980) on simple and intensive agricultural societies around the world, concluded that adult women in intensive agricultural societies average 10.8 working hours per day, as opposed to 6.7 in simple agricultural societies; and that women in intensive agricultural societies spend more time working indoors than women in simple agricultural societies (5.9 vs. 2.9 hours per day). In both types of society, women spend an average 4.5 hours per day working outdoors, so outdoor work doesn't decrease—rather, indoor work markedly increases.

   Ember's findings contradict the notion that "biological" reasons are causal factors in the male/female division of labor among intensive agriculturalists. Men do not take to the plow and women to the home because of men's greater physical strength or women's "natural" role as mothers. Rather, the division of labor along male/female lines is a widespread cultural solution to the problem of increased workloads and accelerated birthrates that accompanied the adoption of more sophisticated agricultural techniques.

2) Changing means and strategies of attaining wealth, status and prestige, as well as reconfigurations within the overall structure of economic exchange, may have contributed to a decline in female status (Bolger 1994). This is suggested by the end of personal exchange networks such as the picrolite networks of the Middle Chalcolithic, which are likely to have been organized and controlled by women. As the relations of production began to be reorganized in terms of membership in corporate kinship groups, personal exchange networks were replaced by corporate control of resources, with the family, rather than individuals, as chief producers and beneficiaries. Moreover, as inheritance within lineages is transmitted vertically, through paternal or maternal lines, it restricts access to material wealth, and circumscribes other forms of economic and social privilege. If, on the basis of cross-cultural data, we may infer that patrilineages were operative in prehistoric Cyprus and, following Frankel, that residency was virilocal (Frankel 1978), men would have enjoyed greater access to social and economic prerogatives, and women would have been increasingly restricted in their ability to own or inherit property and other forms of wealth. It should be noted, however, that the emergence of a more highly stratified society during the later phases of the Bronze Age is associated with the rise to power of powerful and wealthy elites that included women as well as men.

3) Ethnographic research has shown that changes in modes of kinship and production can be correlated to changes in the relations of reproduction (Peletz 1995: 353–54 with references). These approaches emphasize the social context of reproduction by distinguishing its biological and cultural aspects (Holy 1996: 56). While only the mother-child relationship is needed for successful biological reproduction of the species once a woman has successfully been fertilized, the reproduction of individuals capable of full social life involves recognition by society at large. Cross-cultural analysis of modern pre-state societies has shown that in almost every society a person is eligible to become a fully fledged member of the community only if he or she has a socially recognized mother and father. In this way, the family becomes the only acceptable means by which the necessity for the replacement of mortal members of a social group is met.

  The importance attached to the social context of reproduction can often be discerned in the archaeological record through iconographic portrayals of women and children. Olsen (1998), for example, has recently proposed a sharp distinction in gender constructs between Minoan and Myceanean society, with Minoan iconography failing to associate women with children and Mycenaean iconography stressing mother-child relations. She concludes that "this represents, if not a fundamental difference in gender construction between Minoan and Mycenaean societies, at the very least a fundamentally different approach to a gendered social role (Olsen 1998: 390)." In third millennium Cyprus, women's reproductive roles were re-defined within the context of emerging family structures (Bolger 1996). Moreover, restrictions on female sexual behavior, which often accompany new social demands involving the restriction of kin and legitimization of heirs, probably became more stringent as society attained higher levels of sedentarization. These and other changing definitions of "appropriate" social behavior are linked to the intensification of agriculture and the corporate ownership of land, which require a means of passing on inheritance to socially recognized heirs.

4) The need to establish paternity and to recognize offspring socially has an impact upon the role of children as well. With the emergence of lineages and intensification of agriculture, reproductive strategies are likely to have evolved in accordance with newly emerging forces of economic production. In agricultural societies, children are valued as laborers and as future partners in marriage with members of other corporate groups. Yet there is a tendency at the same time to regard children as commodities, reducing their status in much the same way as that of women. In Cyprus, this impact can perhaps be measured by the end of birthing symbolism and the decline in numbers of grave goods associated with child burials during the Late Chalcolithic. Unwanted children may have been put to death, as infanticide in traditional societies lacking adequate methods of birth control usually occurs during conditions of economic exigency; infanticide can also result from unwanted pregnancies due to illegitimacy (Mays 1993). While infant burials, including neonates, form a substantial proportion of the Chalcolithic mortuary record, we have no way of knowing whether these deaths occurred naturally or deliberately nor do we have evidence on the sexes of the deceased infants that figure so largely in graves of Chalcolithic date. Outside Cyprus, several cases of infanticide have been identified in the archaeological record (Mays 1993; Smith and Kahila 1992), but they have thus far failed to establish sex-linked biases, owing largely to the difficulty of sexing infant skeletons. Ethnographic evidence has shown, however, that infanticide is more likely to be practiced on females in cultures where women's economic input is undervalued and female status is low (Smith and Smith 1994).

  But children do more than simply reflect changing social constructs. As "learners and practicers of gender" (Deverenski 1997) they are the repositories and transmitters of appropriate gender behavior. Through processes of enculturation, children learn to imitate and assimilate the values of their elders; later, as adults, they will pass those values on to the next generation. Children and childhood, frequently marginalized in the archaeological literature, are fundamental to our understanding of changing gender constructs since they contribute actively to the transmission of gender ideologies. Engendering the prehistoric past, therefore, requires an appreciation of children as agents in cultural change and the "archaeology of children and childhood," long neglected by scholars, needs to be put at the forefront of future archaeological research (cf. Moore and Scott 1997).

GENDER AND MORTUARY RITUAL DURING THE BRONZE AGE

While group burials are first attested in the Late Chalcolithic period, it was only later, during the Early Bronze Age, that the practice of burying the deceased in large communal cemeteries separate from their associated settlements became standard mortuary practice (fig. 9). The appearance of larger burial populations within tombs is a trend that continues into the Middle and Late Cypriot periods and may indicate the expression of longer-term descent relations during the course of the later 3rd and 2nd millennia (Keswani 1989: 500). Unfortunately, there is very little evidence concerning the human populations buried in these tombs as most were excavated early in the last century prior to the adoption of modern excavation methods. These early campaigns did not, as a rule, gather information on sexes or ages of the deceased, nor did they focus on health issues such as stress, diet, and disease. On the other hand, there is good evidence for construction techniques and architecture of the tombs, as well as for the position and alignment of bodies and the range and quantities of associated grave goods. While such evidence has been used to support models of low or incipient socio-economic differentiation (Keswani 1989; Davies 1997), little scholarly attention has been focussed upon the kinship structures implied by the number, size, chronology and arrangement of tombs within these large mortuary complexes.

Cemeteries of the Early Bronze Age consisted of large networks of chamber tombs cut into bedrock and furnished with long rectangular *dromoi*, limestone slabs used as blocking stones, and single or multiple burial chambers (fig. 10). Although these tombs are larger and more elaborate than their earlier counterparts and were used over longer periods of time, they can be linked in a general sense to the earlier chamber tombs from Kissonerga. Ancestral links are ritually reinforced by the repeated use and re-use of tombs over many generations, presumably by members of the same kinship group. Grave goods, such as spiral earrings, annular shell pendants, and biconical spindle whorls, also recall those from burials at Kissonerga Periods 4–5 (Peltenburg 1991). Dikaios, who excavated five tombs of the Philia culture at Philia-*Vasiliko* between 1942 and 1951, noted that some of the tombs had been reused and that previous occupants had been swept "unceremoniously" to the back of the chamber; the reuse of tombs gradually became a common custom, leading to multiple burials (Dikaios 1962: 160–65).

At Vounous near Bellapais, excavations by Dikaios, Schaeffer and Stewart during the 1930s revealed a total of 164 tombs of EC–MC date (Dikaios 1940; Schaeffer 1936; Stewart and Stewart 1950). They are similar in architectural form to those of Philia but appear to have involved more complex mortuary rituals. According to Stewart, the dead at Vounous were laid out in orderly arrangements, with the first burials placed in the west of chamber, to the right of the entrance, and later in back, with respect maintained for previous dead. Finds in these tombs, including bronze spiral earrings, annular shell pendants and incized, biconical spindle whorls, once again link these tombs to the final phases of Kissonerga, but the size of this cemetery, the re-use of tombs over many generations, and the degree of reverence shown for ancestral dead, suggest the emergence of social groups with more sharply defined communal interests.

In some of the more elaborate tombs at Vounous, the deceased were accompanied by figurines and coroplastic scenes that reflect some of the emerging gender constructs discussed above. These include

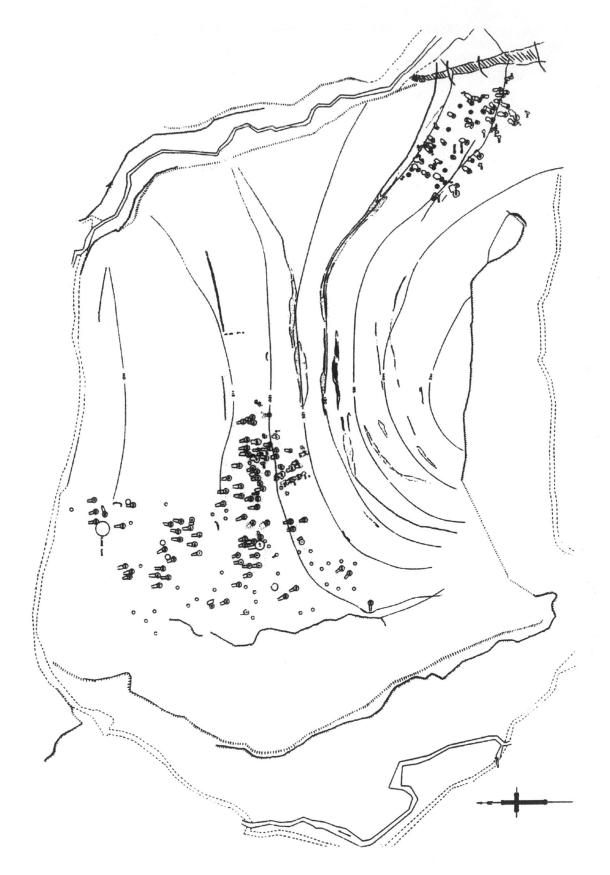

Figure 9. Plan of the Early Bronze Age Cemetery at Bellapais-Vounous. After Stewart (1950).

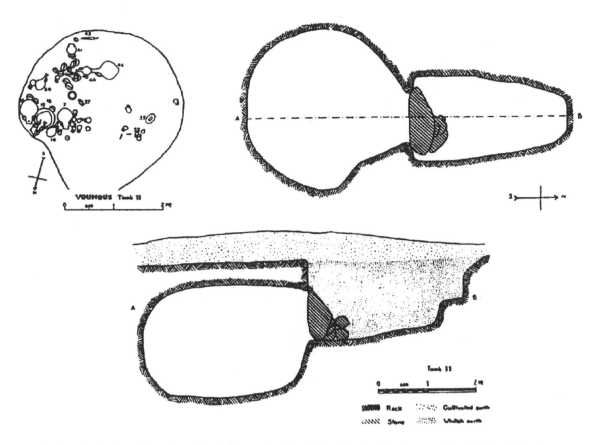

*Figure 10. Plan and section of Early Bronze Age Tomb 11 at Bellapais-*Vounous. *After Dikaios (1940).*

adult female figures holding or nursing children (fig. 6), men and women as husband-and-wife pairs, and complex scenes of everyday activities, with divisions of labor along gender lines sometimes in evidence (described in detail in Morris 1985: chapter 3 and Karageorghis 1991: chapter 3). While serving as indicators of increasing levels of social hierarchy and of sex-linked divisions within society, these compositions underscore the collective nature of productive labor and locate the processes of production and reproduction firmly within the context of family and household groups. Recent discoveries of figurines in settlement contexts at Marki-*Alonia*, dated to EC III, broaden the function and meaning of these objects by indicating their use among the living as well as their burial with the dead (Frankel and Webb 1996: 187–88).

As symbols of "ideal" social behavior, these images of women and men laboring harmoniously together may, in fact, have served to mask underlying tensions that had begun to surface as the result of changes in traditional social and economic roles. Even the concept of complementarity, which connotes a relative degree of equality between the sexes, embraces categories of difference and alterity. In this paper I have tried to show some of the ways in which the social reconstruction of gender, which becomes highly visible in material culture at the end of the Early Bronze Age, can be traced to indigenous social transformations that first began to manifest themselves during the Middle Chalcolithic period. Within an overall framework of advancing social complexity in Cyprus during the 3rd millennium B.C., it is significant that changes in gender constructs first emerged within a social milieu that was still in other respects relatively egalitarian, and that they appear to have anticipated the emergence of state-level society on the island by a millennium or more.

ACKNOWLEDGMENTS

I would like to thank Demos Christou for granting me permission to refer to unpublished material from Souskiou-*Vathyrkakas* and Eddie Peltenburg for allowing me to make use of mortuary data from Kissonerga-*Mosphilia* prior to the publication of the final site report. Dorothy Lunt very kindly supplied me with information on aging and sexing of skeletal material from Kissonerga and Souskiou.

REFERENCES

Bolger, D.
1994   Engendering Cypriot Archaeology: Women's Roles and Statuses before the Bronze Age. *Opuscula Atheniensia* 20: 9–17.
1996   Figurines, Fertility and the Emergence of Complex Society in Prehistoric Cyprus. *Current Anthropology* 37.2: 365–73.

Boserup, E.
1970   *Woman's Role in Economic Development*. London: Allen and Unwin.

Christou, D.
1989   The Chalcolithic Cemetery 1 at Souskiou-*Vathyrkakas*. Pp. 82–94 *in Early Society in Cyprus*, ed. E. Peltenburg. Edinburgh: Edinburgh University.

Davies, P.
1997   Mortuary Practice in Prehistoric Bronze Age Cyprus: Problems and Potential. *Report of the Department of Antiquities of Cyprus*: 11–26.

Deverenski, J.S.
1997   Engendering Children, Engendering Archaeology. Pp. 192–202 in *Invisible Peoples and Processes: Writing Gender and Childhood into European Archaeology*, eds. J. Moore and E. Scott. London and New York: Leicester University.

Dikaios, P.
1940   *Excavations at Vounous-Bellapais in Cyprus, 1931–32*. Oxford: Society of Antiquaries of London.
1962   The Stone Age of Cyprus. Pp. 1–204 in *The Swedish Cyprus Expedition* IV.1A: *The Stone Age and the Early Bronze Age in Cyprus*. Lund: Swedish Cyprus Expedition.

Ember, C.R.
1983   The Relative Decline in Women's Contribution to Agriculture with Intensification. *American Anthropologist* 85: 285–304.

Frankel, D.
1978   Pottery Decoration as an Indicator of Social relationships: a Prehistoric Cypriot Example. Pp. 147–60 in *Art in Society*, eds. M. Greenhalgh and J. V. S. Megaw. London: Duckworth.

Frankel, D., and Webb, J.
1996   *Marki-Alonia: An Early and Middle Bronze Age Town in Cyprus. Excavations 1990–1994*. Studies in Mediterranean Archaeology 123:1. Jonsered: Åströms.

Frankel, D.; Webb, J.; and Eslick, C.
1996   Anatolia and Cyprus in the Third Millennium B.C.E.: A Speculative Model of Interaction. Pp. 37–50 *in Cultural Interaction in the Near East*, ed. G. Bunnens. Louvain: Abr-Nahrain Suppl. Series, Vol. 5, Department of Classics and Archaeology, University of Melbourne. Melbourne: University of Melbourne.

Harris, M.
1971   *Culture, Man and Nature: An Introduction to General Anthropology*. New York: Thomas W. Crowell.

Holy, L.
1996   *Anthropological Perspectives on Kinship*. Chicago: Pluto.

Karageorghis, V.
1991   *The Coroplastic Art of Ancient Cyprus*. Vol. 1: *Chalcolithic - Late Cypriot I*. Nicosia: A.G. Leventis Foundation.

Keswani, P.
1989   Mortuary Ritual and Social Hierarchy in Bronze Age Cyprus. Unpublished Ph.D. Dissertation, University of Michigan.

Knapp, A.B.
1993   Social Complexity: Incipience, Emergence and Development on Prehistoric Cyprus. *Bulletin of the American Schools of Oriental Research* 292: 85–106.

Manning, S.W.
1993   Prestige, Distinction and Competition: the Anatomy of Socioeconomic Complexity in Fourth to Second Millennium B.C.E. Cyprus. *Bulletin of the American Schools of Oriental Research* 292: 35–58.

Mays, S.
1993   Infanticide in Roman Britain. *Antiquity* 67: 883–88.
Minge-Klevana, W.
1980   Does Labor Time Decrease with Industrialization? A Survey of Time Allocation Studies. *Current Anthropology* 21: 279–87.
Moore, J., and Scott, E., eds.
1997   *Invisible People and Processes: Writing Gender and Childhood into European Archaeology.* London and New York: Leicester University.
Morris, D.
1985   *The Art of Ancient Cyprus.* Oxford: Phaidon.
Niklasson, K.
1991   *Early Prehistoric Burials in Cyprus.* Studies In Mediterranean Archaeology 96. Jonsered: Astrom.
Olsen, B.A.
1998   Women, Children and the Family in the Late Aegean Bronze Age: Differences in Minoan and Mycenaean Constructions of Gender. *World Archaeology* 29, 3: 80–92.
O'Shea, J. M.
1984   *Mortuary Variability: An Archaeological Investigation.* Orlando: Academic.
Peletz, M.G.
1995   Kinship Studies in Late Twentieth-Century Anthropology. *Annual Review of Anthropology* 24: 343–72.
Peltenburg, E.
1991   Kissonerga-*Mosphilia*: A Major Chalcolithic Site in Cyprus. *Bulletin of the American Schools of Oriental Research* 282/283: 17–35.
1992   Birth Pendants in Life and Death: Evidence from Kissonerga Grave 563. Pp. 27–36 in *Studies in Honour of Vassos Karageorghis*, ed. G.C. Ioannides. Nicosia: Society of Cypriot Studies.
1993   Settlement Continuity and Resistance to Complexity in Cyprus, ca. 4500–2500 B.C.E. *Bulletin of the American Schools of Oriental Research* 292: 9–23.
Peltenburg, E. and Project Members
1985   *Lemba Archaeological Project(Cyprus) I: Excavations at Lemba-Lakkous, 1976–1983.* Studies in Mediterranean Archaeology 70:1. Göteborg: Åströms.
1991   *Lemba Archaeological Project(Cyprus) II.2: A Ceremonial Area at Kissonerga.* Studies in Mediterranean Archaeology 70: 3. Jonsered: Åströms.
1998   *Lemba Archaeological Project (Cyprus) II.1A: Excavations at Kissonerga- Mosphilia, 1979–1992.* Studies in Mediterranean Archaeology 70: 2. Jonsered: Åströms.
Sanday, P.
1973   Toward a Theory of the Status of Women. *American Anthropologist* 75: 1682–1700.
Schaeffer, C.F.A.
1936   *Missions en Chypre.* Paris: Geuthner.
Smith, E.A., and Smith, S.A.
1994   Inuit Sex-ratio Variation: Population Control, Ethnographic Error or Sex Bias. *Current Anthropology* 35: 595–624.
Smith, P., and Kahila, G.
1992   Identification of Infanticide in Archaeological Sites: a Case Study from the Late Roman-Early Byzantine Periods at Askalon, Israel. *Journal of Archaeological Science* 19: 667–75.
Stewart, E., and Stewart, J.
1950   *Vounous 1937–38: Field Report on the Excavations Sponsored by the British School of Archaeology at Athens.* Lund: Gleerup.

ENGENDERING THE BUILT ENVIRONMENT: HOUSEHOLD AND COMMUNITY IN PREHISTORIC BRONZE AGE CYPRUS

JENNIFER M. WEBB

Department of Archaeology
School of Archaeological and Historical Studies,
La Trobe University
Bundoora, Victoria 3083, Australia
jenny.webb@latrobe.edu.au

The household is a fundamental element of social organization and the domain in which behavioral relationships such as those of age and gender are established, maintained and reproduced. Household archaeology, if it is to be effective in the real world of the prehistoric Cypriot Bronze Age, needs to develop strategies to overcome problems of recognition arising from the density of occupation and the conjoined nature of the final architectural systems at many sites, high rates of artefact curation and the differential effects of discard and abandonment behavior. A relatively large exposure of Early Cypriot III/Middle Cypriot I domestic architecture is now available at Marki-Alonia. This allows us to take up the challenge of recognizing gender and other culturally determined codes of behavior in architectural remains and residual household assemblages. This paper examines methodological and other issues involved in understanding the organization and use of built space and the social relations of production in households and settlements from the remote past.

> Microscale archaeology of the social relations of production in prehistory—the study of residential architecture and household organization and production—is an essential prerequisite for an engendered prehistory and, I would argue, any kind of social archaeology. (Tringham 1991a: 125)

Gender is a major concern of post-processual archaeology. Numerous studies have shown the cultural construction of gender to be a fundamental structuring principle in human behavior, a form of patterned asymmetry with visible material and ideological correlates in the archaeological record (Gero and Conkey 1991; Walde and Willows 1991; Claassen 1992; di Leonardo 1991). Feminist theory has also had a significant impact on archaeological theory and gender issues within the archaeological workplace (Yellen 1983; Gero 1983, 1985, 1988, 1993; Wylie 1991, 1993; Kramer and Stark 1988; Claassen 1994; Nixon 1994; Beck and Head 1990; du Cros and Smith 1993; Webb and Frankel 1995a, 1995b: Balme and Beck 1995; Hays-Gilpin and Whitley 1997; Moore and Scott 1997). Despite an exponential increase in the number of books and articles devoted to the subject, however, explicit recognition of gender relationships in the remote past has proved elusive.

In Cypriot prehistory, gender and the social construction of gender roles and statuses have recently become the subject of explicit debate (Åström 1992; Bolger 1992, 1993, 1994, 1996, 1997; Frankel 1993a; 1997; Peltenburg 1994; Hamilton 1994; in press; Knapp and Meskell 1997). To date, these studies have drawn almost exclusively upon the enigmatic database of anthropomorphic figurines and modeled compositions. One current approach sees these as reflecting a radical re-ordering of gender relations from the Chalcolithic to the Bronze Age, with a significant loss of status for Bronze Age Cypriot women. Hence Peltenburg's reassessment of the Vounous model, which argues that the compositional structure of the bowl reflects a hierarchy expressive of a new social ideology, resulting from a restructuring of power and social conventions during the Early Cypriot transition (Peltenburg 1994). The one apparently female participant in the scene, on this view, stands at the base of the hierarchical construct, symbolizing prosperity, fertility and vitality—while the 18 remaining figures engage in the "adult world of decision-making males" (Peltenburg 1994: 160). Bolger (1993, 1994, 1996) also argues for a fundamental alteration of gender constructs within the trajectory of social and political change accompanying the development of social complexity in Cyprus. More specifically, she suggests that the patriarchal family emerged during the Bronze Age, leading to an ideological decline in female status and the creation of structures "in which women's roles were increasingly restricted and social and economic inequalities became institutionalised" (Bolger 1996: 371).

These analyses draw heavily on cross-cultural generalizations that link changes in gender roles to transformations in socio-cultural ranking and stratification. In these schemata, hierarchical gender relations are assumed to be a by-product of increased levels of social, political and economic inequality. This evolutionary paradigm and the essentialist or homogenising approach to gender that it implies need to be tested rigorously against the full range of empirical data (di Leonardo 1991; Conkey and Gero 1997: 418–20). Attempts to engender broad societal processes by reference only to symbolic representations and idealized constructs are also problematic. Gender and other interpersonal relations are arguably better viewed from a perspective that focuses on the historical specificity of women's and men's lives and an examination of 'everyday' behavior and contingent, short-term and small-scale processes. The most appropriate analytical unit for this purpose, as persuasively argued by Tringham (1991a, 1991b, 1994, 1995), is that of the household.

The household is a fundamental element of social organization and the basic maintenance unit in most human societies (Bender 1967; Yanagisako 1979; Netting et al. 1984; Wilk and Rathje 1982; Wilk and Ashmore 1988; Wilk 1989; MacEachern, Archer and Garvin 1989; Samson 1990; Santley and Hirth 1993; Blanton 1994). While household structure and composition take varied forms, and may variously be constituted at different times in the domestic cycle, they consistently combine residential and economic aspects and involve the cooperative acquisition, pooling and consumption of resources. Households are thus both "the most common social component … and the smallest and most abundant activity group" in a community (Wilk and Rathje 1982: 618), constituting the level at which individuals articulate most directly with each other and with economic, ecological and subsistence processes. Both households and communities are also socially constructed realities (Duncan 1981; Quilter 1989: 476; Spain 1992), their residues reflecting significant behavioral relationships within and between households. Recognition of household units in archaeological settlements is therefore critical to understanding past forms of social and economic organization as well as socio-personal relationships, such as those of age and gender, which were established, maintained and reproduced at the household level.

The purpose of this paper is to examine the potential of household analysis as a means of understanding domestic organization and, more specifically, gender relations in prehistoric Bronze Age Cyprus.

ARCHITECTURAL HOUSEHOLDS

Recent excavations have uncovered large areas of Early and Middle Bronze Age domestic archi-tecture at Marki-*Alonia* (Frankel and Webb 1996a; 1996b; 1997) and Alambra-*Mouttes* (Coleman et al. 1996) in the northeastern foothills of the Troodos and at Sotira-*Kaminoudhia* (Swiny 1985; 1989) in the southwest—adding significantly to a settlement record previously known only from limited exca-vations at Alambra-*Mavroyi* (Gjerstad 1926: 19–27), Kalopsidha-*Tsaoudhi Chiftlik* (Gjerstad 1926: 27–37) and Ambelikou-*Aletri* (Merrillees 1984). Of these, Marki provides the largest horizontal expo-sure and the observations that follow are derived from this site, although they apply equally to Alambra and Sotira. Occupation at Marki began during the Philia and continued through the Early Bronze Age until the end of MC I. Philia architectural remains have not yet been located (Webb and Frankel 1999). Those of EC I and II are well attested but were largely demolished by later construction (Frankel and Webb 1997: 85–87, fig. 1). The EC III and MC I system (ca. 2000–1800 B.C.E.), however, is well preserved over an excavated area of approximately 1000 m^2 (fig. 1). It allows us, for the first time, to address issues of household structure, use and continuity, and the organization and reproduction of domestic space.

The identification of individual house units is a fundamental first step in household archaeology. At Marki this raises interpretive problems that impact significantly on our ability to infer detailed living patterns at the site. Because of the density of occupation and the conjoined nature of the final, MC I architectural system, discrete household units cannot be isolated on straightforward architectural grounds. Recognition of households is also constrained by the fact that individual rooms were differ-entially reused—often confusing or distorting stratigraphic relationships within and between units—and by a horizontal shifting as opposed to vertical accumulation of construction, which frequently led to the full or partial removal of previous building or remodeling episodes. The archaeological record for much of the EC III and MC I exposure is a palimpsest or "time series accumulation" (Hirth 1993: 24) of changing patterns of household structure, use and composition, spanning decades or even centuries of residential occupation.

As a result of this complex history of building and rebuilding, it is not possible to isolate and investigate household structure across this landscape at any single point in time. We can, however, identify a broad-scale compendium of at least six stages of construction and remodeling through a careful examination of differential building strategies, wall joins, abutments and overlays and locational analysis of doorways, load-bearing walls and access routes (fig. 2). This results in a complex strati-graphic sequence, comprising construction, expansion, partitioning, localized replacement and aban-donment, reorienting and the infilling of open spaces. This provides an insight into architectural pro-cesses and allows a number of general observations about house morphology and domestic behavior—the latter reflecting intergenerational changes in the size, composition and social structure of house-holds, which may in turn be linked with the establishment, expansion and fissioning of nuclear or extended families (Goody 1958; Tourtellot 1988; Banning and Byrd 1989: 528–29).

The architectural system seen in the excavated area at Marki shows a clear sequential development from spatially discrete, freestanding rectangular structures comprised of three or more rectilinear rooms to densely packed household units in which interior spaces were progressively partitioned or remod-elled and open areas infilled and converted into new household units. The incremental nature of this sequence resulted in a significantly greater density of occupation in this part of the site and a substan-tial increase in the ratio of built to unbuilt space over time. By MC I most, if not all, households shared external walls with neighbors, impacting on visibility, access and the possibility of further reorganiza-tion. The apparent lack of a canonical house form may also be related to the incremental structure of the architectural system. A site characterized by lengthy and continuous occupation is unlikely to produce standardized house modules but rather *ad hoc* additions to and modification of existing build-ings, with more significant reorganization restricted by the effect on surrounding households. At the

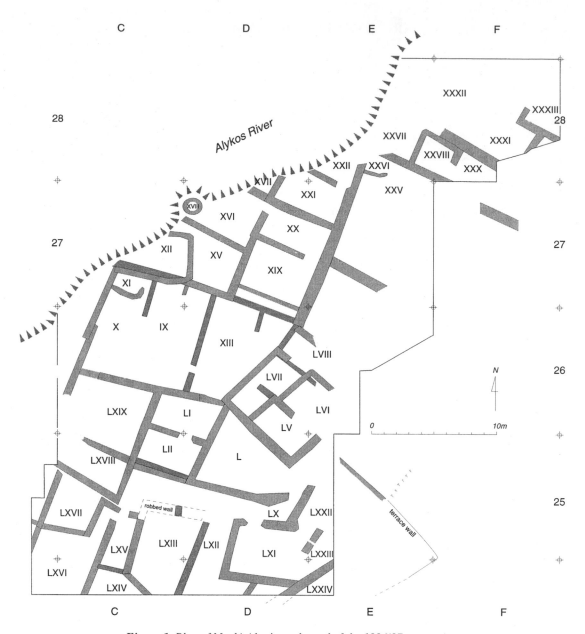

Figure 1. *Plan of Marki-*Alonia *at the end of the 1996/97 excavations.*

same time the resulting conjoined system is likely to have given rise to specific sets of behavioral conventions, designed to regulate social interaction between individuals and within and between contiguous households.

EC III to MC I architecture at Marki is also marked by significant energy investment in planning and construction and by continued in-place rebuilding. This is apparent in the partial removal of earlier structures and deposits and the dumping in some areas of up to one meter of leveling fill to provide a well-drained foundation for walls and floors—and in the use of non-local calcarenite wall blocks transported to the site from a distance of at least 10 km (Xenophontos 1996: 18). Resulting households may be inferred to have been designed for prolonged use, suggesting an anticipation of household continuity and the intergenerational transmission of built property.

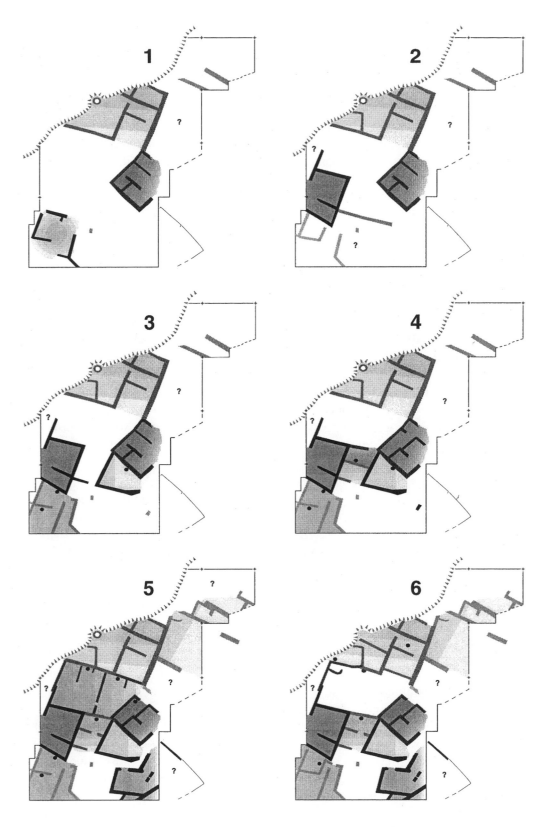

Figure 2. *Schematic plans showing six successive stages of construction, expansion, partitioning, localized replacement and abandonment of EC III–MC I households at Marki-Alonia.*

BEHAVIORAL HOUSEHOLDS

Moving from architectural households to behavioral households raises further issues of recovery and interpretation (Hirth 1993: 21). Reconstruction of room function and identification of activity areas is normally based on the spatial patterning of the material record of production and consumption left on house floors and in associated disposal areas (Kent 1984; 1987; Kramer 1982; Ciolek-Torrello 1989; Daviau 1993). At Marki, however, normal discard behavior resulted in little accumulation of refuse either within or adjacent to households. The by-products of manufacture and consumption appear, instead, to have been removed to communal middens. As a result, the distribution of refuse has no spatial association with individual houses and cannot be used to establish specific patterns of domestic activity (Webb 1995, 1998, in press; Frankel and Webb 1996a: 48–52).

In addition, both localized and final abandonment of the houses at Marki involved the removal of almost all usable objects, including storage jars, foodstuffs and possibly construction materials. Little remains on house floors, and these residual assemblages are comprised almost entirely of fragmentary or exhausted rather than fully functional items. The differential effects of abandonment behavior are also evident. Some artefact types, notably those which could readily be replaced at the new household site (such as expedient stone tools), are over-represented, while others involving greater energy investment or made of non-local or re-cyclable materials are under-represented or absent. The location of objects left behind may also have been affected by dismantling and post-abandonment activities such as scavenging and looting, further distorting the systemic integrity and spatial patterning of this material.

These cultural formation processes inhibit the recognition of activity areas through contextual analysis of artefact residues and production debris. Non-portable installations, however (in particular hearths, benches, storage bins and pot emplacements), are well preserved. The spatial patterning and co-occurrence of these facilities, together with the distribution of residual artefacts, provide an important indication of the range of domestic tasks which defined autonomous households at Marki and allow a number of additional but, again very general, observations.

- Household units at Marki are characterized by widely distributed, small-scale, private domestic storage of foodstuffs, typically in jars or pithoi set in shallow plaster and pebble-lined floor depressions or in three-sided rectangular bins lined with fired mudbrick. Plastered floor depressions are commonly located in discrete rows along walls in rooms without hearths. Rectangular bins, on the other hand, are consistently associated with hearths and may have provided short-term storage for more immediate needs. There is no evidence for communal, supra-household or external storage facilities, suggesting that economic risk and control of subsistence production and storage were maintained at the individual household level.

- Cooking was also a small-scale, intra-household activity. Small built hearths, surrounded by low semicircular kerbs of plaster or stone, are located in designated kitchen areas and associated with benches, bins, hobs, cooking pots and serving vessels. The only oven identified was also located inside a house. There is no evidence for inter-household or communal sharing of food resources, suggesting that both production and consumption networks were restricted to immediate household members.

- The household also served as the primary unit for domestic production and maintenance of textiles, ceramics and lithics and the processing of foodstuffs. Clay spindle whorls and loomweights and metal and bone needles were recovered from most units. Even more common are stone querns and rubbers used for grinding cereals. Broad-based arguments for household pottery production (Frankel 1988, 1991, 1993b) are supported by the widespread recovery of clay and stone burnishing tools, sherds with mend holes and over-fired and "non-professionally" made vessels. On-site knapping of chert and the manufacture of ground stone tools are also indicated in a number of rooms.

In sum, the depositional complexity of the excavated remains at Marki and the depletion of systemic inventories through curate and discard strategies and abandonment processes, limit our ability to make fine-scale interpretations of this landscape and restrict us, for the moment, to fairly broad observations on household structure and domestic organization. These, nonetheless, allow us to infer a relatively stable household regime, primarily organized to meet the needs of subsistence agricultural production and the maintenance of domestic technology and the coresidential unit. Both craft production and agricultural activity appear to have been principally organized at the household level, with most or all households engaged in a similar range and scale of subsistence, maintenance and reproduction tasks. This is visible in co-occurring sets of non-portable installations as well as, less reliably, in the depleted artifact assemblages. While household organization may have involved regular collaboration between related household groups, neither production nor storage beyond specific consumption needs is evident. Households appear to have been small-scale, autonomous economic and co-residence units, engaged in a common, relatively restricted and recurring set of production and maintenance activities. There are few or no significant distinctions in house size or complexity and as yet no non-residential structures which might have served a supra-household or integrative communal function.

INTRODUCING WOMEN AND GENDER

Our observations so far have taken the co-residential unit as the basic element of analysis. They suggest a relatively egalitarian society, at least in terms of differential wealth and the control and distribution of resources at the household level. Whether, however, this apparent symmetry in inter-household relationships was matched by a symmetry in relationships within the household is another question. Can we link elements of this archaeological assemblage to specific sub-sets of the co-residential unit, and, in particular in the present context, to women? If so, how do we move from the recognition of sex-linked activities to an understanding of the social construction of gender and gender relations?

At this point we need to turn to the representational data. A series of Red Polished Ware vessels with modeled decoration are both contemporary with the architectural system at Marki and in many cases probably come from the associated cemeteries (Karageorghis 1991a: 117–27, pls. 65–85). They carry small-scale scenic compositions, modeled in the round. These suggest that certain tasks were consistently performed by women. Women are repeatedly represented as active agents in one or other of three major capacities—as lovers or partners, as mothers (or child-minders) and as a source of productive labor. This last category includes specific depictions of grinding (e.g., Karageorghis 1991a: pls. 70, 75), pounding (e.g., Karageorghis 1991a: pls. 74.3, 77.1), baking (e.g., Karageorghis 1991a: pls. 74.2, 85.5) and perhaps pot-making (Karageorghis 1991b). Where sexual characteristics are indicated, the participants are exclusively female.

If we integrate these images with the artifact residues and non-portable facilities from Marki and elsewhere, we can locate most, if not all, of these female activities within the household. We can, in other words, populate our prehistoric houses with women "busily grinding, kneading, washing, baking and giving birth" (Morris 1985: 281). This does not, however, constitute an engendering of the built environment. There is more to gender than merely finding men and women in the archaeological record. The study of gender is "not as simple as digging down until we come upon a big stone penis or vulva" (Lesick 1997: 39).

The modeled vessels, however, allow us to go a little further. The repeated portrayal of women in secondary food processing activities and the lack of overlap between male and female tasks as depicted on these vases infers a sexual division of labor in which both men and women had consistent gender identities that were systematically related to their productive roles. Within the household, these divisions probably served primarily as a dimension of economic production and reproduction, with men engaged in agricultural work and animal husbandry and women in the transformation of the resulting products and raw materials into useful objects for consumption and storage as well as in a wider array of activities required for the maintenance and reproduction of the family unit. On this reading, the modeled vessels represent a clear gender dichotomy. It might further be suggested that on those pots where sex is not explicitly indicated, the participants were identified as male or female by virtue of the tasks they are engaged in—that is, it is possible that certain activities were so categorically gendered that the depiction of primary sexual characteristics was not necessary (task allocation rather than biological sex being the primary iconographic referent of gender). These modeled scenes may, indeed, not only reflect gender categories, as these were experienced by the people who made and viewed these pots, but have informally served to maintain and reproduce gender identity as a social fact.

The strict and complementary divison of labor in economic production implied by the modeled vases and on the ground at Marki is characteristic of small-scale agrarian societies. It does not, however, necessarily reflect power relationships within the household or translate to opposition and separation in other areas of social relations. In some small-scale agrarian societies, the interdependent role of men and women in production results in a conceptual union between male and female rather than the identification of opposed gender groups (Hingley 1990: 132 with references). In others, sex-based divisions in economic production were accompanied by significant differentials in access to resources and other socio-economic asymmetries between men and women. Which, if either, was the case in Cyprus?

At this point, both the archaeological visibility of gender and the social evolutionary approach to gender relations, which predicts male control over surplus production, private property and labor in prehistoric Bronze Age Cyprus, become problematic. At the moment, the domestic landscape at Marki does not allow reliable inferences about the relative status of men and women either within or beyond the household. To identify activities regularly performed by women and locate these spatially in the domestic domain may "add faces" to the landscape (Tringham 1991a), but it has in itself no necessary predictive value with regard to economic and authority structures and social interaction. At the microscale level of the archaeological household, the institutionalized asymmetries in gender status and authority structures identified by Bolger (1993, 1994, 1996) and Peltenburg (1994) are not, or at least not as yet, visible. Nor are such reified constructs of gender relations likely to account for the full variability of social action experienced within such elemental behavioral units.

CONCLUSION

The question of whether gender behavior, status and attitudes (as opposed to sex and sex-based differences) can reliably be inferred from the material remains of settlement sites like Marki-*Alonia* remains an open question. The methodological and conceptual issues involved in demonstrating gender visibility continue to present a major challenge.

This paper has provided an initial glimpse into domestic behavior at Marki and given rise to a number of broad observations about households, women and gender. With the help of the modeled vessels, we can imaginatively reconstruct our houses as "containers of women" (Duncan 1981) and speak of gender categories defined and maintained through contemporary images of reproduction and labor. To go further and assume gender-based asymmetries in resource control, decision making and ritual and the existence of patriarchal family structures is to go beyond the current household evidence and deny the possibility of varying or alternative patterns of gender dynamics.

Continued study of the built environment may, however, provide a new pathway to gender visibility and allow us formally to test current approaches to gender based on assumed links between the relative status of women and developments in subsistence practice and social complexity. This approach considers general behavioral systems rather than items assumed to be symbolic markers and is based on direct observation of the material conditions in which gender relationships were negotiated and reproduced. The built environment is unique among all artifact types in that it retains the context of its original use and carries encoded information about individual and group interactions. Behavior-environment studies (studies that explore the interactive relationship between human behavior and the built environment) have demonstrated "a direct observable relationship between behavioural responses and the organization of built spaces" (Sandars 1988: 496; see also Holford 1964; King 1980; Pearson and Richards 1994; Pfeiffer 1980; Preziosi 1979a, 1979b). Because the formation and use of the built environment embody behavioral decisions that reflect more general cultural values (Sandars 1985; 1988, 1989; Schaar 1990; Jameson 1989, 1990), it is also a direct physical reflection of *habitus*—that is, it embodies durable learned behavior reflective of group identity and of the inter-generational transmission of habitual action common to all members of a group (Bourdieu 1977). If we are to study gender with full regard to its spatial and temporal context and the cultural and historical specificity of women's and men's lives, an archaeology of the household and of the social relations of domestic production will need to be at the foreground of the enquiry.

The excavated area at Marki, although the largest available from any site of the prehistoric Bronze Age in Cyprus, is as yet insufficient to build a detailed model of gender behavior. A larger sample should allow more reliable inferences—provided it contains enough information to identify the normal range of variability with regard to gender and other categories of difference such as age, rank and wealth. In view of what we now know of the size and morphology of houses at Marki and the depositional complexity of the site, this will require at least twice the horizontal exposure we currently have. Only this scale of data collection might allow us to move beyond general observations and use the social patterning of domestic space to infer more significant aspects of male/female and other interpersonal relations.

To return, finally, to a point of broader significance. Gender, as a category of relationship and identity, is distinct from wider social structures. There need not at any time in the past have been a simple correspondence between the relative status of men and women and community-wide disparities in wealth, rank and authority. We need to disarticulate gender from broader social process and demonstrate rather than assume that personal relationships of domination and subordination are a byproduct of increased social, political and economic inequality. "There is," to quote Hodder, "nothing essential about gender, or about a contextualized approach to gender" (1997: 78). Assumptions based on modern constructs of ethnographically-known societies and symbolically complex subsets of material culture (such as figurines) need to be tested against the full range of empirical data and, in particular, against those elements of the archaeological record which reflect everyday behavioral systems.

ACKNOWLEDGMENTS

Excavations at Marki-*Alonia* are directed by David Frankel and Jennifer Webb and funded by the Australian Research Council. I am grateful to David Frankel for helpful comments and suggestions at various stages in the development of this paper and his close collaboration in the production of fig. 2. I also acknowledge the assistance of the Australian Research Council, which enabled me to attend the *Engendering Aphrodite* conference in March 1998, while holding an Australian Research Council Fellowship.

REFERENCES

Åström, P.
1992   Approaches to the Study of Women in Ancient Cyprus. Pp. 5–8 in *Acta Cypria. Acts of an International Congress on Cypriote Archaeology Held in Göteborg on 22–24 August 1991*, Part 2, ed. P. Åström. Jonsered: Åströms.

Balme, J., and Beck, W.
1995   *Gendered Archaeology. Proceedings of the Second Australian Women in Archaeology Conference*, eds. J. Balme and W. Beck. Research Papers in Archaeology and Natural History 26. Canberra: ANH Publications, Research School of Pacific and Asian Studies, Australian National University.

Banning, E. B., and Byrd, B. F.
1989   Renovations and the Changing Residential Unit at 'Ain Ghazal, Jordan. Pp. 525–33 in *Households and Communities. Proceedings of the Twenty-first Annual Conference of the Archaeological Association of the University of Calgary*, ed. S. MacEachern, D. J. W. Archer, and R. D. Garvin. Alberta: University of Calgary.

Beck, W., and Head, L.
1990   Women in Australian Prehistory. *Australian Feminist Studies* 11: 29–48.

Bender, D.
1967   A Refinement of the Concept of Household, Families, Co-residence, and Domestic Functions. *American Anthropologist* 69: 493–504.

Blanton, R. E.
1994   *Houses and Households. A Comparative Study. Interdisciplinary Contributions to Archaeology*. New York: Plenum.

Bolger, D. L.
1992   The Archaeology of Fertility and Birth: A Ritual Deposit from Chalcolithic Cyprus. *Journal of Anthropological Research* 48: 145–64.
1993   The Feminine Mystique: Gender and Society in Prehistoric Cypriot Studies. *Report of the Department of Antiquities of Cyprus*: 29–41.
1994   Engendering Cypriot Archaeology: Women's Roles and Statuses before the Bronze Age. *Opuscula Atheniensia* 20: 9–17.
1996   Figurines, Fertility, and the Emergence of Complex Society in Prehistoric Cyprus. *Current Anthropology* 37: 365–73.
1997   Reply to D. Frankel, On Cypriot Figurines and the Origins of Patriarchy. *Current Anthroplogy* 38: 85–86.

Bourdieu, P.
1977   *Outline of a Theory of Practice*. Cambridge: Cambridge University.

Ciolek-Torrello, R.
1989   Households, Floor Assemblages and the 'Pompeii Premise' at Grasshopper Pueblo. Pp. 201–208 in *Households and Communities. Proceedings of the Twenty-first Annual Conference of the Archaeological Association of the University of Calgary*, eds. S. MacEachern, D. J. W. Archer, and R. D. Garvin. Alberta: University of Calgary.

Claassen, C., ed.
1992   *Exploring Gender Through Archaeology: Selected Papers from the 1991 Boone Conference*. Monographs in World Archaeology 11. Madison, WI: Prehistory.

Claassen, C.
1994   *Women in Archaeology*. Philadelphia: University of Pennsylvania.

Coleman, J. E.; Barlow, J. A.; Mogelonsky, M. K.; and Schaar, K. W.
1996   *Alambra. A Middle Bronze Age Settlement in Cyprus. Archaeological Investigations by Cornell University 1974–1985*. Studies in Mediterranean Archaeology 118. Jonsered: Åströms.

Conkey, M. W., and Gero, J. M.
1997   Programme to Practice: Gender and Feminism in Archaeology. *Annual Review of Anthropology* 26: 411–64.

Daviau, P. M.
  1993   *Houses and Their Furnishings in Bronze Age Palestine. Domestic Activity Areas and Artefact Distribution in the Middle and Late Bronze Ages.* Sheffield: Sheffield Academic.
di Leonardo, M.
  1991   Introduction: Gender, Culture and Political Economy. Feminist Anthropology in Historical Perspective. Pp. 1–48 in *Gender at the Crossroads of Knowledge: Feminist Anthropology in the Post-Modern Era*, ed. M. di Leonardo. Berkeley and Los Angeles: University of California.
du Cros, H., and Smith, L., eds.
  1993   *Women in Archaeology. A Feminist Critique.* Occasional Papers in Prehistory 23. Canberra: Department of Prehistory, Research School of Pacific Studies, Australian National University.
Duncan, J. S.
  1981   From Container of Women to Status Symbol: The Impact of Social Structure on the Meaning of the House. Pp. 36–59 in *Housing and Identity. Cross-cultural Perspectives*, ed. J. S. Duncan. London: Croom Helm.
Frankel, D.
  1988   Pottery Production in Prehistoric Bronze Age Cyprus: Assessing the Problem. *Journal of Mediterranean Archaeology* 1: 27–55.
  1991   Ceramic Variability: Measurement and Meaning. Pp. 241–53 in *Cypriot Ceramics: Reading the Prehistoric Record*, eds. J. A. Barlow, D. L. Bolger and B. Kling. Philadelphia: University of Pennsylvania.
  1993a   Is This a Trivial Observation? Gender in Prehistoric Cyprus. Pp. 138–42 in *Women in Archaeology. A Feminist Critique*, eds. H. du Cros and L. Smith. Occasional Papers in Prehistory 23. Canberra: Department of Prehistory, Research School of Pacific Studies, Australian National University.
  1993b   Inter- and Intra-site Variability in Prehistoric Bronze Age Cyprus: Types, Ranges, Trends. *Bulletin of the American Schools of Oriental Research* 292: 59–72.
  1997   On Cypriot Figurines and the Origins of Patriarchy. *Current Anthropology* 38: 84.
Frankel, D., and Webb, J. M.
  1996a   *Marki Alonia. An Early and Middle Bronze Age Town in Cyprus. Excavations 1990–1994.* Studies in Mediterranean Archaeology 123:1. Jonsered: Åströms.
  1996b   Excavations at Marki-*Alonia*, 1995–96. *Report of the Department of Antiquities of Cyprus*: 51–68.
  1997   Excavations at Marki-*Alonia*, 1996–97. *Report of the Department of Antiquities of Cyprus*: 85–109.
Gero, J. M.
  1983   Gender Bias in Archaeology: A Cross-cultural Perspective. Pp. 51–57 in *The Socio-Politics of Archaeology*, eds. J. M. Gero, D. Lacy and M. L. Blakey. Anthropological Research Report 23. Amherst: University of Massachusetts.
  1985   Socio-politics of Archaeology and the Woman-at-home Ideology. *American Antiquity* 50: 342–50.
  1988   Gender Bias in Archaeology: Here, Then, and Now. Pp. 33–43 in *Resistances to Feminism in Science and the Health Care Professions*, ed. S. V. Rosser. London: Pergamon.
  1993   The Social World of Prehistoric Facts: Gender and Power in Paleoindian Research. Pp. 31–40 in *Women in Archaeology. A Feminist Critique,* eds. H. du Cros and L. Smith. Occasional Papers in Prehistory No. 23. Canberra: Department of Prehistory, Research School of Pacific Studies, Australian National University.
Gero, J. M., and Conkey, M. W., eds.
  1991   *Engendering Archaeology: Women and Prehistory.* Oxford: Blackwell.
Gjerstad, E.
  1926   *Studies on Prehistoric Cyprus.* Uppsala: Uppsala Universitets Årsskrift.
Goody, J. R., ed.
  1958   *The Developmental Cycle in Domestic Groups.* Cambridge: Cambridge University.
Hamilton, N.
  1994   A Fresh Look at the 'Seated Gentleman' in the Pierides Foundation Museum, Republic of Cyprus. *Cambridge Archaeological Journal* 4: 302–12.
  2000   Ungendering Archaeology: Concepts of Sex and Gender in Figurine Studies in Prehistory. Pp. 17–30

in *Representations of Gender from Prehistory to the Present. Proceedings of the Conference on Gender and Material Culture Held at Exeter University, July 1994,* eds. M. Donald and L. Hurcombe. Studies in Gender and Material Culture Series. London: Macmillan.

Hays-Gilpin, K., and Whitley, D. S. eds.
1997   *Reader in Gender Archaeology.* New York: Routledge.

Hingley, R.
1990   Domestic Organisation and Gender Relations in Iron Age and Romano-British Households. Pp. 125–47 in *The Social Archaeology of Houses,* ed. R. Samson. Edinburgh: Edinburgh University.

Hirth, K. G.
1993   The Household as an Analytical Unit: Problems in Method and Theory. Pp. 21–36 in *Prehispanic Domestic Units in Western Mesoamerica. Studies of the Household, Compound, and Residence,* eds. R. S. Santley and K. G. Hirth. Ann Arbor: CRC.

Hodder, I.
1997   Commentary. The Gender Screen. Pp. 75–78 in *Invisible People and Processes. Writing Gender and Childhood into European Archaeology,* eds. J. Moore and E. Scott. New York: Leicester University.

Holford, W.
1964   *The Built Environment. Its Creation, Motivations and Control.* London: Tavistock.

Jameson, M.
1989   Domestic Space in the Greek City-state. Pp. 92–113 in *Domestic Architecture and the Use of Space. An Interdisciplinary Cross-Cultural Study,* ed. S. Kent. Cambridge: Cambridge University.
1990   Private Space and the Greek City. Pp. 171–95 in *The Greek City State from Homer to Alexander,* eds. O. Murray and S. Price. Oxford: Clarendon.

Karageorghis, V.
1991a   *The Coroplastic Art of Ancient Cyprus.* Vol. I: *Chalcolithic-Late Cypriote I.* Nicosia: A. G. Leventis Foundation.
1991b   A Middle Bronze Age Scenic Composition: Copper Leaching or Pot-making? Pp. 33–37 in *Cypriote Terracottas. Proceedings of the First International Conference of Cypriote Studies,* eds. F. Vandenabeele and R. Laffineur. Brussels-Liège: A.G. Leventis Foundation, Vrije Universiteit Brussel, Université de Liège.

Kent, S.
1984   *Analyzing Activity Areas: An Ethnoarchaeological Study of the Use of Space.* Albuquerque: University of New Mexico.
1987   *Method and Theory for Activity Area Research: An Ethnoarchaeological Approach.* New York: Columbia University.

King, A. D., ed.
1980   *Buildings and Society: Essays on the Social Development of the Built Environment.* London: Routledge and Kegan Paul.

Knapp, A. B., and Meskell, L.
1997   Bodies of Evidence on Prehistoric Cyprus. *Cambridge Archaeological Journal* 7: 183–204.

Kramer, C.
1982   Ethnographic Households and Archaeological Interpretation. Pp. 663–76 in *Archaeology of the Household: Building a Prehistory of Domestic Life,* eds. R. Wilk and W. Rathje. *American Behavioural Scientist* 25.

Kramer, C., and Stark, M.
1988   The Status of Women in Archaeology. *Anthropology Newsletter* 29, 9: 11–12.

Lesick, K.
1997   Re-engendering Gender: Some Theoretical and Methodological Concerns on a Burgeoning Archaeological Pursuit. Pp. 31–41 in *Invisible People and Processes. Writing Gender and Childhood into European Archaeology,* eds. J. Moore and E. Scott. New York: Leicester University.

MacEachern, S.; Archer, D. J. W.; and Garvin, R. D., eds.
1989   *Households and Communities. Proceedings of the Twenty-first Annual Conference of the Archaeological Association of the University of Calgary.* Alberta: University of Calgary.

Merrillees, R. S.
1984   Ambelikou-*Aletri*: A Preliminary Report. *Report of the Department of Antiquities of Cyprus* 1–13.
Moore, J., and Scott, E., eds.
1997   *Invisible People and Processes. Writing Gender and Childhood into European Archaeology.* New York: Leicester University.

Morris, D.
1985   *The Art of Ancient Cyprus.* Oxford: Phaidon.
Netting, R.; Wilk, R. R.; and Arnould, E. J.
1984   *Households: Comparative and Historical Studies of the Domestic Group.* Berkeley: University of California.

Nixon, L.
1994   Gender Bias in Archaeology. Pp. 1–23 in *Women in Ancient Societies. An Illusion of the Night*, eds. L. J. Archer, S. Fischler, and M. Wyke. London: Routledge.

Pearson, M., and Richards, C., eds.
1994   *Architecture and Order: Approaches to Social Space.* London: Routledge.
Peltenburg, E. J.
1994   Constructing Authority: The Vounous Enclosure Model. *Opuscula Atheniensia* 20: 157–62.
Pfeiffer, T.
1980   Behaviour and Interaction in Built Space. *Built Environment* 6: 35–50.
Preziosi, D.
1979a   *Architecture, Language and Meaning: The Origins of the Built Environment and its Semiotic Organisation.* The Hague: Mouton.
1979b   *The Semiotics of the Built Environment. An Introduction to Architectonic Analysis.* London: Indiana University.

Quilter, J.
1989   Households and Societies in Preceramic Peru, Paloma and El Paraiso. Pp. 469–77 in *Households and Communities. Proceedings of the Twenty-first Annual Conference of the Archaeological Association of the University of Calgary*, eds. S. MacEachern, D. J. W. Archer, and R. D. Garvin. Alberta: University of Calgary.

Samson, R., ed.
1990   *The Social Archaeology of Houses.* Edinburgh: Edinburgh University.
Sandars, D. H.
1985   Ancient Behaviour and the Built Environment: Applying Environmental Psychology Methods and Theories to Archaeological Contexts. Pp. 296–305 in *Environmental Change/Social Change*, eds. S. Klein et al. Washington, D.C.: EDRA.
1988   Architecture—the Neglected Artifact. Pp. 489–98 in *Problems in Greek Prehistory. Papers Presented at the Centenary Conference of the British School of Archaeology at Athens, Manchester, April 1986,* eds. E. B. French and K. A. Wardle. Bristol: Bristol Classical.
1989   Behavioural Conventions and Archaeology: Methods for the Analysis of Ancient Architecture. Pp. 43–72 in *Domestic Architecture and the Use of Space. An Interdisciplinary Cross-Cultural Study*, ed. S. Kent. Cambridge: Cambridge University.

Santley, R. S., and Hirth, K. G., eds.
1993   *Prehispanic Domestic Units in Western Mesoamerica. Studies of the Household, Compound, and Residence.* Ann Arbor: CRC.

Schaar, K. W.
1990   Aegean House Form: A Reflection of Cultural Behaviour. Pp. 173–82 in *L'Habitat Egéen Préhistorique*, eds. P. Darcque and R. Treuil. *Bulletin de correspondance hellénique* Supplement 19. Athens: École Française d'Athènes.

Spain, D.
1992   *Gendered Spaces.* Chapel Hill: University of North Carolina.

Swiny, S.
  1985   Sotira-*Kaminoudhia* and the Chalcolithic-Early Bronze Age Transition in Cyprus. Pp. 115–24 in *Archaeology in Cyprus 1960–1985*, ed. V. Karageorghis. Nicosia: A. G. Leventis Foundation.
  1989   From Round House to Duplex: A Re-assessment of Prehistoric Bronze Age Society. Pp. 14–31 in *Early Society in Cyprus*, ed. E. Peltenburg. Edinburgh: Edinburgh University.

Tourtellot, G.
  1988   Developmental Cycles of Households and Houses at Seibal. Pp. 97–120 in *Household and Community in the Mesoamerican Past*, eds. R. R. Wilk and W. Ashmore. Albuquerque: University of New Mexico.

Tringham, R.
  1991a   Households with Faces: The Challenge of Gender in Prehistoric Architectural Remains. Pp. 93–131 in *Engendering Archaeology: Women and Prehistory*, eds. J. M. Gero and M. W. Conkey. Oxford: Blackwell.
  1991b   Men and Women in Prehistoric Architecture. *Traditional Dwellings and Settlement Review* 3: 9–28.
  1994   Engendered Places in Prehistory. *Gender, Place and Culture* 1: 169–203.
  1995   Archaeological Houses, Households, Housework, and the Home. Pp. 79–107 in *The Home: Words, Interpretations, Meanings and Environments*, eds. D. Benjamin and D. Stea. Aldershot: Avebury.

Walde, D., and Willows. N. D., eds.
  1991   *The Archaeology of Gender. Proceedings of the Twenty-second Annual Conference of the Archaeological Association of the University of Calgary*. Calgary: Archaeological Association, University of Calgary.

Webb, J. M.
  1995   Abandonment Processes and Curate/Discard Strategies at Marki-*Alonia*, Cyprus. *The Artefact* 18: 64–70.
  1998   Lithic Technology and Discard at Marki, Cyprus: Consumer Behaviour and Site Formation in the Prehistoric Bronze Age. *Antiquity* 72: 796–805.
  2000   Curation, Expediency and Discard. The Ground Stone Industry at Marki-*Alonia*. Pp. 261–79. *Praktika. Proceedings of the Third International Congress of Cypriot Studies, Nicosia, 16–20 April 1996*, Vol. 1, ed. G. Ioannides and S. Hadjistyllis. Nicosia: Society of Cypriot Studies.

Webb, J. M., and Frankel, D.
  1995a   "This Fair Paper, This Most Goodly Book." Gender and International Scholarship in Cypriot Archaeology, 1920–1991. Pp. 34–42 in *Gendered Archaeology. Proceedings of the Second Australian Women in Archaeology Conference*, eds. J. Balme and W. Beck. Research Papers in Archaeology and Natural History 26. Canberra: ANH Publications, Research School of Pacific and Asian Studies, Australian National University.
  1995b   Gender Inequity and Archaeological Practice: A Cypriot Case Study. *Journal of Mediterranean Archaeology* 8: 93–112.
  1999   Characterising the Philia Facies. Material Culture, Chronology and the Origin of the Bronze Age in Cyprus. *American Journal of Archaeology* 103: 3–43.

Wilk, R. R., ed.
  1989   *The Household Economy. Reconsidering the Domestic Mode of Production*. Boulder: Westview.

Wilk, R. R., and Ashmore, W., eds.
  1988   *Household and Community in the Mesoamerican Past*. Albuquerque: University of New Mexico.

Wilk, R. R., and Rathje, W. L., eds.
  1982   *Archaeology of the Household: Building a Prehistory of Domestic Life. American Behavioural Scientist* 25.

Wylie, A.
  1991   Gender Theory and the Archaeological Record: Why is There No Archaeology of Gender? Pp. 31–54 in *Engendering Archaeology: Women and Prehistory,* eds. J. M. Gero and M. W. Conkey. Oxford: Blackwell.
  1993   Workplace Issues for Women in Archaeology: The Chilly Climate. Pp. 245–58 in *Women in Archaeology. A Feminist Critique*, eds. H. du Cros and L. Smith. Occasional Papers in Prehistory 23. Canberra: Department of Prehistory, Research School of Pacific Studies, Australian National University.

Xenophontos, C.
  1996   Environment and Resources. Pp. 16–18 in *Marki Alonia. An Early and Middle Bronze Age Town in Cyprus. Excavations 1990–1994*, D. Frankel and J. M. Webb. Studies in Mediterranean Archaeology 123:1. Jonsered: Åströms.

Yanagisako, S.
  1979   Family and Household. The Analysis of Domestic Groups. *Annual Review of Anthropology* 8: 161–207.

Yellen, J. E.
  1983   Women, Archaeology and the National Science Foundation. Pp. 59–65 in *The Socio-Politics of Archaeology*, eds. J. M. Gero, D. Lacy, and M. L. Blakey. Anthropological Research Report 23. Amherst: University of Massachusetts.

PART THREE

GENDER AND SOCIAL ORGANIZATION
(LATE BRONZE AGE–MEDIEVAL)

WINE, WOMEN AND SONG: DRINKING RITUAL IN CYPRUS IN THE LATE BRONZE AND EARLY IRON AGES

LOUISE STEEL

Department of Archaeology
University of Wales, Lampeter
Ceredigion SA48 7ED, Wales
l.steel@lamp.ac.uk

This paper traces the transmission of alcohol from the Near East to Cyprus during the 4th or 3rd millennium B.C. and explores how this exotic, luxury commodity was integrated within funerary ceremony as a means of social distinction. It reviews the extant evidence for female participation in ceremonial feasting on Cyprus during the Late Bronze and Early Iron Ages as a means of evaluating the relative position of women in Cypriot society. Finally, the paper argues for a transformation in social organization at the end of the Late Bronze Age with profound implications for the role of women in society.

This paper examines the relative position of adult males and females of a select social class (the elite) in Cyprus during the Late Bronze Age and the earliest period of the Early Iron Age. Late Bronze Age Cyprus was characterized by a flourishing and sophisticated urban society with extensive external trading contacts (Keswani 1989b, 1993, 1996). A wealthy, urban-based elite group had emerged whose position was apparently based on control of the island's mineral and agricultural resources and external trade (Keswani 1993; Manning and de Mita 1997: 102, 108–15). This group was able to amass substantial concentrations of wealth in the form of luxury imported exotica, which they deposited in funerary assemblages in large quantities (Keswani 1989b: 68–70). Beyond the fact that it comprised a stratified society with large urban centers (Negbi 1986; Keswani 1993; 1996; Knapp 1996), Late Cypriot social organization remains elusive and gender relations, in particular, have been ignored in the archaeological literature. At the end of the Late Bronze Age, Cyprus, along with the rest of the eastern Mediterranean, suffered a series of major disruptions (Sandars 1985; Iacovou 1989; 1994; Karageorghis 1992; 1997). These disruptions are usually associated with population movements, in particular from the Aegean. In Cyprus, this period is characterized by a major demographic transformation illustrated by a massive shift in settlement pattern (Iacovou 1989, 1994). Novel elements in the archaeological record, such as the appearance of warrior burials, imply that from LC IIIA, and during the earlier part of the Iron Age in particular, social position to some extent was judged on military prowess (Keswani 1989b: 67–68; Coldstream 1989: 329; Catling 1995). Such changes would imply shifting dynamics in social organization and were presumably particularly disruptive in the sphere of gender relations.

Only limited resources are available for an investigation of gender relations, broadly speaking both male/female and adult/subadult groups, in Cyprus during the Bronze and Iron Ages. Anthropological studies of skeletal remains would apparently offer the best scope for investigation although there are problems of bias (Bright 1995a, 1995b; Mee 1998). Otherwise, only limited iconographic and textual sources have survived, and these contain an enormous gender bias. Ancient textual sources tend to privilege male activities and roles, distorting the picture of past social structures. The Sumerian King List, for example, cites the male rulers of the early Mesopotamian city states, but there is no comparable document listing important female roles within these early city states—priestesses or queens, for example, are not listed. Egyptian equivalents to the King List (such as the Turin Papyrus and the Palermo Stone) likewise distort the picture of ancient Egypt, where the royal line passed through the female. This gender bias has been exacerbated by modern scholarly readings of the material. Our reluctance to identify female figures on Mycenaean pictorial vases, despite the predominance of females in other Minoan-Mycenaean artistic media, is a case in point. Ironically, even though the only figures depicted seated on a throne in a Late Bronze Age Aegean context are female, de Jong's reconstruction of the Pylos *megaron* showed a male *wanax* figure on the throne (Rehak 1995: 109). Likewise, there has been a tendency among archaeologists to ascribe particular objects found in funerary contexts either to males or females on the basis of certain preconceived notions of what would have been appropriate activities for either sex during antiquity, e.g., jewelry and toilet articles are often associated with females and military equipment with males. However, there are numerous examples of female burials that are equipped with impressive arrays of weapons and armor and also frequently with other artifacts decorated with martial iconography that usually are considered more appropriate for males. Particularly noteworthy is a high-status female burial of LM IIIA date in Tholos A at Archanes equipped with a bull and horse sacrifice, ten bronze vases and an ivory footstool decorated with warriors' heads and figure-of-eight shields (Sakellarakis and Sakellarakis 1991: 72–85, figs. 49, 59–61).

Females are not entirely excluded from ancient documents, and representations of females are common in a variety of artistic media and in a rich variety of contexts. They are frequently depicted in purely domestic contexts. Nevett, however, highlights problems interpreting scenes depicting female activities both outside the domestic context and within the realm of the *gynaikon* on Classical pottery from Athens (Nevett 1999: 11–12, 16, 19–20). She argues that many of these scenes will represent an idealized account of female roles within Classical Athens, focusing on a particular social stratum rather than reflecting the full range of female activities.

GENDER RELATIONS

Gender is not a simple biological fact but a social construct that encompasses more variables than simplistic opposites of male and female. Attempts to "engender" archaeology, therefore, need to move beyond "the biological determinism that is implicit in many models of sex role differentiation" (Conkey and Gero 1991: 8). The aim is not to identify past activities in the archaeological record and then employ ethnographic parallels or anthropological data simply to attribute specific roles to either sex in a monolithic, unchanging system. Gender roles and relations are defined by different cultural groups in specific ways, and simple cross cultural generalizations in a binary system of opposition are insufficient for extrapolating gender roles from the archaeological record. The danger of attributing specific activities to either sex is demonstrated by the example of the 19th century Tswana of southern Africa. In an apparent contradiction of European expected social roles, the females of the Tswana were responsible for "male" jobs, such as the construction of houses and tending the fields, whereas the men worked within the apparent "female" domestic arena where they made clothing for both sexes (Comaroff 1996: 25).

Regardless of biological sex, an individual might be attributed different gender status as he/she progresses through life, from pre-pubescent groups, to fully sexual adults, to a final non-sexual stage at the end of life. Stears, for example, discusses changing funerary iconography for females in Classical Athens that reflect differing attitudes and gender relations for women according to their age and sexual or marital status (Stears 1995: 118–26). Other gender groups might include those outside the normal set of gender relations governing the rest of society, such as the virginal status of priests, priestesses, monks and nuns in certain societies. Nevertheless, in the absence of detailed epigraphic or iconographic data, the scope of this paper is limited to a broad examination of male and female activities within the Cypriot Late Bronze Age and Early Iron Age.

Gender relations might be explored through a simplistic analysis of mortuary data to examine the wealth deposited with separate groups of individuals, such as males, females, adults, and sub-adults. Certainly, both females and subadults might be buried with large quantities of luxury objects and possible status symbols, but there is no evidence that either group could acquire these in its own right. Accumulation of wealth with subadults is usually taken as evidence of a society in which status was inherited and not ascribed (Binford 1972: 234; Brown 1981: 28–29), and the wealthy burial of females could be interpreted as familial wealth, possibly a dowry (Goring 1989: 103–4), since richly ornamented females could be considered suitable vehicles for the display of male wealth and social status. In Classical Athens, for example, it has been suggested that the elaborate burial of a young female might reflect her value to a wealthy and prominent family and her ability to increase the family's wealth and status through a favorable marriage alliance (Stears 1995: 117). Elaborate burials of females, therefore, cannot simplistically be equated with female wealth, access to and/or control over specific economic resources, and a concurrent elevated socio-political status.

Consequently, patterns of male and female funerary wealth *per se* might not be the best indication of the relative role and position of men and women in Late Cypriot society. Instead, closer examination of certain activities usually assumed to be gender specific and associated with a male elite might be a more precise indicator of actual gender relations during the Late Cypriot period and Early Iron Age. One such activity that leaves considerable evidence in the archaeological record is ritualized or ceremonial drinking of alcohol. Analysis of the evidence for drinking ritual in Cyprus might determine whether this was a gender specific activity and what impact, if any, the disruptions at the end of the Late Bronze Age had on Cypriot gender relations.

DRINKING RITUAL

Consumption of food and drink outside the immediate domestic environment is more than a simple strategy for subsistence and can often acquire very important cultural and symbolic significance. In the public arena, this is a statement of social relations and a means of defining and maintaining group relations (Sherratt 1997b: 405), and, therefore, is one of the environments in which we might expect gender relations to play an important role. It is generally assumed that in most cultural contexts, women are largely responsible for the preparation of food. In circumstances where women control the production and distribution of foodstuffs, they will, in general, enjoy high status. However, certain labor-intensive and symbolic foods as well as more prestigious and non-essential or exotic elements of the diet are more likely to be appropriated by men with a resultant decline in the position of women (Hastorf 1991: 134–35). This is evident in the production and consumption of alcoholic beverages.

Ancient societies probably first discovered alcohol in the 4th millennium B.C. (Sherratt 1997a: 391). The earliest alcoholic beverage known to man was probably beer, and its production is attested in Egypt and Mesopotamia from the beginning of history (Stager 1985: 175). This drink was either strained or was drunk through a siphon (Evans 1930: fig. 140a; Dikaios 1936/37: figs. 2–3). Viticulture appears to pre-date the unification of Egypt, occurring probably in ca. 3100 B.C. The wealthy chieftain's tomb U-j of Predynastic date from Abydos contained large quantities of imported Palestinian storage jars which resin analyses have shown to have contained wine (T. Wilkinson, personal communication), and wine was quickly adopted as the elite drink of Egypt and Syro-Palestine in the Early Bronze Age (Stager 1985: 174–79; Herscher 1997: 30). Once the delights of alcohol were discovered, it spread with seeming rapidity across the eastern Mediterranean, Anatolia and the Aegean, and then into northern Europe. This advance can be seen through the development of new ceramic forms comprising a variety of drinking and serving vessels in a prescribed set, often elaborately decorated or imitating metallic forms (Sherratt 1997a: 391).

Sherratt (1997a) has charted other novel features in the archaeological record that appear to accompany the spread of alcohol: the appearance of differential burial practices and a select group of richly equipped burials, in particular male warrior burials; the development of long-distance trade, especially in search of metals; and the development (in Europe) of international ceramic styles associated with serving and consumption of food and drink, perhaps best-illustrated by the Beaker phenomenon (Sherratt 1997a: 378, 385, 387). We can, thus, conclude that when alcohol appeared, it was appropriated by an exclusive social group defined by military prowess and generally assumed to be predominantly male. The ceremonial (and cultic) connotations of this new commodity very probably derived from the exotic nature and intoxicating properties of alcohol (Sherratt 1997a: 391–92). Numerous studies indicate that rituals and ceremonies associated with consumption of alcoholic beverages and its associated equipment were valued social elements and were eagerly adopted and modified by population groups throughout the Near East and Europe during antiquity. Meadows, for example, analyzes the transmission of such elements as part of a Romanized lifestyle to elite groups beyond the Roman frontiers (Meadows 1999: 105–6).

The production of wine was labor-intensive, entailing control over the management and cultivation of vineyards and the actual processing involved in wine manufacture. The final product was, no doubt, beyond the reach of most members of society, both male and female. In the Mycenaean world, Cavanagh (1998: 111) notes that wine was "a powerfully symbolic substance," the production and consumption of which were closely controlled by the palace administration (Palmer 1995: 278). It is not surprising that, following the collapse of the palaces, we see the disappearance of large-scale wine consumption as an integral element of Mycenaean funerary practices (Cavanagh 1998: 111). As noted above, elements of diet (such as wine) that were labor-intensive in production and symbolic and/or prestigious in function in most social contexts are more likely to have been controlled by men rather than women (Hastorf 1991: 134–35).

In ancient societies, therefore, alcohol was highly symbolic. Its consumption was probably surrounded by taboos and very likely involved conspicuous display in exclusive rituals and ceremonies: an exclusively male form of entertainment or hospitality involving the controlled and socially acceptable use of a mild stimulant as a social lubricant (Sherratt 1997a: 389). The majority of society—the non-elite, sub-adults and possibly women—appear to have been excluded from these rituals. Textual evidence from the Near East refers to the *marzeah*, an association of prominent men whose main activity appears to have been drinking in ceremonies specifically associated with communion with the ancestors, a cult of the dead designed to legitimize and maintain the authority of the living (Barnett 1985: 1–6; Carter 1995: 300, n.54). Descriptions of the *marzeah* and the Greek *symposium* (Murray 1983), another male-specific activity with aristocratic connotations (Carter 1995: 305), give us some idea of the contexts in which these drinking rituals occurred with other associated activities, such as feasting, that were accompanied by musicians and epic recitals. These feasts often took place in specialized locations, either ritual or secular, as in the dining room of the Greek Iron Age or the large halls of the Mycenaean megaron and the elite residences of LH IIIC (Deger-Jalkotzy 1994: 21). While men are frequently depicted drinking at these occasions (Evans 1930: 140a; Langdon 1989: fig. 13; Gubel 1993: fig. 3), women were only admitted as servers, dancing girls, or courtesans and not as participants in their own right. Accounts of these activities have colored our view of the participants of these rituals, obscuring the possible existence of ceremonies not recorded in texts (but known in other cultures) in which rich and varied permutations of gender relations were performed. Iconographic evidence from Minoan Crete, for example, provides tantalizing evidence that some women might have had a role in drinking and feasting ceremonies. The Camp Stool fresco of LM IIIA date from Knossos shows both men and women seated and drinking from chalices (Evans 1936: fig. 323). This is paralleled by the scene of the lyre player adorning the walls of the throne room in Pylos (Carter 1995: 295–96, fig. 18.8). Carter has implicitly related the activities depicted on the LM IIIA Ayia Triadha sarcophagus, in which women are major participants, to the early transmission to the Aegean of feasting and drinking accompanied by epic poetry recitals and music (Carter 1995: 294–95, figs.18.7a–c). This accords with the apparent high status or general prominence of females within Minoan palatial society according to iconographic evidence, such as the prominence of females in the Grand Stand fresco (Evans 1930: figs. 28–34, pls. 16–17). Indeed, in Minoan and Mycenaean art, seated figures drinking are generally females and seated females (usually interpreted as goddesses) are often recipients of offerings of food and drink (Evans 1936: figs. 322, 329b, 331). In a recent discussion of representations of male and female figures of authority in the Bronze Age Aegean, Rehak notes that female figures are more typically represented in artistic media. From this he suggests that women played an important role in ceremonial banqueting within the context of the Mycenaean megaron structures (Rehak 1995: 109–12). Thus, it seems plausible that gender relations more complex than the simple male-warrior equation were an important element in the drinking ceremonies of certain ancient cultures. The activity of drinking appears to be identified with an elevated social class, but the possibility that women might have participated cannot be ignored.

BRONZE AGE CYPRUS

Herscher (1997) has recently suggested that ritualized drinking, presumably of wine, and "aristocratic" or elite feasting first appeared in Cyprus by EC III–MC I. Its appearance is best illustrated by the tombs at Vounous and is attested by the development of elaborate drinking equipment in Red Polished ware, dominated by large spouted bowls (the central element of the drinking set, for mixing wine). Alongside this new ceramic drinking set there is evidence for large-scale funerary feasting in the form of plentiful cattle bones, a pattern that contrasts sharply from domestic contexts in which goat and pig dominate. The new elements of funerary ritual are associated with elaborate, differentiated burials of an emergent elite group and so would appear to fit into the model developed by Sherratt. It is notable that from their inception in Cyprus, feasting and ceremonial drinking of alcohol have very specific funerary associations, either as elements of a lifestyle that were deemed appropriate for inclusion in elite burials or as the residues of actual funerary feasts on the part of the mourners.

Manning, however, places the introduction of alcohol to Cyprus somewhat earlier, at the Chalcolithic/EC transition and fixes it into the wider context of the spread of alcohol from the Near East to the Aegean and northern Europe alongside the emergence of elite groups (Manning 1993: 45). In this respect, the high concentration of decorated wares associated with the storing, serving and consumption of liquids, possibly alcohol, found in the exceptionally large Middle Chalcolithic structure (Building 206 or the "Red Building") at Kissonerga-*Mosphilia* is worthy of comment (Bolger 1998: 125–26; Peltenburg 1998: 248). These, it has been suggested "may have served as symbols of wealth and conspicuous consumption" (Bolger 1998: 125), possibly as some form of high-status group feasting of symbolic significance (Peltenburg 1998: 248). This would imply that feasting incorporating an alcoholic beverage was introduced to Cyprus as early as the Chalcolithic period, when there is no evidence for its association with funerary ritual.

In the Late Cypriot period, we see evidence for the continuation of ceremonial drinking in the form of the deposition in tombs of elaborate ceramic drinking services in the Base Ring, White Slip and Bichrome wheelmade wares, the centerpieces of which were large kraters used for mixing wine (Morris 1985: pls. 25, 27, 30–31; South et al. 1989: figs. 43, 48–52; Steel 1998). As in the Middle Cypriot period, ceremonies involving alcohol consumption and ritual feasting in the Late Cypriot period were closely controlled by the elite. The evidence for these activities is found in the urban polities around the coastal fringes of the island. Although there is some evidence for emulation of this activity in the form of Plain ware and White Painted ware kraters deposited in less wealthy tomb assemblages, especially at Enkomi (Keswani 1989b: 64), it is unclear whether this refers to actual participation in drinking rituals by people who were not members of the elite group. Perhaps, alternatively, it had simply become accepted that a burial should be accompanied by a certain range of goods including a krater and thus need not be evidence for dissemination of drinking and feasting beyond a very select and selective group. It might indicate, however, that LC society was far less bounded than that of many contemporary cultures in the eastern Mediterranean and that group membership and social relations were fairly fluid.

As the Late Cypriot period progressed, ceremonial drinking was increasingly formalized and standardized across the island. Of particular note is the move away from the indigenous drinking services in the Base Ring and White Slip wares to the more exotic Mycenaean kraters which are often decorated with elaborate pictorial scenes (Steel 1998). The Mycenaean wine krater decorated in a distinctive and socially exclusive pictorial style, a semiology only understandable to the aristocratic class of the Late Bronze Age eastern Mediterranean, was widely disseminated in the Levant, from Atchana and Ugarit in the north, to Tell el-Ajjul in the south, and as far inland as the temple site of Amman (Steel 1999). It was not part of a standardized drinking set. The choice of drinking cup, either Mycenaean or local, was highly individual, but the krater itself can be identified as the central element of an international, eastern Mediterranean drinking complex.

As in the preceding MC period, the material evidence for ceremonial drinking on Cyprus in the Late Bronze Age appears to have a specific funerary connotation or at least is mainly known from funerary remains, although there is some evidence for the use of ceremonial drinking equipment and feasting in non-funerary contexts. Particularly noteworthy is the deposit of meat-bearing caprine bones found in a pit or latrine in the administrative, public area of Kalavasos-*Ayios Dhimitrios* together with the components of a fine Mycenaean dinner service, the apparent residue from elite feasting (South 1988: 227–28). Keswani has also noted signs of wear and abrasion on Mycenaean kraters from Cypriot tomb groups, suggesting they had a history of use within the settlement before being finally deposited in the tomb (Keswani 1989a: 562).[1] Such ceremonial drinking and feasting was no doubt an important means for constructing and maintaining group identities and relations. The strong funerary connotations of this activity suggest that it was associated with an ancestor cult to confirm legitimacy on the authority of the Cypriot elite in much the same way as the *marzeah* in the Levant.

A number of questions arise concerning the organization of elite drinking in a Late Cypriot context: whether or not this activity was gender specific: what groups were given access to drinking sets; whether an individual was buried with a drinking set that he/she had used it in life or whether it was simply an expression of the wealth and position of the family overall. Moreover, the question of whether the iconography of the Mycenaean krater was gender specific (i.e., possible chariot and agonistic scenes being reserved for males and other scenes for females) is particularly interesting. The famous "Zeus Krater" from Swedish Tomb 17 at Enkomi, for example, was decorated with a chariot scene (Gjerstad 1934: pl. 87.1, no. 61; pl. 147.11) and accompanied a male burial (Fischer 1986: 36). Unfortunately, much of the relevant data comes from tomb groups excavated at the end of the last century from sites such as Enkomi, Kourion and Maroni (Murray 1900; Walters 1900; Johnson 1980; Crouwel and Morris 1987; Manning and Monks 1998), with resultant gaps in information concerning burial assemblages and their associated skeletal remains. Moreover, it is unclear to what extent the inhabitants of Cyprus and the cities on the Levantine coast exercised any real choice over the iconography of Mycenaean pictorial kraters.

There is some evidence, however, that might suggest female participation in ceremonial drinking. First, there is the wealthily equipped Tomb 11 from Kalavasos-*Ayios Dhimitrios* (Goring 1989) which contained three adult females and several child and infant remains. Among the ceramic assemblage was a fine Mycenaean krater decorated with swimming fish (Crouwel and Morris 1987: 43, no. 9), perhaps confirming differing choices of iconography for males and females. The unusual horns-of-consecration krater from Kalavasos-*Ayios Dhimitrios* Tomb 13, which depicts a seated female inside a shrine (Steel 1994: figs. 2, 4), is also associated with a female burial (South 1998). Secondly, there is an Aegeanizing cylinder seal from Idalion which depicts two female figures and a male with various items of drinking equipment (Karageorghis 1982: fig. 47). While there are wealthy Late Cypriot child burials, such as the three infants and child in Kalavasos-*Ayios Dhimitrios* Tomb 12, whose grave furniture included a silver Hittite figurine (South 1998: pl. 19.1), there is no evidence that subadults took part in this activity or were equipped with an elite drinking set at death. However, the children in Kalavasos Tomb 12 were equipped with a large Monochrome krater (South 1998), which was possibly a substitute for the high status Mycenaean pictorial krater. Although not conclusive, the evidence from Kalavasos might suggest that women of high status were allowed to participate in ceremonial drinking or that it was at least considered appropriate to provide them with drinking equipment at burial.

Ritualized consumption of wine within a funerary context does not appear to be a gender specific activity on Cyprus during the Late Bronze Age. Bearing in mind the social context in which such activities are believed to have occurred elsewhere in prehistoric Europe (Sherratt 1997a), this has significant ramifications for Late Cypriot gender relations, at least at the higher end of the social spectrum, and may be indicative of some form of high status held by women in their own right in Late Cypriot society. The funerary context of drinking ritual in Cyprus and the limited evidence for female participation might imply that high status females were not excluded from ceremonies designed to legitimize group membership.

THE END OF THE BRONZE AGE

The dramatic upheavals at the end of the Late Bronze Age—mass destructions from the Aegean to the coast of the Levant, the disappearance of palace-based economies from the Aegean, central Anatolia, and parts of the Levant, the breakdown of large-scale, long-distance trade, and presumably widespread population movements (Sandars 1985)—are associated with major disruptions to the socio-political fabric of the region. Cyprus appears to have undergone two major periods of upheaval, the first in the 12th century, after which Cypriot culture continued and flourished with very little overall change but with possible infiltration of new ethnic groups (Iacovou 1989; Karageorghis 1992, 1997), and the second in the 11th century, which involved a fundamental overhaul of the geopolitical and socio-economic structure of the island (Iacovou 1989, 1994; Steel 1993, 1996: 288; Rupp 1998: 213). The new society which emerged in LC IIIB–CG I was largely characterized by warrior burials and what have been described as "Homeric" lifestyles (Coldstream 1989; Catling 1994, 1995). In Cyprus, we see the earliest normalization of what was to become the Iron Age warrior feasting equipment, standard throughout the Aegean: bronze cauldrons and sets of obeloi accompanied by iron knives, swords, spears, and dirks (Catling 1995). Presumably, such transformations, and in particular the emergence of an explicitly militaristic warrior class which defined itself through warfare, hunting, feasting and drinking, would have had considerable repercussions on gender relations.

Major changes in drinking ceremonies can be postulated as early as the 13th–12th centuries B.C. with a move away from the Mycenaean drinking set to bronze drinking equipment, deposited in tombs from LC IIC and increasingly in LC IIIA (Keswani 1989b: 65). This may reflect changing spheres of economic and political influence, with Cyprus coming into closer contact with Egypto-Palestine where similar equipment is apparent in elite burials and settlement contexts in the southern Levant at sites such as Tell el-Ajjul, Megiddo, Deir el-Balah, and as far inland as Tell es-Sa'idiyeh from the 13th century B.C. (Petrie 1933: pl. 8.14–16; Pritchard 1968: 103–4; Dothan 1979: figs. 38–42, 148–51; Tubb 1995: pl. 9.1). It also seems to reflect shifting gender relations, as in Cyprus this equipment seems mainly to be associated with males. Perhaps as early as the late 13th century we can chart the emergence of an elite warrior class on the island. By the late 11th or early 10th century B.C., the structures of the proto-Iron Age city kingdoms of Cyprus were established (Steel 1993),[2] and alongside this we see the development of a distinctive burial kit characterized by spectacular bronze feasting equipment: *obeloi*, bronze cauldrons, and occasional bronze tripods, LC IIIA heirlooms (Catling 1988). To some extent this developed from the equipment buried in LC IIIA tombs.

There is a continuous underlying trend that extends back in time to the earliest Cypriot consumers of alcohol in the Early-Middle Cypriot period. In Cyprus this activity always appears to have had a very specific funerary connotation, and so the disruption to funerary feasting in Greece that Cavanagh notes following the collapse of the Mycenaean palaces does not affect Cyprus during the period of social and political upheaval at the end of the Late Bronze Age (1998: 111). While there is no apparent change in context of ceremonial consumption of alcohol between the Bronze Age and Iron Age in Cyprus, the status of the individuals involved appears to be explicitly related to their role as warriors. The pictorial style of Proto White-Painted and White-Painted pottery that developed in the 11th century B.C. reflects the aristocratic and warlike concerns of this social class (Sherratt 1992: 331–33). This is essentially a "macho" style depicting men in aristocratic pursuits such as hunting (Iacovou 1988: figs. 45, 77–78), seafaring (Iacovou 1988: figs. 10, 11), horse riding (Iacovou 1988: figs. 19, 21, 50), and drinking (Iacovou 1988: figs. 34, 36). In addition, there are musicians (Iacovou 1988: fig. 70), who, no doubt, offered the entertainment and epic recitals at feasts. This world is not too distant from that described in Homer's *Odyssey*, and the Proto White Painted-White Painted I pictorial style has been related explicitly to the transmission of an Aegean warrior class and its epic poetry to Cyprus (Deger-Jalkotzy 1994: 21). Sherratt suggests that the style is a means of marking membership of a particular elite social group whose rank was based on the military prowess and hunting skills of its male members (Sherratt 1992: 333). It is noteworthy that the 11th century pictorial style has no representations of females. In contrast, while females are not overly represented on the Mycenaean pictorial style, neither are they entirely absent (Walters 1900: fig. 127; Vermeule and Karageorghis 1982: pls. 3.2,10–12; 5.2–3; Steel 1994: figs. 2, 4; Steel 1998: notes 58–60). The implication might be that the socio-economic and political changes at the end of the Late Bronze Age really did have a dramatic impact on gender relations and, in particular, on the status and activities of upper class females.

There is only limited and tenuous evidence for elite female participation in drinking ceremonies in the 11th century B.C., most notably from Kourion-*Kaloriziki* Tomb 40. This tomb housed a richly furnished burial, equipped with one of the most elaborate displays of military equipment (McFadden 1954: pls. 25–26) and a fine bronze drinking set, comprising at least one, and possibly a pair of bronze amphorae, a bronze strainer, possibly a pair of bronze tripods, together with a set of ceramic drinking vessels (McFadden 1954: pls. 21–23, 27). This is usually thought to be a male-female joint burial, possibly even a form of *suttee* (McFadden 1954: 134; Hood 1973: 40–41; Catling 1995; Steel 1995a: 23), but the only (cremated) skeletal remains recovered by excavation are those of an adult female (McFadden 1954: 133). The tomb was looted, and the possibility that the cremated remains of a male burial had been removed along with the fine bronze amphora in the Cyprus Museum should not be ignored. In other cases where fine bronze drinking sets were deposited in 11th–10th century tomb groups, most notably the fine array of equipment in Tombs 49 and 58 from Palaepaphos-*Skales* (Karageorghis 1983: pls. 60–63, 89) and Tomb 39 in Kourion-*Kaloriziki* (Benson 1973: pl. 41), these were associated with male burials. These burials stand out from contemporary burials throughout Cyprus, not only in terms of the wealth of their elaborate funerary gifts but also for the increased expenditure in construction of the tomb facility (Steel 1995b). Limited osteological reports are insufficient to resolve what burial assemblages were specifically male or female in the LC IIIB–CG I periods, a problem compounded by the re-use of tombs for successive interments. Present evidence suggests, however, that the typical feasting equipment comprising bronze vessels, occasional tripods and *obeloi*, which were usually associated with the trappings of elaborate military display, remained firmly in the male arena.

While Kourion-*Kaloriziki* Tomb 40 implies female access to these high status accoutrements, the obvious problems surrounding the excavation of the tomb and the provenance of many of the looted objects attributed to this tomb group (Goring 1995; Steel 1996: 297–98) suggest that any conclusions drawn on the basis of this tomb group alone are highly suspect.

Following the disruptions at the end of the Late Bronze Age, there seems to be considerable evidence for a transformation in male-female relations based on the high status attributed certain males linked specifically to their roles as warriors. This is reflected not only in the close association of drinking equipment with male burials and warrior equipment but also in the development of a new iconographic form used to decorate ceramic versions of the metal drinking sets and depicting a host of aristocratic, male activities. Females largely appear to be excluded from these activities, and the only relationship between a female and the drinking set and military paraphernalia that can be demonstrated is unclear and from a looted tomb. The impetus for this change in gender relations might be attributed to two related phenomena, the unsettled economic and socio-political conditions of the 12th–11th centuries B.C., and the assumed influx of a new population including large elements from the Aegean during the same period (Iacovou 1989; Karageorghis 1992; Deger-Jalkotzy 1994).

CONCLUSIONS

From its introduction to Cyprus in EC III–MC I (or earlier), there is considerable evidence that ritualized consumption of wine (or some other alcoholic drink) was explicitly associated with funerary ritual, suggesting that it was used specifically as a means for group legitimization through exclusive rituals centered on membership of ancestral groups. While in other parts of the ancient world this activity seems to be exclusively associated with male elites and warriors, in Cyprus during the Late Bronze Age there is limited evidence for female participation in such activities. This might imply that certain females were not excluded from activities relating to the elite status of their kinship or family group in contrast to the situation in contemporary, neighboring societies.

At the transition to the Iron Age, however, there is evidence for major upheavals in the socio-economic and political structure of Cyprus and, as a corollary, on the gender relations of Cypriot society. This is first evident as early as the late 13th century B.C. with changes in the drinking equipment deposited in tombs, possibly reflecting a shift in emphasis of the Cypriot cultural and economic sphere away from Ugarit and the cities of the northern Levant to the Egyptian sphere of influence in southern Palestine. This drinking equipment is explicitly associated with military paraphernalia from the 12th–11th centuries B.C. as standard elements of a warrior's equipment. The high social position enjoyed by certain females of Late Cypriot society was apparently eclipsed by the emergence of this warrior class and other areas of "elite" culture, such as the newly developed pictorial style, seem to corroborate the implied shifting relationship between males and females on Cyprus at the transition to the Iron Age.

ACKNOWLEDGMENTS

I would like to thank the organizers of the Engendering Aphrodite conference for all their encouragement and patience with the completion of this paper and my *BASOR* reviewers for their helpful comments. Much of the research was carried out at Kalavasos-*Ayios Dhimitrios*, and I am very grateful to Professor Ian Todd and Alison South for access to this ceramic material and for their help. I would also like to thank the School of Classics, Trinity College, Dublin, which facilitated the final stages of this research under the East Mediterranean Studies Programme.

NOTES

1. Use wear analysis of Middle Cypriot Red Polished pottery likewise indicates that it was not made specifically as a funerary ware but was used extensively in the settlement before being deposited in tombs (Dugay 1996).

2. Rupp, however, dates the emergence of the Cypriot Iron Age city kingdoms to the 8th century B.C., postulating a series of chiefdoms for the LC IIIB–CG I/II periods (1998: 216–17).

REFERENCES

Barnett, R. D.
1985   Assurbanipal's Feast. *Eretz-Israel* 18: 1–6.

Benson, J. L.
1973   *The Necropolis of Kaloriziki*. Studies in Mediterranean Archaeology 36. Göteborg: Åströms.

Binford, L.
1972   Mortuary Practices: Their Study and Their Potential. Pp. 208–43 in *An Archaeological Perspective*, ed. L. Binford. New York and San Francisco: Seminar.

Bolger, D.
1998   The Pottery. Pp. 93–132 in *Lemba Archaeological Project II.1A. Excavations at Kissonerga-Mosphilia, 1979–1992.*, ed. E. Peltenburg. Studies in Mediterranean Archaeology 70:2. Göteborg: Åströms.

Bright, L.
1995a   A Possible Case for the Practice of Abandonment During the Late Cypriot and Cypro-Geometric Periods. Pp. 35–43 in *Klados. Essays in Honour of J. N. Coldstream*, ed. C. Morris. London: Institute of Classical Studies.
1995b   Approaches to the Archaeological Study of Death with Particular Reference to Ancient Cyprus. Pp. 62–74 in *The Archaeology of Death in the Ancient Near East*, eds. S. Campbell and A. Green. Oxbow Monograph 51. Oxford: Oxbow.

Brown, J. A.
1981   The Search for Rank in Prehistoric Burials. Pp. 25–37 in *The Archaeology of Death*, eds. R. Chapman, I. Kinnes, and K. Randsborg. Cambridge: Cambridge University.

Carter, J. B.
1995   Ancestor Cult and the Occasion of Homeric Performance. Pp. 285–312 in *The Ages of Homer. A Tribute to Emily Townsend Vermeule*, eds. J. B. Carter and S. Morris. Austin: University of Texas.

Catling, H. W.
1988   Workshop and Heirloom: Prehistoric Bronze Stands in the East Mediterranean. *Report of the Department of Antiquities of Cyprus*: 69–91.
1994   Cyprus in the Eleventh Century B.C.–an End or a Beginning? Pp. 133–40 in *Cyprus in the 11th Century B.C.*, ed. V. Karageorghis. Nicosia: A. G. Leventis Foundation.
1995   Heroes Returned? Subminoan Burials from Crete. Pp. 123–36 in *The Ages of Homer. A Tribute to Emily Townsend Vermeule*, eds. J. B. Carter and S. Morris. Austin: University of Texas.

Cavanagh, W.
1998   Innovation, Conservatism and Variation in Mycenaean Funerary Ritual. Pp. 103–14 in *Cemetery and Society in the Aegean Bronze Age*, ed. K. Branigan. Sheffield: Sheffield Academic.

Coldstream, J. N.
1989   Status Symbols in Cyprus in the Eleventh Century B.C. Pp. 325–35 in *Early Society in Cyprus,* ed. E. Peltenburg. Edinburgh: University of Edinburgh.

Comaroff, J.
1996   The Empire's Old Clothes: Fashioning the Colonial Subject. Pp.19–38 in *Cross-Cultural Consumption: Global Markets, Local Realities*, ed. D. Howes. New York: Routledge.

Conkey, M. W., and Gero, J. M.
1991   Tensions, Pluralities, and Engendering Archaeology: An Introduction to Women and Prehistory. Pp. 3–30 in *Engendering Archaeology: Women and Prehistory*, eds. J. M. Gero and M. W. Conkey. Oxford: Blackwell.

Crouwel, J. H., and Morris, C. E.
1987   An Early Mycenaean Fish Krater from Maroni, Cyprus. *Annual of the British School at Athens* 82: 37–46.

Deger-Jalkotzy, S.
1994   The Post-Palatial Period of Greece: An Aegean Prelude to the 11th Century B.C. in Cyprus. Pp. 11–29 in *Cyprus in the 11th Century B.C.*, ed. V. Karageorghis. Nicosia: A. G. Leventis Foundation.

Dikaios P.
1936/37   An Iron Age Painted Amphora in the Cyprus Museum. *Annual of the British School at Athens* 37: 56–72.

Dothan, T.
1979   *Excavations at the Cemetery of Deir el-Balah*. Qedem 10. Jerusalem: Hebrew University.
Dugay, L.
1996   Specialized Pottery Production on Bronze Age Cyprus and Pottery Use-wear Analysis. *Journal of Mediterranean Archaeology* 9: 167–92.
Evans, A.
1930   *The Palace of Minos. A Comparative Account of the Early Successive Stages of the Early Cretan Civilization as Illustrated in the Discoveries at Knossos*. Vol. 3. London: Macmillan.
1936   *The Palace of Minos. A Comparative Account of the Early Successive Stages of the Early Cretan Civilization as Illustrated in the Discoveries at Knossos*. Vol. 4. London: Macmillan.
Fischer, P. M.
1986   *Prehistoric Cypriot Skulls*. Studies in Mediterranean Archaeology 75. Göteborg: Åströms.
Gjerstad, E.
1934   *Swedish Cyprus Expedition*. Vol. 1: *Finds and Results of the Excavations in Cyprus 1927–1931*. Stockholm: Swedish Cyprus Expedition.
Goring, E.
1989   Death in Everyday Life: Aspects of Burial Practice in the Late Bronze Age. Pp. 95–105 in *Early Society in Cyprus*, ed. E. Peltenburg. Edinburgh: University of Edinburgh.
1995   The Kourion Sceptre: Some Facts and Factoids. Pp. 103–10 in *Klados. Essays in Honour of J. N. Coldstream*, ed. C. Morris. London: Institute of Classical Studies.
Gubel, E.
1993   The Influence of Egypt on Western Asiatic Furniture and Evidence from Phoenicia. Pp.139–51 in *The Furniture of Western Asia Ancient and Traditional*, ed. G. Herrmann. Mainz: von Zabern.
Hastorf, C. A.
1991   Gender, Space and Food in Prehistory. Pp. 132–59 in *Engendering Archaeology: Women and Prehistory*, eds. J. M. Gero and M. W. Conkey. Oxford: Blackwell.
Herscher, E.
1997   Representation Relief on Early and Middle Cypriot Pottery. Pp. 25–36 in *Four Thousand Years of Images on Cypriote Pottery. Proceedings of the Third International Conference of Cypriote Studies. Nicosia, 3–4 May 1996*, eds. V. Karageorghis, R. Laffineur, and F. Vandenabeele. Nicosia: A. G. Leventis Foundation.
Hood, S.
1973   Mycenaean Settlement in Cyprus and the Coming of the Greeks. Pp. 40–50 in *The First International Symposium, "The Mycenaeans in the Eastern Mediterranean,"* ed. V. Karageorghis. Nicosia: Department of Antiquities.
Iacovou, M.
1988   *The Pictorial Pottery of Eleventh Century B.C. Cyprus*. Studies in Mediterranean Archaeology 78. Göteborg: Åströms.
1989   Society and Settlements in Late Cypriot III. Pp. 52–59 in *Early Society in Cyprus*, ed. E. Peltenburg. Edinburgh: University of Edinburgh.
1994   The Topography of Eleventh Century B.C. Cyprus. Pp. 149–64 in *Cyprus in the Eleventh Century B.C.*, ed. V. Karageorghis. Nicosia: A. G. Leventis Foundation.
Johnson, J.
1980   *Maroni de Chypre*. Studies in Mediterranean Archaeology 59. Göteborg: Åströms.
Karageorghis, V.
1982   *Cyprus from the Stone Age to the Romans*. London: Thames and Hudson.
1983   *Palaepaphos Skales. An Iron Age Cemetery in Cyprus*. Ausgrabungen in Alt-Paphos auf Cypern 3. Konstanz: Universitätsverlag.
1992   The Crisis Years: Cyprus. Pp. 79–86 in *The Crisis Years: The 12th Century B.C.*, eds. W. A. Ward and M. S. Joukowsky. Dubuque: Kendall/Hunt.
1997   Hearths and Bathtubs in Cyprus: A "Sea Peoples" Innovation? Pp. 276–82 in *Mediterranean Peoples in Transition. Thirteenth to Early Tenth Centuries B.C.E. Studies in Honor of Professor Trude Dothan*, eds. S. Gitin, A. Mazar and E. Stern. Jerusalem: Israel Exploration Society.

Keswani, P. S.
1989a   *Mortuary Ritual and Social Hierarchy in Bronze Age Cyprus*. Unpublished Ph.D. Dissertation, University of Michigan.
1989b   Dimensions of Social Hierarchy in Late Bronze Age Cyprus: An Analysis of the Mortuary Data from Enkomi. *Journal of Mediterranean Archaeology* 2: 49–86.
1993   Models of Local Exchange in Late Bronze Age Cyprus. *Bulletin of the American Schools of Oriental Research* 292: 73–83.
1996   Hierarchies, Heterarchies, and Urbanization Process: the View from Bronze Age Cyprus. *Journal of Mediterranean Archaeology* 9: 211–50.

Knapp, A. B.
1996   Settlement and Society on Late Bronze Age Cyprus: Dynamics and Development. Pp. 54–80 in *Late Bronze Age Settlement in Cyprus: Function and Relationship*, eds. P. Åström and E. Herscher. Studies in Mediterranean Archaeology Pocket-book 126. Jonsered: Åströms.

Langdon, S.
1989   The Return of the Horse Leader. *American Journal of Archaeology* 93: 185–201.

Manning, S. W.
1993   Prestige, Distinction, and Competition: the Anatomy of Socioeconomic Complexity in Fourth to Second Millennium B.C.E. *Bulletin of the American Schools of Oriental Research* 292: 35–58.

Manning, S. W., and de Mita, F. A.
1997   Cyprus, the Aegean, and Maroni-*Tsaroukkas*. Pp. 103–41 in *Cyprus and the Aegean in Antiquity*. Nicosia: Department of Antiquities.

Manning, S. W., and Monks, S. L.
1998   Late Cypriot Tombs at Maroni-*Tsaroukkas*, Cyprus. *Annual of the British School at Athens* 93: 297–351.

McFadden, G.
1954   A Late Cypriote III Tomb from Kourion Kaloriziki, No. 40. *American Journal of Archaeology* 58: 131–42.

Meadows, K.
1999   The Appetites of Households in Early Roman Britain. Pp. 101–20 in *Dwelling in the Past: the Archaeology of Household Activities*, ed. P. M. Allison. New York: Routledge.

Mee, C.
1998   Gender Bias in Mycenaean Mortuary Practices. Pp. 165–70 in *Cemetery and Society in the Aegean Bronze Age*, ed. K. Branigan. Sheffield: Sheffield Academic.

Morris, D.
1985   *The Art of Ancient Cyprus*. Oxford: Phaidon.

Murray, A. S.
1900   Excavations at Enkomi. Pp. 1–54 in *Excavations in Cyprus*, eds. A. S. Murray, A. H. Smith, and H. B. Walters. London: British Museum.

Murray, O.
1983   The Greek Symposium in History. Pp. 257–72 in *Tria Corda. Scritti in Onore di Arnald Momigliano*, ed. E. Gabba. Como: Edizione New.

Negbi, O.
1986   The Climax of Urban Development in Bronze Age Cyprus. *Report of the Department of Antiquities of Cyprus*: 97–121.

Nevett, L. C.
1999   *House and Society in the Ancient Greek World*. New Studies in Archaeology. Cambridge: Cambridge University.

Palmer, R.
1995   Wine and Viticulture in the Linear A and B Texts of the Bronze Age Aegean. Pp. 269–85 in *The Origins and Ancient History of Wine*, eds. P. E. McGovern, S. J. Fleming, and S. H. Katz. Amsterdam: Gordon and Breach.

Peltenburg, E., ed.
1998   *Lemba Archaeological Project II.1A. Excavations at Kissonerga-Mosphilia,1979–1992*. Studies in Mediterranean Archaeology 70:2. Göteborg: Åströms.

Petrie, F.
1933   *Ancient Gaza III. Tell el Ajjul.* London: British School of Archaeology in Egypt.
Pritchard, J. B.
1968   New Evidence on the Role of the Sea Peoples in Canaan at the Beginning of the Iron Age. Pp. 99–
          112 in *The Role of the Phoenicians in the Interaction of Mediterranean Civilizations*, ed. W. A.
          Ward. Beirut: American University.
Rehak, P.
1995   Enthroned Figures in Aegean Art and the Function of the Mycenaean Megaron. Pp. 95–118 in *The
          Role of the Ruler in the Prehistoric Aegean*, ed. P. Rehak. Aegeum 11. Liège: Université de Liège,
          Histoire de l'art et archéologie de la Grèce antique; Austin, TX: University of Texas, Program in
          Aegean Scripts and Prehistory.
Rupp, D. W.
1998   The Seven Kings of the Land of Ia', a District on Ia-ad-na-na: Achaean Bluebloods, Cypriot Parve-
          nus or Both? Pp. 209–22 in *STEFANOS. Studies in Honor of Brunilde Sismondo Ridgway*, eds. K. J.
          Hartswick and M. C. Sturgeon. Philadelphia: University Museum, University of Pennsylvania.
Sakellarakis, J., and Sakellarakis, E.
1991   *Archanes.* Athens: Ekdotike Athenon S.A.
Sandars, N. K.
1985   *The Sea Peoples. Warriors of the Ancient Mediterranean.* Revised edition. London: Thames and Hudson.
Sherratt, A.
1997a   Cups that Cheered: The Introduction of Alcohol to Prehistoric Europe. Pp. 376–402 in *Economy
          and Society in Prehistoric Europe. Changing Perspectives*, compiled by A. Sherratt. Edinburgh:
          Edinburgh University.
1997b   The Ritual Use of Narcotics in Later Neolithic Europe. Pp. 403–30 in *Economy and Society in Pre-
          historic Europe. Changing Perspectives*, compiled by A. Sherratt. Edinburgh: Edinburgh University.
Sherratt, E. S.
1992   Immigration and Archaeology: Some Indirect Reflections. Pp. 316–46 in *Acta Cypria. Acts of an
          International Congress on Cypriote Archaeology Held in Göteborg on 22–24 August, 1991*, Part 1.2,
          ed. P. Åström. Studies in Mediterranean Archaeology Pocket-book 117. Göteborg: Åströms.
South, A. K.
1988   Kalavasos-Ayios Dhimitrios 1987: An Important Ceramic Group from Building X. *Report of the
          Department of Antiquities of Cyprus*, Part 1: 223–28.
1998   Kalavasos-Ayios Dhimitrios 1992–1996. *Report of the Department of Antiquities of Cyprus*: 151–75.
South, A. K., Russell, P., and Keswani, P. S.
1989   *Kalavasos-Ayios Dhimitrios. Ceramics, Objects, Tombs, Specialist Studies*, ed. I. Todd. Studies in
          Mediterranean Archaeology 71:3. Göteborg: Åströms.
Stager, L.
1985   The Firstfruits of Civilization. Pp. 172–87 in *Palestine in the Bronze And Iron Ages: Studies in
          Honour of Olga Tufnell*, ed. J. N. Tubb. London: University of London.
Stears, K.
1995   Dead Women's Society: Constructing Female Gender in Classical Athenian Funerary Sculpture. Pp.
          109–31 in *Time, Tradition and Society in Greek Archaeology. Bridging the Great Divide*, ed. N.
          Spencer. New York: Routledge.
Steel, L.
1993   The Establishment of the City Kingdoms in Iron Age Cyprus: An Archaeological Commentary. *Re-
          port of the Department of Antiquities of Cyprus*: 147–56.
1994   Representations of a Shrine on a Mycenaean Chariot Krater from Kalavasos-Ayios Dhimitrios, Cyprus.
          Annual of the British School of Archaeology at Athens 89: 201–11.
1995a   Challenging Preconceptions of Oriental "Barbarity" and Greek "Humanity": Human Sacrifice in the
          Ancient World. Pp. 18–27 in *Time, Tradition and Society in Greek Archaeology. Bridging the Great
          Divide*, ed. N. Spencer. New York: Routledge.
1995b   Differential Burial Practices in Cyprus in the 11th Century BC. Pp. 199–205 in *The Archaeol-

ogy of Death in the Ancient Near East, eds. S. Campbell and A. Green. Oxbow Monograph 51. Oxford: Oxbow.

1996   Transition from Bronze to Iron at Kourion: A Review of the Tombs from Episkopi-Bamboula and Kaloriziki. *Annual of the British School at Athens* 91: 287–300.

1998   The Social Impact of Mycenaean Pottery in Cyprus. *Annual of the British School at Athens* 93: 285–96.

1999   Wine Kraters and Chariots: The Mycenaean Pictorial Style Reconsidered. Pp. 803–11 in *MELETEMATA: Studies in Aegean Archaeology Presented to Malcolm H. Wiener as He Enters his 65th Year*, Vol. 3, eds. P. Betancourt, V. Karageorghis, R. Laffineur, W.-D. Niemeier. Aegeum 20. Liège: Université de Liège; Austin: University of Texas.

Tubb, J. N.

1995   An Aegean Presence in Egypto-Canaan. Pp. 136–45 in *Egypt, the Aegean and the Levant: Interconnections in the Second Millennium B.C.*, eds. W. V. Davies and L. Schofield. London: British Museum.

Vermeule, E., and Karageorghis, V.

1982   *Mycenaean Pictorial Vase Painting*. Cambridge, Massachussetts: Harvard University.

Walters, H. B.

1900   Excavations at Curium. Pp. 57–86 in *Excavations in Cyprus*, eds. A. S. Murray, A. H. Smith, and H. B. Walters. London: British Museum.

CYPRIOT WOMEN OF THE ARCHAIC PERIOD: EVIDENCE FROM SCULPTURE

LONE WRIEDT SØRENSEN

Institute of Archaeology and Ethnology
University of Copenhagen
Vandkunsten 5, DK 1467, Denmark
LWS@coco.ihi.ku.dk

Our knowledge of Cypriot women during the Archaic period is limited. The large number of statues and figures of stone and terracotta provides the best source of information, and the present paper offers a survey of the female image and its changes through the period in question. According to the available evidence, it is suggested that certain elements characterize either men or women, others seem to be shared by both sexes from the beginning, and others still relate first to the male image and then seem to pass on to the female image. It is also suggested that some of the figures, male as well as female, may be connected to rites of passage.

Over the past few years, several volumes dealing with women in antiquity have appeared, but most contributions have focused on topics ranging from the Classical to the Roman periods or on mythological aspects (for instance Hawley and Levick 1995; Koloski-Ostrow and Lyons 1997). With respect to sex and gender, the Archaic period has received less attention, and thus our knowledge of women, including their roles and status in the Archaic societies of the island, is extremely limited. With its geographical position, the island constituted a link between the Greek world and the Near East, and close connections existed in both directions. The population is often described as Cypro-Greek, Cypro-Phoenician or "Eteo-Cypriot," without clear distinctions being made, but the use of different types of script indicates a mixed population. According to contemporary Assyrian sources, the island was divided into kingdoms (Karageorghis 1982: 129), and the structure of the societies seems, therefore, to compare better with the kingdoms in the Near East than with the Greek *poleis*. We may assume that a hierarchic order existed also among women and that some women belonging to the elite may have been powerful, but we do not know the extent of their possibilities. In this context, the information available from Persia should be kept in mind. Here some of the royal women had certain powers in family matters, traveled freely, and owned and controlled estates. Moreover, various titles were used not only for royal but also for non-royal women, indicating, for example, that women of the workforce could obtain superior positions (Brosius 1996).

Such evidence is not available from Cyprus where tomb finds and sculpture, including terracottas, represent the two major sources of information. However, as the dead were buried in collective tombs, it is often difficult to distinguish between the different burial assemblages, and the lack of systematic sex identifications of the skeletons poses further obstacles. Useful information can, no doubt, be deduced from burial assemblages, but the present paper focuses on the information drawn from the female image. The large stone statues represent a point of departure, but as many of them are fragmentary, often with the heads alone preserved, references are also made to statuettes and terracottas in order to fill in the gaps. Large stone statues were dedicated in sanctuaries, presumably by the elite of the local kingdoms. Male statues seem to be more numerous than female statues, and from the beginning, both beardless men and men with a short or a long beard were made, indicating that age differentiation was important in the male image (Sørensen 1994: 87). The same phenomenon cannot be detected among the female statues, and not only because age, as such, was not expressed at this early period. Nothing else by way of dress or hairdo implies different ages or statuses as was the case in Greece, where the bride and the married woman were distinguished by covering the head with a veil or a mantle (Vérilhac and Vial 1998: 297, 307). Although the sculptures do not represent portraits of women, the present analysis provides us with some idea of how they themselves or the society wished or allowed them to be presented in public. In addition, references are made to male statues, as a study of women based upon representations makes little sense without a comparison with contemporary male images.

GODS OR MORTALS?

Cypriot male statues are generally interpreted as representations of mortal men, while some of the female statues are referred to as images of the Great Goddess (J. Karageorghis 1977; Hermary 1989: 400). The female statues in question wear a tall headdress decorated with floral motifs or a combination of floral motifs and relief figures of sphinxes, winged figures and Hathor heads on pillars (fig. 1). I have argued against a divine interpretation in another context (Sørensen 1994), but some of the

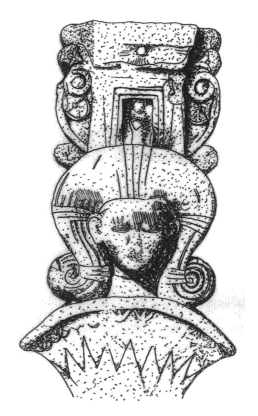

Figure 1. Female with calathos.
Hermary (1985: fig. 19).

Figure 2. Hathor capital.
Hermary (1989: no. 807).

aspects may be repeated here. During the Archaic period, images easily identified as gods and demi-gods were known. Small figures of Astarte, Dea Gravida, Zeus Ammon and Herakles are well-known examples, and stone statues of Zeus Ammon and Herakles are documented from the later 6th century B.C. (Hermary 1989: 299, 305, 394). In earlier stone sculpture, however, the repertoire of deities is limited. Best known are the so-called Hathor capitals, showing only the head of the goddess (fig. 2; Hermary 1985: 199; 1989: 396) and her male associate, Bes, who could also be represented in an abbreviated form as a head placed on a pedestal (Hermary 1989: 295). Both deities were also depicted in other media in Cyprus. On a sherd from a local amphora, a Hathor capital is painted between human figures leading a sacrificial animal towards it (Hermary 1985: fig. 26). This scene provides evidence that offerings took place in connection with these capitals. Pillars and aniconic stones, known from the Near East, were also used as cult symbols in various sanctuaries of the island (V. Karageorghis 1976: 98; Gjerstad 1935: 651, figs. 261–62; Maier 1985: pls. 13, 3–4 and 6). The material seems to indicate that divine aspects were clearly expressed when needed, and it is, therefore, likely that not only anony-mous statues of men but also those of women represent mortals.

DRESS AND ACCESSORIES: CULT OR STATUS?

The production of large statues started during the 7th century B.C. in the Cypriot and Greek societ-ies, but certain differences may be noticed over and above their stylistic particulars. While the Greeks produced both standing and seated statues (Adams 1978), Cypriot statues of the Archaic period are all standing. Males as well as females are dressed, and the naked youth, the *kouros*, which was very popular in Greece, was not produced in Cyprus.

Little attention is directed towards the body shape in Cypriot sculpture; the back is often treated in-sufficiently in contrast to the heads, which are of-ten elaborately executed. In fact, the similarities concerning body shape and dress fashion some-times make it difficult to identify Cypriot statues with regard to sex. Today the presence or absence of either beard or jewelry may be the only sex in-dicator, but perhaps the painted decoration, which is now mostly lost, once helped to emphasize cer-tain differences. The variety of dress for the early female statues is particularly limited in compari-son to that of men. Female statues are clothed in a long garment with sleeves, and their hair is cov-ered with what looks like a veil or a wig. Some-times there seems to be a "diadem" below the veil, lifting it up above the forehead; as Hermary has suggested, this may be a later trait (Hermary 1989: no. 639). Some of the statues wear a headgear re-sembling a wreath (fig. 3), which has also been interpreted as a turban (Ergülec 1972: pl. 3; Cesnola 1885: pl. 15:18; Hermary 1989: 400; V. Karageorghis 1993: 93). The combination of a veil and a wreath/turban is also seen on some of the heads in the British Museum dating to about the middle of the 6th century B.C. (Pryce 1931: C 271– C 273).

Figure 3. *Female with a wreath/turban. Hermary (1989: no. 811).*

Figure 4. *Male with turban.*
Pryce (1931: no. C 79).

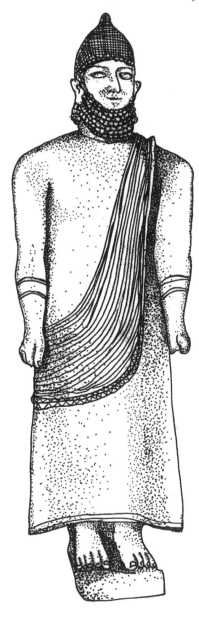

Figure 5. *Male with conical cap.*
Cesnola (1885: no. 407).

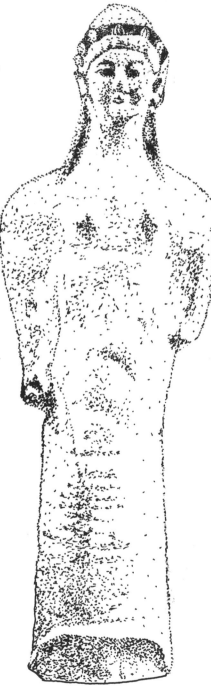

Figure 6. *Female with pointed cap.*
Karageorghis (1993: pl. 59, 2).

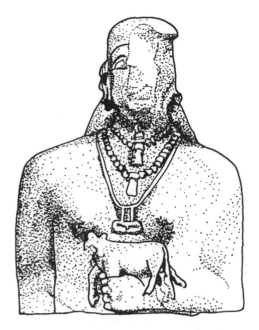

Figure 7. *Female with scarab seals. Westholm (1937b: pl. 185).*

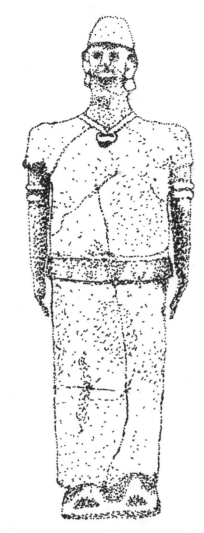

Figure 8. *Male with scarab seal, Karageorghis (1993: pl. 13, 2).*

However, as known from many male statues, the wig-like hairstyle was not reserved for the female image. Men are also shown wearing it alone or in combination with a turban, a conical or pointed cap, or a band. Turbans are mostly worn by bearded men (fig. 4; V. Karageorghis 1978: pl. 28:38; 1993: nos. 68–70) and are sometimes referred to as *mitra*, which according to Herodotus (7.90) were worn by Cypriot kings. By analogy, it could be argued that a turban-like headgear also distinguished important women in the Cypriot kingdoms. This interpretation seems to be contradicted by the fact that some statues of beardless males and even female musicians are shown wearing this type of headgear (Pryce 1931: C 22; V. Karageorghis 1993: 88; Hermary 1989: no. 790). However, these representations appear to be later, and we cannot rule out the possibility that the significance of this headgear changed through time. The conical cap was exclusively worn by Cypriot men through most of the Archaic period (fig. 5; Hermary 1989: 22; V. Karageorghis 1993: 86), but during the second part of the 6th century B.C., a pointed cap adorned with a wreath was introduced. It was used by both men and women, as demonstrated by terracottas from Mersinaki (fig. 6), and it may have been of a hieratic character as suggested by V. Karageorghis (1993: 87, pl. 59: 2–4).

Early female statues are often characterized by impressive jewelry. The so-called ear-caps and large necklaces are the most conspicuous elements with clear connotations of wealth and status (fig. 7). Some of these statues also wear one or more scarab seals in a string around the neck (Westholm 1937b: pl. 185; V. Karageorghis 1993: 97). Since none of the stone sculptures of men seems to be wearing these items, it would be tempting to conclude that they were only used in a female context. In contrast, two beardless male terracottas from Ayia Irini wear a scarab seal in a short string around the

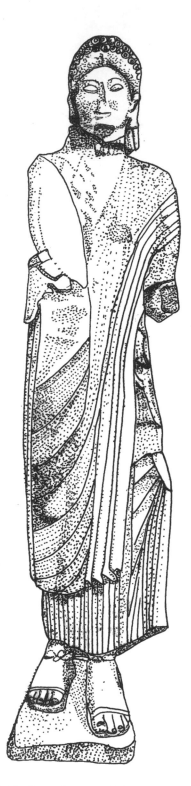

Figure 9. The Vouni Kore. Westholm (1937a: pl. 51).   *Figure 10.* Male with a wreath. Cesnola (1885: no. 453).

neck (fig. 8; V. Karageorghis 1993: pl. 13: 48–49). They demonstrate an early appearance of this iconographic feature in terracotta for male statues, but a continuation is not documented in stone examples. Scarab seals may have continued to be associated with women throughout the 6th century B.C., for they reappear in the female image by the end of that century and are represented in superimposed rows or in bundles (Yon 1974: 121; Hermary 1989: nos. 815 and 818; Nielsen 1983: no. 40). According to Lagarce (1976: 171), scarab seals have a talismanic function and, worn in a specific way, become sacred emblems of a fertility goddess, her priestesses, or her adorants. Yon (1974: 121) holds a similar view, referring to the scarab seals as emblems of cult function before they turned into mere amulets in connection with the so-called temple boys. Some women in Cyprus may have been entitled to use seals for secular purposes as was the case in Persia (Brosius 1996: 50), but in Cyprus the interpretation as amulets and cult emblems is better documented. In Cyprus they were deposited in tombs for protection of the dead, and a terracotta figure of the so-called goddess with uplifted arms wearing a scarab seal painted in a string around the neck supports its identification as a cult emblem (Lagarce 1976: 170, fig. 6).

As a result of Greek influence during the later part of the 6th century, less conspicuous jewelry was introduced, and female images also began to wear a diadem or a simple fillet around the head (for the general development, see Yon 1974: 123). The fillet was also used by men and mostly by beardless men, perhaps even at an earlier date (Hermary 1989: nos. 71, 72), but the diadem, which adorned some of the Greek *korai*, was also reserved for women in Cyprus, who apparently combined it with both the old-fashioned local dress and the newly introduced Greek dress fashion (Hermary 1989: nos. 676–82). The Vouni *kore* (fig. 9; Westholm 1937a: pl. 51) is considered a good example of the so-called Cypro-

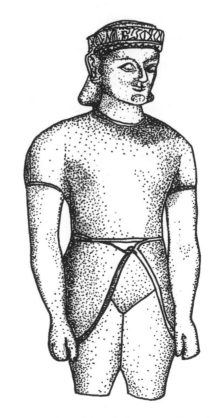

Greek style. Although she looks very Greek in other respects, her mantle is draped like that of Ionian male statues from about the middle of the 6th century B.C. (Boardman 1978: fig. 84). Male statues in Cyprus also adopted the Greek mantle style (fig. 10; Hermary 1989: no. 535), but in a male context this way of wearing the mantle is not a novelty. This is demonstrated by numerous figures in stone and terracotta (Hermary 1989: nos. 33–35; V. Karageorghis 1978: pls. 12, 20:1), but unlike the later statues, the mantle is often draped around the right arm. Here it seems that a piece of clothing originally belonging to men was taken over by female iconography in its Greek transformation. The band tied around the head of the Vouni *kore* is decorated with rosettes, elements which are not associated with earlier stone statues of women. However, some terracottas demonstrate that a headgear decorated with rosettes was not entirely absent from the early Archaic female imagery in Cyprus (V. Karageorghis 1993: 93). According to the decoration of the Hathor capitals, the rosette was also associated with this goddess in Cyprus (Hermary 1985: 683), and in the Near East it symbolized the goddess Ishtar (Barnett 1975: 90). Here, as well as in Egypt and Greece, the rosette has been interpreted as a symbol of fertility or as

Figure 11. Male with band of rosettes. Cesnola (1885: no 13).

an erotic symbol (Koch-Harnack 1989: 169). In the Near East, headgear with rosettes was reserved for the elite (Hermary 1989: 44), and in a Greek context the rosette is seen also as a symbol of male power (Koch-Harnack 1989: 30). In Cyprus, rosettes are connected, in particular, with statues of men wearing a broad band around the head, a bodice, and shorts, all of which may be decorated with rosettes (fig. 11) (Hermary 1989: 44; Sørensen 1994: 82). It has been suggested that this type of statue corresponds to the Greek *kouros*, but since both beardless men and men with a short beard are dressed in this fashion, different age groups are probably represented. A Cypriot terracotta group shows two figures dressed in this manner; they appear together with a large bull, which they are probably leading to sacrifice (V. Karageorghis 1976: fig. 114). Statues of men with large beards are not depicted dressed in this way. The specific costume may, therefore, signify younger men and older boys taking part in some kind of rite of passage, and as argued below, it is possible that a similar interpretation of the rosette is valid in a female context.

A series of statue heads dating to the late 6th and early 5th centuries B.C. are often considered images of the Great Goddess because they wear a more elaborate headgear that is usually called a *kalathos* (Hermary 1982). In several instances it is decorated with two or three tiers of rosettes, but more complicated arrangements, including lotuses and palmettes or palmette trees, are also shown in combination with sphinxes and other figures (fig. 1; Hermary 1982). On some of the *kalathoi*, the decorative elements seem to have been applied to a system of strings indicated by incised lines (e.g., Hermary 1982: pl. 37:1–2). A gold diadem found in a tomb below one of the rooms in the northwest palace at Nimrud may help illustrate how they were made (Matthiae 1997: 50). The decoration, which consists of a mixture of flowers and figures like some of the Cypriot pieces, is applied to a simple system of wires. The diadem was found in the tomb of a woman called Yabaya, perhaps the consort of Assurnasirpal III or Sargon II. It demonstrates that, nominally in Assyria, this type of headgear could be worn by elite women. In Greece, mortal women were also represented with a tall headdress decorated with flowers. The inscription on the base of a *kore* statue with a headdress like the Cypriot ones informs us that the statue represents Phrasikleia who died a maiden (Stewart 1990: 22). The headdress, which is decorated with alternating buds and half-open lotus flowers, may carry a symbolic reference to her unmarried status (Stewart 1997: 115). We may, therefore, suggest the possibility that the rosette, representing the flower in full bloom, was associated with Cypriot maidens ready for marriage.

Unfortunately, only the heads of the statues with *kalathoi* are preserved, yet smaller figures provide additional information. They illustrate that figures were not dressed identically nor were there any particular garments indicated to emphasize that they formed a special group. On the contrary, they are dressed like figures wearing other types of headgear. Above the long dress, the mantle may cover both shoulders (Yon 1974: no. 106; Nielsen 1983: no 40); alternatively, it may cover the left shoulder and extend below the right arm and across the body (Hermary 1989: no. 815). Both arrangements are Greek and were used by men and women in Greece as well as in Cyprus. Other figures with *kalathoi* wear a mantle that covers either the entire body or most of it and is draped around the body from the front (Hermary 1989: nos. 818). In Cyprus, this type of mantle seems to have been reserved for women and has no parallels among Greek statues. Another Greek mantle type, the diagonal mantle, which is well known from the Acropolis *korai* (Brouskari 1974: no. 680) also appeared in Cypriot female imagery. It is not documented in large stone statues in Cyprus, but it is worn by smaller figures, however, it is not always rendered correctly (Yon 1974: type II; Hermary 1989: nos. 682 and 686). In Cyprus, it was used in combination with a fillet, a diadem, or the Greek *kekryphalos* (Yon 1974: no. 44; Hermary 1989: 682; Westholm 1937a: pl. 59). By the beginning of the 5th century B.C., the *kekryphalos* became very popular in Cyprus (Yon 1974: 66), but according to the female statues, Cypriot women created their own version by adding a string of flowers mostly in the shape of rosettes (Hermary 1989: no. 701). During the 5th century, it was also decorated at times with a wreath of leaves (Hermary 1989: no. 719). This combination is seen in Greek vase painting ca. 500 B.C. (Boardman 1975: fig. 27), but since the wreaths are made of ivy leaves and worn by naked prostitutes participating in a symposium, they convey a different message. In Cyprus, many statues of bearded and beardless males are shown with wreaths of leaves around their heads from about the middle of the 6th century onwards (fig. 10). The leaves are not always easy to identify, and several types, but not the ivy, have been suggested (Cassimatis 1982). Within the Cypriot context, it is possible that this adornment passed from male to female imagery. At the same time, a new development seems to have taken place primarily among the male statues. The wreath of leaves may now be combined with buds, or in some cases with a separate wreath or diadem decorated with flowers below it (fig. 12; Hermary 1989: 124, 201). Sometimes rosettes are shown, but another type of flower (perhaps a narcissus) seems to have been more popular.

Figure 12. *Male with wreath and "diadem." Hermary (1989: no 245).*

CONCLUSION

This survey indicates that during the Archaic period, specific traits were in some cases related to both male and female statues. In other instances, however, certain elements were initially typical of male statues but subsequently appeared also in female imagery. Moreover, when new elements were introduced, some of the older elements disappeared from the male images. This is not an isolated phenomenon. In Athens, for example, parasols, fans and perhaps flywhisks, which are well-known Oriental male status symbols, became associated with the Athenian female image in vase painting during the Classical period (collected by Miller 1997: 192). A modern-day example of the same phenomenon is the adoption of trousers and jackets by women in western societies, although the underlying motivations are entirely different.

Statues cannot simply be equated with reality, however, and in real life differences between men and women, whether rich or poor, may have been emphasized by the types of material used for dress and headgear. For instance, wreaths of real flowers and leaves could be worn by everybody, but it is possible that wreaths and bands made of precious metal were actually used by the elite for festive occasions, despite the fact that they are only known as funerary jewelry (Laffineur 1992: pl. 9, T354, 120).

Another factor that must be taken into consideration is the religious context in which the Cypriot statues were produced and used, and the extent to which the depictions of both female and male images were influenced by this context should not be underestimated. This is supported by representations of musicians. As mentioned above, male and female musicians are shown with a turban-like headgear, and female musicians also wear elaborate dress, large jewelry, scarab seals and *kalathoi* (Hermary 1989: no.791; Ohnefalsch-Richter 1893: pl. 12:5). The many figures of musicians show that they played an important role in Cyprus as they did in other ancient societies. The high regard for music in Archaic Greece, for instance, is underlined by the fact that it was not uncommon that members of the nobility were skilled in playing the lyre (West 1992: 25).

According to the material evidence, a peaceful, dignified expression was chosen for the statuary, which conveys an expression of power. It is noteworthy, though, that the warrior aspect is seldom expressed by the stone statues (V. Karageorghis 1993: 89), considering the often troubled situation of the island. Another issue pertains to the reception of Greek style and dress fashion during the later 6th century B.C. Although Greek fashion was a Mediterranean-wide phenomenon (Ridgway 1985: 7), the impact in Cyprus is perhaps better described as an example of "foreign accent" than "foreign language" (Lurie 1981: 7–8, 84–86), as the Greek elements were often combined with local characteristics. However, the specific needs for the reception of Greek fashion in Cyprus deserve further analyses, as factors pertaining to external politics, social structure, and internal constraints have to be taken into consideration.

Nonetheless, the above survey of Archaic Cypriot statuary shows that from the beginning, attention not only focused on both males and females, but males and females were represented according to the same basic principles with an emphasis on formal appearance. It could perhaps be argued that women were basically considered important as wives and daughters, and that impressive representations of them were conceived as supplementary illustrations of the importance of men. This view appears to be contradicted by the images, however. Although the large jewelry worn by the female statues may be interpreted according to this point of view, other characteristic traits, which were either shared with male statues from the onset or were gradually taken over from them, indicate that women were not just male appendages.

In conclusion, the statues and statuettes that have been considered in this paper represent a large group of imagery from Archaic Cyprus that we might call "public images." However, it should not be forgotten that the contemporary production of handmade terracottas provides a very different and informal picture of humans engaged in activities such as bread baking and childbirth, where the attention focuses on action (J. Karageorghis 1991).

REFERENCES

Adams, L.
1978　　*Orientalizing Sculpture in Soft Limestone*. BAR Supplementary Series 42. Oxford: British Archaeological Reports.

Barnett, R. D.
1975　　*A Catalogue of the Nimrud Ivories with Other Examples of Ancient Near Eastern Ivories in the British Museum*. London: British Museum.

Boardman, J.
1975　　*Athenian Red Figure Vases. The Archaic Period*. London: Thames and Hudson.
1978　　*Greek Sculpture. The Archaic Period*. London: Thames and Hudson.

Brosius, M.
1996　　*Women in Ancient Persia (559–331)*. Oxford Classical Monographs. Oxford: Clarendon.

Brouskari, M. S.
1974　　*The Acropolis Museum: A Desciptive Catalogue*. Athens: Commercial Bank of Greece.

Cassimatis, H.
1982　　A propos de couronnes sur les têtes masculines en calcaire de Chypre. *Report of the Department of Antiquities of Cyprus:* 156–63.

Cesnola, L. P. di
1885　　*A Descriptive Atlas of the Cesnola Collection of Cypriote Antiquities in the Metropolitan Museum of Art, New York*. Vol 1. Boston: Osgood.

Ergülec, H.
1972　　Large-Sized Cypriot Sculpture in the Archaeological Museums of Istanbul. Studies in Mediterranean Archaeology 20:4. Göteborg: Åströms.

Gjerstad, E.
1935　　Ayia Irini. Pp. 642–824 in *The Swedish Cyprus Expedition*. Vol. 2: *Finds and Results of the Excavations in Cyprus 1927–1931*. Stockholm: Pettersons.

Hawley, R., and Levick, B.
1995　　*Women in Antiquity: New Assessments*. New York: Routledge.

Hermary, A.
1982　　Divinités Chypriotes, 1. *Report of the Department of Antiquities of Cyprus*: 164–73.
1985　　Un nouveau chapiteau hathorique trouvé à Amathonte. *Bulletin de correspondance hellénique* 109: 657–99.
1989　　*Catalogue des antiquités de Chypre. Sculptures*. Musée du Louvre. Départment des antiquités orientales. Paris: Éditions de la Réunion des musées nationaux.

Karageorghis, J.
1977　　*La grande déesse de Chypre et son culte*. Lyons: Maison de l'Orient.
1991　　La vie quotidienne à Chypre d'apres les terres cuites d'époque géometrique et archaïque. Pp. 149–169 in *Cypriot Terracottas. Proceedings of the First International Conference of Cypriote Studies, Brussels-Liège-Amsterdam, 1989*, eds. F. Vandenabeele and R. Laffineur. Brussels-Liège: A. G. Leventis Foundation, Vrije Universiteit Brussels, Université de Liège.

Karageorghis, V.
1976　　*Kition: Mycenaean and Phoenician Discoveries in Cyprus*. London: Thames and Hudson.
1978　　A "Favissa" at Kazaphni. *Report of the Department of Antiquities of Cyprus*: 156–93.
1982　　*Cyprus from the Stone Age to the Romans*. London: Thames and Hudson.
1993　　*The Coroplastic Art of Ancient Cyprus*. Vol. 3: *The Cypro-Archaic Period. Large and Medium Size Sculpture*. Nicosia: A. G. Leventis Foundation.

Koch-Harnack, G.
1989　　*Erotische Symbole. Lotusblüte und gemeinsamer Mantel auf antiken Vasen*. Berlin: Mann.

Koloski-Ostrow, A. O., and Lyons, C. L., eds.
1997　　*Naked Truths. Women, Sexuality, and Gender in Classical Art and Archaeology*. New York: Routledge.

Laffineur, R.
1992　　Bijoux et Orfèvrerie. Pp. 1–32 in *La Nécropole d'Amathonte. Tombes 113–36*. Vol. 6: *Bijoux, armes,*

verres, astragales et coquillages, squelettes, eds. V. Karageorghis, O. Picard, and C. Tytgat. Études chypriotes 14. Nicosia: A. G. Leventis Foundation, École Française d'Athènes.

Lagarce, E.
1976   Remarques sur l'utilisation des scarabées, scaraboïdes, amulettes et figurines de type égyptien à Chypre. Pp. 167–182 in *Fouilles de Kition.* Vol. II: *Objets égyptiens et égyptisants. Scarabées, amulettes et figurines en pâte de verre et en faïence, vase plastique en faïence. Sites I et II, 1959–1975,* eds. G. Clerc, V. Karageorghis, E. Lagarce and J. Leclant. Nicosia: A. G. Leventis Foundation.

Lurie, A.
1981   *The Language of Clothes.* New York: Random House.

Maier, F. G.
1985   *Alt-Paphos auf Cypern. Ausgrabungen zur Geschichte von Stadt und Heiligtum 1966–1984.* Mainz am Rhein: von Zabern.

Matthiae, P.
1997   Gli assiri. L'arte e la potenza. *Archaeologia Viva* 65 n.s. (Sept): 50–55, 59–63.

Miller, M. C.
1997   *Athens and Persia in the Fifth Century BC. A Study in Cultural Receptivity.* Cambridge: Cambridge University.

Nielsen, A. M.
1983   *Cypriote Antiquities in the Ny Carlsberg Glyptotek, Copenhagen.* Studies in Mediterranean Archaeology 20:8. Göteborg: Åströms.

Ohnefalsch-Richter, M.
1893   *Kypros, die Bibel und Homer.* Berlin: Asher.

Pryce, F. N.
1931   *Catalogue of Sculpture in the Department of Greek and Roman Antiquities of the British Museum.* Vol. 1, 2: *Cypriote and Etruscan.* London: Oxford University.

Ridgway, B. S.
1985   Late Archaic Sculpture. Pp. 1–17 in *Greek Art. Archaic into Classical. A Symposium held at the University of Cincinnati 1982,* ed. C. G. Boulter. Leiden: Brill.

Sørensen, L. W.
1994   The Divine Image? Pp. 79–89 in *Cypriot Stone Sculpture. Proceedings of the Second International Conference of Cypriote Studies. Brussels-Liége 1993,* eds. F. Vandenabeele and R. Laffineur. Brussels-Liège: A. G. Leventis Foundation, Vrije Universiteit Brussels-Université de Liège.

Stewart, A.
1990   *Greek Sculpture. An Exploration.* New Haven and London: Yale University.

Stewart, A.
1997   *Art, Desire and the Body in Ancient Greece.* Cambridge and New York: Cambridge University.

Vérilhac, A. -M., and Vial, C.
1998   *Le Mariage Grec du V^{ie} siècle AV. J.- à l'epoque d'Auguste. Bulletin de correspondance hellénique,* Supplément 32. Athènes: École Française d'Athènes.

West, M. L.
1992   *Ancient Greek Music.* Oxford: Clarendon.

Westholm, A.
1937a   Vouni: The Palace. Pp. 111–292 in *The Swedish Cyprus Expedition.* Vol. 3: *Finds and Results of the Excavations in Cyprus 1927–1931.* Stockholm: Pettersons.
1937b   Arsos. Pp. 583–600 in *The Swedish Cyprus Expedition.* Vol. 3: *Finds and Results of the Excavations in Cyprus 1927–1931.* Stockholm: Pettersons.

Yon, M.
1974   *Un depôt de sculptures archaïques. Salamine de Chypre* V. Paris: de Boccard.

EVIDENCE OF GENDER AND FAMILY RELATIONS IN A TOMB OF THE CYPRO-ARCHAIC I PERIOD

MARIA HADJICOSTI

Department of Antiquities
The Republic of Cyprus
The Cyprus Museum
1097 Nicosia, Cyprus

The burial rites of the Cypro-Archaic I period mainly involved inhumations with a variety of grave goods, most of which were probably the personal possessions of the deceased. A clear picture about gender, the wealth and status of different individuals, and of women compared to men can be obtained in a few instances where tombs have been found unlooted with undisturbed contexts. One of the best examples of this kind of evidence is Tomb 1 at Mari, excavated in 1991 in the middle of Mari village in Larnaka District. As far the morphology of the tomb is concerned, the Mari tomb presents, at least for the ordinary cemeteries of the Cypro-Archaic I period, an unusual interior arrangement of the rock-cut chamber with regularly cut benches along three of its sides. Compared with other tombs of ordinary Cypro-Archaic cemeteries, it is obvious that an effort was made to accentuate the status of the buried family, especially the male individual, by means of an elaborately arranged and abundantly furnished post-mortem habitation. Analysis of the human skeletal remains indicates the position of each member of the family within the tomb, and this must, to a great extent, reflect the role of the deceased in real life. The dominant role of the male individual, not only in the close environment of his family but within the broader limits of the community and perhaps outside it, as well as the dominant position of his wife in the household, is amply attested by the funerary offerings. The unlooted condition of the tomb and its form provide us with valuable information concerning the community-wide organization of burial customs at this time. It also furnishes evidence concerning the gender and social and economic status of the deceased in addition to the economic capacity of the Mari region in the Cypro-Archaic I period.

Archaeological evidence for gender, family relations, and the socio-economic conditions of a particular community falls generally into various categories. It has already been noted that the most obvious evidence is that provided by burials (Ehrenberg 1989: 23), although settlement sites, sanctuaries, and isolated works of art may also provide valuable information. The present paper examines burial evidence with a view to better understanding the gender and family relations of the Cypro-Archaic period. It focuses on one particular tomb of the Cypro-Archaic I period uncovered in Mari Village, located 3 km southwest of the village of Kalavassos in the Vasilikos valley and not very far from Amathus (Hadjicosti 1997). The unlooted condition of the tomb, as well as its form and contents, provide us with valuable information concerning the community-wide organization of burial customs, the gender, social and economic position of the deceased, and the economic capacity of the Mari region during the Cypro-Archaic I period.

Although the intention here is not to examine thoroughly the question of gender in the burials of the Cypro-Archaic I period, as it would be an ambitious task requiring a detailed study of both the published and unpublished tombs, some general observations on Cypriot burials can provide a brief review of the topic. Burial rites in the Cypro-Archaic I period, not unlike the other periods of Cypriot history, mainly consist of inhumations with a variety of grave goods. Most of the latter were probably the personal possessions of the deceased, although in some instances the quantity and quality of the offerings indicate the existence of workshops specializing in the production of pottery intentionally made to be deposited in tombs. The surprisingly elaborate pottery shapes and decoration of earlier periods, which sometimes make the vessels unsuitable for use in everyday life, as well as the poor quality of vessels (made of unbaked clay and exhibiting deformations on their bodies) in at least three tombs from Nicosia-*Agioi Omologites*, indicate a pottery production oriented to satisfy this practice (Hadjicosti 1993: 190–91).

Observations on tombs and burial customs are closely dependent on the state of preservation of the tombs and the detailed presentation of the architectural and artifactual remains. The majority of Cypriot tombs, not only of the Cypro-Archaic period, but of all periods, present a disturbed context on account of one or more of the following factors: the habit of the population of reusing the tombs for multiple burials over a long period of time, the poor preservation of the tombs due to damp conditions, and systematic looting. Thus, the clearest picture about gender, the wealth and status of different individuals, and the position of women compared with men can only be obtained from tombs that have not been looted and are in an undisturbed context. Even so, in the great majority of the publications treating Cypriot tombs and cemeteries, the study of the skeletal remains is absent, and discussions are usually oriented to the status of the deceased and the social differentiation based exclusively on the presence or absence of precious grave goods and imports. Bolger's observation that "very little skeletal material from any period of Cypriot prehistory has been aged and sexed" is valid for all periods of Cypriot history (Bolger 1993: 32). The analysis of the human bones is the only factor that indicates the position of each member of the family within the tomb, and this must, to a great extent, reflect the role of the deceased in real life.

From this point of view, Mari Tomb 1 is a rare example of a case in which the ages and sexes of the occupants have clearly been established. The skeletal remains of the tomb, although incomplete due to the collapse of the tomb roof as well as to weathering of some skeletal elements, have been analyzed in detail by Sherry C. Fox, who kindly accepted our invitation to undertake their study (Fox 1997). Results of the analysis provide information that the occupants of the tomb consist of "a robust male (Individual A) of at least 26 years of age with osteoarthritis, a gracile adult female (Individual B) of short stature (approximately 155.7 cm in height), and a 4–5 year old child (Individual C)" (Fox 1997: 265). The child was identified among the remains of the female skeleton upon the examination of the bones, while the position of the two adult individuals was clearly defined during the excavation and will be discussed below in connection with the architecture and the grave goods.

THE TOMB AND ITS CONTENTS

Mari Tomb 1 is the first unlooted tomb excavated so far in the area of Mari. It was discovered in 1991 in the middle of the village (Cadastral Plan 55/28.1, Plot 72) during consolidation works carried out on the small, old building that houses the office of the mayor of the small community of Mari (fig. 1).

As far as the morphology of the tomb is concerned, it displays an elaborate interior arrangement (fig. 2), which does not, however, compare in any way with the built "royal" tombs of the same period. It is a rock-cut chamber tomb consisting of a trapezoidal chamber with rounded corners, a rather long entrance with a stomion blocked by a large worked limestone slab and a dromos, which has not been excavated. The entrance, oriented to the east, opens into the tomb approximately on the longitudinal

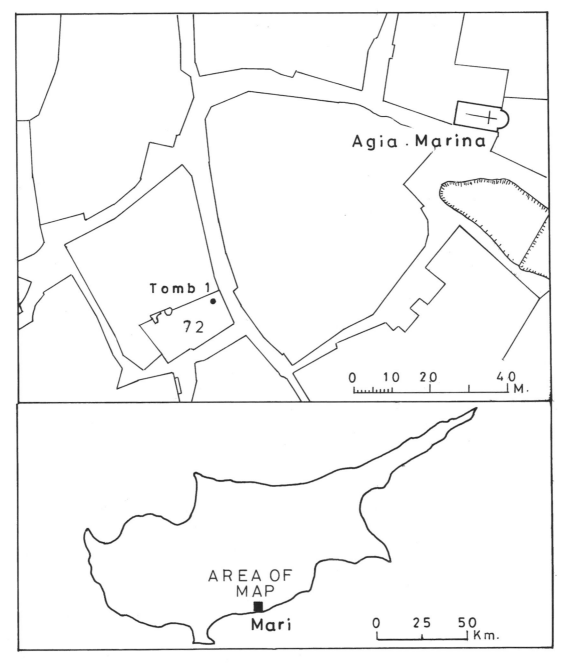

Figure 1. *Cadastral Plan showing the area of Mari Tomb 1 and map of Cyprus showing the area of Mari village.*

axis of the chamber. In terms of the ordinary tombs of the Cypro-Archaic I period, Tomb 1 presents an unusual interior arrangement of the chamber with fairly regularly cut benches along three sides. One bench along the west side, opposite the entrance, is narrower and higher than the other two and served for the deposition of the grave gifts. The other two, along the north and south sides, received the deceased. The male skeleton was found on the north bench and those of the woman and the child on the south bench. Both adults were deposited in a dorsal position, with both hands alongside the body and the head oriented toward the entrance of the chamber.

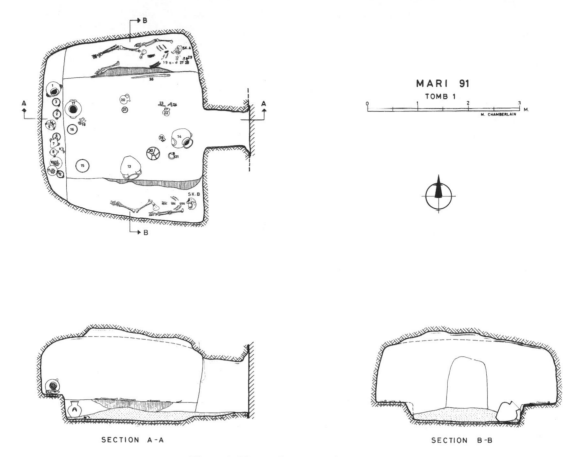

Figure 2. *Plan and sections of Mari Tomb 1.*

The contents of the chamber were found intact, apart from the damage caused by moisture and the collapse of the tomb roof. Large limestone blocks covered the large amphorae, which were deposited in the central area of the chamber; three of the amphorae were found broken. Roof collapse had damaged the edges of the two lower benches. Some bones were found on the floor, as were a number of small vessels and the metal objects which had evidently fallen from their original position along the left side of the man on the north bench and the right side of the woman on the south bench.

Neither the quantity nor the quality of the grave goods gives the impression of extraordinary wealth and indicates, rather, that the contents of the tomb represent the personal belongings of the deceased persons. The grave goods consist of the following items: five large storage amphorae, the largest of which, nos. 13 and 14, were placed closer to the female burial; a small number of bowls, small jugs, a lamp and four metal objects found on the floor of the chamber but evidently fallen from their original position during the collapse of the benches as mentioned above; twelve items consisting of amphoriskoi, jugs and bowls found *in situ*, placed in a row on the higher bench along the west side of the chamber; and finally, an iron ring, three small worked stones, a small fragment of an unidentified bronze object and three artifacts of unusual type, the only items found on benches and all placed near the face of the adult male on the north bench (Hadjicosti 1997: 253–58, pls. 50–54). The metal objects excavated on the floor (a bronze bowl, no. 21; an iron knife, no. 23; a fragmentary bronze fibula, no. 24; and an iron sword, no. 25) were found closer to the male burial (Hadjicosti 1997: fig. 4, pl. 54), while three of the vessels on the higher bench, bowls nos. 10–11 (Hadjicosti 1997: pl. 53) and amphoriskos no. 8 contained pebbles, perhaps a substitute of food, and were deposited closer to the female burial.

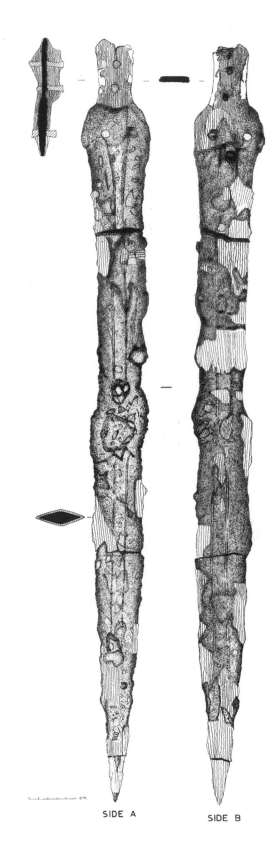

SIDE A   SIDE B

Figure 3. *Iron sword no. 25, photograph.*   **Figure 4.** *Iron sword no. 25, drawing.*

From the above description it is apparent that most of the artifacts are ceramic. The pottery classes consist entirely of Gjerstad Type IV (Gjerstad 1948: 48–91 and 184–206), represented by White Painted, Bichrome, Bichrome Red, Black-on-Red and Plain White ware; only a single specimen of foreign Phoenician ware of an early date is present. Four of the decorated bowls are of an extremely high quality, and some of the amphoriskoi and jugs are connected with Amathusian styles. The classification of the pottery places the contents of the tomb within the mature phase of the Cypro-Archaic I period, in the second half of the 7th century B.C. and not long after 650 B.C. (Hadjicosti 1997: 261).

Of greatest interest are, undoubtedly, the metal objects. The iron sword no. 25 (figs. 3–4), found immediately below the north bench near the left side of the male individual, represents one of his valuable belongings. It is 82.0 cm long without the pommel. The blade is leaf-shaped with a low midrib and parallel grooves on either side. On the blade there are traces of the scabbard, which must have been of wood covered with leather, and at two points there are clearly visible traces of a leather strap preserved across the blade. The elaborately rendered hilt has a rectangular upper terminal and broad splaying shoulder. At the end of the hilt is a horizontal iron border with a hemispherical recess at the center, very similar to that on the sword from Tamassos. Most probably the recess served to receive the button of the scabbard, traces of which are still preserved just below this point. On the hilt are remains of ivory plates, which were fixed by means of four bronze rivets, the heads of which were covered by a thin layer of silver. A new element in the technique of this kind of sword is the rectangular sheet of silver that covers the parallel edges of the hilt without any soldering.

The Mari sword represents a fine addition to the repertoire of long Cypriot swords. Swords of this type have been uncovered at Kouklia-*Palaepaphos*, Kourion, Amathus, Idalion, Tamassos, Nicosia, Enkomi, Salamis and perhaps Lapithos and Marion (Snodgrass 1964: 93–113; 1981), areas where Cypriot kingdoms flourished. As far as the classification is concerned, the Mari sword belongs to Type III in Snodgrass' classification (Snodgrass 1964: 102; 1981) and represents the third complete specimen of the type, together with the sword from Salamis (Karageorghis 1967: 38, no. 95; Karageorghis

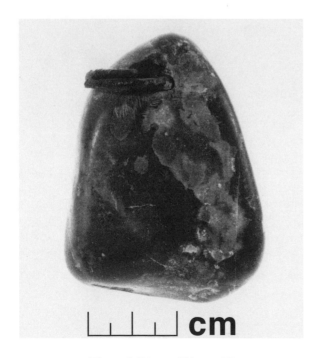

Figure 5. River pebble no. 27.   *Figure 6.* Bronze artifact no. 28.

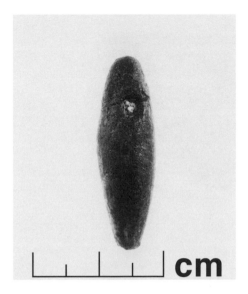

Figure 7. *Bronze artifact no. 29.*

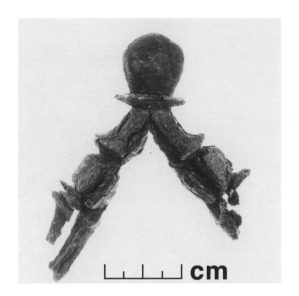

Figure 8. *Fragmentary iron fibula no. 24.*

1967: 43, pls. 45, 129:95) and the shorter one from Tamassos (Masson 1964: 227–30, figs. 16–17; Karageorghis et al. 1999: 108–9). Both were found in "royal" tombs. A few fragments belonging to swords of the same type are of unknown provenance. Similar long swords also appear on bronze statuettes of warriors, such as the examples from Salamis (Karageorghis 1973: 14, no. 188, pls. G and 103–105, 257; 19, no. 129; pls. 101–102) and on pictorial representations on vases (Karageorghis and Des Gagniers 1974: 65). A connection between this sword type and warriors or high-ranking officials is supported by the discoveries in the "royal" tombs mentioned above. The Mari sword, although found in an ordinary tomb, indicates the dominant role of the male, not only in his immediate environment, but also in the broader limits of the community and perhaps outside it. Some unique objects, nos. 27–29 (Hadjicosti 1997: 258, fig. 4, pl. 54), found on the bench near the face of the deceased support this notion. A pyramidal, dark colored river pebble, no. 27 (fig. 5) with a bronze suspension ring, as well as the two bronze artifacts, no. 28 (fig. 6) and no. 29 (fig. 7), hanging from lead rings, might be net-weights, bullets, weights or just pendants with some kind of symbolism signifying the status of the dead person. As far as we know, they have no parallels in Cyprus and may have been imported from a neighboring country, perhaps Egypt.

Another bronze object that may be interpreted as a status symbol is the extraordinarily large fibula, no. 24 (Hadjicosti 1997: 256, fig. 4, pl. 54; *infra* fig. 8), which was found closer to the male individual. It represents a well-known Cypriot type (Buchholz 1986) found in many different places in Cyprus as well as abroad, but this is the first time that contextual evidence from a tomb can assign this kind of fibula to a male. The rest of the metal objects, the bronze bowl, no. 21, and the iron knife, no. 23 (Hadjicosti 1997: 256, fig.4, pl. 54; *infra* figs. 9–10), are of common types but not without interest. It is worth noting that long iron swords have been found in "royal" or rich tombs together with chariot accessories and horses' gear as in Salamis (Karageorghis 1967: 31, 33), with a helmet and a scepter as in Tamassos (Masson 1964: 230–31) or in combination with the bronze bowl in Nicosia (Flourentzos 1981: pl. 16: 25).

Bronze fibulae have also been found in comparatively rich tombs with horses' gear and a knife at Kouklia-*Alonia* (Karageorghis 1963: 270–3, fig. 9; 280, fig. 20); together with an iron knife in the same tomb (Karageorghis 1963: 280, no. 23, fig. 21); with an iron knife and a bronze bowl in Idalion

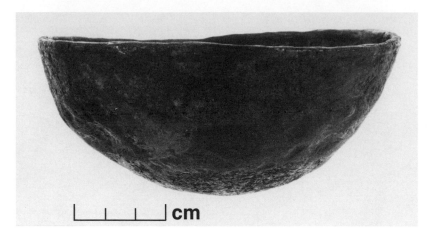

Figure 9. Bronze bowl no. 21.

(Karageorghis 1964: 47, fig. 13) and with an iron knife in Ayios Athanasios (Karageorghis 1986: 820, fig. 13).

Thus, it is interesting to observe that all these four types of object, namely the long sword, knife, bronze bowl and fibula, have been found together only in Mari Tomb 1, where they are associated with a male. Does this perhaps signify the existence of more or less uniform burial equipment for Cypriot warriors or high-ranking officials?

CONCLUSIONS

From the above discussion it is evident that the context of the Mari tomb defines the role of the female individual through the status of the accompanying male. The archaeological evidence, in combination with the damage patterns and condition of the bones, indicates that the bodies were very likely placed in the chamber simultaneously, and the sexing and age of the skeletal remains suggest, to a great extent, that the other bodies represent the familial relations of the dead. Furthermore, the undisturbed context of the tomb, the designation of the position of each member of the family by the analysis of the skeletal remains, and the morphology of the tomb, as well as the quality and quantity of the grave-goods, provide substantial evidence for the examination of the role of the deceased in real life. The male, deposited on the bench to the right of the entrance and surrounded by his precious belongings, was either a warrior or a high-ranking official, perhaps connected with the army. He must have played an important role in the political and economic activities of a thriving community in the Vasilikos valley, presumably under the control of the kingdom of Amathus. His position within society must have ensured a good economic status for his family. The woman, on the other hand, was deposited on the bench to the left of the entrance without precious grave goods and even without the jewelry that one would expect to accompany the wife of an important member of a thriving community (despite the lack of reliably sexed skeletons from tombs, sculpture shows that elaborate jewelry was frequently worn by women during this period). Perhaps the absence of jewelry indicates that the funeral took place at a time of social unrest, an assumption that is also supported by the simultaneous burials in the tomb. The deposition of the child near her right side accentuates the woman's role as mother, suggesting that motherhood in the Cypro-Archaic I period constituted the primary role of women in the family and in society at large. In addition, the placement of the large amphorae representing food containers and the vessels containing pebbles, perhaps a substitute for food, close to her side of the chamber,

Figure 10. *Iron knife no. 23.*

accentuates her dominant role in the household and ultimately indicates her secondary role in the social and political events of the community.

Although we must be aware, of course, of the weaknesses inherent in conclusions based on a single example, this very rare case of a well-identified family group from the Cypro-Archaic period suggests many interesting possibilities regarding the roles of men and women in ancient Cypriot society. Hopefully, further discoveries of well-preserved tombs, with studies of skeletal material, will be able to throw more light on the questions raised here.

REFERENCES

Bolger, D.
1993   The Feminine Mystique: Gender and Society in Prehistoric Cypriot Studies. *Report of the Department of Antiquities of Cyprus*: 29–41.

Buchholz, H. -G.
1986   Ein Kyprischer Fibeltypus und seine auswärtige Verbreitung. Pp. 223–45 in *Cyprus Between the Orient and the Occident: Acts of the International Symposium Held in Nicosia, 8–14 September 1985*, ed. V. Karageorghis. Nicosia: Department of Antiquities.

Ehrenberg, M.
1989   *Women in Prehistory*. London: British Museum.

Flourentzos, P.
1981   Four Early Iron Age Tombs from Nicosia Old Municipality. *Report of the Department of Antiquities of Cyprus*: 115–28.

Fox, S. C.
1997   The Human Skeletal Remains from Tomb 1, Mari Village, Larnaka District, Cyprus. Pp. 264–66 (Appendix) in Hadjicosti, M. The Family Tomb of a Warrior of the Cypro-Archaic I Period at Mari. *Report of the Department of Antiquities of Cyprus*.

Gjerstad, E.
1948   *The Swedish Cyprus Expedition*. Vol. 4, 2: *The Cypro-Geometric, Cypro-Archaic, and Cypro-Classical Periods*. Stockholm: The Swedish Cyprus Expedition.

Hadjicosti, M.
1993   The Late Archaic and Classical Cemetery of Agioi Omologites, Nicosia, in the Light of New Evidence. *Report of the Department of Antiquities of Cyprus*: 173–93.
1997   The Family Tomb of a Warrior of the Cypro-Archaic I Period at Mari. *Report of the Department of Antiquities of Cyprus*: 251–63.

Karageorghis, V.
1963   Une Tombe de Guerrier à Palaepaphos. *Bulletin de correspondance hellénique* 87: 265–300.
1964   Excavations in the Necropolis of Idalion, 1963. *Report of the Department of Antiquities of Cyprus*: 28–113.
1967   *Excavations in the Necropolis of Salamis, I*. Nicosia: Department of Antiquities.
1973   *Excavations in the Necropolis of Salamis, III*. Nicosia: Department of Antiquities.
1986   Chronique des fouilles et découvertes à Chypre en 1985. *Bulletin de correspondance hellénique* 110: 823–907.

Karageorghis, V., and Des Gagniers, J.
1974   La Céramique Chypriote de Style Figuré. Âge du Fer (1050–500 av. J.-C.). Rome: Instituto per gli Studi Micenei ed Egeo-Anatolici.

Karageorghis, V., Vassilika, E., and Wilson, P.
1999   *The Art of Ancient Cyprus in the Fitzwilliam Museum, Cambridge*. Nicosia: The Fitzwilliam Museum and A. G. Leventis Foundation.

Masson, O.
1964   Kypriaka. Recherches sur les Antiquités de Tamassos. *Bulletin de correspondance hellénique* 88: 199–233.

Snodgrass, A.
1964   *Early Greek Armour and Weapons, from the End of the Bronze Age to 600 B.C.* Edinburgh: Edinburgh University.
1981   Early Iron Swords in Cyprus. *Report of the Department of Antiquities of Cyprus*: 129–34.

CHILDBIRTH IN IRON AGE CYPRUS: A CASE STUDY[1]

MARIANNE VANDERVONDELEN

Neerpedestraat 382
B-1070 Brussels, Belgium

Using sculptures in terracotta for the 6th century B.C. and those in stone for the middle of the 5th through the 3rd century B.C. that have already been studied and partly interpreted in an earlier paper, the author wishes to place the theme of childbirth into the broader historical, religious and social contexts of Cyprus and to trace behavioral patterns of both women and men in this matter. No Cypriot written sources inform us on this, and the theme can only be approached through iconographic material. Therefore, Greek texts and epigraphic evidence are extremely important, as the theme of childbirth is also known iconographically in Greece during the 4th and 3rd centuries B.C. The Cypriot sculptures of that period show that Greek influence impacted on style but also on the type of representation. However, as the Cypriot context of the various sculptures is completely different from the Greek, caution is required. Indeed, Cypriot representations mostly come from sanctuaries, while Greek representations belong to funerary contexts. Therefore, we are possibly dealing with different social and religious views. This implies that we need to take a closer look at various different facets: the deities, both male and female, involved with childbirth; the dedicators of those sculptures; the image, role and position of women and midwifery in Cypriot society; and last, but not least, the attitude of Cypriot men towards childbirth, midwifery, and women, in general.

This paper examines the role of childbirth in Iron Age Cyprus by investigating the broader historical, religious and social contexts of Cyprus during this period.[2] It also looks for related behavioral patterns of both sexes at the time of childbirth. Representations of childbirth from Iron Age Cyprus are rather rare, although childbirth can be regarded as a very important moment in the lives of women and as a crucial factor for the survival of the community.

Anthropological studies have shown that societies lacking social insurance need full-grown children who can care for their elderly parents. Nevertheless, as infant mortality was substantial, as archaeological evidence demonstrates (e.g., Olynthos, see Robinson 1942: 166, 169–70),[3] a woman in ancient society had to endure a number of pregnancies in order to insure that there would be sufficient offspring to care for herself and her husband when they became elderly. Corvisier has suggested that women in ancient Greece had to give birth to an average of 4.6 children each in order to maintain the same population; he based his opinion on the estimates given by anthropologists working among the Gainj, a tribe of Papua New Guinea, and the Dobe !Kung bushmen of the Kalahari desert in southern Africa (Corvisier 1985: 161–66). According to Sallares, however, this assessment only represents a minimum, for different parts of Greece were thought to have different fertility rates, as a passage from Theophrastus, cited by Sallares, suggests (Sallares 1991: 137).[4]

In reality, we hardly know anything about the population of Cyprus during the Iron Age since Cypriot textual and archaeological evidence is absent. Although Cyprus is mentioned in Greek literature (Hadjioannou 1971, 1973, 1975, 1977, 1978),[5] we still know little about Cypriot social organization in the Iron Age and almost nothing about family structure. We do know, of course, that kingdoms arose in Iron Age Cyprus which probably comprised ranked classes within a well-defined hierarchical structure. It seems logical that in such a society, a king, or at least members of the elite, would wish to pass on their social achievements and territorial claims to their legitimate heirs and that marriage was involved in this process. This view presupposes the existence of a patrilineal society, by which we mean that a father can transfer his property to his own children. Judging from the slight evidence we have for Iron Age Cyprus, we can probably conclude that it was a patriarchal society.

The subject of childbirth in Cyprus is known to us from the story of Paeon the Amathusian (3rd century B.C.?),[6] reported in Plutarch's *Theseus*. The subject is also known from a number of sculptures in terracotta and stone.[7] Terracottas with known provenance date from the 6th century B.C. and were found in the cave of Empros Temenon at Lapithos. The stone sculptures in soft limestone date from the middle of the 5th century to the 3rd century B.C., while those found at the "temple" of Golgoi-*Ayios Photios* have been dated stylistically from the end of the fourth to the beginning of the 3rd century B.C. A fragmentary piece was found by the Swedish Cyprus Expedition at the palace site of Vouni. It was uncovered under the floor of Room 69 in the southwest kitchen courtyard, and it may derive from Level 3, which was thrown in as a substructure for the floor of Period 4; therefore, this fragment can be dated to before Period 4 and from 450–440 B.C. onwards.[8] The fragment was found together with a male head (V378) assigned by Gjerstad to Style IIIB (Gjerstad et al. 1937: 149–50, 188–89, 197, 228, 286, 289–90).

At the moment of childbirth, a woman can choose to deliver her child in a variety of positions. The iconographic material attests that in Iron Age Cyprus a parturient woman most frequently chose to give birth while sitting in a chair, perhaps already a kind of obstetrical chair, or while sitting on an assistant's lap. Only one sculpture (BM 1855.11–1.26), if it is authentic, shows that childbirth could take place while lying on a bed (Pryce 1931: 132, fig. 210, no. C412; Vandervondelen 1997: 278). The standing position for childbirth is similarly attested by a single terracotta (Louvre AO 22858; see Gourevitch 1988: 47).

The only written source for childbirth in Cyprus is the myth of Theseus and Ariadne as reported by Paeon the Amathusian, cited by Plutarch (Plutarch, *Theseus* 20). The version of the myth relates the homeward voyage of Theseus, as reported by Paeon, who describes a behavior that can be identified as the ritual couvade. We will focus here on the first part of the myth, which ends with Ariadne's death in childbirth:

> Theseus, on his homeward voyage from Crete, was overtaken by a storm at sea and was brought to Cyprus. Ariadne, pregnant and sea-sick, disembarked, while Theseus trying to save his ship drove again seawards. The native women received Ariadne and took great care of her. When the pangs of childbirth arrived, they sympathized with her suffering and helped her. Ariadne died, not being able to deliver the child. (Emended from Hadjioannou 1978: 107; see also Aupert 1984: 22)

The first part of the myth indicates the risks of childbirth for a woman; it also suggests that only women were involved in childbirth and that there was a genuine solidarity among them.

Nevertheless, male physicians existed in Cyprus. They are documented from the 5th century B.C. onwards (Foster, Kanada, and Michaelides 1988: Table 4); however, we do not know whether they were involved with childbirth. That male physicians were sometimes called in when complications at childbirth occurred is, nonetheless, attested by the Hippocratic treatises, although these treatises, which date from the end of the 5th through the 4th century, never actually describe a delivery. This does not necessarily mean that male physicians were not present at the delivery, but it is apparent that childbirth was more of a woman's business, and the Hippocratic treatises rely clearly on female lore (Demand 1994: 19, 23, 38, 47, 53, 63). The iconographic evidence shows that women—relatives, neighbors or "professional" midwives—provided the only relief available to a parturient woman seized by labor pains.

We have to wait for Soranus' *Gynaecia* (Rome, 1st century A.D.) to find a description of an actual delivery. Soranus is one of the very few sources who reports the process of childbirth. The passage, intended as instruction for midwives, is important as it is the only evidence we have for behavioral patterns at childbirth besides the sculptural representations (Lefkowitz and Fant 1982: 224–25). When comparing Soranus' instructions with the stone sculptures that we will soon focus on, it seems obvious that the literary prescriptions picture an old female tradition of childbirth care. The first of Soranus' directions is the need for a birthing stool (the defining element of the first sculptural iconographic group): "If no birthing stool is available the same arrangement can be made if the parturient sits on a woman's lap" (Lefkowitz and Fant 1982: 224). His second instruction mentions the use of a couch: "two couches, the one made up with soft coverings for rest after giving birth, the other hard for lying down on between labor pains" (Lefkowitz and Fant 1982: 224), and it is the couch that defines our second iconographical group. Soranus' other recommendations concern the midwife and her assistants:

> Three women should stay ready who are able gently to calm the fears of the woman who is giving birth, even if they do not happen to have experience in childbirth. Two should stand on the sides, and one behind her so that the mother does not lean sideways because of the pain. ... the midwife ... should sit down below, beneath and opposite the mother ... When the infant tries to come out, the midwife should have a cloth in her hands to pick him up. (Lefkowitz and Fant 1982: 224–25)

As far as we know, no professional midwives are attested in Cyprus. Nevertheless, while describing the sculptures, I will use the term "midwife" to indicate the woman sitting in front of the mother. "Midwife" will refer to any female relative or neighbour.

The stone sculptures were probably made by local artisans, but we have no evidence for this. The sculptures in the round were carved from rectangular blocks of soft limestone with the following maximum dimensions: height ca. 16 cm; length ca. 21 cm; width ca. 10 cm. The high reliefs are larger, but they are too fragmentary to allow us to give even approximate dimensions. The fact that the sitting women are always portrayed taller than the standing ones seems a technical rather than an iconographic feature.

The first group of sculptures portrays women in the act of labor. The pregnant woman sits on a kind of obstetrical chair, reclining backwards against a standing female assistant. In front and below her sits a midwife. Different moments in the delivery are depicted in the several representations. On one example, MMA 74.51.2698 (fig. 1; Cesnola 1885: 435, pl. 66), the moment after delivery is illustrated: the midwife holds the baby in her arms while the exhausted mother reclines; her dress appears to have slipped away, leaving her breasts uncovered. The hair and clothes of the parturient woman are loose, as prescribed by ancient texts. This rather elaborate piece shows that the artist preferred to represent the obstetrical chair as a pouf with cushions and drapery. This would have rendered his task technically easier because he did not have to sculpt the chair's complete design.

Less elaborate pieces of the same group, Autun V.11 and BM 1869.6–8.54 (fig. 2; Decaudin 1987: 9, no. 12; Pryce 1931: 131, fig. 208, no. C410), are roughly shaped, but they show the same pattern as the previous one. They depict the full delivery, with the midwife leaning over and positioned between the legs of the parturient woman. In the case of Louvre AM 3368, the baby's head is visible between its mother's legs. The midwife, however, seems to be missing, as in Louvre AM 3028. In both cases the piece is broken off at the midwife's side, so it is not clear whether a midwife was ever actually depicted (Hermary 1989: 442–43, nos. 914 and 915).

BM 1866.1–1.334 (figs. 3, 4) is quite different from the previous examples and shows the parturient woman sitting on the attendant's lap, while both are sitting on an obstetrical chair with cushions.

Figure 1. Limestone sculpture representing a childbirth scene. New York, Metropolitan Museum of Art, 74.51.2698. Photo courtesy of Dr. J. Mertens.

Figure 2. Limestone sculpture representing a childbirth scene. London, British Museum, 1869.6-8.54. Photo courtesy of Dr. R. Senff.

Figure 3. *Limestone sculpture
representing a childbirth scene.
London, British Museum, 1866.1-
1.334. Photo courtesy of Dr. R. Senff.*

The midwife, who kneels in front of them, leans forward in order to receive the baby. This scheme, a pregnant woman sitting on the lap of the woman behind her and both sitting on a chair with a midwife in front, was already used in a terracotta group Louvre MNB 118, which dates from the 6th century B.C. (Pryce 1931: 131, fig. 209, no. C411; Caubet 1992: 131, 140, fig. 5a). However, as the majority of terracottas show, this scheme was not common practice. Normally, the woman sits on the attendant's lap and a midwife may or may not sit in front of her (Bossert 1951: 10, no.156; 52; 156; Karageorghis 1981: 155, CM B55, CM B56). It does seem clear, however, that the use of an obstetrical chair became standard or at least more common in the 4th to 3rd centuries B.C. It is, thus, remarkable that BM 1866.1.1.334 still shows the parturient woman sitting on the attendant's lap while sitting on a chair. There seems no real need for the chair.

The second group of stone sculptures picture a woman reclining on a couch. Louvre AM 3068 (Hermary 1989: 442, no. 913) shows a woman with a swollen belly lying on a couch and supported from behind by an attendant. The hair of both women is loose. It is difficult to determine which moment of childbrith is being portrayed here: it could be a woman reclining between the pangs of labor before giving birth or the sculpture may show the moment after the delivery. Equally, the representa-

Figure 4. Limestone sculpture
representing a childbirth scene.
London, British Museum, 1866.1-
1.334. Photo courtesy of Dr. R. Senff.

tion may be that of the actual moment of delivery. The only sculpture that certainly portrays a delivery
on a couch, if it is authentic, is BM 1855.11–1.26 (fig. 5). Here, the woman lies on a bed with the head
of the midwife raised between her legs. Stylistically, their heads belong to the Arsinoë 3 type, dated by
Pryce to the end of the 3rd century B.C. (Pryce 1931: 132, fig. 210, no. C412). Nevertheless, it is clear
that for the actual delivery, the sitting position was preferred in the 4th and 3rd centuries B.C., with an
increasing use of the obstetrical chair. The chair must have facilitated the delivery.

But where was the man—the husband—at the crucial moment? Was he involved in some way, and
if so, how? The sculptures do not answer these questions, but we may find indications of his behavior
in the second part of the myth told by Paeon the Amathusian:

> When Theseus returned, he found Ariadne dead and gave money to the locals to dedicate her sacrifices.
> During the sacrifice at the second of the month Gorpiaïos, a young man lies down and imitates the cries
> and movements of women during the pangs of labour. (Emended from Hadjioannou 1978: 107; see also
> Aupert 1984: 22)

Figure 5. *Limestone sculpture representing a childbirth scene. London, British Museum, 1855.11-1.26. Photo courtesy of Dr. R. Senff.*

This account of a man miming a childbirth once a year presents a classic example of ritual couvade. There is also the suggestion of the survival of an older tradition, perhaps an old Cypriot behavioral pattern. This ritual was probably no longer practiced when Paeon related it (possibly in the 3rd century B.C.) as the account indicates the ritualized form of the act along with an accompanying myth. At any rate, the ritual and myth at least preserved the memory of the couvade. We do not know when the custom became an institutionalized ritual, but we do know that it was a ritual performed on the second of the month Gorpiaïos and that the performance probably took place in Amathus near the mythical site of Ariadne's tomb (Aupert 1984: 22). It is uncertain whether this ritual and the custom of couvade were restricted locally to Amathus or were common to the whole of Cyprus. The mention of ritual couvade, referring perhaps to an old Cypriot tradition, is, nevertheless, an indication of a more or less egalitarian gendered society, as recent anthropological studies of existing ethnic groups tend to show. Malinowski (1963: 68, 107, 140 , 157) has stated the following with regard to couvade:

1) Couvade can be interpreted as a genuine concern on the part of a husband to share his wife's pregnancy taboos, to avert the evil eye, to ward off other dangers at childbirth, and to take an active role in the care of offspring.

2) Couvade indicates a solidarity between man and woman.

3) In performing the couvade and other customs, the man works for the welfare of his wife and children. By miming the pangs, the headaches, the fears and shivers he shows that he has a number of legal and magical obligations to fulfill. However, he is not allowed to attend the

delivery due to a variety of social, magical and moral regulations; only close kinswomen are permitted to assist the parturient woman.

4)   A couvade also individualizes the relationship between the actual parents and their children.

If we follow Malinowski's statements regarding couvade and if we assume that the couvade existed in Cyprus, the logical conclusion would be that at one time—perhaps even in historical times—relatively egalitarian gendered relations existed in Cyprus, either on the local or perhaps on a larger, regional scale. Given our scant understanding of the history of Iron Age Cyprus, the question remains open, but the mention of this ritual couvade is the first tangible element we have of a behavioral pattern concerning both sexes and perhaps the entire community.

The second element that can contribute to our understanding of the behavioral patterns of the community is a contextual analysis of the iconographic material. Unfortunately, most of the sculptures with known provenance were uncovered in the course of excavations conducted during the 19th century. While we know, for example, that some of the terracotta representations were found in the cave of Empros Temenon at Lapithos, we have to rely on Walters's assumption, based on associated finds, that the context to which they belonged was ritual (Walters 1903: 22). We also know that most of the stone sculptures discussed here come from the "temple" of Golgoi-*Ayios Photios*. The sculptures in the Louvre Museum and in the Museum of Autun were recovered from the southwest corner of the "temple" by Duthoit in 1862 during the Vogüé Mission, but Duthoit, failing to recognize the building as a temple, managed to destroy the whole corner with his trenches (Cesnola 1877: 151; Foucart-Borville 1985: 24–25, 55).[9]

The childbirth sculpture (fig. 1; MMA 74.51.2698) was found in 1870 by Cesnola who described its context as follows (Cesnola 1877: 158–60) :

> Near the north entrance, between the first and second rows of large square blocks or pedestals, was another kind of votive offering consisting of little stone groups of women holding and sometimes suckling babes, and of cows and other animals similarly occupied with their young.[10] Another group, badly defaced, consisted of four persons, one holding a newly borne babe, while the mother extended upon a sort of chair, her face still convulsed by pain, has her head supported by an attendant. Another group, in no better preservation, exhibited a scene in the vaccine race [sic].[11]

Cesnola stresses further, "In the close proximity of these offerings was found the base or lower part of a cone in blue granite, which Mr. Georges Colonna-Ceccaldi recognizes as a fragment of the symbol of Venus [sic]."

It seems clear from the above that Cesnola was in some ways impressed by "the order which was evident in the original arrangement of the sculptures in this temple, the statues … and the different votive offerings classed according to their nature, and probably placed before their appropriate divinities." Even if Cesnola subsequently mixed up some of the temple sculptures, he recognized that there was a certain pattern and an original arrangement in their locations. Moreover, Cesnola is our only source for Golgoi, and we have only one very fragmentary sculpture from a scientific excavation from that site.

As stated earlier, it was the Swedish Cyprus Expedition that uncovered V406 (fig. 6) below the floor of Room 69 at the palace of Vouni in Room 66. The latter dates stratigraphically from the third building period onwards when it formed part of the southwest kitchen courtyard. Only in the fourth building period was the room separated from the courtyard by a wall to become a proper room. There may be a correlation with the reconstruction of the palace and the construction of the Athena sanctuary to the southwest of the palace, as the temple is close to the outer wall of Room 69 (Gjerstad et al. 1937: 110).[12] However, the question remains open, even if we consider the fact that other sculptures in stone and terracotta were also found in the courtyard.

Figure 6. Two views of a fragment in limestone representing two torsos of women clinging together belonging to a childbirth scene. Stockholm, Medelhavsmuseet, V 406. Photo by M. Vandervondelen.

We may, nevertheless, wonder why people would make an appeal to the gods by dedicating such sculptures in sanctuaries. There must certainly be a correlation between the dedication of sculptures and the high rate of mortality among women of childbearing age, i.e., between 15 and 45 years. It is not so much maternal mortality that plays a major part, but the fact that during pregnancy the woman's immune defences are weakened against diseases, such as malaria, tuberculosis, smallpox, etc., frequent among the general population. The Hippocratic treatises report that a malaria attack during childbirth is always fatal. As Sallares has rightly stressed, the average woman's immune system is likely to be depressed for several years as a result of pregnancy. There is also the risk of childbirth and more specifically, the postpartum complications like puerperal infection, toxemia, and hemorrhage (Demand 1994: 71, 75–86; Sallares 1991: 130–32, 236–37). It is, therefore, understandable that women undergoing childbirth looked to the gods for assistance.[13] The appeal could have taken any form. The only tangible evidence for this in Cyprus is the dedication of terracottas in the cave of Empros Temenon and a number of stone sculptures in the sanctuary at Golgoi. These could, however, represent various things, as there is no inscription that specifies the favor being requested. Consequently, these votive offerings could be an appeal to the gods for offspring or a safe delivery, or they could represent an offer of thanks following a successful childbirth.[14]

It would seem logical that women, rather than men, offered sculptures to the gods, but we can neither confirm nor deny this because of the lack of information. Neither do we know anything about the attendance of either sex at sanctuaries, but as we are dealing with a tradition of couvade, it is possible that a man could make such a dedication as well.[15] On the other hand, childbirth was a woman's business in Cyprus as the myth related by Paeon clearly shows. It, thus, seems more likely that it was a woman, either alone or with her nearest kinswomen, who made the dedication.

The deities involved in childbirth are not easy to trace in Cyprus. For the cave of Empros Temenon we have no inscriptions. The sanctuary at Golgoi is dedicated to Apollo and Zeus, although according to the inscriptions, Apollo is clearly the principal deity of the sanctuary. However, an inscription, known earlier but now lost, mentions both Demeter and Apollo (Masson 1961: 280; Masson 1971: 327, no. 5). Greek texts also refer to an "Aphrodite Golgia," and a dedication to "the Paphian" was found on the arm of the "Priest with Dove" from the *bothros*. According to Pausanias, her cult would be older at Golgoi than at Paphos (Pausanias 8.5.2). Ancient authors even considered Golgoi as one of Aphrodite's most important cult centers on the island (Meyer 1979; Bennett 1980: 308; Masson 1961:

283, no. 262). An over-lifesize statue of Aphrodite and Eros, dating from the 4th century B.C., was also found in the temple (Cesnola 1885: pl. 107). So it is likely that in addition to male deities or, perhaps, a male deity with diverse aspects associated with Apollo, Zeus Ammon, Heracles and Pan, a female deity was worshipped at Golgoi as well. We can assume that the childbirth groups, *kourotrophoi*, isolated cows, cows suckling calves, and perhaps temple-boys were dedicated to her since the motif of the cow suckling a calf was borrowed from the iconography of the Isis-Hathor cult, evoking in this animal form Isis-Hathor suckling Horus. The deity is also called *Kourotrophos*, as the above mentioned votive offerings attest, and it is more likely to be female since a male deity can only be a *kourotrophos* in connection with upbringing and educational functions (Hadzisteliou-Pryce 1978: 199, 201). That the deity is female and worshipped as "Protectress of Childbirth" and *Kourotrophos* is confirmed by her assimilation with Demeter in the lost inscription cited above. Demeter, herself, was in some parts of the Greek world an old mother goddess and worshipped as "Protectress of Childbirth" and *Kourotrophos* (Bennett 1980: 292, 308, 317; Kern 1901).[16]

Further evidence on the character of the deity of Golgoi is offered not only by the votive offerings mentioned above that were uncovered in the "temple" of Golgoi but also by the ritual of the couvade as reported in the myth related by Paeon the Amathusian in which the ritual includes a sacrifice performed for Ariadne who is worshipped as "Protectress of Childbirth." Ariadne is mostly assimilated with the old Cypriot mother goddess (Hadzisteliou-Pryce 1978: 98, 100; Hermary 1989: 442; Fauth 1979; Papaxenopoulos 1981: 54). The testimony of the ancient authors and the existence of the epithet "Golgia" attest that Golgoi was a place of worship of the old Cypriot mother goddess. The latter is also documented by the epithet "Paphia" found on the arm of the "Priest with Dove" from the *bothros*. We can, therefore, conclude that Golgoi was a place of worship of the ancient Cypriot mother goddess and was probably associated there with her male counterpart, as at other Cypriot sanctuaries.

The location of this cult dedicated to the "Protectress of Childbirth" and *Kourotrophos* is not easy to trace in the "temple" of Golgoi. We know, however, that in the southwest corner Duthoit found the childbirth groups associated with *kourotrophoi*, cows, cows suckling calves and temple-boys. It is also very likely, though not absolutely certain, that the childbirth group in the Metropolitan Museum of Art (MMA 74.51.2698) was found near the north entrance situated near the western wall of the "temple." We do not know, however, where Aphrodite's life-size statue was located.

While, on the one hand, the cult dedicated to a "Protectress of Childbirth" and *Kourotrophos* was chthonic in nature, it was also concerned with life—from the cradle to the grave. Therefore, the ritual must have served certain social functions. It appears to have offered an emotional support to women and parents, but it also provided a meeting place for mothers, nurses and children (Hadzisteliou-Pryce 1978: 219). Even if we have no clues as to the nature of the ritual linked to the dedication of these votives, we can easily imagine the emotional support women could have drawn from offering those statuettes in a sanctuary. We can also imagine its social significance for the whole community.

Unfortunately, we can not make such an analysis for the cave of Empros Temenon at Lapithos, as too much information is lacking. The presence of childbirth groups could, nonetheless, indicate a female deity concerned with childbirth or a ritual connected with childbirth performed in the cave. I would like to suggest that the terracottas from which the baby can be removed could have served as models for initiation rites concerning childbirth.[17]

In conclusion, many questions remain, but with the evidence cited above we can now begin to reconstruct some of the behavioral patterns related to childbirth in Iron Age Cyprus. The iconographical material, together with textual evidence, demonstrate that childbirth was women's business and that women preferred the sitting position for delivering children. In view of the serious risks to mother and infant during childbirth, we have also found evidence for two important behavioral patterns that concerned the community as a whole: the first is the evidence for ritual couvade and the second the dedication of the statuettes in the "temple" of Golgoi and the terracottas in the cave of Empros Temenon at Lapithos. The deity invoked in the ritual couvade and in the offering of the statuettes from Golgoi is the old Cypriot mother goddess worshipped as "Protectress of Childbirth" and *Kourotrophos*. With regard to evidence for gender relations, the evidence for ritual couvades suggests that Cyprus may once have been a relatively egalitarian society with few gendered divisions; ritual couvades may, thus, preserve both the memory of the custom of couvade and the equality of relations between the sexes.

NOTES

1. I would like to thank Dr. J. Mertens, Dr. V. Tatton-Brown, and Ms. M.-L. Winbladh for their kind permission to publish the photographs of the following sculptures: 74.51.2698, Metropolitan Museum of Art, New York, The Cesnola Collection, purchased by subscription 1874–76; 1869.6–8.54, 1866.1–1.334 and 1855.11–1.26, British Museum, London, courtesy of the Trustees of the British Museum; and V 406, Medelhavsmuseet, Stockholm. I am also indebted to Ms. A. Ulbrich and Ms. M. G. Weir who kindly discussed the subject with me. This paper is intended as a complementary study to a more iconographical one. It also is an opportunity to correct the dating of V 406 and to specify the deity involved with childbirth. For a complete list of bibliography of the terracottas and stone sculptures representing childbirth, see Vandervondelen 1997.

2. For the representations of childbirth dating from the Chalcolithic period but not considered in this paper, see E. Peltenburg et al. 1988: 48–49; Peltenburg and Goring 1991.

3. Further knowledge will be provided by the study of Dr. L. Preston-Day of the human bones found at the Iron Age cemetery of Vrounda, Crete.

4. Sallares cites Theophrastus, H.P., which appears to refer to the *Historia plantarum* (Theophrastus, *Hist.Pl.*, 9.18.10–11, ed. Wimmer).

5. See the exhaustive work of K. Hadjioannou, Ἡ ἀρχαια Κύπρος εἰς τὰς Ἑλληνικὰς Πηγάς, Vol. 1 (1971), Vol. 2 (1973), Vol. 3A (1975), and Vol. 3B (1977).

6. For an approximate date for Paeon of Amathus, see Aupert 1984: 16.

7. An entry on the terracottas is available in Vandenabeele 1988: 31; see also Vandervondelen 1997: 273, notes 7–9; and Vandervondelen 1997 for a detailed entry and full iconographical study of the stone sculpture.

8. The palace at Vouni was destroyed by fire and definitively abandoned in 390/380 B.C. (Gjerstad et al. 1937: 288).

9. His letter of 24 March 1862 states, "Voici quinze jours que je suis fixé à Athienou … La semaine dernière, j'ai payé 1000 Fr à mes hommes. C'est énorme d'autant plus que les résultats que j'ai obtenu sont presque nuls. A Iorgos (aujourd'hui Golgoï) point sur lequel M. de Vogüé avait beaucoup espéré, je n'ai rencontré que des fondements en blocage mal fait, pas une pierre de taille. Quant au fragments plus ou moins beaux de sculptures, il n'en faut pas parler." This passage seems to refer to the "temple," as we know from Cesnola that only the foundations of the "temple" were made of rubble and that the superstructure was made of sundried mudbrick (Cesnola 1877: 139, 163; Foucart-Borville 1985: 24–25).

10. All animals are now identified as cows and calves, but in some cases doubts remain (Hermary 1988: 18; 1989: 458).

11. Unfortunately, this bovine birthing scene seems to be lost and cannot be traced as no illustration is provided. However, no such scene is published in Cesnola 1885.

12. I would like to thank M. G. Weir for this interesting suggestion.

13. For divine helpers in Greece, see Demand 1994: 87–88.

14. Offerings of hair and clothes, unlike in some parts of Greece, were never attested in Cyprus. For Greek examples and their meaning, see Demand 1994: 88–90; Hadzisteliou-Pryce 1978: 103 and 211.

15. It is interesting to note that in Brauron in Attica, men offered their sandals to Artemis-Iphigeneia (Hadzisteliou-Pryce 1978: 211).

16. Artemis is also worshipped as a Protectress of Childbirth in some parts of the Greek world, as in Brauron (see above note). In an earlier article, I also identified the female statue (Cesnola 1885: no. 844, pl. 116) as a possible statue of Artemis. However, since there is not enough evidence to identify the statue correctly, I prefer not to pursue the hypothesis that at the temple site of Golgoi, Artemis could have been assimilated with the old Cypriot mother goddess, worshipped as a Protectress of Childbirth.

17. I would like to thank F. Vandenabeele and. M. Kyriacou for this suggestion.

REFERENCES

Aupert, P.
1984   Les auteurs anciens. Pp. 11–56 in *Amathonte* 1: *Testimonia* 1. *Etudes chypriotes* 4, eds. P. Aupert and M.-Chr. Hellmann. Ecole Française d'Athènes Mémoire 32. Paris: Éditions Recherche sur les Civilisations.

Bennett, C. G.
1980   *The Cults of the Ancient Greek Cypriotes*. Unpublished Ph.D. Dissertation, University of Pennsylvania.

Bossert, H.
1951   *Altsyrien*. Die altesten Kulturen des Mittelmeeres 3. Tübingen: Wasmuth.

Caubet, A.
1992   The Terracotta Workshops of Idalion during the Cypro-Archaic Period. Pp. 128–51 in *Acta Cypria. Acts of an International Congress on Cypriote Archaeology Held in Göteborg on 22–24 August 1991*, Part 3, ed. P. Aström. Jonsered: Astroms.

Cesnola, L.
1877   *Cyprus : Its Ancient Cities, Tombs, and Temples*. London: Murray.
1885   *A Descriptive Atlas of the Cesnola Collection of Cypriote Antiquities in the Metropolitan Museum of Art, New York*. Vol.1. Boston: Osgood.

Corvisier, J. -N.
1984   *Santé et société en Grèce ancienne*. Paris: Economica.

Decaudin, A. J.
1987   *Les antiquités chypriotes dans les collections publiques françaises*. Nicosia: A. G. Leventis Foundation.

Demand, N.
1994   *Birth, Death and Motherhood in Classical Greece*. Baltimore: The John Hopkins University.

Fauth, W.
1979   *S.v.* Aphrodite, col. 429 in *Der Kleine Pauly. Lexikon der Antike*, eds. K. Ziegler and W. Sontheimer. Stuttgart: Druckenmüller.

Foster, G. V.; Kanada, K.; and Michaelides, D.
1988   A Roman Surgeon's Tomb from Nea Paphos, Part 2: Ancient Medicines, By-Products of Copper Mining in Cyprus. *Report of the Department of Antiquities of Cyprus*, Part 2: 229–34.

Foucart-Borville, J.
1985   La correspondance chypriote d'Edmond Duthoit (1862 et 1865). Centre d'Etudes chypriotes. *Cahier* 4: 3–60.

Gjerstad, E.; Lindros, J.; Sjöqvist, E.; and Westholm, A.
1937   *The Swedish Cyprus Expedition*. Vol. 3: *Finds and Results of the Excavations in Cyprus 1927–1931*. Stockholm: Swedish Cyprus Expedition.

Gourevitch, D.
1988   Grossesse et accouchement dans l'iconographie antique. *Dossiers de l'archéologie* 123: 42–48.

Hadjioannou, K.
1971   Ἡ ἀρχαία Κύπρος εἰς τὰς Ἑλληνικάς Πηγάς, Vol. 1. Nicosia: Holy Archbishopric of Cyprus.
1973   Ἡ ἀρχαία Κύπρος εἰς τὰς Ἑλληνικάς Πηγάς, Vol. 2. Nicosia: Holy Archbishopric of Cyprus.
1975   Ἡ ἀρχαία Κύπρος εἰς τὰς Ἑλληνικάς Πηγάς, Vol. 3A. Nicosia: Holy Archbishopric of Cyprus.
1977   Ἡ ἀρχαία Κυπρος εἰς τὰς Ἑλληνικάς Πηγάς, Vol. 3B. Nicosia: Holy Archbishopric of Cyprus.
1978   On Some Disputed Matters of the Ancient Religion of Cyprus. *Report of the Department of Antiquities of Cyprus*: 103–110.

Hadzisteliou-Pryce, T.
1978   *Kourotrophos. Cults and Representations of the Greek Nursing Deities*. Leiden: Brill.

Hermary, A.
1988   Nouvelles découvertes sur la mission Vogüé de 1862. Centre d'Etudes chypriotes. *Cahier* 10.2: 15–20.
1989   *Musée du Louvre. Département des antiquités orientales. Catalogue des antiquités de Chypre. Sculptures*. Paris: Editions de la Réunion des musées nationaux.

Karageorghis, V.
1980   *Ancient Cyprus. 7000 Years of Art and Archaeology*. Baton Rouge, LA: Louisiana State University.

Kern, O.
1901   *S.v.* Demeter, col. 2750 in *Paulys Realencyclopädie der classischen Altertumswissenschaft*, ed. G. Wissowa. Stuttgart: Druckenmüller.

Lefkowitz, M. R., and Fant, M. B.
1982   *Women's Life in Greece and Rome. A Sourcebook in Translation*. London: Duckworth.

Malinowski, B.
1963   *Sex, Culture and Myth*. London: Hart-Davis.

Masson, O.
1961   *Les inscriptions chypriotes syllabiques. Recueil critique et commenté*. Paris: de Boccard.
1971   Kypriaka IX. Recherches sur les antiquités de Golgoi. *Bulletin de correspondance hellénique* 95: 305–34.

Meyer, E.
1979   *S.v.* Golgoi, col. 843 in *Der Kleine Pauly. Lexikon der Antike*, eds. K. Ziegler and W. Sontheimer. Stuttgart: Druckenmüller.

Papaxenopoulos, A.
1981   *Zypriotische Medizin in der Antike*. Pattensen: Wellm.

Peltenburg, E.; Bolger, D.; Goring, E.; and Elliott, C.
1988   Kissonerga Mosphilia 1987: Ritual Deposit, Unit 1015. *Report of the Department of Antiquities of Cyprus*, Part 1: 43–52.

Peltenburg, E., and Goring, E.
1991   Terracotta Figurines and Ritual at Kissonerga-Mosphilia. Pp. 17–26 in *Cypriote Terracottas. Proceedings of the First International Conference of Cypriote Studies, Brussels-Liège-Amsterdam, 29 May–1 June, 1989*, eds. F. Vandenabeele and R. Laffineur. Brussels-Liège: A. G. Leventis Foundation, Vrije Universiteit Brussel, and Université de Liège.

Pryce, F. N.
1931   *Catalogue of Sculpture in the Department of Greek and Roman Antiquities of the British Museum. Vol 1, 2: Cypriote and Etruscan*. London: Trustees of the British Museum.

Robinson, D. M.
1942   *Excavations at Olynthus. Vol. 11: Necrolynthia. A Study in Greek Burial Customs and Anthropology*. Baltimore: The John Hopkins University.

Sallares, R.
1991   *The Ecology of the Ancient Greek World*. London: Duckworth.

Vandenabeele, F.
1988   Kourotrophoi in the Cypriote Terracotta Production from the Early Bronze Age to the Late Archaic Period. *Report of the Department of Antiquities of Cyprus*, Part 2: 25–34.

Vandervondelen, M.
1997   L'accouchement à Chypre dans l'Antiquité. Etude de sculptures. Pp. 271–88 in *Studia Varia Bruxellensia 4. In honorem Aloysi Gerlo*, eds. R. Desmet, H. Melaerts and C. Saerens. Leuven: Peeters.

Walters, H. B.
1901   *Catalogue of the Terracottas in the Department of Greek and Roman Antiquities in the British Museum*. London: Trustees of the British Museum.

"SAINTED LADIES AND WICKED HARLOTS": PERCEPTIONS OF GENDER IN MEDIEVAL CYPRUS

IOANNA CHRISTOFORAKI

Institute of Archaeology
University of Oxford
36 Beaumont Street
Oxford OX1 2PG, United Kingdom
joanna.christoforaki@archaeology.ox.ac.uk

This paper examines perceptions of gender in medieval Cyprus. Research is inevitably based on texts written by men since female self-expression was extremely rare. The binary thought of medieval times, which perceived women as either "good" or "evil," is tested on three women connected with the island of Cyprus. The "good" woman is represented by St. Helena, who epitomized female piety, was strongly entrenched in the family, and practically asexual. On the contrary, a sexually active and attractive woman was powerful and, therefore, "evil." Queen Eleanora of Aragon possessed this kind of power and was presented as a temptress and a witch. Another woman perceived as "evil," mainly by western historians, was Helena Palaiologina who assumed significant political power and, thus, surpassed her traditionally assigned role in medieval society. Male perceptions of gender were presented as the natural, god-given order and consequently shaped female identity, thus perpetuating the male-dominant cultural reality of medieval times.

In memory of Constantinos Balaskas

THEORETICAL CONSIDERATIONS

Forms of binarism are present in human thought from earliest times. "Thought has always worked through opposition" claims the feminist writer Hélène Cixous (Cixous and Clement 1986: 63). Dualisms in philosophy and religion (subject and object, god and man, temporal and eternal) are the foundation of entire world-views (Selden 1989: 55). We tend to perceive the world in antithetical pairs, where the subordinate term is seen as inferior, more problematic or less acceptable than the dominant.

Such binary oppositions are fundamental to structuralist thought. Structuralists have argued that binary oppositions are instrumental to human language, cognition and communication. They are used to mark differences in an otherwise apparently random sequence of features and thus give shape to our experience (Selden 1989: 56). Any binary opposition, such as nature and culture, logos and pathos, man and woman, comprises two terms that are classified hierarchically, so that the second term is assumed to be derivative from and inferior to the first. Class, race and sexuality are fundamental determinants of binary thought, widely accepted in our culture. Couples such as black/white, middle-class/working class, straight/gay are examples of hierarchical binary oppositions (Eagleton 1996: 148).

The literary critic looks at binary oppositions operating within a text, either consciously or unconsciously employed by the author. These oppositions may structure the text and be integral to its ideological concerns. The way these oppositions are constructed, the meaning they contain, what is revealed or hidden by them, and how to separate these antithetical couples are important considerations. Feminists have found this subject relevant because of their belief that binary thinking upholds patriarchy. They, therefore, have a vested interest in understanding and dismantling the process of binary thought (Eagleton 1996: 146).

Binary oppositions are often culturally constructed. One such crucial determinant is gender, which results in a pairing valid through the centuries, namely male/female. The ongoing battle between these two sides is a power struggle where, in patriarchal culture, the masculine side is dominant. Although the biological distinction between male and female seems to be part of the natural order, feminists have challenged the apparently "natural" opposition between masculine and feminine, arguing that it is an essentially cultural one. The attributes we tend to assign to each term (masculine equals strong, feminine equals submissive, and so on) are not universal but culturally variable. Feminist criticism has argued that sex and gender are two very different things. Whereas sex is the biological difference between women and men, gender is a cultural construction that can be deconstructed in order to understand and analyze a society. Feminist critique has shown that men have defined meanings and values according to their perceptions, excluding anything that is outside their immediate experience. Gender roles are presented as sex roles and justified as natural, god-given and unchangeable. Such gender systems promote and value male attributes and activities as superior: men are the "norm," women are the "other." Consider this passage by John Ruskin, in which all male activities are valued as superior against inferior female performance:

> Now their [men's and women's] characters are briefly these. The man's power is active, progressive, defensive. He is eminently the doer, the creator, the discoverer, the defender. His intellect is for speculation and invention; his energy is for adventure, for war, and for conquest, wherever war is just, wherever conquest is necessary. But the woman's power is for rule not for battle and her intellect is not for invention or creation but for sweet ordering, arrangement and decision. She sees the qualities of things, their claims and their places. Her great function is praise: she enters into no contest, but infallibility adjudges the crown of the contest. By her office and place, she is protected from all danger and temptation. The man, in his rough work in open world, must encounter all peril and trial: to him, therefore, the failure, the offence, the inevitable error: often he must be wounded, or subdued, often misled, and always hardened. But he guards the woman from all this: within his house, as ruled by her, unless she herself has sought it, need enter no danger, no temptation, no cause of error or offence. This is the true nature of home: it is the place of Peace, the shelter, not only from all injury but from all terror, doubt and division (Ruskin, 1864: 59).

Such a hierarchy of vices and virtues is clearly a cultural construct with no basis in nature. Sometimes it is not only the actual activity performed by a person but the sex of the performer that determines whether the activity is valued or not, and this is true even if the same activity is performed by both sexes. Adultery, as we shall see, for example, in the course of this article, is a source of pride for men and can be excused, but it is unforgivable for women. Male activities are always recognized as more important than female, and a patriarchal cultural system gives authority and value to the roles and activities of men.

A challenge to patriarchal binary thought is deconstructive criticism, which dismantles the pattern of binary oppositions, consciously or unconsciously formulated, in the act of reading. A deconstructive reading tries to bring out the logic of the text's language as opposed to the logic of the author's claims. It undoes the hierarchic binary oppositions and uncovers the trace of otherness within what seems single and self-identical (Belsey and Moore 1989: 251). It teases out the text's implied presuppositions and points out the inevitable contradictions in them (Jefferson and Robey 1982: 118). As Catherine Belsey observes,

> the aim is to locate the point of contradictions within the text, the point at which it transgresses the limits within which it is constructed and breaks free of the constraints imposed by its own realist form. Composed of contradictions, the text is no longer restricted to a single, harmonious authoritative reading. Instead it becomes plural, open to re-reading, no longer an object for passive consumption but an object for work by the reader to produce meaning (Belsey 1980: 104).

Deconstruction does not see such textual contradictions as faults or examples of loss of control by the author. The text does not compose a unified entity. On the contrary, such "cracks" in the text are points of greater interest and can be used as avenues of access for the reader.

Deconstruction is not interested in reversing the hierarchy. Such a reversal (for example, valuing passivity over activity or the personal and domestic over the public) is insufficient since it would still be locked into binary thinking. Deconstruction involves itself in an endless dismantling of hierarchies. According to Raman Selden,

> a deconstructive reading begins by noting the hierarchy, proceeds to reverse it and finally resists the assertion of a new hierarchy by displacing the second term from a position of inferiority to one of superiority … A deconstructive reading would go on to recognize that the couplet cannot be hierarchised in either direction without "violence" … Deconstruction can begin when we locate the moment when a text transgresses the laws it appears to set up for itself. At this point the text goes to pieces, so to speak. (Selden 1989: 90)

In an attempt to unravel perceptions of gender in Cyprus during the Middle Ages, emphasis will be placed on the ways that feminine identities were constructed and ideal female roles presented as the norm. Deviations from the accepted role models will be examined in contrast to the established patriarchal value system. Before embarking on this line of research, it is worth pausing briefly to introduce some general medieval perceptions of gender.

MEDIEVAL PERCEPTIONS OF GENDER

Female self-expression was extremely rare, if not non-existent, in medieval times. Anna Komnena's history, the *Alexiad*, was the only book written by a woman throughout the history of Byzantium, while the writings of Christine de Pizan and Margery Kempe in the West were exceptions that confirmed the rule. We do not and cannot know how medieval women perceived themselves since our knowledge comes almost exclusively from men. Historical accounts as well as laws, legal documents, hagiographical sources, and works of art were produced by men. The attitudes and assumptions enshrined in such texts were unavoidably male, and even texts that were supposedly about women ultimately reveal more about men than women. All such works were also the products of their society, both reflecting and reproducing what was normal and correct. As Leslie Brubaker succinctly states, "narrative text was an élite male genre," and the fact that these texts have survived and come down to us is a demonstration that they espoused ideas acceptable to the later men who had them copied (Brubaker 1997: 53). Inevitably then, what contemporary research can only examine is how *men* perceived *women* and how male perceptions shaped female identity, thus perpetuating the male-dominant cultural reality of the time (Smythe 1997: 150).

Christian attitudes towards women were ambivalent. On the one hand, there was the statement in the Old Testament that God created humankind, both male and female, in his image, while on the other there was the portrayal of Eve as causing the original sin by succumbing to the temptation of the serpent. Furthermore, although Christ's disciples were all male, it was a woman, the Virgin Mary, who was chosen as the instrument of salvation by giving birth to Christ. Accordingly, women were usually perceived in two polarized ways. On the one hand, there was Eve, the epitome of evil since the expulsion from paradise, while on the other figured the pious Virgin, who, being a woman of absolute purity and humility, was to redeem humanity from all evil as the second Eve. The female descendants of Eve were held responsible for the loss of paradise and were routinely castigated as temptresses and sinners, rebellious and undisciplined (Grössinger 1997: 1; Galatariotou 1985: 59–61).

The dominant ideology of the time recognized a number of ideal roles for secular women. The most powerful of all was that of the mother, who had a duty to care for her children and to nurture and prepare them for life. Motherhood was pleasing to God, and a good mother spent much of her time in prayer for her children. Being a mother was the only sphere in which women were granted overt power. Another role was that of the wife, who was expected to be in love with her husband, a feeling she could only nurture within the marital relationship. Women who could not control their passion or committed adultery were denounced and criticized. The ideal wife was not supposed to participate in politics, and her only public role was restricted to acts of patronage. Finally, the ideal sister and daughter were both supposed to be loyal and serve the family (Hill 1999: 78, 85, 87, 93).

Conversely, there was the image of the woman as an instrument of the devil, inferior and evil. This view took shape in the writings of St. Paul as well as in the ideas and practice of monasticism. The early Church Fathers of the 4th and 5th centuries C.E. in particular were responsible for creating the image of the woman as a temptress, for men fled the world with its temptations and led a life of extreme asceticism in the desert. Evil to them was identified with the flesh. As ascetic ideals flourished and monasticism became the refuge of men, the concept of the woman as the supreme temptress came into being. She was the greatest obstacle in the way of salvation (Power 1975: 16). The medieval woman was described as

> a crawling worm, the daughter of mendacity, the enemy of peace; she was frivolous, garrulous and licentious. Above all she was addicted to luxury and expense. She loaded herself with jewellery, powdered her face, painted her cheeks with rouge, scented her garments and thus made herself into a deadly trap to seduce young men through all their senses. No amount of wealth was sufficient to satisfy a woman's desires. Day and night she thought of nothing but gold and precious stones, of purple cloth and embroidery, of ointments and perfumes. She was the friend and organ of the devil, the source of all evil, a shameless and wild beast, a poisonous snake, a thesaurus of dirt, a sexual trap which is insatiable. (Mango 1980: 226)

Women were seen as disruptive, as a source of disorder, able to lead men astray. They were thought of as being weak, irrational, emotional and always receptive to evil influences. That was why they had to be watched over by men, protected, guarded, led, as the power of rational thinking was by nature stronger in men.

Such views were the products of a certain society, both reflecting and reproducing what was considered normal and acceptable. Since society was predicated on and around men and male values, men were the positive members and women were the Other. Any expectations built up around women, however, were (and still are) culturally constructed and, as such, can be deconstructed because they are not natural. If the ideal stereotype of who a woman should be and how she should behave is juxtaposed to her actual behavior, we can then begin to understand the workings of the female presence and power within the framework of male authority.

WOMEN OF CYPRUS

In considering male perceptions of gender in Cyprus, the text of the chronicle of Leontios Machairas will be used as a focal point. As the expressed opinion of any age depends on the persons and the classes who happen to articulate it, it is important to give a general outline of the history of Cyprus in this period before we proceed to the author and his life.

Cyprus was an outpost of Byzantium until 1192 when, after a short spell under Richard the Lionheart and the Templars, it passed to the Lusignans, a dynasty that originally came from Poitou in France but had long been settled in the Levant and the Latin kingdom of Jerusalem. The island remained in their hands until 1489 when it became a Venetian colony.

The first century after the foundation of the kingdom of Cyprus in 1196 was a time of forced symbiosis between the two main ethnic and religious groups of the island, the Frankish rulers and the local Cypriot population. In contrast, the period from 1291 to 1369 was the most prosperous age in the history of medieval Cyprus. It was an era of unprecedented power and wealth that transformed the insular kingdom into an independent state and established its political presence in the area of the eastern Mediterranean. However, the devastating war with the Genoese from 1372–74 and the repeated invasions by the Mamluks of Egypt during 1424–1426 crippled the kingdom morally as well as financially. It was a matter of time before Cyprus lost its independence and became a Venetian territory.

Leontios Machairas was born in Cyprus between 1360 and 1380. He was the son of Stavrinos Machairas, an educated member of the Greek bourgeoisie of the period. His family was close to the Frankish rulers of the island and was actively involved in the Lusignan royal court. His father participated in the grand council of nobles, the *Haute Cour*, and Leontios himself served as secretary to a member of the nobility, Sir John de Nores. A relative of his was tutor to King Peter II while another member of the extended family, Sir George Bili, held the post of governor of Cyprus (Anaxagorou 1998: 12–13). His chronicle, entitled *Recital Concerning the Sweet Land of Cyprus*, covers the history of the island from the arrival of St. Helena in Early Christian times until the death of King John II in 1458 A.D. His opinions essentially reflect the views of a small but vociferous aristocratic minority on the island.

The personalities of three women, related to Cyprus but not Cypriot themselves, will be examined through the writings of men in order to explore male attitudes towards gender. The first is St. Helena, mother of the Emperor Constantine who passed by the island on her way to the Holy Land. The other two are Queen Eleanora of Aragon, the Spanish wife of Peter I (1359–1369), and the Greek Helena Palaiologina, the second wife of King John II (1432–1458). It is unfortunate that contemporary written sources do not contain references to local Cypriot women.

In medieval times a major cultural construction of femininity was the concept of the "good woman." A strong association of the good woman was with the family. She was firmly entrenched in a family structure, and her identity was defined in relation to a male (Grössinger 1997: 147; Galatariotou 1985: 78–81). This meant that she was almost without exception presented as either the mother, wife, daughter or sister of a male (Mentzou-Meimari 1982: 433–43). She was not perceived independently as a woman but as a close relative of a man, and in the absence of a father or a husband she became the daughter and bride of Christ (Galatariotou 1985: 79). She was thus deprived of her sexuality and became asexual. This leads to another important component of the good woman, the negation of her sexuality. A good woman was preferably a virgin, a widow or simply of very advanced age. She was good precisely because she had ceased to be a woman. Another of her vital characteristics was her association with religious works. She usually came from an aristocratic family and could therefore afford to build a church, found a monastery, or order illuminated manuscripts and painted panels as luxury gifts or for private use (Grössinger 1997: 147; Galatariotou 1988: 263–90; Buchthal and Belting 1978).

A woman who fulfilled the above criteria was St. Helena, mother of Constantine I and the most famous pilgrim to the Holy Land (Drijvers 1993; Pohlsander 1995). She came from the uppermost echelons of the Constantinopolitan elite and although not a Cypriot herself, she was nonetheless directly linked to the island since she stopped there on her way to Jerusalem. The idea of the family was celebrated in the person of Helena by her role as mother of Constantine. Her perception as mother of the first Christian emperor and her long celibate life together with her advanced age promoted an essentially asexual image of her. She supplied the model and was at the same time the utmost representative of female elite piety (Brubaker 1997: 56–59, 62–64). In accordance with this image, she was credited with a number of commissions and endowments in the Holy Land,

> And straightway she departed and went to Jerusalem; and with much labor and at great cost and danger she found the Holy Cross and the two crosses of the two thieves besides, and the nails and the crown of the thorns and thirty-six gouts of the blood of the Lord ... And the sainted lady Helena was filled with wonder at the sight and made them build many churches in Jerusalem in the name of the Living God and of the Life-giving Cross, all new from the foundations; and some she finished and for others she left money for the people to finish them. (Machairas 1932: §5; hereafter the date of 1932 is given, referring to the Dawkins translation)

According to the same chronicle, she also founded two churches on Cyprus:

> And when they had arrived and cast anchor by the land, she brought out the chest and the two crosses and ate meat at Vasilopotamos. And when she had finished eating, she lay down, being wearied by the sea, and fell asleep; and she saw a dream, that a young man said to her: 'My lady Helena, as you did at Jerusalem, building many churches, so do here also, for it is commanded that in this same land men shall dwell until the end of all things, and it shall not be destroyed for all ages. And build a church in the name of the Venerable and Life-giving Cross, and put in it of the Holy Wood which you have with you.' And she awoke and rose up from her sleep ... and she built a church of the Holy Cross, and set in the heart of the cross a fragment of the Holy Cross. Afterwards she saw a pillar of fire which reached from the earth to the sky, and went to see the marvel, and found on the bank of the river one of the four small crosses. And a voice from heaven said to her: 'Helena, cause a church to be built here in this very place, the name of which is Togni.' And she built a church of the Holy Cross, and a bridge for men to pass over. And she overlaid the said cross with silver, gold, and pearls ... And when she had finished her buildings, she embarked in her galley and went to Constantinople. (Machairas 1932: §9)

Machairas places Helena almost at the very beginning of his chronicle. However, although the story revolves around Helena and her journey to the Holy Land, her son takes precedence over her. Helena's name gets mentioned only after Constantine has already been referred to twice (Machairas 1932: §§ 3–4). She is introduced as the mother of her son and is furthermore presented as fulfilling Constantine's order when embarking on her pilgrimage. Her role in this expedition is exposed as passive, as she "received a command from her son to go to seek for the Holy Cross in Jerusalem" (Machairas 1932: §4). She goes to great pains to ensure that her son is informed about her discovery as soon as possible by building

> towers from Jerusalem to Constantinople, so that each should be able to see the next, and that there should be men upon them to keep guard day and night, and they should be ready as soon as they see fire or smoke at Jerusalem, each one to act immediately so that, when the Holy Cross should be found, a beacon should be raised so as to be seen from tower to tower, that the emperor might know the day when his mother found the Holy Cross. And thus it was done, in this way: the hour the blessed Helena found the Holy Cross, at that hour her son the emperor heard of the tidings. Now let us turn to St. Helena. (Machairas 1932: §6)

This account confirms the up-to-then created impression that the discovery of the Holy Cross should really be attributed to Constantine. The mastermind behind this crusade is Constantine, whereas Helena was a mere instrument of his will. In the eyes of Machairas, Helena was the epitome of the good woman: pious and obedient, dependant and asexual. The cultural core of her goodness, however, was essentially her lack of power. Good women were never depicted as holding or exercising power; they did not stand alone in the narrative or act independently from a male. Powerful females equalled evil females (Galatariotou 1985: 62–63).

An element routinely linked with female power was sexuality. What men feared most was the uncontrollable force of sexual arousal. It was female sexual power that lured Adam into temptation and brought destruction upon mankind. Subsequently, undisciplined passion and carnal desire were always strongly criticized. Sexuality was the most common and serious accusation raised against women and the sexually attractive woman was seen as spiritually and morally corrupt (Grössinger 1997: 2, 4, 15; Galatariotou 1985: 71–72).

In Cypriot female prosopography, the archetypal sensual seductress was Eleanora of Aragon, wife of the flamboyant King Peter I (A.D. 1359–1369). Probably the most famous passage in the chronicle of Machairas is the one recounting how the king always carried with him the queen's night-dress and slept with it in his arms:

> Even as I have told you already of the love which the king had for the queen, so for the love which he had he promised that, wherever he was, he would take her shift to lay it at night in his arms when he slept, and he made his chamberlain always bring with him the queen's shift, and had them put it in his bed. And if one say, "Seeing that he had such love for her, how was it that he had two mistresses?" This he did on account of his great sensuality, because he was a young man. (Machairas 1932: § 242)

However, Eleanora's profile as sketched by Machairas is far from attractive. He repeatedly calls her wicked and godless, and his description of the tortures that the king's lover, Joanna l'Aleman, was subjected to in her hands reinforce her image as an essentially evil woman.

> Now we leave the story of that dog the sultan and let us pass to another, that of the queen, whose name was Eleanora, the wife of the aforesaid king Peter. Even as you know that the demon of fornication assails the whole world, so he beguiled the king, and the good king fell into sin with a noble lady, whose name was Joanna l'Aleman, the wife of sir John de Montolif, the lord of Khoulou: and the king had left her eight months with child. And when the king went for the second time to France, the queen sent and brought her to the court. And when she came before her she insulted her with shameful words and said to her: "Wicked harlot, (it is you who) separate me from my husband." And the lady was silent. (Machairas 1932: §234)

Her treatment of Joanna reveals a cruel and vindictive woman, driven by passion, not reason, and the most degenerate instincts. In Machairas' own words,

> the queen gave orders to her women, and they threw her [Joanna] on the ground, and by her orders they brought a great marble mortar and set it upon her womb, and they pounded a measure of salt in it, to make her miscarry of the child … and they brought a handmill and stretched her out on the ground and put it on her womb, and they held her firmly and ground two measures of flour upon her womb; and still she did not miscarry. And the queen maltreated her in many ways, with fumigations, with nettles, with evil-smelling drugs and other torments; and the child in her womb grew all the stronger … .she [the queen] told all the midwives, that if they do not take the child away from her as soon as she is delivered, and bring it to the queen and she hears of it, she will cut off her head. And thus it was done, and we do not know what happened to the child, the pure innocent. (Machairas 1932: §234)

The image of Eleanora emerging from the description of Machairas conforms to the stereotypical image of the witch. The witch was the "ultimate seductress, the heiress of all generic Eves" (Cixous and Clement 1986: 6). Witches were thought to be sexually promiscuous (and Eleanora is known to have had a lover), degenerate in thoughts and deeds, and plotting against innocent people. The picture of Eleanora as a witch is supported by her paramedical activities to kill her enemy's innocent, unborn child. Witches, already from classical times as the examples of Circe and Medea indicate, were experts in the manufacture of poison but also of love filters. The accusation of witchcraft was another expression of misogyny because the power of the witch was seen as a threat to the established order (Galatariotou 1985: 63–65). She presented the utmost threat as she healed against the Church's canon, performed abortions, and favored extra-marital love. She brought disorder into the regularity of everyday life and challenged authority (Cixous and Clement 1986: 4–5).

In the chronicle of Machairas, men are usually seen as victims of the bewitching sexual power possessed by women. Although both Peter and Eleanora had adulterous affairs, it is always the woman who is more severely criticized than the man. The extra-marital affairs of Peter are blamed on the "demon of fornication," who is "the beginner of all trouble," "assails the whole world" and thus made "the good king fall into sin" (Machairas 1932: §§ 234, 239). And that the king kept two lovers, when he supposedly was so infatuated with his own wife, "this he did on account of his great sensuality, because he was a young man" (Machairas 1932: §242). Even the queen's lover is presented as a passive victim of her powers of seduction and Eleanora is to take all the blame:

> Again let us return to what happened on account of the queen's wrongdoing. The beginner of all trouble, the demon of fornication, entered into the heart of messire John de Morphou the Count of Roukha, and very great love came upon him for the queen: and he used many shifts, and gave so much to the go-betweens, that he carried the affair through from the beginning to the end, and they came together. And the affair was made known to all the town, namely that so lawless a deed had been done, and all the people were speaking of nothing else, so much that even the street boys were talking about it. (Machairas 1932: § 239)

The vulnerability of men in love is aptly described in the following passage:

> Learn then from me what befalls men who love women and believe what they say. For women love men furiously; then they try to get rid of them; and give them magic potions to drink, with ten thousand wicked tricks; and they wheedle them, and finally for a mere word they kill them. And they do as the she-bear does: when she is on heat, she fondles her mate, the male animal; and when he has covered her and she is off heat, then she kills him. But the love of a man goes very deep; for his love for the woman waxes little by little until a perfect love is brought to the perfect end, or his hate waxes little by little until he leaves her completely. But the ladder of a woman's love has but one step: if she loves you, she practices a thousand wicked wiles to make you love her, and right in the midst of them she kills you. And if she hates you, she tries to get rid of you, and nothing will stop her. (Machairas 1932: §576)

Eleanora was even accused that her affair caused the murder of her husband by yet another man whom she supposedly tried to seduce, unsuccessfully this time:

> And sir Thibald (turned and) reviled the queen and said to her: "Stinking and wicked harlot, you wanted me to have you and for this you sent me word, and I refused to do a shameful deed in the house of my lord, and it is for this that you strike me with this cruel death, because you were always a wicked harlot, and you were the cause of killing your husband the good king Peter, that you might go whoring with the Count of Roukha." (Machairas 1932: §575)

In a very schematic way, men are perceived as good and women as evil; men are innocent victims, whereas women are blood-thirsty seductresses. Interestingly enough, this is one of the few instances in which women assume an active role instead of passively being subjected to the wishes of men. Inevitably, this kind of behavior is condemned by being presented not as merely sinful but criminal.

Power is perceived as evil because it is a threat to the established order; it clashes with the interests of those who exercise authority in a social system. Female power, especially political power expressed in a male society against a patriarchal structure, is unavoidably seen as threatening and potentially destructive. This is why the third and last woman to be discussed here has been attacked by both Cypriot and non-Cypriot authors.

Helena Palaiologina was the second wife of John II (A.D. 1432–1458) and reached Cyprus in 1442. She was the daughter of Theodore Palaiologos, despot of Morea and younger brother of two Byzantine emperors, John VIII (A.D. 1425–1448) and Constantine XI (A.D. 1448–1453) (Hill 1948: 527). This was the first time that the Lusignans were linked to the imperial family of the Palaiologoi, and because Helena was a Greek Orthodox, she was accused as being hostile to the Latin church on Cyprus. She was also charged as responsible for changing the Latin rite to the Greek and giving almost all offices to the Greeks (Hill 1948: 527, note 2). Pope Pius II vehemently condemned Helena for her support to the Greek church (Vacalopoulos 1972: 278–79). He described her as "ingeniosa et cordata mulier, verum Graeca instituta perfidia, Latinis inimica sacris et Romanae hostis ecclesiae" (Hill 1948: 527, note 2). Her endowment to the monastery of George of Mangana with 15,000 ducats a year was regarded as extravagant generosity in impoverished times (Machairas 1932: §711).

The truth is that Helena was only half Greek. Her mother, Cleopa Malatesta, was an Italian who kept her faith to the Roman Catholic dogma, and her brother was the Latin archbishop of Patras. There is no substantial evidence to support that she actively promoted the Greek church over the Latin. Her alleged support to refugees from Constantinople after the fall of the city to the Turks in 1453, no matter how plausible, cannot be proven concretely. Her attempts to promote her own candidate as archbishop of Cyprus against the will of the pope failed in the end (Hill 1948: 1090–92). The widely debated process of "hellenization" that she has so much been both accused and credited for, was already in process before she even arrived to Cyprus (Richard 1987: 400–403; Christoforaki 1997: 89–90).

What did she do, then, to deserve such vitriolic attacks from her contemporaries? The answer is succinctly provided by a modern author, George Hill, in his *History of Cyprus*. He writes: "Not content with exerting her influence in the way in which strong-minded wives are wont to do, she sought official recognition as regent of the kingdom and secured it from the High Court" (Hill 1948: 528). In other words, Helena surpassed her traditional role as spouse of the king and assumed power that was beyond her prescribed part. She actively seized politicalpower and exercized it, although her husband was still alive and in good health. Even worse, the king apparently consented to this arrangement. Pope Pius II described her as behaving not only as queen but also as king and practically governing the island single-handedly (Vacalopoulos 1972: 279). According to his account,

> non tam reginam quam regem egit; regnumquem ipsa gubernavit, magistratus veteres deposuit, novos instituit, sacerdotia pro suo arbitrio ordinavit, et, eliminato Latinorum ritu, Graecanicum superinduxit, belli pacisque leges dixit. Viro satis fuit convivari, deliciisque affluere, atque in hunc modum universa insula in potestatem Graecorum rediit. (Hill 1948: 528, note 1)

Although there might be some element of exaggeration in his description, the reason for discontent is obvious: a female active in male territory is a threat. She has to be exorcized as evil so as not to function as a female role model.

Helena also failed in the main duty of a wife to produce a son and an heir for the kingdom. She only had two daughters, Cleopatra, who died in infancy, and Charlotte. There was, however, an illegitimate heir by the king's mistress, Marietta of Patras. According to the chroniclers of the time, Helena was so jealous of her rival that she attacked her so violently that she cut off her nose. In the meantime, the king "took indescribable pleasure in watching two such brave Amazons contending for his love" (Hill 1948: 529 and note 2).

Eleanora of Aragon and Helena Palaiologina are the two prime examples of the construction of evil women in Cypriot historiography. The power they wielded, be it sexual or political, has always been perceived as evil, and is further evidenced by Sir George Hill, who pairs the two women together in his *History*. When introducing Helena, he writes: "Helena was ... in vindictiveness ... hardly surpassed by Queen Eleanor" (Hill 1948: 527).

It is only by "reading between the lines" that we can analyze and understand medieval perceptions of gender and unveil the stereotypes that women assume in men's writings. It is not surprising that male perceptions of femininity followed the pre-requisites of a patriarchal society. Women, unless dependent and obedient, were ostracized as evil and dangerous. This cultural construct had become so deeply entrenched that it was considered as the natural, god-given order. Male narratives not only reflected this reality but also contributed to their perpetuation. Cypriot historiography could be no exception.

ACKNOWLEDGMENTS

I wish to extend my warmest thanks to Dr. Nancy Serwint for her continuous encouragement and moral support to an "alien" Byzantinist. I would also like to acknowledge the pioneering work of Dr. Catia Galatariotou, whose research on gender in medieval Cyprus has provided the inspiration for this article. I am also most grateful to Dr. Liz James for reading an early draft of this paper and making helpful comments.

REFERENCES

Anaxagorou, N.
1998   *Narrative and Stylistic Structures in the Chronicle of Leontios Machairas*. Nicosia: A. G. Leventis Foundation.

Belsey, C.
1980   *Critical Practice*. London: Methuen.

Belsey, C., and Moore, J., eds.
1989   *The Feminist Reader: Essays in Gender and the Politics of Literary Criticism*. London: Macmillan.

Brubaker, L.
1997   Memories of Helena: Patterns in Imperial Female Matronage in the Fourth and Fifth Centuries. Pp. 52–75 in *Women, Men and Eunuchs. Gender in Byzantium*, ed. L. James. London: Routledge.

Buchthal, H., and Belting, H.
1978   *Patronage in Thirteenth-Century Constantinople. An Atelier of Calligraphy and Book Decoration*. Dumbarton Oaks Studies 16. Washington, D.C.: Dumbarton Oaks Center for Byzantine Studies.

Christoforaki, I.
1997   Η τέχνη στην Κύπρο την εποχή του Λ. Μαχαιρά και του Γ. Βουστρώνιου. Pp. 87–96 in *Πρακτικά Συμποσίου: Λεόντιος Μαχαιράς και Γεώργιος Βουστρώνιος. Δύο χρονικά της μεσαιωνικής Κύπρου. Λευκωσία, 21 Σεπτεμβρίου 1996*, ed. L. Loizou. Nicosia: A. G. Leventis Foundation.

Cixous, H., and Clement, C.
1986   *The Newly Born Woman*. Trans. by B. Wing from French. Minneapolis: University of Minnesota.

Drijvers, J. W.
1993   *Helena Augusta*. Leiden: Brill.

Eagleton, M.
1996   *Working with Feminist Criticism*. Oxford: Blackwell.

Galatariotou, C.
1985   Holy Women and Witches: Aspects of Byzantine Conceptions of Gender. *Byzantine and Modern Greek Studies* 9: 55–96.
1988   Byzantine Women's Monastic Communities: The Evidence of the Typika. *Jahrbuch der Österreichischen Byzantinistik* 38: 263–90.

Grössinger, C.
1997   *Picturing Women in Late Medieval and Renaissance Art*. Manchester Medieval Studies. New York: Manchester University.

Hill, B.
1999   *Imperial Women in Byzantium 1025–1204: Power, Patronage and Ideology*. Harlow, Essex: Longman.

Hill, G.
1948   *A History of Cyprus*. Vol. 3. Cambridge: Cambridge University.

Jefferson, A., and Robey, D. eds.
1982   *Modern Literary Theory: A Comparative Introduction*. London: Batsford.

Machairas, L.
1932   *Leontios Makhairas, Recital Concerning the Sweet Land of Cyprus entitled 'Chronicle'*. Vol. 1. Ed. and trans. R. M. Dawkins. Oxford: Clarendon.

Mango, C.
1980   *Byzantium. The Empire of New Rome*. London: Weidenfeld and Nicholson.

Mentzou-Meimari, K.
1982   Η παρουσία της γυναίκας στις ελληνικές επιγραφές από τον 4ο μέχρι τον 10ο αιώνα. *Jahrbuch der Österreichischen Byzantinistik* 32.2: 433–43.

Pohlsander, H.
1995   *Helena: Empress and Saint*. Chicago: Univeristy of Chicago.

Power, E.
1975   *Medieval Women*. Cambridge: Cambridge University.
Richard, J.
1987   Culture franque et culture grecque. Le royaume de Chypre au XVe siècle. *Byzantinische Forschungen* 11: 339–415.
Ruskin, J.
1864   *Sesame and Lilies*. London: Dent.
Selden, R.
1989   *Practising Theory and Reading Literature: An Introduction*. Hemel Hemstead: Harvester Wheatsheaf.
Smythe, D. C.
1997   Women as Outsiders. Pp. 149–67 in *Women, Men and Eunuchs. Gender in Byzantium*, ed. L. James. London: Routledge.
Vacalopoulos, A.
1972   Une reine grecque de Chypre mal comprise par les historiens: Hélène Paléologine (1442–1458). Pp. 277–80 in *Πρακτικά του Πρώτου Διεθνούς Κυπρολογικού Συνεδρίου. Λευκωσία, 14–19 Απριλίου 1969*, Τομ. 2, ed. A. Papageorgiou. Nicosia: Εταιρεία Κυπριακών Σπουδών.

PART FOUR

GENDER, IDENTITY AND ETHNICITY

SOCIAL STRATIFICATION, GENDER AND ETHNICITY IN THIRD MILLENNIUM CYPRUS

DAVID FRANKEL

Department of Archaeology
La Trobe University
Bundoora 3083, Australia
d.frankel@latrobe.edu.au

There are two main approaches to explaining the change from the Chalcolithic to the Bronze Age in Cyprus. One emphasizes internal developments in social complexity, the other suggests the arrival on the island of whole communities and the maintenance of separate ethnic groups for some generations. Recent discussions have attempted to integrate gender as a significant element in this debate, mainly in terms of the relative status of women and men, seen in a context of increased social stratification. A view of the 3rd millennium in terms of contrasting ethnic identities suggests the need to disassociate the question of gender relationships from the nature of social organization and technology and to consider other ways in which gender can contribute to archaeological explanation.

INTRODUCTION

Despite a general agreement that gender is a major structuring principle of society, archaeologists continue to have difficulty in developing appropriate ways to incorporate this dimension of social identity and relationship into general models or explanations. This is partly because gender may be constructed in many different ways and intersects with other dimensions of age, ability, wealth and status to define either individual or corporate identity. In this paper, I set a discussion of gender into a broader context, linking aspects of domestic and industrial (presumably gendered) behavior to other markers of social identity in mid-3rd millennium B.C.E. Cyprus.

Archaeologists dealing with prehistoric Cyprus have considered gender in several different ways. These range from the more simple (division of labor), to the more complex (mechanisms of social interaction) and the most fundamental (basis of social organization and power). Several approaches have been used, singly, in combination, or associated with other material and arguments.

Biological Analyses

Insofar as gender may be equated with sex (and apart from a few regularly quoted exceptions, this is by far the most common practice), there is no good evidence provided by the identification of the sex of buried individuals to suggest any significant difference in mortuary treatment between male and female burials or demonstrable differences in different cultural contexts. This may partly be because taphonomic and other factors have so adversely affected burials that our samples are not adequate to identify consistent patterns of mortality, health, status or custom.

Anthropomorphic Figurines

Anthropomorphic figurines have provided by far the most fertile grounds for discussion. A well-known array of free-standing figures, genre models, pendants and other representations form the starting point for numerous contrasting interpretations. They may be reading at many different levels ranging from the superficial (direct representations of activities) to the deeply symbolic (manifestations of embedded structures in society). Given the inherent ambiguities and complexities in any such material, these analyses, more often than not, impose rather than extract meaning.

Behavioral Models

Archaeological constructs of gender-based activities and social behavior often link broad general analogues with a variety of objects and patterns. These, too, may impose meaning and limit concepts of appropriate gender-roles to those most common cross-culturally but can have the advantage of explicitly articulating bridging arguments.

One important arena where all these data sets and approaches intersect is the 3rd millennium B.C.E., a time that saw considerable and relatively rapid change in Cyprus and which has given rise to much past and current scholarly debate. This involves the definition and assessment of different archaeological entities and closely linked attitudes and approaches to explanations for variation and change. In this paper, I would like to rehearse aspects of these debates and consider to what extent a gendered view can be developed or can contribute to an understanding of developments in social organization and cultural change—seen by some as the key issues in archaeological analysis.

THE CHALCOLITHIC BACKGROUND

In reviewing evidence from both excavations and surveys, Peltenburg has developed broad models of Late Neolithic and Chalcolithic social organization and its evolution from the 4th and 3rd millennia B.C.E He argues that occasional examples of control beyond the individual household suggest the development of structured hierarchies at intervals, with fluctuations between simpler *managed inequalities* and more complex *intensified inequalities* at each site—episodes within a cyclical process of social reproduction (1993: Table 1). Increases in site numbers, together with the discontinuities of occupation and shifts in settlement within sites, provide the basis for suggesting general regulatory mechanisms operating to maintain a relatively low level of formal hierarchy. As the scale of inequality intensified, settlement fissioning took place. This social fragmentation and the establishment of new settlements, or shifting locations of control within existing settlements, served to regulate the degree of structured asymmetry, with population centers remaining below a fairly low threshold of social inequality.

Although Peltenburg rejects an ecological explanation for this pattern of cyclical intensification and fissioning, it is possible to argue that even in the better-watered river valleys of southwestern Cyprus, hoe-based agriculture imposed limits on population density and distribution. This may, however, have led to increased inequality where individuals or groups were able to develop greater control of limited resources, at least in the short term.

A key difference between the Chalcolithic and the Bronze Age is an economy characteristic of the Secondary Products Revolution, involving the use of animals for traction power and in other ways (Sherratt 1981). The arrival of new animals on the island, especially cattle and donkeys, are the most obvious sign of this. The new use of ox-drawn ploughs transformed agricultural practice, leading to a higher level of productivity and production and more extensive cultivation than was possible for Chalcolithic farmers. While lands just north of the Troodos, with low rainfall, were clearly of less value to Chalcolithic hoe-based agriculturalists, they were far more suitable for Bronze Age agricultural technology. These areas had, in addition, the advantage of being close to copper deposits, an irrelevant resource for Cypriots before the mid-3rd millennium. The greater productivity of Bronze Age farming technology not only allowed settlement in previously marginal areas but also allowed settlements of larger size to develop. The question remains whether settlement (population?) size is necessarily correlated with complexity, differentiation and stratification.

MODELS OF INCREASED SOCIAL STRATIFICATION

These elements are emphasized in the models of change currently adopted by scholars such as Knapp and Manning who prefer an evolutionary progress toward increasing social differentiation with the emergence of social elites during the Early Bronze Age (Knapp 1993, 1994; Manning 1993). Both argue, for example, that increases in the relative size of settlements not only show a growth in the scale of communities and intensity of production but are also correlated with increased social complexity (Manning 1993: fig. 3; Knapp 1993: figs. 1–3). In examining the Chalcolithic–Bronze Age transition, Manning presents a general model of a consistent, although not simply linear, increase in the scale of social complexity (1993: fig. 4). While accommodating Peltenburg's arguments for limits to settlement size and social complexity in the Chalcolithic—a pattern of fluctuating levels of inequality—his diagram suggests that during the Bronze Age these limits were continually relaxed. The increase in scale of settlement and population brought about by the greater efficiencies of the Secondary Products Revolution are here seen to lead inevitably to increases in social complexity.

Knapp (1993, 1994) and Manning (1993) both favor a primary role for internal processes in initiating these changes. Manning, for example, picks up some elements of Sherratt's general model to suggest that emergent elites signal their status by, among other things, the acquisition of foreign exotica to display and enhance their status. New forms of pottery, which mark the earliest facies of the Bronze Age, are thus interpreted as luxury items, restricted to the elite (the characteristic tall jugs with cut-away spouts thus represent elite drinking parties). The introduction of cattle to the island is also explained by competitive emergent elites seeking out and importing prestigious innovations. In this case it was an economically significant innovation where the investment of capital in acquiring animals was speedily recouped and enhanced as the innovators increasingly established their dominance over less competitive neighbors.

Other evidence is adduced by these and other scholars in support of such views of greater status differentiation and hence power asymmetry in the Early and Middle Bronze Age. Knapp emphasises the role of metal objects in burial contexts as a measure of differential displays of wealth by some individuals or families (1993, 1994). The well-known model from Vounous is seen by both Manning (1993) and Peltenburg (1994; cf. Knapp 1996) as symbolically representing such an hierarchy of power with the seated male figure at the apex.

AN EGALITARIAN BRONZE AGE?

Social organization during the prehistoric Bronze Age, however, is still a matter of debate, and alternative views of Early Cypriot society and its development are possible. While the longevity and rebuilding of houses at Marki argue for the inter-generational reuse of settlement space, paralleled by probable maintenance of family tombs, there is little substantial evidence for social stratification or accumulated wealth. Bronze Age architecture displays little differentiation in scale or quality of housing, at least as seen in the few excavations at settlements of the period. The size, location and probable number of storage facilities at Marki suggests that storage was at the household, rather than suprahousehold or community level (Webb, this volume). Pottery was—at least so I have previously argued—produced at a household level of production, with minor regional variations which reflect degrees of inter-site connections and relationships (Frankel 1974, 1988; Frankel and Webb 1996: 110–11). Although some tombs are larger than others and some have a slightly higher ratio of grave-goods to burials, there is insufficient evidence to sustain an argument for patterned inequalities at most sites, with the possible exception of Lapithos (Davies 1997). Unless concentrations of metalwork in some tombs are assumed to represent wealth, power or status, there are no identifiable symbols of power or prestige.

In this way, one may view Early and Middle Bronze Age society as made up of independent but inter-related villages of self-sufficient agro-pastoralists, with few or no standardized or overt symbols of status and power or clear indications of differential wealth or control of resources. There is no evidence to suggest a pattern of fluctuating intensity of social inequality as suggested for the Neolithic and Chalcolithic but rather a stable system which, once established, lasted for at least 500 years. It was only toward the end of the Middle Bronze Age that there may have been a slow, incremental growth in social differentiation.

GENDER AND STATUS

Discussions of gender, power and status in prehistoric Cyprus often involve a series of linked arguments. Especially important are those that link the degree of formal stratification, or complexity of society, and asymmetries along gender lines (e.g., Bolger 1994). Even if later 3rd millennium Cypriot society was more complex and more hierarchically ordered than that of the Chalcolithic, this parallelism needs to be demonstrated rather than assumed.

In attempting to engender the process of change between the Chalcolithic and the Bronze Age, Bolger (1996) adopts the general model of development of a more hierarchical society advocated by Knapp and Manning. Parallel to the putative growth of social or political elites is an (inevitable?) asymmetry in gender relations: Chalcolithic gender equality replaced by Bronze Age patriarchal dominance. In brief, Bolger suggests that Chalcolithic women, often depicted in poses suggestive of pregnancy and/or childbirth, should be seen as filling the ideological role of *genetrix*. Both in practice and in social ideology, they were in control of their destinies and reproduction—equals within an egalitarian society. By contrast, some images of Bronze Age women are taken to mean that women were ideologically cast in the role of *mater*, long-suffering mothers, subordinated to men (Bolger 1996). As I have argued elsewhere, this reading of the evidence provided by models is fraught with difficulties of many kinds, both intrinsic to the figurines and in the extrinsic context provided by different views of Bronze Age society (Frankel 1997).

However, other discussions imply a similar low status for Bronze Age women. In contrast to the limited role for women—procreation—represented in Chalcolithic images, Early and Middle Bronze Age genre models display a wide array of activities—so many that some have taken this to reflect their inferior status *vis-à-vis* men (e.g., Morris 1985: 281). There is, however, no *necessity* to see in this material any evidence that women had a restricted or subordinate role. While it is possible to identify activities carried out by women, this says little about gender relationships (cf. Frankel 1993).

Analysis of other material may also build on broad models of gendered behavior to raise issues of group and personal identity and interaction. In earlier studies (Frankel 1974, 1978, 1988), I have argued that if pottery manufacture was primarily organized at a household level, it was probably in the hands of women. If this were the case, then the patterns of ceramic similarity within and between sites can provide a map of the scale of social interaction. In addition, any such movement of potters, bringing techniques and styles from one place to another, would have facilitated other aspects of technology transfer and social interaction and exchange. If this chain of argument is valid, then we need to understand the mechanisms that allowed, encouraged or forced women to relocate. It is possible to read into this "exchange" of women an implication of male dominance. This is, however, not necessarily the case. In a somewhat similar scenario, Bolger sees an equivalent movement of women in the Chalcolithic in a more positive light and not simply as "pawns in an increasingly intricate game of patriarchal politics" (1994: 14).

Both with regard to pottery and other material, Bolger suggests that Chalcolithic women's high social standing can be inferred from their skills in craft production. Even if this were a valid line of argument, it would not serve to differentiate between the Chalcolithic and the Bronze Age, for both societies display material culture of similar quality (however that may be measured).

In an associated analysis of Neolithic and Chalcolithic life expectancy, Bolger suggests a decline in women's health during the early 3rd millennium, although the very small sample size detracts from the force of this argument. This analysis cannot easily be applied to Bronze Age populations, as the current limited data available on sex and age of skeletons does not at present provide any basis for identifying a significant difference between men and women in health status or longevity. Moreover, there is no necessary reason why health and longevity need be closely correlated with other aspects of social organization and stratification.

GENDER AND ETHNICITY

The introduction of gender into the discussions noted above essentially treats women as a *category*. A broader engendering of archaeology needs to move beyond this and to see this dimension of society in other ways. This may be illustrated by considering again the issue of the origins of the Bronze Age cultural system.

The Bronze Age is archaeologically distinguished from the Chalcolithic in many ways. Apart from newly introduced animals and agricultural technology noted above (with important implications for the range and scheduling of activities and products), there are significant differences in many items of material culture and technology. Among the many, commonly observed, differences are:

- Pottery techniques and decoration are distinctive, while new shapes represent new needs and ways of handling vessels. This is most efficiently explained by the arrival of people with a different potting tradition.
- Terracotta spindle whorls and loomweights, which represent the introduction of low-whorl spindles and vertical warp-weighted looms similar to those common in Anatolia. The particular mode of handling whorls and setting up looms is also best explained by positing the movement of spinners and weavers (Frankel and Webb 1996: 193–95; Frankel and Webb 1998; Webb and Frankel 1999).
- The appearance of direct fire-boiling cooking pots and associated hobs demonstrate different methods of preparing food, implying a different cuisine.
- Multi-roomed rectilinear architecture, which shows a clearly distinct concepts, design and techniques of construction from the circular single units of the Chalcolithic. These have major implications for many aspects of inter-personal relationships and relationships within the settlement.

These do not represent markers of status brought in by newly emergent elites but a wide array of everyday domestic items and actions. It is clear that the range of activities represented—especially those related to domestic crafts—represent those carried out by all sectors of society, women as well as men. This provides a basis for arguing that these introductions of normal everyday ways of doing things signal the arrival on the island of communities. In other words, the differences in material culture that mark the Bronze Age in Cyprus were initiated by the migration to the island by groups of people probably from southwestern Anatolia (Frankel et al. 1996; cf. Peltenburg 1996). These groups established and maintained a significantly different *habitus sensu* (Bourdieu 1977) from that of the indigenous Chalcolithic communities (Frankel and Webb 1998; Webb and Frankel 1999; Frankel 2000).

We have, in effect, an argument for a migration based on a more comprehensive view of behavior, representing the activities of both women and men carrying out the everyday tasks that combine into the defining *habitus* of an ethnic group.

As these components of the earliest (Philia) facies of the Early Cypriot Bronze Age overlapped in time with the Late Chalcolithic, it is appropriate to envisage two distinct behavioral, technological and economic systems on the island. For several generations, at least, these ethnic communities maintained fundamentally different ways of working and organizing tasks and society. Any differences that may be observed in practical, ideological or other aspects of gender definition and relationships may, therefore, be seen as part of two distinctive patterns of organizing society and the demands of different economic and social systems. This makes no assumptions about the relative degree of social stratification or any asymmetry of wealth, status or power within either community.

If such a model can be sustained, then 3rd millennium Cyprus becomes an especially interesting site—a site where we can begin to see a series of processes by which migrant groups moved into new areas and established themselves, adapting to their new surroundings. The concurrent responses by the indigenous Chalcolithic communities are of equal interest. The different agricultural practices and technologies of new settlers may have minimized competition with the main concentrations of Chalcolithic population, as they targeted areas undesirable for non-metal using, hoe-based agriculturalists. But the presence on the island of new peoples and new technologies had its effects. The breakdown of the old values which Peltenburg perceives in the Late Chalcolithic may be symptomatic of a gradual exposure to new peoples, ideas and technologies. At the same time, one might suggest that the ability of individuals during the Chalcolithic to control more limited agricultural production would have been undermined by the availability of alternative, more efficient farming practices and the opening up of previously unproductive regions.

Adaptation and acculturation by settlers and indigenous communities over several generations—perhaps several centuries—eventually led to a situation where the whole island became, archaeologically, Bronze Age, with no material trace of the indigenous culture. The unstable, but perhaps self-regulating fluctuations in scale of complexity, which seem to have characterized Chalcolithic societies in the 4th millennium B.C.E, are not apparent in the Bronze Age of the mid-3rd to early 2nd millennia. There is no clear evidence of a continual increase in either productive efficiency or in social complexity for at least 500 years. Different mechanisms of social reproduction, ones that encouraged maintenance of a uniform system, appear to have been in operation.

The explanation for these changes and developments will require a complex series of interrelated elements and approaches, involving both historical contingency (initial migration), economic and technological influences (settlement size and location) and culture process (adaptation and assimilation; Frankel in press). The origin, development and maintenance of varied cultural systems involves all parts of communities and has implications for gender relationships. Investigating this dimension of 3rd millennium B.C.E history is one of the challenges for archaeologists of the third millennium C.E. But in order to meet this challenge, we need to explicate clearly in what way, and at what scale, we can perceive gender in the past and build it into broader explanations.

DISASSOCIATING GENDER

Several issues arise from this brief review of aspects of 3rd millennium Cyprus. These are all linked by a common element—the need to disassociate gender from other dimensions of social relationships and historical process.

Social Organization and Gender Status and Relationships

Even if we could clearly distinguish between a more egalitarian Chalcolithic social formation and a more hierarchical prehistoric Bronze Age system, there is no necessary reason why the relative status of men and women need be correlated with this difference.

Gender-based Division of Labor and Relative Status

A wide array of activities can be demonstrated from the variety of terracotta models of the prehistoric Bronze Age. There is, however, little need to see a significantly different allocation of tasks to that characteristic of Chalcolithic communities. Specific activities or particular ways of carrying out equivalent tasks may have differed, but this does not imply a difference of relative status between men and women.

Explaining 3ʳᵈ Millennium Differences

In the place of an evolutionary model, linking changes in work practices, status and relative degree of social hierarchy, we can argue for an alternative agent of change. Historically contingent events, rather than broad evolutionary processes, provide an alternative and challenging mode of explanation. In the place of a more-or-less inevitable evolution of society toward greater complexity (and an essentialist correlation of greater social differentiation and the suppression of women), we may perceive the differences between the prehistoric Bronze Age communities and Chalcolithic communities as indicative of two distinct ethnicities (Frankel 2000). This may provide a particularly appropriate scale at which to analyse this prehistoric material.

On a broader front, one may question whether the issue of gender relationships and the relative status of men and women is the most appropriate way to develop a gendered archaeology. If we now identify contemporary ethnic groups in 3ʳᵈ millennium Cyprus and focus on the mechanisms by which cultural differences were first maintained and later dissolved, then questions of evolving status and hierarchy become less relevant than those of social intercourse. Can we begin to address the process of acculturation and assimilation in prehistory by considering it in terms of gender?

ACKNOWLEDGMENTS

In preparing this paper I have, as usual, benefited from continuous discussions with Jenny Webb as well as from her specific advice. Susan Lawrence and Caroline Bird read and commented on a draft of this paper.

REFERENCES

Bolger, D. L.
1994   Engendering Cypriot Archaeology: Women's Roles and Statuses before the Bronze Age. *Opuscula Atheniensia* 20: 9–17.
1996   Figurines, Fertility, and the Emergence of Complex Society in Prehistoric Cyprus. *Current Anthropology* 37: 365–73.

Bourdieu, P.
1977   *Outline of a Theory of Practice*. Cambridge: Cambridge University.

Davies, P.
1997   Mortuary practice in Prehistoric Bronze Age Cyprus: Problems and Potential. *Report of the Department of Antiquities of Cyprus*: 11–26.

Frankel, D.
1974   *Middle Cypriot White Painted Pottery: An Analytical Study of the Decoration*. Studies in Mediterranean Archaeology 42. Göteborg: Åströms.
1978   Pottery Decoration as an Indicator of Social Relationships: A Prehistoric Cypriot Example. Pp. 147–60 in *Art in Society*, eds. M. Greenhalgh and J. V. S. Megaw. London: Duckworth.
1988   Pottery Production in Prehistoric Bronze Age Cyprus: Assessing the Problem. *Journal of Mediterranean Archaeology* 1, 2: 27–55.
1993   Is this a Trivial Observation? Gender Roles in Prehistoric Bronze Age Cyprus. Pp.138–42 in *Women in Archaeology: A Feminist Critique,* eds. H. du Cros and L. Smith. Canberra: Occasional Papers in Prehistory No. 23, Department of Prehistory, Research School of Pacific Studies, Australian National University.
1997   On Cypriot Figurines and the Origins of Patriarchy. *Current Anthropology* 38: 84.
2000   Migration and Ethnicity in Prehistoric Cyprus: Technology as *habitus. European Journal of Archaeology* 3:167–87.
in press Becoming Bronze Age. Acculturation and Enculturation in Third Millennium B.C.E. Cyprus. In *The Transmission and Assimilation of Culture in the Near East*, ed. J. Clarke.

Frankel, D., and Webb, J. M.
1996   *Marki Alonia. An Early and Middle Bronze Age Town in Cyprus. Excavations 1990–1994*. Studies in Mediterranean Archaeology 123:1. Jonsered: Åströms.
1998   Three Faces of Identity: Ethnicity, Community and Status in Bronze Age Cyprus. *Mediterranean Archaeology* 11: 1–12.

Frankel, D.; Webb, J. M.; and Eslick, C.
1996   Anatolia and Cyprus in the Third Millennium BCE. A Speculative Model of Interaction. Pp. 37–50 in *Cultural Interaction in the Ancient Near East*, ed. G. Bunnens. Abr-Nahrain Supplementary Series Vol. 5, Department of Classics and Archaeology, University of Melbourne. Melbourne: University of Melbourne.

Knapp, A. B.
1993   Social Complexity: Incipience, Emergence, and Development on Prehistoric Cyprus. *Bulletin of the American Schools of Oriental Research* 292: 85–106.
1994   The Prehistory of Cyprus: Problems and Prospects. *Journal of World Prehistory* 8, 4: 377–453.
1996   The Bronze Age Economy of Cyprus: Ritual, Ideology, and the Sacred Landscape. Pp. 71–106 in *The Development of the Cypriot Economy from the Prehistoric Period to the Present Day*, eds.V. Karageorghis and D. Michaelides. Nicosia: The University of Cyprus and the Bank of Cyprus.

Manning, S. W.
1993   Prestige, Distinction, and Competition: The Anatomy of Socioeconomic Complexity in Fourth to Second Millennium B.C.E. Cyprus. *Bulletin of the American Schools of Oriental Research* 292: 35–58.

Morris, D.
1985   *The Art of Ancient Cyprus*. Oxford: Phaidon.

Peltenburg, E.
  1993   Settlement Discontinuity and Resistance to Complexity in Cyprus ca. 4500–2500 B.C.E. *Bulletin of the American Schools of Oriental Research* 292: 9–24.
  1994   Constructing Authority: The Vounous Enclosure Model. *Opuscula Atheniensia* 20: 157–62.
  1996   From Isolation to State Formation in Cyprus, c. 3500–1500 B.C. Pp. 17–44 in *The Development of the Cypriot Economy from the Prehistoric Period to the Present Day*, eds. V. Karageorghis and D. Michaelides. Nicosia: The University of Cyprus and the Bank of Cyprus.
Sherratt, A.
  1981   Plough and Pastoralism: Aspects of the Secondary Products Revolution. Pp. 261–306 in *Pattern of the Past. Studies in Honour of David Clarke*, eds. I. Hodder, G. Isaac, and N. Hammond. Cambridge: Cambridge University.
Webb, J.M., and Frankel, D.
  1999   Characterising the Philia Facies. Material Culture, Chronology and the Origin of the Bronze Age in Cyprus. *American Journal of Archaeology* 103: 3–43.

SEXUAL AMBIGUITY IN PLANK FIGURES FROM BRONZE AGE CYPRUS

LAUREN E. TALALAY

Kelsey Museum of Archaeology
University of Michigan
434 South State Street
Ann Arbor, Michigan 48109
talalay@umich.edu

TRACEY CULLEN

Hesperia
American School of Classical Studies at Athens
6–8 Charlton Street
Princeton, New Jersey 08540
tc@ascsa.org

Embedded in most interpretations of the meaning, use, and function of Bronze Age Cypriot plank-shaped idols is the notion that they were viewed as female by the ancient users. In many cases, however, characteristics clearly attributable to males or females are absent. The readiness with which scholars impose a binary sexual identification on figurines has deterred them from investigating whether the ancient users and makers of these images conceived of more fluid or multiple constructions of sex and gender. We suggest that plank figures were intended to project sexual ambiguity and may have held a multiplicity of meanings within the context of an emerging hierarchical society. The ambiguity inherent in a multivalent symbol may have been particularly appropriate in the context of mortuary ritual, in which mystification and transformation play important roles.

> The social body constrains the way the physical body is perceived .... There is a continual exchange of meanings between the two kinds of bodily experience so that each reinforces the categories of the other. As a result of this interaction the body itself is a highly restricted medium of expression. (Douglas 1973: 93)

Cypriot plank figures, the first of which was discovered in 1913, have been the focus of discussion and debate among scholars for the last two decades. Despite studies ranging from the descriptive and typological to the analytic and synthetic, scholars have yet to agree on the possible origin, function, and meaning of these enigmatic images. While most archaeologists suggest that the distinctive form of the Cypriot plank figure originated in Chalcolithic or Early Bronze Age Anatolia (Åström 1972: 253; Flourentzos 1975: 32; Orphanides 1983: 37–38; Belgiorno 1984: 16),

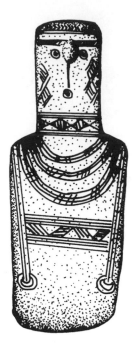

Figure 1. Single-headed Plank Figure. Lapithos, Tomb 201. Red Polished Ware. Ht. 0.27 m. After Morris (1985: fig. 178).

Figure 2. Plank Figure Attached to Vessel. Vounous, Tomb 71. Red Polished Ware. No scale given. After Morris (1985: fig. 242).

Figure 3. Cradled Plank Figure. No Provenance. Red Polished Ware. Ht. 0.16 m. After Morris (1985: fig. 237).

Figure 4. Double-headed Plank Figure. Dhenia. Red Polished Ware. Ht. 0.28 m. After Morris (1985: fig. 218).

others flatly reject external inspiration, arguing instead for indigenous development (e.g., Morris 1985: 136). Interpretations of the figures' imagery also reflect divergent opinions, ranging from Mother God-desses and fertility charms to "hydria-headed" monsters and symbolic marriage contracts connected to women's status in society (see, e.g., Åström 1972; Flourentzos 1975; J. Karageorghis 1977; Merrillees 1980; Orphanides 1983, 1988; Belgiorno 1984; Morris 1985; Mogelonsky 1991; a Campo 1994; Hamilton 1994, 2000; Lubsen Admiraal 1994; and Knapp and Meskell 1997).

In an effort to understand plank figures, most archaeologists have cast these images as monolithic, attempting to construct a single, overarching explanation for their meaning and function. They often attribute a definite sexual identity—usually female—to the figures as well. We argue that such an approach has constrained scholars, limiting them to narrowly defined discourses and precluding valu-able lines of research (see also Knapp and Meskell 1997; Hamilton 2000). The ethnographic record demonstrates clearly that the function, use, and meanings of anthropomorphic figures are complex and dynamic (Ucko 1968, 1996; Talalay 1993, 2000; Bailey 1996; Haaland and Haaland 1996; Hamilton 1996). As nuanced symbols, they can elicit various and changing readings over the course of their lifetime. The impulse of archaeologists to impose a binary sexual identification on plank figures seems especially dubious. Only a few of the planks actually exhibit characteristics that permit unproblematic identifications as male or female. Rather than argue for a specific meaning tied to a specific sexual identity for these figures, we would like to suggest the possibility that they were intended to project sexual ambiguity and may have held a multiplicity of meanings within the context of an emerging hierarchical society. Moreover, the ambiguity that has so confounded modern scholars may have played an important role within the context of mortuary ritual.

THE SAMPLE

Archaeologists have devised various typologies for plank figures: a Campo (1994), for example, focuses on three basic categories, freestanding images (n=78; fig. 1), plank figures attached to vessels (n=15; fig. 2), and plank figures in the form of cradled infants (n=11; fig. 3), while Morris is more inclusive, seeing the controversial comb or brush figures as well as slab figures as part of the same tradition (Morris 1985: 137–49). Most freestanding figures have a single head, though multiheaded examples are also found (n=23; fig. 4). The figures all appear to date from the final phase of what is traditionally termed the Early Cypriot (EC) period into the Middle Cypriot (MC) period (ca. 2000–1700 B.C.; Prehistoric Bronze Age 2 in Knapp's revised chronology [Knapp 1994: 381; Knapp and Meskell 1997: 184]). Approximately two-thirds of the plank figures in a Campo's sample derive from burials while the contexts of the remaining third are unknown. The majority of plank figures are fash-ioned from clay, primarily in Red Polished Ware and to a lesser extent in White Painted Ware. A few stone idols are also included in the corpus.

Whereas the flattening involved in the production of a plank figure simplified the outline of the human form, the designs on clay planks are anything but reductionist. Many figures are richly deco-rated with incised geometric patterns that exhibit striking parallels to motifs selected by EC–MC pot-ters. Indeed, several archaeologists have minimized the importance of the figures' form, arguing that the decorative elements were the focus of production, function and meaning (e.g., a Campo 1994: 119).

The incised designs on both single- and multiheaded planks denote a range of attributes. Readily recognizable are bodily features such as eyes, eyebrows, mouths, noses, hair, and ears. Details of what may be dress and ornamentation typically include headbands, necklaces, scarfs or shawls, and waist-bands, although these designs can also be read as tattoos, scarifications, or body paint. Sexual charac-teristics such as breasts are depicted in a third of a Campo's sample (a Campo 1994: 199–208) and portrayals of male or female genitalia are extremely rare. *Kourotrophoi* holding either cradled or non-cradled infants comprise a small part of the sample (16 percent); often, but not invariably, the "parental" image is depicted with breasts.

The freestanding planks range in height from 0.10 m to 0.70 m, with an average of approximately 0.25 m (excluding the apparently anomalous 0.70 m figure). The catalogue compiled by a Campo includes 40 complete or nearly complete planks, including 29 single-headed images that average nearly 0.22 m in height (range 0.10–0.29), nine double-headed pieces averaging 0.26 m (range 0.19–0.30), one complete triple-headed example measuring 0.25 m, and the 0.70 m figure, an undecorated stone example from an unusually large and richly provided tomb at Lapithos-*Vrysi tou Barba* (hereafter, Lapithos; Gjerstad et al. 1934: 147; a Campo 1994: 199–208). The figures' substantial size and often elaborate decoration suggest that planks required, if not special expertise, at least several hours to produce and finish.

ARCHAEOLOGICAL CONTEXT

Plank figures derive principally from burials in the northern and north-central parts of Cyprus. Of the 78 freestanding examples in a Campo's corpus (1994: 62, Table 6; see also pp. 109–14), 39 were recovered from tombs in the Lapithos area (most from Lapithos: Gjerstad et al. 1934; Myres 1946), 22 from unknown contexts, seven and six respectively from burials at Dhenia-*Kafkalla* (Frankel 1983) and Bellapais-*Vounous* B (hereafter, Vounous; Schaeffer 1936; Dikaios 1940), two from Nicosia-*Ayia Paraskevi* (Ohnefalsch-Richter 1893), and one each from Alambra-*Mouttes* (Orphanides 1983) and Nicosia-*Tamassos* (Belgiorno 1984: 20–21; fig. 7.2). Excluded from a Campo's sample is a single fragmentary plank from Lapithos recovered during excavations sponsored by the University Museum of the University of Pennsylvania (Herscher 1975: 47). Multiheaded figures come primarily from Lapithos and Dhenia-*Kafkalla*, with none reported from the nearby site of Vounous.

The mortuary context in which most plank figures have been found must be regarded cautiously, given the overwhelming funerary bias of the archaeological record for this span of Cypriot prehistory. There is, in fact, no good evidence that plank figures were exclusively manufactured for use in tombs. Indeed, several figures found in tombs at Lapithos were worn, chipped, or repaired, suggesting prolonged use prior to their placement in burials (see, e.g., Gjerstad et al. 1934: 92, no. 93; 93, no. 20). This observation accords well with Dugay's assertion made on the basis of use-wear analysis, that pottery deposited in tombs of this period had been used previously in a domestic context (Dugay 1994: 123, cited in Davies 1997: 16). Moreover, fragments have been reported recently from settlements: at least two from Alambra-*Mouttes* (Mogelonsky 1996: 199–205; fig. 49, E1, E11), one from Ambelikou-*Aletri* (Belgiorno 1984: 19; V. Karageorghis 1991a: 56, no. 8; pl. 22.1), and three from Marki-*Alonia* (Frankel and Webb 1996: 187–88; fig 8.3, P3674, P6360, AP8). Also convincing is the recent discovery of a plank figure with mend-holes from Marki-*Alonia*. The piece had broken, was mended, and then broke again before it was discarded in the settlement (Frankel and Webb 1996: 188). The mended Marki plank and the condition of select examples from Lapithos may indicate that plank figurines were not casually discarded or removed from circulation in domestic contexts. As valued objects, they may, as Webb (1992: 90) points out, "have been endowed with symbolic, magical or apotropaic validity, a status not inconsistent with their occasional use as grave goods and votives."

Within funerary contexts, the precise association of plank figures with the remains of the deceased and other grave goods can rarely be determined. Many of the chamber tombs at Lapithos and Vounous, which provide the most complete contextual evidence, have been subject to flooding, ground inundation, and looting. The practice of multiple and successive burial, with earlier burials often being pushed aside to make room for later ones, further complicates interpretation. Human bones were seldom preserved sufficiently to allow identification of the age or sex of an individual or sometimes even the number of individuals present in a given chamber. In those instances when an osteologist could identify such attributes, poor excavation records often prevented association of the deceased with particular grave goods (Fischer 1986: 5). Several excavators have worked at Lapithos—Myres and Buxton in 1913 (Myres 1946), Markides in 1917 (Gjerstad 1926), Gjerstad and his colleagues in 1927–1931 (Gjerstad et al. 1934), and Hill in 1931–1932 (Herscher 1975)—and it is difficult to correlate the records from the different areas of excavation. This is particularly unfortunate since the number and types of plank figures differ strikingly from one excavation report to the next: Myres' and Markides' samples appear to be dominated by double-headed planks; the tombs excavated by the Swedish project contained exclusively single-headed examples; and the 38 tombs excavated by the University Museum yielded only a single fragment.

The sex of the deceased has generally been inferred from associated or nearby grave goods rather than from skeletal indicators. Necklaces, for example, have been attributed routinely to females and axes to males. The few osteological determinations have sometimes overturned such facile gender-linked attributions. At Lapithos, a woman 18 to 24 years of age was buried in Tomb 322B with bronze weapons, glass paste beads, spindle whorls, a small plank figure (possibly from a vessel), and the skeletal remains of a horse (see Fischer 1986: 29, who refers to the deceased as an "Amazon"). Other tombs also present assemblages that resist stereotypical attributions, such as single burials at Vounous accompanied by knives and spindle whorls (Webb 1992: 90). The number of plank figures in a given chamber rarely conforms to the number of individuals interred. Tomb 18 at Lapithos, for example, contained three plank figures and seven burials—one of which we know was an adult male—but poor documentation makes it impossible to associate the planks with a particular burial (Gjerstad et al. 1934: 58; Fischer 1986: 30). Another plank figure at Lapithos was found beneath a skull in a fragmentary burial in a niche in Tomb 306B, accompanied by 53 glass paste beads (Gjerstad et al. 1934: 60). Although one might be tempted to identify the dead as female, any attribution in the absence of study by a physical anthropologist is suspect. The osteological analysis of the young woman buried in Tomb 322B at Lapithos, mentioned above, provides the only secure evidence for the sex of an individual buried with a plank figure.

Plank figures are found in less than a tenth of Cypriot tombs, according to Webb (1992: 90), and purportedly in rich and poor graves alike. At Lapithos, 11 of the 37 excavated plank figures occur in large, lavishly furnished tombs with abundant metal objects. The remaining examples, although not in opulent burial contexts, were in every instance accompanied by metal goods such as daggers, knives, pins, axes, and rings, and sometimes precious items of gold, silver, and faience as well (a Campo 1994: 113; Keswani 1989: Table 6.1). The absence of figurines from tombs lacking copper or bronze grave goods (a quarter of the tombs in the Lapithos cemetery, according to Davies 1997: 20) and their presence in four of the five largest and wealthiest tombs (scored on the basis of number and range of metal goods) may point to a link with elite interments, a possibility discussed more fully below.

FUNCTION AND MEANING

Plank figures, like other prehistoric figurines in the Mediterranean and Near East, have elicited a range of interpretations, including representations of Mother Goddesses or priestesses associated with a cult of the Great Goddess (J. Karageorghis 1977: 57–60), symbols meant to ensure the continuity of human existence (Merrillees 1980: 184), Cypriot versions of Egyptian *ushabtis* that serve the dead in various capacities, especially sexual (Åström 1972: 254; Orphanides 1983: 45; Belgiorno 1984: 15–17), and charms that were perhaps tucked into women's garments to ensure fertility or successful births (Morris 1985: 161–62). The plank-like shape of the figures has suggested to some that a wooden prototype was represented in miniature, perhaps a *xoana* that stood in sanctuaries (V. Karageorghis 1991b: 11). Other suggestions have included the argument that the decorative elements, particularly the facial incisions, signaled aspects of a woman's marriage (or marriageable) status, her social background, or her membership in a specific family or clan (a Campo 1994: 164–72). Bolger has situated the planks within the broader landscape of prehistoric Cypriot figurines, viewing them as part of an ideological shift that marks a gradual loss of status for women between the Neolithic and the Bronze Age; in earlier periods, she argues, women are prized for their procreative abilities, whereas by the Bronze Age, they are depicted more often in the role of caretaker (Bolger 1993, 1996).

Most of these interpretations are based on the assumption that plank figures are representations of females. In the absence of explicit sexual notations, however, scholars have recently questioned the sexual coding of plank figures. Hamilton (2000), for example, cautions that our determination of the figures' sex is distorted by modern cultural filters and that the sex of plank figures may not have been of primary importance to the makers. Knapp and Meskell (1997: 189) also propose that the depiction of sex *per se* was not of central relevance to the function of these figures, further suggesting that the images served to construct and characterize persons rather than categories, salient identities rather than classes of people (cf. also Bailey 1994, 1996 for interpretations of prehistoric figurines as individuals). Although these arguments are plausible, the absence of explicit sexual indicators in many planks may represent not merely disinterest on the part of the makers, but a deliberate emphasis on sexual ambiguity.

SEXUAL AMBIGUITY

Ambiguity—be it sexual or other—defines a quality that is indeterminate, vague, or imprecise. It can also, however, connote that which is paradoxical. Unlike binary frameworks, ambiguity accommodates conflicting or contradictory discourses. From our particular western, ethnocentric perspective, the iconography of prehistoric Cypriot figurines has a decidedly paradoxical or ambiguous side. As several scholars have observed, some Neolithic and Chalcolithic figurines appear to embody both male and female biological attributes (Hamilton 1994, 2000; Knapp and Meskell 1997). Well-known examples from Sotira-*Arkolies* (Swiny and Swiny 1983) and Lemba-*Lakkous* (Karageorghis, Peltenburg, and Flourentzos 1990: catalogue no. 12) can be read as sexually dimorphic, with their phallic heads and female bodily attributes. An ideology of sexual duality or equivocalness thus appears to have been an established tradition on Cyprus well before the production of plank figures. Already in the Chalcolithic, if not earlier, these condensed and encoded models of the human form relayed a kind of multivocality. It has also been suggested that at least two Bronze Age Cypriot figures might represent hermaphrodites: one in White Painted Ware from the Nicosia-*Ayia Paraskevi* burials, and another now in Glasgow (see Morris 1985: 157; Hamilton 1994, 2000; Knapp and Meskell 1997: 195–96 for brief comments and illustrations; also Morris 1985: fig. 233 for a White Painted figurine that displays small breasts, a penis, and a cradled child). As discussed by Bonnie MacLachlan elsewhere in this volume, androgyny resurfaces much later in myths, depictions, and rituals related to Cyprian Aphrodite, who often appears as a bearded female. Although it is possible that the sex or gender of the Early and Middle Bronze Age plank figures was signaled by attributes such as decoration, design, or dress, it is just as likely, given the tradition on Cyprus of representing sexually equivocal images, that the sexuality of these images was intended to be ambiguous, if not androgynous.

Whereas Neolithic and Chalcolithic images such as the seated example from Sotira-*Arkolies* and the "Lemba Lady" projected a sexual duality by subsuming both sexes in one image, the Early Bronze Age Cypriot craftsmen or women struck upon a different solution, expressing a sexual ambiguity in the plank figures by *concealing* rather than *revealing* certain attributes. The simplified and very flattened form of the plank became a kind of blank canvas or palette that was easily and quickly reproduced. Rather than indicate duality, however, the artist used the canvas to connote a sexual continuum by submerging any clear coding of biological attributes. Such lack of explicit coding would not necessarily have rendered these images neuter or asexual but rather would have opened the door for the user to impose a range of sexual or gendered identities on the piece—or none at all. Figures could have served different functions without concern on the part of the user as to whether a male or female image was required. Such iconographic fluidity is expressed in another context by the *nkisi* figures of western Equatorial Africa; these images are designed without sexual attributes but take on different sexes or genders depending on the particular circumstances of their use (Greub 1988: 38–50). In the Cypriot case, the maker chose to indicate clearly the sex of the image on select pieces, but in most examples the sex (and/or gender) is not clearly specified.

The depiction of sexual ambiguity in prehistoric figurines is not confined to Cyprus. Though rare, examples of possibly androgynous images have been attributed to Neolithic Greece (Gallis and Orphanidis 1996: 180, 186, 187) and the Tisza culture in Hungary (Korek 1987: 55). In addition, pendants that can be read either as male phalluses with testicles or as the upper bodies of females— depending on how they are viewed or held—have been recovered from Upper Palaeolithic levels in France (Kehoe 1991) and later Neolithic levels in Greece (Lambert 1981: fig. 284; Sampson 1992: figs. 25.1; 27).

Texts from the ancient Near East and Mediterranean also contain intriguing references to inter-sexual individuals, gender transformers, and rituals involving the inversion of gender roles. A Mesopotamian text of a New Year's festival describes specially dressed individuals who approach the goddess Inanna with their right side covered in male clothing and their left in women's dress. The procession also includes women holding male weapons and men carrying hoops—emblems usually associated with females. The precise meaning of this ritual remains a mystery, but it is interesting to note that Inanna is sometimes referred to as the goddess who can change men into women and women into men (Leick 1994: 157–59). In classical mythology, the most famous intersexual individual was Hermaphroditus, who is mentioned by several ancient writers including Theophrastus (*Char.* 16.10) and Ovid (*Met.* 4.285–388) and not infrequently depicted in Hellenistic and Roman art (Delcourt 1966; Ajootian 1997). Other references to gender transformations in Graeco-Roman literature can be found in the myth of Teiresias, who was metamorphosed into a woman and then back to a man (Ovid, *Met.* 3), the story of Iphis, who was originally a girl and then transformed into a boy (Ovid, *Met.* 9), and in Pliny's *Natural History* (7.4.36). Pliny writes of a girl changed into a boy at Casinum, a woman from Argos who married a man but then developed masculine traits and took a wife, and an African woman transformed into a man on his/her wedding day. Transvestism is documented in Greek vase painting, drama, and literature during the Archaic and Classical periods, with cross-dressing most often portrayed as part of festivals, *rites de passage* including weddings and coming-of-age ceremo-nies, and sacrifices (see Miller 1999 for a full treatment of transvestism in Archaic and Classical Greece). While none of these examples has a direct bearing on Bronze Age Cyprus, they serve to remind us that the nature of sexual and gendered identities in the ancient world was probably more fluid than traditional scholarship has allowed.

It should not be surprising that images such as the Cypriot plank figures would encode a range of iconic signals that have multiple references. The ethnographic record contains many instructive paral-lels, including examples from Melanesian society where male bodies are seen as ideologically encom-passing female parts (and vice versa), and where appendages on images and cult houses can be read as both breasts and phalluses (Strathern 1988: 122–32). Equally telling is the well-known example of the modern Walbiri of central Australia, who use concentric circles to signify a woman's vagina, as well as a waterhole, campsite, totemic location, or gateway onto the other world (Leach 1973: 223; Munn 1973; cf. also Turner 1967: 28 for the layers of meaning associated with the milk tree in Zambian ritual). For the plank figures, this kind of flexibility could accommodate the notion of individualizing identities, as Knapp and Meskell (1997) have proposed, though we suspect that an emphasis on collec-tive or group identity is more aligned with the ethos of the earlier Cypriot Bronze Age, particularly since many of these images were recovered from collective or multiple burials.

The sexual ambiguity of classic plank figures is also evident in the multiheaded examples (fig. 4). The concept of multiplicity is not uncommon in the art of Bronze Age Cyprus: duplicating motifs, a kind of "visual stammer," occur frequently on pottery and figurines. Multiheaded planks comprise nearly 30 percent of the freestanding sample (a Campo 1994: 199–208) and exhibit the same repertoire of bodily and facial decorations as their single-headed companions. Several of the single-headed images, when viewed from the back, are decorated as if they were intended as double-headed portrayals (e.g., Belgiorno 1984: fig. 11.1–2; pl. 8), underscoring a similarity between these two types of images that must have been intended by the makers.

Some archaeologists have been quite literal in their interpretations of these curious images, suggesting that they pertained to twins and the desire for multiple births (Morris 1985: 145) or represented a double-faced version of the Great Goddess (J. Karageorghis 1977: 60) or a male and female couple, possibly a *hieros gamos* (V. Karageorghis 1991a: 91; cf. Herscher 1997: 28 for human pairs shown in relief on pottery). Given what we can glean from the ethnographic record, however, these pieces may have functioned on a more metaphorical plane, akin, for example, to the Egyptian idea of multiple parts of the "soul" or the Dinka belief that the living are always tethered to a ghostly counterpart. Recently, Schmandt-Besserat (1998) has suggested that the spectacular twin-headed images from the Neolithic site of Ain Ghazal in Jordan may be related to later texts that refer to double-headedness as a divine symbol of infinite beauty, ultimate wisdom, and vision. Whether the Cypriot multiheaded examples are in any way similar is not known, but Schmandt-Besserat's proposal cautions us not to be too literal in our interpretation of these fanciful images.

PLANK FIGURINES IN SOCIOPOLITICAL CONTEXT

Mary Douglas has aptly observed that "the social body constrains the way the physical body is perceived" (1973: 93). While the "social body" of the Cypriot Bronze Age is still imperfectly understood, a consideration of the plank figures' contexts of deposition and the sociopolitical landscape at the time of their production may give us clues about their function.

The earlier part of the Bronze Age is generally characterized as a time of emerging social complexity, the roots of which can be seen in the Chalcolithic period. The number and size of known sites increase in the Bronze Age, suggesting a rise in population, presumably with accompanying social tensions. The introduction of the plough and cattle led to a transformation of subsistence practices, with the possibility of generating greater agricultural surpluses, some of which could be used for ceremonial feasts. Equally important, the exploitation of copper resources in the Troodos foothills provided a basis for acquiring and displaying wealth. The development of metallurgy, with its restricted sources and requirements of technological expertise, was probably organized and controlled by an emerging elite, whose power and influence may be manifest in the lavish grave goods found in some tombs at Lapithos and Vounous. Imported goods from the neighboring mainland as well as Egypt and Crete appear in very limited numbers, probably exchanged for Cypriot copper, and bolstering the status of those who participated in overseas contact (for various and not always concordant discussions of emerging social complexity in the EC–MC period, see Knapp 1990, 1993, 1994; Held 1993; Manning 1993; Peltenburg 1996; Keswani 1989; Frankel 1988; Swiny 1989; and Philip 1991).

The preference for collective burial seen at this time—with groups of adults and children buried together, sometimes in a single ceremony, and other times in succession—suggests an emphasis on group or family identity. Tombs, presumably marked, were often used over several generations; in the period during which planks were deposited, chambers commonly held three or more inhumations (Davies 1997: 19, 21 fig. 3). At Lapithos, plank figures occur most often in tombs containing four to ten individuals, though six planks were discovered in Tomb 313, which held as many as 26 burials and abundant grave goods. A familial tie among the individuals buried within single chambers has not been demonstrated, but it is clearly a possibility and would imply an emphasis in the community on ancestral authority and lines of descent.

In a reexamination of the complex depositional history of the interments at Lapithos, Keswani (1989: 227–28, 231–33) has suggested that some of the Lapithos burials may be secondary, with the body of the deceased first buried in *pithoi* or shallow pits found above many of the chamber tombs. In this way, she explains several troubling aspects of the Lapithos cemetery: the uneven preservation and disarticulation of bones within single tombs and the apparent occurrence of simultaneous multiple burials. Periodic mortuary celebrations may have been enacted in which corpses were exhumed and reinterred in the collective chambers. At a time in which political and social alliances were shifting, the occasion of the funeral would have served to consolidate the status of a given group—with accompanying feasts, a rich display of goods, and homage paid to ancestors. The extended period of time between the initial burial and subsequent reinterment would have allowed kin groups to accumulate the necessary resources such as livestock, copper objects, and ceramics (Keswani 1989: 229–33). Herscher has also stressed the possible importance of mortuary ritual in Early and Middle Bronze Age Cyprus. Based on a convergence of evidence, she proposes that Cypriot practice may have anticipated the Near Eastern institution of the *marzeah*, which is attested in several Ugaritic texts and consisted of lavish banqueting, drinking, mourning the dead, and memorializing deceased ancestors (Herscher 1997: 32–35; cf. Schmidt 1996: 144–47, 245–49, however, who questions the association of the *marzeah* with mortuary rites or ancestor practices).

The absorption of the individual into a collective whole may thus be implied by secondary burial rites at Lapithos, at the same time that clear differences in the size and furnishings of the tombs underscore social divisions. Keswani (1989: Table 6.2) and Davies (1997: 20) have both documented a close correlation among tomb size, number of inhumations, and metal grave goods at Lapithos. The uneven distribution of the many hundreds of metal finds is striking: a mere six percent of intact tomb chambers yielded 55.4 percent of metal artifacts (Davies 1997: 20; cf. Swiny 1989: 25, Table 2.2). Metal axes, typically an item of prestige, were found in only a handful of tombs. While there is no secure evidence for fixed, hierarchical ranking, the differences in tomb size and furnishings suggest that mortuary ritual played a critical role in legitimating differences in status among competing groups.

We noted above that the plank figures from the Lapithos tombs (the majority of known figures) were accompanied in every case by metal grave goods. As conspicuous symbols of social prestige, metal objects, particularly weapons, are good examples of what Knapp calls "paraphernalia of power" (Knapp 1993: 100). It would not be surprising to find an emerging elite seeking new ideological symbols that could broadcast or reinforce their burgeoning status. Plank figures might be appropriate insignias for an emerging class: their size and distinctive and often elaborate decoration create a bold visual statement, even if they did not require extensive expertise or materials to create. Moreover, a possible connection with contemporary Anatolian figures would lend an exotic aura to these images, reinforcing the strength of a new symbol. These new emblems may also have served as symbols of group identity, with specific reference to ancestral authority. Within the tombs at Lapithos, in which collectivity and perhaps family ties were stressed, the plank figures might have constituted generic ancestor images, their schematized form and sexual ambiguity capable of accommodating male, female, and other identities. None of these possibilities—markers for an emerging elite, symbols of group identity, or ancestor images—is excluded by the discovery of planks in settlement contexts.

PLANK FIGURINES AS RITUAL SYMBOLS

Our intention has been to stress the sexual ambiguity and probable multivalence of plank figures, though we favor interpretations that take into account the mortuary context in which so many have been found. The evidence for often elaborate funerary ceremonies in the tombs of the Lapithos and

Vounous cemeteries, with feasting and drinking and a wide range of grave goods deposited with the dead, provides a backdrop against which to consider these images. Ritual is commonly acknowledged as an effective strategy for social empowerment, closely linked to structures of political power and their legitimation. The formalization that attends ritual practice has been shown to be particularly effective in promoting social solidarity within closed, hierarchical societies or societies in which traditional authority dominates (Douglas 1973: 178–79; Bloch 1977: 289). The Cypriot mortuary evidence strongly suggests social inequalities nested within a collective ideal. Within such a context, ritual is likely to have played an important role in formalizing and legitimizing the authority of competing social groups.

The wide spectrum of interpretations proposed for plank figures may not solely be the result of our 20th century perspective on Bronze Age practice. The contradictions embodied in these figures and, to our eyes, the ambiguity of purpose and sexual identity accord well with the demands of ritual. Mystification and ambiguity are critical aspects of ritual practice, and ritual symbols, as Turner pointed out long ago (1967: 27–29), unify and condense many disparate meanings within a single form. The consequence is an eternal "deferral of signification," inviting speculation and varied personal responses from participants (Bell 1992: 106). Ritual symbols can promote solidarity within a community while being understood in diverse ways by the members of that community; indeed, ambiguity may be key to the symbol's effectiveness (see Bell 1992: 183–84 for several examples). Such symbols are thus inherently fuzzy or ambiguous, and deliberately multireferential. By virtue of their ambiguity, they help create an arena starkly opposed to that of everyday living and yet intimately shaped by social realities.

To grasp the range of meanings embodied by plank figures, we suspect that we need to comprehend more fully the processes involved in the adoption of new social roles and the use of emblems both by groups and individuals during a time of increasing social complexity. The role that these images played in mortuary ritual is central to interpretation: plank figures may well have been valued possessions of the dead or the mourners, but they also may have carried a particular meaning appropriate to the circumstances of the individual burial. Although we probably will never identify that specific meaning, the schematic form, rich decoration, sexual ambiguity, and fantastic aspect of the plank figures would have made these objects potent symbols within a funerary context.

Death and burial represent the ultimate rite of passage, and many have acknowledged the peculiar liminal state of the corpse between the moment of death and final burial, paralleling the state of the mourners as they gradually relinquish the dead (Van Gennep 1960). Turner writes that "liminality is the realm of primitive hypothesis, where there is a certain freedom to juggle with the factors of existence" (1967: 106). Although sexual distinctions may have been drawn sharply in kin-based communities, within the liminal state they no longer would have applied in the same fashion, being recombined into other, often fantastic guises. The plank figures may have contributed to the ritualization of burial, providing in material form a reference to the human body (male, female, or other), divine or ancestral authority, and community unification—a correlation of levels of experience within symbolic formations explored most thoroughly in other contexts by Douglas (1973: 136–52).

Most interpretations of plank figures suffer from an urge to minimize the complexity of these images. Plank figures were palimpsests that surely evinced dominant, secondary, and even tertiary meanings in much the same way that, for example, the Virgin Mary does in our society. This most hallowed of images can be read on several levels: as the Mother of Jesus, a symbol of motherhood, a symbol of sexual purity, and an embodiment of miracles and the overriding power of faith. Planks may well have served different functions in domestic and funerary contexts. Their relative rarity in both contexts cannot be cited as evidence that they were of little ideological significance.

The imposition of gendered identity on Cypriot plank figures seems to us to impose a specificity of interpretation that is rarely warranted and to overlook a sexual ambiguity that may well have been intended by the artist and of complex significance and efficacy within a ritual context. The coincidence of these images with metal finds in the Lapithos tombs, perhaps with secondary burials of both men and women, may imply that plank figures conveyed a cultural message that subsumed male and female and stressed instead the collectivity and ancestral ties of the community, a message of particular power for an emerging elite.

ACKNOWLEDGMENTS

A preliminary version of this paper was presented in March 1998 at the conference "Engendering Aphrodite: Women and Society in Ancient Cyprus," hosted by the Cyprus American Archaeological Research Institute in Nicosia. We are grateful to Diane Bolger and Nancy Serwint for their hospitality and for organizing and coordinating this conference so smoothly. We would also like to thank Ellen Herscher for her provocative and helpful comments on an earlier draft. Finally, we express our unambiguous appreciation to Steve Bank and Mehmet Rona for their support, and to the University of Michigan, which kindly provided funding for travel to Cyprus.

REFERENCES

a Campo, A. L.

1994   *Anthropomorphic Representations in Prehistoric Cyprus: A Formal and Symbolic Analysis of Figurines, c. 3500–1800 B.C.* Studies in Mediterranean Archaeology Pocket-book 109. Jonsered: Åströms.

Ajootian, A.

1997   The Only Happy Couple: Hermaphrodites and Gender. Pp. 220–42 in *Naked Truths: Women, Sexuality, and Gender in Classical Art and Archaeology,* eds. A. O. Koloski-Ostrow and C. L. Lyons. London: Routledge.

Åström, P.

1972   *The Swedish Cyprus Expedition.* Vol. 4.1B: *The Middle Cypriot Bronze Age.* Lund: Swedish Cyprus Expedition.

Bailey, D. W.

1994   Reading Prehistoric Figurines as Individuals. *World Archaeology* 25: 321–31.

1996   The Interpretation of Figurines: The Emergence of Illusion and New Ways of Seeing. *Cambridge Archaeological Journal* 6: 291–95.

Belgiorno, M. R.

1984   Le statuette antropomorfe cipriote dell'età del Bronzo. Parte I: Gli idoli del Bronzo Antico III–Bronzo Medio I. *Studi micenei ed egeo-anatolici* 25: 9–63.

Bell, C.

1992   *Ritual Theory, Ritual Practice.* New York: Oxford University.

Bloch, M.

1977   The Past and the Present in the Present. *Man* 12: 278–92.

Bolger, D.

1993   The Feminine Mystique: Gender and Society in Prehistoric Cypriot Studies. *Report of the Department of Antiquities of Cyprus*: 29–41.

1996   Figurines, Fertility and the Emergence of Complex Society in Prehistoric Cyprus. *Current Anthropology* 37: 365–73.

Davies, P.

1997   Mortuary Practice in Prehistoric Bronze Age Cyprus: Problems and Potential. *Report of the Department of Antiquities of Cyprus*: 11–26.

Delcourt, M.

1966   *Hermaphroditea: Recherches sur l'être double promoteur de la fertilité dans le monde classique.* Collection Latomus 86. Brussels: Latomus.

Dikaios, P.

1940   The Excavations at Vounous-Bellapais in Cyprus, 1931–32. *Archaeologica* 88 (2nd series 38): 1–174.

Douglas, M.

1973   *Natural Symbols: Explorations in Cosmology.* New York: Vintage Books.

Dugay, L.

1994   Pottery Use-Wear Analysis: A Comparison of Cemetery and Settlement Pottery from Prehistoric Bronze Age Cyprus. Unpublished M.A.Thesis, La Trobe University.

Fischer, P. M.

1986   *Prehistoric Cypriot Skulls.* Studies in Mediterranean Archaeology 75. Göteborg: Åströms.

Flourentzos, P.

1975   Notes on the Red Polished III Plank-shaped Idols from Cyprus. *Report of the Department of Antiquities of Cyprus*: 29–35.

Frankel, D.

1983   *Corpus of Cypriote Antiquities 7: Early and Middle Bronze Age Material in the Ashmolean Museum, Oxford.* Studies in Mediterranean Archaeology 20. Göteborg: Åströms.

1988   Pottery Production in Prehistoric Bronze Age Cyprus: Assessing the Problem. *Journal of Mediterranean Archaeology* 1.2: 27–55.

Frankel, D., and Webb, J. M.

1996   *Marki Alonia. An Early and Middle Bronze Age Town in Cyprus. Excavations 1990–1994.* Studies in Mediterranean Archaeology 123. Jonsered: Åströms.

Gallis, K., and Orphanidis, L.

1996   *Figurines of Neolithic Thessaly* 1. Athens: Academy of Athens, Research Center for Antiquity.

Gjerstad, E.

1926   *Studies on Prehistoric Cyprus*. Uppsala Universitets Årsskrift 1.Uppsala:A.-B.Lundequistska Bokhandeln.

Gjerstad, E.; Lindros J.; Sjöqvist, E.; and Westholm, A.

1934   *The Swedish Cyprus Expedition*. Vol. 1: *Finds and Results of the Excavations in Cyprus, 1927–1931*. Stockholm: Pettersons.

Greub, S.

1988   *Expressions of Belief: Masterpieces of African, Oceanic, and Indonesian Art from the Museum voor Volkenkunde, Rotterdam*. New York: Rizzoli.

Haaland, G., and Haaland, R.

1996   Levels of Meaning in Symbolic Objects. *Cambridge Archaeological Journal* 6: 295–300.

Hamilton, N.

1994   A Fresh Look at the "Seated Gentleman" in the Pierides Foundation Museum, Republic of Cyprus. *Cambridge Archaeological Journal* 4: 302–12.

1996   The Personal is Political. *Cambridge Archaeological Journal* 6: 282–85.

2000   Ungendering Archaeology: Concepts of Sex and Gender in Figurine Studies in Prehistory. Pp. 17–30 in *Representations of Gender from Prehistory to the Present*, eds. M. Donald and L. Hurcombe. New York: St. Martin's.

Held, S. O.

1993   Insularity as a Modifier of Cultural Change: The Case of Prehistoric Cyprus. *Bulletin of the American Schools of Oriental Research* 292: 25–33.

Herscher, E.

1975   New Light from Lapithos. Pp. 39–60 in *The Archaeology of Cyprus: Recent Developments*, ed. N. Robertson. Park Ridge, NJ: Noyes.

1997   Representational Relief on Early and Middle Cypriot Pottery. Pp. 25–36 in *Four Thousand Years of Images on Cypriote Pottery. Proceedings of the Third International Conference of Cypriote Studies, Nicosia, 3–4 May 1996*, eds. V. Karageorghis, R. Laffineur, and F. Vandenabeele. Nicosia: A. G. Leventis Foundation.

Karageorghis, J.

1977   *La grande déesse de Chypre et son culte*. Lyons: Collection de la Maison de l'Orient.

Karageorghis, V.

1991a   *The Coroplastic Art of Ancient Cyprus*. Vol. 1: *Chalcolithic–Late Cypriote I*. Nicosia: A. G. Leventis Foundation.

1991b   The Coroplastic Art of Cyprus: An Introduction. Pp. 9–15 in *Cypriote Terracottas. Proceedings of the First International Conference of Cypriote Studies, Brussels–Liège–Amsterdam, 29 May–1 June 1989*, eds. F. Vandenabeele and R. Laffineur. Brussels: A. G. Leventis Foundation.

Karageorghis, V.; Peltenburg, E. J.; and Flourentzos, P.

1990   *Cyprus before the Bronze Age: Art of the Chalcolithic Period*. Malibu: The J. Paul Getty Museum.

Kehoe, A.

1991   No Possible, Probable Shadow of Doubt. *Antiquity* 65: 129–31.

Keswani, P.

1989   Mortuary Ritual and Social Hierarchy in Bronze Age Cyprus. Unpublished Ph.D. Dissertation, University of Michigan.

Knapp, A. B.

1990   Production, Location, and Integration in Bronze Age Cyprus. *Current Anthropology* 31: 147–76.

1993   Social Complexity: Incipience, Emergence, and Development on Prehistoric Cyprus. *Bulletin of the American Schools of Oriental Research* 292: 85–106.

1994   The Prehistory of Cyprus: Problems and Prospects. *Journal of World Prehistory* 8: 377–453.

Knapp, A. B., and Meskell, L.

1997   Bodies of Evidence on Prehistoric Cyprus. *Cambridge Archaeological Journal* 7: 183–204.

Korek, J.
1987   Szegvar-Tuzkoves: A Settlement of the Tisza Culture. Pp. 47–60 in *The Late Neolithic of the Tisza Region*, ed. L. Talas. Budapest: Szolnok.

Lambert, N.
1981   *La grotte préhistorique de Kitsos (Attique), missions 1968–1978*. Paris: Ecole française d'Athènes.

Leach, E.
1973   Levels of Communication and Problems of Taboo in the Appreciation of Primitive Art. Pp. 221–34 in *Primitive Art and Society*, ed. A. Forge. New York: Oxford University.

Leick, G.
1994   *Sex and Eroticism in Mesopotamian Literature*. New York: Routledge.

Lubsen Admiraal, S. M.
1994   Bronze Age Plank Figures in the Zintilis Collection in Amsterdam. Pp. 23–35 in *Cypriote Stone Sculpture. Proceedings of the Second International Conference of Cypriote Studies, Brussels–Liège, 17–19 May 1993*, eds. F. Vandenabeele and R. Laffineur. Brussels: A. G. Leventis Foundation.

Manning, S. W.
1993   Prestige, Distinction, and Competition: The Anatomy of Socioeconomic Complexity in Fourth to Second Millennium B.C.E. Cyprus. *Bulletin of the American Schools of Oriental Research* 292: 35–58.

Merrillees, R. S.
1980   Representations of the Human Form in Prehistoric Cyprus. *Opuscula Atheniensia* 13: 171–84.

Miller, M. C.
1999   Reexamining Transvestism in Archaic and Classical Athens: The Zewadski Stamnos. *American Journal of Archaeology* 103: 223–53.

Mogelonsky, M. K.
1991   A Typological System for Early and Middle Cypriot Anthropomorphic Terracotta Figurines. *Report of the Department of Antiquities of Cyprus*: 19–36.
1996   Terracotta Figurines. Pp. 199–205 in *Alambra: A Middle Bronze Age Settlement in Cyprus*, by J. E. Coleman et al. Studies in Mediterranean Archaeology 118. Jonsered: Åströms.

Morris, D.
1985   *The Art of Ancient Cyprus*. Oxford: Phaidon.

Munn, N.
1973   The Spatial Presentation of Cosmic Order in Walbiri Iconography. Pp.193–220 in *Primitive Art and Society*, ed. A. Forge. New York: Oxford University.

Myres, J. L.
1946   Excavations in Cyprus, 1913. A Bronze Age Cemetery at Lapithos. *Annual of the British School at Athens* 41: 78–85.

Ohnefalsch-Richter, M.
1893   *Kypros, the Bible and Homer*. London: Asher.

Orphanides, A. G.
1983   *Bronze Age Anthropomorphic Figurines in the Cesnola Collection at the Metropolitan Museum of Art*. Studies in Mediterranean Archaeology Pocketbook 20. Göteborg: Åströms.
1988   A Classification of the Bronze Age Terracotta Anthropomorphic Figurines from Cyprus. *Report of the Department of Antiquities of Cyprus*: 187–99.

Peltenburg, E. J.
1996   From Isolation to State Formation in Cyprus, c. 3500–1500 B.C. Pp. 17–43 in *The Development of the Cypriot Economy: From the Prehistoric Period to the Present Day*, eds. V. Karageorghis and D. Michaelides. Nicosia: University of Cyprus and Bank of Cyprus.

Philip, G.
1991   Cypriot Bronzework in the Levantine World: Conservatism, Innovation and Social Change. *Journal of Mediterranean Archaeology* 4: 59–107.

Sampson, A.
1992   Late Neolithic Remains at Tharrounia, Euboea: A Model for the Seasonal Use of Settlements and Caves. *Annual of the British School at Athens* 87: 61–101.

Schaeffer, C. F. A.

1936   *Missions en Chypre, 1932–1935*. Paris: Librairie orientaliste Paul Geuthner.

Schmandt-Besserat, D.

1998   Neolithic Art and Symbolism at Ain Ghazal. Pp. 582–84 in Archaeology in Jordan, by V. Egan and P. M. Bikai. *American Journal of Archaeology* 102: 571–606.

Schmidt, B. B.

1996   *Israel's Beneficent Dead: Ancestor Cult and Necromancy in Ancient Israelite Religion and Tradition*. Winona Lake, IN: Eisenbrauns.

Strathern, M.

1988   *The Gender of the Gift: Problems with Women and Problems with Society in Melanesia*. Berkeley: University of California.

Swiny, H. W., and Swiny, S.

1983   An Anthropomorphic Figurine from the Sotira Area. *Report of the Department of Antiquities of Cyprus*: 56–59.

Swiny, S.

1989   From Round House to Duplex: A Re-assessment of Prehistoric Cypriot Bronze Age Society. Pp. 14–31 in *Early Society in Cyprus*, ed. E. J. Peltenburg. Edinburgh: Edinburgh University.

Talalay, L. E.

1993   *Deities, Dolls, and Devices: Neolithic Figurines from Franchthi Cave, Greece*. Excavations at Franchthi Cave, Greece 9. Indianapolis: Indiana University.

2000   Archaeological Ms.conceptions: Contemplating Gender and the Greek Neolithic. Pp. 3–16 in *Representations of Gender from Prehistory to the Present*, eds. M. Donald and L. Hurcombe. New York: St. Martin's.

Turner, V.

1967   *The Forest of Symbols: Aspects of Ndembu Ritual*. Ithaca, NY: Cornell University.

Ucko, P. J.

1968   *Anthropomorphic Figurines of Predynastic Egypt and Neolithic Crete*. Royal Anthropological Institute, Occasional Paper 24. London: Szmidla.

1996   Mother, Are You There? *Cambridge Archaeological Journal* 6: 300–304.

Van Gennep, A.

1960   *The Rites of Passage*. Chicago: University of Chicago.

Webb, J. M.

1992   Funerary Ideology in Bronze Age Cyprus: Toward the Recognition and Analysis of Cypriot Ritual Data. Pp. 87–99 in *Studies in Honour of Vassos Karageorghis*, ed. G. C. Ioannides. Nicosia: A. G. Leventis Foundation.

ALTERING THE BODY: REPRESENTATIONS OF PRE-PUBESCENT GENDER GROUPS ON EARLY AND MIDDLE CYPRIOT "SCENIC COMPOSITIONS"

ELINOR C. RIBEIRO

Department of Archaeology
Faculty of Letters and Social Sciences
University of Reading
Whiteknights
Reading RG6 2AA, United Kingdom
e.c.ribeiro@reading.ac.uk

This paper is concerned with one of the multiple gender groupings that are apparent in the Early and Middle Cypriot "scenic composition" ceramic vases: a group consisting of pre-pubescent children. Gender groups are, in traditional societies, frequently demarcated according to age and sexual/reproductive status as well as biological sexual orientation. In prehistoric contexts, children and infants are frequently subsumed by the binary biological groups of adult male and female identities. This paper attempts to remedy this deficit by examining the unsexed human figures on Cypriot "scenic compositions." Traditional societies often disregard pre-pubescent or pre-sexual children as "people;" in contrast, when they attain puberty and full sexual roles, they may assume a mode of dress or body decoration that draws attention to their "newly-invented" sexual regions. It will be argued that the absence of sexual organs on several of the human figures on these ceramic vessels indicates a similar state of affairs: that pre-pubescent figures have "absent" or invisible sexual regions, whereas sexually mature human figures on these vessels have clearly represented sex organs. Thus, a pre-sexual gender group, children, can be said to exist within Early and Middle Cypriot representations.

Taking gender as a process that is constructed as a relationship or sets of relationships, necessarily embedded within other cultural and historical institutions such as status, class, ethnicity, and race, means that gender cannot be understood simply in terms of male and female activities. (Gero and Conkey 1991: 9)

Gender is multiple: It is not restricted to the binary opposites of male and female biological groups, nor, as the quotation above asserts, to the analyses of male and female activities nor to Cartesian dualities of "male" and "female" attributes. While gender groups in many cultures are often largely based upon biological dichotomy, considerations of gender also rest upon marital status, reproductivity, sexuality, social standing and age.

Initial considerations of gender in the archaeological record have tended to focus upon representations of female forms and on female roles in prehistory (Wylie 1991: 38–39). This approach, initially stemming from feminist impulses to "redress" the imbalance inherent in the perceived androcentric approach to archaeology, has, nonetheless, had an ultimately limiting effect on gender work in archaeology, creating a gynocentric bias in many analyses (Wylie 1991: 39–40; Gero and Conkey 1991: 18). Thus, gender work today must stress the importance of focusing on the relationships between groups socially determined by their sex, age, experience, sexuality, ethnicity and status, as none of these determinatives are divisible in most societies. Gender work, in other words, is no longer merely a matter of "adding women and stirring." Bearing this in mind, I wish to address the question of children and infants in the Early and Middle Cypriot ceramic record. As stated above, gender groups are often demarcated in terms of age as well as biological difference. In analyses that claim to acknowledge children in prehistoric contexts, one of two scenarios often ensues: 1) the child may often be subsumed by either the male or the female identities that are enshrined in a binary model of sexual and gender relations, or 2) the child is defined as "female" or in terms of the Feminine in archaeological and ethnographic analyses, and thus is often rendered "invisible" or negligible in the archaeological record (Baker 1997: 183).[1] I intend to view the children that I am going to discuss as belonging to and representing a separate gender/social group from that of adult men and women.

EARLY AND MIDDLE CYPRIOT SCENIC COMPOSITIONS

"Scenic compositions" is the term given to a relatively small but prominent genre of Early and Middle Cypriot Red Polished Ware pottery that bears complex plastic decoration in the form of human figures engaged in various activities.[2] Analysis of this intriguing genre has generally—with a few significant exceptions—been restricted to interpretations of these scenes as depictions of "everyday life" (for whom or for which sectors of society?) and "ritual activity."[3] A prominent example is Morris' work on prehistoric Cypriot pottery, which, although intended for the art-historically minded lay person, has, nonetheless, proved to be extremely influential (Morris 1985). Morris succumbs to the understandable temptation to read direct reflections of Early Cypriot life from the figural art of the period:

> By far the most interesting works of art to survive from the prehistoric period of Cyprus are those which depict scenes from daily life. This is because, by definition, we have no written records from this early phase of the island's story, and any artefacts which depict human activities are therefore of great value. (Morris 1985: 264)

He, like Karageorghis (1991), views scenic compositions primarily as grave goods that would either make the deceased feel at home through the depiction of familiar activities and scenes (Morris 1985: 264) or, more directly, would serve the deceased in the afterlife, in the same way that Egyptian *ushabtis* are often viewed. While it cannot be denied that the provenance (when traceable) of these vessels and of most plank figurines is a funerary one, it has to be remembered that funerary rituals are not always strictly limited to death and the deceased nor are grave goods always exclusively connected with the grave. Graveside activities, therefore, and the objets connected to graves, should be viewed in the context of the society that displays them, rather than merely of the deceased. Notably, Peltenburg's recent paper re-examining the Vounous Bowl views the vessel as a model of a stratified society, from the point of view of the ruling elite (Peltenburg 1994). These scenes of human activity should, therefore, be viewed within the context of political ideologies; they enshrine encoded (to the modern viewer) messages about the way in which the prestige pottery-commissioning elite wished to be viewed. However, unlike Peltenburg, I intend to focus on the treatment of specific age-related gender groups on these vessels.

The scenes on the pottery seem, at first, to show a wide range of human activities, apparently divided in terms of sex group—that is, biological males and females. Women are taken to be those figures that have clearly defined breasts and, very occasionally, an incision at the groin; men are taken to be the figures that have clearly depicted penises. Work done on these vessels that takes its starting point from these binary divisions goes on to discuss male metallurgical processing and animal husbandry and female grain processing and bread making—these are the most commonly given interpretations of the depicted activities (Morris 1985; Karageorghis 1991). Such interpretations may very well be correct, but they fail to take into consideration the fact that such activities are not restricted to either sex group or that very often, the physical sex of the participants is unclear or simply not depicted at all. In some cases (for example, the Kalavassos Bowl), these unsexed figures appear on the same vessels as figures with clear sexual definition, thus ruling out the possibility of individual artistic foibles on the part of the potter (Table 1). I would argue that this group of figures, those without physical sexual attributes, constitutes a Third Sex and separate gender grouping—that of pre-pubescent children.

Sex grouping and sexual attributes are evidently of great interest to Early and Middle Cypriot society. Figures on pots and plank figurines are universally shown as being naked, though often with

Table 1. Sexed and unsexed figures in Scenic Compositions (SC 1-10, as preserved).

VESSEL	MALE	FEMALE	UNSEXED/ INFANT
SC 1	4	0	6
SC 2	1	0	0
SC 3	2	6	1
SC 4	0	0	5
SC 5	3	3	1
SC 6	0	2 (?)	7
SC 7	0	0	4
SC 8	2	4	6
SC 9	0	1	17
SC 10	1	1	0

extensive and elaborate body decoration and jewelry, belts and headbands. The deliberate depiction of a naked society indicates a need to draw attention, even to create, visual distinctions between the biological sexes and to demarcate possible gender divisions based upon genital difference. The sexual organs are often shown prominently, the posture of an individual figure perhaps even modeled to display them. A large jug from the Morris collection (SC 2) bearing models of animals and a male figure (fig. 1) demonstrates this. A male figure, clearly, if not monumentally endowed, sits among a collection of pottery vessels and deer and is possibly involved in animal husbandry, even in milking the deer. On a Red Polished bowl, also in Morris' collection (SC 1), a similar conjunction of images presents itself: clearly defined male figures and deer, and there may be a specific iconographic link between adult men and deer. The Sevres Jar (SC 3) bears some of the clearest sexual definitions in the genre. On one side, several male figures stand next to a pottery vessel mimicking the shape of the Sevres Jar itself. On the other side of the vessel, there are modeled a group figures with breasts— therefore, women—engaging in some sort of trough-related activity, possibly kneading dough or clay. Two of these women are given prominence by dint of their larger breasts and bellies and by their placement above the other figures, up by the neck of the jar. These three vessels (SC 1, 2 and 3) display the standard depiction of sexual organs; however, the majority of scenes include figures whose sex is indeterminate—wholly absent. It is a representative group of these figures that I will review next.

SEXUAL AMBIGUITY IN SCENIC COMPOSITIONS

A large Red Polished bowl from Marki (SC 1) bears several human figures that are engaged in activities that are separated by the two sides of the bowl. On one side, accompanied by a male deer and a smaller quadruped (a fawn or dog) are a pair of male figures, their sexual organs well defined. However, a set of far less clearly defined human figures is modeled on the other side of the vessel. Only one of those has a penis; the others have neither penis nor breasts. Even observed in profile, no sexual characteristics can be discerned and no significant damage to the figures is recorded. In spite of this, these latter figures are commonly taken to be female merely because they are in compositional opposition to the males on the other side of the bowl, and Morris explicitly states that the unsexed figures must be female because of their *lack* of sexual differentiation, regardless of the frequent depiction of figures with breasts in this genre (Morris 1985: 273).[4] Another Red Polished bowl from Marki (SC 9) again shows a number of human figures at work in front of troughs. With one exception, they are not given sexual organs or any individual characterization. The characterized figure stands at the end of one of the troughs and has indications of breasts and what is probably an infant modeled against "her" chest (fig. 2). If this were a female figure, then why would the potter have depicted her as the only human figure with sexual characteristics out of a possible 18 on the vessel?

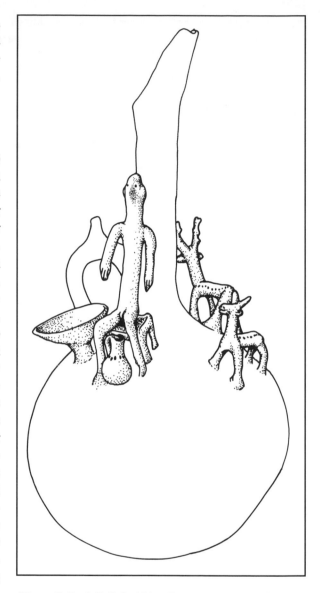

Figure 1. Drab Polished Blue Core jug (Morris Collection, SC 2).

A large Red Polished bowl from Kalavasos (SC 5) bears a set of very complex and densely modeled human figures, animals and vessels. A collection of rather elongated human figures is engaged in a fairly wide range of activities; a group is grinding a substance in a large trough; other figures are kneading a lumpy substance in a bowl; one stands in front of what is probably an oven; animals are loaded with panniers and led; and several human figures sit "embracing" on a "bench" beside the handle of the bowl (fig. 3). This "embracing man and woman" motif—both in relief and as here, modeled in three dimensions—appears to be an abiding one on these vessels, and care is usually taken to distinguish between male and female, as here.[5] However, existing beside this sexually differentiated couple are less sexually defined human figures. Of an original six individuals at work around a trough, only two remain entire (fig. 4). One of these, the one on the right, is female as defined by her clay pellet

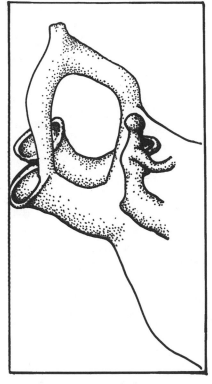

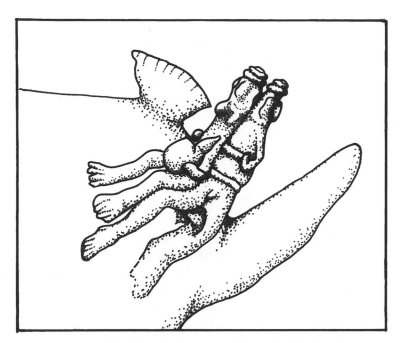

Figure 2. *Red Polished bowl (Marki, SC 9); detail.*

Figure 3. *Red Polished bowl (Kalavassos, SC 5); detail.*

Figure 4. *Red Polished bowl (Kalavassos, SC 5); detail.*

breasts. The other, in contrast, has no sexual features whatsoever. The other (missing) figures may also have been without sexual differentiation. What, then, are we to make of these figures, working side by side at the same activity but apparently of different sexual, and possibly gender, groups? It contradicts readings of these vessels that seek to establish activity-related gender groups and suggests that the "barriers" that may be thought to demarcate Early and Middle Cypriot social life are not as impermeable as they initially seem to be.

Finally, I wish to focus on the Red Polished bowl from the Pierides Collection (SC 8). This vessel depicts a series of modeled scenes that are among the more complex of this genre. The vessel, like the Sevres Jar, exhibits some human figures with modeled sexual features alongside unsexed figures, thus emphasizing the contrast between those with less characterization and those with established sexual identity. Two manifestly female figures, modeled on a larger scale than the other figures, dominate one side of the bowl. The first woman has a massively swollen belly, presumably indicating advanced pregnancy since, with one other exception, none of the other female figures on this vessel have swollen bellies (fig. 5). Her breasts, though damaged, are rather larger than they tend to be on these vessels, and very unusually, her genitals have been indicated by a deep vertical incision, as the illustration shows. The only other female figure to have a swollen stomach is modeled further along the same side of the vessel (fig. 6). Again, she has a vertical incision indicating genitals from which a small clay pellet emerges; she is being shown in the act of giving birth. These sexed figures are modeled alongside at least three other unsexed figures. Two of these appear to be subverting the established stereotype of the "embracing male and female" motif that was discussed above. Here, a pair of figures is placed to the right of the first pregnant woman, and like other couples in the genre, they are embracing—that is, they both face outwards and have their arms around each other. However, unlike other embracing couples on other vessels, they are of no specified sex in that neither of them has sexual organs. Since this vessel already depicts a clear distinction between male and female and seems particularly preoccupied with sexual and reproductive functions, this initially appears to be strange. A third figure, working with some sort of pounder or grinder at a trough, also lacks any sexual characteristics. Finally, next to, and possibly belonging to a male and female couple, is an infant in some sort of swaddling or cradle (fig.

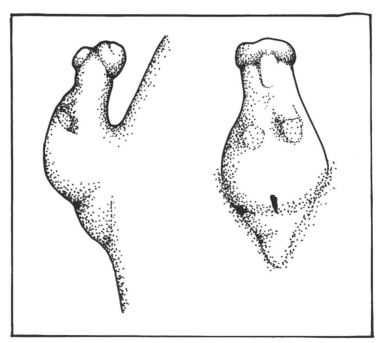

Figure 5. *Red Polished bowl (Pierides Collection, SC 8); detail.*

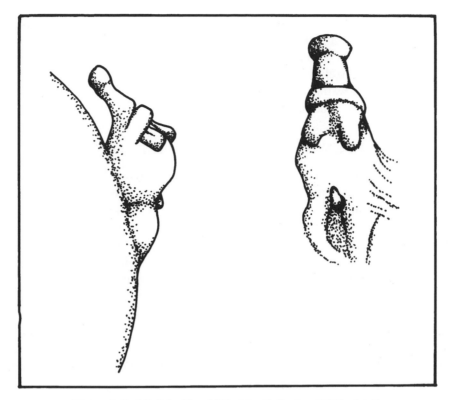

Figure 6. *Red Polished bowl (Pierides Collection, SC 8); detail.*

Figure 7. *Red Polished bowl (Pierides Collection, SC 8); detail.*

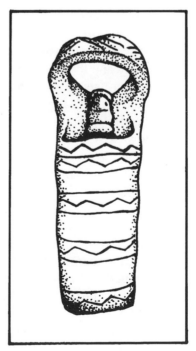

Figure 8. *Red Polished Cradle Figurine (Hadjiprodromou Collection, C1).*

7). Depictions of infants presented thus are common in the Early and Middle Cypriot repertoire but are more commonly associated with plank figurines or modeled individually in the genre of plank figurines (fig. 8). The infant is, like other figures without sexual differentiation, unsexed, and although there at first seems to be no correlation between the more mature-looking unsexed human figures and this young one, I will try to show that to the contemporary gaze they may be viewed as belonging to the same gender group, or at least as being excluded from adult male and female gender groupings.

ETHNOLOGY AND BODY ALTERATION

At this point, it may be expedient to bring in several ethnological examples of the treatment and view of pre-pubescent children. I do not want to rely upon any one case study here nor imply that the circumstances of these examples can or should be transferred directly onto Early and Middle Cypriot social life. The ethnographies are used to demonstrate the ways comparative evidence can shed new light on familiar ceramic material and to suggest an alternative interpretation of these vessels. Many cultures base their primary gender distinctions upon the various biological and social stages of life rather than simply defining a human by their static sex group, male or female, for their entire life. Indeed, studies of such cultures remind us that biological sex is *never* static throughout life. In many instances, pre-pubescent children are regarded neither as male or female but as a third sex , or pre-sex, until they reach puberty and become fully reproductive adults. The individual does not exist as either man or woman until this happens, and as I shall show, some cultures name their pre-pubescent children by the same term, whether boy or girl, until puberty is reached. Once this has happened, there are almost always immediate personal implications. The new woman may be seen as being ready for marriage and reproduction; the new man may instantly be inducted into adult male society, start hunting, eating, joking and living with the adult men.

Often, in the case of both biological sexes, the clothing, jewelry and body decoration that are now permitted reflect this change from non-sexed child to sexually functioning woman or man. Before this transformation is complete, however, the newly-pubescent groups very often will have to undergo some sort of ceremony, which generally has circumcision or genital alteration, often combined with permanent body decoration at its core. This alteration or decoration serves publicly to write the experience of puberty and the transition to maturity onto the body of the individual initiate. It also serves, by altering the genitals, to *recreate* the individual as a fully sexual woman or man. The dramatic—and traumatic—nature of these extremely painful acts may be seen as "re-birthing" the participant in a public and social way. The alteration of the genitals can thus be read as the public acknowledgement of them; they now exist *socially* as they did not before puberty and its associated ceremony.

The *Luba* and *Hembu* cultures of Zaire practice an unusual from of female genital alteration at puberty: Rather than removing flesh, they elongate the labia laterally (Neyt 1993; Fraser and Cole 1972). The pubescent girl is also scarified on her abdomen and lower stomach and this decoration is added to at certain important stages in her lifetime. These particular markings are strictly associated with "femaleness," rather than with pre-pubertal "non-sexness." The Body becomes the biography of the individual, charting the periods during which she reaches puberty, marries, gives birth, and becomes, once again, non-reproductive.

In another part of the world entirely—Manam Island, Papua New Guinea—pubescent girls and their families celebrate the onset of menstruation with a protracted, linked set of rites termed *Imoaziri* (Lutkehaus 1995). "The *Imoaziri* period is literally transitional between the phases of asexuality and sexuality, a time when a young girl is no longer a child but not yet *socially recognised as a sexually active adult woman*" (Lutkehaus 1995: 197; my italics). The phase *aine imoaziri* is taken to mean both the rites themselves and the girl who has just started to menstruate. This linking of biological event and social celebration/recognition of it is borne out by the fact that some parents delay the rites until they have sufficient food for the concluding feast, even if their daughter has *already begun* to menstruate. It seems that the social recognition of menarche actually serves to *create* the biological event. "A girl who had started to menstruate before her *Imoaziri* rites had been performed was not socially recognised as sexually mature (i.e., she was not considered to be, or referred to as, a *barasi*, a woman capable of childbearing)" (Lutkehaus 1995: 186).

A Manam girl undergoing the transition from childhood to reproductive woman will observe various taboos and rituals associated with the newly menstruating, but her biological state is manifested socially by the radical changing of her appearance. She is given several newly-made banana-leaf skirts by a group of young women who have already reached the menarche; these she wears during the entire *imoaziri* ritual period and they are also worn by adult Manam women during menstruation. Over the next few days, the initiate receives a set of *cicatrices*, raised permanent scarification on her chest and back. These are performed in a social atmosphere, and there is a sense that the visual participation of the adult onlookers again serves to create the event. She is thus marked out as a fully-reproductive woman in ways that her society will read and understand; her changed physical appearance, the skirts and scarification all embody the biological changes that she is undergoing and the socially ordained gender group that she will now inhabit. Prior to this, she was, like all pre-pubescent Manam girls and boys, named as *nimoalala*, which literally means "naked." This term is used both to describe a pre-sex gender group where sexual organs have not yet become recognized and to stress that an initiate becomes "clothed" in adult scarification, body decoration and certain items of adult clothing. Lutkehaus suggests "that these rites are also concerned with promoting the transition of boys and girls from an androgynous state of childhood to the genderized, hence sexually differentiated, state of masculine or feminine adulthood" (Lutkehaus 1995: 196).

Lastly, tying these themes together, I will look briefly at Henrietta Moore's groundbreaking gendered study of the Marakwet and Endo in Kenya (Moore 1986). The Marakwet have a complex system of ordering gender and social groups, and these are largely dependent upon age. Social, productive and political activities are acted out within and as part of these groups, which are defined by whatever period of recent historical time an individual was circumcised. The chronology of these age groups is astronomically ordained and remains open to new initiates for about 15 years each. While the roles of post-pubescent adults differ between the sexes, the male and female age sets are characterized by the common dictate that puberty, and ultimately marriage and reproductivity, *create* the adult man and woman.

> Prior to initiation, an individual is thought to be a "child" because he or she has not yet assumed the social status and responsibilities of an adult. The transition to full adult status is a two-stage process, of which initiation is the first stage, and marriage the second. Initiation legitimises the individual's right to marry and have children. This is a crucial point for the Endo, because mature social status is dependent upon having children. A man who has no children is not truly a man, and a barren woman is a person without purpose or worth. (Moore 1986: 61)

Pubescent boys and girls are circumcised at around the age of 15, and this physical genital alteration itself, along with admission to an age set, rather than the actual physical process of puberty, marks the transition to adulthood even though this status must be proved later on by having children. Before puberty, the child is regarded neither as male or female but is called *lakwe*, which simply means "child." The word has non-sexual connotations that we, who encourage sexual conformity from a very early age, may have problems fully appreciating. It is concerned with the nullity of a child's sexuality and biological sexual identity.

> Circumcision for boys marks the assumption of full "personhood" or male individuality ... circumcision also entitles a man to marry. In other words, it is the beginning of his right to control land, livestock

and women. For a woman, circumcision marks the transition to fully procreative being. It is the social creation of her sexuality and fertility. (Moore 1986: 63)

It can be seen, then, that very often the importance of becoming a fully sexual and mature adult is enshrined in the *creation*—by alteration—of the genitals, and often also by the decoration of the body at puberty in a way that relates to society's structured perception of puberty and adulthood. It can even be argued that public rituals enacted at puberty are themselves seen as agents of the transition between child and adult.

PRE-PUBERTY AND ADULTHOOD IN THE SCENIC COMPOSITIONS

It may now seem rather far-fetched to attempt to relate the points discussed above to Early and Middle Cypriot pottery. Within the context of the scenic compositions, the selective absence of sexual characteristics in some cases and not in others has, I feel, been established. I would go on to argue that this is wholly deliberate and that the deliberate absence of sexual organs on some human figures and the deliberate presence of them on others indicates a state of affairs similar to those discussed in the section above that dealt with ethnographical genderizations. In other words, Early and Middle Cypriot society had a similar attitude to the setting out of age-related gender groups. While no genital alteration can be determined on these small-scale figures, the selective absence of sexual differentiation may point to the physical immaturity of those figures that are unsexed. In the same way that the *alteration* of the genitals in ethnographic examples can be read as "creating" the sexual organs along with the new, gendered, adult persona of the individual, the bestowing of male and female sexual organs on these figures can be read as similarly "creating" sexual adulthood. The unsexed individuals should, therefore, be regarded as a separate gender group—a pre-pubescent "pre-sex."

READING CHILDREN INTO THE RECORD

So the question must, once more, be asked: How should we view children on these complex vessels? Infants, hitherto the only recognized non-adults on these pots, have a tradition of being regarded as *attributes* of femininity rather than being viewed in their own right.[6] A figure holding a child, whether it is a plank figure or from one of the scenic compositions, is automatically regarded as "female," even if it has no female sexual characteristics.[7] Thus, women are defined by their reproductive status only, and children, as Baker (1997) discusses, are rendered "invisible" through their identification as the attribute of female fertility. Even individual models of infants may be viewed within the constraints of a simplistic model based on female fertility (fig. 8). Worse yet, this model is very often expanded to imply a matriarchal ideology and a set of ritual beliefs based on a "Great Goddess" cult, and everything that this is taken to imply about gender and society (Meskell 1995). Women may, thus, be recognized in the archaeological and ceramic record but within the strictly limiting constraints of the "Mother Goddess." This state of affairs prevails despite the obvious and marked change in Cypriot iconography at the time of the transition between the Late Chalcolithic and Early Cypriot phases (e.g., Bolger 1996; Manning 1993). Visual depictions change from a Chalcolithic focus or exploitation of the image of the "fertile female" icon,[8] to a far less exclusively female-oriented range of images in the Early Bronze Age: bulls, male figures, more complex "ritual" activity, drinking, and the depiction of industrial and subsistence activities that are enacted by both biological sexes. Pottery vessels themselves have changed radically, and there is a new preoccupation with vessels that pour and libate liquids and that can hold an individual person's drink,[9] in other words, the type of Early Bronze Age "drinking kit" that appears throughout the Aegean and Mediterranean at this time, with all the connotations of feasting and social drinking that *this* implies. There has been an obvious shift in ideologies, and the scenes on the scenic compositions have been formulated both to create the new ideologies, and to enshrine and legitimize them.

Bearing this in mind, I suggest an alternative way of viewing the children and infants on these vessels. The emergence of a new elite requires a change in iconography, one that at once articulates and legitimizes the new claims that are being made on land and power (Manning 1993 and Peltenburg 1996). The appearance of collective burials with rich grave goods used over several generations in the Early Cypriot period shows us at least two things: 1) that a section of society was demonstrating a hereditary progression of power, and 2) that, by physically imposing these family tombs on the Early Cypriot landscape, this newly-risen elite was laying claim both to the land and to a (spurious) assertion that their lineage had *always* occupied this position of power. This constitutes a re-ordering of local history and landscape. The use of complex, ideological pottery at graveside ritual would further serve to emphasize the restructuring of social life and iconography by the newly-emerged ruling elite, in a context (burial) that visibly demonstrated the new claims made on land.

In circumstances such as these, the iconographic representation of infants and children on status pottery and ceramic figurines represents more than simple notions of a generic female fertility; they represent the "next generation" of the ruling elite and emphasize the incorruptible continuity and strength of lineage.

ACKNOWLEDGMENTS

I would like to thank Diane Bolger and Nancy Serwint for accepting my paper for what proved to be an immensely enjoyable conference, and the other conference participants, for stimulating conversation. A travel bursary from the Department of Archaeology, Reading University, made it possible for me to come to Nicosia, and I thank the department for their generosity. Finally, I thank Sturt Manning for reading a draft of this paper and offering comments. He has tolerated what has proved to be a protracted distraction from my thesis and supported my interest in it, for which I am extremely grateful.

NOTES

1. Baker discusses "invisibility" and children at length in the opening chapter of a section that deals with childhood and gender in Moore and Scott (1997).

2. I shall be referring to the pots discussed by their commonly used names relating to site origin or current collection and also by the "Scenic Composition" number given to them by Karageorghis (1991).

3. A significant exception to this trend is provided in a recent paper by Peltenburg, which explores the composition of the "Vounous Enclosure Bowl" as an articulation of power by the ruling elite of a stratified society, with each human figure in his or her place, and the possible singling out of a prominent and elite key individual (Peltenburg 1994). Naomi Hamilton (this volume) suggests a female-based communal organization of labor and productivity, based on the groups of figures engaged in various productive activities on these bowls.

4. Ironically, Morris' reading of this Scenic Composition is, ostensibly, a feminist one; he interprets the female figures as literally slaving over hot bread-ovens, while the male figures are involved in copper leaching (a process in copper production), which process, Morris states, involves about as much activity as watching paint dry (Morris 1985: 274).

5. The "embracing male and female" motif should, perhaps, be taken as a single iconic convention and has an obvious correlation with double-headed and dual-bodied plank figurines. However, while the plank figurines may be taken plausibly as representations of a hermaphrodite or dually sexual group/concept, or of ambiguous sexuality (see Talalay and Cullen, this volume) the "embracing male and female" motif, as it appears on these vessels, seems to represent two separate individuals, although perhaps together representing a single ideological concept. More work needs to be done on this iconic convention.

6. For example, Peltenburg identifies the figure next to the bulls on the Vounous Bowl as female because "she" is holding an infant and, thus, is identified by this attribute (Peltenburg 1994).

7. Talalay and Cullen (this volume) show that only about 30 percent of plank figurines have breasts, yet they are almost universally defined as "female."

8. E.g., Hodder 1990.

9. Vessels with multiple spouts from this period appear to enshrine the actual *concept* of pouring and drinking without necessarily being of practical use.

REFERENCES

Baker, M.
 1997   Invisibility as a Symptom of Gender Categories. Pp. 183–91 in *Invisible People and Processes: Writing Gender and Childhood into European Archaeology,* eds. J. Moore and E. Scott. London: Leicester University.

Bolger, D.
 1996   Figurines, Fertility and the Emergence of Complex Society in Prehistoric Cyprus. *Current Anthropology* 37: 365–73.

Fraser, D., and Cole H. M.
 1972   *African Art and Leadership.* Madison: University of Wisconsin.

Gero, J. M., and Conkey, M. W., eds.
 1991   *Engendering Archaeology: Women and Prehistory.* Oxford: Blackwell.

Hodder, I.
 1990   *The Domestication of Europe.* Oxford: Blackwell.

Karageorghis, V.
 1991   *The Coroplastic Art of Ancient Cyprus.* Vol.1: *Chalcolihic-Late Cypriote I.* Nicosia: A. G. Leventis Foundation.

Lutkehaus, N. C.
 1995   Gender Metamorphosis: Female Rituals As Cultural Models in Manam. Pp. 183–204 in *Gender Rituals:Female Initiation in Melanesia,* eds. N. C. Lutkehaus and P. B. Roscoe. London: Routledge.

Meskell, L.
 1995   Goddesses, Gimbutas and "New Age" Archaeology. *Antiquity* 69: 74–86.

Manning, S. W.
 1993   Prestige, Distinction and Competition: The Anatomy of Socioeconomic Complexity in Fourth to Second Millennium B.C.E. Cyprus. *Bulletin of the American Schools of Oriental Research* 292: 35–58.

Moore, H. L.
 1986   *Space, Text and Gender: An Anthropological Study of the Marakwet of Kenya.* Cambridge: Cambridge University.

Moore, J., and Scott, E., eds.
 1997   *Invisible People and Processes: Writing Gender and Childhood into European Archaeology.* London: Leicester University.

Morris, D.
 1985   *The Art of Ancient Cyprus.* Oxford: Phaidon.

Neyt, F.
 1993   *Luba: aux sources du Zaire.* Paris: Musée Dapper.

Peltenburg, E. J.
 1994   Constructing Authority: The Vounous Enclosure Model. *Opuscula Atheniensia* 20: 157–62.
 1996   From Isolation to State Formation in Cyprus, c. 3500 to 1500 BC. Pp. 17–43 in *The Development of the Cypriot Economy from the Prehistoric Period to the Present Day,* eds. V. Karageorghis and D. Michaelides. Nicosia: The University of Cyprus and the Bank of Cyprus.

Wylie, A.
 1991   Gender Theory and the Archaeological Record: Why Is There No Archaeology of Gender? Pp. 31–54 in *Engendering Archaeology: Women and Prehistory,* eds. J. M. Gero and M. W. Conkey. Oxford: Blackwell.

WOMEN AND AEGEAN IMMIGRATION TO CYPRUS IN THE 12ᵗʰ CENTURY B.C.E.

SHLOMO BUNIMOVITZ AND ASSAF YASUR-LANDAU

Department of Archaeology and Ancient Near Eastern Studies
Tel Aviv University
P.O.B. 39040, Ramat Aviv
Tel Aviv 69978, Israel
bunimov@post.tau.ac.il
assafy@post.tau.ac.il

The place of women in ancient migrations is a topic that has barely been investigated in the archaeology of the 2ⁿᵈ millennium B.C.E., a time of widespread immigration in the Mediterranean region. Of particular interest are the geographical and ethnic origins of women who may have participated in the immigration movements evidenced in the archaeological record of the period. Was the immigrating population composed of both men and women or only of men later marrying local women? What was the influence of mixed marriages on the behavioral patterns reflected in the material culture?

In this study, we shall look for the footprints of women in the 12ᵗʰ century B.C.E. Aegean immigration to Cyprus at the site of Maa-Palaeokastro. The data from this site and from related sites on Cyprus will be analyzed using a threefold strategy: 1) We shall review the place of women in modern migrations according to anthropological literature; 2) we shall examine the place of women in the Greek colonization of the 1ˢᵗ millennium B.C.E. using evidence of textual sources and archaeological evidence; and 3) we shall analyze an archaeological assemblage attributed to 12ᵗʰ century B.C.E. Aegean immigrants at the site of Ashdod in Israel.

There is a wide consensus among students of the transition from the Late Bronze period to the Iron Age on Cyprus that a Greek immigration to the island took place within the first half of the 11ᵗʰ century B.C.E., i.e., during Late Cypriot IIIB period (see Iacovou 1989; Karageorghis 1990: 29–32; Sherratt 1992; and most articles in Karageorghis, ed. 1994). According to these and other scholars, the island experienced an urban breakdown from the end of the Late Cypriot IIC to the end of the Late Cypriot IIIA (Karageorghis 1990; 1992). This settlement upheaval was followed during the Late Cypriot IIIB period by the abandonment of old burial grounds and the establishment of new sites and cemeteries. Many of the new cemeteries are distinguished by Mycenaean-style chamber tombs with long *dromoi*, while most of the newly founded sites boast Greek foundation legends (Gjerstad 1944; Iacovou 1989; 1994; Demetriou 1989; Karageorghis 1994; Deger-Jalkotzy 1994; Vanschoonwinkel 1994; Catling 1994). It is certainly not accidental that the first concrete evidence for a Greek speaking population on the island—the famous inscribed *obelos* from the cemetery of Palaepaphos-*Skales* (Masson and Masson 1983)—also belongs to the 11ᵗʰ century B.C.E.

However, the hellenization of Cyprus was not the outcome of a single event but the result of a long and complex process involving recurrent migrations to the island. Already in the early 12ᵗʰ century B.C.E., "Achaean" immigrants, recently equated with the so-called Sea Peoples of Ramesses III, seem to have settled on Cyprus (Muhly 1984: 51–53; Mazar 1985: 104–6; Karageorghis 1990: 27–30; 1992).

If the idea of a series of migrations to Cyprus during the 12th–11th centuries B.C.E. is tenable, then one may wonder about the place of women in these migrations. Was the emigrating population composed of both men and women or only of men later engaged with local women? And what was the influence of such mixed marriages on the behavioral patterns of the immigrants? It should be remembered that the famous Medinet Habu reliefs of Ramesses III, which depict the Sea Peoples, include not only male warriors but also women and children (Dothan 1982: 5–7; Sweeney and Yasur-Landau 1999). Was the same true for the supposed settlement of Sea Peoples on Cyprus? Furthermore, does this picture of complete migrant families fit other early Iron Age immigrations to the island? Concerning the conjectured 11th century B.C.E. Greek migration to Cyprus, two very different views have been recently expressed. While Catling (1994) is inclined to connect the immigrants with the wandering Heroes whose exploits fill the books of the *Odyssey*, Coldstream (1994) has suggested that whole families, and even whole communities, were included in the Greek expeditions to Cyprus.

This short review of questions and rival hypotheses about the place of women in the Aegean-based migrations to Cyprus at the end of the Bronze Age demonstrates the need to engender these migrations. Paraphrasing Conkey and Gero (1991: 5), we would like to "find" women in the archaeological contexts of the above mentioned migrations and identify their participation in the gender relations, gender ideologies and gender roles involved (for other recent gender-oriented studies in the Aegean and Cyprus see Åström 1992; Bolger 1994; Marinatos 1995; Kopaka 1997; Nordquist 1995; 1997; Barber 1997). Such a project demands a close scrutiny of the relevant archaeological data within a theoretical framework related to the structure and composition of migrations. Adopting this strategy we shall present: 1) a few insights about women and migrations extracted from anthropological studies of contemporary migrations, 2) textual sources and archaeological evidence concerning the Greek colonization of the first millennium B.C.E., and 3) an analysis of an archaeological assemblage attributed to 12th century B.C.E. Aegean immigrants at the site of Ashdod in Israel. In light of these insights, we shall look for the "footprints" of women in the Achaean/Sea Peoples migration to Cyprus at the site of Maa-*Paleokastro*, considered to be a bridge-head established by these immigrants. This three-fold examination will conclude with a comparative discussion of the place of women within the 11th vs. 12th centuries B.C.E. Aegean migrations to Cyprus.

WOMEN IN CONTEMPORARY MIGRATIONS

The recent re-emergence of migration as a legitimate cultural process after three decades of discredit and neglect by both processual and post-processual archaeology (see Adams, Van Gerven, and Levy 1978; Anthony 1990; Chapman and Hamerow 1997) opens the door for the study of its gendered aspects. According to Anthony, when migration is conceived as a structured human behavior, it exhibits a few distinctive characteristics (1990: 899–905; 1997: 23–25). First and foremost, it is an information-dependent process. Negative stresses in the home region are not enough to initiate migration, and factors such as transportation costs, obstacles *en route*, and positive information about attractions in the destination region are essential. Long-distance migration is, therefore, a successive process starting with the activity of "scouts"—merchants, mercenaries, craft specialists, and other agents—who collect information on social conditions and resource potentials and relay it back to the potential migrants. These pre-migration informants are then followed by single migrants and later by settling families.

Many examples embedded within the anthropological and sociological literature of migrations indicate that uncertainties and lack of information concerning the destination, reception, and potential hardships on arrival may confine the first fleet of immigrants to unmarried young men, and husbands leaving their women behind (see Anthony 1990: 902 with references; Leonard 1992: 23; Branigan

1984: 50; for case studies related to ancient Greek colonization, see below). However, there are also examples of pioneer women who represent the first in their family to have emigrated when they were single or left their husbands behind (Kadioglu 1994: 539; Sorensen 1994: 104). These cases may result in mixed marriages between migrant males and local women or vice versa (Barbara 1994: 573; Stolcke 1994: 14; Branigan 1984: 50). Such intermarriages may find their most revealing expression in domestic assemblages of material culture. Thus, for example, excavations conducted at St. Augustine, Florida, of 18th century houses belonging to the descendants of an Indian woman who had married a Spanish soldier showed a mixed cultural heritage: while architecture was heavily influenced by Spanish styles, the vessels for food preparation and cooking were entirely of Indian manufacture (Fairbanks 1976: 166).

A slightly different picture is seen in the intermarriages of Punjabi immigrants and local Hispanic women in California at the beginning of the century. With regard to language and children's names, the domestic domain was mainly Hispanic (Leonard 1992: 131). On the other hand, cooking was both Mexican and Punjabi since husbands or their unmarried compatriots had taught the Hispanic women Punjabi foodways and food taboos (Leonard 1992: 75, 129).

Although these ethnographic examples from recent, well-documented migrations should not be taken as direct parallels to our case study, they attract attention to possible processes and types of interaction that *may* have occurred in migrations of the more remote past. This possibility will be examined further below using ethnohistoric accounts and archaeological materials.

WOMEN IN THE GREEK COLONIZATION OF THE FIRST MILLENNIUM B.C.E.

Moving in time to the era of Greek colonization, textual sources make it clear that most of the Greek colonists were males who subsequently established families by marrying women of indigenous stock (Pomeroy 1975: 34; Graham 1982: 147). According to Herodotus (1.146), when the Ionian settlers came to Miletus, they took no wives with them but on arrival slew the Carian men and married their womenfolk. In other places, such as Thera and Cyrene, intermarriages were conducted more peacefully, but differences in dietary customs forced men and women to live on different foods (4.186). Even when Greek settlers brought their women with them, as in the case of the Minyans who migrated to Laconia from Lemnos, they soon married Spartan wives and gave their women to local husbands (4.146).

An analysis of personal ornaments from the cemetery of Pithekoussai, which demonstrate a clear preference for the local artistic tradition, indicates that most, if not all, of the Greek colonists' women were natives (Coldstream 1993: 90–94; 1994: 145–46; for a different view, see Graham 1982: 147–48). It is interesting, however, that in the 7th century B.C.E. Greek enclave at Tell Sukas, a certain *Pesakore,* whose name was inscribed on a clay whorl, must have originated from a Greek land (Coldstream 1993: 98). Other Greek women seem to have emigrated to Syracuse since their names were located at the colony's cemetery (Graham 1982: 148).

Can these insights about the place of women in contemporary and ancient Greek migrations shed light on their role within the Aegean settlement on Cyprus at the beginning of the 1st millennium B.C.E.? As already mentioned, in the "Land Battle" relief of Ramesses III, five carts carrying women and children are depicted among the Sea Peoples' charioteers and warriors. A recent iconographic analysis (Sweeney and Yasur-Landau 1999) has shown, on the basis of Egyptian artistic conventions, that a few of the women appear to be Canaanite. The manner of depiction of other women on the relief, however, has no parallels in Egyptian art and may hint at their Aegean origins. If this were the case, it would appear that at least some of the Sea Peoples were women who migrated from their homeland together with their families. We believe that the presence of both the Aegean and indigenous women can be gauged in the material culture assemblages from the bridgeheads established by the Sea Peoples on the Coastal Plain of Israel and on Cyprus.

AEGEAN AND CANAANITE WOMEN AT PHILISTINE ASHDOD

The first stage of the Sea Peoples settlement in Israel is known mainly from excavations at three sites of the famous Philistine Pentapolis—Ashdod, Ekron/Tel Miqne, and Ashkelon (Dothan and Dothan 1992; Stager 1991, 1995; Dothan 1995, 1998). Our discussion will concentrate on the finds from Ashdod since this is the only site that has been published in final form.

Most of the Canaanite city of Stratum XIV at Ashdod, including its Egyptian-Canaanite governmental residences, was destroyed in an intense conflagration. The new settlers of Stratum XIIIb, associated with the Philistines, used part of a ruined public building for habitation. Two zones of occupation were discerned over this so-called "Governor's Residency" (Dothan and Porath 1993:11–12, 53–55, and plans 8–9). In the northern zone, five small rooms replaced a spacious courtyard, while the southern zone remained much the same as in the former residency. The excavators interpreted one of the small rooms as a potter's workshop and storeroom due to a large group of Mycenaean IIIC1 *skyphoi* found there and ascribed cultic purposes to a few installations found in both zones (Dothan and Porath 1993: 12, 54).

Our interpretation, which has been detailed elsewhere (Bunimovitz and Yasur-Landau 1999), conceives of both zones of occupation as a single functional unit divided into a public or official unit in the south and a service subunit to the north (fig. 1). The more monumental, southern unit included a large hall furnished with a hearth, an innovation brought by the newcomers. Similar assembly halls are known now also from Ekron/Tel Miqne and Tel Qasile (Dothan 1995: 42–45; 1998: 155–58; Mazar 1986: 3–6; Stager 1995; see also Karageorghis 1998). Serving vessels were stored in the adjacent smaller sub-unit to the north, and food preparation was carried out in a nearby open courtyard equipped with a hearth. Of great importance is the fact that cooking was conducted mainly in Aegean-style cooking jugs (Dothan and Porath 1993: 58, 63, and figs. 15.5; 17.4–5; 23.5–7), which were probably put directly over the hearth. These finds imply a different cuisine than the Canaanite one (Yasur-Landau 1992; Killebrew 1998: 397). Moreover, the serving vessels, which seem to comprise a set for ten people, included Mycenaean IIIC1 *skyphoi,* mixing bowls, and spouted jugs (Dothan and Porath 1993: figs. 14–15)—undoubtedly a typical Aegean wine service (Stager 1995: 108; Mountjoy 1993: 122; Tournavitou 1992: 209–10). However, the presence of shallow, open-mouth Canaanite cooking-pots may indicate that Canaanite dietary customs were also practiced in the residency. It therefore seems that food as well as wine, prepared in the northern service quarters, was brought into the more official part of the building and consumed there. The bipartite division of the architectural units into domestic vs. public/official is further enhanced by the fact that spindle whorls and typical Aegean loom weights were found only in the northern quarters (Dothan and Porath 1993: figs. 13.14–15, 17, 18.3–7, 24.3–5; for the loom weights, see Stager 1995: 346, pl. 6). Since most of the domestic activities bear an Aegean stamp, we may conclude that they were conducted by Aegean women. Nevertheless, the Canaanite affinities that characterize some of these activities seem to reflect the reality behind the Medinet Habu relief, namely the coexistence of migrant and indigenous women.

The attribution of cooking and weaving to women at Ashdod may be disputed as reflecting contemporary androcentric bias. However, in many documented ethnographic and ethnohistoric contexts, women are often reported to be in charge of the preparation and serving of food, as well as of weaving (Hastorf 1991:134 with references; Brumfiel 1991). Moreover, the making of textiles, including weaving, was a predominantly female occupation in ancient and pre-industrial societies. While male weavers are also known, they occur less frequently and are usually associated with non-domestic production of textiles (Barber 1991: 283–93). Evidence from the Linear B archives concerning textile production is limited, of course, to the palatial industry (Nordquist 1997: 534), yet even there it was predominantly women's occupation. The best-known references are to the children of (a group of?) women weavers (*i-te-ja-o*; PY Ad 684; Aura Jorro 1985: 288–89) and to two single male weavers from Knossos

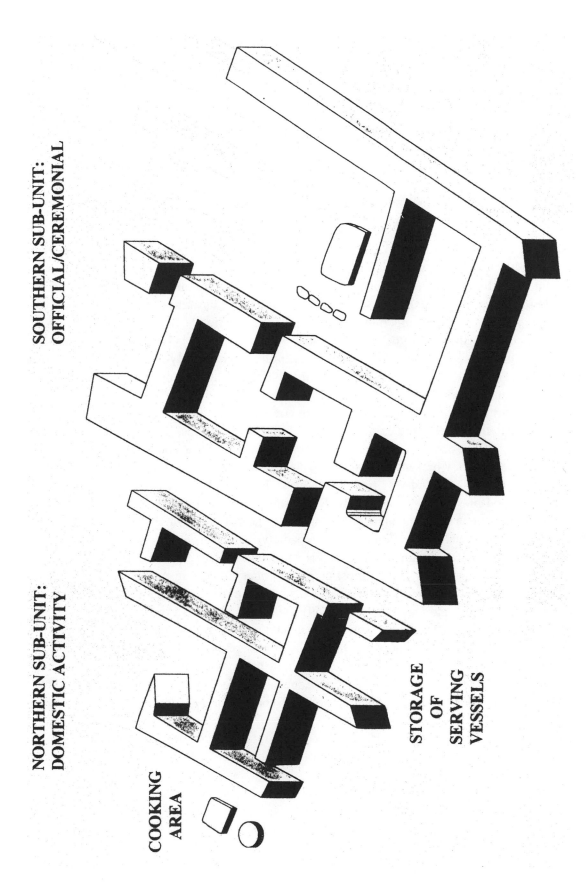

SOUTHERN SUB-UNIT:
OFFICIAL/CEREMONIAL

NORTHERN SUB-UNIT:
DOMESTIC ACTIVITY

STORAGE
OF
SERVING
VESSELS

COOKING
AREA

Figure 1. Ashdod, Area G, Stratum XIIIb. After Dothan and Porath (1993: plans 8–9).

and Pylos (*i-te-u*; Barber 1991: 283; KN An 1516.9; PY Un 1322.3; Aura Jorro 1985: 289). Other tasks connected with weaving, such as making borders and weaving edges to cloth, were also carried out by women (Barber 1991: 283).

In general, we maintain that the picture similar to that emerging from Ashdod is also true for the Achaean/Sea Peoples settlement on Cyprus. However, as one of us has recently argued (Bunimovitz 1998), we should expect a much more variable situation on the island than in Israel due to the conspicuous differences between the Late Bronze sociopolitical organization of these regions. Sociopolitical factors in Cyprus appear to have allowed for a more flexible and peaceful reaction toward the Aegean newcomers.

AEGEAN AND ETEOCYPRIOT WOMEN IN CYPRUS

Maa-*Palaeokastro*, a site situated on a desolate promontory on the west coast of Cyprus, is considered to be the most celebrated example of a 12th century B.C.E. Achaean/Sea Peoples bridgehead on the island (Karageorghis and Demas 1988; Karageorghis 1990: 21–26). Disconnected from the mainland by formidable fortifications and exhibiting non-Cypriot elements in its architecture and material culture, this unique settlement offers important evidence for the migration of Aegeans to Cyprus. However, as already noted by the excavators, Maa provides evidence for local Cypriot elements as well. The excavators thus envisage there a cooperative venture between Mycenaeans and Cypriots (Karageorghis and Demas 1988: 262–66; Karageorghis 1990: 26). This idea can be further elaborated in light of the insights gained from Ashdod.

In the central part of Area III, three major building complexes were exposed. Based on structural unity, building orientation, access routes, and associated finds and features, Buildings II and IV were associated together with the adjacent rooms and open spaces (Karageorghis and Demas 1988: 58, plan 8). Interestingly enough, they present a behavioral pattern similar to the one shown by us to exist at Ashdod. As evident from a diversity of finds, Area 96 and Room 76 at Maa should be considered primary areas for food preparation, servicing both Building II and Building IV (fig. 2). Each of the latter appears to constitute a domestic unit containing a large hearth room which may be conceived of as a Mycenaean assembly hall in the Homeric sense, namely, a spacious room for communal dining, drinking, banqueting and story-telling (Karageorghis and Demas 1988: 58–62). Indeed, Mycenaean IIIC1 *skyphoi* and drinking cups were the most common pottery shapes in Area III, and a standard "dinner-set" comprised of the two was inferred from the presence of a few of such pairs in one of the hearth rooms (Karaegorghis and Demas 1988: 58–59). Moreover, almost all the cooking-pots at Maa are Aegean in style, identical with the cooking jugs that accompany the Mycenaean IIIC1 fine ware at Philistia (e.g., Karageorghis and Demas 1988: pl. 51, lower row; pl. 60: 692, 578; pl. 80: 336, 374; pl. 153: 350, 358). The presence of Aegean women, hinted at by the cooking pots, is further confirmed by the fact that all the loom weights found at Maa are Aegean in style (Karageorghis and Demas 1988: 220, 222, 225, 227–28, 239–41, 248; pl. 56, upper row; pls. 64–65; pl. 111, upper row, where they are referred to as "clay reels").

A different picture is revealed in the large urban centers on the south coast of the island where the Aegean immigrants seem to constitute only a portion of the population. Thus, for example, at Kition and Enkomi, cooking was conducted mainly in local cooking-pots (e.g., Karageorghis 1985: pl. 4: 659/1; Dikaios 1969: pl. 65: 11; pl. 83: 37; see also Dikaios 1969: pl. 121: 10, 15, 27; Todd 1989: 6, fig. 10), while the loom weights show a mixture of the local pyramidal types and the flat, unperforated Aegean types (e.g., Karageorghis 1985: 35, n.1; pls.117, 129–30; Dikaios 1969: 460–61, 465–67, 472–74, pls. 134: 34; 146: 3; 147: 51).

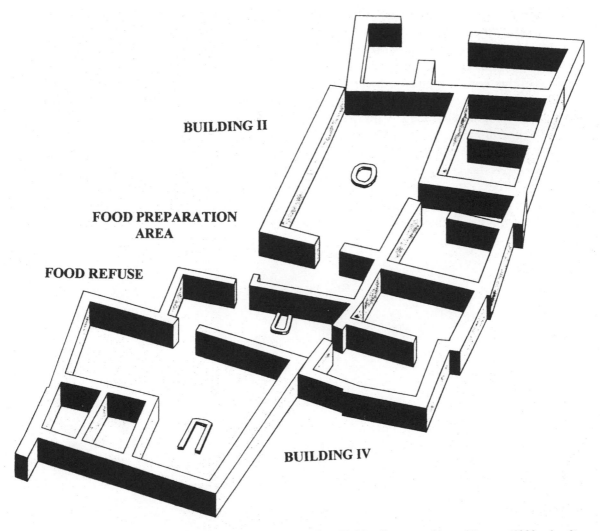

Figure 2. Maa-Palaeokastro, *Buildings II and IV, Area III, Floor II. After Karageorghis and Demas (1988: plan 8).*

ENGENDERING THE 11ᵀᴴ CENTURY B.C.E. MIGRATION TO CYPRUS

The engendering of the 11th century B.C.E. Greek migration to Cyprus is definitely a complex issue. First and foremost, there is a severe dearth of information from the new habitation sites that replaced the Late Cypriot centers. Unlike the latter, which were abandoned in antiquity and therefore easily located and excavated in the 20th century, the main new sites lie below historical cities and were, to a large extent, eliminated by subsequent habitation over the course of many centuries (Iacovou 1994: 150). All gender-related data, therefore, comes from burials. Thus, for example, the tombs of the Greek settlers at Palaepaohos-S*kales* contain fibulae and long pins of wholly Aegean character, suggesting that women were also included in the expeditions of the immigrants (Coldstream 1994: 146; see, however, Hadjicosti this volume).

Strikingly, gender ideology in Cyprus during the 11th century B.C.E. creates a very different impression about the Greek migration to the island. As is well known, most of the Late Cypriot IIIB sites that formed the nuclei of the Greek historical kingdoms on the island boast foundation legends attributing their foundation to Achaean heroes stranded on the island while attempting to return home from the

Trojan War (Gjerstad 1944; Demetriou 1989; Vanschoonwinkel 1994; Catling 1994: 137). The same "heroic" spirit was identified by Iacovou (1988: 76; 1997: 63, 66–67) and Sherratt (1992: 331–38) in scenes depicted on Cypriot pictorial pottery of the 11th–10th centuries B.C.E. These scenes commemorate various "macho" activities such as hunting, deep-sea fishing, horse riding and drinking, and at least some of them can be connected with Greek male society. In such image-projection scenes there was no place for the women that accompanied the heroes to their new homes on the island, and modern research has lost sight of them. Only further "women-oriented" research on the archaeological materials from 11th century B.C.E. Cyprus will make them reappear.

In this short discussion we have tried to engender the migrations to Cyprus during the 12th–11th centuries B.C.E. Archaeology can provide important evidence about the human composition of these migrations. Moreover, by overcoming past and present ideologies, which ignore the women involved in this cultural process, it can rescue both the migrating and the local womenfolk from oblivion. Thus, it can shed light on their role as active agents in the culture change that reshaped Cyprus at the close of the Bronze Age.

REFERENCES

Adams, W. Y.; Van Gerven, D. P.; and Levy, R. S.
 1978   The Retreat from Migrationism. *Annual Review of Anthropology* 7: 483–532.
Anthony, D. W.
 1990   Migration in Archaeology: The Baby and the Bathwater. *American Anthropologist* 92: 895–914.
 1997   Prehistoric Migration as Social Process. Pp. 21–32 in *Migrations and Invasions in Archaeological Explanation*, eds. J. Chapman and H. Hamerow. BAR International Series 664. Oxford: British Archaeological Reports.
Åström, P.
 1992   Approaches to the Study of Women in Ancient Cyprus. Pp. 5–8 in *Acta Cypria. Acts of an International Congress on Cypriote Archaeology held in Göteborg on 22–24 August 1991*, Part 2, ed. P. Åström. Studies in Mediterranean Archaeology Pocket-Book 117. Jonsered: Åströms.
Aura Jorro, F.
 1985   *Diccionario Griego-español, Anejo I. Diccionario micénico, 1*. Consejo Superior de Investigaciones Cientificas, Madrid.
Barbara, A.
 1994   Mixed Marriages. Some Key Questions. *International Migration* 32: 571–85.
Barber, E. J. W.
 1991   *Prehistoric Textiles. The Development of Cloth in the Neolithic and Bronze Ages, with Special Reference to the Aegean*. Princeton: Princeton University.
 1997   Minoan Women and the Challenges of Weaving for Home, Trade, and Shrine. Pp. 515–19 in *TEXNH. Craftsmen, Craftswomen and Craftsmanship in the Aegean Bronze Age*, eds. R. Laffineur and P. P. Betancourt. *Aegaeum* 16.
Bolger, D.
 1994   Engendering Cypriot Archaeology: Women's Roles and Statuses before the Bronze Age. *Opuscula Atheniensia* 20: 9–17.
Branigan, K.
 1984   Minoan Community Colonies in the Aegean? Pp. 49–52 in *The Minoan Thalassocracy. Myth and Reality*, eds. R. Hägg and N. Marinatos. Stockholm: Swedish Institute in Athens.
Brumfiel, E. M.
 1991   Weaving and Cooking: Women's Production in Aztec Mexico. Pp. 224–51 in *Engendering Archaeology: Women and Prehistory*, eds. J. M. Gero and M. W. Conkey. Oxford: Blackwell.
Bunimovitz, S.
 1998   Sea Peoples in Cyprus and Israel: A Comparative Study of Immigration Processes. Pp. 103–13 in *Mediterranean Peoples in Transition. Thirteenth to Early Tenth Centuries BCE*, eds. S. Gitin, A. Mazar, and E. Stern. Jerusalem: Israel Exploration Society.
Bunimovitz, S., and Yasur-Landau, A.
 1999   Behavioral Aspects of 12th Century B.C.E. Aegean Immigrants in Palestine and Cyprus. Paper presented at the conference "Material Culture, Society and Ideology: New Directions in the Archaeology of the Land of Israel," Bar-Ilan University, Ramat, Israel.
Catling, H. W.
 1994   Cyprus in the 11th century B.C. - An End or a Beginning? Pp. 133–40 in *Proceedings of the International Symposium "Cyprus in the 11th Century B.C.,"* ed. V. Karageorghis. Nicosia: A. G. Leventis Foundation.
Chapman, J., and Hamerow, H., eds.
 1997   *Migrations and Invasions in Archaeological Explanation*. BAR International Series 664. Oxford: British Archaeological Reports.
Coldstream, J. M.
 1993   Mixed Marriages at the Frontiers of the Early Greek World. *Oxford Journal of Archaeology* 12: 89–108.
 1994   What Sort of Aegean Migration? Pp. 143–46 in *Proceedings of the International Symposium "Cyprus in the 11th Century B.C.,"* ed. V. Karageorghis. Nicosia: A. G. Leventis Foundation.
Conkey, M. W., and Gero, J. M.
 1991   Tensions, Pluralities, and Engendering Archaeology: An Introduction to Women and Prehistory. Pp.

3–30 in *Engendering Archaeology: Women and Prehistory*, eds. J. M. Gero and M. W. Conkey. Oxford: Blackwell.

Deger-Jalkotzy, S.
1994   The Post-Palatial Period of Greece: An Aegean Prelude to the 11th Century B.C. in Cyprus. Pp. 11–30 in *Proceedings of the International Symposium "Cyprus in the 11th Century B.C.,"* ed. V. Karageorghis. Nicosia: A. G. Leventis Foundation.

Demetriou, A.
1989   *Cypro-Aegean Relations in the Early Iron Age.* Studies in Mediterranean Archaeology 83. Göteborg: Åströms.

Dikaios, P.
1969–71   *Enkomi 1948–1958,* Vols. 1–3b. Mainz am Rhein: von Zabern.

Dothan, M., and Porath, Y.
1992   *Ashdod 5: Excavations of Area G.* ʿAtiqot 23. Jerusalem: Israel Antiquities Authority.

Dothan, T.
1982   *The Philistines and Their Material Culture.* Jerusalem: Israel Exploration Society.
1995   Tel Miqne-Ekron: The Aegean Affinities of the Sea Peoples' (Philistines') Settlement in Canaan in Iron Age I. Pp. 41–59 in *Recent Excavations in Israel. A View to the West,* ed. S. Gitin. Archaeological Institute of America Colloquia & Conference Papers No. 1. Dubuque: Kendall/Hunt.
1998   Initial Philistine Settlement: From Migration to Coexistence. Pp. 148–61 in *Mediterranean Peoples in Transition. Thirteenth to Early Tenth Centuries BCE,* eds. S. Gitin, A. Mazar, and E. Stern. Jerusalem: Israel Exploration Society.

Dothan, T., and Dothan, M.
1992   *People of the Sea. The Search for the Philistines.* New York: Macmillan.

Fairbanks, C. H.
1976   Spaniards, Planters, Ships and Slaves. *Archaeology* 29: 164–72.

Gjerstad, E.
1944   The Colonization of Cyprus in Greek Legend. *Opuscula Archaeologica* 3: 107–23.

Graham, A. J.
1982   The Colonial Expansion of Greece. Pp. 83–162 in *The Cambridge Ancient History,* Vol. 3, Part 3, eds. J. Boardman, I. E. S. Edwards, N. G. L. Hammond, and E. Sollberger. 2nd ed. Cambridge: Cambridge University.

Hastorf, C. A.
1991   Gender, Space, and Food in Prehistory. Pp. 132–59 in *Engendering Archaeology: Women and Prehistory,* eds. J. M. Gero and M. W. Conkey. Oxford: Blackwell.

Iacovou, M.
1988   *The Pictorial Pottery of Eleventh Century B.C. Cyprus.* Studies in Mediterranean Archaeology 79. Göteborg: Åströms.
1989   Society and Settlement in Late Cypriot III. Pp. 52–59 in *Early Society in Cyprus,* ed. E. Peltenburg. Edinburgh: Edinburgh University.
1994   The Topography of 11th Century B.C. Cyprus. Pp. 149–64 in *Proceedings of the International Symposium "Cyprus in the 11th Century B.C.,"* ed. V. Karageorghis. Nicosia: A. G. Leventis Foundation.
1997   Images in Silhouette: The Missing Link of the Figurative Representations on Eleventh Century B.C. Cypriote Pottery. Pp. 61–71 in *Four Thousand Years of Images on Cypriote Pottery,* eds. V. Karageorghis, R. Laffineur, and F. Vandenabeele. Brussels, Liège, and Nicosia: A. G. Leventis Foundation, Vrije Universiteit Brussel, and Universite de Liège.

Kadioglu, A.
1994   The Impact of Migration on Gender Roles: Findings of Field Research in Turkey. *International Migration* 32: 533–60.

Karageorghis, V.
1985   *Excavations at Kition 5. The Pre-Phoenician Levels.* Nicosia: Department of Antiquities of Cyprus.
1990   *The End of the Late Bronze Age in Cyprus.* Nicosia: Pierides Foundation.

1992   The Crisis Years: Cyprus. Pp. 79–86 in *The Crisis Years: The 12th Century B.C.*, eds. W. A. Ward and M. S. Joukowsky. Dubuque: Kendall/Hunt.

1994   The Prehistory of an Ethnogenesis. Pp. 1–9 in *Proceedings of the International Smposium "Cyprus in the 11th Century B.C.,"* ed. V. Karageorghis. Nicosia: A. G. Leventis Foundation.

1998   Hearths and Bathtubs in Cyprus: A "Sea Peoples" Innovation? Pp. 276–82 in *Mediterranean Peoples in Transition. Thirteenth to Early Tenth Centuries B.C.E.*, eds. S. Gitin, A. Mazar, and E. Stern. Jerusalem: Israel Exploration Society.

Karageorghis, V., ed.
1994   *Proceedings of the International Smposium "Cyprus in the 11th Century B.C."* Nicosia: A. G. Leventis Foundation.

Karageorghis, V., and Demas, M.
1988   *Excavations at Maa-Palaeokastro 1979–1986*. Nicosia: Department of Antiquities of Cyprus.

Killebrew, A.
1998   Ceramic Typology and Technology of Late Bronze II and Iron I Assemblages from Tel Miqne-Ekron: The Transition from Canaanite to Philistine Culture. Pp. 379–405 in *Mediterranean Peoples in Transition: Thirteenth to Early Tenth Centuries B.C.E.*, eds. S. Gitin, A. Mazar, and E. Stern. Jerusalem: Israel Exploration Society.

Kopaka, K.
1997   "Women's Arts - Men's Crafts"? Towards a Framework for Approaching Gender Skills in the Prehistoric Aegean. Pp. 521–31 in *TEXNH. Craftsmen, Craftswomen and Craftsmanship in the Aegean Bronze Age*, eds. R. Laffineur and P. P. Betancourt. *Aegaeum* 16.

Leonard, K. I.
1992   *Making Ethnic Choices. California's Punjabi Mexican American*. Philadelphia: Temple University.

Marinatos, N.
1995   Formalism and Gender Roles: A Comparison of Minoan and Egyptian Art. Pp. 577–85 in *Politeia: Society and State in the Aegean Bronze Age*, eds. R. Laffineur and W. -D. Niemeier. *Aegaeum* 12.

Masson, E., and Masson, O.
1983   Les Objets Inscrits de Palaepaphos-*Skales*. Pp. 410–15 in V. Karageorghis, *Palaepaphos-Skales. An Iron Age Cemetery in Cyprus*. Ausgrabungen in Alt-Paphos auf Cypren 3. Konstanz: Universitatsverlag Konstanz.

Mazar, A.
1985   The Emergence of the Philistine Material Culture. *Israel Exploration Journal* 35: 95–107.

1986   Excavations at Tell Qasile, 1982–1984: Preliminary Report. *Israel Exploration Journal* 36:1–15.

Mountjoy, P. A.
1993   *Mycenaean Pottery. An Introduction*. Oxford University Committee for Archaeology Monograph No. 36. Oxford: Oxford University Committee for Archaeology.

Muhly, J. D.
1984   The Role of the Sea Peoples in Cyprus during the LC III Period. Pp. 39–56 in *Cyprus at the Close of the Late Bronze Age*, eds. V. Karageorghis and J. D. Muhly. Nicosia: A. G. Leventis Foundation.

Nordquist, G.
1995   Who Made the Pots? Production in the Middle Helladic Society. Pp. 201–207 in *Politeia: Society and State in the Aegean Bronze Age*, eds. R. Laffineur and W.-D. Niemeier. *Aegaeum* 12.

1997   Male Craft and Female Industry: Two Types of Production in the Aegean Bronze Age. Pp. 533–37 in *TEXNH. Craftsmen, Craftswomen and Craftsmanship in the Aegean Bronze Age*, eds. R. Laffineur and P. P. Betancourt. *Aegaeum* 16.

Pomeroy, S. B.
1975   *Goddesses, Whores, Wives and Slaves*. New York: Schoken Books.

Sherratt, S. E.
1992   Immigration and Archaeology: Some Indirect Reflections. Pp. 316–47 in *Acta Cypria. Acts of an International Congress on Cypriote Archaeology Held in Göteborg on 22–24 August 1991*. Part 3, ed. P. Åström. Studies in Mediterranean Archaeology Pocket-Book 117. Jonsered: Åströms.

Sørensen, N. N.
  1994   Roots, Routs and Transitional Attractions: Dominican Migration, Gender and Culture Change. Pp.
              104–18 in *Ethnicity, Gender and the Subversion of Nationality*, eds. F. Wilson and B. F. Frederiksen.
              The European Journal of Development Research 6.2. London: Cass.
Stager, L. E.
  1991   When Canaanites and Philistines Ruled Ashkelon. *Biblical Archaeology Review* 7, 2: 24–43.
  1995   The Impact of the Sea Peoples in Canaan (1185–1050 BCE). Pp. 332–48 in *The Archaeology of
              Society in the Holy Land*, ed. T. E. Levy. London: Leicester University.
Stolcke, V.
  1994   Invaded Women: Sex, Race and Class in the Formation of Colonial Society. Pp. 7–21 in *Ethnicity,
              Gender and the Subversion of Nationality*, eds. F. Wilson and B. F. Frederiksen. The European Jour-
              nal of Development Research 6.2. London: Cass.
Sweeney, D., and Yasur-Landau, A.
  1999   Following the Path of the Sea Persons: The Women in the Medinet Habu Reliefs. *Tel Aviv* 26: 116–45.
Todd, I.A., ed.
  1989   *Vasilikos Valley Project 3: Kalavasos-Ayios Dhimitrios 2*. Studies in Mediterranean Archaeology
              71:3. Göteborg: Åström
Tournavitou, I.
  1992   Practical Use and Social Function: A Neglected Aspect of Mycenaean Pottery. *Annual of the British
              School at Athens* 87: 181–210.
Vanschoonwinkel, J.
  1994   La presence grecque à Chypre au XIe siecle av. J.-C. Pp. 109–31 in *Proceedings of the International
              Symposium "Cyprus in the 11th Century B.C.,"* ed. V. Karageorghis. Nicosia: A. G. Leventis Foundation.
Yasur-Landau, A.
  1992   The Philistine Kitchen - Foodways as Ethnic Demarcators. P. 10 in *Eighteenth Archaeological Con-
              ference in Israel, Abstracts*. Tel Aviv: Israel Exploration Society/Israel Antiquities Authority. (Hebrew).

THE (ETHNO)GYNOGRAPHIC GAZE:
THE BLACK FEMALE ON DISPLAY
IN ANCIENT CYPRIOT ART

DENA GILBY

Endicott College
Art & Design Division
376 Hale Street
Beverly, MA 01915
dgilby@endicott.edu

In 1988, following the pioneering work of Frank Snowden, Jr., Vassos Karageorghis published a catalog of Cypriot works representing Africans. Of the 52 entries, whose dates range from the Middle Bronze Age through the Roman period, five portray black women. All of the latter are either small-scale statuettes and figurines or so-called luxury items. Based on hairstyle and facial features, a terracotta head from Marion that represents a non-Cypriot type may be a Nubian woman. Not only do the examples range greatly chronologically, but they also come from a variety of sites on Cyprus. It appears that in representing black women, Cypriot and Greco-Roman artists exaggerated and stereotyped African women giving them large, bulbous lips, tight kinky hair and flat, broad noses. The cultural theorist Homi Bhabha provides the viewer with an avenue of interpretation when he states that one must move from "the identification of images as positive or negative, to an understanding of the process of subjectification made possible (and plausible) through stereotypical discourse." Thus, by examining images of black women in Cypriot art from a variety of places and periods, we may gain a greater understanding not only of male-female interactions, but also of Cypriot attitudes toward non-Cypriots and processes of objectification of the African female. Such an analysis adds to the ever-increasing pool of information about the ways in which groups both exclude and include others in the development of national, cultural and ethnic identities. Hence, though on a small scale, these "precious" objects speak to large cultural issues.

Did I complain just now that you get served different wines? You drink different water. Some Gaetulian messenger or the bony hand of a black Moor will give you your cup, someone you would prefer not to meet at midnight. (Juvenal, *Satires* 5.51–54)

How and why does Cypriot art represent the black female body? In 1988, following the line of inquiry opened through the pioneering work of Frank Snowden, Jr., Vassos Karageorghis published a catalog of Cypriot works that represent Africans (Haley 1993: 23–43; Karageorghis 1988; Snowden 1970, 1976, 1983, 1997). All of the items are either small-scale or luxury objects. Of the 52 entries, whose dates range from the Middle Bronze Age through the Roman period, five (that is,

10 percent) of these portray African women. Based on hairstyle and facial features, a not-yet-fully-published terracotta head fragment from Marion that represents a non-Cypriot type may be a Nubian woman. While this is about the same percentage of images of Africans in Greco-Roman art in general (Snowden in 1976 notes that 18 out of 170 objects discussed [or just over 10 percent] are images of black women), it is still a statistically small sample. If viewed within the context of the processes of stereotyping and the development of what may be termed a visual ethnogynography (visual definition of the African female), this small sample of objects serves as a starting point for interpretations of complex ethnic interactions in antiquity. I have not made the purpose of this study the search for depictions of African women; rather, using Karageorghis' catalog, I have interpreted what is already extant. Therefore, this paper investigates and offers tentative hypotheses about Cypriot images of black African women, raises issues of interpretation, and endeavors to connect the Cypriot rendition of African women to the Mediterranean traditions of a visio-cultural ethnogynography or enscripting of African women.

The evidence for black Africans abroad comes predominantly from male writers (both ancient and modern) treating African males. Herodotus (2.152, 154) tells the reader that mercenary male Ethiopians were in Egypt and Snowden confidently states, "Finally, the Greco-Roman image of blacks, even if at times idealized or not always based on historical fact, must have had an enormous impact on the day-to-day attitudes toward blacks" (Snowden 1983: 58). Interpretation of the primary evidence, almost all of which treats male Africans, is further complicated because the Greco-Roman images of African women are predominantly of non-elite women, at times represented as serving vessels, which are also common to Cyprus. The assertion is that "day-to-day attitudes towards blacks" were impacted, allowing for Africans to attain high status in Greco-Roman societies. Even if this implication is theoretically true, it is true for men only. Because the images of women are those of non-high status people, the hypothesis that blacks could attain high status does not hold true for African women in the Greco-Roman world or on Cyprus. Two fundamental questions must guide interpretive strategies: What, if any, are the special problems of imaging black African women in non-African contexts? What effect does the Cypriot ethnogynograph have on the conception of the black African female?

There is no direct evidence that representations of African women correspond to the activities of their actual lives. However, non-mythological representations of men in Cypriot art often display figures performing daily or ritual acts that appear to correlate, in a generalized manner, with the reality of their daily existence (Dikaios 1961, see especially pls. 4, 5 and 18; Karageorghis 1969; 1976; 1981; 1988; Tatton-Brown 1997). Representations of African women, moreover, appear to convey what the philosopher of art Ellen Dissanayake has termed the "training perception of reality": learning how to represent objects and people in a manner that corresponds to the world, both on the actual and metaphorical levels (Dissanayake 1984: 36). Given that the sample size of objects depicting African women is statistically small, one can only make a highly speculative hypothesis. However, the activities of African women in Cypriot art appear to be correlative to those of men, thus locating African women in a variety of activities but rarely in what could be regarded as the activities of elites.

In the larger Greco-Roman context, two instances in which a black woman of power is portrayed are the Andromeda myth (not appearing in extant Cypriot images of African women) and images of Cassiopeia. These two African royal figures are invariably represented with stereotypically Mediterranean features and "Persian" dress, although both were purportedly Ethiopian (Boardman, 1989: figs. 166, 169).[1] For instance, the Late Roman mosaic from the House of Aion at Paphos displays an image of Cassiopeia (Daszewski 1985; Liebeschuetz 1995).[2] She is not physically differentiated from other females in the scene; that is, physically she is neither Nilotic nor Nubian African. The depiction of African royalty as ethnically Greco-Roman, in combination with the pedestrian activities and lack of mythological scenes involving African women in Cypriot art, suggests that the conception of roles for African women in Cyprus was limited.

Ivory Weight

An ivory weight dating to the 14th century B.C.E. exemplifies the continuous process of encoding that seems to be a key feature of Cypriot images of African women. It stands 3.4 cm in height and weighs 13.8 gms (Karageorghis 1988: 10, no. 3). Found at the eastern coastal city of Enkomi, it is now in the Cyprus Museum (registered as Enkomi 59–145). This small head depicts a woman with long, loose hair. She possesses no adornments, suggesting she is of non-elite status. The features, like other weights, are "naturalistically" depicted according to ancient Cypriot Greek standards: "Flat nose, thick lips, swollen cheeks" (Karageorghis 1988: 10).[3] Unlike a similar Cypriot object dating to the 13th century B.C.E. and found at Kalavasos-*Ayios Dhimitrios* (Courtois 1983: 120), this figure appears not to be of "pure" or what has been called a "Nubian African" type but is rather of mixed ethnicity or the so-called "Nilotic African" model (see Beardsley 1929; Snowden 1970 and 1976 for delineation of types). Her hair is smooth and fine, and her features, while African, are less exaggerated than many other Africans displayed in Cypriot art. The tombs at Enkomi during this period yielded high quality pottery of Mycenaean IIIA style. Additionally, since trading with Egypt and the Syro-Palestinian coast was developing at this time, it is not surprising that the general features of this figure appear somewhat Egyptian (Cline 1994: 61; Karageorghis 1981: 44).[4] A practical and utilitarian object such as a weight, therefore, can perhaps be viewed as an apt metaphor for Cypriot attitudes towards African women when observed within the context of other images of African women, especially in clay.[5]

Artifacts of Clay

There are three works formed from clay in Karageorghis' catalog: one dates to the Cypro-Archaic II (600–475 B.C.E.) period, one to the Hellenistic period (Hellenistic I: 325–150 B.C.E.; Hellenistic II: 150–50 B.C.E.), and one to the Roman period (Roman I: 50 B.C.E.–150 C.E.; Roman II: 150–250 C.E.; Roman III: from 250 C.E.; Karageorghis 1988: 28, 44–45, 52–53 nos. 17, 37, 49). The Cypro-Archaic II piece is a *kourotrophos* that stands 24.4 cm high (Cyprus Museum C238). Her mold-made head possesses a thick bush of hair, divided into horizontal rows, everted lips and a flat, broad nose.[6] While the object is of uncertain provenance, given the material and size of the piece, it was most likely created for a sanctuary and was perhaps found in a *bothros* (a shallow discard pit in the vicinity of a sanctuary). The subject of this piece clearly follows traditions evident in the prehistoric periods of Cyprus (Karageorghis 1976: 112–13; 194–95). Additionally, the style and materials of this piece resemble both groups of terracottas depicting childbirth and Archaic votives from a variety of sites, most notably Ayia Irini. The "midwifery" scenes found at Karavas and the sanctuary at Lapithos (excavated in 1897), date to the 6th century B.C.E. and range in height from eight to twelve cm (Cyprus Museum, Nicosia, nos. B48, B54, B56, B65). Each depicts a group of two or more figures, one of which gives birth. However, as with many of the Bronze Age *kourotrophoi*, the faces of these figures are, for the most part, pinched pieces of clay or imprecise globs of clay that represent eyes, nose and mouth (Karageorghis 1976; Spiteris 1970; Tatton-Brown 1997). The artists in these cases appear unconcerned with representing their features, possibly because they are ethnically Cypriot. The African figure holds a child of indeterminate ethnicity in her hands. Although Karageorghis (1988: 28) labels the piece "Mother and Child," this work does not necessarily depict a mother with her infant but could be a concubine or nurse.

Here, then, is a presentation of the nurturing caregiver (mother or other). That the figure lacks jewelry—a feature common to almost all depictions of Cypriot women—suggests that this image is of a person of non-elite status. It would be simple to dismiss the piece as a mother and child. However, to impose the nuclear family model of past interpretations onto this piece would be to ignore the extended household, a conglomerate household (male head, female head, children, slaves and servants) that seems to have characterized some of the past cultures of the Mediterranean (Cox 1999; Dixon 1992;

Gardner and Wiedemann 1991; Gardner 1998; Patterson 1998; Rawson 1987; Rawson and Weaver 1997). Moreover, although I include the piece as an image of a woman, the lack of breasts may, in fact, indicate that the figure is a male, and, in that case, clearly not a biological mother. Again, the identification of this figure as female seems to rest more on Western notions of gender roles than on visual evidence. If it is male, can we assume that it represents the father, a low-status member of the household, or a type of household member for which there is no contemporary equivalent?

An item, recently unearthed at Marion and not yet fully published, also dates to the Archaic period and provides some tantalizing evidence of Nubian women worshippers or priestesses on Cyprus. The figure is almost lifesize (24.05 cm high x 16.5 cm wide, with a depth of 18 cm for the extant fragment) and possibly depicts a Nubian female wearing a diadem. Discovered in a *bothros* that lies to the east of the Peristeries sanctuary, the piece is irregularly broken at the neck, indicating that it is not an insert but rather was part of a terracotta statue. No other fragments from the *bothros* have been definitively assigned to this piece. It seems to date to the 6th century and Serwint believes that a date in the fourth quarter of the 6th or even early 5th century fits the stylistic elements of the fragment.[7] The fragment is in good condition, missing only several locks of hair (the hair was applied separately) and the tip of the nose. The head bears traces of red, yellow and black pigment. The overall features of the head suggest that the figure may have belonged to a statue representing a dedicant or perhaps a priestess (similarly see Casson 1970; J. Karageorghis 1999; V. Karageorghis 1993, 1995, 1996, 1998; Morris 1985; Tatton-Brown 1997). Like many Cypriot artworks, the non-Cypriot features on this piece are exaggerated: "parallel rows of clay with a chevron pattern" that express a curly hair texture (Serwint, personal communication). Since the hair is unusual and extremely elaborate, the artist's intention seems to be to differentiate this figure from those images of Cypriots with "corkscrew" curls, represented by "a clay roll incised along a continuous diagonal" (Nancy Serwint, personal communication). While depicted in an exaggerated and somewhat stereotyped manner, this head is intriguing and, combined with Cyprus Museum C238, suggests that if African women were living on Cyprus during the Archaic period, they were integrated into the Cypriot religious and household communities (Nancy Serwint, personal communication; see also Serwint 1992).

A fragment of a terracotta figurine, which Karageorghis has dated as possibly Hellenistic, stands 4.4 cm high. Now in the Cyprus Museum (MNB 88), its provenance is unknown. This molded piece possesses the now-familiar broad nose, full lips and ample cheeks of Cypriot depictions of Africans, regardless of gender. The properties of the clay itself, as well as the smooth surface, are two indications that the object is an import. This fragment provides small, but tantalizing evidence that Cypriots were exposed to the Greco-Roman works that the features of this piece suggest, with perhaps the concomitant transmission of Greco-Roman philosophies about foreigners. With this in mind, the object appears to be the only representation of a clearly matronly African woman in Cypriot art as the hairstyle indicates. As an import item, this piece could be more expensive than locally manufactured items and would be status-enhancing for the owner (Corrigan 1998; Douglas and Isherwood 1996). Since this object lacks a provenance, its general features as a mold-made, small-scale figurine suggest that a likely context for this image is that of a votive, visible to those dedicating objects at a sanctuary. As a votive, the object stands eternally in the sanctuary and would have become an extension of its owner. Thus, the object may have been valued as a form of ostentatious display that allowed its owner to express a cosmopolitanism (Corrigan 1998; Douglas and Isherwood 1996; Pollitt 1986: 1, 10–13).

A brown-glazed jug, termed Magenta Ware in Cyprus after its distinctive slip, is of Roman date and completes the ceramic pieces under consideration. It stands 19 cm high and was found in a tomb at Limassol (Limassol District Museum, no. 1092). The vessel is mold-made and in extremely good condition. Two horizontal rows of curls frame the forehead, and the features are a broad nose, wide lips and high cheeks—the conventional attributes of Africans. Karageorghis points out that this object can be compared to head vases of African men, especially that illustrated by Snowden (1976: fig. 328).

Head vases with Africans, barbarians, satyrs and women were not uncommon in the Mediterranean world, especially during the 6th century and later. Perhaps they indicate some view or attitude about the nature of "others," i.e., that they were there to service the locals. As Lissarague postulates in *The Aesthetics of the Banquet* (1990), such images of "exotics" aided in evoking discussion about the other by elite males at symposia (also Michaelides 1997 with references). Placed in the tomb, this object may become an eternal *ushabti* to service the dead, even if not depicting a servant originally.

Jewelry

The last item is a piece of jewelry, probably a necklace finial because it is perforated vertically (Karageorghis 1988: 44–45, number 38; Paphos District Museum, no. 2983/9). It dates to the Hellenistic period, is made of garnet, and stands 1.2 cm high. The eyes were inlaid with another material, and although it does not have hair, the flat nose and thick lips suggest, if not explicitly establish, its African ethnicity. It is comparable to such objects as the earrings from Pantikapaion and the pendant from Santa Eufemia (Williams and Ogden 1994: 163, fig. 103; 206–208, fig. 139). Found in Tomb 31 at Nea Paphos, the Cypriot piece apparently hung from a woman's or man's neck to serve as an apotropaic image to avert evils for the deceased. Like the other images we have seen from Cyprus, this figure has no jeweled adornments. In the funerary context, this object can be compared to such images as Medusa, hunchbacks, and dwarves whose thematic significance lies in their physical deformity or mental fierceness as the locus of their magical power (Snowden 1976: 195, fig. 244; Williams and Ogden 1994: 208, fig. 139). Like the object illustrated by Snowden, this may be a male image and not a female. Nevertheless, this face is so unlike a typical Cypriot's that magical qualities may have been attached to it.

DISCUSSION AND CONCLUSIONS

Studies of Africans within the Greco-Roman world, like early feminist studies of these ancient cultures, have attempted to uncover presence from relative absence, in this instance, of Africans in Greece and Rome. Corollary studies of images of blacks strive to analyze what those images say about African-Greek and African-Roman relationships (Sherwin-White 1970; Snowden 1970, 1976, 1983, 1997). While feminist studies have concluded that the status of women in the Mediterranean was generally low or, at least, that the roles of women were limited (Archer, Fischler, and Wyke 1994; Cameron and Kuhrt 1983; Conkey and Spector 1984; Fantham, et al. 1994; Pomeroy 1975; Scott 1994; Skinner 1986), Snowden and others conclude that the status of Africans could be relatively high (Hannaford 1996; Kern-Foxworth 1994: 62; Snowden 1997: 120; Thompson 1989). This presents a seemingly irrevocable dilemma in the interpretation of images of African women. The classicist Shelley Haley believes that Africans, including African women, were highly regarded in the Greco-Roman world. She even criticizes Snowden's translation of *Moretum* 31–35 (an Augustan poem of unknown authorship) as indulging in 20th century stereotyping and offers an alternate and more flattering translation (Haley 1993: 30).

The objects from Cyprus that have been presented above indicate both gender difference and the dichotomy between the literary and the artistic materials. The Cypriot works, on the whole and in combination with Greek and Roman images of the physical characteristics of black African women, appear to draw upon theories of ethnography that later writers, such as Xenophanes and the Hippocratic corpus, utilize. For instance, Xenophanes, in Fragment 16, recognizes their "black faces" and "flat noses." Herodotus calls them "wooly-haired" (7.70) and Diodorus (3.8.3) attributes differences between Greeks and "Ethiopians" (the term Greeks applied to all Africans, regardless of physical differences) to environment. This environmental theme is carried to its conclusion in the Hippocratic corpus (*Airs, Waters, Places* 3-6). While some of the Cypriot objects discussed in this paper pre-date these writers and were largely created by a people more used to ethnic diversity because of their strategic position within the Mediterranean, the ethnographic, observational aesthetic of the Cypriot works appears similar to mainland Greek and Roman visual conceptualization of the African.

In examining depictions of African women on Cyprus, Snowden focuses on the issue of whether there was racial prejudice in antiquity. In his view, social relations between African and Mediterranean peoples were equitable. The idea of equitability has dominated the interpretation of images of Africans in antiquity. Such a conclusion appears inevitable from examination of the literary evidence, such as Homer's statement that the Ethiopians are a blameless people (*Iliad* 1.423), but is rarely supported completely from examination of visual evidence. Although Snowden has collected and described the visual evidence, it is only recently that he has emphasized the existence of a preponderance of figures performing activities drawn from the occupations and activities of lower classes: acrobats, dancers, *hetairai*, musicians and servants (Snowden 1997). One is led to conclude, as Snowden has in his most recent article, that "Like many others, slaves or adventurous migrants, Ethiopians engaged in occupations at the lower end of the economic scale, and those with special qualifications found a place for their talent and industry" (Snowden 1997: 120). In this excerpt, Snowden is speaking of African men. He continues in this vein to the end of the article, discussing mercenaries, kings, the playwright Terence, priests and monks.[8] Where are the women in this discussion? Snowden's lack of detailed visual analysis serves to over-simplify and ungender representations of Africans in the Mediterranean world and reduces complex relationships between and among genders and ethnicities.[9]

While there is no evidence that color was the basis of lack of status of African women, the material objects are very careful to portray the ethnicity and gender of African women, suggesting that both are somehow important to the content of the works for Cypriots (Hannaford 1996; Snowden 1970; 1976; 1983; 1997; Thompson 1989). According to Snowden (1976: 242):

> Negroes may look alike to those critics who have regarded most Negroes in Greek and Roman art as repetitions of a few "typical" blacks, but such an opinion overlooks the many individualized Negroes we have seen. Even in the Roman period, artists working in Hellenistic traditions were not always blind to the interesting anthropological characteristics of Negroes whom they encountered. Motifs were at times repeated, but the freshness and vitality of the Negroes portrayed often suggest that the models were contemporaries of the artists.

Yet Cypriot depictions of African women do fall within a rubric of what constitutes the physical attributes of Africans, and they mostly represent Africans involved in activities (or incorporated into utilitarian objects) that suggest a non-elite status, as is common in Greco-Roman art in general. This is not to say the works have no individuality; indeed, the ivory weight (Karageorghis 1988: no. 3) and the figurine head fragment (Karageorghis 1988: no. 37) are probably African-Mediterranean mixes, as evidenced by their loosely-flowing hair (for ancient literary corroboration, see Aristotle, *De generatione animalium* 1.18.722a; *Historia animalium* 7.6.586a). The other depictions have varying physical and emotional characteristics: the *kourotrophos* emphasizes nurturing (Karageorghis 1988: no. 17), the necklace finial magical protection (Karageorghis 1988: no. 38), and the head vase serviceability to the deceased (Karageorghis 1988: no. 49). Yet all these objects appear as types rather than true individuals.

Definitions of the Greek words *ethnos* and *grapho*, moreover, provide clear evidence that Cypriot conceptions of African women can be viewed as ethnogynographies of difference. Combining *ethnos*, "a race, tribe … a nation, people" with *grapho*, "to draw lines with a pencil, to sketch, draw, paint … to inscribe" (Liddell and Scott 1989: 195, 145, respectively) and *gyne*, "woman," one can examine the gaze of Cypriot Greeks historically, aesthetically and socially. This ethnogynographic gaze attempts to enscript black African females' physical form and to conscript them to non-elite status, either by their activities or by means of the objects' original utilitarian functions. Such encoding leads, inevitably, to a totalizing view of black African women and one that fits within accepted social roles for women on Cyprus and in the Mediterranean as a whole.

What meanings can the viewer derive from all these images? In the first place, the paucity of material evidence suggests a dearth of African women on Cyprus.[10] This is underscored by the fact that two of the objects may be representations of males and another two were imported items. One is left with two works, the Marion head fragment and the Roman head vase from Limassol, as the only Cypriot-manufactured work representing African women (and the head vase could be based on male physiognomy). Is the viewer to conclude that artists were creating the works *ex nihilo* or from male models? How did African-Mediterranean types arise on Cyprus, if one believes that the two biracial figures in some way represent an actual situation? Is one to imagine that there were African colonists on the island? The material evidence does not support this. It seems more likely that the pattern was the one Herodotos conveys (2.30.1): Mercenaries settle and intermarry with the local population, as deserters to Ethiopia state that wherever their genitals are, so are their wives and children. This does not negate the idea that the images themselves are ethnogynographs—these images exist and still enforce a code that defines African women—however, they possess weak implications for actual social relations between Africans and Cypriots.[11]

When viewed as a group, these images of black African women move the viewer, in the words of cultural theorist Homi Bhabha, from "the identification of images as positive or negative, to an understanding of the process of subjectification made possible (and plausible) through stereotypical discourse" (Bhabha 1990: 71–88). The process is clearly displayed, like African women, in the common themes and repetitive physical motifs of the representations. Moreover, it is located in the types of items found on Cyprus: generally small, common forms that could be used daily in many instances. These are works that can go anywhere, are easily buried with the deceased, and can transmit meaning in a deceptively simple way so the viewer may not even be conscious of the evocative nature of the material. This formulaic process leads to an almost total obliteration of the African female as an individual, and she becomes an unknown and unknowable figure: she is an ethnogynographic cypher. The lack of documents from Cyprus that deal with African women reinforces this obscuring of the complex nature of African females and their relations within Cypriot society at different periods and times. However, by examining images of black women in Cypriot art from a variety of periods, times, and contexts, viewers discover the filter of those who merely represent, but are not members of, the class or ethnicity or gender of those portrayed. This ethnogynograph reveals something about the tastes of patrons at least, if not about the actuality or even existence of African women on Cyprus. These objects speak about Cypriot attitudes toward non-Cypriots and processes of objectification of the African female's physical characteristics. Even in the case of imports, owners of these objects must have felt that they expressed some characteristic akin to indigenous Cypriot mores to have bought them and, in certain cases, to have had them buried alongside themselves. It is clear from both the subjects and types of objects that the general categorization of these women is as nurturers: physically, if one accepts the *kourotrophos* as an image of daily life, and metaphorically for the male and female dead (as protective, magical objects). These types, contexts, and iconographies display blacks involved in what may be described as typical, daily "women's" activities, and in most cases they possess emphatic African features. Thus, one may think of the poet Juvenal's musing in the quotation from the *Satires*, cited at the beginning of the essay, about the black body. Admittedly, that passage speaks of a male servant, but the material evidence from Cyprus bears out that the ethnogynograph of Africans and the conception foreigners seem determinedly non-elite. What this implies is that the Cypriots or non-Cypriot ruling elites, either through personal experience or reports, were creating or purchasing objects developed from an ethnogynography to present the physical attributes of African women within the Cypriot world. One can only speculate as to why they did this; perhaps it was because these items were regarded as exotica, emblems of the cosmopolitanism of the owner (Veblen 1994).

The placement of those images of known provenance in tombs does not tell us that Africans in Cyprus were placing them within their own tombs, for the other materials are clearly of predominantly Cypriot or Greco-Roman character. These images, therefore, cannot be said to be generalized images of the deceased. Rather, there is an intimation that these are similar to *ushabti* images: while the person was alive, the objects were curiosities or exotica. Once the owner died, such figures became an aid to the deceased. This furnishes further evidence that, within the context of the Cypriot Greek world, African women had little power. Instead, African women's status in Cyprus, according to these images, seems in keeping with that of the average, non-elite or foreign female, at least during the historical period. What the artist—whether Cypriot, Greek or Roman—projected was a variety of detail within the ethnogynographic code of the African woman.

It is hoped that this brief analysis has contributed to the ever-increasing pool of information about the ways in which groups both exclude and include others in the development of national, cultural and ethnic identities. These items are not epitaphs; rather, they speak obliquely of their makers' and owners' intentions, feelings, and views of ethnicity. Although they exist on a small scale, these "precious" objects can, after all, reveal in a limited way the attitudes toward African women by the ethnically diverse inhabitants of Cyprus.

ACKNOWLEDGMENTS

I would like to thank Nancy Serwint, Director of CAARI, and Diane Bolger, whose conference allowed me to present my findings on the image of African woman in the art of Cyprus. I would also like to thank those who read and commented on drafts of this manuscript: Amy Damico and Louise Hitchcock. I am also indebted to the anonymous readers of this paper for their many invaluable editorial suggestions.

NOTES

1. Both date to the Classical period. One is a hydria, unearthed in Vulci, Italy (London, British Museum E169); the other is a pelike (Boston, Museum of Fine Arts 63.6223).

2. I thank D. Michaelides for bringing this reference to my attention.

3. Karageorghis states, additionally, that this piece resembles Zairean and Yoruban gaming pieces, such as those of The Menil Collection in Houston. He further remarks on its similarity to Amarna Period works from Egypt. The implied suggestion of African production or influence is intriguing and merits further study, but it is beyond the scope of this essay.

4. There appears to have been a surge of crafts workers from abroad at this time, as evidenced by Aegeo-Oriental seals and the occurrence of the Aegean niello technique on a silver bowl from Enkomi, as well as the afore-mentioned pots. A rhyton from Kition, moreover, exhibits a combination of Aegean, Cypriot, Near Eastern and Egyptian motifs (Karageorghis 1976; Karageorghis 1981; Merrillees 1968; Spiteris 1970).

5. For the use of weights as funerary gifts, consult the recently excavated Cypro-Archaic I tomb at Mari (see Hadjicosti paper, this volume).

6. The image exhibits the stylistic hellenizing traits used by artists during this period of Assyrian, and later, Egyptian hegemony over Cyprus.

7. Princeton University Excavation Registry number R9913/TC3078. I thank Nancy Serwint for generously sharing information about this fragment with me (N. Serwint, personal communication, January 31, 2000).

8. Snowden (1970: 187–88) notes that the terracottas depict lower classes, in keeping with occupations of foreigners in the Greco-Roman world; however, he quickly dwells on the few instances of high ranking individuals depicted, thus negating the preponderance of evidence from which one draws the inference that most Africans were relegated to the lower social rungs (as were most foreigners, in general).

9. In this regard, his work can be likened to early American feminist studies that attempted to locate the worship of the Great Goddess to a time of a pre-patriarchal egalitarianism in society. Recent scholarship, how-

ever, has clearly demonstrated that the existence of a primary female goddess does not correlate to or suggest matriarchy. So, too, the depiction of Africans in Greco-Roman art does not presuppose relationships between Africans and Greeks, Romans or Cypriots.

10. Indeed, material remains throughout the island from a variety of periods lack evidence of one of the key markers of migrant women: cooking pots and utensils indigenous to the immigrant group. Hence, even if African women were living on Cyprus, they do not appear to have been female heads of households who could determine the utensils and foods prepared for the *oikos*.

11. This may be so even if Herodotus (2.182.1 and 7.90.1) relates that Amasis conquered Cyprus and that the Cypriots considered their community, as evidenced through troops, being made up of Salamians, Athenians, Arcadians, Ethiopians and native Cypriots.

REFERENCES

Archer, L.; Fischler, S.; and Wyke, M., eds.
 1994   *Women in Ancient Societies: "An Illusion of the Night."* New York: Routledge.
Beardsley, G.
 1929   *The Negro in Greek and Roman Culture. A Study of the Ethiopian Type.* Baltimore: Johns
           Hopkins University.
Bhabha, H.
 1990   The Other Question: Difference, Discrimination and the Discourse of Colonialism. Pp. 71–88 in *Out
           There: Marginalization and Contemporary Cultures*, eds. R. Ferguson, M. Gever, T. Minh-ha and C.
           West. Cambridge, MA: MIT.
Boardman, J.
 1989   *Athenian Red Figure Vases: The Classical Period.* London: Thames and Hudson.
Cameron, A., and Kuhrt, A., eds.
 1983   *Images of Women in Antiquity.* Detroit: Wayne State University.
Casson, S.
 1970   *Ancient Cyprus: Its Art and Architecture.* Westport, CT: Greenwood.
Cline, E.
 1994   *Sailing the Wine-Dark Sea.* Oxford: BAR International Series 591. Oxford: British Archaeological
           Reports.
Conkey, M., and Spector, J.
 1984   Archaeology and the Study of Gender. *Advances in Archaeological Method and Theory* 7 : 1–38.
Corrigan, P.
 1998   *The Sociology of Consumption.* New York: Sage.
Courtois, J.-C.
 1983   "Le trésor de poids de Kalavassos-Ayios Dhimitrios 1982." *Report of the Department of Antiquities
           of Cyprus*: 117–30.
Cox, C.
 1999   *Household Interests: Property, Marriage Strategies and Family Dynamics in Ancient Athens.*
           Princeton: Princeton University.
Daszewski, W.
 1985   *Dionysus der Erloser: griechische Mythen im spatantiken Cypern.* Mainz am Rhein: von Zabern.
Dikaios, P.
 1961   *A Guide to the Cyprus Museum.* 3rd rev. ed. Nicosia: Department of Antiquities of Cyprus.
Dissanayake, E.
 1984   Does Art Have Selective Value? *Empirical Studies of the Arts* 2, 1: 35–49.
Dixon, S.
 1992   *The Roman Family.* Baltimore: Johns Hopkins University.
Douglas, M., and Isherwood, B.
 1996   *The World of Goods: Towards an Anthropology of Consumption.* New York: Routledge.
Fantham, E.; Foley, H.; Kampen, N.; Pomeroy, S.; and Shapiro, H. A.
 1994   *Women in the Classical World: Image and Text.* New York: Oxford University.
Gardner, J.
 1998   *Family and Familia in Roman Law and Life.* Oxford: Clarendon.
Gardner, J., and Wiedemann, T.
 1991   *The Roman Household: A Sourcebook.* New York: Routledge.
Hadjicosti, M.
 1997   The Family Tomb of a Warrior of the Cypro-Archaic I Period at Mari. *Report of the Department of
           Antiquities of Cyprus*: 251–63.
Haley, S. P.
 1993   Black Feminist Thought and Classics: Re-membering, Re-claiming, Re-empowering. Pp. 23–43 in
           Feminist Theory and the Classics, eds. N. S. Rabinowitz and A. Richlin. New York: Routledge.

Hannaford, I.
1996   *Race: The History of an Idea in the West*. Baltimore: The Johns Hopkins University.
Karageorghis, J.
1999   *The Coroplastic Art of Ancient Cyprus*. Vol. 5 (B): *The Cypro-Archaic Period Small Female Figurines. Figurines Moulées*. Nicosia: A. G. Leventis Foundation.
Karageorghis, V.
1969   *The Ancient Civilization of Cyprus*. New York: Cowles Education Corporation.
1976   *The Civilization of Prehistoric Cyprus*. Athens: Ekdotike Athenon.
1981   *Ancient Cyprus: 7,000 Years of Art and Archaeology*. Baton Rouge: Lousiana State University.
1988   *Blacks in Ancient Cypriot Art*. Houston: The Menil Foundation.
1993   *The Coroplastic Art of Ancient Cyprus*. Vol. 3: *The Cypro-Archaic Period Large and Medium Size Sculpture*. Nicosia: A. G.Leventis Foundation.
1995   *The Coroplastic Art of Ancient Cyprus*. Vol. 4: *The Cypro-Archaic Period Small Male Figurines*. Nicosia: A. G.Leventis Foundation.
1996   *The Coroplastic Art of Ancient Cyprus*. Vol. 6: *The Cypro-Archaic Period Monsters, Animals and Miscellanea*. Nicosia: A. G.Leventis Foundation.
1998   *The Coroplastic Art of Ancient Cyprus*. Vol. 5 (A): *The Cypro-Archaic Period Small Female Figurines. Handmade/Wheelmade Figurines*. Nicosia: A. G. Leventis Foundation.
Kern-Foxworth, M.
1994   *Aunt Jemima, Uncle Ben and Rastus*. Westport, CT: Greenwood.
Leibeschuetz, W.
1995   Pagan Mythology in the Christian Empire. *International Journal of the Classical Tradition* 2, 2: 193–209.
Liddell, H. G., and Scott, R.
1989   *A Lexicon: Abridged from Liddell and Scott's Greek-English Lexicon*. Oxford: Clarendon.
Lissarrague, F.
1990   *The Aesthetics of the Greek Banquet: Images of Wine and Ritual*. Princeton: Princeton University.
Merrillees, R. S.
1968   *The Cypriote Bronze Age Pottery Found in Egypt*. Lund: Åströms.
Michaelides, D.
1997   Magenta Ware in Cyprus Once More. Pp. 137–43 in *Four Thousand Years of Images on Cypriote Pottery*, eds. V Karageorghis, R. Laffineur, and F. Vandenabeele. Nicosia: A. G. Leventis Foundation.
Morris, D.
1985   *The Art of Ancient Cyprus*. Oxford: Phaidon.
Patterson, C.
1998   *The Family in Greek History*. Cambridge, MA: Harvard University.
Pollitt, J. J.
1986   *Art in the Hellenistic Age*. Cambridge: Cambridge University.
Pomeroy, S.
1975   *Goddesses, Whores, Wives and Slaves: Women in Classical Antiquity*. New York: Schocken Books.
Rawson, B.
1987   *The Family in Ancient Rome: New Perspectives*. Ithaca: Cornell University.
Rawson, B., and Weaver, P.
1997   *The Roman Family in Italy*. Oxford: Clarendon.
Scott, E.
1994   *Those of Little Note: Gender, Race and Class in Historical Archaeology*. Tucson: University of Arizona.
Serwint, N.
1992   The Terracotta Sculpture from Ancient Marion: Recent Discoveries. Pp. 382–426 in *Acta Cypria: Acts of an International Congress on Cypriote Archaeology Held in Göteborg on 22–24 August 1991*, Part 3, ed. P. Åström. Studies in Mediterranean Archaeology Pocket-Book 117. Jonsered: Åströms.
Sherwin-White, A. N.
1970   *Racial Prejudice in Imperial Rome*. Cambridge: Cambridge University.

Skinner, M.
  1986   Rescuing Creusa: New Methodological Approaches to Women in Antiquity. *Helios* 13, 2: 1–8.
Snowden, Jr., F.
  1970   *Blacks in Antiquity*. Cambridge, MA: Harvard University.
  1976   Iconographical Evidence on the Black Populations in Greco-Roman Antiquity. Pp. 133–245 in *The Image of the Black in Western Art,* Vol.1, ed. J. Vercoutter et al. New York: William Morrow.
  1983   *Before Color Prejudice*. Cambridge, MA: Harvard University.
  1997   Greeks and Ethiopians. Pp. 103–26 in *Greeks and Barbarians*, eds. J. Coleman and C. Walz. Bethesda, MD: CDL.
Spiteris, T.
  1970   *The Art of Cyprus*. New York: William Morrow.
Tatton-Brown, V.
  1997   *Ancient Cyprus*. London: British Museum.
Thompson, L.A.
  1989   *Romans and Blacks*. Oklahoma City: University of Oklahoma.
Veblen, T.
  1994   *The Theory of the Leisure Class*. Reprint edition. New York: Penguin.
Williams, D., and Ogden, J.
  1994   *Greek Gold: Jewelry of the Classical World*. New York: Abrams.

PART FIVE

GENDER, TECHNOLOGY AND MATERIAL CULTURE

WOMEN'S KNIVES

CAROLE MCCARTNEY

Lemba Archaeological Research Centre
Pafos District
Cyprus
carole@spidernet.com.cy

On the basis of blade form and ethnographic analogy, Stekelis (1961) suggested a gender difference for tools belonging to the chipped stone assemblage from the Ceramic Neolithic type-site of Sotira-Teppes. While recently challenged in light of new evidence, Cypriot Neolithic chipped stone assemblages have typically been described as containing few elements traditionally associated with "male" activities such as arrowheads for hunting or warfare and large, well made bifaces used in forest clearance or sophisticated formal core technologies. Cypriot assemblages are, instead, dominated by tool types generally associated with domestic activities such as food gathering and preparation, and are produced by less complex core technologies often ascribed to women. The following paper will investigate whether we can assign such gender associations to the production and utilization of chipped stone technology by considering some of the formal, technical and functional aspects of the artifacts themselves as well as the contexts from which they derive.

The study of chipped stone has long been a largely male preserve, focusing on androcentric topics such as achievement in knapping skills or the trade of prestige materials like obsidian. Similarly, replication studies often assume gender orientations associated with a generalized "man-the-hunter" ideology predominant in prehistoric research. Thus we see men felling trees, killing game and butchering animal carcasses, while in the female domain women work skins with flint scrapers (Gero 1991: 165–69). In Cyprus, chipped stone analysis is still largely typological, a necessity in a region where fully published assemblages are few and the technology poorly understood. The published literature provides a limited number of use-wear analyses and context distributions, but we are still far from a complete understanding of the role played by this technology in the society of prehistoric Cyprus. A large amount of research currently in progress for most of the key Neolithic assemblages in Cyprus, however, promises interesting results in the near future.

Although the study of complex symbolism linked to Cypriot chipped stone does not seem possible on the basis of current evidence, our understanding of this artifact type need not remain devoid of social value. Much can already be said about how this major industry was organized within Neolithic society. While concepts such as "gender identity" or "gender ideology" may not be appropriate to the study of Cypriot chipped stone, ideas can be tested in the area of "gender roles" (Conkey and Spector 1984: 15). As Conkey and Spector indicate, "task differentiation" is more complex than the simple association of particular tool types with either men or women, involving social, temporal and spatial dimensions (Conkey and Spector 1984: 25–28). We can investigate how various performance related parameters such as activity type, raw material utilization and activity context were structured in the industry, changing a passive artifact type into an active technology within the total socio-cultural sys-

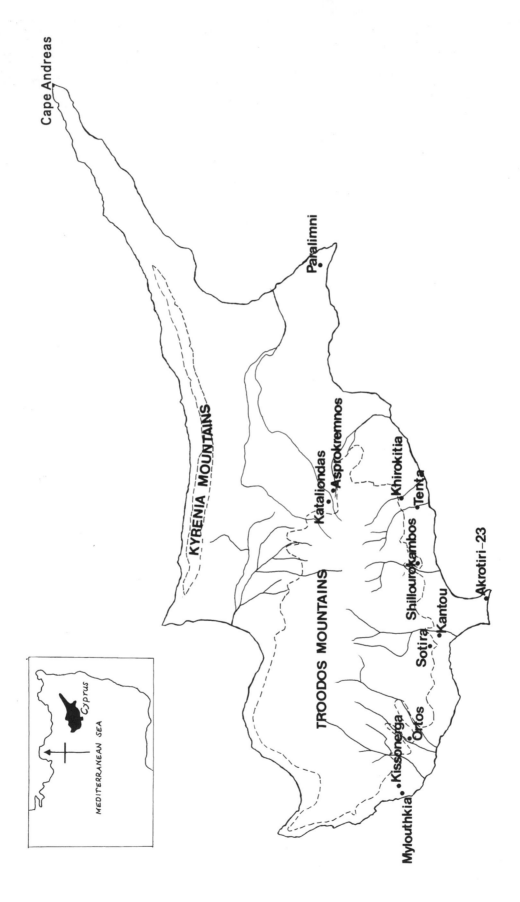

Figure 1. Map showing locations of sites discussed in text.

tem. The first part of this paper focuses on an early attempt to engender the study of chipped stone in Cyprus, and thus accounts for the title, "Women's Knives." Continuing with the theme of "knives," but looking at the whole of the Neolithic period, I then consider how cutting implements were integrated within a possible system of social organization.

Stekelis's contribution to the Sotira report represents the first and only specific reference to gender in the study of Cypriot chipped stone (Stekelis 1961: 231–32). In it, he distinguished between "pointed" blades, interpreted as male knives, and "squarish" blades (sometimes exhibiting luster) attributed to women. This typological distinction at Sotira was supported by analogy with ethnographic evidence from modern Aboriginal peoples in Australia. Stekelis inferred that, in general, the Sotira blades functioned for domestic and agricultural work of all kinds, particularly cutting.

The typological distinction between pointed and squarish blade tools drawn by Stekelis, however, is neither simple nor consistent, and the subjective nature of that distinction is readily apparent. First, the terms "pointed" and "squarish" cover tools with variable amounts of secondary retouch, particularly in the more common squarish blade category (figs. 1, 2). Unretouched blades of various shapes and sizes were also included in both tool types. Secondly, the inclusion of examples exhibiting "luster" (or gloss) with other non-lustrous squared blades represents a conflict with the conventional differentiation between glossed elements (commonly referred to as "sickles") and utilized blade tools (referred to as "knives"). Without entering in detail into the complex issue of the meaning of style, we need to mention the concept in reference to Stekelis's association between the Australian knives and the blade tools defined in his Sotira typology. It seems problematic to transfer the stylistic concept of one culture directly to another distinctly unrelated one. Instead, it is more likely that stylistic preferences varied from one society to the next, and, equally if not more probably, that the various pointed and squarish

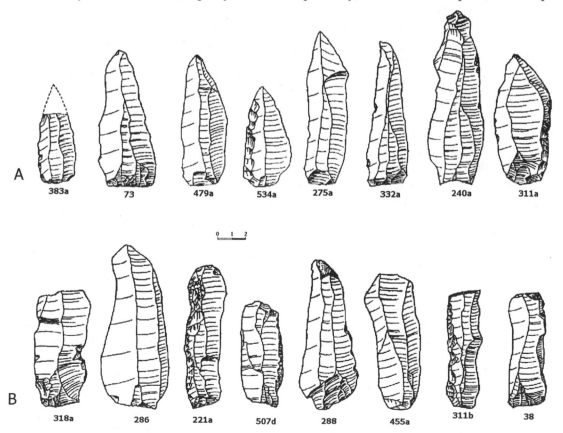

Figure 2. A) Sotira "Pointed" and B) "Squarish" blades. Redrawn from Dikaios (1961: pls. 116–18).

blades found within the Sotira assemblage were selected on the basis of situational performance related characteristics (Binford 1986: 183–85).

With regard to technology, blades, according to the accepted metric definition of the term, vary widely in shape. In a formal core technology like that employing the Naviform reduction strategy diagnostic of the Pre-Pottery Neolithic industry throughout the Near East, the blades produced vary widely in form, depending on their relationship to the overall strategy of core shaping, utilization and maintenance (Wilkie and Quintero 1994: 35–41, Table 1, pl. 5). Studies of blade technology typically focus on the systematic production of blades, showing low curvature, roughly parallel sides and uniformity of size. Successful application of technique is interpreted in terms of a flat distal end profile rather than edge delineation, with both pointed and squared blades typically produced from the same core (Wilkie and Quintero 1994: 41, 57; Clark 1985). While opposed platform cores were used to maintain the production of long parallel-sided blades, single platform cores, sometimes conical in shape, could facilitate the production of greater numbers of pointed blades. In Aceramic Neolithic Cyprus, both opposed platform and single platform cores were utilized for blade production, with single platform cores becoming increasingly prominent during the later Aceramic period and into the subsequent Ceramic Neolithic (Le Brun 1981: 32; 1987: 297; 1993: 71; M. Cauvin 1984: 85; Guilaine 1995: 24; McCartney 1998a: 87–88; personal observation). Shifts in core reduction strategy, however, were not matched by a corresponding change in blade outline form. In addition, as the bidirectional dorsal scar configurations on many of the Sotira blades (including pointed examples) suggest, more than one core reduction method continued into the Ceramic Neolithic (fig. 2; Dikaios 1961: pls. 116–18).

Beyond etic typological and technical considerations, the strongest criticism of Stekelis's gender-based interpretation rests in the ideological implications of ethnographic analogy. In the study of chipped stone from archaeological contexts, ethnographic and ethno-archaeological studies of modern aboriginal peoples in Australia and Papua New Guinea are frequently cited (Hayden 1977; White, Modjeska and Hipuya 1977; Binford 1986). Though such analogies may be of value when considered on a generalized pan-cultural level, specific references that include symbolic value without a direct historical relationship between the cultures being compared are invalid (Charlton 1981: 133–39). Thus, while it may be profitable to test whether particular blade forms were selected according to specific preferences, there is no direct evidence for inferring a gender rather than individual role in such selection (e.g., White, Modjeska and Hipuya 1977; Binford 1986: 179–80). The Australian analogy used by Stekelis fails at the direct historical level but also at the general level since much of the gender association is inextricably linked with symbolic attributes particular to the Aboriginal culture system. For example, the particular stone used in male knives is charged with unique symbolic significance (Taçon 1991: 194–205). Specific stones are considered to be extremely powerful when derived from sources linked to the highly developed ancestor cosmology of the Aboriginal culture. Importantly, the status and power males derive from such stones must not be "contaminated" by female associated objects. It is the inherent power in the stone that gives the Australian knives their special value. Thus, the main performance role of the Aboriginal knives is symbolic, with the more mundane, functional aspects being secondary (see, e.g., Binford 1986: 181–82, in which a "fighting" knife becomes a portable tool kit). It is speculative, at best, to consider associating particular Cypriot stone types with the same cosmological place significance found in the Aboriginal example although as we shall see below, the selective utilization of raw materials is evident within the Cypriot Neolithic.

Perhaps most importantly, context fails to provide the necessary symbolic associations for "male" and "female" spheres. The general plan of structures at Sotira, marked to illustrate the presence of pointed blades (A), squarish knives and other blades (B), other retouched tools (C), and core and debitage materials (D), demonstrates that all artifact categories can be found within the same individual structure (fig. 3). In all cases, pointed blades were found together with squarish blades. This

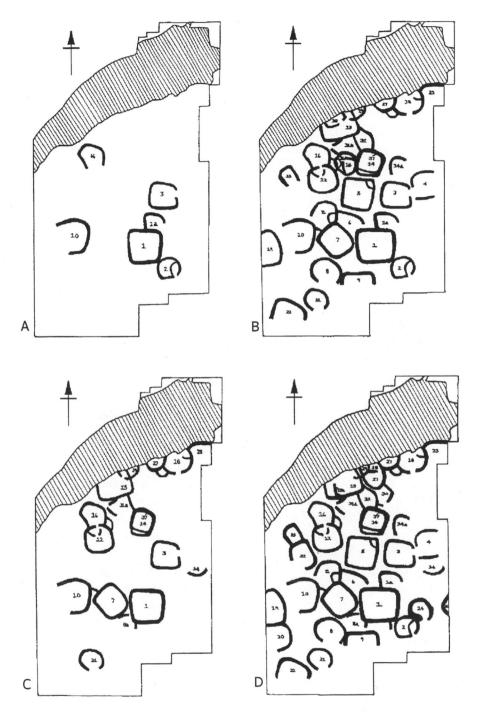

Figure 3. *Sotira general plan. Redrawn from Dikaios (1960: pl. 10): A) structures with "pointed" blades, B) structures with "squarish" blades, C) structures with other retouched tools, D) structures with cores and flake debitage.*

directly contradicts the context restrictions suggested by the Australian analogy where contact with female knives results in the "contamination" of their male counterparts. Male knives in Aboriginal culture are so susceptible to contamination by female tools and activities that specialized "male" camps exist totally removed from domestic site contexts where female activities are performed (Taçon 1991:

204–5; Binford 1986: 187–88). The evidence from Sotira, like the general ubiquity of cutting implements at all Neolithic sites in Cyprus, argues against such a strict gender/tool type association. Instead,
it seems worth considering tool type differences and diversity on the basis of chronology and site type,
and the results of such endeavors can be used to suggest a more generalized pattern of social organization for the Cypriot chipped stone industry during the Neolithic.

New data from a variety of Aceramic and Ceramic Neolithic sites in Cyprus have begun to provide
greater chronological depth and increased assemblage variety. By considering tool types, diversity and
context, we can begin to demonstrate a more complex picture of social organization and chipped stone
utilization than typically allowed in earlier interpretations of the Neolithic period in Cyprus. For example, the paucity of projectiles and bifacial axes in the chipped stone industry has been used to deny
links between Cyprus and Neolithic cultures elsewhere in the Near East (M. Cauvin 1984: 85; Le Brun
1986: 74; 1993: 71). Such tools are typically attributed to men in both manufacture and use, although
examples of women making arrowheads and hunting can be found, particularly in agricultural societies (Gero 1991: 170, 175). While chipped stone axes seem to have been supplanted by the ubiquitous
ground stone examples, the lack of projectiles has been surprising considering the importance of wild
deer to the Neolithic economy of the island (e.g., Croft 1991: 67–69). Highly diagnostic examples of
this tool group have, however, appeared in assemblages collected from open-air sites such as Akrotiri-
Vounarouthkia ton Lamnion East (= "Akrotiri site 23"), Parekklisia-*Shillourokambos* (early phases A
and B) and the early phase sample at Kalavasos-*Tenta* (see Swiny 1988: 10–11, fig. 4:1; Guilaine 1995:
24; Briois, Gratuze and Guilaine 1997: 95–97). Similarly, with at least one pressure flaked obsidian
example from Khirokitia-*Vounoi* as well as other broken or incomplete pressure retouched projectiles
belong to samples from short-term Aceramic occupations at Kissonerga-*Mosphilia* and Kissonerga-
Mylouthkia (well 116), the presence of this retouch technique can no longer be doubted (Betts 1987:
13; Christou 1994: 664; McCartney 1998b: 277; in press). While a limited number of crude projectile
examples were recovered from the settlement sites like Cape Andreas-*Kastros*, the more frequent association of well-made projectiles with pressure retouch seems to occur at sites lacking permanent stone
architecture (Le Brun 1981: 25, fig. 25: 5–6). The differential association of projectiles begins to
suggest something of a distinction between the "domestic" utilization of chipped stone technology at
settlement sites and a "non-domestic" aspect at open-air type-sites. In suggesting such a dichotomy
between "domestic" and "non-domestic" spheres, I do not refer to the restrictive and out-dated paradigms of domestic = female and public = male that frequently have been adopted in the ethnographic
literature (Strathern 1980; Conkey and Spector 1984: 18–19). Gero's discussion of the likelihood of
particular women being visible in domestic contexts seems overly strict since we have no direct evidence excluding male activity from domestic contexts and should not assume that women were not
involved in the activities performed at open-air sites (Gero 1991: 169). Instead, as Gero goes on to
note, we cannot assume a gender-based division of labor. Thus, the terms "domestic" and "non-domestic"
used here simply indicate contextual spheres that distinguish the performance of activities carried out in
association with stone structures at permanent settlement sites versus the organization of activities,
particularly industrial, at other types of Neolithic sites (Conkey and Spector 1984: 10; Gero 1991: 170).

The tool group that dominates many Neolithic assemblages in Cyprus represents implements with
sharp, acute angled edges that appear to have been used for a variety of cutting activities (fig. 4). We
may include a variety of tools in this group, such as implements traditionally viewed as sickles, knives,
backed and/or truncated blades and unretouched but utilized blades and flakes. Chronological changes
in style associated with this generalized tool group are marked most clearly by the glossed pieces.
Diminutive blade segments exhibiting gloss at an oblique angle to the tool edge have been used to
define the early phase B at Shillourokambos, parallels for which can also be seen in the assemblage
from Tenta (Guilaine 1995: 24, fig. 10:1–8; Briois, Gratuze and Guilaine 1997: 95–97; see also *infra*
fig. 4:1). Later Aceramic glossed pieces, made on larger blades and sometimes backed and/or trun-

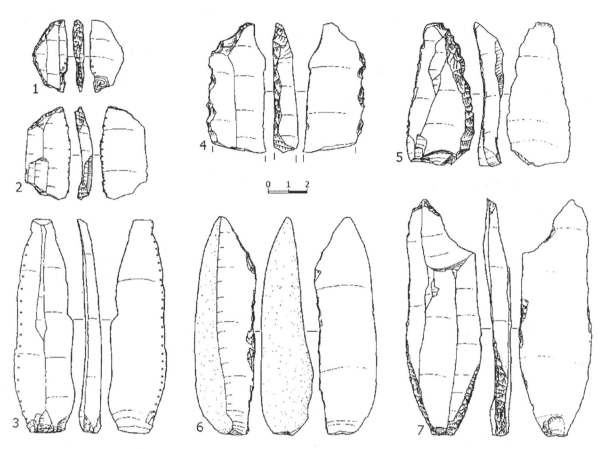

Figure 4. *Cutting group tools, all examples from Tenta: 1) glossed piece with angled gloss, 2) bi-truncated glossed piece, 3) unretouched glossed piece, 4) backed and truncated piece, 5) inverse retouched blade, 6) utilized blade with natural back, 7) "tanged" flake.*

cated, exhibit gloss parallel to the blade edge. Tools of this type have been found in a number of assemblages including the later Aceramic phase at Shillourokambos, Khirokitia, Tenta, Cape Andreas and Kholetria-*Ortos* (Le Brun 1981: 53–55, figs. 18–21; M. Cauvin 1984: 85; Guilaine 1995: 16; Simmons 1996: 35; see also *infra* fig. 4:3). Arched or straight backed blades without gloss, as well as unretouched blades or flakes exhibiting edge damage consistent with longitudinal "cutting" or "sawing" motions and typically associated with tools used as knives, are common to all assemblages (Tringham et al. 1974: 188; see also below). Large "tanged" blades or flakes have been found both at settlement sites such as Khirokitia and Tenta and sites lacking permanent stone architecture like Ortos and Ayia Varvara-*Asprokremnos*. Many of these tanged artifacts exhibit edge damage consistent with other cutting tools commonly interpreted as "knives" (Stekelis 1961; 1953: 411; Simmons 1996: 35–36; McCartney 1998a: 88; see also *infra* fig. 4:7). During the Ceramic Neolithic, cutting tools continued to be made on blade forms, but the occurrence of secondary retouch in the assemblages from Sotira, Paralimni-*Nissia* and Kantou-*Kouphovounos* appears to be reduced (e.g., fig. 4:3 = Tenta ceramic period; Dikaios 1961: pls. 116–18; Mantzourani 1996: fig. 12). Ceramic Neolithic retouch may have been used more frequently to resharpen cutting tools than for deliberately backing or shaping tools as seen during the earlier Aceramic Neolithic.

Use-wear evidence from Khirokitia is significant to the definition of a cutting tool group, demonstrating cereal gathering as expected but also the cutting or shaving of other plants, notably reeds and

fresh wood (Coqueugniot 1984: 90–93). Use-wear experimentation from Tenta suggests a high proportion of cutting soft materials such as meat and fresh skin (Hordynsky 1997). Related functional
studies from broadly contemporary sites on the Levantine mainland show cutting edges associated
with a variety of domestic activities such as basketry, the cutting of reeds for mat making, thatching,
bedding, and the collection of cereals, fodder and medicine plant materials (see, for example, Anderson-Gerfaud 1983: 86–97; 1994: 63–64; Perlis and Vaughan 1983: 209). According to Jacques Cauvin,
tool use changed during the Neolithic with traditional forms being used for an expanded variety of
tasks associated with agricultural economies. Tool group uses became more diversified to include new
technologies such as wool-working and cereal processing, while similar tools forms could also be used
in specialized ways in association with specific ecological contexts (J. Cauvin 1983: 263, 268–69).
These ideas are particularly relevant to the discussion of social organization in the chipped stone industry suggested here. Differences between settlements and open-air sites in Aceramic Neolithic Cyprus
have previously been interpreted as representing a more fully agricultural Neolithic in contrast to a
"para-neolithic" exhibiting a more broad spectrum subsistence base (Morris and Watkins 1974: 74).
This population distinction, however, contradicts the cultural uniformity demonstrated by the chipped
stone industry. Aceramic assemblages from sites lacking formal architecture, such as Asprokremnos,
Kataliondas-*Kourvellos*, Ortos and the early phases at Shillourokambos, contain numerous artifacts
belonging to the cutting tool group but also many notches, denticulates, burins and scraper forms less
dominant in the settlement site assemblages (Watkins 1979: 18–19; Guilaine 1995: 24; Simmons 1996:
40, Table 2; McCartney 1998a: 88–89; see also fig. 5). Truncations were associated with "sickle"
elements at Khirokitia, but at least one example was shown by use-wear analysis to have been used for

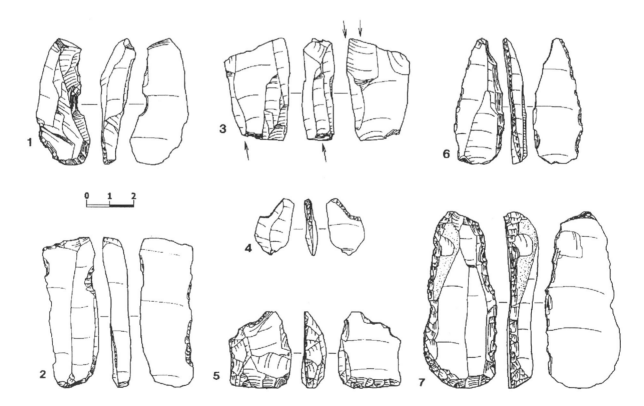

*Figure 5. Other retouched tools, all examples from Kataliondas: 1) burin, 2) backed blade with lateral notch, 3) blade
with alternating retouch, 4) notched flake, 5) backed and truncated piece, 6) end scraper with lateral notch, 7) truncated
blade with lateral notches, 8) double end scraper with bilateral retouch.*

scraping fresh hide (M. Cauvin 1984: 85; Coqueugniot 1984: 92). Hordynsky has observed that one main difference in tool morphology leading to differential utilization is variation in the edge angle. Tools with more acute edge angles, like those suggested for the "cutting" tool group, were associated with cutting activities, while more obtusely angled tools like scrapers and truncations were employed for scraping (Hordynsky 1997). Thus, functional variation on a context specific basis is suggested by assemblages from non-settlement sites such as Kataliondas with its dominant scrapers and truncations and Asprokremnos with its high proportion of burins (McCartney 1998a: 88–89). The abundance of animal bone, ground stone, antler and chipped stone tools and debris demonstrate the wealth of collecting and processing activities carried out at open-air sites (Watkins 1979: 15–20; Lehavy 1980: 205–206, 209; Guilaine 1995: 24–25). In contrast, the construction and maintenance of stone and mud-built structures, plant processing, food preparation and other domestic and craft activities are evidenced at sites with permanent architecture. A similar pattern may well have continued into the Ceramic Neolithic period, considering the contrast represented by pits and silos containing ceramics at Shillourokambos, Tenta and Khirokitia versus Sotira, Paralimni and Kantou with their abundant permanent architecture. Erosional forces, however, may account for part of the latter difference, while some of the ceramics may be dated to the Early Chalcolithic (Dikaios 1961; Todd 1987: 18; Guilaine 1995: 25; Mantzourani 1996).

Finally, it is worth noting that the raw materials used in assemblages from the main Aceramic settlement sites (Tenta, Khirokitia and Cape Andreas) were dominated by local "Lefkara-translucent" cherts which are of moderate quality but generate sharp, tough blade edges (Le Brun 1981; personal observation). Local cherts were also utilized at non-domestic sites, but the latter are more frequently dominated by fine-grained "Lefkara-basal" and cryptocrystalline varieties of chert, both of which fracture more controllably than the more quartz-like Lefkara-translucent type cherts. Thus, at Kataliondas and Shillourkambos (recent phase), Lefkara-basal cherts are most common, with silicified umbers representing a unique, though less frequent, local favorite at Kataliondas (Guilaine 1995: 14–15; personal observation). Similarly, at Shillourokambos (early phase A and B), Asprokremnos and Aceramic Mylouthkia, high quality, translucent red-brown cryptocrystalline cherts were worked to a high degree of craftsmanship (Guilaine 1995: 14–15; McCartney 1998a: 87; in press). At Ortos, the assemblage was dominated by high quality black "Moni" cherts, occurring in great abundance local to the site (Simmons 1996: 35). It seems likely, therefore, that differences represented by the dominant tool types in both the domestic and non-domestic Aceramic period assemblages were partly governed by the quality of cherts locally available and that one reason for the existence of some open-air sites may be attributed to the local presence of superior quality chert. During the Ceramic Neolithic, raw materials seem to have been preferentially selected for blade production. According to simple color distinctions, the majority of all blades (68.1 percent) at Sotira were made on light brown, light gray or buff raw materials. Conversely, the majority of flakes (72.3 percent) were made on dark brown, red-brown, and gray/dark gray materials. The cores (74.3 percent) and "non-cutting" tools (62.1 percent) also demonstrate greater use of the darker colored cherts. Importantly, however, cores and debitage of both material color groups were found within the same house contexts, and approximately one-third of the blades were produced with the darker colored raw materials. Thus, the distinction recently made between a "specialist" blade and generalized flake production for the Kantou assemblage seems unlikely at Sotira (Mantzourani 1996: 23). Instead of reiterating the stereotypical model by which women are typically and arbitrarily attributed with the "less skilled" flake core technology, we should first consider context and whether specific raw materials exhibit mechanical differences that enhance the performance of either blades or flakes (see Gero 1991: 169 although Gero 1991: 176 suggests, in contradiction to her earlier statement, that we focus on "expedient" flake-based assemblages and keep away from highly retouched tools). The use of high quality translucent cryptocrystalline cherts in the production of blade tools at Paralimni supports the Sotira pattern (personal observation).

The discussion of a social organization in the technology of chipped stone in Neolithic Cyprus is necessarily preliminary, raising hypotheses that can be tested as more data become available. By categorizing different aspects of task differentiation, it seems possible to illustrate how the technology of chipped stone on the basis of performance was more integrated within the total social system than normally granted. While not defining this technology as one governed by either men or women, it is readily apparent that much of the production and utilization of chipped stone, particularly cutting activities, took place within domestic contexts. Non-domestic site assemblages often show other dominant tool types. The technology of chipped stone was consistently employed in or between the densely packed structures at both Aceramic and Ceramic Neolithic sites, as well as at occupations lacking permanent architecture. Considering the total array of Neolithic evidence, the organizational differences demonstrated by this technology suggest gender integration rather than exclusively male or female differentiated activities (Harris 1980). On a pragmatic level, the chipped stone industry of Neolithic Cyprus suggests that males and females may be thought of as a single economic unit. Like many modern farming societies, males and females, in spite of possible status loaded associations, must work as an integrated unit in order to create a viable economic whole.

LIST OF SITES

Akrotiri site 23 = Akrotiri-*Vounarouthkia ton Lamnion* East
Asprokremnos = Ayia Varvara-*Asprokremnos*
Cape Andreas = Cape Andreas-*Kastros*
Kantou = Kantou-*Kouphovounos*
Kataliondas = Kataliondas-*Kourvellos*
Khirokitia = Khirokitia-*Vounoi*
Kissonerga = Kissonerga-*Mosphilia*
Mylouthkia = Kissonerga-*Mylouthkia*
Ortos = Kholetria-*Ortos*
Paralimni = Paralimni-*Nissia*
Shillourokambos = Parekklisia-*Shillourokambos*
Sotira = Sotira-*Teppes*
Tenta = Kalavasos-*Tenta*

REFERENCES

Anderson-Gerfaud, P.
1983   A Consideration of the Uses of Certain Backed and "Lustered" Stone Tools from Late Mesolithic and Natufian Levels of Abu Hureyra and Mureybet (Syria). Pp. 77–105 in *Traces d' Utilisation sur les outils Néolithiques du Proche Orient*, ed. M. C. Cauvin. Travaux de la Masion de l'Orient 5. Paris: Masion de l'Orient.
1994   Reflections on the Significance of Two PPN Typological Classes in the Light of Experimentation and Microwear Analysis: Flint "Sickles" and Obsidian "Çayönü Tools". Pp. 61–82 in *Neolithic Chipped Stone Industries of the Fertile Crescent*, eds. H. G. Gebel and S. K.Kozlowski. Studies in Early Near Eastern Production, Subsistence and Environment 1. Berlin: Ex Oriente.

Betts, A.
1987   The Chipped Stone. Pp.10–14 in "Excavations at Kissonerga-Mosphilia, 1986" by E. Peltenburg and Project Members. *Report of the Department of Antiquities of Cyprus*: 1–18.

Binford, L.
1986   An Alyawara Day: Making Men's Knives and Beyond. *American Antiquity* 51: 547–62.

Briois, F.; Gratuze, B.; and Guilaine, J.
1997   Obsidiennes du Site Néolithique Précéramique de Shillourokambos (Chypre). *Paléorient* 23.1: 95–112.

Cauvin, J.
1983   Typologie et Fonctions des Outils Prehistoriques: Apports de la Tracéologie a un Vieux Débat. Pp. 259–74 in *Traces d´Utilisation sur les outils Néolithiques du Proche Orient*, ed. M. C.Cauvin. Travaux de la Masion de l´Orient, 5. Paris: Maison de l'Orient.

Cauvin, M. C.
1984   L'outillage lithique de Khirokitia (Chypre) et le Levant. Pp. 85–87 in *Fouilles récentes à Khirokitia (Chypre) 1977–1981*, ed. A. Le Brun. Paris: Editions Recherche sur les Civilisations.

Charlton, T. H.
1981   Archaeology, Ethnohistory and Ethnology: Interpretive Interfaces. Pp. 129–76 in *Advances in Archaeological Method and Theory* 4, ed. M. Schiffer. London: Academic.

Christou, D.
1994   Chroniques des Fouilles et Découvertes Archéologiques à Chypre en 1993. *Bulletin de correspondance hellénique* 18: 647–93.

Clark, J. E.
1985   Platforms, Bits, Punches and Vises: A Potpourri of Mesoamerican BladeTechnology. *Lithic Technology* 14, 1: 1–15.

Conkey, M. W., and Spector, J. D.
1984   Archaeology and the Study of Gender. Pp. 1–38 in *Advances in Archaeological Method and Theory* 7, ed. M. Schiffer. London: Academic.

Coqueugniot, E.
1984   Premiers Éléments Concernant L´Utilisation des Outils de Silex de Khirokitia (Chypre) Campagne de 1981. Pp. 89–96 in *Fouilles Récentes à Khirokitia (Chypre) 1977–1981*, ed. A. Le Brun. Paris: Editions Recherche sur les Civilisations.

Croft, P.
1991   Man and Beast in Chalcolithic Cyprus. *Bulletin of the American Schools of Oriental Research* 282/283: 63–79.

Dikaios, P.
1961   *Sotira*. Philadelphia: The University of Pennsylvania.

Gero, J. M.
1991   Genderlithics: Women's Roles in Stone Tool Production. Pp. 163–93 in *Engendering Archaeology: Women and Prehistory*, eds. J. M. Gero and M. W. Conkey. Oxford: Blackwell.

Guilaine, J.; Coularou, J.; and Carrère, I.
1995   L'Etablissement Neolithique de Shillourokambos (Parekklisha, Chypre) Premiers Résultats. *Report of the Department of Antiquities of Cyprus*: 11–32.

Harris, O.
1980   The Power of Signs: Gender, Culture and the Wild in the Bolivian Andes. Pp. 70–94 in *Nature, Culture and Gender*, eds. C. MacCormack and M. Strathern. Cambridge: Cambridge University.
Hayden, B.
1977   Stone Tool Functions in the Western Desert. Pp. 178–88 in *Stone Tools as Cultural Markers*, ed. R. V. S. Wright. Canberra: Australian Institute of Aboriginal Studies.
Hordynsky, L.
1997   Working Units in Stone Tool Assemblages in Neolithic Cyprus. Paper presented at the annual meeting of the American Schools of Oriental Research, Napa, CA.
Le Brun, A.
1981   *Un site Néolithique Précéramique en Chypre: Cap Andreas-Kastros*. Recherche sur les grandes civilisations, Mémoire 5, Etudes néolithiques. Paris: Editions Association pour la diffusion de la pensée française.
1986   Cap Andreas-Kastros et Khirokitia. Pp. 73–80 in *Archaeology in Cyprus 1960–1985*, ed. V. Karageorghis. Nicosia: A. G. Leventis Foundation.
1987   Le Néolithique Précéramique de Chypre. *L'Anthropologie* 91.1: 283–316.
1993   Recherches sur le Néolithique Précéramique de Chypre: Les fouilles du Cap Andreas-Kastros et de Khirokitia. Pp. 55–80 in *Kinyras, Archéologie Française à Chypre*, ed. M. Yon. Travaux de la Maison de l'Orient, 22. Lyon: Maison de l'Orient.
Lehavy, Y. M.
1980   Excavations at Dhali-Agridhi: 1972, 1974, 1976. Pp. 204–43 in *American Expedition to Idalion, Cyprus 1973–1980*, eds. L. Stager and A. M. Walker. Oriental Institute Communications, 24. Chicago: University of Chicago.
Mantzourani, E.
1996   Ekthesi Apotelesmaton tis Anaskafis sti Thesi Kantou-Koufovounos Kata tis Periodous 1994–1995. *Report of the Department of Antiquities of Cyprus*: 1–28.
McCartney, C.
1998a   Preliminary Report on the Chipped Stone Assemblage from the Aceramic Neolithic Site of Ayia Varvara Asprokremnos, Cyprus. *Levant* 30: 85–90.
1998b   Chipped Stone Report. Pp. 249–93, in *Lemba Archaeological Project, Cyprus II.1B: Excavations at Kissonerga-Mosphilia*, ed. E. Peltenburg. Occasional Paper 19. Edinburgh: University of Edinburgh.
in press   The Chipped Stone Assemblage. In *Lemba Archaeological Project, Cyprus III.1: Excavations at Kissonerga-Mylouthkia 1977–1995*, ed. E. Peltenburg. Studies in Mediterranean Archaeology 70:4. Göteborg: Åströms.
Morrison, I., and Watkins. T.
1974   Kataliondas-Kourvellos: A Survey of an Aceramic Neolithic Site and its Environs in Cyprus. *Palestine Excavation Quarterly* 106: 67–75.
Perlès, C., and Vaughan, P.
1983   Pieces lustrées, travail des Plantes et Moissons a Franchthi (Grèce) (Xème-IVème mill. B.C.). Pp. 209–24 in *Traces d'utilisation sur les Outils Néolithiques du Proche Orient*, ed. M. C. Cauvin. Travaux de la Masion de l'Orient, 5. Paris: Masion de l'Orient.
Simmons, A. H.
1996   Preliminary Report on Multidisciplinary Investigations at Neolithic Kholetria-Ortos, Paphos District. *Report of the Department of Antiquities of Cyprus*: 29–44.
Stekelis, M.
1953   The Flint Implements from Khirokitia. Pp. 409–15 (Appendix 1) in *Khirokitia: Final Report on the Excavations of a Neolithic Settlement in Cyprus on Behalf of the Department of Antiquities 1936–1946*, ed. P. Dikaios. Oxford: Oxford University.
1961   The Flint Implements. Pp. 230–34 (Appendix 2) in *Sotira*, ed. P. Dikaios. Philadelphia: The University of Pennsylvania.
Strathern, M.
1980   No Nature, No Culture: The Hagen Case. Pp. 174–222 in *Nature, Culture and Gender*, eds. C. MacCormack and M. Strathern. Cambridge: Cambridge University.

Swiny, S.
1988   The Pleistocene Fauna of Cyprus and Recent Discoveries on the Akrotiri Peninsula. *Report of the Department of Antiquities of Cyprus*: 1–11.

Taçon, P. S. C.
1991   The Power of Stone: Symbolic Aspects of Stone Use and Tool Development in Western Arnhem Land, Australia. *Antiquity* 65: 192–207.

Todd, I. A.
1987   *Vasilikos Valley Project 6: Excavations at Kalavasos-Tenta* 1. Studies in Mediterranean Archaeology 71:6. Göteborg: Åströms.

Tringham, R.; Cooper, G.; Odell, G.; Voytek, B.; and Whitman, A.
1974   Experimentation in the Formation of Edge Damage: A New Approach to Lithic Analysis. *Journal of Field Archaeology* 1: 171–95.

Watkins, T.
1979   Kataliondas-*Kourvellos*: The Analysis of the Surface-Collected Data. Pp. 12–20 in *Studies Presented in Memory of Porphyrios Dikaios*, eds.V. Karageorghis et al. Nicosia: Lion's Club.

White, P. J.; Modjeska N.; and Hipuya I.
1977   Group Definitions and Mental Templates: An Ethnographic Experiment. Pp. 380–90 in *Stone Tools as Cultural Markers*, ed. R. V. S. Wright. Canberra: Australian Institute of Aboriginal Studies.

Wilke, P., and Quintero, L.
1994   Naviform Core-and-Blade Technology: Assemblage Character as Determined by Replicative Experiments. Pp. 33–60 in *Neolithic Chipped Stone Industries of the Fertile Crescent*, eds. H. G. Gebel and S. K. Kozlowski. Studies in Early Near Eastern Production, Subsistence and Environment 1. Berlin: Ex Oriente.

GENDER, ECONOMY AND CERAMIC PRODUCTION IN NEOLITHIC CYPRUS

JOANNE CLARKE

School of World Art Studies and Museology
University of East Anglia
Norwich NR4 7TJ, United Kingdom
joanne.clarke@uea.ac.uk

Theoretical model building has long been part of archaeological method. However, archaeologists must be wary of modern constructs and biases that can limit the application of models in archaeological interpretation. Gender and social theory are two areas where theoretical models have played a significant role in interpretation, but they are also most susceptible to modern bias. This paper considers two aspects of early archaeological theory pertaining to the role of women in early prehistoric society. The first concerns the assumption that women were the primary producers of pottery, and the second concerns the assumption that stylistic variation is determined by the movement of women potters in exogamic community structures. Using evidence from Ceramic Neolithic Cyprus, this paper attempts to deconstruct previous biases regarding the role of women and the dynamics of social interaction in prehistoric society.

EARLY THEORETICAL CONSTRUCTS

During the 1960s and 1970s, Deetz (1965, 1968), Whallon (1968), Longacre (1968, 1970), and Hill (1968, 1970) formulated a series of hypotheses to explain patterns of diversity in ceramic design within and between sites. Their theories, which were designed to account for intra- and inter-site diversity in early agro-pastoralist North American societies, were based upon arbitrary assumptions concerning descent patterns and post-marital residence arrangements and can be summarized as follows:

1) Women made pots.
2) Techniques of pottery manufacture and decoration were learned before marriage and passed down from mother to daughter.
3) The degree to which designs diffuse is directly proportional to the amount of interaction between individuals.
4) All households made the pottery they used.

The Deetz/Longacre model presumed that a matrilocal endogamous or exogamous society, where there is little contact between potters, is characterized by a non-random distribution of ceramic designs. In other words, in societies where women stay within the village unit after marriage, there should be homogeneity in ceramic designs within the village, but between village units there should be diversity in ceramic design. Conversely, in a patrilocal exogamous society where women move to the husband's village after marriage, new female potters continually bring new ideas into the

251

village, and there should be greater heterogeneity of designs within villages and greater similarity between villages.

Although Longacre's work in the Kalinga district of the northern Philippines enabled him to modify and refine his original theories, his general premises did not alter radically. On the basis of his ethnographic work, Longacre (1981, 1991), in conjunction with Graves (1991), argued that intra-site, inter-site, and inter-regional variation in ceramics was the result of female manufacturers conveying different messages within and between sites. Decorative motifs on vessels display some intra-site variation, but this, they argued, was due to the female artisans taking "pride in their work" (Graves 1991: 112–43). Alternatively, between regions there is marked variation in vessel morphology and design as certain regions will form "peace pacts" with other regions, resulting in strong regional solidarity. Graves (1991: 119) has argued that the marked variation in ceramic design between villages and regions "does not reflect the material manifestations of individuals exchanging information … but rather, they serve as subtle icons for individuals linked to a common polity." Here we see a greater degree of causality introduced into Longacre's model, but it is still predicated on the assumption that women are usually the sole producers of pottery and design similarity will vary in accordance with female social dynamics.

In an unrelated but relevant study, Dean Arnold argued that subsistence patterns and pottery manufacture were closely tied to gender (1985: 102). Division of labor, particularly pottery production within agro-pastoralist and complex societies, was governed by what he called "scheduling conflicts" dictated by seasonally related patterning of subsistence tasks. Arnold argued that,

> For part-time, seasonal potters, pottery making is primarily a household craft. Because the potter probably seldom has the capital (cash or goods) to set up structures used only for pottery making, the potter's house serves a number of important uses. Since females tend to be closely attached to the household by the requirements of pregnancy, infant care and other household tasks, they have an advantage in performing tasks (like making pottery) that can be accomplished within the household. Females are at a disadvantage in undertaking tasks which must be performed away from the household because of household and childcare responsibilities, and pottery making is relatively monotonous, does not require great concentration, can be carried out in spite of interruptions and can be easily resumed. It is easily compatible with household chores like cooking and women can easily make pots in the house in their spare moments.
>
> As traditional subsistence strategies (like agriculture and hunting) were reduced and ultimately eliminated by population pressure, pottery making would become the primary activity for livelihood. In this situation male potters would become more involved in the pottery making process and eventually would replace female potters, since the use of females for making pottery on a part-time basis is related to the female advantage in making pottery in a household. (Arnold 1985: 102)

Not surprisingly, the theories of Longacre et al. and Arnold have been the subject of a good deal of criticism during the last twenty years. Implicit in the Deetz/Longacre model (even with Longacre's later modifications) are a number of *prima facie* assumptions that preclude the action of other forces, both external and internal, acting upon social interactive systems, and which would more than likely produce a different set of cultural traits. Perhaps the most blatant of all assumptions is that women are usually the primary producers of pottery in household industries. In order for the Deetz/Longacre model to be useful, it must be applicable to other archaeological contexts. However, it is rare that either identical or similar dynamics exist in any two social interactive systems. The very fact that Longacre revised his earlier model indicates that he, too, understood the general flaws inherent in building models with narrow parameters. Ethnographic and archaeological studies undertaken by Plog (1978, 1980) and Hodder (1978, 1979) have illustrated that it cannot arbitrarily be assumed that women made pots nor can it be assumed that there is direct correlation between the degree of similarity in ceramic design and female social dynamics.

In the same way, Arnold's theories on economic and subsistence strategies have been shown to have inherent biases. Wright argues that pottery can be both a male and female craft, with women usually integral to its production and that there is also little basis for the stereotype that when pottery is produced for non-household consumption, women no longer participate in it (1991: 199). Rather, it appears that although there clearly are societies in which women do not produce pottery, there are many others where the production of pottery is divided into a series of related tasks, such as forming, firing and decorating, and that both women and men are involved in these tasks.

In a further study on the production of stone tools, Gero indirectly opposes Arnold's viewpoint by arguing that universal prescriptions placed on subsistence tasks are widely debated, and in fact rejected today, especially in reference to generalizations such as "women's roles" or "women's experiences" (1991: 171). Many agro-pastoralist societies, as with societies today, are characterized by extended family structures where child care and responsibility for the old is spread amongst siblings, cousins and marital partners. Women are not always pregnant and, therefore, not always tied to the household unit, and infants do not have to be breast-fed by the biological mother but can and often are fed by nursemaids. Moreover, older children and other family members often look after weaned infants in societies where the mother is required to carry out subsistence tasks outside the village unit.

Ultimately, the models of Deetz, Longacre, Whallon, and Hill in the first instance, and Arnold in the second instance, highlight the theoretical inconsistencies of archaeological interpretation with regard to both gender based divisions of labor in prehistoric subsistence strategies, and socio-cultural interactive patterning.

All this being said, there is no doubt that women may have frequently been the primary producers of pottery in early agro-pastoralist societies and that the manufacturing of pottery was subject to scheduling conflicts brought about by seasonal constraints of weather and other subsistence efforts. Given the fact that design variation in the ceramics of Neolithic Cyprus is so distinctive, one tends to suspect that some form of highly structured social and economic interaction was taking place, particularly when other material culture items are almost without variation across the island. The question is whether, in this instance, we can attribute stylistic patterning to female potters and their movement through intermarriage or some other form of social connection. In order to test whether women made pottery in Ceramic Neolithic Cyprus, it is necessary to identify what other tasks women might have been involved in on a day-to-day and seasonal basis and, in addition, what roles men were playing in seasonal subsistence pursuits.

Social interaction and, by extension, regional variation are closely tied to subsistence activities in early farming societies, and it is assumed in this paper that the seasonal patterning of subsistence related tasks, including the production of pottery, contributed to the scheduling and structure of village production and maintenance. In this one respect, therefore, the argument of Arnold (in which he maintains that early village life would have been subject to the seasonal scheduling of activities) is assumed to be correct. However, this does not necessarily mean that males and females were participants in scheduling conflicts that forced certain activities be carried out by one or the other sex. Rather, it is more likely that a range of social interactions occurred that contributed to a much more dynamic arrangement of activity sharing.

In order to identify the types of subsistence activities that were being undertaken, we turn now to the economic evidence from the Ceramic Neolithic period in Cyprus. It is important to keep in mind, however, that this evidence can only determine how and when pottery may have been manufactured. In order to determine whether women were the primary producers of pottery, evidence for design variation in the ceramics will be compared with the Deetz/Longacre model and other recent stylistic models in order to discern the most likely patterns of social interaction. Ultimately, the object is to determine whether women can be identified in the archaeological record and, if so, whether there is accompanying evidence for post-marital residence arrangements that might explain diversity in ceramic design.

CERAMIC NEOLITHIC CYPRUS

Ceramic Neolithic Cyprus is characterized by a non-hierarchical, agro-pastoralist, essentially "closed" society that demonstrates little or no contact with the mainland at this time. Peltenburg (1978; 1982a) noted that ceramic Neolithic sites fall into two distinct categories based upon variation in the execution of designs on painted pottery:

1) Sites characterized by a predominantly red-on-white design tradition (Dikaios 1962: fig. 35; Peltenburg 1982b: fig. 70–76; Watkins, personal communication).

2) Sites characterized by a predominantly combed and red monochrome painted design tradition (Dikaios 1953: pls. 72–78; Dikaios 1961: pls. 58–73, 80–83).

These two ceramic categories can be separated geographically into two broad geographical regions:

1) A northern, red-on-white region, encompassing all of the sites north of the Kyrenia Range, the Morphou Bay area and the Paphos Region.

2) A southern, combed and red monochrome painted region, encompassing all of the sites around the Coastal Gateway between the Paphos Region and the Southern Chalk Plateaus, and the South Central Southern Chalk Plateaus.

When broadly contemporaneous assemblages are compared, variation is not detectable in any other aspect of the material culture.

Despite the differences in decoration, the pottery tradition is essentially homogeneous. Although red-on-white is favored in the north and west of the island, and combed and red monochrome painted are favored in the south-central region, there is overlap between the two regions with combed and red monochrome painted appearing in varying quantities in the north and vice versa. This homogeneity is most clearly evident in the range of limited vessel shapes. Pottery technology does not vary between sites (Peltenburg 1978: 66), and vessels are handmade and, in most instances, coil-built.

Neolithic pottery is, without exception, from settlements. Within settlements there is some variation in the type of contexts in which the pottery is found. Most of the pottery comes from domestic contexts, such as house floors and work surfaces, and is often smashed *in situ* beside hearths and preparation areas (Peltenburg 1975). These observations support the theory that Neolithic pottery was associated with the day-to-day aspects of subsistence, including the preparation of food, cooking, serving and eating.

Evidence from the analysis of fabrics (Clarke 1998: 140) indicates that pottery, by and large, was made within individual villages. Therefore, it is likely that pottery was manufactured by the household for the household. Habitation units were mono-cellular structures with domestic fixtures and fittings on the floors and around the walls. Deposition patterns on the floors of structures suggest that most of the economic activities (cooking, food preparation, craft production, and storage) were carried out within and around the habitation units. Sleeping areas are hypothesized as being above ground level (Peltenburg 1978: 62) or outside the buildings. Therefore, the socio-economic division within the village structure was most likely based on one family unit per house, with members of the family manufacturing pottery according to its own needs.

Although it cannot be ruled out that some seasonal production of surplus was practiced, intra-site settlement plans and burial practices indicate an absence of craft specialization. Likewise, the absence of large "storage" vessels, common in the subsequent Chalcolithic period (Bolger 1988), argues against the production of surplus at this early date.

Evidence for social ranking or differential economic strategies is absent throughout most of the Ceramic Neolithic period. The comparative uniformity in both size of habitation units, as well as patterns of deposition on house floors, indicate that households produced pottery for similar domestic purposes. Peltenburg has looked at the density of objects on hut floors at Ayios Epiktitos-*Vrysi* and concluded that there is differentiation between the North Sector and the South Sector, with the North Sector displaying a greater density of objects and larger building dimensions than the South Sector (1993: 10). Peltenburg's results suggest that at Ayios Epiktitos-*Vrysi* at least there may have been increasing differentiation of wealth as the settlement expanded. However, Peltenburg is quick to point out that

> the differences must be set against the background of standardized internal fixtures, especially the normal range of domestic and craft items (and that this) prevents us from describing either Sector as a specialized quarter. The evidence rather suggests that most buildings are generalized habitations in which all major domestic activities including consumption and manufacture took place. (Peltenburg 1985: 61)

Ceramic Neolithic Cyprus is characterized by communities that engaged in mixed farming and herding, the gathering of sea and land molluscs, and the controlled management and hunting of deer (Croft 1991: 65; Kyllo 1982: 82; Legge 1982). Wheat, barley, lentils and pulses were cultivated, and the presence of grinders and saddle querns suggests that grains were ground into meal. Tree fruits, such as figs, were also grown and wild grapes and olives and a number of grasses were collected (Kyllo 1982: 415–36). Faunal remains are dominated by the basic domesticates and commensals of early sedentary communities. The domesticated ovicaprids (*Ovis orientalis and Capra hircus*) and domesticated pig (*Sus scrofa*) and fallow deer predominate in the faunal record.

Ceramic Neolithic populations inhabited small villages and campsites and carried out a range of activities associated with a mixed farming economy. Villages were located in areas where water was readily accessible and soils were fertile. The availability of optimum arable land in Cyprus was not unlimited in the early prehistoric period, and settlements aggregated along river courses or around perennial springs. Peltenburg (1982b: 13) quotes a radius of 2–3 km as the average catchment area per village for grazing and farming, and presumably village catchment areas overlapped. The management of deer would have involved some traveling into the foothills of the Kyrenia and Troodos ranges and areas of poorer grazing away from the central village zone: Therefore, inhabitants of more distant villages presumably came into contact with each other on a regular basis. Subsistence activities would have been carried out on a seasonal basis. The wild cereals, characteristic of the Near East, would have grown through the winter months and would have been harvested in the spring (Sherratt 1980: 315). Animal husbanding would have been an activity that required most effort in the winter and spring when new animals were born and milk was available (Davis 1984). The very hot, dry summer months in Cyprus may have forced farmers to move their herds into the cooler mountain foothills where late growing grasses and perennials would still be available, although there is little evidence in support of a transhumant economy. However, in many regions the cooler upland areas are close enough to the major sites that seasonal transhumance would not have been necessary, but foraging trips (Binford 1996) and regular periods away from villages were probably part of the seasonal subsistence strategy.

Presumably, the absence of storage vessels in Ceramic Neolithic contexts indicates that seasonal storage of cereals or other food products was not part of the economic strategy of Neolithic populations. Therefore, resources were probably supplemented by the addition of collected plants (Hastorf 1991) and, of course, hunting forays. This is, in fact, one aspect of foraging that Binford singles out as being characteristic of some foraging systems—what he has called "encounter of strategy." He describes this as a hunting trip where several *"men"* (my italics) leave the residential base, establishing overnight camps from which they move out in search of game. If they succeed in their hunting endeavors and if the body size of the animal is large or the distance to camp is great and the temperature is warm, they may elect to dry the meat in the field and transport processed meat back to camp (Binford 1996: 44).

Binford outlines a number of characteristics of different foraging activities (1996: 41–46). Of particular interest are those aspects which resemble Neolithic subsistence strategies. He notes that one distinctive characteristic of a foraging strategy is that foragers typically do not store foods but gather foods daily (Binford 1996: 41). Although herd survival would have been important for meat and other products, deer would have been hunted all year round, providing a regular source of energy in the leaner summer months. Using this model, the pattern of Ceramic Neolithic subsistence strategies could be one of intensive activity in the winter and spring, with village populations involved in activities that would keep them most often within the agricultural catchment area. During the summer and autumn months, food would be scarcer and foraging trips would be more regular. Craft production would be higher due to better weather conditions because ceramic production and presumably house construction requires long, dry spells (London 1987; London, Egoumenidou, and Karagcorghis 1990). The scheduling of agricultural activities undertaken in the winter and spring would require that tasks, such as the production of pottery and general village repairs and maintenance, would be confined to the seasons when subsistence strategies needed less input.

Arnold states:

> Because the environmental variables of temperature, wind velocity and relative humidity affect the drying of pottery, weather and climate can have a profound effect on the success of pottery production …. Pottery making is ideally a dry weather craft; cold and damp weather and climate provide a significant limiting factor for pottery production. The most favourable weather and climatic conditions for pottery production thus occur during a time of sustained sunshine, warm temperatures, little or no rainfall and low relative humidity. (Arnold 1985: 62–71)

Furthermore, Gero has argued that although stone tool technology is usually assumed to be a male domain:

> females comprised approximately half of all prehistoric populations, and these women carried out productive activities at prehistoric sites. We suspect, moreover, that women were especially visible and active in household contexts where they played significant roles in household production and household management …. As women work in association with such living areas, they need tools for the tasks they carry out. Although the kinds of tools women need would clearly vary from culture to culture and from task to task, it is inconceivable that they sat and waited for a flake to be produced, or that they set out each time to borrow one. Women clearly required ready access to efficient working edges in their routine work, and they must have manufactured them as needed. (Gero 1991: 169–70)

It is likely that in Ceramic Neolithic Cyprus, women were also involved in the production of stone tools (see McCartney, this volume). It is illuminating to note that Ceramic Neolithic Cyprus is devoid of any tool form that can categorically be associated with a hunting function. More specifically, the ubiquitous flakes and blades were more likely used for the daily activities of food preparation and the manufacturing of household items.

Therefore, there is no direct evidence in Neolithic Cyprus for a structured division of labor between men and women, whereby men make stone tools and women make pots. Although there is ethnographic analogy to suggest women were the primary manufacturers of pottery in agro-pastoralist societies, there is also an abundance of ethnographic cases where the opposite is the case. Furthermore, there is also substantial evidence that labor divisions exist on a shared basis with both men and women undertaking different aspects of the manufacturing process (Wright 1991). The fact that the manufacture of pottery would have been seasonally confined to a narrow window of time when food collection and production activities were at an ebb suggests that all able-bodied members of the village unit would have worked at village maintenance and craft production. Likewise, intensive activity in the winter and summer months would have required greater human input than just the men of the village. There is, thus, no reason *not* to presume that both men and women were engaged in similar horticultural and domestic tasks, including the production of pottery.

Personal and group relationships in the Ceramic Neolithic period would have been influenced by economic and subsistence factors. Interaction within and between sites is likely to have been structured around the seasonal activities of the village. Within individual villages, group maintenance would have been fundamental to the survival of the village, and seasonal subsistence tasks would have been rigidly followed to ensure continuation of the population. Competition for resources within site clusters would have governed the types of relationships that existed between villages.

Evidence for agro-pastoral practices in the Ceramic Neolithic period conform to the model established by Sherratt (1980) for restricted, selective agricultural exploitation in which early agro-pastoralists occupied only a narrow zone of maximum productivity in an essentially small scale though locally intensive systems of cultivation. While in some places this was capable of supporting nucleated communities, in others it produced a pattern of hamlets following the exploited zone (Sherratt 1980: 315).

Sherratt also maintains that such early horticultural systems would always have been spatially restricted, with locally high population levels but wide intervening, uncultivated areas and with little potential for local growth without radical changes in technique. The main pattern of growth would be first by rapid budding-off and export of population, followed by expansion into smaller and smaller patches of the appropriate high-yielding soils within the occupied area (1980: 318).

Exploitation of intensive agricultural zones in this way should exhibit features indicative of interaction and regional diversity. In the first instance, Sherratt's suggestion that population growth brought a rapid "budding-off" of population followed by expansion into smaller and smaller patches of high-yielding soils is in accordance with the pattern of settlement expansion and dislocation hypothesized by Peltenburg for the Neolithic/Chalcolithic transition. Essentially, as Neolithic populations expanded, new settlements broke-off and established themselves in areas within the optimum agricultural catchment area. Site clusters such as the northern group of Ayios Epiktitos-*Vrysi*, Klepini-*Troulli*, and other small scale settlements on the north coast, and the Kalavasos sites in the south ecotone zone attest to this pattern of intensive exploitation of the best arable land. This process could have occurred fairly rapidly; therefore, little evidence would be visible in the archaeological record for temporal divisions and discontinuities between sites.

In stylistic terms, this pattern of settlement dislocation is called stylistic drift. Binford has described stylistic drift in the following manner:

> With demographic increases daughter populations are likely to bud off from the parent communities with the result that random sampling error may arise in relation to some attribute classes, consequently covariation relationships should overlap in regular spatial patterns discernible in radiating linear distributions. (Binford 1963: 93)

"WOMAN" THE POTTER

In order to test the theories of Deetz and Longacre outlined above against evidence suggesting that women were not the sole producers of pottery in ceramic Neolithic Cyprus, some simple frequency calculations were undertaken on the design motifs of three Neolithic sites. The task was to identify whether there was significant design variation within and/or between villages and whether this variation was concomitant with the Deetz/Longacre model. This would not prove that women made pots, but it would help to identify the types of interaction taking place between sites.

Three sites were required for testing; these were located in reasonable distance from one another and produced similar types of pottery. The sites chosen were Ayios Epiktitos-*Vrysi* and Klepini-*Troulli* on the Kyrenia coast and Philia-*Drakos* A in the Morphou Bay region. The original motif frequency counts from Philia-*Drakos* A and Ayios Epiktitos-*Vrysi* were used in the analysis, and an identical classification system was applied to the total sherd assemblage from Klepini-*Troulli* stored in the Cyprus Museum. It was also necessary to compare sites that were broadly contemporaneous in order to limit temporal diversity. Therefore, only the pottery from the Middle Phase at Ayios Epiktitos-*Vrysi*,

Phase 3 at Philia-*Drakos* A, and Levels 260–40 in Pit A at Klepini-*Troulli* were included in the analysis (Clarke 1992: 9).

The two hypotheses tested were:

1) Whether Ayios Epiktitos-*Vrysi*, Klepini-*Troulli* and Philia-*Drakos* A exhibited homogeneity or diversity in ceramic designs within the individual assemblages.

2) Whether there was similarity or diversity in ceramic designs between the three assemblages.

In order to test whether the assemblages showed intra-site homogeneity or diversity, relative frequencies of different motif groups were tabulated for each site and the results compared between sites. Six of the most common motif groups were compared on the basis of their relative frequency of occurrence within individual assemblages. These were ripple patterns (Group 2), straight lines and bands (Group 14), wavy lines and bands (Group 6), reserved circles (Group 9), targets (Group 15), and concentric V's and ladders (Group 16). Sites with evenly spread frequencies of most of the six motif groups could be said to have heterogeneous assemblages because of the greater diversity in the types of motifs found. Sites with only one or two motif groups could be said to have greater homogeneity within the ceramic assemblage.

Fig.1 gives a percentage breakdown of the six major motif groups at the three sites. Klepini-*Troulli* shows the most marked homogeneity within the assemblage. The most common motif group is the broad straight band or lines and this group accounts for 66 percent of the total motif count of the Pit A sample. There is no ripple design; wavy lines are rare, but circles and targets are common. Ayios Epiktitos-*Vrysi* and Philia-*Drakos* A, on the other hand, have a much more even spread of design variation. All of the six groups are represented and both sites have a relatively even spread of at least four of the six motif groups. Where reserved circles are more common at Ayios Epiktitos-*Vrysi*, straight lines and bands are more common at Philia-*Drakos* A. Ayios Epiktitos-*Vrysi* and Philia-*Drakos* A are almost identical in the degree to which both ceramic assemblages exhibit heterogeneity. If we take all three sites together, there is greater diversity between Ayios Epiktitos-*Vrysi* and Klepini-*Troulli* (which are less than 5 km apart) than between Ayios Epiktitos-*Vrysi* and Philia-*Drakos* A.

In order to ensure that the motifs included in the sample did not determine the pattern of variation, all twenty-two motif groups as recorded by Peltenburg (1982b) at Ayios Epiktitos-*Vrysi* and Watkins (personal communication) at Philia-*Drakos* A were compared. The results are presented in fig. 2 as a percentage frequency bar graph.

In this instance, even those motifs that appeared at only a single site have been included. The graph shows a much greater degree of heterogeneity in the motif groups represented at Philia-*Drakos* A and Ayios Epiktitos-*Vrysi*, supporting the results presented in fig. 1. Although the smaller sample size from Klepini-*Troulli* has some degree of influence upon the percentage patterning, particularly with regard to the range of motifs found, it cannot explain the disproportionately high representation of one motif group over another.

How then can this be interpreted? If we consider the results above in relation to the Deetz/Longacre model, sites that show internal homogeneity should be characteristic of matrilocal residence rules and sites that show internal heterogeneity should be characteristic of patrilocal residence rules. Moreover, those sites that are geographically proximate and are in regular contact with one another should exhibit inter-site similarity, while those sites that are at some distance from one another should exhibit a greater degree of diversity. The homogeneous character of the Klepini-*Troulli* assemblage would thus argue for a matrilocal residence rule, while the heterogeneity of the Ayios Epiktitos-*Vrysi* and Philia-*Drakos* A assemblages would evince a patrilocal residence rule. However, given that Klepini-*Troulli* and Ayios Epiktitos-*Vrysi* are less than 5 km apart and, therefore, more likely to be in regular contact with each other than the more distant Philia-*Drakos* A, it is unlikely that two different forms of social patterning existed. Moreover, as we have seen above, there is greater similarity between Ayios Epiktitos-*Vrysi* and Philia-*Drakos* A than between Ayios Epiktitos-*Vrysi* and Klepini-*Troulli*.

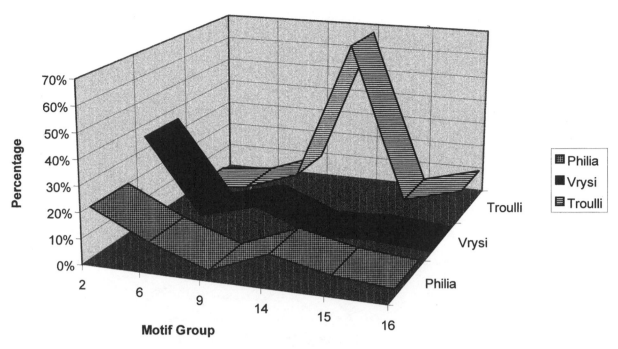

Figure 1. *Percentage frequencies of six common motif groups at Ayios Epiktitos-*Vrysi, *Philia-*Drakos A, *and Klepini-*Troulli.

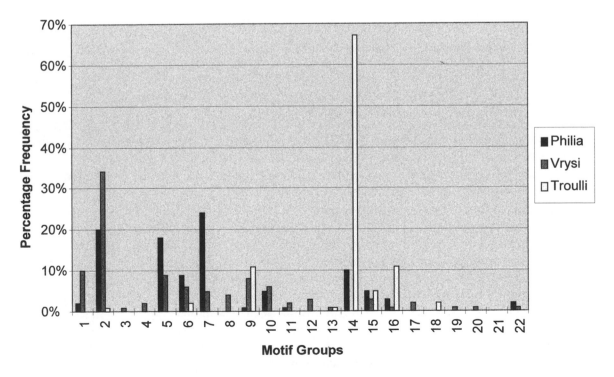

Figure 2. *Percentage frequency distribution of all twenty two-motif groups at Philia-*Drakos A, *Ayios Epiktitos-*Vrysi *and Klepini-*Troulli.

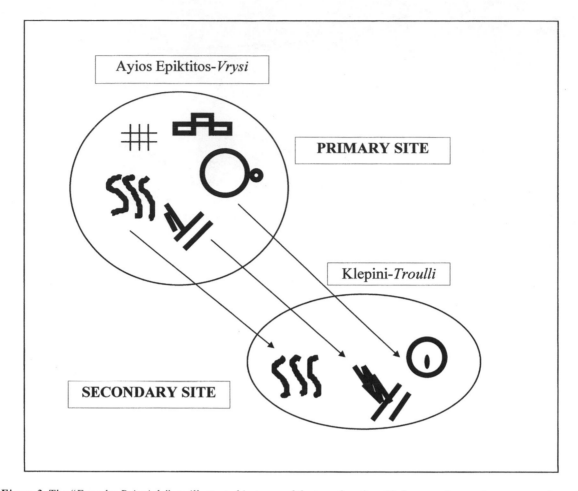

Figure 3. *The "Founder Principle" as illustrated in terms of the transfer of motifs from a primary site to a secondary site.*

TOWARDS A NEW MODEL OF DESIGN VARIABILITY

Inconsistencies between ceramic design diversity in the Cypriot Neolithic sample and the expected pattern of design diversity outlined in the Deetz/Longacre model suggests another explanation. The disparity between Klepini-*Troulli* and Ayios Epiktitos-*Vrysi* indicates that similarity in design is not necessarily governed by the degree of interaction or distance between sites. In fact, the patterns of diversity fit relatively well with the model for settlement budding-off as suggested by Sherratt. As fig. 3 visually demonstrates, pronounced heterogeneity in the Ayios Epiktitos-*Vrysi* and Philia-*Drakos* A motif repertoire would be expected if both were primary sites within their site clusters. Secondary, smaller sites might be expected to have a more homogeneous motif repertoire because their motifs would have been derived from the repertoire of the primary site; certain motifs could have been discarded, forgotten, or not painted by the artisans who moved. This model is similar in idea to the "Founder Principle," which Held has used in his argument for cultural involution at the end of the Aceramic Neolithic (1992, 1993). However, now we are dealing with evolutionary processes in technology and design rather than evolutionary processes in biogeography and human genetics. Held's theory was based upon early suggestions that a founding population would bring with it only part of the parent gene pool because it represented only a fraction of the original population. In the same way, only a fraction of the Ayios Epiktitos-*Vrysi* motif repertoire is found at Klepini-*Troulli*. It could easily be argued at this point that Held's model for cultural retardation presupposes little or no contact between the founding population and the parent population subsequent to the initial breakaway, and that no further outside influence altered the pattern of development. This is obviously not the case with sites that are no more than 3 km apart, and it has been argued that interaction did indeed take place. However, the dynamics of stylistic variation are significantly removed from that of cultural and biogeographical isolation. In the instance of Ayios Epiktitos-*Vrysi* and Klepini-*Troulli*, it is not inconceivable that the differences between pottery design were maintained for reasons other than those naturally occurring through evolutionary processes. Whether this was brought through the action of the Ayios Epiktitos-*Vrysi* inhabitants upon the smaller site of Klepini-*Troulli* or that the Klepini-*Troulli* inhabitants wished to maintain their individuality remains uncertain. The fact is that throughout the Ceramic Neolithic phase, these two sites exhibit significant design variation that is at odds with early assumptions about social interaction.

In conclusion, it is very likely that design diversity in other regions of Ceramic Neolithic Cyprus can eventually be explained in the same way. What is fairly assured is that diversity in this instance is not the result of post-marital residence patterns, that it does not follow the Deetz/Longacre model of expected design similarity based upon the ratio of female social dynamics, and that there is absolutely no evidence to suggest that women were the sole producers of pottery.

REFERENCES

Arnold, D. E.
1985   *Ceramic Theory and Cultural Process.* Cambridge: Cambridge University.
Binford, L. R.
1963   Red Ochre Caches from the Michigan Area: A Possible Case of Cultural Drift. *Southwestern Journal of Anthropology* 19: 89–108.
1996   Willow Smoke and Dogs' Tails: Hunter-Gatherer Settlement Systems and Archaeological Site Formation. Pp. 39–60 in *Contemporary Archaeology in Theory: A Reader*, eds. R. W. Preucel and I. Hodder. Oxford: Blackwell.
Bolger, D. L.
1988   *Erimi-Pamboula: a Chalcolithic Settlement in Cyprus.* BAR International Series 443. Oxford: British Archaeological Reports.
Clarke, J. T.
1992   The Ceramic Neolithic of Northern Cyprus. *Centre d'Etude Chypriotes* 17: 1–22.
1998   *Regional Variation in the Ceramics of Neolithic Cyprus: Implications for the Socio-Economic and Cultural Dynamics of a Prehistoric Island Society.* Unpublished Ph.D. Dissertation. University of Edinburgh.
Croft, P. W.
1991   Man and Beast in Chalcolithic Cyprus. *Bulletin of the American Schools of Oriental Research* 282/283: 63–79.
Davis, S. J. M.
1984   The Advent of Milk and Wool Production in Western Iran: Some Speculations. Pp. 265–78 in *Animals and Archaeology. Vol. 3: Early Herders and their Flocks*, eds. J. Clutton-Brock and C. Grigson. BAR International Series 202. Oxford: British Archaeological Reports.
Deetz, J.
1965   *The Dynamics of Stylistic Change in Arikara Ceramics.* Urbana: University of Illinois.
1968   The Inference of Residence and Descent Rules from Archaeological Data. Pp. 41–48 in *New Perspectives in Archaeology*, eds. L. R. Binford and S. R. Binford. Chicago: Aldine.
Dikaios, P.
1953   *Khirokitia.* Monograph of the Department of Antiquities of Cyprus. Oxford: Oxford University.
1961   *Sotira.* Philadelphia: University of Pennsylvania.
1962   Troulli. Pp. 63–72 in *The Swedish Cyprus Expedition. Vol. 4, 1A: The Stone Age and Early Bronze Age in Cyprus*, eds. P. Dikaios and J. Stewart. Lund: Swedish Cyprus Expedition.
Gero, J. M.
1991   Genderlithics: Women's Roles in Stone Tool Production. Pp. 163–93 in *Engendering Archaeology: Women and Prehistory*, eds. J. M. Gero and M. W. Conkey. Oxford: Blackwell.
Graves, M. W.
1991   Pottery Production and Distribution among the Kalinga: A Study of Household and Regional Organization and Differentiation. Pp. 112–43 in *Ceramic Ethnoarchaeology*, ed. W. A. Longacre. Tucson: University of Arizona.
Hastorf, C. A.
1991   Gender, Space and Food in Prehistory. Pp. 132–59 in *Engendering Archaeology: Women and Prehistory*, eds. J. M. Gero and M. W. Conkey. Oxford: Blackwell.
Held, S. O.
1992   Colonization and Extinction on Early Prehistoric Cyprus. Pp. 104–64 in *Acta Cypria: Acts of an International Congress on Cypriote Archaeology,* Part 2, ed. P. Åström. Studies in Mediterranean Archaeology Pocket-book 117. Jonsered: Åströms.
1993   Insularity as a Modifier of Cultural Change: The Case of Prehistoric Cyprus. *Bulletin of the American Schools of Oriental Research* 292: 25–33.
Hill, J. N.
1968   Broken K Pueblo: Patterns of Form and Function. Pp. 103–42 in *New Perspectives in Archeology*, eds. S. R. Binford and L. R. Binford. Chicago: Aldine.

1970   *Broken K Pueblo: Prehistoric Social Organization in the American Southwest.* University of Arizona, Anthropological Papers 18. Tucson: University of Arizona.

Hodder, I.
1978   The Maintenance of Group Identities in the Baringo District, Western Kenya. Pp. 47–73 in *Social Organization and Settlement: Contributions from Anthropology, Archaeology and Geography*, eds. D. Green et al. BAR International Series (Suppl.) 47. Oxford: British Archaeological Reports.
1979   Economic and Social Stress and Material Culture Patterning. *American Antiquity* 44: 446–54.

Kyllo, M.
1982   The Botanical Remains. Pp. 90–95 in *Vrysi: A Subterranean Settlement in Cyprus: Excavations at Prehistoric Ayios Epikitito-Vrysi, 1969–1973*, ed. E. J. Peltenburg. Warminster: Aris and Phillips.

Legge, A. J
1982   The Vertebrate Fauna. Pp. 76–90 in *Vrysi: a Subterranean Settlement in Cyprus: Excavations at Prehistoric Ayios Epikitito-Vrysi, 1969–1973*, ed. E. J. Peltenburg. Warminster: Aris and Phillips.

London, G. A.
1987   Cypriote Potters: Past and Present. *Report of the Department of Antiquities of Cyprus*: 319–22.

London, G. A.; Egoumenidou, F.; and Karageorghis, V.
1990   *Traditional Pottery in Cyprus.* Mainz: von Zabern.

Longacre, W. A.
1968   Aspects of Prehistoric Society in East-Central Arizona. Pp. 89–102 in *New Perspectives in Archaeology*, eds. L. R. Binford and S. R. Binford. Chicago: Aldine.
1970   *Archaeology as Anthropology: A Case Study.* University of Arizona, Anthropological Papers 17. Tucson: University of Arizona.
1981   Kalinga Pottery: An Ethnoarchaeological Study. Pp. 49–66 in *Pattern of the Past*, ed. I. Hodder. New York: Cambridge University.
1991   Sources of Ceramic Variability among the Kalinga of Northern Luzon. Pp. 95–111 in *Ceramic Ethnoarchaeology*, ed. W. A. Longacre. Tucson: University of Arizona.

Peltenburg, E. J.
1975   Ayios Epiktitos-*Vrysi*: Preliminary Results of the 1969–1973 Excavations at a Neolithic Coastal Settlement in Cyprus. *Proceedings of the Prehistoric Society* 41: 17–45.
1978   The Sotira Culture: Regional Diversity and Cultural Unity in Late Neolithic Cyprus. *Levant* 10: 55–74.
1982a   *Recent Developments in the Later Prehistory of Cyprus.* Studies in Mediterranean Archaeology Pocketbook 16. Göteborg: Åströms.
1982b   *Vrysi: A Subterranian Settlement in Cyprus: Excavations at Prehistoric Ayios Epikitito Vrysi, 1969–1973.* Warminster: Aris and Phillips.
1985   Pattern and Purpose in the Prehistoric Cypriot Village of Ayios Epiktitos-*Vrysi.* Pp. 46–64 in *Chypre, La vie quotidienne de l'antiquité à nos jours*, ed. Musée de l'Homme. Paris: Musée de l'Homme.
1993   Settlement Discontinuity and Resistance to Complexity in Cyprus, ca. 4500–2500 B.C.E. *Bulletin of the American Schools of Oriental Research* 292: 9–23.

Plog, S.
1978   Social Interaction and Stylistic Similarity: A Re-analysis. Pp. 143–82 in *Advances in Archaeological Method and Theory* 1, ed. M. Schiffer. New York: Academic.
1980   *Stylistic Analysis.* Cambridge: Cambridge University.

Sherratt, A.
1980   Water, Soil and Seasonality in Early Cereal Cultivation. *World Archaeology* 11, 3: 313–30.

Whallon, R.
1968   Investigations of Late Prehistoric Social Organisation in New York State. Pp. 223–44 in *New Perspectives in Archaeology*, eds. L. R. Binford and S. R. Binford. Chicago: Aldine.

Wright, R. P.
1991   Women's Labor and Pottery Production in Prehistory. Pp. 194–223 in *Engendering Archaeology: Women and Prehistory*, eds. J. M. Gero and M. W. Conkey. Oxford: Blackwell.

WOMEN POTTERS AND CRAFT SPECIALIZATION IN A PRE-MARKET CYPRIOT ECONOMY

GLORIA ANNE LONDON

Burke Museum
Seattle, WA
galondon@earthlink.net

The origins of pottery craft specialization are assessed in terms of why people might choose to specialize in a high-risk low-return seasonal industry. Reconstruction of the production technique is a necessary component to understand the allocation of labor and overall organization of the industry. Discussion of the role women potters played in prehistoric Cyprus in both pre-market and complex societies follows. Craft specialization in pottery appears in neighboring countries prior to the 2nd millennium B.C.E. and it probably did in Cyprus as well.

It has long been assumed that pottery manufacture was one of many innovations occurring in the Neolithic period, along with the domestication of plants and animals and the emergence of sedentism. It was also thought that initially pottery was made in each Old World Neolithic household by domestic potters until a subsequent stage when craft specialization evolved in association with market economies in "complex societies." The invention of pottery and the concept of craft specialization are subjects worthy of reevaluation, especially in terms of the role of women during the pre-market era. The term "pre-market" refers to the lack of a market as the driving force of the economy rather than the absence of sites serving as periodic market places. The role of women in pottery manufacture and the organization of the industry primarily during the 3rd and 2nd millennia pre-market economy are the subjects discussed here.

THE EARLIEST APPEARANCE OF POTTERY

Recent research demonstrates that the link between ceramics, sedentism and agriculture is tenuous at best. In cultures worldwide, the earliest pottery is found in association with water-side economies of non-sedentary people who continue to gather foods rather than grow them. This is true for the 9th century B.C.E. Jomon culture of Japan (Aikens 1995: 19), for Egypt (Close 1995: 28), and for the Sudan (Haaland 1997; Haaland and Magid 1995). The earliest pottery in the American southwest is likewise not associated with early agriculture since the first known pots date a millennium after the adoption of maize and squash (Crown and Wills 1995: 242). Along the coastal strip of the Levant, submerged Neolithic sites (Galili and Nir 1993; Nir 1997) might have similar evidence. The same holds for Cyprus.

In *The Emergence of Pottery* (Barnett and Hoopes 1995), most contributors agree that women were involved with the transformation of clay into containers from the very beginning due primarily to the role of women in gathering foods. Murdock and Provost demonstrate cross-culturally that it is women who gather wild plants, a necessary element of the diet, both in foraging societies and mixed economies (1973). In most societies, women are responsible for the various activities associated with vegetal food preparation, processing, and cooking. Clay pots enabled cooking the foods, such as seeds and shellfish, gathered by women. In cooked form, some of the foods became more palatable, more digestible, softer, less toxic (e.g., barley) and suitable for all, including babies. Cooking meat rendered fat from the bones. Fibers could be removed as a result of cooking. Grains and legumes could be fermented in clay pots. Seeds harvested could be stored in water-tight clay pots that would prevent germination during storage. Neither pests nor rodents could penetrate a clay pot in contrast to less satisfactory permeable and perishable pits and baskets. The cultigens could eventually enhance the diets of women and children in particular. Speth reports that women typically receive lower quantities and less desirable parts of animal meat among so-called egalitarian foraging communities (1990). As a consequence, Crown and Wills infer that cooking foods led to the enrichment of the diet for women and children since in most societies women cook food as well as care for their young with the help of female members of the extended family (1995: 250). Women consequently distribute cooked food to children and other females to improve their caloric intake, unlike animals caught and distributed by men.

In assessing recent research on the link between ceramics and food preparation, Longacre concludes that women were instrumental in the invention of pottery, one of the few technologies women ever controlled (1995: 278–79). This is not to exclude men entirely, but simply to note a predominance of women in the manufacture of clay containers since they had the most to gain from their use. The employment of clay containers in association with food, including processing, fermenting, storing, and cooking, leads to the conclusion that women were also involved in the transformation of wild plants into cultigens. The association between women and the gathering and preparing of grains, fruits, legumes, etc. places females in the context of converting wild plants into edible foods, which account for 60 to 90 percent of the normal diet. This vital work contrasts with an earlier idea that women were involved with the domestication of plants as a result of tending shrines of the Mother Goddess in Cyprus as noted by Dawson in 1928 (quoted in Stone 1976: 18).

CRAFT SPECIALIZATION IN THE MANUFACTURE OF POTTERY

Craft specialization, a term normally juxtaposed with complex societies, also deserves reassessment. It was Childe who articulated the idea that one aspect of a complex society is the generation and distribution of surplus foodstuffs to crafts people and others whose involvement with religious, political, and social affairs prevents them from producing their own food (1942: 241). Craft specialization is generally considered to belong to the broad spectrum of activities characteristic of a controlled, formal, organized economic and political system of both state and non-state societies. In this sense, specialization, like the earliest use of pottery, has been understood as one element of a larger array of features typical of certain levels of society. Rather than equate specialized production to a specific level of social complexity, it is becoming clearer that economic specialization can be associated with a wide range of levels of complexity (Clark and Parry 1990). For pottery, Rice notes that specialization can manifest itself at different levels of sociopolitical complexity and does not imply intensification of production (1996: 179), i.e., greater investment of labor and resources or the ratio effects of scale, efficiency and mass production. Specialization need not result in intensification since specialization and standardization of pottery wares are distinct processes. The social and behavioral sources of variability of wares produced by craft specialists result from the structure of the labor force and production techniques (Hardin 1991; London 1991b; and Longacre 1991).

Craft specialists normally fabricate artifacts of metal, stone (including semi-precious minerals and rocks), bone, cloth, and clay as both utilitarian and luxury goods. Most products (seals, cult objects, mirrors, jewelry, figurines, etc.) are costly, prestige, luxury items, often small in size and worthy of trade on the international market. Usually the raw material itself is valuable. Pottery alone exhibits none of these features. No one has ever amassed a fortune making pottery. Selling (rather than making) pottery was possibly more rewarding, but it was not without risks. Ceramic containers were always of low value and cost, especially the utilitarian forms used in daily life. Even red Attic wares were never considered expensive, except when found far from their place of manufacture (Pucci 1983: 110). Throughout the Roman period, pottery was never a major element of the ancient economy, and when it was traded long-distance, it was transported along with foodstuffs packed between the amphorae (Pucci 1983: 109; 111–12). Copper, in contrast, starts with a valued raw material found in limited distribution that can be repeatedly smelted and melted until the desired results are achieved. Clay pots that underfire in the kiln can be refired, but nothing helps a cracked pot.

Pottery production requires a low initial investment if potters dig their own clay from the ground, find their own fuel and make whatever tools they use. It is dirty work and risky. Pots break even before they are fired. Damp weather can cause them to collapse, and the activities of children and pets can be harmful. Pots crack in the firing and can be damaged during kiln unloading or in transporting to customers. Given its fragility and low value, pottery was normally not a major trade item unless it held something of value. Some pots may have been traded for their attractively decorated surfaces, such as the Cypriot White Slip wares which were sent abroad, especially to the Levant where the poor clays do not favor pottery painting. Therefore, pottery production falls outside the normal parameters or qualifiers for an export item worthy of controlled production.

Why then specialize in pottery production? Ceramic containers were a necessary part of the ancient household in that they were multi-functional, water-tight, pest resistant, non-perishable, reusable containers in which a wide variety of foods could be processed, fermented, detoxified, and stored. Cemeteries of all periods reveal the need for pottery as funerary objects. These factors made pottery a necessity, but a risky affair with low economic returns. Specialization in pottery was not a choice, but a necessity for some. The low status of potters at times results from undertaking hard, dirty, unpredictable, low paying work others would prefer to avoid. Rather than deliberately choosing to specialize in pottery, people might do so on account of a lack of other resources, such as land on which to grow food, or a husband to work the fields. In situations of dire stress, women working in their own homes might specialize in pottery, something that everyone needs but that they might not want to make. It is not only dirty, risky work, it is also time-consuming due to the preparation of the clay, shaping the pots, gathering of the wood, and constructing a kiln if necessary. Given the nature of pottery manufacture, it is a task people avoid, if possible. Although the raw materials are of relatively low cost, so is the value of the finished products, despite the enormous risks. Unfired pots are always at risk and can easily be damaged by animals, children, or water. Pots can misfire or break if dropped at any time.

In two geographically distant communities of craft specialists, male potters are known to have left the ceramics industry periodically and permanently once they found more lucrative employment. Both in Kornos, Cyprus and in the Filipino town of Gubat, men could earn more money as day laborers or factory workers than as potters. The Paradijon potters belong to one of two landless groups of people in Gubat. To support themselves, the second group turned to the sea to fish, thereby using another resource that is free and available for the taking, yet seasonal and not without risk. As such it is comparable to clay. In Gubat, the potters, in fact, paid a small percentage of their wares to the landowner from whose land the clay was taken, but there were no other costs (London 1991b: 187). It is feasible that in antiquity landless people would similarly exploit low cost raw materials to engage in an activity that the majority of the population prefers to avoid due to the high risk and low return. The perception of pottery making as a low status occupation underscores the undesirability of the work.

The alternative to craft specialization is household domestic production, described as "an ideal type, and is probably rare or non-existent" (Pool 1992: 283). Although part of the hypothetical reconstruction of the ancient ceramic industry, it finds few parallels ethnographically. Even if pottery production can be characterized as "domestic," i.e., made and used within the household, there is normally some gift-giving and at times sales or barter, as among the Kalinga of Luzon Island in the Philippines (Graves 1991; Longacre 1991: 109). Allen characterizes Native American Iroquois pottery as household production (1992: 134). Women in each household make and use their own pottery. But if households consist of a number of families, household production involves some specialization. One woman might produce for the entire household or, within a given village, just a few women might produce pots for everyone (Allen 1992: 142). There are various possibilities rather than a strict definition of domestic versus specialists and within each category there are distinctions. Intensified domestic production borders on craft specialization. Specialized craft potters can work in the confines of their homes and courtyards, in a separate workspace, or in factories and still fall under the general rubric of specialized production although the scale of production is not large. All three can co-exist and might be visible archaeologically in the variety of wares found at most archaeological sites.

POTTERY IN THE ARCHAEOLOGICAL RECORD

As the most malleable of all ancient materials, clay objects embody the work of individual crafts people to a greater extent than stone, metal, bone, or wood. Archaeologists rely on changes in clay artifacts to establish relative chronologies on account of the relatively rapid changes in vessel morphology and surface treatment and the desire for regional conformity of material culture within cultural boundaries for each archaeological period. Modifications in form and finish are due to frequent use of pottery in daily life, the ease with which it breaks, and the relative low cost of replacing damaged pieces. There is an anomaly, however, in that potters are considered to have been conservative in terms of technology and hesitant to change, yet it is new vessel shapes and decoration that signal short term changes from one archaeological period to the next. In the search for spatial and temporal discontinuity between each period, some regional differences have been defined, but there is less acknowledgment of the more subtle differences on the next smaller level: identification of wares made in contemporaneous yet distinct workshops or households within each region. Differences representing the individuality of potters and workshops can be detected in virtually all aspects of the manufacturing technique—clays, firing, overall vessel proportions, and surface treatment decoration. On the broad regional level, cultural boundaries and ideologies mitigate stylistic change. In contrast, there is a tendency toward individuality and non-conformity at the level of the workshop or specific potter, since each potter is different, because the pots are handmade, and due to what Wright describes as the "flexibility of cultural rules" (1986: 18).

Although archaeologists can date pottery to specific archaeological periods, few conclude that similar looking pottery came from the same workshop unless a pot is signed by the potter, a situation that does not normally prevail for the pre-Hellenistic world. In contrast, Hennessey (1973) and Herscher (1972, 1973, 1991) have used stylistic and morphological features to identify the work of individual potters for Middle Bronze Age pottery in Cyprus. The significance of the subtle differences discernible at the macroscopic level and/or with the aid of precise measurements, differentiates the work of individual potters and/or workshops. Initially archaeologists searched for similarities between pottery excavated at different sites. Building on that research, current emphasis can shift to the more subtle differences in ceramics and their implications in terms of the organization of the ancient pottery industry, the allocation of the labor force, and the potters themselves. Understanding and describing manufacturing techniques directs attention to labor organization, as seen in the work of Stewart (1962), Frankel (1974, 1981, 1988), Herscher (1972, 1973), Herscher and Fox (1993), Merrillees (1979), and Knapp (1986, 1990, 1992, 1993).

A focus on labor organization coincides with an emphasis on investigating individuals in ancient societies. Material culture makes ancient history more pluralistic than epigraphic sources, since with few exceptions mundane activities are rarely the subject of texts or artwork, regardless of whether men or women are involved. Of all the names of painters and potters written on pottery of the Classical period, none appear in Classical literary sources (Austin and Vidal-Naqet 1977: 115). Since the work of crafts people was hardly a subject considered appropriate for literature, they are best represented by their craft as long as they worked in a non-organic medium. Mesopotamian texts dealing with the state, palatial, and well-organized merchant traders who controlled industries are exceptions (Renger 1984). Given that pottery is indestructible, pots, tool assemblages, permanent equipment, and work spaces afford the opportunity to investigate the organization of the industry based on the archaeological remains.

THE RESIDUES OF POTTERY PRODUCTION

Pottery Production Locations

Ideally, production locations reveal evidence of the social context of pottery manufacture, the scale of the industry, and the degree of specialization if preservation is good. Yet production sites are rare, a fact often attributed to their placement outside or on the boundaries of habitation areas (Wood 1990: 33; Knapp 1989: 137). Ethnoarchaeological fieldwork, however, provides ample evidence of craft specialists who produce market oriented wares in the courtyards of their homes (London 1989b: 224–25), and the same may have prevailed in antiquity. Three separate specialized work spaces are known in Cyprus. They include LC II Atheniou (Dothan and Ben-Tor 1983), 14th century Sanidha (Todd, Hadjicosti, et al. 1991; Todd et al. 1992), a workshop that appears to be independent of any settlement (Herscher 1991: 61), and Morphou-*Toumba tou Skourou*, where deposits imply a production work space (Vermeule and Wolsky 1990).

Tosi (1984: 26) has stated that since pottery production involves fixed facilities, such as kilns, one should find archaeological remains of the industry in the absence of deliberate reuse of the materials. However, in Cyprus (London 1989a: 75) and Egypt (Nicholson and Patterson 1985), defunct kilns are dismantled to reuse the space and bricks. Wasters are ground into grog for use in the construction industry, while larger sherds provide a hint of color in traditional stone buildings (London 1989b: 221). For the Cypriot rural ceramics industry, the low rate of loss due to misfires also accounts for a dearth of sherds (London 1989a: 76).

Production locations elsewhere occur both in and outside settlements. In Athens, the potters' quarter of the Kerameikos extends inside and outside the city walls (Wisseman 1994: 25). At Sarepta in Lebanon, an industrial quarter existed from the LB II through the Persian period (Anderson 1987; 1989: 197). Earlier production locations include those of the Turanian basin, straddling Iran and India where Bronze Age pottery was made both within and beyond the settlement areas (Tosi 1984: 29). In Baluchistan, at the 2nd millennium B.C.E. site of Mehrgarh, kilns and workspaces are associated with dwellings (Wright 1991: 210–11). At Tell el-Hayyat in the Jordan Valley, a MB II potter's kiln has been excavated within the village rather than outside (Falconer and Magness-Gardiner 1984; Magness-Gardiner and Falconer 1994).

Ethnoarchaeological evidence provides case studies of craft specialists who work in close proximity to houses as in Cyprus (London 1989a: 73; London, Egoumenidou, and Karageorghis 1989: 63) and Mexico (Stark 1984: 6). In Cyprus, traditional craft specialists work within their courtyards in Ayios Dhimitrios (Marathasa), Kaminaria, and Kornos and in a separate workspace created by the Kornos Pottery Cooperative (London 1989a; London, Egoumenidou, and Karageorghis 1989). Modern factories producing molded and wheel-thrown table wares co-exist nearby close to and within city limits.

Tools, Raw Materials, and Pottery

Non-stationary equipment consisting of organic, reused, worn artifacts leaves no trace. Even durable pieces of equipment are not normally found where they were used due to the seasonality of the industry and the multi-functional use of space in the household setting. Nor are raw materials stored from year to year among traditional craft specialists worldwide.

At most ancient sites, a diversity of wares indicates the work of different potters, each working with a specific clay to produce a variety of containers. Potters normally learn to work with one type of clay. Good clay for one potter is bad clay for anyone else who does not know how to use it. Potters who produce large containers from heavily tempered clays were probably not the same people who made small shapes fabricated from finer clays. This implies multiple co-existing workshops, perhaps organized differently in terms of size, location, and personnel, and including men, women and children. One useful way to analyze organization of the industry is to assess the production steps in pottery making.

INTERRUPTED TECHNIQUE OF MANUFACTURE

It is often assumed that until pottery was thrown on a wheel, pottery manufacture was trivial and easy. The oversimplification of hand made versus wheel made pottery minimizes interest in those who did the work, how they did it, or how they were organized. There are perhaps ten ways to produce a pot, and within each technique there are variations. Potters today, both modern and traditional, use the same techniques as in the past, and although the times, aesthetics, and economy have changed, the clay remains the same. The ethnoarchaeological examples referred to most often here deal with craft specialists who produce market-oriented utilitarian wares seasonally in Cyprus (London 1986; 1987a; 1987b; 1989a; 1989b; 1991a; and London, Egoumenidou, and Karageorghis 1989), Jordan (London and Sinclair 1991) and the Philippines (London 1985; 1991b). The cross-cultural studies of potters in three different countries who use locally available raw materials to produce shapes comparable in function to ancient pottery offer a glimpse of craft specialists who work under some of the same constraints as their ancient counterparts.

Whether production occurs in individual homes, workshops or factories, it often involves an interrupted technique of manufacture. This method breaks down the stages of work and responsibilities while allowing, enabling, and encouraging the participation of non-professional potters. Normally, after each stage of working the wet clay, there is an obligatory drying period before the next stage can be rendered. As a result, potters work on many pots at any given time as they wait for others to dry. Non-professionals perform secondary tasks not requiring the skills of trained potters, such as preparing clay, adding accessory pieces, cutting holes into flower pots, incense burners, stoves, etc., and decorating surfaces.

PERSONNEL AND ALLOCATION OF LABOR

In terms of personnel, the relevant issues include number and gender of potters and precisely who qualifies as a potter. The latter is significant since pottery production entails clay procurement, clay processing (cleaning, adding or extracting non-plastics etc., mixing with water and kneading), shaping the pot, drying, decorating, firing, and distribution of the finished product. As noted above, shaping the pot can be further broken down to allow the participation of more than one hand on a pot. Work can stop on a pot that can be covered or wrapped until the next day. However, there are times when the clay is too dry to wait or a firing must occur to meet an order. In such instances, every member of the household is called to help with the finishing touches especially surface treatment.

It is possible to determine those aspects of pottery manufacture plausibly rendered by the unskilled learners, apprentices, non-potters or members of the extended family. To do so requires distinguishing between primary (shaping and thinning) and secondary forming and finishing work, such as adding accessories and decoration although at times the surface treatment, especially burnishing, is part of the primary forming work (Franken 1973; Franken and London 1995). Handles that stand askew on carefully shaped pottery (in contrast to well attached, carefully placed handles of even thickness) signal the hand sof unskilled workers. Non-professionals are essential to a production line manufacture, but they are not potters. Whereas professional potters can perform the work of their assistants, the latter are not qualified to render the primary forming work of the potter. The assistants who work irregularly are critical to the viability of the industry in that they free the potters to concentrate on the primary forming work. Their participation minimizes labor costs.

Number of Potters

How many potters would there have been any given time in prehistoric Cyprus? Would it have been necessary, practical, or beneficial to have pottery made in each household or in each village? For 5th century B.C.E. Athens, there were only 200–300 potters, pot painters, and assistants at any one time (Webster 1972). If craft specialists were operative in ancient Cyprus, it is likely that pottery was not made in each village or town but was one of the artifacts bartered for other essential commodities, especially foodstuffs. The degree of ecological diversity of Cyprus encourages and demands trade between the highlands, foothills, plains and coastal area. Bolger comments on the potential impact of geography on the history and settlement patterns of Cyprus (1989). Given the diversity of the flora, fauna, and landscape, people might have moved within the island not only to collect copper, but also to benefit from the food sources restricted to the higher elevations as well as the cooler summer temperatures of the foothills and mountains. Periodic inter-regional fairs would have afforded the opportunity to exchange and barter pots for foodstuffs to store over the winter months, just as they did in the late 20th century. Until the mid-20th century, Kornos potters traveled from their lowland village up to the foothills for part of the summer where they made pottery to be bartered for winter food supplies. Families returned annually to the same village. At times a Kornos family would settle in the foothills, as at Klirou where they could make pottery from local clays until the potter died (Hampe and Winter 1962: 79; London 1989a: 69).

Potter's Gender

There is no way to determine from a pot if a male or female potter made it. Depictions of people making pots include men and women (London 1987a: 320; Walz 1985); however, the overall number of examples throughout the Middle East and Mediterranean is paltry, as are illustrations of washing clothes, weaving, sewing, or other activities often associated with women's work. Pottery making, if viewed as a cottage industry carried out in the home during the dry season, becomes simply another facet of women's seasonal work, much like preparing foods for the winter. Hankey has suggested, on the basis of contemporary examples, that Late Cypriot potters could have been women who produced for a clientele beyond their immediate community (1983: 171). Cross-cultural ethnographic studies demonstrate that both men and women make pottery, but women predominate when it is carried out in the household workspace (Murdock and Provost 1973: 206). Consequently, home-based production locations in antiquity are likely to have involved women. In the absence of identifiable pottery production locations for prehistoric Cyprus, it is probable that women potters worked in their household courtyards. Due to the seasonal nature of pottery production, unless a site was destroyed during the summer, nothing would remain *in situ*. This implies that either all sites were abandoned or destroyed during the winter and/or that pottery production was made in a limited number of households. Had it been a regular activity practiced in each house, one would expect something to remain.

EVIDENCE OF CRAFT SPECIALIZATION IN PREHISTORIC CYPRUS

Chalcolithic Period

The Chalcolithic monochromes of western Cyprus display a certain morphological similarity despite an army of names referring to different surface treatments, such as Glossy Burnished, Red Monochrome Painted and Black Topped (Peltenburg 1991: 13). Surfaces are greatly dependent on firing: burnished treatment if overfired will lack a sheen; an overly hot fire can cause paint to drip, be masked by the slip, or become mottled (Franken and London 1995: 217–18). Perhaps despite the apparent variety of surface finishes, the vessel morphology betrays some element of craft specialization. The results of the replication work for Lemba Chalcolithic wares can address this issue (Shiels 1988).

Early and Middle Cypriot Bronze Age

Early Cypriot Red Polished (Philia) pottery found island-wide displays uniformity of fabric for pots found in all regions of the country (Bolger 1991: 34). This might imply improved pyrotechnology as well as a more limited number of production locations than for the Late Chalcolithic given the decreased variation in fabric. Ware categories for the Kaminoudhia material were collapsed by Swiny (1991: 39), who raises the issue of firing as a factor contributing to the superficial variation in the sherds, which could belong to a single ware. Refiring tests in which all sherds are brought up to the same temperature might cause the "different fabrics" and finishes to suddenly look alike.

Improved pyrotechnology is implied by Frankel's (1994) study of surface color of Red Polished wares in which he demonstrates that there is no significant difference between the colors of pottery from three sites. He attributes this to a technology common to all potters and the ability to select and fire raw materials to achieve a desired effect. It is plausible that either fewer centers of production were involved than in the previous period or there was a different organization of industry that included specialists who traded their wares beyond the region as well as potters who continued to produce for a more localized clientele. The impetus to trade outside to adjacent areas derives from the uneven distribution of resources throughout the island. The distribution of Philia Ware, along the coast, along rivers in the northwest, and the Troodos Mountain periphery, could reflect interaction among people in diverse environmental settings. Trade in closed vessels of Brown Polished (EC III–MC I) and Red Polished III wares, possibly forerunners of the LC opium exchange (Herscher 1991: 48), imply specialist production for intra-island trading. Middle Bronze Age trade to the Levant (Amiran 1969: 121) and Egypt (Merrillees 1968) involving substances contained in clay pots presumably required a regularized, reliable source of pottery, most likely the work of craft specialists.

Evidence that potters selected specific clay mixtures to create particular vessel types has been demonstrated for the Alambra Red Polished pottery (Barlow and Idziak 1989). At different contemporaneous sites, potters purposefully chose a non-calcareous clay to shape cooking pots, a calcareous clay for a variety of forms, and a mixture of the two clays for jugs (Barlow 1991). The latter clay suits closed containers since it cleans water by absorbing the carbonates, which results in the white deposit on vessel interiors. Large bowls were made of the non-calcareous clay (Barlow 1991: 55). Clear association between vessel type and clay recipe implies craft specialization rather than domestic production.

For the Middle Cypriot Red Polished and White Painted wares, Frankel (1974) has recorded stylistic similarities among nearby sites but a drop off in similarities as distance increases. This could indicate that pottery was made by specialists at each site or at a single site belonging to a cluster or region. In the first scenario, the bulk of pottery at any single site would come from the potter(s) producing at the site, whereas exchange due to periodic barter would introduce pottery from nearby villages into each site of the region. Common to all the pots would be the overall shape that results from a specific fabrication process while surface treatment and nuances in the manufacturing techniques would show greater variation. In other words, vessel morphology follows the well-established manufacturing technique whereas surface treatment is susceptible to individual manipulation.

In his assessment of Middle Cypriot wares, Frankel equates craft specialization with a stratified society and complex structure as opposed to a "simpler society" in which kinship ties rather than institutional associations and relationships prevail (1988: 32). Although Frankel favors domestic household production, his assertion that eastern White Painted ware jugs exhibit great similarity and simplicity of decoration "perhaps indicative of a greater degree of mass production" (Frankel 1988: 44) contradicts domestic production unless one favors a mix of specialist and domestic potters. Yet Frankel has preferred household production due to the lack of standardization (Frankel 1988: 29; 50; Frankel and Webb 1996: 111). This criterion, however, is not an ideal measure of craft specialization (London 1991b). Standardization within vessel size, shape and surface does not consider the behavioral and social sources of variation in pottery produced in an interrupted technique by craft specialists who allocate non-essential work to non-potters. Among craft specialists, especially those dealing with a distant or foreign clientele as in the Late Cypriot Age, it is the non-professionals who perform the secondary tasks like painting and other surface treatments on which archaeologists rely to construct ceramic typologies, in addition to considerations of shape and fabric. Rather than focus on the stylistic attributes, more attention to the manufacturing technique both the primary and secondary work, would help better to understand the allocation of the labor force involved with pottery production and account for variation in the finish.

Late Cypriot Bronze Age

Cypriot White Painted ware found in the Levant provides an interesting case study of diversity within a single ware type and the work of craft specialists (London 1986: 511). Characteristic of Cypriot exports found in the Levant and Egypt are busy painted patterns belonging to the Pendant Line Style, Cross Line Style and White Painted V Style. A single exception is one example of a White Painted Fine Line vessel (Maguire 1991: 64). The latter pots are well made and decorated with fine, clean patterns carefully painted and attributable to the work of a professional. Known examples are found throughout Cyprus rather than abroad (Maguire 1991: 61). In contrast, the Pendant and Cross Line Styles, characterized by busy repetitive patterns accomplished with short strokes or a few wide bands, are regional styles that predominate on exported wares. These reveal the work of non-specialists who painted pots made by professional potters for international trade. Less decoration does not necessarily mean less time-consuming or cost-efficient efforts; on the contrary, the opposite can be true. Multiple short strokes of a busy, poorly rendered pattern become cost-effective if painted by a non-potter who enables the professional potter to carry on with the essential primary forming work (London 1986: 511). The variety of White Painted V wares and the differential distribution within Cyprus (north, south, and central) and abroad imply that there were separate, regional, contemporaneous styles in use to supply different markets (Maguire 1991: 61, 64).

In an assessment of "handmade" and "wheelmade" Late Cypriot Plain White wares, Keswani measured overall vessel proportions to investigate the degree of standardization found in funerary wares with the aim of addressing organization of the industry (1991). She concludes that since certain morphological types display greater standardization than others, there were multiple workshops in operation (1991: 211). In contrast, variation in specific types can be attributed to the presence of non-professionals in the same workshop of professional potters, especially if the pots were assembled in pieces in an interrupted technique of manufacture. For kraters, the reduced standardization could result from their larger size and shape since big shapes display more variation than smaller pieces (Longacre, Kvamme, and Kobayashi 1988: 107). Open forms like kraters are easier to construct than closed forms and could have been made by less skilled workers. Overall, the relative absence of diversity within the

800 Enkomi tomb pots implies the work of craft specialists. Keswani proposes that while certain workshops at Enkomi and Angastina produced those wares, other potters, perhaps itinerants, continued to produce coarser, utilitarian jugs, bowls, basins, and storage vessels implying a multi-facetted ceramics industry (1991: 116).

The concept that craft specialists might have supplied ancient Cypriots with pottery in the Chalcolithic, Early Cypriot and Middle Cypriot periods might seem daunting, but such potters would not be the earliest craft specialists. Vitelli (1993; 1995: 60) presents data from Franchthi cave for Neolithic Greek pottery craft specialists. Early Minoan pottery of the pre-palatial era in Crete is considered another example (Day and Wilson 1996). Neolithic pottery from Jericho exhibits a wealth of potting knowledge including the use of grog to temper pottery (the best tempering agent to this day), kiln firing attaining at least 800 degrees C for one hour, fine slip application and burnishing (Homès-Fredericq and Franken 1986: 51–53). The quality of fine burnished wares, in contrast to the coarser wares at Jericho, suggests craft specialization. As a result, it would be exceptional if specialization in pottery production did not appear prior to the Late Cypriot Bronze Age.

Certain White Painted V wares were designed with export to the Levant and Egypt in mind while others were made for the more demanding Cypriot market. Local clientele are more vocal than a distant unseen clientele. The international arena created a foreign market for pottery traded for its aesthetic value and as a container for precious items in the cargo of ships carrying more valuable commodities. With the surge in demand for Cypriot painted pottery, the response was specialized production sites, away from habitation sites and the household courtyard, and perhaps an increase in male participation. To create a more cost-efficient production line, separate workshops and factories arose employing a larger number of people to shape and decorate the hand built wares. Concentration of the work under one roof, preferably adjacent to the clay source, enabled better control over production costs. Craft specialists produced handmade pottery for export and trade. Only one other strategy could enhance production—the adoption of a fast wheel to throw the shapes. The sole advantage of wheel thrown pottery is the ability to create inexpensive wares faster than by hand. This technological change, which was soon to follow, requires a large market exemplified by the distribution of Cypro-Geometric pottery throughout the Levant.

CONCLUSION

Women potters controlled the ceramics industry from its inception, given their roles related to food gathering, plant domestication, vegetal food cooking, processing, preserving, and caring for their families. The need to store foods was an important factor in the need for clay pots. Given the association between women and vegetal food and in the absence of distinct pottery production locations outside habitation areas, it can be inferred that women made pottery in their homes for use by their families and at times for sale. There is no reason to exclude men as potters. Nor does the evidence suggest that each Chalcolithic, Early or Middle Cypriot Age household made the pottery it used. Once Cyprus entered the Middle Bronze Age international market, the increased need for pottery forced trades people to consider faster ways to produce painted pottery during the short dry season. New strategies include constructing separate workspaces at some distance from habitation sites and eventually the production of wheel thrown wares. Distant markets of voiceless clientele allowed shortcuts in the work, especially in the surface treatment, which increasingly became the task of non-professionals. Whether or not the move to separate workspaces was accompanied by a decrease in the number of women involved in the industry is unclear. Perhaps the role of women changed, while some remained potters and others became pottery painters. Given the increased role of trade in the Late Cypriot Age economy, changes permeated the social sphere and altered the world of women forever.

Does it matter if pottery was made by women in each household in each village or by women specialists? Only if it helps to reevaluate the ancient industry and the society in which it operated, which includes the contribution of women. Potters and pot decorators were instrumental not only in providing essential durable containers necessary for many aspects of life; they also were responsible for the maintenance of styles, heritage, and tradition. If craft specialization involves a diverse labor force, meaning non-professionals including women apprentices and family members, standardization alone will not necessarily measure specialization. Could a small local and/or regional population support a pottery specialist in a pre-market economy when kin-based ties predominated in the absence of political and institutional organizations? The answer is affirmative given the seasonal nature of the work limited to the period of dry weather. Craft specialization is not dependent on a complex society. Pottery specialization explains the overlapping regional variations of prehistoric wares. It is evidence of interaction and exchange among the different geographic regions of Cyprus. In antiquity, women were a dominant factor in the production of trade pottery, whether made by hand or thrown on the wheel.

ACKNOWLEDGMENTS

My thanks to Dr. Nancy Serwint, Dr. Diane Bolger, and the entire CAARI staff for organizing the symposium on the role of women in antiquity. Dr. Judith Baroody, Director of the American Center, and Mr. Daniel Hadjittofi, Director of the Fulbright Commission in Nicosia, also have my gratitude. Fieldwork described here could not have been achieved without the help of my hosts in Kornos, the potters and friends to whom I extend my deepest appreciation. Comments of Ellen Herscher and anonymous reviewers who read the paper are gratefully acknowledged. Herscher suggests that the Sanidha workshop would qualify for a summer work place for potters living elsewhere and could be an ancient example of early 20th century potters from Kornos who retreated to villages of the Troodos foothills seasonally. My thanks to Robert Merrillees for equating the Sanidha workshop with a production location for export wares given the predominance of sherds with imprecisely painted patterns in contrast to the finer version used locally. To this day, any White Slip sherd excavated in Israel or Jordan constitutes a precious and treasured find.

REFERENCES

Aikens, C. M.
1995   First in the World: The Jomon Pottery of Early Japan. Pp. 11–21 in *The Emergence of Pottery*, eds. W. K. Barnett and J. W. Hoopes. Washington, D.C.: Smithsonian Institution.

Allen, K. M. S.
1992   Iroquois Ceramic Production: A Case Study of Household-Level Organization. Pp. 133–54 in *Ceramic Production and Distribution*, eds. G. J. Bey and C. A. Pool. Boulder: Westview.

Amiran, R.
1969   *Ancient Pottery of the Holy Land*. Ramat Gan: Massada.

Anderson, W. P.
1987   The Kilns and Workshops of Sarepta (Sarafand, Lebanon): Remnants of a Phoenician Ceramic Industry. *Berytus* 35: 41–66.
1989   The Pottery Industry at Phoenician Sarepta (Sarafand, Lebanon), with Parallels to Kilns from Other East Mediterranean Sites. Pp. 197–215 in *Cross-craft and Cross-cultural Interactions in Ceramics*, eds. P. E. McGovern, and M. R. Notis. Ceramics and Civilization 4. Westerville, OH: American Ceramic Society.

Austin, M. M., and Vidal-Naquet, P.
1977   *Economic and Social History of Ancient Greece: An Introduction*. Translated and revised by M. M. Austin. Berkeley: University of California.

Barlow, J.
1991   New Light on Red Polished Ware. Pp. 51–57 in *Cypriot Ceramics: Reading the Prehistoric Record*, eds. J. Barlow, D. Bolger and B. Kling. Philadelphia: University of Pennsylvania Museum.

Barlow, J., and Idziak, P.
1989   Selective Use of Clays at a Middle Bronze Age Site in Cyprus. *Archaeometry* 31: 66–76.

Barnett, W. K., and Hoopes, J. W., eds.
1995   *The Emergence of Pottery*. Washington, D.C.: Smithsonian Institution.

Bolger, D. L.
1989   Regionalism, Cultural Variation and the Culture-Area Concept in Later Prehistoric Cypriot Studies. Pp. 142–52 in *Early Society in Cyprus*, ed. E. Peltenburg. Edinburgh: University of Edinburgh.
1991   Early Red Polished Ware and the Origin of the "Philia Culture." Pp. 29–35 in *Cypriot Ceramics: Reading the Prehistoric Record*, eds. J. Barlow, D. Bolger and B. Kling. Philadelphia: University of Pennsylvania Museum.

Childe, G.
1942   *What Happened in History*. Reprinted 1952. Harmondsworth: Penguin.

Clark, J. E., and Parry, W. J.
1990   Craft Specialization and Cultural Complexity. *Research in Economic Anthropology* 12: 289–346.

Close, A. E.
1995   Few and Far Between: Early Ceramics in North Africa. Pp. 23–37 in *The Emergence of Pottery*, eds. W. K. Barnett and J. W. Hoopes. Washington, D.C.: Smithsonian Institution.

Crown, P. L., and Wills, W. H.
1995   Economic Intensification and the Origins of Ceramic Containers in the American Southwest. Pp. 241–54 in *The Emergence of Pottery*, eds. W. K. Barnett and J. W. Hoopes. Washington, D.C.: Smithsonian Institution.

Day, P. M., and Wilson, D. E.
1996   Reassessing Specialization in Prepalatial Ceramic Production. Paper presented at the 6th International Aegean Conference, Craftsmen, Craftswomen and Craftsmanship in the Aegean Bronze Age. Philadelphia.

Dothan T. K., and Ben Tor, A.
1983   *Excavations at Atheniou, Cyprus 1971–1972*. Qedem 16. Jerusalem: Hebrew University, Institute of Archaeology.

Falconer, S. E., and Magness-Gardiner, B.
1984   Preliminary Report of the First Season of the Tell el-Hayyat Project. *Bulletin of the American Schools of Oriental Research* 255: 49–74.

Frankel, D.
1974   *Middle Cypriot White Painted Pottery: An Analytical Study of the Decoration*. Studies in Mediterranean Archaeology 42. Göteborg: Åströms.
1981   Uniformity and Variation in a Cypriot Ceramic Tradition: Two Approaches. *Levant* 13: 88–106.
1988   Pottery Production in Prehistoric Bronze Age Cyprus: Assessing the Problem. *Journal of Mediterranean Archaeology* 1, 2: 27–55.
1994   Color Variation on Prehistoric Cypriot Red Polished Pottery. *Journal of Field Archaeology* 21: 205–19.
Frankel, D., and Webb, J. M.
1996   *Marki Alonia. An Early-Middle Bronze Age Town in Cyprus. Excavations 1990–1994*. Studies in Mediterranean Archaeology 123. Jonsered: Åströms.
Franken, H. J.
1973   Ring Burnished Bowls from the 7th Century B.C. in Palestine. Pp. 144–48 in *Symbolae Biblicae et Mesopotamicae Francisoco Mario Theodoro De Liagre Bohl*, eds. M. A. Beek et al. Leiden: Brill.
Franken, H. J., and London, G. A.
1995   Why Painted Pottery Disappeared at the End of the Second Millennium B.C.E. *Biblical Archaeologist* 58: 214–22.
Galili, E., and Nir, Y.
1993   The Sub-merged Pre-Pottery Neolithic Water Well of Atlit-Yam Northern Israel, and its Paleoenvironmental Implications. *The Holocene* 3: 265–70.
Graves, M. W.
1991   Pottery Production and Distribution among the Kalinga: A Study of Household and Regional Organization and Differentiation. Pp. 112–43 in *Ceramic Ethnoarchaeology*, ed. W. A. Longacre. Tucson: University of Arizona.
Haaland, R.
1997   Emergence of sedentism: new ways of living, new ways of symbolizing. *Antiquity* 71: 374–85.
Haaland, R., and Magid, A. A.
1995   *Aquatic Sites along the Rivers Nile and Atbara, Sudan*. Bergen: Alma Mater.
Hampe, R., and Winter, A.
1962   *Bei Töpfer und Töpferinnen in Kreta, Messenien und Zypern*. Reprinted 1976. Mainz: von Zabern.
Hankey, V.
1983   The Ceramic Tradition in Late Bronze Age Cyprus. *Report of the Department of Antiquities of Cyprus*: 168–71.
Hardin, M.
1991   Sources of Variability at Zuni Pueblo. Pp. 40–70 in *Ceramic Ethnoarchaeology*, ed. W. A. Longacre. Tucson: University of Arizona.
Hennessy, J. B.
1973   Cypriot Artists of the Early and Middle Bronze Age. Pp. 10–22 in *The Cypriot Bronze Age*, ed. J. M. Birmingham. Australian Studies in Archaeology 1. Sydney: Department of Archaeology, University of Sydney.
Herscher, E.
1972   A Potter's Error. Aspects of Middle Cypriote III. *Report of the Department of Antiquities of Cyprus*: 22–34.
1973   Red-and Black Polished Ware from the Western Karpas. *Report of the Department of Antiquities of Cyprus*: 62–71.
1991   Beyond Regionalism: Toward an Islandwide-Middle Cypriot Sequence. Pp. 45–50 in *Cypriot Ceramics: Reading the Prehistoric Record*, eds. J. Barlow, D. Bolger and B. Kling. Philadelphia: University of Pennsylvania Museum.
Herscher, E., and Fox, S. C.
1993   A Middle Bronze Age Tomb from Western Cyprus. *Report of the Department of Antiquities of Cyprus*: 69–80.
Homès-Fredericq, D., and Franken, H. J., eds.
1986   *Pottery and Potters-Past and Present: 7000 Years of Ceramic Art in Jordan*. Tübingen: Attempto.

Keswani, P. S.
1991   A Preliminary Investigation of Systems of Ceramic Production and Distribution in Cyprus During the Late Bronze Age. Pp. 97–118 in *Cypriot Ceramics: Reading the Prehistoric Record*, eds. J. Barlow, D. Bolger and B. Kling. Philadelphia: University of Pennsylvania Museum.

Knapp, A. B.
1986   Production, Exchange, and Socio-political Complexity on Bronze Age Cyprus. *Oxford Journal of Archaeology* 5, 1: 35–60.
1989   Complexity and Collapse in the North Jordan Valley: Archaeometry and Society in the Middle-Late Bronze Ages. *Israel Exploration Society* 39, 3–4: 129–48.
1990   Production, Location, and Integration in Bronze Age Cyprus. *Current Anthropology* 31: 147–76.
1992   Bronze Age Mediterranean Island Cultures and the Ancient Near East, Part I, *Biblical Archaeologist* 55, 2: 52–72.
1993   Social Complexity: Incipience, Emergence and Development on Prehistoric Cyprus. *Bulletin of the American Schools of Oriental Research* 292: 85–106.

London, G. A.
1985   Decoding Designs: The Late Third Millennium B.C. Pottery from Jebel Oa'aqir. Unpublished Ph.D. Dissertation, University of Arizona.
1986   Response to M. Hagstrum, Measuring Prehistoric Ceramic Craft Specialization: A Test Case in the American Southwest. *Journal of Field Archaeology* 13, 4: 510–11.
1987a   Cypriote Potters: Past and Present. *Report of the Department of Antiquities of Cyprus*: 319–22.
1987b   Regionalism in Traditional Cypriote Ceramics. *Newsletter of Pottery Technology* 5: 125–36.
1989a   On Fig Leaves, Itinerant Potters, and Pottery Production Locations in Cyprus. Pp. 65–80 in *Cross-craft and Cross-cultural Interactions in Ceramics*, eds. P. E. McGovern. and M. R. Notis. Ceramics and Civilization 4. Westerville, OH: American Ceramic Society.
1989b   Past Present: The Village Potters in Cyprus. *Biblical Archaeologist* 50: 219–29.
1991a   Ethnoarchaeological Evidence of Variation in Cypriot Ceramics and its Implications for the Taxonomy of Ancient Pottery. Pp. 221–35 in *Cypriot Ceramics: Reading the Prehistoric Record*, eds. J. Barlow, D. Bolger and B. Kling. Philadelphia: University of Pennsylvania Museum.
1991b   Standardization and Variation in the Work of Craft Specialists. Pp. 182–204 in *Ceramic Ethnoarchaeology*, ed. W. A. Longacre. Tucson: University of Arizona.

London, G. A.; Egoumenidou, F.; and Karageorghis, V.
1989   *Traditional Pottery in Cyprus*. Mainz: von Zabern.

London, G. A., and Sinclair, M.
1991   An Ethnoarchaeological Survey of Potters in Jordan. Pp. 420–28 in *Madaba Plains Project 2*, eds. L. Herr et al. Berrien Springs, MI: Andrews University.

Longacre, W. A.
1991   Sources of Ceramic Variability Among the Kalinga of Northern Luzon. Pp. 95–111 in *Ceramic Ethnoarchaeology*, ed. W. A. Longacre. Tucson: University of Arizona.
1995   Why Did they Invent Pottery Anyway? Pp. 277–80 in *The Emergence of Pottery*, eds. W. K. Barnett and J. W. Hoopes. Washington, D.C.: Smithsonian Institution.

Longacre, W. A.; Kvamme, K. L.; and Kobayashi, M.
1988   Southwestern Pottery Standardization: An Ethnoarchaeological View from the Philippines. *The Kiva* 53, 2: 101–12.

Magness-Gardiner, B., and Falconer, S. E.
1994   Community, Polity, and Temple in a Middle Bronze Age Levantine Village. *Journal of Mediterranean Archaeology* 7, 2: 127–64.

Maguire, L. C.
1991   The Classification of Middle Bronze Age Painted Pottery: Wares, Styles ... Workshops? Pp. 59–66 in *Cypriot Ceramics: Reading the Prehistoric Record*, eds. J. Barlow, D. Bolger and B. Kling. Philadelphia: University of Pennsylvania Museum.

Merrillees, R. S.
1968   *Cypriote Bronze Age Pottery in Egypt*. Studies in Mediterranean Archaeology 17. Lund: Åströms.

1979   Pottery Trade in Bronze Age Cyprus. *Report of the Department of Antiquities of Cyprus*: 114–34.
Murdock, G. P., and Provost, C.
1973   Factors in the Division of Labor by Sex: A Cross-cultural Analysis. *Ethnology* 12: 203–25.
Nicholson, P., and Patterson, H.
1985   Pottery Making in Upper Egypt: An Ethnoarchaeological Study. *World Archaeology* 17: 222–39.
Nir, Y.
1997   Middle and Late Holocene Sea-levels along the Israel Mediterranean Coast—Evidence from Ancient Water Wells. *Journal of Quaternary Science* 12: 143–51.
Peltenburg, E.
1991   Toward Definition of the Late Chalcolithic in Cyprus: The Monochrome Pottery Debate. Pp. 9–20 in *Cypriot Ceramics: Reading the Prehistoric Record*, eds. J. Barlow, D. Bolger and B. Kling. Philadelphia: University of Pennsylvania Museum.
Pool, C. A.
1992   Integrating Ceramic Production and Distribution. Pp. 275–313 in *Ceramic Production and Distribution,* eds. G. J. Bey and C. A. Pool. Boulder: Westview.
Pucci, G.
1983   Pottery and Trade in the Roman Period. Pp. 105–17 in *Trade in the Ancient Economy*, eds. P. Garnsey, K. Hopkins and C. R. Whittaker. London: Hogarth.
Renger, J.
1984   Patterns of Non-institutional Trade and Non-commercial Exchange in Ancient Mesopotamia at the Beginning of the Second Millennium B.C. Pp. 31–123 in *Circulation of Goods in Non-Palatial Context in the Ancient Near East*, ed. A. Archi. Rome: Instituto per gli studi Micenei ed Egeo-Anatolici.
Rice, P. M.
1996   Recent Ceramic Analysis: 2. Composition, Production, and Theory. *Journal of Anthropological Archaeology* 4: 165–201.
Shiels, J.
1998   Sherds as Evidence: The Replication of Archaeological Ceramics in Cyprus. *Bulletin of Primitive Technology* 15: 49–53.
Speth, J. D.
1990   Seasonality, Resource Stress, and Food Sharing in So-Called "Egalitarian" Foraging Societies. *Journal of Anthropological Archaeology* 9: 148–88.
Stark, B. L.
1984   An Ethnoarchaeological Study of a Mexican Pottery Industry. *Journal of New World Archaeology* 6: 4–14.
Stewart, J. R. B.
1962   The Early Cypriote Bronze Age. Pp. 203–391 in *The Swedish Cyprus Expedition*. Vol. 4, 1A: *The Stone Age and Early Bronze Age in Cyprus*, eds. P. Dikaios and J. Stewart. Lund: Swedish Cyprus Expedition.
Stone, M.
1976   *When God Was a Woman*. New York: Dorset.
Swiny, S.
1991   Reading the Prehistoric Record: A View from the South in the Late Third Millennium B.C. Pp. 37–43 in *Cypriot Ceramics: Reading the Prehistoric Record*, eds. J. Barlow, D. Bolger and B. Kling. Philadelphia: University of Pennsylvania Museum.
Todd, I., Hadjicosti, M., et al.
1991   Excavations at Sanida 1990. *Report of the Department of Antiquities of Cyprus*: 37–74.
Todd, I., et al.
1992   Excavations at Sanida 1991. *Report of the Department of Antiquities of Cyprus*: 75–112.
Tosi, M.
1984   The Notion of Craft Specialization and its Representation in the Archaeological Record of Early States in the Turanian Basin. Pp. 22–52 in *Marxist Perspectives in Archaeology*, ed. M. Spriggs. Cambridge: Cambridge University.

Vermeule, E. D. T., and Wolsky, F. Z.
   1990   Toumba tou Skourou: A Bronze Age Potters' Quarter on Morphou Bay in Cyprus. Cambridge, MA:
               Harvard University, Museum of Fine Arts.
Vitelli, K. D.
   1993   Power to the Potters. Comment on Perles' "System of Exchange and Organization of Production in
               Neolithic Greece" [*JMA* 5: 115–641]. *Journal of Mediterranean Archaeology* 6: 247–57.
   1995   Pots, Potters, and the Shaping of Greek Neolithic Society. Pp. 55–63 in *The Emergence of Pottery*,
               eds. W. K. Barnett and J. W. Hoopes. Washington, D.C.: Smithsonian Institution.
Walz, C.
   1985   Ethnographic Analogy and the Gender of Potters in the Late Bronze Age. *Report of the Department
               of Antiquities of Cyprus*: 126–32.
Webster, T. B. L.
   1972   *Potter and Patron in Classical Athens*. London: Methuen.
Wisseman, S. U.
   1994   From Pots to People: Ceramic Production in the Ancient Mediterranean. Pp. 17–40 in *Ancient Tech-
               nologies and Archaeological Materials*, eds. S. U. Wisseman and W. S. Williams. Langhorne, PA:
               Gordon and Breach.
Wright, R. P.
   1986   The Boundaries of Technology and Stylistic Change. Pp. 1–20 in *Ceramics and Civilization* 2, ed. W.
               D. Kingery. Columbus, OH: American Ceramic Society.
   1991   Women's Labor and Pottery Production in Prehistory. Pp. 194–223 in *Engendering Archaeology*,
               eds. J. M. Gero and M. W. Conkey. Oxford: Blackwell.
Wood, B. G.
   1990   *The Sociology of Pottery in Ancient Palestine*. Journal for the Study of the Old Testament/American
               Schools of Oriental Research Monograph 4. Sheffield: Journal for the Study of the Old Testament.

CHANGES IN THE WORKPLACE:
WOMEN AND TEXTILE PRODUCTION
ON LATE BRONZE AGE CYPRUS

JOANNA S. SMITH

Department of Art History and Archaeology
Columbia University
826 Schermerhorn Hall, MC 5517
New York, NY 10027
jss245@columbia.edu

Elizabeth Barber's discussions of "women's work," or women's involvement in the produc-
tion of textiles in the prehistoric Aegean and surrounding regions, are important contributions
to our understanding of the roles of women in antiquity (1991, 1994). In this paper I explore
the roles of women in the production of textiles on Late Bronze Age Cyprus (ca. 1650 to 1050
B.C.) and consider some of the ways in which increasing social complexity affected "women's
work." Archaeological, textual, and ethnographic evidence from or about Cyprus, as well as
comparative pictorial and textual information from neighboring regions such as the Aegean,
Egypt, Anatolia, and the Near East, contribute to a model for how textiles were produced
during the Late Bronze Age. Because different technologies and locations are important clues
to determining whether women or men performed different tasks in textile production, the
model accounts for not only who was doing what kind of work, but also how the work was done
and where. Using textile production on Cyprus as a case study, I summarize what there is to
know about textile production prior to the Late Cypriot IIC period (13ᵗʰ century B.C.) and focus
on the site of Kition from Late Cypriot IIC to the end of the Late Bronze Age in the 11ᵗʰ century
B.C. Kition preserves detailed evidence both for domestic and non-domestic areas of textile
manufacture. Differences in the work performed in these areas over time suggest that as the
locations of textile production diversified, so too did the workforce that made them, involving
men as well as women.

Economic growth and political change during the Late Bronze Age of Cyprus (ca. 1650 to 1050 B.C.) had a profound effect on the inhabitants of the island. When the dynamics of daily life in settlements across the island extended beyond their previously known limits during the 13ᵗʰ century B.C., or the Late Cypriot (LC) IIC period, some people to some extent must have altered the way in which they lived and worked. This paper explores how changes in the complexity of Late Cypriot society at that time affected the roles of women and men in one fundamental form of work, the manufacture of textiles.

Although usually invisible in the form of cloth to archaeologists working on Cyprus and in many other Mediterranean areas, textiles were an indispensable part of the material culture of the ancient world. They were staple goods used to make clothing; they were needed for sea transport when used to create sails; and they were markers of status not only in the form of garments, but also as woven objects for display, such as tapestries. Textile arts in the Late Bronze Age Aegean and neighboring regions have been shown to be more often the result of women's rather than men's efforts (Barber 1991, 1994). Women worked at spinning, weaving, sewing, and finishing textiles in the home as well as sometimes outside the home in supervised workshops (Van De Mieroop 1989: 63–64, 67). On Cyprus during the LC IIC period, cloth went from being solely a product of home manufacture to something that was both made in the home and in workshops, probably administered by a central authority.

In order to give "faces" (Tringham 1991: 94) to those who worked in these areas and created the now largely invisible textile arts of Late Bronze Age Cyprus, I will look to archaeological, textual, and ethnographic evidence from or about Cyprus as well as comparative pictorial and textual information from neighboring regions such as the Aegean, Egypt, Anatolia, and the Near East. By considering the full context of textile production (Ehrenberg 1989: 19), not only which tasks were allocated to whom, what fabrics were made, and what tools were used, but also, and perhaps most importantly, where activities occurred when they were assigned to different individuals, whether female or male, we can create a model that allows us to some extent to determine whether women's roles on Cyprus changed along with shifts that occurred in society generally (Brumfiel 1991: 245).

It is not possible to detail all that there is to know about Cypriot textiles from the Late Bronze Age and previous periods in this one paper. Instead, I summarize what there is to know about textile production prior to the LC IIC period in order to show that it existed, took place within the home, and fits generally within the model that women performed the work. Then, for the period from LC IIC to the end of the Late Bronze Age, the LC IIIB period in the 11th century B.C., I focus on the site of Kition as a case study of task differentiation in textile production. Throughout five Late Bronze Age "Floors," Areas I and II at Kition preserve detailed evidence both for domestic and non-domestic areas of textile manufacture. Differences in the work performed in these areas suggest that as the locations of textile production diversified, so, too, did the workforce that made them, involving men as well as women.

In order to reach this conclusion, it is necessary to oversimplify the nature of changes that took place across Cyprus at that time (Keswani 1996) and accept that the unusually well-preserved information from Kition serves as a representative sample for the period. There are indications from other sites to suggest that the evidence for workshop production of cloth from Kition is not unique, although the scale of production at Kition may have been unusually large and some of the specific work that took place was probably different, involving large scale dye works. Textile production outside the home did exist at other LC IIC and later sites such as Maroni, Enkomi, and Idalion. These discoveries contribute to the general pattern of increased division of labor and increased administrative complexity, both considered hallmarks of Cypriot urban life between ca. 1300 and 1050 B.C. However, at this time only Kition provides enough evidence to suggest who performed the work outside the home.

TASK DIFFERENTIATION: BUILDING A MODEL

A model based on task differentiation (Spector 1982; Conkey and Spector 1984; Brumfiel 1991) can be useful for identifying men and women in the archaeological record, but in its construction we must recognize that there may be tasks we cannot label as "male" or "female." In attempting to create a model for prehistoric Cypriot textile production, it is important to consider that, both in the past and in the present, each activity that contributes to a finished piece of cloth was performed in some cases by both men and women. In order to use the archaeological, textual, and ethnographic information at our disposal to construct a reasonable model of task differentiation that is applicable to the evidence from Kition and can lead to some form of gender distinctions, we must take into account a variety of factors. Not only must we consider who was doing the work, but also what was being made, what tools and facilities were used, where the work took place, whether production was for the home or a wider range of consumers, and how often the work was performed. Once all of these factors are taken into account, it is possible to construct a model that suggests who did what kind of work in only a few stages of the production process.

An inquiry into task differentiation cannot begin with the evidence left behind in areas where textiles were produced on Cyprus. During the Late Cypriot period there are no images of textiles or textile workers, nor are there any written records of workers' activities. Except for a few fragments of textiles that have survived, all that we have are the tools used in production. An individual loom weight or spindle whorl alone does not tell the story of who created the textiles of Late Bronze Age Cyprus. Prior to an investigation of debris left behind in areas of production, direct and indirect evidence for who did the work needs to be evaluated in order to build the model we will use when looking at the tools left behind. Direct evidence from Cyprus exists in the form of burials in which the deceased were buried with the tools of a particular trade. Indirect evidence is available by making analogies with evidence for textile production from contemporary or nearly contemporary ancient societies as well as ethnographic studies of Cypriot textile production during the 19th and early 20th centuries A.D.

Burials

Using burial evidence to differentiate among tasks performed by men and women requires accurately sexed skeletal remains found in primary context in association with a tool or tools used to perform a particular activity. Even when remains of this nature are preserved, the archaeologist must determine whether the objects buried with the deceased reflect something about who or what the person was in life (Ucko 1969; Ehrenberg 1989: 29). Objects placed in graves may have many sources and many meanings; for example, some may reflect the status of the family as a whole rather than the individual, while others may be objects made to accompany the person only in death. It is rare that personal objects are found *in situ* with a skeleton as they were worn or used in life (e.g., Marcus 1993).

Tools used to create textiles, such as spindle whorls and loom weights of terracotta, are commonly assumed to be objects placed in burials because they were used in life by the deceased. I accept this assumption, for these terracotta artifacts are utilitarian, easily reproduced and replaced, and with little or no intrinsic value (Appadurai 1986). Still, while spindle whorls and loom weights of terracotta found in burials probably indicate tasks performed by the deceased in life, it is too speculative to use them as gender indicators in the absence of a significant quantity of sexed skeletal information (Fischer 1986: 42).

Identifying the sex of a skeleton by means of physical characteristics is more accurate than (Fischer 1986: 43) and preferable to using artifactual evidence (Ehrenberg 1989: 30–31). However, sexed skeletal information is frequently unavailable, either because the bones were not sufficiently preserved after their burial in the ground or were not sufficiently recorded during, and studied after, their excavation. In Cyprus, the number of sexed skeletons increases with new discoveries, for it is now standard to include physical anthropological studies in excavation reports (e.g., Angel 1972; Schwartz 1974; Moyer 1989). Studies of prehistoric populations on the island are not new (e.g., Charles 1962; Domurad 1986) and form part of the increasing number of studies of mortuary practices for the period (e.g., Keswani 1989; Niklasson 1991; Davies 1997). However, few studies have attempted to determine artifactual associations with sexed skeletal remains (Fischer 1986), largely because most burials are multiple interments (Keswani 1989: 502–3) and are often looted or otherwise disturbed, making it impossible to isolate individuals and the artifacts with which they were buried. Exceptions do exist (e.g., Goring 1989; Niklasson 1983), making it possible to isolate some general patterns.

Fischer found that the small sample of spindle whorls in Early and Middle Cypriot tomb assemblages is associated exclusively with females (1986: 42). Evidence for the Late Cypriot period can not be added to this pattern because there are almost no whorls found in burials, a pattern that itself demands further inquiry. Late Cypriot stone and ivory objects most often identified as whorls are more likely parts of pins or buttons based on an analysis of their weights, dimensions, and wear marks. A survey of the literature shows that few loom weights are found in tombs, including those of the Late Cypriot period (Åström 1972: 586). Those that do come from tombs, such as at Kition (e.g., Karageorghis 1974: 33, 93), can not be associated with single sexed skeletons (Schwartz 1974). Other artifacts interpreted as textile manufacturing tools found in burials follow the same inconclusive pattern. On the whole, the direct evidence for task differentiation as seen in burial evidence from Cyprus is inconclusive for the Late Cypriot period.

Comparative Evidence

By making a series of relational analogies, or a composite analogy (Wylie 1985: 106), with contemporary or near contemporary ancient societies and 19th and early 20th century modern Cypriot society, we can construct a model that will help us explain who produced textiles during the Late Bronze Age of Cyprus. In this effort, we are constructing a model for production, not for consumption or distribution (Peacock 1982: 7), that takes into account the full context of that production. Although textiles must have been passed on to consumers and used in a variety of ways, any statements about these processes remain almost entirely hypothetical on account of the paucity of textile remains on Cyprus. For the production of textiles during the Late Cypriot period, however, we have plentiful evidence in the form of tools and installations that can be viewed against the proposed model.

Archaeologists who work with pottery production have constructed models of craft production that are a useful start for this inquiry (e.g., van der Leeuw 1977; Peacock 1982: 7–8; Arnold 1991: 92–95; Sinopoli 1991: 99). Although these definitions of craft production do not contain indicators of task differentiation for textile production, they can be adapted for that purpose (fig. 1). These definitions of pottery production already contain several of the criteria needed in order to consider the full context of textile production, for they define where work takes place, how often work is performed, and for whom work is done. To these we need to add what work occurs and how it was done as well as who carried it through.

Four systems of production appear in fig. 1, adapted from earlier models of pottery production. They summarize the results of what we know about textile manufacture from the comparative evidence presented below. The word specialist is avoided, for all producers who perform tasks in the production of textiles can be considered specialists in their craft, although they may work with varying frequency (Brumfiel and Earle 1987: 5) and produce different products in different locations, using different tools. The possibility that producers were obliged to provide at least some work for a central authority (Brumfiel and Earle 1987: 5; Arnold 1991: 94–95) concerns both the consumers and the producers, but it does not affect the location, product, and frequency of the work or the tools used. Because this factor does not have any bearing upon the information visible in the archaeological record (fig. 1, boldface and italic) of Cyprus for the Late Bronze Age, we cannot confirm that attached or tethered specialists existed, although we can postulate their existence by analogy with other cultures (see below).

At first glance, the four general models in fig. 1 appear to make the search for gender distinctions among different tasks impossible. However, once the comparative evidence is divided into separate tasks, such as spinning, weaving, washing, and dyeing, patterns emerge that allow us to determine for some tasks in some locations whether it is more likely that a man or a woman was the producer, using certain tools, in a specific location, and even of a probable product. Comparative evidence that we can use to make fig. 1 task-specific exists in the form of a few ancient textual references concerning Cyprus, contemporary or near contemporary pictorial and textual evidence from neighboring regions, and ethnographic studies of textile production in 19th and early 20th century Cyprus.

Location	Product	Frequency	Tools Used	Consumers	Producers
Household Production	**domestic context, possibly in designated space**	*variety, possibly on speciality items*	part-time work	**movable; not permanent installations, mobile tools**	household	women, some men
Household Industry	**domestic context, possibly in designated space**	*variety, possibly on speciality items*	part-time work	**movable; not permanent installations, mobile tools**	household and beyond; possibly for central authority	women, some men; possibly tethered to central authorities
Workshop Industry	**designated space outside of or in addition to domestic context**	*specialty items, probably a variety*	full-time work	**permanent installations, some mobile tools**	society; possibly for central authority	women and men; possibly tethered to central authority
Large-scale Industry	**designated space outside of domestic context**	*specialty items, probably a variety*	full-time work	**permanent installations, some mobile tools**	society; possibly for central authority	men and women; possibly tethered to central authority

Figure 1. Models of Textile Production. Boldface: visible in archaeological record directly in association with areas of production. Italic: possibly visible in archaeological record, but often not directly associated with production. Normal: must be inferred through analysis of archaeological record and use of model.

Ancient Textual References. Ancient textual references concerning Cyprus do not contain records of women on Cyprus who worked in any capacity related to textile production. However, if we consider that the Late Bronze Age place name Alashiya is connected with Cyprus, we do know that outside of Cyprus at Ugarit, an Alashiyan female and her apprentices receive an allotment of a vessel (Walls 1996b: 39), indicating that in some way, women from Alashiya performed a service for a central authority, possibly as attached or tethered specialists.

Specifically connected with textile production, there are three texts that mention men, all of which are post-Bronze Age in date. Two of the texts are epitaphs from Marion (Polis) that date to the late 4th century B.C. One man was a *knapheus* (Masson 1985: 88), or a fuller, someone who cleaned textiles. A second man was a *porphureus* (Masson 1985: 87), meaning a person involved in the production of purple made from the shells of the murex. Copious murex shells were discovered in Polis in a 6th century B.C. context (Smith 1997: 90–91). The production of purple dye on Cyprus is also attested by Pliny (*NH* 34.98) in the 1st century A.D. (Wallace and Orphanides 1990: 148). The third reference dates to the 2nd or 3rd century A.D. (Athenaeus, 2.48b) and mentions two men as famous weavers, known at Delphi and compared in caliber to an "artist" from Egypt, also male (Wallace and Orphanides 1990: 249).

None of these texts indicates the locations where these men worked or how the textile production was organized. However, because the professions of the two men buried in Polis were important enough to be placed on their tombstones, we can infer that they worked more or less full-time, the one as a fuller, the other as a dyer. At least they worked with a high enough frequency in those professions to have their work become part of their identity. Similarly, the weavers were of international renown, which suggests that they worked as weavers also on a full-time basis. If it is correct that these men, a fuller, a dyer, and two weavers, all worked more or less full-time in these capacities, we can hypothesize, using the models in fig. 1, that it is most likely that they worked outside the home.

Pictorial and Textual Evidence. Pictorial and textual evidence for textile producers during the Late Bronze Age comes from the Aegean, Egypt, Anatolia, and other parts of the Near East. Most of the images and inscriptions were made for high authorities such as pharaohs, kings, palace administrators, or merchants serving those authorities. Work that took place in the home under the model of "household production" is rarely recorded in any of these sources, although there are some Egyptian references (Barber 1991: 288–89) that support the idea that women produced textiles in the home. In spite of this less well-defined area of our knowledge, the images and texts generously illustrate details in the other models of production outlined above (fig. 1).

Production that can be defined as "household industry" involved mainly women as producers. The Linear B tablets from Knossos and Pylos attest to workers whose location of work was probably the home (Killen 1984; Barber 1991: 285) but who were obliged to provide some products for a palace authority. Most of the workers recorded are female. They are specified as combers, spinners, weavers, border makers, and sewers. Men are also listed, but their activities are limited to possibly weaving and definitely sewing (leather) and fulling (Barber 1991: 283–84). Prior to the Late Bronze Age, written records from the Assyrian trading colonies show that Assyrian women produced textiles in the home while men acted as the middlemen between the producers and the Anatolian consumers (Veenhof 1972; Barber 1991: 287). Evidence for "household industry" supports the idea that women were involved in most of the production tasks, including spinning and weaving, while men performed only a few tasks, most notably washing or fulling.

A similar division between those who spin and weave and those who wash is found in Egypt (Barber 1991: 285–86). However, unlike the Aegean and Assyrian evidence, the evidence from Egypt informs us primarily about production in workshops that appear to be located outside the home. This evidence comes from models, paintings, and reliefs (Barber 1991: 285–86) as well as texts, such as from the New Kingdom site of Gurob (Thomas 1981). Using the models above, we can most accurately define the work portrayed in these scenes as a "workshop industry." Similar work done outside the home by women who worked in groups under supervisors is attested at Sumer (Van De Mieroop 1989: 67).

Another form of "workshop industry," which was more restricted in its purpose and can perhaps be classified as "large-scale industry," existed in Egypt in which the weavers were male, not female (Barber 1991: 286). These men wove only for the elite, including the Pharaoh, using a specific loom, the large and heavy vertical two-beam loom called the "tapestry" loom (Barber 1991: 286). In this form of production, the product, tools used, consumers, and producers are all narrowly defined, setting this special case apart from the more common production of textiles in Egypt by women.

There are many tasks involved in the production of textiles, from the cultivation of the fiber to the distribution of the cloth, but the tasks of spinning, weaving, and washing present the patterns that are most relevant to what can be evaluated in the archaeological record of Cyprus. Based on this brief survey of comparative contemporary evidence, we can say that women did the majority of weaving, but if the weaving took place outside the home, it is possible that male weavers were active. Spinning was done largely by women, although Barber notes one young boy spinning alongside women who worked outside the home (1991: 286). Åström records that in Classical Greece flax was sometimes spun by men as well as women while wool was always spun by women (1970: 17). Washing, on the other hand, at least washing or fulling done for a central authority or in a workshop context, was done by men. Similarly, in Classical Greece, fulling done outside the home was undertaken by men, while inside the home it was the task of women (Åström 1970: 16).

Another task that leaves traces in the archaeological record of Cyprus but is not listed in the texts or portrayed in the images summarized above, is dyeing. Fullers who used foul smelling substances, such as urine, do appear in those sources. The dyer also used urine in addition to other foul smelling dyestuffs. Barber comments that dyers were viewed with "revulsion" in antiquity due to the smells from their work (Barber 1991: 239). Forbes also mentions "the sorry lot" of a dyer based on a papyrus from ca. 2000 B.C. that mentions the "stink" of his hands (1954: 249). It appears that most dyers were male. I have been unable to find a reference to a female dyer for the Bronze Age, although they may well have dyed fibers and fabrics in the home as they did in the recent past (see below). Women, or at least girls, certainly collected dyestuffs such as saffron in the Aegean (Barber 1991: 316). Possibly the professional dyer and fuller were one and the same person in some cases, using similar noxious substances; their areas of work are difficult to distinguish in the archaeological record (Barber 1991: 240).

Evidence for textile producers. Evidence for textile producers in the Cypriot ethnographic record, mainly from the 19th and early 20th centuries, is rich. Although most everyday textile production is now mechanized and performed outside the home in factories, handicraft traditions of Cyprus survived in many parts of the island. Some traditional crafts have formed the basis for ethnographic studies in recent years and some even continue today, although today handmade cloth increasingly is produced solely for the tourist trade rather than for everyday use on the island.

In Cyprus, mechanized "large-scale" industrial facilities for textile production exist alongside non-mechanized "household production," "household industry," and "workshop industry" forms of production (Papademetriou 1993a: 9; 1993b: 17). In factories, men and women both work outside the home (Filaktou and Ioannides 1992: 80–83). The shift towards more mechanized and fewer handmade textiles is just one of the several changes in textile production between the past and the present. Whereas in the past the warp-weighted loom was in use, Cyprus now uses the horizontal loom (Papademetriou 1993b: 18), which requires no weights. For hand spinning, Cypriots use the high-whorl spindle, whereas in the Bronze Age they used the low whorl spindle (Frankel and Webb 1996: 193–94). Moreover, the scale of production has changed enormously. The types of textiles produced now include cotton and silk cloths (Pieridou 1959; Papademetriou 1995) in addition to the linen and woolen weaves known from antiquity (e.g. Åström 1965; see below).

Scholars who study Cypriot textiles consider that the non-mechanized handicraft work of the island preserves a more "traditional" structure (Pieridou 1960: 107) because it is done by hand in the home. Three forms of modern production, "household production," "household industry," and "workshop industry," are comparable to ancient textile production because they preserve similar systems, locations, and frequencies of production and use similar, although not identical, tools. The products are different because they include fabrics not made in the Mediterranean during the Bronze Age. Likewise, consumers are also different, living as they do in an industrial society within a world economy. However, because the organization of the production is similar, gender distinctions that exist among different tasks in the making of textiles by hand may reasonably be compared to those that existed in the past.

For just about every stage in the production of textiles, one can generally associate particular tasks with either women or men. Cypriot women, not men, normally engage in weaving, embroidery, and sewing (Pieridou 1960: 107). Women usually work in the home, while men work in shops (Pieridou 1960: 107). However, there are instances where that pattern is interrupted. For example, men participate in home industry, especially as reelers in silk production (Papademetriou 1995: 59–77). Below I review only the four tasks that were noted as useful for the model of task differentiation using Late Bronze Age comparative evidence: spinning, weaving, washing, and dyeing.

Spinning is normally done by women (Ohnefalsch-Richter 1913: 19–20; Papademetriou 1995: 79–105). When men spin fibers, it is to make string rather than thread (e.g., Kasdaglis 1990: fig. 56), but men also appear as spinners in census lists, with no listing of their location of work (Christodoulou 1959: 105). Spinning is often a portable activity, as is the manufacture of cord or rope, a heavy, thick product often made by men, although women also made it (Christodoulou 1959: 143).

Hand weaving on a loom is normally done by women (Ohnefalsch-Richter 1913: 19–20; Pieridou 1960: 107; Papademetriou 1993b: 18, 21; Papademetriou 1995: 79–105) and was one of their main occupations until recent memory (Pieridou 1959: 53). Men, however, also weave in the home, mainly in the Troodos mountain region, but usually they weave only on large, heavy looms and make thick woolen beddings, sacks (Christodoulou 1959: 105), and bags that are used for agricultural purposes

(Papademetriou 1993a: 11; 1993b: 21). A few men among a majority of women are also listed as weavers in census lists (Christodoulou 1959: 105), but the location of their work is not stated.

I was unable to find specific references in the ethnographic record to fullers who wash cloth. Possibly related is the messy job of boiling and washing the silk-worm cocoons and eventually reeling their threads, a task always performed by men on Cyprus, even in home production, although the prior handling of the cocoons to separate them from the branches of trees is often done by women (Papademetriou 1995: 59–77). The related activity of cloth dyeing, also using often poisonous and certainly noxious chemicals, is performed on Cyprus by women in home industry (Pieridou 1961: 128; Papademetriou 1995: 87), but by men in dye workshops located outside the home (Ohnefalsch-Richter 1913: 274–75).

Women's only occasional involvement with dyeing, as it would be in the home, or even non-involvement, as it would be with specialized dye workshops, may be due to the hazardous fumes that stem from the dye process and can lead to miscarriage in pregnant women (Mary Dabney, personal communication). Although I have not been able to find reference to a taboo concerning women and dyestuffs in the Mediterranean or Near East (women's contact with a dye such as saffron was in fact encouraged in ancient Greece because of its medicinal effects on menstrual pain; Barber 1994: 115–16, 162), taboos do exist in other cultures where women are kept separate from locations of dye work during pregnancy and menstruation because it is thought that their presence will harm the outcome of the dye work (Bühler 1942: 1602).

A model for task differentiation in textile production. A model for task differentiation in textile production emerges from the evidence available and may be applied to the patterns preserved in the Cypriot archaeological record. Because this model incorporates both the tools used in the production of textiles and the locations where textiles are produced, it is suitable for the patterned evidence from Cyprus, which consists almost exclusively of tools used in production in settlement contexts.

When spinning, weaving, and other textile production activities occur in the home, the producers are almost always female. This is true both for "household production" and "household industry" systems. Exceptions to this general rule do exist but are often regionally specific, as in the case of men who weave heavy textiles in the Troodos mountain range, or limited to certain activities, such as silk reeling. In the Late Bronze Age Aegean, washing also appears to have been done by men, perhaps within the structure of "household industry."

From the archaeological record of Late Bronze Age Cyprus, we can not know for whom the textiles were produced or in what quantity, so we are not able to distinguish between the two forms of "household" production. We can, however, generally identify "domestic production" or evidence for textile production that occurs within areas interpreted as "dwellings" (Wilk and Rathje 1982: 718), as opposed to areas set aside as activity specific "workshops" (see below). When we find artifacts associated with the tasks of spinning and weaving in primary contexts in "dwellings," it is reasonable to propose that women performed the work in those areas. Other evidence, such as for washing or dyeing, is less gender-specific and is not useful as part of a model of task differentiation in domestic areas.

When textile production occurs outside the home, often it is still women who spin and weave, especially in "workshop industry" situations. However, men also weave on a large scale, perhaps in systems better defined as "large-scale industry," as they did in Egypt on the "tapestry" loom, and men engage in the messy and smelly activities of fulling and dyeing in workshops outside the home. From the evidence available within non-mechanized textile production, there is no evidence for women who served as full-time dyers in workshops located outside the home, and there is almost no evidence that women served as fullers in similar capacities (e.g., Lefkowitz and Fant 1992: 220). Both women and men worked outside the home and are depicted seemingly in the same context (cf. Barber 1991: 286), but we do not know whether they worked in the same space or in separate areas. Women's textile work was sometimes supervised by a female and sometimes by a male (Van De Mieroop 1989: 63).

Archaeologically it is difficult to distinguish between "workshop industry" and "large-scale indus-try" on Cyprus, unless one decides upon an arbitrary indicator of scale that might separate the two. For the purposes of this study, I make no attempt at such a distinction, for there is no pattern that might suggest what scale is "large" enough for separating the two. What we can do is isolate areas in the archaeological record that can be defined as use-specific "workshops." These areas differ from activity areas in "dwellings" used for textile production because those in "workshops" are devoted permanently to the activity, whereas those in "dwellings" are temporary, allowing for the use of the space for other activities. Often the only way to determine that these workshops existed is by means of permanent installations that would have prevented the use of the space for anything but textile manufacture. Evidence for spinning and weaving in these areas is less useful than evidence for fulling and dyeing for making gender distinctions among tasks performed. While it is possible that the weaving was per-formed by either women or men, it is probable that all fulling and dyeing activities in "workshops" were performed by men.

An earlier predictive statement for distinguishing some male and female roles in textile production appeared in Elizabeth Barber's now standard book, *Prehistoric Textiles*:

> It seems … that we may expect to find men becoming involved with the weaving when something new is being added to the technology, and/or when new prestige goods are being developed and exploited fairly rapidly … Otherwise we must expect the women to be doing the spinning and weaving while they tend their children. (Barber 1991: 291)

Although this statement refers more to the cloth produced than the archaeologically recognizable tools and locations, it adds to the generally described picture above that suggests that women performed most activities in textile production in a variety of contexts, while men were limited to specific activi-ties, most of which occurred outside the home.

IDENTIFYING TEXTILE PRODUCTION IN THE ARCHAEOLOGICAL RECORD OF LATE BRONZE AGE CYPRUS

Areas of production with debris from manufacturing processes have been found at several Late Cypriot sites, including areas of metallurgical, ceramic, and textile production. When an area was used for a specific activity, whether permanently or temporarily, we expect to find groups of features and artifacts connected with this activity in greater numbers than in other parts of a site. Production fre-quency and regularity, the time and space needed for work, the residues left by the activity, and how many people were involved generally affect the preservation of features and artifacts connected with craft activity (Arnold 1991: 103).

Areas where craft activity took place on a large scale and in permanent installations are easier to identify than those where the activity occurred at a smaller scale in temporary locations. In addition, it is easier to identify areas of production for crafts, such as metal working, that leave large quantities of durable materials in the archaeological record, than it is to identify those from crafts, such as textile production, whose products would leave little trace archaeologically on Cyprus. Both the raw materi-als used in textile production and the finished textiles perish easily in archaeological context due to the effects of environmental transformation processes. They only survive in extreme climatic conditions. Wooden looms used to weave textiles also rarely survive.

What we can recognize archaeologically are the tools used to make textiles (Tzachili 1990: 380). During the Cypriot Bronze Age, the warp-weighted loom was used, a device that leaves behind in the archaeological record its weights, which are often made of clay. In addition, we have whorls used for spinning, bone tools used for beating in the weft of textiles, clay reels, possibly used for belt-cord or band making (Barber 1997: 516–17), installations used for fulling and dyeing, and even remains of dyestuffs, detergents, and bleaches. The evidence for textiles is very extensive (Barber 1991: xxi) and this one includes the main items from Cyprus considered in this paper.

When trying to reconstruct textile production from these remains, we find that activities that are spatially restricted (Arnold 1991: 101) are more successfully identified in the archaeological record with a group of tools and a specific place. Those that were easily portable are harder to isolate within a specific area. Spinning, band weaving, and rope making (Barber 1991: 69; 1997: 515–16) are spatially flexible (Arnold 1991: 100). Tasks that must take place in a fixed location, at least for the duration of the activity, include weaving on a loom and the washing and dyeing of fabrics. However, looms may be packed up and "moved." Dyeing and washing containers and racks may be portable and stored away once the activity is completed.

Fibers and Textiles

Fibers woven for textiles in Cyprus during the Late Bronze Age are wool and flax. While cotton displaced sugar cane as a major crop on the island during the Medieval period, there is no evidence for its ancient growth and use (Christodoulou 1959: 136–38). Similarly, silk was cultivated later (Papademetriou 1995). Recently hemp was a main product of Paphos and Morphou (Christodoulou 1959: 144), although its use during antiquity on Cyprus is unknown. Elsewhere in the Mediterranean, hemp was used in the Bronze Age for rope and sails (Barber 1991: 15). On Cyprus in antiquity, sheep were bred not only for their meat (Nobis 1985: 424–25), but also for wool (e.g., Halstead 1977; Croft 1996: 219) as they are still today (Christodoulou 1959: 189). Flax was a product particularly of the Morphou district, both during the 20th century (Christodoulou 1959: 142–43) and in the past when Soli produced flax (Mitford 1980b: 1327) administered by the company of Zeno during the 3rd century B.C. (Mitford 1980a: 256–57).

Fragments of textiles from ancient Cyprus are few. The oldest preserves only a fossilized form of a likely vegetable product from the Neolithic period at Khirokitia (Le Brun 1994: 299). Fragments of cloth from the Early through Late Bronze Ages are mainly of flax (Jacobsthal 1956: 115; Åström 1965; Pieridou 1967; Frankel and Webb 1996: 198), although there is also possible evidence of wool (Åström 1965: 112; Pieridou 1967; Frankel and Webb 1996) from an Early Cypriot tomb at Lapithos (Gjerstad et al. 1934: 42f.). Purple dyed textiles are known from Salamis in the Iron Age where impressions of purple-dyed fabrics were discovered (Karageorghis 1967: 40, 53, no. 167, pl. 37.4–6, 74). Purple wool from the 3rd to 1st century B.C. was found in the same area (Granger-Taylor, Jenkins, and Wild 1989).

A few written sources suggest that Late Bronze Age Cyprus produced linen and woolen textiles, sometimes colored purple, not only for local consumption, but also for export east and west. From written evidence that survives from Bronze Age Anatolia, Syria, the Levant, and the Aegean, we know that Alashiya, if that place equates in some way with Cyprus, was a source of linen (Beckman 1996: 33) and slightly later in the Iron Age, a source of purple wool (Walls 1996a: 59). In the Linear B texts, a possible "Cypriot" type of wool is also attested (Bennet 1996: 57–58).

Tools and Installations

The textile production activities that can be reconstructed from remains in the archaeological record on Cyprus, and which are significant for the model of task differentiation outlined above, are spinning, weaving, washing, and dyeing. Evidence for these activities exists in the form of whorls, weights that hung on warp-weighted looms, vats with traces of detergents and dyes, ground stone tools for preparing dyestuffs, and interior and exterior spaces where these objects are preserved and the work was probably performed.

Spinning. Spinning thread requires no tool other than the hand but often uses a stick, or spindle, to which a weight, or whorl, is attached, at the top, the bottom, or even somewhere in the middle of the shaft. Whorls, being made of durable materials such as clay and stone, frequently survive in the archaeological record. However, it can be difficult to determine whether objects are whorls, beads, or other centrally pierced objects (Liu 1978; Swiny 1986: 99).

When studying a potential whorl it is important to (1) look for wear marks consistent with spinning, such as wear around one end of the hole, the other side of the whorl having been protected by the spun fiber (Frankel and Webb 1996: 194); (2) measure the diameter, for that will help to reconstruct the tightness of the spin (Barber 1991: 53) and, generally, an object less than 2 cm in diameter is more likely to be a bead than a whorl (Liu 1978; Barber 1991: 51); (3) determine whether the object is symmetrical about its perforation; (4) measure the size of the central hole, generally no larger than 1 cm in diameter (Barber 1991: 52), for it often tapers to accommodate the shape of the spindle; and (5) measure the weight of the whorl, the highest weight being in the range of 150 gms; whorls ca. 10 gm or lighter were probably more appropriate for cotton and too light for spinning wool and flax (Barber 1991: 51–52, note 9).

Generally, heavier whorls have larger diameters and greater perforations for placement on thick spindles. Spinning with these whorls produces heavier, thicker fibers. Similarly, lighter whorls tend to have smaller diameters and narrower perforations for placement on thinner spindles. Spinning with these whorls produces lighter, more tightly spun fibers (Barber 1991: 52; Frankel and Webb 1996: 195).

On modern Cyprus, the high-whorl spindle is used and, until recently, was thought to have been used on Cyprus in antiquity as well (Pieridou 1967: 27; Swiny 1986: 99). However, a study of whorls from the Early Cypriot III–Middle Cypriot I site of Marki-*Alonia* shows that the low-whorl spindle was used during the Bronze Age (Frankel and Webb 1996: 193–94), placing that period within a tradition of spinning known in the Levant, Europe, the Aegean, and Anatolia. The high whorl, by contrast, is characteristic of ancient Egypt and Mesopotamia (Barber 1991: 53; Frankel and Webb 1996: 194).

Many objects of terracotta, stone, bone, and ivory found in Late Cypriot contexts have been classified as whorls (P. Åström 1972: 585–86, 598–99), based on their small size and central perforations. While many of the objects identified as whorls of terracotta fit the criteria for whorls laid out above,

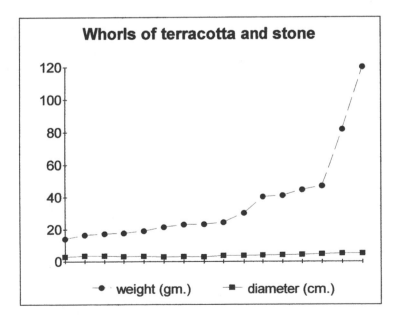

Figure 2. Whorls of terracotta and stone from Kition Areas I and II by weight and diameter.

Enkomi,
Dikaios   5749/6

Enkomi,
Dikaios   6032/1

Figure 3. *Pair of pyramidal loom weights bearing the same ring impression, from P. Dikaios' excavations at Enkomi, nos. 5749/6 and 6032/1. Drawing by the author.*

most of the objects of stone and all of the bone and ivory examples fall short of the definition because of details of their wear marks, their weights, their perforations, or a combination of factors. They are more accurately categorized as beads, buttons, and parts of pins.[1]

Objects thought to be whorls that I have handled and studied in detail come from Kition (Karageorghis 1985a). In size, shape, and material they are no different from similar objects at other sites and may be taken as representative of the range of objects classified as whorls for the Late Bronze Age of Cyprus. Pieces that can be defined as whorls using the criteria set out above are mostly of terracotta (Karageorghis 1985a: nos. 288, 433/4e, 557, 710/1, 863/1, 946, 2042, 2635, 5077, 5080, 5084, 5112), but they are also made of chalk, sandstone, and melagabbro (Karageorghis 1985a: 423/2, 5050, 5116). These whorls, with the exception of the one made of melagabbro (no. 5116), are clearly made by hand in an irregular, but functional way. They are generally spherical, biconical, or hemi-spherical, with little attempt at decoration. Some are even made of unfired clay. As artifacts they are expedient, suited for the purpose of spinning, but with little intrinsic value and easily replaced (fig. 2).

Weaving. Weaving can require several tools, especially when using the warp-weighted loom. Quantities of loom weights attest to the existence of the warp-weighted loom on Bronze Age Cyprus. Other possible evidence is a motif suggestive of a warp-weighted loom that appears in the impression of a single ring on a pair of loom weights from the LC IIIA period at Enkomi (fig. 3; Dikaios 1971: nos. 5749/6 and 6032/1, pls. 146.6a and 146.2, 3). A similar motif exists in Linear A (Barber 1991: 92). In addition to loom weights, artifacts found consistently in Late Cypriot contexts that were probably used by weavers are clay "reels" (L. Åström 1972: 518; P. Åström 1972: 587), possibly used to make belt cords (Barber 1997: 516–17; Barber 1999: 58–60), and pointed bone tools (Smith 1993; 1994: 57–60), originally classified as styli (P. Åström 1972: 608). For the purposes of this study, only loom weights are considered, for we not only understand their purpose, but their study can reveal something about the type of textiles they were used to produce.

When studying a potential loom weight, it is important to (1) look for wear marks consistent with their use on a loom (Frankel and Webb 1996: 198), such as wear on the sides where weights bumped and banged against one another with the movement of the loom; (2) locate the method of attachment for the warp fibers, such as a hole that may preserve wear to indicate that it hung heavily upon a fiber passed through it; (3) measure the weight of the object, which can indicate something about the textile woven on the loom; and (4) note the shape of the object, which although possibly unrelated to its function (Tzachili 1990: 383), may be useful for studies of different ethnic groups (Barber 1991: 299–310), or have some bearing on the type of cloth that was woven.

Generally, the use of light weights produces light fabrics and the use of heavy weights produces heavy fabrics (Barber 1991: 104). However, textiles woven on a warp-weighted loom vary by width as well as weight (Barber 1991: 104), making it important not only to know the weights of the objects hung from the loom, but also their quantity and arrangement. A weaver could use the same set of weights to produce a narrow, heavy fabric or a wide, light-weight fabric by varying the number of warp fibers attached to a single weight (Barber 1991: 96). Ideally, one needs sets of weights, preferably found in a row as they were positioned on the loom (Barber 1991: 93). When not on a loom, a set of weights was generally stored away as a group (Barber 1991: 102). Often sets consist of a few heavy or many light weights (Barber 1991: 104). Normally, fewer weights were used for narrower cloths and many for wider (Barber 1991: 104).

Loom weights used during the Late Cypriot period are mostly made of terracotta, low-fired, or unbaked clay and are pyramidal or rectangular in shape with a hole at the top (fig. 4; L. Åström 1972: 517, types 1–2). A flat, circular type with a central hole also existed (fig. 5; L. Åström 1972: 517, type 3). Terracotta or unbaked clay weights of pyramidal shape were in continuous use from the Early Cypriot period into the Iron Age (Frankel and Webb 1996; Swiny 1986: 107–108; P. Åström 1972: 586). Weights of this shape generally preserve evidence for wear around their corners and in and around their holes, supporting their classification as objects that hung from cords on a loom (fig. 4). Disc-shaped or "donut"-shaped weights first appear in the LC IIC period and are almost always made of low-fired or unbaked clay, although terracotta examples do exist. Because of their unfired state, weights of this sort do not often preserve the same wear marks as the terracotta, pyramidal variety (fig.

Figure 4. Pyramidal loom weights from Kition Area II, nos. 5141 and 5191. Photo by the author.

Figure 5. Disc-shaped loom weights from Kition Area II, nos. 5053, 5061A–H, 5064, 5065, 5065A, 5101, and 5112.
Photo by the author.

Figure 6. Rope impressions (ca. 1 cm in width) on disc-shaped loom weights from Kition Area I, nos. 1054.1–5.
Photo by the author.

5). Several "donut" weights from Kition preserve rope impressions on their surfaces (fig. 6) but not generally through their holes.

Washing (fulling). Washing (fulling) is a major activity in textile production. Substances such as wool need to be cleaned of the dirt and natural grease from the sheep. Woven textiles need finishing work such as bleaching. Washing involves the use of detergents and bleaches. Soap is a combination of vegetable or animal fat and an alkali such as wood ash or potash (Forbes 1954: 260; Hodges 1964: 170). Hot, soapy water not only cleaned the cloth but was used in the felting process of woolen fabrics (Hodges 1964: 145). Bleaches include various decolorizing agents such as ammonia.

A major component of soap is the fat from animal bone that comes from degreasing bones by boiling them in water (Lewkowitsch and Warburton 1959: 846). Potash combined with the fat from degreased bones leaves behind a greasy, almost clay-like substance. Sometimes potash is even mixed with clay when bleaching linen fabrics (Forbes 1954: 260). Fuller's earth is, of course, a form of clay (Hodges 1964: 145). Once bones were degreased, they could be carbonized to make a substance that decolorizes. Carbonized bone, when calcined in air, forms bone ash, a substance used in refining metals (Lewkowitsch and Warburton 1959: 846).

Dyeing. Dyeing fibers and fabrics was also a major component of textile production. However, it was not simply a dye that was required. A mordant to "fix" the dye was needed as well as tools such as grinding stones to prepare the dye and vats in which to do the work. Several vegetable, mineral, and other natural dyes were available in Cyprus in antiquity. Purple dye from the murex was exploited on the island during the Late Bronze Age. Several crushed, fresh murex have been found at Hala Sultan Tekke as well as other sites on Cyprus and in the Mediterranean basin (Reese 1979/80, 1985: 348–49; 1987). Red and yellow ochres are other dye sources that survive in the archaeological record (Elliott 1985: 301, 304). Pounders, grinders, and other stone tools that could have been used to prepare dye-stuffs abound during the Late Cypriot period (e.g., Elliott 1985).

Mordants used to fix the dyed colors include substances such as ammonia or urine (Barber 1991: 236, 239), which do not survive in the archeological record, and hydrated or slaked lime (Barber 1991: 237–38), which may leave residues behind. Metal salts, such as alum, also used to fix dyes, are available on Cyprus (Bear 1963: 43). The island was known as a resource for alum during the Late Bronze Age (Pliny, *NH* 35.52.183–84; Barber 1991: 238). Another way of using metal salts as mordants is to throw scraps of metal, such as copper, into the dye vat, a practice that may preserve archaeologically-visible traces (Barber 1991: 238–39).

Textile Production Before the LC IIC Period

Although the earliest evidence for a woven textile on Cyprus dates to the Neolithic period (Le Brun 1994: 299), the earliest evidence for spinning and weaving tools dates to the Early Cypriot period. There are several whorls in Cypriot archaeological literature that date to the Early and Middle Cypriot periods, but very few come from non-funerary contexts. Even fewer loom weights are known from that period. However, a significant addition to our knowledge of this subject is the recent publication of the Early Cypriot III to Middle Cypriot I site of Marki-*Alonia,* in which is a detailed account of evidence for spinning and weaving activity at the site, including the weights of the objects and comments on use wear in addition to the usual dimension, shape, and material descriptions (Frankel and Webb 1996: 192, 198). The remains come from domestic contexts.

Comparable evidence comes from the nearby Middle Cypriot site of Alambra-*Mouttes,* also published recently (Coleman et al. 1996), where whorls and weights have also been found in domestic contexts. Another settlement site with well-preserved and recorded evidence for spinning and weaving is Episkopi-*Phaneromeni*, which dates to the Late Cypriot I period (Swiny 1986). Swiny was the first to publish whorls and loom weights from Cyprus along with records of their weights, recognizing the value of these artifacts for our reconstruction of past textile production (1986: 98–108).

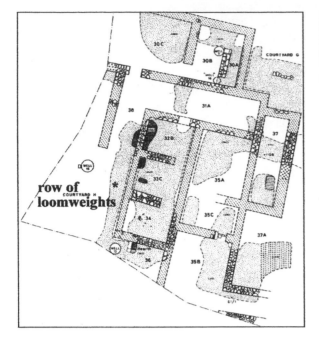

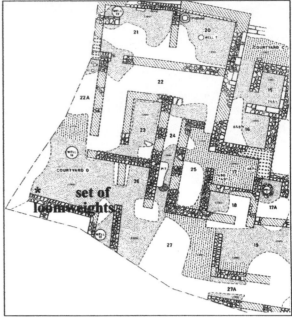

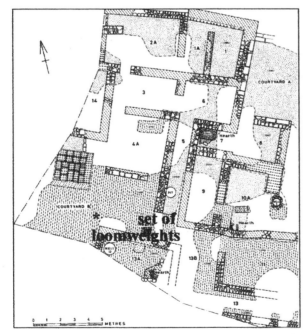

Figure 7. *Kition Area I, Floors IIIA (top left), II (top right), and I (bottom left), showing locations of sets and rows of loomweights found in courtyards. Adapted from Karageorghis (1985b: pls. 9, 14, and 17).*

Evidence for spinning shows that a number of fibers of different weights were spun (Frankel and Webb 1996: 192–95). Whorls range in weight from 20–30 and up to 95 gm each. The sample size for loom weights is small, but from what is available it is possible to begin a reconstruction of weaving on warp-weighted looms. Loom weights from Marki are more than 1000 gm each (Frankel and Webb 1996: 197–98). The excavators suggest that small numbers of weights were used to make heavy, dense cloth at the site (Frankel and Webb 1996: 198). By contrast, later weights at Episkopi fall into three groups, ca. 220, 550, and 1000 gm (Swiny 1986: 107–8), presenting a wider range of weights, probably for weaving a wider variety of fabrics. Weights continue to decrease in weight and increase in variety towards the end of the Late Bronze Age, as at Kition (see below), suggesting that the range of fabrics produced increased over time.

All evidence for textile production prior to the Late Cypriot IIC period comes from domestic contexts, indicating that spinning and weaving took place in the home. Although washing and dyeing must have taken place, there is no trace of these activities in the archaeological record thus far. Using the model for task differentiation outlined above and considering Fischer's discovery that Early and Middle Cypriot whorls in tombs are found exclusively with female skeletons (1986: 42), it is reasonable to hypothesize that the evidence for textile production at Marki, Alambra, Episkopi, and other contemporary sites such as Kalopsidha and Enkomi is mostly, if not wholly, representative of women's, not men's, efforts. Whether women produced textiles only for the household or for other consumers is unknown. However, with additional detailed evidence from sites such as Marki that are still under

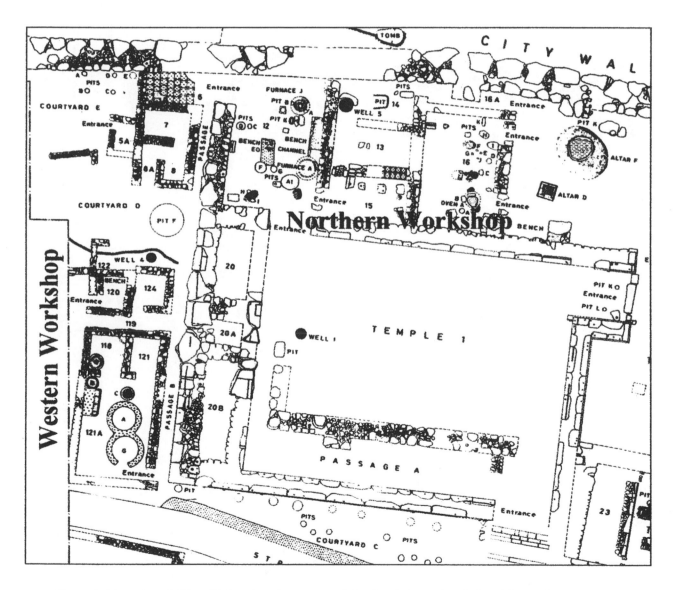

Figure 8. Kition Area II, Floor III, location of western workshop in relation to Temple 1 and the northern workshop.
Adapted from Karageorghis (1985b: plan V).

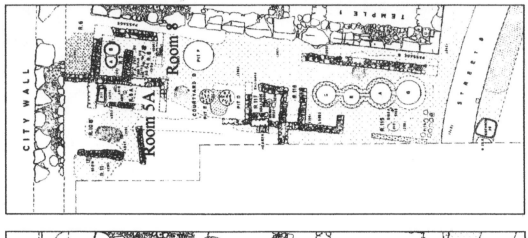

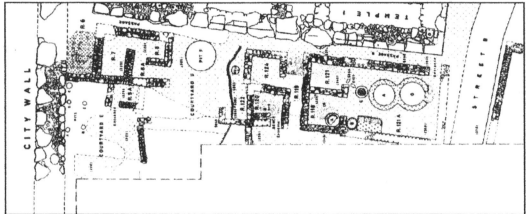

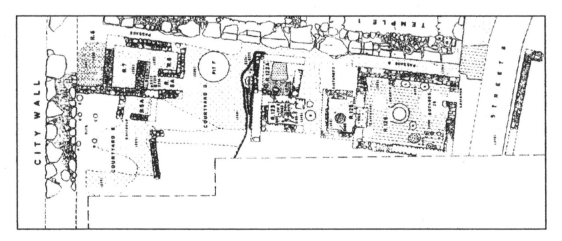

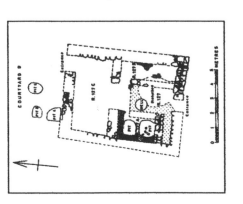

Figure 9. Kition Area II, western workshop. From left to right: Floors IV, IIIA, III, and II, shown at same scale to illustrate the changes in size and layout of the workshop over time. Adapted from Karageorghis (1985b: plans X, XXXII, and XXXIV). Floor II Rooms 5A and 8, locations of two sets of loomweights, labeled. See fig. 13 for details of Floor III Rooms 118 and 121A.

Weight (gm)	Area I	Area II	Weight (gm)	Area I	Area II
20-29	0	1	160-169	2	2
30-39	1	3	170-179	4	0
40-49	6	11	180-189	2	0
50-59	31	18	190-199	0	1
60-69	20	16	200-209	0	1
70-79	16	12	220-229	1	0
80-89	17	7	230-239	1	0
90-99	14	2	270-279	1	2
100-109	11	3	280-289	2	0
110-119	1	7	290-299	1	1
120-129	2	6	300-309	2	0
130-139	3	3	310-319	2	1
140-149	0	2	330-339	1	0
150-159	1	1	350-359	1	0

Figure 10. Loom weights from Kition, Areas I and II, inclusive of Floors IV–I, by weight.

excavation, it may be possible to show that evidence for spinning and weaving occurs in only a few "dwellings" or domestic units at a site. This pattern might suggest that more textile production took place in some households than others, supporting in some cases the existence of "household industry."

Textile Production from LC IIC to LC IIIB

Several sites beginning in the LC IIC period preserve evidence for textile production both in domestic units, as at Enkomi (Courtois 1984: 65–68; Courtois 1988; Barber 1991: 242), and in areas that may be classified as "workshops," or at least areas that appear to be separate from domestic areas at sites such as Idalion (Gjerstad et al. 1935: 517, 556) and Maroni-*Vournes* (Cadogan 1987: 83). The most detailed evidence, however, comes from the site of Kition, in Areas I and II, excavated by the Department of Antiquities of Cyprus (Karageorghis 1985a; Karageorghis and Demas 1985).

Kition Areas I and II. Kition Areas I and II were occupied from some point towards the end of the Late Cypriot IIC period (though see Kling 1989: 68–78), in the 13th century B.C., and continued to operate through a series of five "Floors" into the 11th century B.C., Area I is characterized by relatively small-roomed, mostly rubble-walled structures, with few consistent divisions in the use of space, either within one phase or through time (fig. 7). Space in Area I appears flexible in how it was used, for there are few permanent installations that limit the use of specific areas. I define Area I as "domestic" space, where textile work in the form of "household production" and "household industry" are likely to have occurred, especially during Floors IIIA–I.

By contrast, Area II contains five monumental buildings constructed of ashlar as well as rubble masonry that have been interpreted as temples or ceremonial structures (fig. 8). These specific-use structures stand alongside two areas with smaller rubble-walled buildings called the "northern" and "western" workshops. Consistent divisions in the use of space over time, permanent installations, and large quantities of debris associated with metal working identify the northern buildings as metal workshops. Similarly consistent in organization, the buildings to the west contain permanent installations and large numbers of loom weights and other artifacts used for textile production (fig. 9; Demas 1985: 32–33, 77–81, 112–15, 132–35, 153–57). Eighty percent of all whorls and loom weights from Area II were found in rooms and outdoor spaces associated with the western-workshop area. Whether or not the metal and textile workshops were the sites of "sacred industries" because of their proximity to the temples (Karageorghis 1985b: 253–54), they do stand apart from the remains of craft production found

Context	Location	Quantity	Total weight	Individual weights (gms)	Shape (s) and Materials	Whorls	Fiber/fabric
AREA I							
Floor IIIA: Courtyard H (nos. 421/1-3, 4-6, 422/1, **423a-v**, 423/1a/1-2, 423/1b, 423/4)	outside, probable work area	33 (22 in group, 5 possibly in row)	**group: 1320** row?: 382 (+ 45 gm whorl) other: 504	43(2), 45(1), 50(1), 51(1), 52(2/1), 53(3), 54(1), 55(1), 57(2), 58(1), 62(1/1), 63(1), 66(1), 67(1), 69(1), 72(1/1), 79(1/1), 82(1), 85(1), 87(1), 106(1), 109(1), 172(1)	pyramidal (7); disc (25); conical (1) terracotta (3); low fired/unbaked clay (30)	45 (1)	medium weight fibers; wide light or medium weight fabric?
Floor II: Courtyard D (nos. 432, **433/1a-b, 433/2, 433/3a-d, 433/4a-d, 433/5,** 434a-b, 446/1, 452)	outside, probable work area	17 (11 in group)	**group: 1859** to sides of group: 975 scatter: 168	55(2), 58(1), 70(1), 76(1), 83(1), 84(1), 114(1), 122(1), 220(1), 235(1), 280(2), 295(1), 305(1), 315(1), 355(1)	pyramidal (1); disc (11); square (4); ovoid (1) terracotta (4); low fired/unbaked clay (13)	41 (1)	medium weight fibers; medium weight fabric?
Floor I: Courtyard B (nos. 408/1, **412a-k**)	outside, probable work area	12 (11 in group)	**group: 2029** other: 77	43(1), 77(1), 152(1), 162(1), 166(1), 171(1), 178(1), 179(1), 183(1), 184(1), 275(1), 336(1)	disc (12); low fired/unbaked clay (12)	19 (1)	light weight fibers; light or medium weight fabric?
Floor I: Room 1 (nos. **892/1-4**)	inside, storage	**4 (4 in group)**	**group: 303**	57(1), 65(1), 87(1), 94(1)	disc (4) low fired/unbaked clay (4)		narrow light weight fabric?
Floor I: Room 2a (nos. 970/1, 1021a-b, 1057)	inside, storage	4	scatter: 295	69(1), 72(1), 73(1), 81(1)	disc (4) low fired/unbaked clay (4)		narrow light weight fabric
AREA II							
Floor III: Room 118 (nos. 5053, **5061a-h**, 5064, 5065, 5065A, 5101)	inside, storage	13 (**8 in group**, 4 in second group)	**group: 825** group: 542 other: 149	48(1), 73(1), 75(1), 85(1), 94(1), 112(1), 115(1), 117(1), 120(1), 126(1), 132(1), 149(1), 270(1)	disc terracotta (7); low fired/unbaked clay (6)	120 (1)	heavy weight fibers; medium weight fabric?
Floor III: Room 121A (nos. 5097, 5098, 5107, 5107A)	inside, possible work area	4 (4 in close scatter)	close scatter: 539	105(1), 113(1), 155(1), 166(1)	disc terracotta (1) low fired/unbaked clay (3)		medium weight fabric?
Floor II: Room 5A (nos. 567, 568, 912, 4952)	inside, storage?	4	scatter: 266	43(1), 67(1), 69(1), 87(1)	pyramidal (2); disc (2) terracotta (2); low fired/unbaked clay (2)		narrow light weight fabric?
Floor II: Room 8 (nos. 573, 574, 575, 576, 899, 903, 904, 909, 910)	inside, possible work area	9 (7 in possible row)	clustered near wall - row?: 406 scatter: 145	42(1), 47(1), 51(1), 57(1), 60(1), 63(1), 66(1), 79(1), 86(1)	pyramidal (5); disc (4) terracotta (5); low fired/unbaked clay (4)		light weight fabric?

Figure 11. Sets of loom weights from Kition Areas I and II (all weights in gm). Boldface: weights found together in a group; Italic: weights found together in second group; Underline: weights possibly in row.

in Area I because of their permanent installations and their close connection with what was certainly a center of power at Kition during the Late Cypriot period. Textile production in the form of "workshop industry" or even "large-scale industry" is likely to have taken place in the western workshops.

Spinning at Kition. Spinning at Kition can be reconstructed from sixteen whorls found in Areas I and II. They range from 14 to 120 gm in weight. These fall into light (14–24), medium (30–47), heavy (80), and very heavy (120 gm). Four light and three medium weight whorls come from Area I. The one heavy and one very heavy whorl each come from Area II, along with five light and two medium weight whorls. The discovery of most whorls in fill deposits between floors and the portability of the activity of spinning make it difficult to be sure that a specific area where a whorl was discovered can be associated with that activity. Four whorls, however, were found with sets of loom weights (see below), suggesting that the fibers spun with those whorls were woven with the aid of those weights, giving a greater context to those few whorls. Generally, however, from the weights of the whorls from Areas I and II, it appears that light weight and medium fibers were spun for use in both areas, but heavy and very heavy fibers were only spun for use in Area II.

Weaving at Kition. Weaving at Kition is attested by 242 loom weights, 142 from Area I and 100 from Area II, with both areas preserving a similar range of weights (fig. 10). The heaviest weighs 355 gm, but the majority weigh between 40 and 110 gm. Others weigh more than 100 or 200 gm, and a few more than 300 gm. Several weights were found in fill deposits between floors, making it difficult to determine whether or not they were used in the rooms or other spaces where they were discovered. Of those found in primary deposits on floors, several occur singly or in pairs, indicating little about their use on the loom. Only a few weights may have been found in rows as they fell from looms.

Most informative are weights found together on the floors of single spaces in groups; these may be "sets" or parts of sets, which provide information not only about the weights of the objects hung on an individual loom, but also how many weights were used. Generally between six and thirty weights were used on a single loom when it was set up (Barber 1991: 104). Using Elizabeth Barber's number of four as the smallest number of weights that can be convincingly called a "set" (1991: 104), and looking only at deposits said to be "on floors," nine deposits of weights at Kition are significant, accounting for 100 of the total discovered (fig. 11).

Details of sets from Kition appear in fig. 11. The most striking feature is that the location of weaving in Area I is primarily outside in courtyard spaces (Karageorghis 1985b, pls. 10, 15, 19; Floor IIIA, Courtyard H; Floor II, Courtyard D; Floor I, Courtyard B), whereas in the western workshop it takes place inside, sometimes within large rooms (Karageorghis 1985b, pl. 48; Floor III, Room 121A), but also seemingly within smaller spaces near a doorway, possibly to allow light into the room (Karageorghis 1985b, pl. 34; Floor II, Room 8). Weaving outdoors was common, sometimes taking place on the roofs of buildings (Barber 1991: 101). It is suggestive of part-time work. The temporary work space would be cleared during inclement weather or for the use of the space for other outdoor activities. Weaving indoors could have been on looms permanently set up in a space set aside only for that activity.

Only in two cases were weights found in possible rows to indicate how they were arranged on looms. In Area I, a set was found in a row, but close inspection of that row reveals that only three individual weights were found in a row, the other parts of the row including a chalk whorl and a group of 22 loom weights (fig. 12). Another possible row was found in Area II, but it may represent a suggestive scatter of weights near a wall (Karageorghis 1985b, pl. 34; Floor II, Room 8). What is interesting, however, is that all sets found in probable locations of work rather than storage were found near walls where it would have been logical to set up a loom, leaving the remaining workspace free for the weaver to work and move.

It is difficult to determine the types of fabrics produced from the information preserved. Larger numbers of weights form sets in Area I than in Area II, suggesting that wider fabrics were woven in the

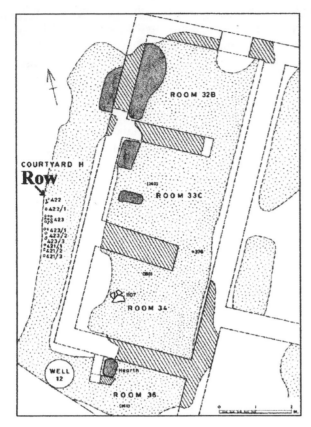

Figure 12. *Kition Area I, Floor IIIA, Courtyard H, with row of loomweights indicated. Adapted from Karageorghis (1985b: pl. 10).*

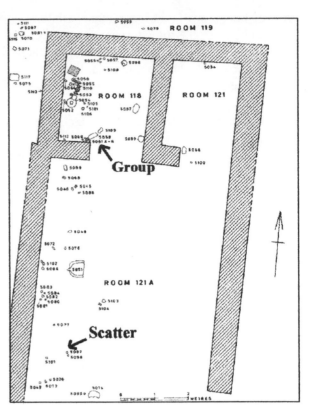

Figure 13. *Kition, Area II, Floor III, western workshop, detail showing objects on floors of Rooms 118 and 121A, group and scatter of loomweights indicated. Adapted from Karageorghis (1985b: pl. 48).*

outside areas, possibly bed linens and other household fabrics. The number and weight of the weights and whorls found with these sets suggest that the fabrics were of light and medium weight. Whorls of greater weight were found in Area II, including one found in a deposit of stored weights (fig. 13; Floor III, Room 118), suggesting that heavier fibers were used in some cases in the western workshops than in domestic contexts. Fabrics of medium and narrow width were produced in Area II, to judge from sets possibly found in a location of work rather than storage. The weight range of individual weights in Area II is similar to Area I, in some cases being lighter, but the weight of fabrics may have been similar in both areas at Kition. Both areas have low or unfired disc-shaped weights that preserve the impression of cords or ropes up to 1 cm in width on their surfaces, suggesting that in some cases ropes were located near or even used in the weaving process.

Washing and dyeing at Kition. Evidence for washing and dyeing at Kition is found only in the western workshop in Area II. Each floor preserves a series of pits and vats, some connected by channels, that increase in number from two to four over time and occupy space first in one and then two separate buildings at the site (fig. 9). Samples of the fills of the vats and other "pits" located in the western workshop area from Floor IV through Floor II were not saved, but descriptions of their contents are suggestive of fulling and dyeing activity.

The contents of these features are: ashes (Demas 1985: 32, 78, 113), black ash (1985: 133), blackwood ash (1985: 112), bones (1985: 113, 132, 133), bone ash (1985: 112, 132, 133), gray clay

Type of Groundstone	Area II, Western Workshop [# (% of) total]	Remainder of Area II [# (% of) total]	Area I, textile working areas [# (% of) total]	Remainder of Area I [# (% of) total]
Quern	5 (100 %)	0	0	0
Grinder/rubber	1 (100 %)	0	0	0
Cupped stone	1 (100 %)	0	0	0
Anvil	1 (100 %)	0	0	0
Slab	1 (100 %)	0	0	0
Pebble	1 (100 %)	0	0	0
Perforated weight	7 (70 %)	3 (30 %)	0	0
Rubber	20 (65 %)	6 (19 %)	1 (3 %)	4 (13 %)
Pounder	6 (50 %)	0	2 (17 %)	4 (33 %)
Perforated disc	2 (50 %)	2 (50 %)	0	0
Grinder/pounder	3 (33 %)	6 (67 %)	0	0
Pestle	1 (9 %)	2 (18 %)	4 (36.5 %)	4 (36.5 %)
Perforated stone	0	0	3 (100 %)	0
Macehead	0	0	1 (100 %)	0
Hammerstone	0	0	1 (25 %)	3 (75 %)
# (% of) Total	49 (51.5 %)	19 (20 %)	12 (12.5 %)	15 (16 %)

Figure 14. Kition, Areas I and II, percentage of ground stone tools in textile production areas. Numbers of artifacts based on information in Elliott (1985).

(1985: 113, 134, 135), gray sandy soil (1985: 78–79), dark soil (1985: 133), red soil (1985: 33, 133), gravel (1985: 78, 113, 134), crushed havara (1985: 134), patches of lime (1985: 113), burnt lime plaster (1985: 113), green staining (1985: 113), fragments of copper (1985: 113), as well as soil (1985: 32), burnt patches (1985: 33), small rubble (1985: 32), and bits of gypsum "floor" (1985: 32).

Bone ash may have been used for refining metals in the northern workshops (Stech, Maddin, and Muhly 1985: 399; Zwicker 1985: 412), but the interpretation of the pits in the western workshop as storage containers for bone ash is unlikely. Instead, the pits or vats in the western workshop appear to contain residues one might expect from a fulling and dyeing workshop. Both of the ingredients for detergent or soap are present, the bones boiled for their fat and ashes, even wood ash. Gray clay and other darkened deposits may even attest to the presence of detergent or bleach. Lime deposits may indicate the use of fixers or mordants by dyers. Likewise, the presence of copper fragments and green staining probably attests to the use of copper salts in the dye process. The use of the vats in the western workshop area for washing and dyeing fibers and fabrics explains the presence of channels connecting the vats and the presence of hearths for heating their contents.

A reciprocal relationship existed between the metal workers and textile producers. Bone degreased for soaps and then made into charcoal could be used in its final stage as bone ash in the metal workshops. Recycled scrap metal (Karageorghis and Kassianidou 1999: 183) from the metal workshop could be used by dyers for fixing dyes. Both crafts also required a water resource. In addition to wells, the area located just beyond the northern boundary of the site where the two workshops are located was a lagoon as early as the 4th century B.C. (Gifford 1985: 385). Shared resources may have led to the close proximity between the two workshops at Kition. It was important also that both be located away from residential areas where noxious fumes from metal work, fulling, and dyeing could have been blown away by the south wind (Karageorghis 1985c: 251–52).

There is very little evidence at Kition for actual dyes. A couple of fresh murex shells were found (Reese 1985: 343) as was some yellow ochre (Elliott 1985, 301) and a cupped stone possibly used for crushing ochre (Elliott 1985: 304). In spite of the lack of dyestuffs, numerous ground stone tools from the western workshops support the identification of that area as a dye works. At Kition, over fifty percent of all ground stone tools were found in the western workshops (fig. 14; Elliott 1985: 301–11). Six forms of tool were found exclusively in those workshops. The balance of ground stone from Area II favors the western workshops over the rest of the area by approximately 70:30. In Area I, areas with identifiable concentrations of textile manufacturing artifacts had almost the same number of groundstone artifacts as other parts of Area I, supporting the hypothesis that activity in that area is less segregated as it contained fewer areas set aside for single activities.

Other features of the western workshop fit what can be expected for a dye workshop (Barber 1991: 239–40). No textiles have been found, although impressions of heavy cords or ropes on loom weights and the so-called "reels" attest to some form of manually worked fiber. Large vessels for steeping have not been found, but holes for inset vessels such as small pithoi attest that they were once there. In one phase, a stone carved drainboard was found (fig.13, no. 5051). The large space within the workshop rooms to the south and in the courtyard to the north would have provided space to hang out fibers and textiles to dry.

Task differentiation at Kition can be identified using the model developed. Weaving and spinning occurred in both domestic and workshop areas at Kition. Permanent washing and dyeing facilities are present, however, only in the workshops. Their presence separates the activities performed in Area I from those in Area II by function, adding to previously noted differences in scale and probable frequency of production. According to the model developed, men must have been involved in textile production in the western workshops, at least as fullers and dyers, if not also as weavers. Using our model, it is also possible that women worked in the western workshops alongside the men. The spinning and weaving technology used is the same as in Area I. There is evidence for some heavier fibers in Area II, but it appears that heavier weaves were produced in Area I, making it difficult to determine who wove based on the textiles produced. In Area I, however, according to the model developed, it is likely that only women produced textiles and that they worked part-time, usually in outdoor spaces.

CONCLUSIONS

Permanent textile workshops operated on Cyprus in the 13th through the 11th centuries B.C. The increase in numbers of textile tools, such as loom weights, during this time probably attests to a larger scale of production in these workshops than had existed previously in Cypriot households. These changes were part of a general Cypriot economic expansion that broadened its role in international commerce as well as diversified its internal economic systems.

During this period, women's roles in a traditionally female set of tasks altered along with the development of workshop industry. Based on the evidence collected here, women were the primary producers of textiles on Cyprus into the Late Bronze Age. Their location of work was in the home, although they may have made cloth both for home consumption and consumers from other households, even from other communities.

In the 13th century B.C., with the addition of non-domestic workshop areas for the production of textiles, the evidence suggests that women were active in household as well as workshop production. In workshops they may have been spinners and weavers. If women continued as weavers and spinners in workshops outside the home such as at Kition, they probably worked there alongside men. At this time men probably began to play a major part in textile arts, not only as fullers and dyers, but also perhaps as weavers. Together they may have produced cloth for sails and even highly decorated textiles for elite consumption (Smith 1999), both of which would have been important parts of Cypriot life at home and abroad.

With this study, not only of the craft of textile manufacture but also the people who were most likely involved, it is possible to begin to understand how women as well as men played significant roles in the expanding Late Bronze Age Cypriot economy. At the same time, however, this study is only part of the beginning of research in this area for Late Bronze Age Cyprus. Other crafts that follow a similar pattern at this time are ceramic, metal, and stone and ivory carving. It may be possible to construct similar models of female and male roles in those crafts that will be useful when compared to that developed for textile production. Furthermore, with changes in the economy, women's roles both as elites and non-elites undoubtedly diversified. Occasional finds such as Tomb 11 at Kalavasos-*Ayios Dhimitrios*, containing two women resplendent with gold (Goring 1989), or scattered textual references such as in *The Report of Wenamun,* in which we find a female leader of Alashiya (Goedicke 1975), may help to lay a foundation for women's roles as elites, even administrators on Cyprus. However, to gain an understanding of the full spectrum of women's, men's, and children's roles, a thorough, gendered study is needed. The present study can only begin to illuminate part of the puzzle.

Archaeologically, we can only identify people as textile producers on a general level. Investigating individual tasks, such as spinning and dyeing, we can sometimes be more specific about the people involved. Whether a task can be interpreted as gender-specific or not, our ability to move from the archaeological identification of the sex of the producer to interpreting the significance of gender roles that operated in the past involves all categories of information. Tasks such as weaving that cannot easily be gendered may be our most important clues to discovering the nature of female/male roles in different segments of a community structure.

An important step towards understanding the usefulness of the comparative evidence for textile producers from other regions and time periods is recognition of exceptions to the model developed. Male spinners and female dyers exist and make it difficult to establish certain gender associations for past activities. However, most tasks for which is it difficult to identify the sex of the producers can be interpreted as more gender-specific once the location of work is defined. Even so, the Late Cypriot systems of textile production, in which both women and men were involved, must have been far more complex than I have been able to reconstruct.

For Late Cypriot textile manufacture, important associations between producers, their products, and consumers are missing. Evidence for centrally-located and probably centrally-controlled cloth production on Cyprus exists only in the form of workshops, such as in Kition Area II, which were devoted to textile crafts. However, "household industry" producers, such as may have existed in Kition Area I, may also have produced textiles for a central authority. Due to the lack of written records and textile products, this relationship cannot be demonstrated at this time.

Careful study of the wealth of information for Late Cypriot textiles that exists among the publications and storage trays full of Late Cypriot textile manufacturing tools may help us to fill the gap created by the absence of text and fabric. This paper has only begun to reveal details of weight patterns and whorls, the possible textiles created, where, and by whom. Further patterns at Kition, patterns at other sites, and patterns among sites through time will provide a larger picture of textile production on Cyprus that may help us to work towards a better understanding of how the producers and their products fit into the functioning of the overall economy for the period.

ACKNOWLEDGMENTS

My study of objects found during the Department of Antiquities of Cyprus excavations at Kition, now housed in the Larnaca District Museum and the Cyprus Museum, took place in 1992 while I was in Cyprus as a Fulbright Scholar. Some of my comments on the material appeared in my dissertation, completed in 1994. This article includes a more detailed analysis of the artifacts associated with textile manufacture than I was able to include in that earlier work. My sincere thanks and appreciation go to the Department of Antiquities for facilitating my study in 1992 and in subsequent years. In connection with my work on the Kition material, in particular I thank then Director Dr. Demos Christou, Curator of Antiquities, Dr. Pavlos Flourentzos, Curator of Monuments, Dr. Maria Hadjicosti, and Keeper of the Larnaca Museum, Mr. Andreas Savva. I also thank Nancy Serwint and Diane Bolger for the opportunity to present this paper in March of 1998 at the conference, Engendering Aphrodite. For inspiring comments on pins, buttons, bones, pregnancy, Cypriot ethnography, and other wide ranging subjects, I thank Alexis Castor, Mary Dabney, Frosso Egoumenidou, Katherina Giesen, and Sherry Fox Leonard. Any inaccuracies or other errors in the text are my own.

NOTE

1. Currently in progress is an article on the reinterpretation of many Late Cypriot objects traditionally interpreted as spindle whorls. From wear patterns, size, shape, and context they are more accurately described as buttons and attachments for dress pins. I plan to submit this article to the *Report of the Department of Antiquities of Cyprus*.

REFERENCES

Angel, J. L.
1972   Appendix B: Late Bronze Age Cypriotes from Bamboula: The Skeletal Remains. Pp. 148–65 in *Bamboula at Kourion: The Necropolis and the Finds*, ed. J. L. Benson. Philadelphia: University of Pennsylvania.

Appadurai, A.
1986   Introduction: Commodities and the Politics of Value. Pp. 3–63 in *The Social Life of Things: Commodities in Cultural Perspective*, ed. A. Appadurai. New York: Cambridge University.

Arnold, P. J., III
1991   *Domestic Ceramic Production and Spatial Organization: A Mexican Case Study in Ethnoarchaeology.* Cambridge: Cambridge University.

Åström, L.
1972   Other Arts and Crafts. Pp. 473–557 in *The Swedish Cyprus Expedition*. Vol. IV, 1D: *The Late Cypriote Bronze Age,* by L. Åström and P. Åström. Lund: The Swedish Cyprus Expedition.

Åström, P.
1965   Remains of Ancient Cloth from Cyprus. *Opuscula Atheniensia* 5: 111–14.
1970   What we Know about Ancient Fibres. Pp. 12–18 in *The Thread of Ariadne: A Study of Ancient Greek Dress,* by E. Gullberg and P. Åström. Studies in Mediterranean Archaeology 21. Göteborg: Åströms.
1972   Relative and Absolute Chronology, Foreign Relations, Summary and Historical Conclusions. Pp. 558–781 in *The Swedish Cyprus Expedition*. Vol. IV, 1D: *The Late Cypriote Bronze Age*, by L. Åström and P. Åström. Lund: The Swedish Cyprus Expedition.

Barber, E. J. W.
1991   *Prehistoric Textiles: The Development of Cloth in the Neolithic and Bronze Ages with Special Reference to the Aegean.* Princeton: Princeton University.
1994   *Women's Work: The First 20,000 Years, Women, Cloth, and Society in Early Times.* New York: W. W. Norton.
1997   Minoan Women and the Challenge of Weaving for Home, Trade, and Shrine. Pp. 515–19 in *TEXNH: Craftsmen, Craftswomen and Craftsmanship in the Aegean Bronze Age II,* eds. R. Laffineur and P. P. Betancourt. Aegaeum 16. Liège and Austin: Université de Liège and Program in Aegean Scripts and Prehistory.
1999   *The Mummies of Ürümchi.* New York: W. W. Norton.

Bear, L. M.
1963   *The Mineral Resources and Mining Industry of Cyprus Bulletin* 1. Nicosia: Republic of Cyprus, Ministry of Communications and Industry, Geological Survey Department.

Beckman, G.
1996   Hittite Documents from Ḫattuša. Pp. 31–35 in *Sources for the History of Cyprus Volume II: Near Eastern and Aegean Texts from the Third to the First Millennia B.C.,* ed. A. B. Knapp. Altamont, NY: Greece and Cyprus Research Center.

Bennet, J.
1996   Linear B Texts from the Bronze Age Aegean. Pp. 51–58 in *Sources for the History of Cyprus Volume II: Near Eastern and Aegean Texts from the Third to the First Millennia B.C.,* ed. A. B. Knapp. Altamont, NY: Greece and Cyprus Research Center.

Brumfiel, E. M.
1991   Weaving and Cooking: Women's Production in Aztec Mexico. Pp. 224–51 in *Engendering Archaeology: Women and Prehistory,* eds. J. M. Gero and M. W. Conkey. Oxford: Basil Blackwell.

Brumfiel, E. M., and Earle, T. K.
1987   Specialization, Exchange, and Complex Societies: an Introduction. Pp. 1–9 in *Specialization, Exchange and Complex Societies,* eds. E. M. Brumfiel and T. K. Earle. Cambridge: Cambridge University.

Bühler, A.
1942   Dyes and Dyeing Methods for Ikat Threads. *Ciba Review* 44: 1597–1603.

Cadogan, G.
1987   Maroni III. *Report of the Department of Antiquities of Cyprus* 1987: 81–84.

Charles, R. -P.
1962   *Le peuplement de Chypre dans l'Antiquité: Étude Anthropologique.* Études Chypriotes II. Paris: de Boccard.

Christodoulou, D.
1959   *The Evolution of the Rural Land Use Pattern in Cyprus.* Bude, Cornwall, England: Geographical Publications.

Coleman, J. E., et al.
1996   *Alambra: A Middle Bronze Age Settlement in Cyprus: Archaeological Investigations by Cornell University 1974–1985.* Studies in Mediterranean Archaeology 118. Jonsered: Åströms.

Conkey, M., and Spector, J.
1984   Archaeology and the Study of Gender. Pp. 1–38 in *Advances in Archaeological Method and Theory* 7, ed. M. Schiffer. New York: Academic.

Courtois, J. -C.
1984   *Alasia III: Les objets des niveaux stratifiés d'Enkomi: Fouilles C. F. -A. Schaeffer (1947–1970).* Paris: Éditions Recherches sur les Civilisations.

1988   Enkomi (Fouilles Schaeffer 1934–1966): Inventaire complémentaire (suite): Les objets en terre cuite et en pierre. *Report of the Department of Antiquities of Cyprus,* Part 1: 307–18.

Croft, P.
1996   Animal remains. Pp. 217–23 in *Marki*-Alonia, *An Early and Middle Bronze Age Town in Cyprus: Excavations 1990–1994,* by D. Frankel and J. M. Webb. Studies in Mediterranean Archaeology 123:1. Jonsered: Åströms.

Davies, P.
1997   Mortuary Practice in Prehistoric Bronze Age Cyprus: Problems and Potential. *Report of the Department of Antiquities of Cyprus* 1997: 11–26.

Demas, M.
1985   The Architecture. Pp. 5–164 in *Excavations at Kition V. The Pre-Phoenician Levels: Areas I and II, Part I,* by V. Karageorghis and M. Demas. Nicosia: Department of Antiquities of Cyprus.

Dikaios, P.
1971   *Enkomi Excavations 1948–1958, Vol. II.* Mainz am Rhein: Philipp von Zabern.

Domurad, M.
1986   *The Populations of Ancient Cyprus.* Unpublished Ph.D. Dissertation, University of Cincinnati.

Ehrenberg, M.
1989   *Women in Prehistory.* London: British Museum.

Elliott, C.
1985   Appendix V: Ground Stone Tools from Kition Areas I and II. Pp. 295–316 in *Excavations at Kition V. The Pre-Phoenician Levels: Areas I and II, Part II,* by V. Karageorghis. Nicosia: Department of Antiquities of Cyprus.

Filaktou, A., and Ioannides, G. K.
1991   Πάφος 1924–1984: Μέσα από το Φακό του Σπύρου Χαρίτου. Nicosia: Popular Bank Cultural Center.

Fischer, P. M.
1986   *Prehistoric Cypriot Skulls.* Studies in Mediterranean Archaeology 75. Göteborg: Åströms.

Forbes, R. J.
1954   Chemical, Culinary, and Cosmetic Arts. Pp. 238–98 in *A History of Technology. Vol. 1: From Early Times to Fall of Ancient Empires,* eds. C. Singer, E. J. Holmyard, and A. R. Hall. New York: Oxford University.

Frankel, D., and Webb, J. M.
1996   *Marki* Alonia, *An Early and Middle Bronze Age Town in Cyprus: Excavations 1990–1994.* Studies in Mediterranean Archaeology 123:1. Jonsered: Åströms.

Gifford, J. A.
1985   Appendix IV: Post-Bronze Age Coastal Change in the Vicinity of Kition. Pp. 375–87 in *Excavations*

at Kition V. The Pre-Phoenician Levels: Areas I and II, Part I, by V. Karageorghis and M. Demas. Nicosia: Department of Antiquities of Cyprus.

Gjerstad, E.; Lindros, J.; Sjöqvist, E.; and Westholm, A.
1934   *The Swedish Cyprus Expedition*. Vol. I: *Finds and Results of the Excavations in Cyprus 1927–1931*. Stockholm: The Swedish Cyprus Expedition.
1935   *The Swedish Cyprus Expedition*. Vol. II: *Finds and Results of the Excavations in Cyprus 1927–1931*. Stockholm: The Swedish Cyprus Expedition.

Goedicke, H.
1975   *The Report of Wenamun*. Baltimore: Johns Hopkins University.

Goring, E.
1989   Death in Everyday Life: Aspects of Burial Practice in the Late Bronze Age. Pp. 95–105 in *Early Society in Cyprus*, ed. E. Peltenburg. Edinburgh: University of Edinburgh.

Granger-Taylor, H.; Jenkins, I. K.; and Wild, J. P.
1989   From Rags to Riches: Two Textile Fragments from Cyprus. Pp. 146–65 in *Cyprus and the East Mediterranean in the Iron Age*, ed. V. Tatton-Brown. London: British Museum.

Halstead, P.
1977   A Preliminary Report on the Faunal Remains from Late Bronze Age Kouklia. *Report of the Department of Antiquities of Cyprus*: 261–75.

Hodges, H.
1964   *Artifacts: An Introduction to Early Materials and Technology*. London: John Baker.

Jacobsthal, P.
1956   *Greek Pins and their Connexions with Europe and Asia*. Oxford: Clarendon.

Karageorghis, V.
1967   *Salamis III: Excavations in the Necropolis of Salamis I*. Nicosia: Department of Antiquities of Cyprus.
1974   *Excavations at Kition I. The Tombs*. Nicosia: Department of Antiquities of Cyprus.
1985a   *Excavations at Kition V. The Pre-Phoenician Levels: Areas I and II, Part II*. Nicosia: Department of Antiquities of Cyprus.
1985b   *Excavations at Kition V. The Pre-Phoenician Levels: Areas I and II, Plans*. Nicosia: Department of Antiquities of Cyprus.
1985c   Religious Aspects. Pp. 240–62 in *Excavations at Kition V. The Pre-Phoenician Levels: Areas I and II, Part I*, by V. Karageorghis and M. Demas. Nicosia: Department of Antiquities of Cyprus.

Karageorghis, V., and Demas, M.
1985   *Excavations at Kition V. The Pre-Phoenician Levels: Areas I and II, Part I*. Nicosia: Department of Antiquities of Cyprus.

Karageorghis, V., and Kassianidou, V.
1999   Metalworking and Recycling in Late Bronze Age Cyprus - the Evidence from Kition. *Oxford Journal of Archaeology* 18: 171–88.

Kasdaglis, E. X.
1990   *Κύπρος: Μνήμη καὶ Αγάπη με το Φάκο του Γιῶργου Σεφέρη*. Nicosia: Popular Bank Cultural Center.

Keswani, P. F. S.
1989   *Mortuary Ritual and Social Hierarchy in Bronze Age Cyprus*. Unpublished Ph.D. Dissertation, University of Michigan.
1996   Hierarchies, Heterarchies, and Urbanization Processes: The View from Bronze Age Cyprus. *Journal of Mediterranean Archaeology* 9: 211–50.

Killen, J. T.
1984   The Textile Industries at Pylos and Knossos. Pp. 49–63 in *Pylos Comes Alive: Industry and Administration in a Mycenaean Palace*, eds. C. W. Shelmerdine and T. G. Palaima. New York: Fordham University.

Kling, B.
1989   *Mycenaean IIIC:1b and Related Pottery in Cyprus*. Studies in Mediterranean Archaeology 87. Göteborg: Åströms.

Le Brun, A.
1994   *Fouilles récentes à Khirokitia (Chypre) 1988–1991*. Paris: Éditions Recherches sur les Civilisations

Lefkowitz, M. R., and Fant, M. B.
1992   *Women's Life in Greece and Rome: A Source Book in Translation*. 2nd ed. Baltimore: Johns Hopkins University.

Lewkowitsch, P. R. E., and Warburton, G. H.
1959   Bone, Industrial Uses of. Pp. 845–46 in *Encyclopedia Britannica: A New Survey of Universal Knowledge*. Vol. 3. Chicago: Encyclopedia Britannica.

Liu, R. K.
1978   Spindle Whorls Part I: Some Comments and Speculations. *The Bead Journal* 3: 87–103.

Marcus, M.
1993   Incorporating the Body: Adornment, Gender, and Social Identity in Ancient Iran. *Cambridge Archaeological Journal* 3: 157–78.

Masson, O.
1985   Eléments de la vie quotidienne dans l'épigraphie chypriote. Pp. 87–89 in *Chypre: La vie quotidienne de l'antiquité à nos jours. Actes du Colloque, Musée de l'Homme*. Paris: Musée de l'Homme.

Mitford, T. B.
1980a   *The Nymphaeum of Kafizin: The Inscribed Pottery*. New York: Walter de Gruyter.
1980b   Roman Cyprus. Pp. 1285–1384 in *Aufsteig und Niedergang der Römischen Welt: Geschichte und Kultur Roms im Spiegel der Neueren Forschung II*, eds. H. Temporini and W. Haase. New York: Walter de Gruyter.

Moyer, C. J.
1989   Human Skeletal Remains. Pp. 58–69 in *Vasilikos Valley Project 3: Kalavasos*-Ayios Dhimitrios *II: Ceramics, Objects, Tombs, Specialist Studies*, by A. K. South, P. Russell, and P. S. Keswani, ed. I. A. Todd. Studies in Mediterranean Archaeology 71:3. Göteborg: Åströms.

Niklasson, K.
1983   Tomb 23: A Shaft-grave of the Late Cypriote III Period. Pp. 169–213 in *Hala Sultan Tekke 8: Excavations 1971–79*, by P. Åström, E. Åström, A. Hatziantoniou, K. Niklasson, and U. Öbrink. Studies in Mediterranean Archaeology 45:8. Göteborg: Åströms.
1991   *Early Prehistoric Burials in Cyprus*. Studies in Mediterranean Archaeology 96. Jonsered: Åströms.

Nobis, G.
1985   Appendix IX: Tierreste aus dem Präphönizischen Kition. Pp. 416–33 in *Excavations at Kition V. The Pre-Phoenician Levels: Areas I and II, Part II*, by V. Karageorghis. Nicosia: Department of Antiquities of Cyprus.

Ohnefalsch-Richter, M. H.
1913   *Griechische Sitten und Gebräuche auf Cypern: mit Berücksichtigung von Naturkunde und Volkswirtschaft sowie der Fortschritte unter Englishcher Herrschaft*. Berlin: Dietrich Reimer.

Papademetriou, E.
1993a   *Cyprus Folk Art: Exhibition Organised on the Occasion of the Commonwealth Heads of Government Meeting, Cyprus, 21–25 October 1993*. Nicosia: Cultural Services, Ministry of Education and Culture.
1993b   Παραδοσιακή Υφαντική καὶ Φορεσιά. Pp. 17–32 in *Κυπριακή Λαϊκή Τέχνη: Πρακτικά Ημερί–δας που διοργανώθηκε από το Ἴδρυμα Πιερίδη στη Λάρνακα στις 23 Μαΐου 1992*, eds. V. Karageorghis, E. Papademetriou, and F. Egoumenidou. Nicosia: Pierides Foundation.
1995   *Μεταξουργία στην Κύπρο: με Αναφορά στη Λάπηθο και τον Καραβά*. Nicosia: Popular Bank Cultural Centre.

Peacock, D. P. S.
1982   *Pottery in the Roman World: An Ethnoarchaeological Approach*. New York: Longman.

Pieridou, A.
1959   Κυπριακή Λαϊκή Ὑφαντική. *Κυπριακαὶ Σπουδαί* 23: 187–214. Pp. 53–81 in *Κυπριακη Λαϊκη Τέχνη* (Δημοσιευματα της Ἑταιρείας Κυπριακῶν Σπουδῶν 6). Nicosia: Society for Cypriot Studies.
1960   Η Λαϊκή Τέχνη στὴ Λευκοσία κατὰ τὸν 18ον καὶ 19ον Αἰώνα. *Φιλολογικὴ Κύπρος* 1960:

102–108. Pp. 107–14 in *Κυπριακή Λαϊκή Τέχνη* (Δημοσιέυματα της Ἑταιρείας Κυπριακῶν Σπουδῶν 6). Nicosia: Society for Cypriot Studies.

1961   Φυτικὲς Βαφικὲς Οὐσίες στὴν Κυπριακὴ Λαϊκὴ Τέχνη. *Φιλολογικὴ Κύπρος* 1961: 177–79. Pp. 125–29 in *Κυπριακή Λαϊκή Τέχνη* (Δημοσιέυματα της Ἑταιρείας Κυπριακῶν Σπουδῶν 6). Nicosia: Society for Cypriot Studies.

1967   Pieces of Cloth from the Early and Middle Cypriote Periods. *Report of the Department of Antiquities of Cyprus*: 25–29.

Reese, D.
1979/80   Industrial Exploitation of Murex Shells: Purple Dye and Lime Production at Sidi Khrebish, Benghazi, (Berenici). *Libyan Studies* 11: 79–93.

1985   Appendix VIII: Shells, Ostrich Eggshells and Other Exotic Faunal Remains from Kition. Pp. 340–415 in Excavations at Kition V. *The Pre-Phoenician Levels: Areas I and II, Part II*, by V. Karageorghis. Nicosia: Department of Antiquities of Cyprus.

1987   Palaikastro Shells and Bronze Age Purple Dye Production in the Mediterranean Basin. *Annual of the British School at Athens* 82: 201–6.

Schwartz, J. H.
1974   Appendix IV: The Human Remains from Kition and Hala Sultan Tekke: A Cultural Interpretation. Pp. 151–62 in *Excavations at Kition I. The Tombs*, by V. Karageorghis. Nicosia: Department of Antiquities of Cyprus.

Sinopoli, C. M.
1991   *Approaches to Archaeological Ceramics*. New York: Plenum.

Smith, J. S.
1993   From Writing to Weaving. *CAARI News* 7: 1–2.
1994   *Seals for Sealing in the Late Cypriot Period*. Unpublished Ph.D. Dissertation, Bryn Mawr College.
1997   Preliminary Comments on a Rural Cypro-Archaic Sanctuary in Polis-*Peristeries*. *Bulletin of the American Schools of Oriental Research* 308: 77–98.
1999   Changes in Warp-weighted Loom Technology in Late Bronze Age Cyprus. Paper presented at the annual meeting of the American Schools of Oriental Research, Boston.

Spector, J.
1982   Male/Female Task Differentiation among the Hidatsa: Toward the Development of an Archaeological Approach to Gender. Pp 77–99 in *The Hidden Half: Studies of Plains Indians Women*, eds. P. Albers and B. Medicine. Washington: University Press of America.

Stech, T.; Maddin, R.; and Muhly, J. D.
1985   Appendix V: Copper Production at Kition in the Late Bronze Age. Pp. 388–402 in *Excavations at Kition V. The Pre-Phoenician Levels: Areas I and II, Part I*, by V. Karageorghis and M. Demas. Nicosia: Department of Antiquities of Cyprus.

Swiny, S.
1986   *The Kent State University Expedition to Episkopi-Phaneromeni. Part 2*. Studies in Mediterranean Archaeology 74:2. Nicosia: Åströms.

Thomas, A. P.
1981   *Gurob: A New Kingdom Town: Introduction and Catalogue of Objects in the Petrie Collection*. Egyptology Today 5. Warminster: Aris and Philipps.

Tringham, R. E.
1991   Households with Faces: The Challenge of Gender in Prehistoric Architectural Remains. Pp. 93–131 in *Engendering Archaeology: Women and Prehistory,* eds. J. M. Gero and M. W. Conkey. Oxford: Blackwell.

Tzachili, I.
1990   All Important yet Elusive: Looking for Evidence of Cloth-Making at Akrotiri. Pp. 380–89 in *Thera and the Aegean World III, Vol. One: Archaeology, Proceedings of the Third International Congress, Santorini, Greece 3–9 September 1989*, eds. D. A. Handy, C. G. Doumas, J. A. Sakellarakis, and P. M. Warren. London: The Thera Foundation.

Ucko, P. J.
1969   Ethnography and Archaeological Interpretation of Funerary Remains. *World Archaeology* 1: 262–77.

Van De Mieroop, M.

1989   Women in the Economy of Sumer. Pp. 53–69 in *Women's Earliest Records From Ancient Egypt and Western Asia*, ed. B. S. Lesko. Atlanta: Scholars.

van der Leeuw, S. E.

1977   Towards a Study of the Economics of Pottery Making. Pp. 68–76 in *Ex Horreo*, eds. B. L. Van Beek, R. W. Brandt, and W. Goeman-van Waateringe. Amsterdam: University of Amsterdam.

Veenhof, K. R.

1972   *Aspects of Old Assyrian Trade and Its Terminology*. Leiden: Brill.

Wallace, P. W. and Orphanides, A. G., eds.

1990   *Sources for the History of Cyprus. Vol. 1: Greek and Latin Texts to the Third Century A.D.* Albany, NY: The Institute of Cypriot Studies, University of Albany, State University of New York and Cyprus College.

Walls, N.

1996a   Biblical Hebrew Texts (post-Bronze Age). P. 59 in *Sources for the History of Cyprus Volume II: Near Eastern and Aegean Texts from the Third to the First Millennia B.C.*, ed. A. B. Knapp. Altamont, NY: Greece and Cyprus Research Center.

1996b   Ugaritic Documents from Ugarit. Pp. 36–40 in *Sources for the History of Cyprus Volume II: Near Eastern and Aegean Texts from the Third to the First Millennia B.C.*, ed. A. B. Knapp. Altamont, NY: Greece and Cyprus Research Center.

Wilk, R. R., and Rathje, W. L.

1982   Household Archaeology. Pp. 617–39 in *Archaeology of the Household: Building a Prehistory of Domestic Life*, eds. R. R. Wilk and W. L. Rathje. American Behavioral Scientist 25 (6).

Wylie, A.

1985   The Reaction Against Analogy. Pp. 63–111 in *Advances in Archaeological Method and Theory* 8, ed. M. Schiffer. New York: Academic.

Zwicker, U.

1985   Appendix VI: Investigation of Samples from the Metallurgical Workshops at Kition. Pp. 403–29 in *Excavations at Kition V. The Pre-Phoenician Levels: Areas I and II, Part I*, by V. Karageorghis and M. Demas. Nicosia: Department of Antiquities of Cyprus.

PART SIX

GENDER AND THE GODDESS

CREATING A GODDESS OF SEX

STEPHANIE LYNN BUDIN

University of Pennsylvania
sbudin@mail.sas.upenn.edu

All too often in discussions of ancient religion, the concepts of fertility and sexuality have been confused. Important goddesses within ancient pantheons have been termed "Mother Goddesses" regardless of their actual maternal status, while iconographic emphasis on breasts, pudenda or hips has been automatically regarded as a manifestation of the fertile nature of females and female deities. As a result, eroticism has been eclipsed, and scholarship has avoided the more "embarrassing" aspects of female divinity, namely the embodiment and power of sexual pleasure as distinct from reproduction.

This paper examines the interplay of sexuality and fertility as these concepts apply to the iconography of Late Cypriot goddess figurines, in particular, the bird-faced figurines of Late Cypriot II and the Bomford figurine of Late Cypriot III. At the end of the Bronze Age, the Greeks came to know and adopt the Cypriot goddess, and she evolved into the Hellenic Aphrodite. Using Cypriot iconography, Near Eastern artistic and literary parallels, and Greek mythology, this paper considers the extent to which the Cypriot goddess was specifically a goddess of sex, separate and distinct from notions of fertility.

There is a fairly consistent tendency in the study of ancient religions to dissociate sexuality from divinity and from power. While goddesses might be "sexy" or "alluring" or "beautiful," these traits are inevitably interpreted as indications of fertility, and female deities become generically defined as "Earth Mothers" or "fertility goddesses" regardless of their unique and individual aspects. This tendency to separate sexuality from divinity, and thus to deny the inherent power within sexuality, is especially prominent in the study of the development of Cypriot religion. J. Karageorghis (1992: 19) claims in her study of Cypriot Chalcolithic cruciform figurines that "it is indisputable that the image of a strongly sexualized woman is promoted here. It is difficult to say whether this is the representation of a goddess of fertility or simply a magic image of the forces of fertility, but the main point is that the image of fertility is identified with woman." When writing about a larger version of these Chalcolithic images, the "Lemba Lady," Tatton-Brown (1997: 48) claims that, "She must have been a fertility charm and may even represent a goddess." The fact that the figurines in question are "sexualized" automatically leads to the assumption that they embody fertility, as if breasts and genitalia could have no other purpose or meaning.

In his interpretation of the Late Cypriot III Bomford figurine, Catling (1971: 29) sees a divinity of Near Eastern derivation who, "in all likelihood … is the same goddess who was later to become the Paphian Aphrodite. In her Bronze Age manifestation, at least, she was doubtless a goddess of fecundity." Once again, the pronounced presence of the sexual attributes (breasts and genitalia) and the possible association with the later Greek goddess of sex leads to the hypothesis that the image in question must be a fertility image. In only a slight contrast to Catling's interpretation, Masson (1973: 115–16) claims that the image may, in fact, be Aphrodite or even Athtart but that ultimately such fertility goddesses would have assimilated and distributed attributes too diverse to allow for an identification with a single deity: "ce type de divinité féminine de la fécondité a dû donner lieu à des assimilations diverses." That the figurine in question is a fertility goddess is implicitly accepted; it is only the possibility that the figurine represents another, or several, of the "fertility goddesses" of the eastern Mediterranean which comes into question.

At the other end of the spectrum lie the interpretations of such authors as Desmond Morris. While recognizing the inherent and ultimately undeniable sexual emphasis of the Late Cypriot II bird-faced and normal-faced figurines (see fig. 1), he removes them from the divine context, eschews fertility interpretations, and instead identifies them solely as *ushabti* figurines, meant to accompany dead men into the afterlife. Moreover, to quote Morris (1985: 166), "If the blatant display of the pubic triangle seems more lusty than bereaved, perhaps they were anticipating a long trip. The deceased might appreciate a few diversions."

Thus it would seem that we have goddesses who are only sexual in order to make the grass grow, while make-shift mortal females are over-sexed in order to keep their "husbands" entertained all the way to Nirvana. Sexuality and desire never coincide with divine status. As such, the power of sexuality, in this case female sexuality, is kept within confined and "safe" limits; the sexual attributes of goddesses merely indicate their power to provide a good harvest or healthy children, while sexuality among mortal women is for the use and benefit of their men.[1]

Thankfully, more recent approaches have been taken in understanding the female figurines that comprise such a large portion of our evidence of the development of Cypriot religion. Diane Bolger and Anna a Campo (Bolger 1993; a Campo 1994) have offered new interpretations of the Chalcolithic and Early Cypriot images, seeing aspects of birth rite, status, and perhaps social interaction within their iconography.

My intention here is to incorporate the idea of sex as divine power and attribute into a re-examination of the Late Cypriot II and III figurines so as to derive a fuller understanding of the meaning of these images in Late Bronze Age Cyprus and also, in its final manifestation, to use this understanding as a foil in determining the evolution and the persona of Aphrodite, the sex goddess *par excellence*. This study will begin by considering the coroplastic evidence for goddesses in Late Bronze Age Cyprus and its correlations with Levantine-Mesopotamian goddess iconography. Having de-

Figure 1. Bird-faced figurine. British Museum, A15. Used with permission from the Trustees of the British Museum.

termined which goddess or goddesses most probably influenced the development of the Cypriot pantheon during this period, the study will proceed to an examination of the artistic and literary evidence concerning the personae of those Eastern deities.

There was a sharp increase of Syrian iconography into the Cypriot repertoire at the turn of the Late Bronze Age, that is, in the brief artistic "dark age" between Middle Cypriot III and Late Cypriot II. In contrast to the Early Cypriot III plank figurines, which became increasingly three-dimensional and naturalistic during the Middle Cypriot period, the normal-faced and bird-faced figurines (fig. 1) of the Late Cypriot II period (our primary evidence for Late Cypriot female divinities) are strikingly innovative in style. The latter are almost identical to Syrian and Mesopotamian terracotta figurines identifiable as the goddesses Athtart (aka Astarte, Ashtart), Ishara, and possibly Inanna/Ishtar.

That these figurines in the Levant represent Athtart, Ishara, or Inanna/Ishtar is manifest on the basis of their relationship with the so-called "Astarte plaques," prevalent throughout the Levant in the Late Bronze Age, and on the basis of textual evidence. The mold-made plaques (fig. 2) show a nude female *en face*, often pointing to her breasts and/or genitalia with her hands or holding floral elements or animals to her sides, and standing atop a lion or, in the southern, Egyptianizing Levant, a horse. The goddess Ishtar is also associated with the lion in her Mesopotamian iconography. Thus, a Levantine goddess standing on a lion may represent either her or her Ugaritic "equivalent" Athtart.[2] In Egypt, Athtart is depicted as a horse and chariot goddess (Leclant 1960), and the portrayal on the horse in southern regions may also indicate this deity. That the mold-made plaques and the bird-faced figurines portray the same deity is clear both from the common distribution of both artifacts and the identical repertoire of arm positions. Both are shown either with arms out to the sides, supporting the breasts, or one arm to the breast and the other indicating the genitalia. The primary difference between the figurines and the plaques is merely the means of production, the one being moldmade and two-dimensional, the other handmade and more three-dimensional.

That Ishara might also be portrayed in the bird-faced figurines is evident in the iconographic and textual materials from Alalakh, one of Cyprus' closest neighbors on the Levantine coast. Such images are represented from Levels XII to I at the site, and thus attest to their continuous presence at Alalakh for over one thousand years without considerable stylistic change (Woolley 1955: 244). In the texts from Alalakh, the two female deities whose names appear consistently and frequently from the 18th century B.C.E. onwards (Levels VII and IV specifically) are Ishtar and Ishara. The latter name is more common in Level IV, and the ideogram IŠTAR may also conceal the name of this goddess (Prechel 1996: 42, 69–70). As the goddesses Ishara and, possibly, Ishtar are evident at Alalakh during the period when the bird-faced figurines are abundant, it would appear that these images are intended to portray these deities.

Since Athtart, Ishtar/Inanna and Ishara, iconographically at least, played such a profound role in the development of the Cypriot goddess, I turn attention to the iconographic and literary attributes of these goddesses and how their personae may have effected the Cypriot iconography and religious ideology. Both Ishtar/Inanna and Ishara are goddesses of war and sex. Athtart (usually in Bronze Age Ugarit accompanying the goddess Anat) is a beautiful goddess of war and hunting. None of them are mother goddesses, and their associations with fertility are negligible.

The evidence for Bronze Age Athtart is slight, as she is typically eclipsed by the more prominent goddess Anat in Ugaritic literature. Nevertheless, her physical appeal is indicated in her iconography, where emphasis is on breasts, genitalia and overall beauty (fig. 2). In literature as well, this comes across in the Epic of Keret, wherein King Keret, demanding his bride, calls out:

> You must give me Lady Huraya,
> The Fair One, your firstborn child!
> Who's as fair as the goddess Anath,
> Who's as comely as Astarte![3]

The goddess is named not in relation to a fertile or maternal bride, but as the highest standard of loveliness.

That Athtart is *not* a mother goddess is evident not only by her lack of children, but also by one of her appellations from Egypt (in an incantation against crocodiles from the Harris Magical Papyrus, dated to the 19th or 20th Dynasties), which calls her and Anat "the two goddesses who are pregnant but do not bear" (Pritchard 1943: 79). There are two potential interpretations for this expression. One is a reference to the sexual relations between these goddesses and Seth, who, being a god of desert and destruction, cannot engender live offspring (Wyatt 1999: 111). Or, one might interpret this as a reference to nubility and a healthy sexuality (a *potential* for pregnancy) on the part of the goddesses that is never actually used in reproduction.

Ishara, a Mesopotamian-Syrian goddess who probably had contact with Cyprus through Late Bronze Age Cypriot trading contacts with Alalakh, possesses a far more erotic character than Athtart. In the *Epic of Gilgamesh*, Gilgamesh and Enkidu first wrestle in a wedding context where "a bed is set up for Ishara; Gilgamesh lies by the maiden in

Figure 2. *Gold "Astarte Plaque" from Ugarit/Ras Shamra. Musée du Louvre, AO 14.714. Used with permission of the Musée du Louvre.*

the night," possibly taking part in some manner of *droit du seigneur* (Prechel 1996: 58). Thus Ishara is identified as a bride, perhaps even as the bridal aspect of Ishtar. A love incantation from the Sargonic period (2334 B.C.E.) invokes the beloved object by the names of Ishtar and Ishara, suggesting a possible separate identity for the two deities and yet a common concern for matters of love and sex (Leick 1994: 195).

The evidence for the sexual nature of Ishtar/Inanna is even greater. While iconography shows her almost exclusively as a war goddess (fig. 3) or as the evening star (Venus), her hymns reveal her strong eroticism and deep concern in sexual affairs. When Inanna is preparing to journey to her bridal bed, her song of joy is not one of impending motherhood but rather in the pleasures of sex. Thus, she sings:

> Bring in my bridegroom,
> Let him come, let him come,
>> Let him bring fine butter and cream!
>> Now my breasts stand up,
>> Now hair has grown on my vulva,
>>> Going to the bridegroom's loins, let us rejoice!
>>> O Baba, let us rejoice over my vulva!
>>> Dance! Dance!
>>> Afterwards they will please him, will please him![4]

Likewise, upon the "death" of Ishtar as related in the tale "Ishtar's Descent to the Underworld," the world of the living suffers as:

Ištar went down into the earth, she does not re-emerge.
From this time (when) Ištar went to the Land of No Return
The ox does not mount the cow, the ass does not impregnate the jenny.
The youth does not impregnate the young woman in the street.
The youth lies in his chamber,
The maid lies on her side. (ll. 86–91)

Rather than taking this passage as evidence of Ishtar's inevitable association with fertility, one must note that in each instance listed, what is bemoaned is not so much the loss of fertility but the sexual intercourse which makes generation possible. Thus, even associations with fertility eventually draw one back to Ishtar's essential dominion over sexuality. As for the goddess's associations with maternity, one need only note that in a religious tradition of almost 3000 years, only one myth, the "Anzu Bird," mentions Ishtar as having a child, in this case the warrior god Sharra.

If the strongly sexualized iconography present in the Late Cypriot II figurines can be attributed to Near Eastern influence, specifically to the deities Athtart, Ishara and Ishtar, and if these Near Eastern goddesses are themselves highly sexualized beings with minimal associations with maternity and fertility, then what we should see in the Late Cypriot II figurines are goddess images embodying sexuality as a power and as an attribute in its own right.

This is not to say, of course, that Athtart and Ishara totally eclipse the indigenous Cypriot tradition, for the latter is strong in itself and most evident in the bird-faced *kourotrophos* figurines of Late Cypriot II. The Syrian versions are almost never shown holding children (it is only later, and further to the south, that the Palestinian versions of these figurines show *kourotrophos* imagery), and we must, therefore, conclude that remnants of older, indigenous roles of this deity are still in place. It is perhaps only in this kourotrophic imagery that a maternal role might be speculated for the Cypriot goddess, as per the arguments of Bolger concerning the iconographic transition from Chalcolithic to Early Bronze Age. Contrasting the Chalcolithic cruciform figurines with the Early Cypriot plank figurines, focus switches from birthing posture to *kourotrophos* imagery, and, thus, from the role of the female as *genetrix* to that of *mater* (Bolger 1996).

Nevertheless, even this remnant of early Cypriot tradition disappears in the few meager scraps of iconography that have come down to us from the Late Cypriot III period (fig. 4). Many traits are common between these and the Late Cypriot II images, notably large noses, flap-ears, button eyes and, most importantly, nudity, with careful emphasis on the sexual characteristics of breasts and pubic triangle. Novel are the medium (bronze), the full modeling in the round and the intended upright

Figure 3. *Mesopotamian seal impression of Ishtar. Oriental Institute of the University of Chicago, A27903. Used with permission of the Oriental Institute.*

posture. Once again, these innovations might be traced to the Near East, especially Ugarit where metal images of the gods were standard practice and eroticized Astarte plaques were common.

In Late Cypriot III, we have highly sexualized female figures totally devoid of *kourotrophos* imagery, and thus it would seem that the final links between the Cypriot goddess and a maternal role disappear. In this light, the claims made by scholars such as Catling and Karageorghis that these images, particularly the Bomford figurine, are meant to portray fertility, specifically the "fertility" of the copper foundries, must be reconsidered. Catling suggested of the Bomford figurine that, "The copper workers looked to her, we may suppose, to ensure the fruitfulness of the mines and even more the smelting furnaces and the processes by which the raw copper is produced" (Catling 1971: 30). In a similar vein, J. Karageorghis (1977: 104–105) argued that "l'Idole de Fécondité chypriote" extended her fertilizing powers to the mineral riches of the earth ("Elle a étendu ses pouvoirs fécondants à la fertilité de la terre en minerai"). By contrast, Knapp (1986: 4), abandoning the concept of fertility in his assessment of the Bomford figurine and her "consort" the Ingot God, suggested rather that "a political elite, established on the island by the Middle Cypriot III–Late Cypriot I era (c.1700–1400 B.C.E.), manipulated and secured their domination over copper production and distribution by utilizing culturally significant symbols such as the 'Ingot God' or the miniature 'votive' ingots." In the absence of fertility iconography, an interpretation of the Bomford figurine favoring elitism over fecundity should be preferred.

It was this style of bronze idol that was in place when the Achaeans, during the "Times of Troubles," began their eastward journey to settle in Cyprus.[5] Moreover, it was probably at this time that the Greeks first encountered the goddess who would become for them Aphrodite, and thus these idols represent in some respects the earliest images identifiable from a Greek perspective as that goddess.[6] Several more years of Iron Age Levantine influence would add further oriental flavoring to the goddess, of course, but the basic iconography was already in place: a female, appearing especially sexual to Greeks unaccustomed to portraying their goddesses in the nude, who maintained control over the island of Cyprus.

This extreme sexualization, with minimal associations to maternity and fertility (even the *kourotrophos* motif was no longer in use), was the defining attribute of Aphrodite. That she is not a maternal goddess is evident in Homeric Hymn V, the only reference to the goddess's encounter with motherhood, where she expresses deeply antipathetic feelings concerning maternity:

> But for me this will be a great disgrace among the
> immortal gods for all days everlasting because of you.
> Before they continually feared my words and wiles, as
> ever I made all the gods mingle with mortal women;
> for all minds were tamed by me.
> But now indeed no longer will my mouth be able to boast
> of this among the immortals, since I greatly erred,
> Wretch, most unblameworthy, having gone out of my mind,
> and I put a child under my belt having lain with a mortal.
> As for him, when indeed he first sees the light of the sun,
> deep-bosomed mountain Nymphs will raise him. (ll. 251–57)

In despair at being pregnant, Aphrodite abandons the child as soon as he is born. This is perhaps not the ideal way to characterize a "mother goddess." It is, of course, possible, if not probable, that part of the regret over this son is his mortality. But one must keep in mind that throughout early Greek mythology, Aphrodite has very few children, and they play virtually no role in the myths of the goddess (other than her encounter with Ankheises, mentioned above). Aphrodite's maternal role is also inevitably constrained; Aineas is used to shame the goddess, and she is unable to save her own daughter Harmonia at the end of Euripides' *Bakkhai* from the wrath of Dionysos. Maternity is not a source or manifestation of Aphrodite's power.

Nevertheless, her power over raw sexuality and desire is explicit. In the same Homeric hymn cited above, the poet extols:

> Muses, relate to me the works of golden-throned Aphrodite,
> of Cyprus, who in deities stirs up sweet desire and
> who subdues the race of mortal men
> and air-borne birds and all wild creatures,
> and as many creatures the mainland rears as does as well the sea.
> To all these are the works of well-crowned Kythera a concern. (ll. 1–6)

Her power over sexuality and desire and, for better or worse, over all of creation is perhaps best expressed in a fragment attributed to Sophocles:

> Children, the Kyprian is not the Kyprian alone, but she is called by many names. She is Hades, she is immortal life, she is raving madness, she is unmixed desire, she is lamentation; in her is all activity, all tranquility, all that leads to violence. For she sinks into the vitals of all that have life; who is not greedy for that goddess? She enters into the swimming race of fishes, she is within the four legged brood upon dry-land, and her wing ranges among birds … among beasts, among mortals, among the race of gods above. Which among the gods does she not wrestle and throw three times? If I may speak out—and I may speak out—to tell the truth, she rules over the heart of Zeus, without spear, without iron. All the plans of mortals and of gods are cut short by the Kyprian.[7] (Lloyd-Jones 1996: 405)

Throughout Greek mythological literature we see the power Aphrodite wields through her control of sex and desire: the Trojan War, the massacre of the Lemnian husbands, the death of Hippolytos, and ultimately the Punic Wars are but a few examples. I sometimes marvel that scholars question her frequent associations with Ares, for she causes more massive destruction than he does.

Sexuality is an independent attribute and, as we have seen, a source of divine power in its own right; it need not be associated with the powers of fertility and maternity. It is manifest in the Near Eastern goddesses Inanna/Ishtar, Ishara, and Athtart, and through their influence, its power becomes increasingly more significant in the devel-

Figure 4. *The Bomford Figurine. Ashmolean Museum of Oxford University, 1971.888. Used with permission of the Ashmolean Museum.*

opment of the Cypriot goddess during the Late Bronze Age. At the end of the Bronze Age, these goddesses are introduced into the Greek pantheon as Aphrodite, a goddess who is neither maternal nor fertility-oriented, but who exercises her power through manipulation of sexuality and desire.

Ultimately, this distinction between fertility, maternity, and sexuality, and the innate power of sexuality itself, are important considerations in the field of both religious and mythological studies, in Cyprus and beyond. Without it many, if not almost all, goddesses collapse into a single entity, a universal "Earth Mother Fertility Goddess," making it impossible to distinguish clearly between different deities in the iconographic and literary repertoires of ancient pantheons and reducing the role of the female to a single archetype. An example of this phenomenon is evident in Simon's study of the goddess Aphrodite (Simon 1985: 229–54), in which Simon sees Aphrodite in the Cycladic figurines of the Early Bronze Age, the gold foil nude females from the Mycenaean shaft graves, the "goddess" under a tree on the gold signet rings from Minoan Crete, and any nude female figure from Geometric times forward in Greek art. This confuses the study of Aphrodite's origins and character by placing the goddess in all Aegean societies in all times and by failing to make distinctions between cultures separated widely in time and space. Likewise, it obscures the study and interpretation of the images grouped together with Aphrodite in this assessment, such as the nude female plaques prevalent in Greece in the 8th and 7th centuries that cannot be identified as Aphrodite or any other specific goddess (Böhm 1990: 134–41). Similar problems of interpretation arise with goddesses of various pantheons, including Athtart and Anat in Ugarit (Walls 1992), Inanna/Ishtar in Mesopotamia (Leick 1994: 55ff.), and even the Norse goddess Freyja (Motz 1993: 97). In iconography, Minoan goddesses with upraised arms come to be called "mother goddesses" due to the exposure of their breasts, in spite of the fact that they are *never* shown in association with children.

In conclusion, it is necessary to recognize the multifarious meanings of erotic attributes as presented in ancient iconography and literature and to appreciate the power of sexuality. Only in this way can the meaning of the various sex goddesses of the ancient world (Aphrodite, Inanna/Ishtar) be fully understood and appreciated, and only in this way can they be distinguished from the other goddesses of their respective pantheons.

NOTES

1. For similar interpretations outside of Cyprus, see Böhm (1990: 134–41) for Greece, and Badre (1980: 155–57) for the Near East.

2. Tablet R.S. 20.24 from Ugarit, a bilingual text from Ugarit which list the names of the gods of Ugarit and their Akkadian/Mesopotamian equivalents, names Athtart as the western equivalent of Ishtar (*'ttrt* = ᵈIŠTAR.*iš-tar*).

3. Translation by Greenstein in Parker 1997: 23.

4. Translation by Jacobsen in Jacobsen 1987: 18.

5. For the various theories and arguments concerning the arrival of the Achaeans in Cyprus at the end of the Bronze Age, see *inter alia*: Burdajewicz 1990: 6ff.; Coldstream 1994; Dikaios 1971: 907ff.; Maier 1973: 69ff.; Maier 1986: 312ff.

6. Concerning the Cypriot origins of Aphrodite, see: Herter 1975; Hill 1940: 80; Karageorghis 1977; Maier and Karageorghis 1984: 101–2, 365. For a counter argument that Aphrodite is derived from an Indo-European Dawn Goddess, see Boedeker 1974; Friedrich 1978; Nagy 1990.

7. Fragment 941. Translation by Lloyd-Jones in Lloyd-Jones 1996: 405.

REFERENCES

a Campo, A. L.
  1994   *Anthropomorphic Representations in Prehistoric Cyprus: A Formal and Symbolic Analysis of Figu-
          rines, c. 3500–1800 B.C.* Jonsered: Åströms.

Badre, L.
  1980   *Les Figurines Anthropomorphes en Terre Cuite à l'Age du Bronze en Syrie.* Paris: Geuthner.

Boedeker, D. D.
  1974   *Aphrodite's Entry into Greek Epic.* Leiden: Brill.

Böhm, S.
  1990   *Die "Nackte Göttin": zur Ikonographie und Deutung unbekleideter weiblicher Figuren in der
          frühgriechischen Kunst.* Mainz: von Zabern.

Bolger, D.
  1993   The Feminine Mystique: Gender and Society in Prehistoric Cypriot Studies. *Report of the Depart-
          ment of Antiquities of Cyprus*: 29–41.
  1996   Figurines, Fertility, and the Emergence of Complex Society in Prehistoric Cyprus. *Current Anthro-
          pology* 37, 2: 365–73.

Burdajewicz, M.
  1990   *The Aegean Sea Peoples and Religious Architecture in the Eastern Mediterranean at the Close of the
          Late Bronze Age.* BAR International Series 558. Oxford: British Archaeological Reports.

Catling, H.
  1971   A Cypriot Bronze Statuette in the Bomford Collection. Pp. 15–32 in *Alasia: Mission Archéologique
          d'Alasia* 4, ed. C. Schaeffer. Paris: Brill.

Coldstream, J. N.
  1994   What Sort of Aegean Migration? Pp. 143–46 in *Cyprus in the 11th Century B.C.*, ed. V. Karageorghis.
          Nicosia: A.G. Leventis Foundation.

Dikaios, P.
  1971   *Enkomi: Excavations 1948–1958.* Vols. 1–3. Mainz: von Zabern.

Edwards, I. E. S.
  1955   A Relief of Qudshu-Astarte-Anath in the Winchester College Collection. *Journal of Near Eastern
          Studies* 14, 1: 49–51.

Friedrich, P.
  1978   *The Meaning of Aphrodite.* Chicago: University of Chicago.

Herter, H.
  1975   Die Ursprünge des Aphroditekultes. Pp. 28–42 in *Kleine Schriften*, ed. E. Vogt. Munich: Fink.

Hill, G.
  1940   *A History of Cyprus.* Vol. 1. Cambridge: Cambridge University.

Jacobsen, T., ed. and trans.
  1987   *The Harps that Once—: Sumerian Poetry in Translation.* New Haven: Yale University.

Karageorghis, J.
  1977   *La grande déesse de Chypre et son Culte: À travers l'iconographie de l'époque néolithique au VIème
          s. a.C.* Lyon: Maison de l'Orient Méditerranéen Ancien.
  1992   On Some Aspects of Chalcolithic Religion in Cyprus. *Report of the Department of Antiquities of
          Cyprus*: 17–27.

Knapp, A. B.
  1986   *Copper Production and Divine Protection: Archaeology, Ideology and Social Complexity on Bronze
          Age Cyprus.* Göteborg: Åströms.

Leclant, J.
  1960   Astarté à Cheval d'après les Representations Égyptiennes. *Syria* 37: 1–67.

Leick, G.
  1994   *Sex and Eroticism in Mesopotamian Literature.* London: Routledge.

Lloyd-Jones, H., ed. and trans.
1996   *Sophocles*. Vol. 3. *Fragments*. Cambridge, MA: Harvard University.
Maier, F. G.
1973   Evidence for Mycenaean Settlement at Old Paphos. Pp. 68–78 in *Acts of the International Archaeo-logical Symposium "The Mycenaeans in the Eastern Mediterranean." Nicosia, 27th March–2nd April 1972*. Nicosia: Department of Antiquities of Cyprus.
1986   Kinyras and Agapenor. Pp. 311–20 in *Acts of the International Archaeological Symposium "Cyprus Between the Orient and the Occident." Nicosia, 8–14 September 1985*, ed. V. Karageorghis. Nicosia: Department of Antiquities of Cyprus.
Maier, F. G., and V Karageorghis.
1984   *Paphos: History and Archaeology*. Nicosia: A. G. Leventis Foundation.
Masson, O.
1973   Remarques sur les cultes Chypriotes à l'époque du Bronze Récent. Pp. 110–21 in *Acts of the Interna-tional Archaeological Symposium "The Mycenaeans in the Eastern Mediterranean." Nicosia, 27th March–2nd April 1972*. Nicosia: Department of Antiquities of Cyprus.
Morris, D.
1985   *The Art of Ancient Cyprus*. Oxford: Phaidon.
Motz, L.
1993   *The Beauty and the Hag: Female Figures of Germanic Faith and Myth*. Wien: Fassbaender.
Nagy, G.
1990   Phaethon, Sappho's Phaon, and the White Rock of Leukas: 'Reading' the Symbols of Greek Lyric. Pp. 223–62 in *Greek Mythology and Poetics*, by G. Nagy. New York: Cornell University.
Parker, S. B., ed.
1997   *Ugaritic Narrative Poetry*. Society of Biblical Literature Writings from the Ancient World Series 9. Atlanta: Scholars.
Peltenburg, E. J.
1992   Birth Pendants in Life and Death: Evidence from Kissonerga Grave 263. Pp. 27–36 in *Studies in Honour of Vassos Karageorghis*, ed. G. Ioannides. Nicosia: Society of Cypriot Studies.
Prechel, D.
1996   *Die Göttin Išhara: Ein Beitrag zur Altorientalischen Religionsgeschichte*. Münster: Ugarit-Verlag.
Pritchard, J.
1943   *Palestinian Figurines in Relation to Certain Goddesses Known through Literature*. New Haven: American Oriental Society.
Simon, E.
1985   *Die Götter der Griechen*. München: Hirmer.
Tatton-Brown, V.
1997   *Ancient Cyprus*. London: British Museum.
Walls, N. H.
1992   *The Goddess Anat in Ugaritic Myth*. Society of Biblical Literature Dissertation Series 135. Atlanta: Scholars Press.
Winter, U.
1983   *Frau und Göttin: Exegetische und ikonographische Studies zum weiblichen Gottesbild im Alten Israel und in dessen Umwelt*. Freiburg, Schweiz: Universitätsverlag; Göttingen: Vandenhoeck & Ruprecht.
Woolley, L.
1955   *Alalakh: An Account of the Excavations at Tell Atchana in the Hatay, 1937–1949*. London: Oxford University.
Wyatt, N.
1999   Astarte. Pp. 109–114 in *Dictionary of Deities and Demons in the Bible*. 2nd edition, eds. van der Toorn et al. Leiden: Brill.

APHRODITE AND HER NEAR EASTERN SISTERS: SPHERES OF INFLUENCE

NANCY SERWINT

School of Art
Arizona State University
Tempe, AZ 85287-1505
nancy.serwint@asu.edu

The goddess worshipped in Cyprus, variously known from inscriptional sources as Wanassa *or* Paphia, *is linked by Homeric and Hesiodic sources to a Greek tradition of the divinity who explicitly embodied sexuality and sensual pleasures. The character of the Cypriot goddess, however, was of abundant complexity, and the various aspects of her persona argue for influence from Near Eastern sources—primarily the Sumerian Inanna and her subsequent manifestations as Ishtar and the Canaanite/Phoenician goddesses Astarte, Anat, and even Asherah. Examination of textual material as well as select iconographic representations suggest that these goddesses encompassed three primary spheres of influences: sexuality, fertility and ferocity. Though decidedly female in the Near Eastern literary and artistic tradition, these goddesses reflected a gamut of roles associated with women and engendered the Cypriot goddess with a spectrum of qualities through which she could be revered for her infinite variety.*

Ever since Aphrodite first stepped forth from the sea onto the shore of Cyprus, the island has claimed the goddess as its own. The ancient authors, following in the tradition first established by Homer and Hesiod, went far in promoting a divinity who possessed seductive charms.[1] Consequently, the canonical representation of the goddess, who embodied carnal pleasure as well as the abundance of life itself, is preserved as part of the Western legacy of the nude goddess, at times coyly enticing with her allurements.[2] As a result, the West knows Aphrodite as voluptuous and sensual and unabashedly physical (fig. 1). But Cyprus in antiquity was far from being Western. Given the circumstances of geography and poised between the Greek world and the civilizations to the East, the island was affected by diverse cultural influences. Certainly the most decisive in the development of the Cypriot Aphrodite were those that came from the East (Burkert 1985: 152–53). Admittedly influenced by the Sumerian Inanna and her later manifestation as Ishtar as well as by the Canaanite/Phoenician goddesses Astarte, Anat, and Asherah, the Cypriot goddess evolved into a divinity with multiple characteristics, and her complexity became one of her trademarks.

This paper will focus on selected aspects of the Cypriot goddess with the discussion fixed on Near Eastern predecessors who engendered her with a multi-faceted personality. The concern will not be so much on iconographic borrowings, a topic that has been treated in depth by other scholars (J. Karageorghis 1977; Sophocleous 1985), nor is there a need to reiterate the extent of eastern influence in Cyprus throughout the Bronze and Iron Ages, a treatment that has already been extensive (V. Karageorghis 1986; Michaelidou-Nicolaou 1987; Tatton-Brown 1989). Rather, the thrust of this paper is to consider textual sources in tandem with images and reconsider characteristics of specific Near

Eastern goddesses whose spheres of influence are reflected in the persona of the Cypriot goddess before the manifestation of the Greek Aphrodite was embraced on the island.[3]

THE NEAR EASTERN CONTEXT

Certainly in Cyprus by the Late Bronze Age and continuing into the Iron Age, the roles played by a female goddess on the island were dictated in large part by earlier Near Eastern counterparts. Anthropomorphic conceptions of Mesopotamian divinities had circulated widely, and various cultures—Akkadian, Babylonian, Assyrian, Canaanite/Phoenician, even Israelite—were indebted to the Sumerian pantheon for their own subsequent creations of divine entities (Gray 1969; Jacobsen 1976; Oppenheim 1977: 174; Friedrich 1978: 12–19; Crowley 1989: 169; Dever 1990). Although the number of Mesopotamian divinities abounded, as attested by the over 3000 names recovered from textual sources (Westenholz 1998: 67; Oppenheim 1997: 194), and although there was a plethora of female deities, by far the most important goddess of ancient Sumer was Inanna.

The name Inanna likely derived from "Nin-ana," meaning "Lady of Heaven." Traditions vary as to her genealogy, but one tradition names her as the daughter of An, the leader of the gods and the ruler of the heavens (Black and Green 1992: 108).[4] Already in that patrimony, Inanna and Aphrodite share a close link in that they both claim

Figure 1. Aphrodite from Soloi. Nicosia, Cyprus Museum, E.510. Courtesy of the Cyprus Museum.

descent from a sky god (Burkert 1992: 97–98, although Burkert draws the equation between Ishtar and Aphrodite). Inanna was worshipped at many different sites, but her chief city was Uruk where her primary shrine, known as E-anna ("the House of Heaven") was located, and her worship there was already known by the late fourth millennium (Westenholz 1998: 73). Her Akkadian name was Ishtar, the name by which she is known in later Assyrian texts.[5]

Like so many other Mesopotamian deities, Inanna had a benign as well as a malevolent aspect, and her spheres of influence were diverse, suggesting that the goddess may reflect the syncretism of different local deities. Indeed, one of her appellations was Nin-me-šár-ra ("Lady of Myriad Offices"), and she was responsible for a diverse range of activities, many seemingly contradictory (Jacobsen 1976: 141). Inanna herself, in the poem generally known as "Inanna and the God of Wisdom" (or "Inanna and the World Order"), cites the many powers she had received from Enki, the god of subterranean waters, magic, and wisdom; the paradoxical pairing of many of those powers is obvious:

> He gave me the high priesthood … godship … shepherdship … descent into the underworld … ascent from the underworld … the dagger and sword … the black garment … the colorful garment … the loosening of the hair … the binding of the hair … the standard … the quiver … the art of lovemaking …

the kissing of the phallus … the art of prostitution … the art of forthright speech … the art of slanderous speech … the art of adorning speech … the cult prostitute … the holy tavern … the holy priestess of heaven … the art of song … the art of the hero … the art of power … the art of treachery … the art of straightforwardness … plundering cities … setting up of lamentations … rejoicing of the heart … deceit … rebellious land … the art of kindness … travel … the secure dwelling place … the feeding pen … the sheepfold … fear … consternation … dismay … the bitter-toothed lion … the kindling of fire … the putting out of fire … the assembled family … procreation … the kindling of strife … counseling … heart-soothing. (Wolkstein and Kramer 1983: 16–18)[6]

Although Inanna had been given divine jurisdiction over many aspects, her authority can be broadly categorized as encompassing three spheres—sexuality, fertility, and military prowess—and it is these primary spheres that become manifest in the Cypriot goddess.

SEXUALITY

It is in the area of sexuality that Inanna's power was epic, almost ferocious, and it is the sexuality of the goddess that is inherited by Ishtar, to some extent by Anat, and certainly by the Canaanite Astarte. In the Sumerian hymns, the focus of Inanna's immense sexual power is her genitalia, the entryway into the womb, which has great significance for the profound benefit of lovemaking with the goddess resulting in fertility.[7] The most explicit descriptions of the goddess's appetite for sex are contained in the poems treating the courtship of Inanna and Dumuzi, the ill-fated shepherd god whom Inanna accepts as her husband only later to consign him to the underworld. As she adorns herself to receive her lover, Inanna proclaims in readiness:

My vulva, the horn,
The Boat of Heaven,
Is full of eagerness like the young moon….
Who will plow my vulva?
Who will plow my high field?
Who will plow my wet ground?
(Wolkstein and Kramer 1983: 37)

The passion of Inanna and Dumuzi is graphically described in the poem "The Courtship of Inanna and Dumuzi," and it is in the famous strophe known as "The Honey Man" where the fulfillment of Inanna is accomplished by the completion of the sexual act by Dumuzi.[8] Satiated and sapped by their night of marathon intercourse of 50 times, Dumuzi assumes the kingship of the land. But what the goddess receives in love, she also annihilates. In the sixth tablet of the *Epic of Gilgamesh*, the hero enumerates the long list of Ishtar's former lovers, but in spurning Ishtar's offer of marriage, Gilgamesh also rebukes her for the destruction of all the men she has previously loved; in retaliation for his refusal, Inanna sends the Bull of Heaven to destroy him (Sandars 1987: 86–87).

Votive offerings dedicated to the goddess were equally graphic. Models of human sexual organs, such as stone phalloi and terracotta female sexual organs, pierced for either suspension or attachment, were found in the temple of Ishtar at Ashur and date to ca. 1350–1000 B.C. (Black and Green 1992: 152 and fig. 124). In the same temple but dating to the 8th and 7th centuries B.C., common votives were small lead plaques showing couples engaged in intercourse; in several instances, the female is positioned on a constructed stand, interpreted as an altar, suggesting the plaque may refer to a sacred rite (Berlin, Staatliche Museen, Vorderasiatisches Museum, VA Ass. 4244, VA Ass. 4245 and VA 5428; Seibert 1973: pls. 76.a–b, 77).

That rite may well be the so-called "sacred marriage" frequently associated with Inanna/Ishtar. Known from textual sources as early as 2000 B.C., the ritual doubtless refers to the union of Inanna and Dumuzi and glorifies the resultant fertility of the natural world as a consequence of the bounty produced from Dumuzi's coupling with the goddess (Jacobsen 1976: 33–47). One of the earliest representations of the sacred marriage, dating to the mid-3rd millennium from Tell Asmar, shows the consummation of the sexual act by a god and goddess on a couch (Frankfort 1939: 75–76, pl. 15l). Clay plaques depicting couples or a female lying on a bed were common votives associated with Inanna/Ishtar, with many found near Ishtar's temple at Ashur (Wolkstein and Kramer 1983: 187, fig. 43; Roaf 1990: 130; Seibert 1973: pls. 27.a–c). Likely commemorating a re-enactment of the sacred marriage celebrated on the last day of the annual autumnal Near Year festival in the Near East, the plaques pictorially record the rite between the reigning ruler and perhaps a priestess impersonating the goddess.[9] Although the figures on the clay plaques are nude, it is significant that the female is usually depicted wearing heavy necklaces. Clearly there is a reference to the textual descriptions of the goddess readying herself for lovemaking with Dumuzi by arranging precious lapis beads about her neck and adorning herself with the agate necklace of fertility (Wolkstein and Kramer 1983: 35).

Inanna/Ishtar's typical iconography is standard and largely remained canonical. She is depicted as a clothed goddess wearing the horned cap of divinity, although variations in representation depended on the specific aspect of the goddess being stressed. Several cylinder seals dating to the first half of the second millennium show a female, interpreted as Inanna/Ishtar (fig. 2), exploiting her nudity by lifting her garment and exposing herself (Collon 1987: 167, 170; nos. 776–78). If the identification of Inanna/Ishtar is accepted, her nudity implies the seductive sexuality of the goddess.[10]

Inanna/Ishtar's pronounced sexuality is echoed by Canaanite/Phoenician goddesses, especially Astarte (Bonnet 1996). Although relatively unknown in the Ugaritic literature, the goddess's sexual proclivities are manifest in Old Testament and Phoenician texts (Gray 1964: 124; Gray 1965: 175–76). The goddess Anat also draws heavily from Mesopotamian influence. As the daughter of El, a sky god as well as the king and father of the gods, Anat partakes of a celestial parentage similar to that of Inanna's descent from An as leader of the Sumerian pantheon. Anat's sexuality is manifest in the Ugaritic texts with her sexual relationship with her brother Baal explicitly drawn in their mating in the form of their cultic animals, bull and cow (Albright 1968; Gordon 1949: UL 76:II:10–36; UL 76:III:2–27; UL 6:2–35; UL 132:1–9; contra Walls 1992: 75; it is telling that in Sumerian hymns, Inanna herself is referred to as a wild cow; see Pritchard 1975: 128–29). That coupling clearly references the sacred marriage long established in Mesopotamian tradition.

In Cyprus, a variety of votives were appropriate to the goddess who was worshipped under various manifestations until the advent of the appearance of the Greek aspect of Aphrodite in the classical period (V. Karageorghis 1997: 225). That the goddess had an association with sexuality is sure, and it is worth recalling that the ancient authors inform that it is Aphrodite, the later persona of the Cypriot goddess, who repeatedly returns to Cyprus and her sanctuary at Paphos after lovemaking (*Hymn. Hom. Aph.* 5.53–67 and Homer *Od.* 8.359–66). The abundance of shells as votive gifts found in several sanctuaries, some of which were devoted to the Cypriot goddess, may carry on the earlier Near Eastern tradition of offerings in the form of the female vulva dedicated to a goddess equated with sexuality. The decided visual similarities between conus and cowrie shells to female genitalia have imbued shells with potent religious and sexual symbolism often equated with fecundity and erotic love (Eliade 1969: 125–50). Perhaps it is due to the tradition of her marine birth or equally to the visual equation between shells and vulva that Pliny (*NH* 32.5) records that shellfish were sacred to Aphrodite in Cyprus. A graphic example of the presence of shells in association with a female deity in Cyprus are the many found on the Late Bronze Age Floor III of Area II at Kition (Reese 1985 and pl. A and pl. 133). Most are cited as the inedible Mediterranean *Conus*, and the fact that some were pierced suggests that they were adapted for wear. Likewise, at the archaic Peristeries sanctuary at Marion (modern Polis) dedicated to a female divinity associated with fertility, 725 examples of shells as registered finds have been tabulated (D. Reese 1996: personal communication; Smith 1997 for discussion of the sanctuary).

Representations of male sexual organs have also been found as votive gifts in Cypriot sanctuaries. In the Limassol-*Komissariato* sanctuary dating to ca. 500 B.C., a terracotta phallus was discovered among the offerings (V. Karageorghis 1977: 61 and pl. 21.19) along with figurines of a phallic nature. The stylistic characteristics of this sanctuary's male and female figurines betray Phoenician influence. Although the identification of the deity as male has been assumed but not confirmed (V. Karageorghis 1977: 66), at most the phallic dedication reveals the cult as one associated with human fertility.[11] The tip of a clay phallus, still bearing traces of red paint and a hollow channel down its shaft, has been found at the Polis-*Peristeries* sanctuary (fig. 3).[12] With that sanctuary conclusively identified as dedicated to a female fertility deity (Serwint 1992: 393), the phallus is a type of offering reminiscent of gifts common to Inanna/Ishtar. That the rite of the Cypriot goddess in her sanctuary at Palaepaphos involved paraphernalia of a sexual nature has been related by ancient authors. Well into the Roman period, Arnobius and Clement of Alexandria both report that one aspect of the cult of Aphrodite involved giving a phallus and salt to the initiated (Arnobius, *Adversus Gentes* V.1; Clement of Alexandria, *Protrepticus* 2.12.13; Maier and Karageorghis 1984: 372).

Figure 2. Hematite seal likely showing Ishtar with upraised skirt in front of a god. Brussels, Musées Royaux d'Art et d'Histoire 0.501. Courtesy of Musées Royaux d'Art et d'Histoire.

In Cyprus there are also echoes of the Near Eastern tradition of the sacred marriage. According to one tradition, Cinyras was credited with the founding of Paphos (Apollodorus, *Bibliotheca* 3.14.3–4) as well as the foundation of the great temple to Aphrodite at Palaepaphos (Tacitus, *Historiae* 2.2–3; Lucian, *De Dea Syria* 9). He served as the high priest of the goddess (Pindar, *Pythian* 2.15–16), as did the Cinyrads after him, but also became her lover (Clement of Alexandria, *Protrepticus* 2.12.13; 2.29). His son, the ill-fated Adonis, was the beloved of Aphrodite but also of Persephone, and after his death he was required to spend part of the year with each goddess (Apollodorus, *Bibliotheca* 3.14.3–4). The concept of Adonis as a vegetation god, whose annual sexual union with Aphrodite renewed the earth's fertility, recalls and parallels the myth of Inanna and Dumuzi.

Although the literary sources reinforce the sexual relationship between Aphrodite-Cinyras and Aphrodite-Adonis, the theme of sacred marriage does not seem to manifest itself in the Cypriot artistic repertoire. However, a clay plaquette depicting a heterosexual couple lying in a bed found in a Middle Cypriot I tomb at Lapithos may reinforce the consequences of sexual union (fig. 4; J. Karageorghis 1977: 56h; Tomb 315 in Gjerstad et al. 1934: 112 and pl. 30.28). The tomb context of the plaquette is tantalizing in its possible similarities to the promise of birth and rebirth, which is the core of the Inanna-Dumuzi myth, the annual passion of Aphrodite and Adonis, and the concept at the very heart of the sacred marriage.

As part of her sexual nature, Inanna/Ishtar was associated with prostitution. In the Lugalbanda Epic, Inanna is named as patron of harlots (Jacobsen 1976: 139–40). Likely the connection was reinforced by the goddess's personification as the planet Venus, the evening star. Ishtar was closely allied with the South Arabian Semitic astral god, Athtar, who was manifest in the planet Venus, the brightest star in the desert sky (Gray 1965: 169–71; Gray 1969: 22), and among her various epithets, Inanna is called "Lady of the Evening" as well as "Lady of the Morning."[13] Consequently, one of the most common attributes of the goddess on cylinders was the presence of stars (Black and Green 1992: 109). From the Old Babylonian Period onwards, the goddess was frequently depicted with astral symbolism and could be surrounded by a star nimbus or more commonly with an eight-pointed star positioned near her (fig. 5; Budin, this volume; Frankfort 1939: 195). Just as prostitutes emerged in the evening, so did the goddess as the evening star. The link between the two is made explicit in the Lugalbanda Epic:

> So as to set the poor folk going at their dances, having (with her light) made the
>   dancing green more pleasant,
> and to make the spots to bed down in more pleasant for the harlot setting out for the alehouse,
> did Inanna, the daughter of Suen,
> like a dancer (proudly) raise her head over the land.
> (Jacobsen 1976: 139–40)

Figure 3. *Clay phallus tip from Polis-*Peristeries *sanctuary. R22384/TC8977, Princeton University Excavations.*

Figure 4. *Red Polished III idol in form of a couple lying in a bed; Tomb 315, Lapithos. From Gjerstad et al. (1934: pl. 30.28).*

In a Neo-Babylonian legal text treating the adoption of the son of a prostitute, Ishtar is named in the oath confirming the transfer of the child (Pritchard 1975: 81), while in a Sumerian hymn, Inanna herself is called a prostitute; part of the text reads:

O harlot, you set out for the alehouse,
O Inanna, you are bent on going into your (usual) window (namely, to solicit) for a lover—
O Inanna, mistress of myriad offices, no god rivals you!
… you, my lady, dress like one of no repute in a single garment,
the beads (the sign) of a harlot you put around your neck.
It is you that hail men from the alehouse!
(Jacobsen 1976: 140)

The many images of a female head framed by a window found at Assyrian palace sites have long been thought to have sexual references (fig. 6). They are consistent in their iconography of window and female head which leads to the possibility that solicitation for sex is suggested (Mallowan 1978: 33; Caubet 1979a: 25). The association between harlot and window continued with Israelite accusations against Jezebel, daughter of King Ethbaal of Sidon and wife of King Ahab for introducing yet again the worship of Canaanite gods into Israel (1 Kings 16.31). Jezebel, trying to seduce King Jehu of Israel as he passed in the street below, met her death painted like a harlot, by being thrown from a window of the royal palace (2 Kings 9.30–33).[14]

The well known clay model of a sanctuary found in the necropolis of Idalion perpetuates the motif of a female head peering out from a window (fig. 7; Caubet 1979b: 95). That the image reflects the practice of temple prostitution is a tantalizing one, all the more so because the practice of ritual sex in the Near East and Cyprus is suggested by textual sources.[15] The well known passage in Herodotus (1.105) recounts a Babylonian custom that each girl, before she married, had to offer herself for sex as required by the rites of the goddess who is equated with Aphrodite; Herodotus (and much later Justin, quoting Pompeius Trogus, *Epitome* 18.5) records that a similar practice occurred at several places in Cyprus. Ennius (*Euhemerus* 134–38) maintains that Aphrodite established the art of prostitution in Cyprus, a tradition that Ovid corroborates in his *Metamorphoses* (10.238–46). That prostitutes were part of the ritual personnel at some Cypriot temples is mentioned in the fourth century marble plaque found on the Acropolis of Kition; it lists sacred prostitutes among barbers, bakers, and scribes assigned to the temple at Kition (Masson and Sznycer 1972: 22–23, esp. 28).

The Idalion shrine may well reference sacred prostitution in the 6th century, but even earlier in the Cypriot artistic corpus there may be an allusion to the practice. A bronze four-sided stand found in Enkomi Tomb 97 and now in London shows on each side a building façade with its upper part pierced by a window divided into two; in each window there is a representation of a woman's face (Catling 1964: 204–205, pl. 33.c; London, British Museum 1897/4–I/1296). Interestingly, there is a possible parallel in the terracotta shrine house found in the Ramesses III Southern Temple at Beth-Shan; in the doorway of one of the shrine houses is a female figure holding doves. Because of the bird attribute, the figure has been identified as a goddess (Rowe 1940: 38, pl. 17.1 and pl. 57.a, 1).

The one aspect of many Near Eastern goddesses that was, perhaps, the most significant was sexuality. Literary testimonia as well as a range of objects connected with the Cypriot goddess and her later manifestation as Aphrodite would suggest that sexuality was also a powerful characteristic of the goddess worshipped in Cyprus. The close parallels seen in various cult offerings—phalloi, shells suggestive of the female vulva, the Lapithos plaquette of the bedded couple, and the iconography of the woman in the window—echo profound sexuality, the sacred marriage, and ritual prostitution. Certainly the Cypriot goddess and her counterpart Aphrodite partook of a longstanding Near Eastern tradition that the island inherited through cultural contacts with the East. In the case of manifest sexu-

Figure 5. Drawing of Ishtar or her cult statue receiving worship, from a cylinder seal of the Neo-Assyrian period. After Frankfort (1939: pl. 33.B).

ality, the gendered role of aggressive sexual partner, usually assigned to males in Near Eastern cultures, was equally assumed by the goddess in Cyprus.

FERTILITY

Indulgent in all things sexual, Inanna/Ishtar was responsible for fertility in its widest sphere. Her title as "vulva of heaven and earth" (Pritchard 1975: 135) embraced productivity on cosmic as well as earthly terms. In the beautiful "Hymn of Enheduanna," Inanna is called the "… queen … Who multiplies (all) living creatures (and) peoples … Life-giving goddess …" (Pritchard 1975: 128–29), while in another hymn, likely recited as part of the ritual of the sacred marriage, Inanna is termed "the holy queen of vegetation" (Pritchard 1975: 202). The most telling display of the power of the goddess over fertility is evidenced in "The Descent of Ishtar to the Nether World" where fertility in all its manifestations ceases after Ishtar enters the portals of Ereshkigal's kingdom (Pritchard 1958: 80–85 and Hooke 1991: 39–41).

Inanna's initial link with fertility emanated from her role as a rain goddess, and it was by this connection that she received the lion as her attribute, which frequently appeared with the goddess on cylinders (see Budin, this volume; Jacobsen 1976: 136–37; Porada 1948: 46). The lion was a common emblem of thunder divinities in the Near East (including Inanna's brother, Ishkur), and its roar was echoed in the crash of the thunderstorm. In the "Hymn of Enheduanna," Inanna is addressed:

With the charging storm you charge,
with the howling storm you howl,
with Ishkur you roar,
with all evil winds you rage!
(Jacobsen 1976: 136)

Elsewhere in the literature, the goddess is termed "the dread storm" (Jacobsen 1976: 136). Rain, coupled with her ample sexuality, guaranteed fertility, and Inanna herself proclaims in a hymn:

I step onto the heavens, and the rain
    rains down;
I step onto the earth, and grass and herbs
    sprout up.
(Jacobsen 1976: 136)

On the famous alabaster Warka Vase from Uruk dating to ca. 3000 B.C. (fig. 8), Inanna's involvement in fertility is shown repeatedly. In the top register, the goddess receives a basket filled with the fruits of the land from a priest, while in lower registers, processions of food offerings and animals as

Figure 6. Ivory panel from Nimrud, showing the "lady at the window." London, The British Museum 118155-6, 118158-9. Courtesy of The British Museum.

Figure 7. Terracotta model of a sanctuary from Idalion with woman in a window. Paris, Louvre N 3293. Courtesy of the Musée du Louvre.

well as teeming plants reinforce the goddess's role in bounty. It is clear that it is Inanna who is represented because of the presence of the looped reed bundles behind the goddess; reed bundles were the pictograph character by which Inanna's name was written in historic times, and baked clay models of gathered reeds are known from Uruk. That it is sexual union with the goddess that guarantees fertility is made clear in several hymns, and the ardent lovemaking with her shepherd-husband causes Inanna to proclaim:

> Before my lord Dumuzi,
> I poured plants from my womb.
> I placed plants before him,
> I poured out plants before him.
> I placed grain before him,
> I poured out grain before him.
> I poured out grain from my womb.
> (Wolkstein and Kramer 1983: 40)

That the Mesopotamian Inanna and Ishtar passed on power over fertility to Canaanite goddesses has long been recognized. The three primary Canaanite goddesses—Asherah, Anat, and Astarte—all had varying associations with fertility with each assuming different aspects of fecundity. Asherah, wife of the great god El, bore 70 sons to her consort and was known as "creatress of the gods" (Westenholz

1998: 79). As a mother goddess who also signified the life-giving force, Asherah was represented as a pole or plank and assumed the position of the Tree of Life (Gray 1964: 76, 123–24; Gray 1969: 72, 74). Perhaps even worshipped as the consort of Yahweh in Israelite popular religion (Dever 1990: 144–45), frequent mention of an *asherah* in the Hebrew Bible either in reference to the Canaanite deity herself or her cult symbol testifies to the pervasive character of her cult and the impact on Israelite belief.

Anat's role in fertility, although variously debated (Walls 1992), would appear profound from her frequent association with fertility of the land in the Ugaritic texts. As the destroyer of Mot (the god of sterility, the underworld, and death, whose murder of Baal resulted in an extended period of earthly drought and famine), it is Anat who finds Baal's body and buries it, thereby making possible the restoration of her brother and allowing for the renewal of the earth's productivity. She avenges Baal's murder by utterly annihilating Mot:

> She seizes the god Môt
> With a sword she cleaves him
> With a *pitchfork* she winnows him
> With fire she burns him
> With millstones she grinds him
> In the fields she plants him
> So that the bird do not eat his *flesh*
> Nor *anyone* destroy his *portion*
> Nor the fowl destroy his portion
> *Flesh* calls to *flesh*.
> (Gordon 1949: UL 49:II.31–37)

It is significant that the specific means used to destroy Mot are those activities that mirror Near Eastern harvest practices and reflect a rite mentioned in the Mishnah as well as by Josephus and Philo (Gray 1965: 69). Elsewhere, Anat promises her own direct intervention in bringing fertility to the land:

> I shall *put bread* [in the earth]
>   [I shall] set *mand rakes*] in the dust
> I shall pour [a peace offering] in the midst of the earth
> A *lib[ation]* in the mids[t of the fi]elds.
> (Gordon 1949: UL 'nt:IV, 66–69)

Astarte's role in fertility stems from her strong association with sexuality. Despite infrequent references to the goddess in the Ugaritic texts, the worship of the goddess was significant especially in Phoenicia and Palestine (Bonnet 1996: 19–51; 56–62). Mention of Ashtoreth (with deliberate misvocalization by Jewish scribes of the name of the Canaanite goddess; see Gray 1968: 175) in Deuteronomy as a noun for offering flocks might suggest the association of the goddess with animal fertility (Deuteronomy 7:13; 28:4, 18, and 51; Pritchard 1943: 69–70).

That there was a conflation of the fertility functions as well as the identities of the three Canaanite goddesses is apparent from the well-known British Museum "Qudshu Stele" likely from Deir el-Medina, dating from Dynasty XIX and representative of other New Kingdom examples of this type (fig. 9). Asherah, the mother goddess so commonly associated with a sacred tree, stands nude with her nakedness likely connoting Astarte. With arms outstretched in the guise of the tree of life, the goddess holds the reviving lotus flower and snakes between the ithyphallic fertility god Min and the Canaanite Reshef, god of life and death. The inscription names her *Qds*, variously translated as "the holy one" (Westenholz 1998: 79 and 204, n. 33) or even "the courtesan" (Riis 1949: 80). She stands on the lion, the symbol of

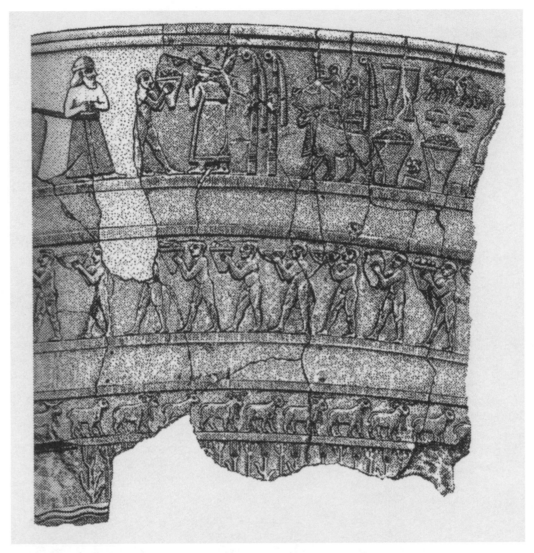

Figure 8. Warka Vase from Uruk, ca. 3100–2900 B.C. Iraq Museum. Reproduced with permission of Andromeda Oxford Limited.

Inanna/Ishtar, although Asherah was frequently associated with lions through her epithet as "the Lion Lady" (Dever 1990: 41). In the register below, the goddess again appears, this time seated, heavily armed and named as Anat (see Negbi 1976: 99–100 and note 34 for discussion of various New Kingdom stelae reflecting the standing Qudshu; also Boreux 1939; Riis 1949: 80–83; Albright 1939: 117; Pritchard 1943: 6–10 and 32–42).

The repetition of Canaanite representations of nude females with established symbols of Mesopotamian iconography suggests an inherited link, even though the identity of the figural type remains debated (Albright 1939; Pritchard 1943; Riis 1949; Gray 1964: 87–88; Barrelet 1968; Negbi 1976: 117; Holland 1977: 134 with bibliography; Badre 1980; and Van der Toorn 1998: 92–95). The famous Tell el-'Ajjul jewelry hoard from the mid 2nd millennium with gold pendants in the shape of female genitalia decorated with a nude goddess (sometimes wearing a necklace) with explicit sexual characteristics as well as eight-pointed star pendants are reminiscent of earlier Near Eastern depictions (fig. 10; Negbi 1970). Similar objects as well as sheet metal representations found at Megiddo, Lachish,

Figure 9. *Qudshu Stele, Dynasty XIX, likely from Deir el-Medina. London, The British Museum EA 191. Courtesy of The British Museum.*

Ugarit, Nahariya, Hazor, and Minet el-Beida (see Budin, this volume) attest to the prevalence of the iconographic type in the Late Bronze Age (Negbi 1970: 95–103).

In Cyprus, the same motifs suggestive of fertility associations continue. Several items from Late Bronze Age Enkomi are telling. A triangular gold pendant with suspension loop from Tomb 32 decorated with a nude female with emphasized breasts and vulva recalls Syro-Palestinian parallels (Murray, Smith and Walters 1969: 19, fig. 37). Similar is another gold sheet pendant with an embossed representation of a nude female set against silver found in Level IIIA (1220/10–1190 B.C.; Dikaios 1971: 463 and 696, inv. 3023; Dikaios 1969: pls. 131.30, 145.3). A small bronze female figurine discovered on Floor II of Room II in Area I in Level IIIB shows a nude woman with cascading hair holding her breasts; the object reflects the Near Eastern nude clay figurine, so emblematic of fertility, as it had survived in Cyprus (Dikaios 1971: 468 and 721, inv. 271; Dikaios 1969: pls. 138.6–8, 145.1–2, 171.52). The gold sheet plaque in the Louvre (fig. 11) of unknown Cypriot provenance and dated to ca. 700 B.C. brilliantly reflects the iconography of nude female standing on top of a lion; the presence of a winged solar disc and an eight-petalled rosette certainly mark the figure as divine (Caubet, Hermary, and Karageorghis 1992: cat. no. 70, p. 68). The bounty of nude terracotta female figurines adorned with jewelry, which are found in so many female sanctuaries, underscores the fertility aspect of the goddess, despite the problematic identification of the figurines themselves (fig. 12).

Preoccupation with human fertility in Cyprus spanned the millennia as a diversity of objects attest, notably the Chalcolithic Kissonerga birthing figurine (Peltenburg 1989: fig. 15.5, 6), the many Middle and Late Bronze Age depictions of kourotrophoi (Caubet, Hermary, and Karageorghis 1992: no. 16, p. 36; no. 29, pp. 44–45), and the frequent archaic period terracotta representations of childbirth (V. Karageorghis 1989: no. 85, p. 86). In Cyprus, the concern for continued abundance of the earth was equally critical, and throughout the Bronze Age the enduring fertility of the copper mines, guaranteeing prosperity for the island, was acute, as was the continuation of the trade of the metal in ox-hide ingots (Knapp 1986). A particularly Cypriot expression of a goddess who insured the abundance of copper finds its form in the "Bomford Goddess" (see Budin, this volume; Oxford, Ashmolean Museum 1971.888). Standing on a copper ingot, as did her male counterpart, the Ingot God from Enkomi, the goddess is ready to receive worship (Catling 1971).[16] Her nudity and heavy jewelry recall a tradition of Near Eastern fertility goddesses, and the placement of the goddess on top of her cult symbol is in keeping with the established Near Eastern convention of deity on sacred token.

Closely linked with sexuality, fertility was a concern of the most powerful Near Eastern goddesses. In Cyprus that concern was expressed in a range of figural representations. Human fertility was evidenced in diverse forms, including a nude female heavily weighted with jewelry, a *kourotrophos* caring for an infant, and a parturient woman ready to give birth. Fertility also extended beyond the human sphere. The fecundity of the land and certain products of the earth's richness were of such consequence on the island that divine protection was invoked in the traditional guise of Near Eastern nudity in conjunction with cult emblem.

MILITARY PROWESS

A third powerful aspect of Inanna/Ishtar was her association with warfare. So potent and deadly was she in this sphere that the Sumerians called battle "the dance of Inanna" (Jacobsen 1976: 137) and "the playground of the goddess." In texts she is variously described as "destroyer of foreign lands" ("Hymn of Enheduanna," Pritchard 1975: 127, 132), "lady of battle" (Vassal Treaty of Esarhaddon 48 [453], Pritchard 1975: 64), and "the one covered with fighting and clothed with terror" (Pritchard 1950: 384). Frequently on cylinders, Inanna and Ishtar are both depicted armed for battle, usually with a mace, scimitars, and arrows (Budin, this volume; Porada 1948: 46; also Frankfort 1939: 130, pl. 20.e; 170, pls. 26.i, 29l; 215, pls. 33.b, c, f, i, k). The goddess was regarded as every aspect of battle, and in a Sumerian hymn, Inanna proclaims:

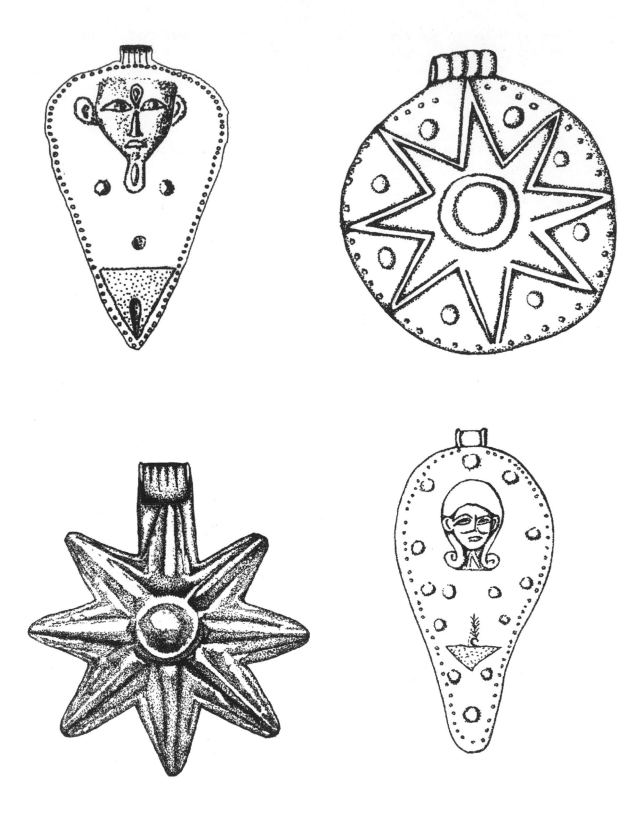

Figure 10. *Various pendants from the Tell el-'Ajjul gold hoard and from Minet el-Beida. After Negbi (1970: pl. 2.4, 7; pl. 3.9; pl. 4.15).*

Figure 11. *Gold sheet plaque depicting nude goddess on lion. Cypro-Geometric III–Cypro-Archaic I, ca. 700 B.C. Paris, Louvre AM 94. Courtesy of the Musée du Louvre.*

Figure 12. *Female figurine of Astarte-type from Polis-Peristeries sanctuary, Cypro-Archaic II. R4404/TC1240, Princeton University Excavations.*

When I stand in the front (line) of battle
    I am the leader of all the lands,
when I stand at the opening of the battle,
    I am the quiver ready to hand,
When I stand in the midst of the battle,
    I am the heart of the battle,
    the arm of the warriors,
when I begin moving at the end of the battle,
    I am an evilly rising flood ...
(Jacobsen 1976: 137)

In Assyria, the warlike character of Ishtar was particularly savage, and representations of Ishtar of Arbela (Pritchard 1954: 177, no. 522) regularly show her with quivers of arrows and scimitar while standing on her lion. Closely allied to the Assyrian king, the goddess destroys his enemies and directs him in battle by means of oracles and dreams (for oracles concerning Esarhaddon, see Pritchard 1975: 168–69; for oracular dreams involving Ashurbanipal, see Pritchard 1975: 170–71). Her ferocity might have derived from association with the South Arabian Semitic god Athtar, who appears as the planet Venus, the heavenly body blazing most brightly, which also was associated with the *ghazzia*, or sudden desert raid (Gray 1969: 22–23).

Of the Canaanite goddesses, it was Anat who was closely associated with the Assyrian Ishtar. Anat's cult was widespread in Egypt (Negbi 1976: 85, note 22 with bibliography), and she was especially revered by the warrior pharaoh Ramesses II, suggesting why her character was extraordinarily fierce in the Ugaritic texts (Gray 1964: 124). In Egyptian references her warlike aspect is frequently cited beginning in Dynasty XIX (Pritchard 1943: 78–79): an inscription from Karnak records that a team of horses of Seti I (1313–1292 B.C.) was called "Anat-is-satisfied;" on an obelisk from Tanit, Ramesses II (1292–1225 B.C.) is called the "suckling of Anat;" his sword is called "Anat-is-victorious;" and the pharaoh's dog is called "Anat-is-protection." An inscription at Medinet Habu dating to the reign of Ramesses III (1198–1167 B.C.) records "Anat and Ashtart are to him a shield."

It is, indeed, in the Ugaritic texts that the ferocity of Anat is most pronounced (Walls 1992) and a common epithet of the goddess in sacrificial and god lists is "Anat the Destroyer."[17] In the Baal and Anat cycle, the goddess lists the various enemies of her brother whom she has destroyed on his behalf (Gordon 1949: UL `nt:III, 34–44, IV, 45–48). The cruelty of Anat and the bloody carnage she is capable of is most extreme in the account of her slaughter of the human enemies of Baal even in her own palace (Gordon 1949: UL `nt:II, 6–35):

> And lo Anath smites in the valley
> Fighting between the two cities
> She smites the people of the s[ea]shore
> Destroys mankind of the sunrise.
> Under her are heads like vultures
> Over her are hands like locusts
> Like thorns of *gwrmn*, the hands of troops.
> She piles up heads on her back
> She ties up hands in her bundle.
> Knee-deep she plunges in the blood of soldiery
> Up to the neck in the gore of troops.
> With a stick she drives out foes
> Against the flank she draws her bow.
> And lo Anath reaches her house
> Yea the goddess enters her palace
> But is not satisfied.
> She had smitten *it* in the valley
> Fought between the two cities
> She hurls chairs at the troops
> Hurling tables at the soldiers
> Footstools at the heroes.
> Much she smites and looks
> Fights and views.
> Anath gluts her liver with laughter
> Her heart is filled with joy
> For in Anath's hand is victory.
> For knee-deep plunges in the blood of soldiery

Up to the neck in the gore of troops.
Until she is sated she smites in the house
Shedding - - - - the blood of soldiery
Pouring the oil of peace from a bowl.
The Virgin Anath washes her hands.
The Progenitress of Heroes, her fingers
She washes her hands in the blood of soldiery
Her fingers in the gore of troops.
(Gordon 1966: 50–51)

A depiction of Anat armed is seen on the bottom of the British Museum Qudshu Stele discussed above, and a possible representation of the goddess in a bronze statuette from Tel Dan dating to the second half of the 2nd millennium B.C. shows a clothed female in a smiting pose (Negbi 1964: pl. 56.a–b). On Roman coins from Ashkelon, Anat *may* be represented as fully armed and dressed as a woman but with a physiognomy that is more male than female (Albright 1968: 112). The androgynous aspect of the goddess is interesting in light of the discussion of the bisexual character of the Cypriot Aphrodite in this volume (see B. MacLachlan).

Astarte also has overt martial characteristics. Her association with military might was such that the Philistines deemed it appropriate to place Saul's armor in her temple (I Samuel 31.10). During the Egyptian New Kingdom, Astarte was prominently named as a war goddess and appeared on many reliefs armed with weapons (javelin and shield or bow and arrows) and sitting on a racing stallion or riding in a speeding chariot (Leclant 1960; Bonnet 1996: 63–67). In the well known seal from Bethel dated to ca. 1300 B.C., Astarte is named in the inscription, stands paired with an armed war god, and wears the plumed Egyptian headdress while brandishing a spear (Pritchard 1954: 303, no. 468). The association of the goddess with warfare is clearly reinforced in the treaty between Esarhaddon, King of Assyria, and Baal, King of Tyre, whereby Astarte is called upon to punish those who violate the treaty by breaking their bows in battle (Pritchard 1975: 53).[18]

The tradition of a female deity associated with militarism continued in Cyprus in different guises. Among the many objects associated with the chariots and vehicles from the dromos of Tomb 79 at Salamis reflecting Phoenician interpretations of Near Eastern motifs, a bronze side pendant of a horse shows in repoussé a winged nude female (fig. 13). Standing on top of her characteristic animal,

Figure 13. Bronze horse side pendant showing winged nude female; from Tomb 79, Salamis. Nicosia, Cyprus Museum 155 + 162. Courtesy of the Cyprus Museum.

a pair of lions each with a calf in its mouth, she holds lions attacked by griffins. Variously identified as Ishtar or Astarte, iconographic parallels are to be found at Gordion, Tell Tainat and abundantly throughout the Near East (Karageorghis 1973: 83–84; pl. 89). Similar images were commonly employed as decoration for horse trappings in northern Syria. Given the importance of that region for the transference of Near Eastern motifs to the west as well as the transmittal of religious iconography and concepts of divinity, the Salaminian horse pendant with a nude goddess as decoration associated with ceremonial military chariots aptly reflects a Cypriot interpretation of a standard Near East convention.

The most demonstrative examples of Aphrodite's association with warfare in Cyprus are the several late representations of the goddess armed with military accoutrements. The almost lifesize marble statue of an armed Aphrodite found in the west wing of the Villa of Theseus in Nea Paphos (fig. 14) shows the nude goddess with a sword belt strapped diagonally across her torso. The remains of a sword handle in the broken right hand indicate that she was brandishing a weapon (Flemberg 1991: 67–71, cat. 2, figs. 12–15; Daszewski 1982: pl. 44.1–2, fig. 1; Daszewski 1994: 155; Hadjioannou and Daszewski

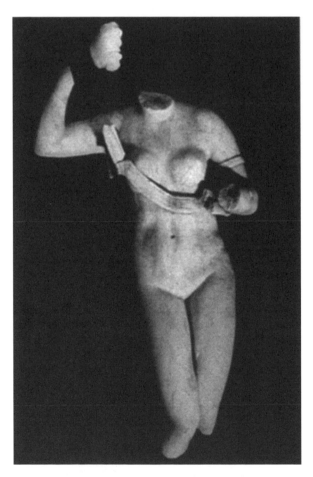

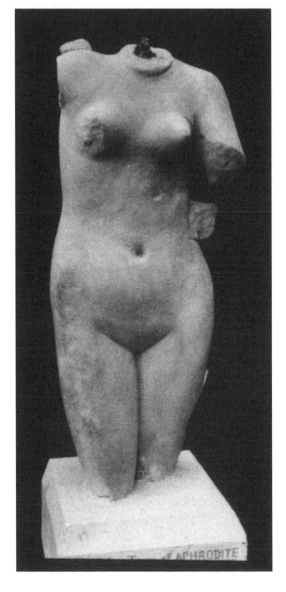

Figure 14 (above). Statue of armed Aphrodite from Villa of Theseus. Paphos, Paphos District Archaeological Museum. Courtesy of the Cyprus Museum.

Figure 15 (right). Statuette of armed Aphrodite from Soloi. Nicosia, Cyprus Museum. Courtesy of the Cyprus Museum.

1983); a late 2nd/early 3rd century A.D. date has been offered. A slightly earlier and smaller version of an armed Aphrodite, also in marble, was discovered at Soloi (fig. 15). Dated to after the middle of the 1st century A.D., the nude goddess wears a baldric obliquely across her back (Flemberg 1991: 87–90, cat. 13, figs. 38–39; Westholm 1936: 108, no. 466, pl. 6.1–2; Gjerstad et al. 1937: 503–504, no. 466, pl. 155.1–2). Like her Paphian counterpart, the Soloi statuette is one of 15 representations derived from the same prototype. Although it has been argued that the earliest extant representation of Aphrodite with military gear dates to the 4th century B.C. and may derive iconographically from her association with Ares, the Greek god of war, there is a strong literary tradition which suggests influence from the Near East.

In the Greek world, Aphrodite had many dimensions, but it was in her title as *Ourania*, the Heavenly Goddess, that she was closely linked with the Near East. Pausanias (1.14.7) says that the Assyrians first instituted worship of Ourania which was later adopted on Cythera, in Cyprus, and by the Phoenicians of Ashkelon, and Herodotus (1.105.3) records that the Cypriot cult of Aphrodite drew its inspiration from Aphrodite Ourania at Ashkelon. Pausanias also says that the cult of Aphrodite Ourania was introduced into Athens by way of the legendary Porphyrion, whose name means "the purple king." Certainly in that name there is reference to the Phoenician murex trade and the diffusion of the eastern aspect of the goddess known to Phoenician merchants traveling west.

In the preceding discussion, one of the most potent aspects of Near Eastern goddesses associated with fertility and sexuality was a profound connection with militarism and warfare which was variously manifested as ferocious violence, barbaric slaughter, and mastery in battle. Those manifestations were iconographically rendered in the Near East by the display of the goddess heavily armed. Literary descriptions of images of Aphrodite armed are numerous (see Flemberg 1991: 29–42 for testimonia), and some suggest that pre-4th century B.C. cult representations of an armed Aphrodite *did* exist in the Greek world (Pausanias 3.23.1; 3.15.10; 3.17.5); their likely appearance as *xoana* adapted from Near Eastern representations has been accepted by most scholars. The Alexandrian lexicographer Hesychios maintains that the epithet of Aphrodite as Ἔγχειος (*s.v.* Ἔγχειος), the goddess armed with a spear, lance, or sword had its origin in Cyprus. Late references comment that the goddess Kypria was widely renowned for her military might (*Anthologia Graeca* 16.173: "To carry quiver and bow and shoot her arrows far into the distance was always the mastery of Kypria;" translation by A. Feldmann).

The military aspect of the Cypriot Aphrodite is assured. Representations of a Near Eastern goddess, such as the one decorating the horse trappings associated with martial gear in Salamis Tomb 79, already bespeak of the recognition in Cyprus of the nude goddess as appropriate in a military context. The Greek literary tradition of Aphrodite named as *Kypris* bearing arms as well as the statement that Aphrodite Ἔγχειος was of Cypriot origin reinforce the connection of the Cypriot Aphrodite with militarism. And the two representations of an armed Aphrodite from Paphos and Soloi should be seen as a continuation of an earlier tradition of wooden *xoana* representing the goddess armed with military gear. The literary tradition strongly asserts that the cult of Ourania, the Heavenly Goddess, was an eastern one and was transmitted to Cyprus and to the Greeks via eastern sources. One facet of Ourania was her warlike nature. In the case of the Cypriot Aphrodite and her martial characteristics, it would seem that the goddess was not only indebted to her Near Eastern predecessors but also may have been instrumental in endowing the Greek Aphrodite with a military aspect.

CONCLUSION

Consideration of the Cypriot goddess reveals that she embraced a complexity of associations, so much so that one might rightly question whether she was one divinity or was conceptualized as many. But to the ancient Cypriots, that complexity was expressed most often in her simple title as *Wanassa*, the Queen or Mistress (Maier and Karageorghis 1984: 358; J. Karageorghis 1977: 109–13). Like many powerful divinities, the Cypriot goddess had jurisdiction over diverse spheres, and the range of her power, touching so many facets of human existence, undoubtedly enlarged the aura of her potency in the eyes of the devoted. If one considers the critical periods of the Late Bronze and Iron Ages and closely examines the areas over which the goddess reigned, it is telling that three of her primary powers, sexuality, fertility, and military prowess, coincided precisely with those wielded by specific Near Eastern goddesses.

The impact of the Sumerian Inanna and her Semitic manifestation, Ishtar, on the Canaanite/ Phoenician goddesses Asherah, Astarte, and Anat is without question. Irrefutable is the fact that elements of Near Eastern cult practice were exercized in Cyprus, such as augury using hepatoscopy, the use of Humbaba masks in ritual, and the practice of sacral foundation deposits employing precious materials (Burkert 1992: 48–49, 53). The epigraphic documentation that Canaanite/ Phoenician goddesses were worshipped in Cyprus (the tablet from Ugarit mentioning Anat and Attort among the gods of Alasia and the ninth century B.C. inscription from Kition referring to Astort as the Phoenician divinity worshipped there; J. Karageorghis 1977: 109) further attests to the presence of the Near Eastern concept of divinity on the island. Certainly the Cypriot goddess evolved by assimilating the characteristics of Near Eastern counterparts.

The relevance of the persona of the Cypriot Aphrodite to the consideration of gender issues in ancient Cyprus is, indeed, significant. Although the roles that the goddess may have assumed in the divine sphere, especially her association with warfare, may not have been ones embraced in totality by women in the mortal domain, nevertheless, the paradigm for female involvement in a range of activities that breached accepted social norms was established. The jurisdiction that the Cypriot goddess exerted over sexuality may well have fostered profound affirmation of the female's role in sexual relations. Clearly the consequences of those relations were manifest in potent fertility, abundance, and productivity, all of which underscored the capacity for female nurturance and sustenance so necessary for survival. And even if the Cypriot goddess aligned herself with violence and martial prowess to a lesser degree than Near Eastern goddesses, still in arming herself with the military accoutrements of the male preserve, the island's goddess defied normative gender roles. In the absence of contemporary texts, it is unfortunate that we will never know what challenge, if any, the goddess may have posed to the current androcentric culture. The combination of vigorous sexuality, potent fertility, and formidable martial skill resulted in a goddess whose gender was ambiguous, and like her Near Eastern sisters, perhaps it was in that ambiguity where her greatest power resided.

ACKNOWLEDGMENTS

I am most grateful to Albert Feldmann for his help in the investigation of the armed Aphrodite, and discussions with Stephanie Budin on aspects of sexuality associated with Near Eastern goddesses have been invaluable. Likewise, I have benefited greatly from dialogue with Charles Sohn on facets of the mythological tradition in the ancient Near East.

NOTES

1. Despite variant mythological traditions involving Aphrodite, the association between the goddess and Cyprus was reinforced by the epithet *Kyprogenia* and the prominence of the name *Kypris* which was the most common poetic name for the goddess. The seductive aspect of Aphrodite is most pronounced in Hesiod *Works and Days* 65–66, *Hymn. Hom. Aph.* 5 and 6, and in Homer *Il.* 3.54, 64, 374f., 5.426, 14.188f. Hesiod *Theogony* 188–206 records the birth of the goddess out of the foam produced from the castrated genitals of Ouranos—an account indebted to earlier cosmogonies but contrary to the tradition of the goddess as the daughter of Zeus and Dione as recorded in Homer *Il.* 5.370–71, 382.

2. The many images of Aphrodite in provocative pose or dress (as well as undress) are well known from

Roman copies after Greek originals. Although the goddess is already treated in the 5th century B.C. in a way suggestive of enticement, as on the front of the "Ludovisi Throne" (Rome, Terme 8570), perhaps on the Parthenon east pediment—if the identification of figure M as Aphrodite reclining in the lap of her mother, Dione, is accepted (figure M; London British Museum), and the Roman copy of the so-called "Aphrodite Fréjus" (Paris, Louvre 525), Praxiteles first exploited the nudity of the goddess in the 4th century with his creation of the "Knidian Aphrodite" (Rome, Vatican 812). Thereafter, representations of Aphrodite unclothed become the standard and create the norm by which the goddess was embraced subsequently by the West ("Aphrodite from Melos," Paris, Louvre 399/400; the "Crouching Aphrodite," Rhodes Museum; and even the "Aphrodite from Soloi," Nicosia, Cyprus Museum E.510; fig. 1).

3. Important provisos for the accurate understanding of Near Eastern divinities are offered by Westenholz (Westenholz 1998: 63–67). On the issue of eastern influence manifested in the evolution of the Cypriot Aphrodite, especially see Bennett 1980; Hermary 1986: 408–9; J. Karageorghis 1977; V. Karageorghis 1981:78–79; and V. Karageorghis 1998: 120–23. Extensive treatment of the Greek Aphrodite's relationship with Near Eastern goddesses has been undertaken and will not be reiterated in this paper, but readers should see Friedrich 1978: especially chapter two, and Flemberg 1991, with abundant bibliography.

Because many primary sources of Near Eastern texts were unavailable in Nicosia where research for this paper was undertaken, the author has had to rely heavily on secondary sources and literary criticism of pivotal texts. Consequently, familiarity with the range of specific textual references to individual deities has been imperative in order to come to terms with the nature of particular goddesses. It is not the intention in this paper to comment on disputed interpretations of controversial texts and rarely do those controversies alter the assessment of the nature of the divinity which this paper aims to establish.

4. An alternative tradition cites Inanna as the daughter of Nanna, the moon god.

5. It has been suggested that the merger of the Semitic Ishtar to the Sumerian Inanna was actively fostered by Sargon and his successors who, due to political motivations during the mid-3rd millennium, were keen to make the Akkadian goddess more admissible to the Sumerians (Westenholz 1998: 74).

6. The poem "Inanna and the World Order" was edited by Gertrud Farber-Flugge as "Der Mythos 'Inanna und Enki' mit besonderer Berücksichtigung der liste der *me*" (Rome: Biblical Institute, 1973). See also Kramer 1972: 64–68.

7. In the poem "Inanna and the God of Wisdom," the delight in the goddess's carnal appeal is clear: "When she leaned against the apple tree, her vulva was wondrous to behold. Rejoicing at her wondrous vulva, the young woman Inanna applauded herself." (Wolkstein and Kramer 1983: 12).

8. "The 'honey-man,' the 'honey-man' sweetens me ever, / my lord, the 'honey-man' of the gods, my favored of the *womb*, / Whose hand is honey, whose foot is honey, sweetens me ever. / Whose limbs are honey sweet, sweetens me ever." (Pritchard, ed. 1975: 203)

9. Various ancient wedding hymns preserve aspects of the sacred marriage with the goddess. The well-known "Iddin-Dagan Text" makes it clear that the king is engaging in the rite as a substitute for the goddess's husband, Dumuzi, and in the case of this specific text, the rite seems to occur in the royal palace at Isin (Jacobsen 1976: 33). Because no exact descriptions of the rite survive, it is unknown whether the rite was purely symbolic or enacted to its conclusion. In the several Sumerian hymns referring to the sexual relation between the king and the goddess, Inanna can be named as the spouse of the king (the "Shulgi Hymn": Pritchard, ed. 1975: 135) and benefits of intercourse with the goddess are listed as long life, a successful reign, and bounty for the land (Pritchard 1975: 199–202).

10. Frankfort (1939: 160, 168) cautions that in Mesopotamian seals, female nudity should be ascribed either to votaries or priestesses and not to goddesses. On the cylinder seals showing the apparent nudity of Inanna/Ishtar cited in this text, it should be noted that the female figure is *not* nude. The gesture of lifting her garment allows the goddess to remain clothed while revealing the provocative aspect of her nature.

11. Several clay phalloi have been found at Kourion, dating to the 7th and 6th centuries B.C. The nature of the entire votive assemblage certainly suggests dedications to a male divinity, either Apollo or possibly Dionysos (Cape 1985; Young and Young 1955: 28, 29 and pl. 11). Also, a stone phallus with cone found along with a pair of stone votive doves was discovered at Amargetti, whose small mudbrick temple has been dated to the Classical period (Hogarth 1888: 171–74). I thank Anja Ulbrich for the references in this note.

12. R22384/TC8977; preserved length = 3.1 cm; preserved width = 2.9 cm; unpublished find.

13. In a Sumerian hymn ("The Lady of the Evening"), Inanna's association with the planet Venus is explicit:
      At the end of the day, the Radiant Star, the Great Light that fills the sky,
      The Lady of the Evening appears in the heavens.
      … My Lady looks in sweet wonder from heaven.
      The people of Sumer parade before the holy Inanna …
      Inanna, the Lady of the Evening, is radiant on the horizon.
      (Wolkstein and Kramer 1983: 101; also see Jacobsen 1976: 138–39).

   Similar sentiments are voiced in a comparable Sumerian hymn ("The Lady of the Morning"):

      When sweet sleep has ended in the bedchamber,
         You appear like bright daylight.
      My Lady looks in sweet wonder from heaven.
         The people of Sumer parade before the holy Inanna …
      Inanna, the Lady of the Morning, is radiant on the horizon.
      (Wolkstein and Kramer 1983: 103).

   14. The name of Jezebel continued to be associated with sexual immorality even in the New Testament; see Revelation 2.20–23.

   15. Imperative reading on the subject of the relationship of sacred prostitution to the cults of Aphrodite is MacLachlan 1992.

   16. Similar to the "Bomford Goddess" is the bronze female figure discovered in the Bairaktar quarter of Nicosia, just north of the D'Avila bastion on the Venetian walls. Found in an area known to have been occupied in the Bronze Age (with possible occupation continuing into the Iron Age), the figure is likely contemporary with the "Bomford Goddess," also is nude and wears a heavy necklace falling between her breasts (Nicosia, Cyprus Museum 1936/VI–18/I; Catling 1964: 257, pl. 44, j).

   17. Anat's aggressive participation in violent acts is variously explained, although many scholars would argue that her cruelty is symbolic of the close relationship she shares with her brother, Baal, who is perhaps to be interpreted as a fertility god. Consequently, Anat's bloodletting may be regarded as imitative magic to induce fertility since blood was regarded as the life-essence in ancient Canaan. Discounting the interpretation of the Myth-Ritual School of Anat's violence as imperative for the establishment of fertility, Walls (Walls 1992: 67) argues strongly that Anat's aggression is necessary in Canaanite myth for guaranteeing the equilibrium of cosmic power and setting up Baal as the king of the gods after his demise at the hand of Mot.

   18. Not only is Astarte invoked in the treaty but likewise Ishtar and Anath-Bethel.

REFERENCES

Albright, W. F.
1939   Astarte Plaques and Figurines from Tell Beit Mirsim. Pp. 107–20 in *Mélanges Syriens Offerts à Monsieur René Dussaud*, Vol. 1. Paris: Librairie Orientaliste Paul Geuthner.
1968   *Yahweh and the Gods of Canaan*. London: Athlone.

Badre, L.
1980   *Les Figurines Anthropomorphes en Terre Cuite à l'Age du Bronze en Syrie*. Paris: Librairie Orientaliste Paul Geuthner.

Barrelet, M. -T.
1968   *Figurines et Reliefs en Terre Cuite de la Mésopotamie Antique*. Paris: Librairie Orientaliste Paul Geuthner.

Bennett, C. G.
1980   *The Cults of the Ancient Greek Cypriots*. 2 vols. Dissertation, University of Pennsylvania. Ann Arbor: University Microfilms.

Black, J., and Green, A.
1991   *Gods, Demons and Symbols of Ancient Mesopotamia*. London: The British Museum.

Bonnet, C.
1996   *Astarté*. Contributi alla Storia della Religione Fenicio-Punica, II. Roma: Consiglio Nazionale delle Ricerche.

Boreux, C.
1939   La stèle C. 86 du Musée du Louvre et les stelès similaires. Pp. 673–87 in *Mélanges Syriens Offerts a Monsieur René Dussaud*, Vol. 2. Paris: Librairie Orientaliste Paul Geuthner.

Burkert, W.
1985   *Greek Religion*. Trans. J. Raffan from German. Cambridge, MA: Harvard University.
1992   *The Orientalizing Revolution. Near Eastern Influence on Greek Culture in the Early Archaic Age*. Trans. M. Pinder and W. Burkert. Cambridge, MA: Harvard University.

Cape, R. W., Jr.
1985   Some Evidence for Dionysiac Activity at Kourion: The Terracotta Hand-Held Phalloi. *Report of the Department of Antiquities of Cyprus*: 312–19.

Catling, H. W.
1964   *Cypriot Bronzework in the Mycenaean World*. Oxford: Clarendon.
1971   A Cypriot Bronze Statuette in the Bomford Collection. Pp. 15–32 in *Alasia* I, ed. C. F. A. Schaeffer. Paris: Mission Archéologique d'Alasia.

Caubet, A.
1979a   *La religion a Chypre dans l'antiquité*. Lyon: Maison de l'Orient.
1979b   Les maquettes architecturales d'Idalion Pp. 94–118 in *Studies Presented in Memory of Porphyrios Dikaios*. Nicosia: Lions Club of Nicosia.

Caubet, A.; Hermary, A.; and Karageorghis, V.
1992   *Art Antique de Chypre au Musée du Louvre*. Paris: Leventis Foundation.

Collon, D.
1987   *First Impressions. Cylinder Seals in the Ancient Near East*. Chicago: University of Chicago.

Crowley, J. L.
1989   *The Aegean and the East. An Investigation into the Transference of Artistic Motifs between the Aegean, Egypt, and the Near East in the Bronze Age*. Jonsered: Åströms.

Daszewski, W. A.
1982   Aphrodite Hoplismene from Nea Paphos. *Report of the Department of Antiquities of Cyprus*: 195–201.
1994   Marble Sculptures in Nea Paphos: Cypriot or Imported? Pp. 153–60 in *Cypriote Stone Sculpture. Proceedings of the Second International Conference of Cypriot Studies in Brussels-Liège 17–19 May 1993,* ed. F. Vandenabeele and R. Laffineur. Brussels and Liège: A. G. Leventis Foundation, Vrije Universiteit Brussels, and Université de Liège.

Dever, W. G.
1990   *Recent Archaeological Discoveries and Biblical Research.* Seattle: University of Washington.
Dikaios, P.
1969   *Enkomi, Excavations 1948–1958,* Vol. 3a. Mainz am Rhein: Phillip von Zabern.
1971   *Enkomi, Excavations 1948–1958,* Vol. 2. Mainz am Rhein: Phillip von Zabern.
Eliade, M.
1969   *Images and Symbols. Studies in Religious Symbolism.* Trans. P. Mairet from French. New York: Sheed and Ward.
Flemberg, J.
1991   *Venus Armata.* Stockholm: Svenska Institutet i Athen.
Frankfort, H.
1939   *Cylinder Seals.* London: Macmillan and Co.
Friedrich, P.
1978   *The Meaning of Aphrodite.* Chicago: University of Chicago.
Gjerstad, E.; Lindros, J.; Sjöqvist, E.; and Westholm, A.
1934   *The Swedish Cyprus Expedition.* Vol. 1: *Finds and Results of the Excavations in Cyprus 1927–1931.* Stockholm: The Swedish Cyprus Expedition.
1937   *The Swedish Cyprus Expedition.* Vol. 3: *Finds and Results of the Excavations in Cyprus 1927–1931.* Stockholm: The Swedish Cyprus Expedition.
Gordon, C. Y.
1949   *Ugaritic Literature.* Rome: Pontificium Institututum Biblicum.
1966   *Ugarit and Minoan Crete.* New York: Norton.
Gray, J.
1964   *The Canaanites.* London: Thames and Hudson.
1965   *The Legacy of Canaan.* 2nd rev. ed. Leiden: Brill.
1969   *Near Eastern Mythology.* Middlesex: Hamlyn.
Hadjioannou, K., and Daszewski, W. A.
1983   The Ἔγχειος Ἀφροδίτη Again. *Report of the Department of Antiquities of Cyprus*: 281–82.
Hermary, A.
1986   Influences orientales et occidentales sur l'iconographie des divinités chypriotes (VIIᵉ–IIIᵉ s. av. J.-C.). Pp. 405–10 in *Acts of the International Archaeological Symposium "Cyprus between the Orient and the Occident" Held in Nicosia from 8–14 September 1985.* Nicosia: Department of Antiquities.
Hogarth, D. G.
1888   Excavations in Cyprus, 1887–88. *Journal of Hellenic Studies* 9: 147–74.
Holland, T. A.
1977   A Study of Palestinian Iron Age Baked Clay Figurines, with Special Reference to Jerusalem: Cave 1. *Levant* 9: 121–55.
Hooke, S. H.
1991   *Middle Eastern Mythology.* Middlesex: Penguin Books.
Jacobsen, T.
1976   *The Treasures of Darkness.* New Haven: Yale University.
Karageorghis, J.
1977   *La grande déesse de Chypre et son culte.* Lyon: Maison de l'Orient Méditerranéen Ancien.
Karageorghis, V.
1973   *Excavations in the Necropolis of Salamis, III.* Nicosia: Department of Antiquities.
1977   *Two Cypriote Sanctuaries of the End of the Cypro-Archaic Period.* Rome: Consiglio Nazionale delle Ricerche.
1981   De l'adaptation et de la transformation de la mythologie grecque à Chypre durant les périodes archaïque et classique. Pp. 77–87 in *Mythologie gréco-romaine, mythologies périphériques. Etudes d'iconographie* (Colloques Internationaux du C.N.R.S. no. 593). Paris: Centre National de la Recherche Scientifique.
1989   *The Cyprus Museum.* Nicosia: C. Epiphaniou.

1997   Greek Gods and Heroes in Cyprus: A Preview of the Problem. Pp. 221–29 in *Greek Offerings: Essays on Greek Art in Honour of John Boardman*, ed. O. Palagia. Oxford: Oxbow Books.

1998   *Greek Gods and Heroes in Ancient Cyprus*. Athens: Commercial Bank of Greece.

Karageorghis, V., ed.

1986   *Acts of the International Archaeological Symposium "Cyprus between the Orient and the Occident" held in Nicosia from 8–14 September 1985*. Nicosia: Department of Antiquities.

Knapp, A. B.

1986   *Copper Production and Divine Protection: Archaeology, Ideology and Social Complexity on Bronze Age Cyprus*. Studies in Mediterranean Archaeology Pocket-book 42. Göteborg: Åströms.

Kramer, S. N.

1972   *Sumerian Mythology*. 3rd ed. Philadelphia: University of Pennsylvania.

Leclant, J.

1960   Astarté à cheval d'après représentations égyptiennes. *Syria* 37: 1–67.

MacLachlan, B.

1992   Sacred Prostitution and Aphrodite. *Studies in Religion* 21, no. 2: 145–62.

Maier, F. G., and Karageorghis, V.

1984   *Paphos. History and Archaeology*. Nicosia: A. G. Leventis Foundation.

Mallowan, M.

1978   *The Nimrud Ivories*. London: The British Museum.

Masson, O., and Sznycer, M.

1972   *Recherces sur les Phéniciens à Chypre*. Centre de Recherches d'Histoire et de Philologie 2; Hautes Études Orientales 3. Geneva: Librairie Droz.

Michaelidou-Nicolaou, I.

1987   Repercussions of the Phoenician Presence in Cyprus. Pp. 331–38 in *Studia Phoenicia V: Phoenicia and the East Mediterranean in the First Millennium*, ed. E. Lipinski. Leuven: Uitgeverij Peeters.

Murray, A. S.; Smith, A. H.; and Walters, H. B.

1969   *Excavations in Cyprus*. London: The Trustees of the British Museum.

Negbi, O.

1964   A Canaanite Bronze Figurine from Tel Dan. *Israel Exploration Journal* 14, 4: 270–71.

1970   *The Hoards of Goldwork from Tell el-'Ajjul*. Studies in Mediterranean Archaeology 25. Göteborg: Åströms.

1976   *Canaanite Gods in Metal*. Tel Aviv: Tel Aviv University, Institute of Archaeology.

Oppenheim, A. L.

1977   *Ancient Mesopotamia*. Rev. edition. Chicago and London: University of Chicago.

Peltenburg, E.

1989   The Beginnings of Religion in Cyprus. Pp. 108–26 in *Early Society in Cyprus*, ed. E. Peltenburg. Edinburgh: Edinburgh University.

Porada, E.

1948   *Corpus of Ancient Near Eastern Seals in North American Collections*. Vols. 1 and 2: *The Collection of the Pierpont Morgan Library*. The Bollingen Series 14. New York: Pantheon Books.

Pritchard, J. B.

1943   *Palestinian Figurines in Relation to Certain Goddesses Known through Literature*. New Haven: American Oriental Society.

1954   *The Ancient Near East in Pictures Relating to the Old Testament*. Princeton: Princeton University.

Pritchard, J. B., ed.

1950   *Ancient Near Eastern Texts Relating to the Old Testament*. Princeton: Princeton University.

1958   *The Ancient Near East. An Anthology of Texts and Pictures*. Princeton: Princeton University.

1975   *The Ancient Near East. Vol. 2: A New Anthology of Texts and Pictures*. Princeton: Princeton University.

Reese, D.

1985   Shells, Ostrich Eggshells and Other Exotic Faunal Remains from Kition. Appendix VIII. Pp. 340–415 in *Excavations at Kition. Vol. 5: The Pre-Phoenician Levels*, by V. Karageorghis. Nicosia: Department of Antiquities.

Riis, P. J.

1949   The Syrian Astarte Plaques and their Western Connections. *Berytus* 9: 69–90.

Roaf, M.
  1990   *Cultural Atlas of Mesopotamia and the Ancient Near East.* New York: Facts on File.
Rowe, A.
  1940   *The Four Canaanite Tempes of Beth-Shan.* Part I: *The Temples and Cult Objects.* Philadelphia: University of Pennsylvania.
Sandars, N. K.
  1987   *The Epic of Gilgamesh.* Rev. ed. Middlesex: Penguin Books.
Seibert, I.
  1973   *Die Frau im alten Orient.* Leipzig: Edition Leipzig.
Serwint, N.
  1992   The Terracotta Sculpture from Ancient Marion: Recent Discoveries. Pp. 382–429 in *Acta Cypria. Acts of an International Congress on Cypriote Archaeology Held in Göteborg on 22–24 August 1991*, Part 3, ed. P. Åström. Jonsered: Åströms.
Smith, J.
  1997   Preliminary Comments on a Rural Cypro-Archaic Sanctuary in Polis-*Peristeries. Bulletin of the American Schools of Oriental Research* 308: 77–98.
Sophocleous, S.
  1985   *Atlas des Représentations Chypro-Archaiques des Divinités.* Göteborg: Åströms.
Tatton-Brown, V., ed.
  1989   *Cyprus and the East Mediterranean in the Iron Age.* London: The British Museum.
Van der Toorn, K.
  1998   Goddesses in Early Israelite Religion. Pp. 83–97 in *Ancient Goddesses*, ed. L. Goodison and C. Morris. London: British Museum.
Walls, N. H.
  1992   *The Goddess Anat in Ugaritic Myth.* SBL Dissertation Series 135. Atlanta: Scholars Press.
Westenholz, J. G.
  1998   Goddesses of the Ancient Near East, 3000–1000 B.C. Pp. 63–82 in *Ancient Goddesses*, ed. L. Goodison and C. Morris. London: British Museum.
Westholm, A.
  1936   *The Temples of Soli.* Stockholm: The Swedish Cyprus Expedition.
Wolkstein, D., and Kramer, S. N.
  1983   *Inanna. Queen of Heaven and Earth.* New York: Harper & Row.
Young, J. H., and Young, S. H.
  1955   *Terracotta Figurines from Kourion in Cyprus.* Philadelphia: University of Pennsylvania Museum.

A DECORATED MIRROR FROM NEA PAPHOS

DEMETRIOS MICHAELIDES

Archaeological Research Unit
University of Cyprus
Kallipoleos 75
1567 Nicosia, Cyprus
dmichael@nautilus.spidernet.net

Bronze mirrors are commonly found in the tombs of Hellenistic and Roman Cyprus. Most of them were deposited in usable condition while others were purposely cut into two or more pieces before burial. The Cypriot examples are usually plain but often carry simple incised linear decoration. More elaborate decoration is rare but not unknown. After a brief discussion of the different basic types of mirrors found on the island, the present paper will concentrate on a rare find from a tomb excavated in Paphos in 1983. This is a small disc-shaped mirror that had a lid decorated in repoussé. Although the mirror is fragmentary and badly preserved, it is still possible to see that it was originally depicted Venus standing and surrounded by Cupids. This is the first mirror of its type to be found on Cyprus, but, in the present context of gender definition, its importance lies in the unusual rendering of the goddess of love. She is depicted as hiding her sexual attributes, and her rather masculine appearance is underlined by the arms she and the Cupids are carrying.

Tomb P.M. 2536 was excavated in April 1983 on plot 321/1 of Kato Paphos, opposite the Paphos Beach Hotel. It was one of 54 tombs investigated on that plot, which were soon after destroyed to make room for a large block of holiday apartments. The tomb was rock-cut and of the atrium type but of a rather unusual plan. Although it was originally used in the Hellenistic period, the burials were later moved to accommodate Roman inhumations. The study of the skeletal remains by Dr. Sherry Fox, to whom I extend my warmest thanks, has shown that the tomb contained at least 39 burials. The grave goods were also numerous, with a total of over 140 objects. There were the usual extravagant quantities of glass and clay unguentaria, as well as cooking pots, amphorae and clay lamps, but also some more unusual items, including bronze fittings and gold jewelry (Karageorghis 1984: 908, figs. 46–49). The tomb and its contents will be published in a programmed study, by the present author, of the rescue work carried out in the necropoleis of Nea Paphos.

The bronze mirror (P.M. 2536/88) discussed here comes from a tomb on the south of the small atrium, opposite the staircase. The tomb had been used at least twice but was found sealed and undisturbed. There was a heap of cremated bones which, according to Dr. Fox, belong to four people: one woman, one man and two non-identifiable individuals. Among the cremated bones, there was a coin, one gold leaf and one golden hoop earring with a gazelle-head terminal. Also probably associated with the cremated bones were a silver spoon, a small bronze hook, a bronze mirror cut in two pieces, and a gold ring with a flat carnelian intaglio (with inventory number P.M. 2536/94 and not 2536/9 as stated in Karageorghis 1984: 908). These early cremations were pushed to the side to make room for the last occupants of the tomb, a woman and a sub-adult of indeterminate sex, both of whom were inhumed.

The objects found among the scattered bones include a complex bronze fitting of unknown nature, three bronze coins and the mirror under discussion.

Although it is now accepted, at least by some scholars, that the presence of a mirror does not necessarily imply the burial of a woman (see, e.g., Richardson 1964: 112; and Van der Meer 1995: 13–27, especially 22–25; Thomson de Grummond and Lambert 1982: 166–68 provide useful references despite being of a different opinion), it can safely be assumed that in the vast majority of instances, as in the present tomb, this must have been the case. Generally speaking, most of the mirrors were in usable condition when deposited with the dead. Others, as the first of the examples in this tomb, were purposely cut into two or more pieces before burial. It is not known what lies behind the intentional breaking of these objects. It must, however, be related to the tradition of "killed swords," a custom that first appeared during the Late Bronze Age and which, it is assumed, aimed at "killing" an object after the death of its owner.

Bronze mirrors are commonly found among the grave goods of Hellenistic and Roman Cyprus. Hitherto, no analytical study of these objects has been published, although Marie-José Chavane's (1990) publication of the Amathus material offers a very good starting point. It is not my intention to present an analysis of Cypriot mirrors here. I will, however, point out the main types in use from the Classical to the Roman periods in order that the uniqueness of the example that will be discussed here can be more easily appreciated.

With the exception of a small number of unusual examples, like a lead, handled mirror decorated with an eagle (Vessberg and Westholm 1956: 112, fig. 33:3) and the mirror with an incised depiction of the Temple of Aphrodite at Palaepaphos (Cesnola 1882: 59, fig. 66; see also pl. 4 for other unusual items), most Cypriot bronze mirrors fall into three main categories. The first of these categories is a standard, earlier form of mirror that is circular with a short, narrow tongue-like projection (Chavane 1990: 11–12, pl. 4:66–73). Such projections must have been inserted into handles made of wood, ivory or bone that have perished. Although the type is known already in the Late Bronze Age, a characteristic form was in use from the end of the Archaic to the Classical and even the Hellenistic periods. The more evolved examples have a small heel at the point where the tongue joins the disc, which sometimes bears linear stylized vegetal decoration (Chavane 1990: 12, pls. 4:74–78, 5:80–83; for a good decorated example from Kouklia, see Karageorghis 1983: fig. 31).

The second large category of objects usually classed as mirrors are simple bronze discs. These have no decoration and can be of different sizes, and their identification as mirrors is often disputed (Chavane 1990: 13–14, pl. 5:85, 87, 89, 94). Some of them, however, have one slightly convex side, and thus it can be argued that they probably were mirrors set in a frame made of wood or some other material that has now perished. A subdivision of this class includes bronze discs with simple incised decoration, usually around the circumference, some of which are equipped with soldered handles (Chavane 1990: 14–15, pl. 5:109; for a good example from Paphos [P.M. 2520/5], see Karageorghis 1984: 905, fig. 35). To this second group also belong flat circular mirrors decorated with small perforated holes all around the circumference (Chavane 1990: 15, pl. 5:110–11; see also Karageorghis 1984: fig. 60, for an example from a tomb in Limassol).

Finally, there is a third category consisting of hinged mirrors. These are flat, circular boxes made of two similar discs that lock into each other like a cosmetic compact. The inside of one of these discs bears the silvery reflective surface—presumably some form of Pliny's *stagnum* (*NH* 33.130; 34.159–60). The discs were usually decorated with concentric circles on the outside, while many are provided with swinging handles, some of which are attached onto the back of the mirror with small Egyptianizing busts (Chavane 1990: 16–18, pls. 5:113, 6:114–122; see also Karageorghis 1984: fig. 36, for a Paphian example). These mirrors appeared in Cyprus towards the end of the Classical period and became particularly popular during Hellenistic and Roman times.

The origin of this type of mirror is believed to have been Greece where, in the second half of the 5th and the 4th centuries B.C., yet another kind of mirror came into use. This was in the form of a round disc

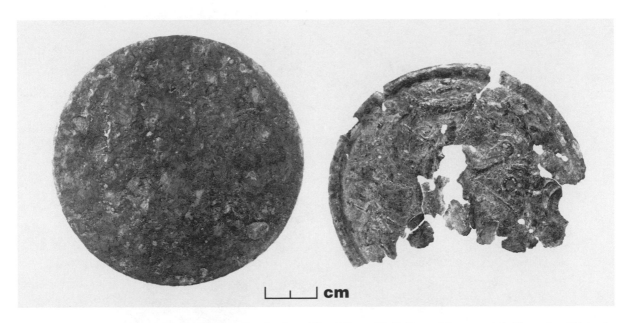

Figure 1. *Mirror and lid, P.M. 2536/88 from Nea Paphos. Disc: 9.7 cm, lid: 9.86 cm. Photograph by Xenophon Michael.*

Figure 2. *Mirror, P.M. 2536/88. Drawing of lid by Glynnis Fawkes.*

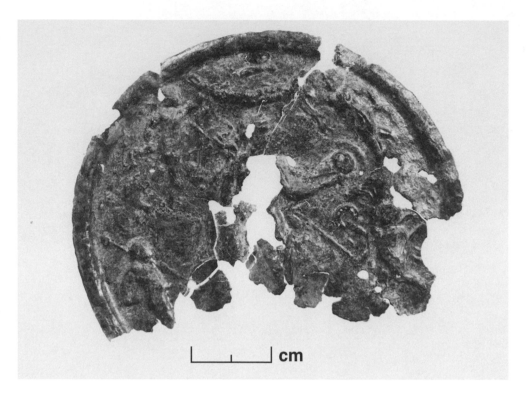

Figure 3. *Mirror, P.M. 2536/88. Photograph by Xenophon Michael.*

without a handle but with a cover attached to the disc by a hinge. In this type of mirror, there was a clear distinction between the two discs, since one was the mirror proper with the reflective surface, and the other the lid, which was often decorated in relief. The decoration of the finer examples usually consisted of a female head or a mythological scene.

The production of such mirrors continued into the Roman period, although the surviving, later examples appear to be less common. These Greek mirrors have roused the interest of scholars, and a number of analytical studies have been published over the years (e.g., Züchner 1942; Schwarzmaier 1997). By contrast, the Roman mirrors of this group, despite their great iconographic interest, have generally been ignored with one important exception: the fundamental study by Zahlhaas (1975).

Decorated mirrors of this kind, dating to the Classical and Hellenistic periods, are unknown in Cyprus. The same was believed to hold true for the Roman period, but the discovery of the Paphos example discussed here shows that this is not the case. The mirror is very poorly preserved (figs. 1–3), and it is a miracle that the lid survives at all, given its extreme thinness. It was, in fact, found in several small, crumbling fragments. The mirror proper is a bronze disc 9.7 cm in diameter and 0.30 cm thick. It is completely flat and plain, and, had the lid not survived, it would not have been possible to identify it with certainty as a mirror, as is the case with many of the items in the second category of mirrors mentioned above. The diameter of the lid is very slightly larger than that of the mirror, 9.86 cm as opposed to 9.7 cm, while the thickness barely reaches 14 mm. It is decorated with a repoussé relief and preserves scanty traces of gilding.

The edge of the lid has a narrow raised band that forms the frame for a scene involving five figures. Because of the very poor state of preservation, only the main lines of the decoration can be discerned. In the center there is a standing figure with its back turned in three-quarter view to the spectator and its left elbow leaning on a short column decorated with garlands. It holds a spear in the left and a crested helmet in the right towards which the diademed head is turned (fig. 4). Above, two flying Cupids hold a garland like a canopy over the head of the central figure. Two other figures fill the lower space (fig. 5). On the right, a Cupid holds a palm-branch(?) and with his right hand raises a filleted crown towards the central figure (fig. 5). On the left, there is an ithyphallic Priapos herm holding a staff(?) over his left shoulder (fig. 6).

There can be no doubt that this is a depiction of Venus bearing arms—an identification that is confirmed by a better preserved, almost identical mirror (fig. 7) of unknown provenance (probably Asia Minor?) now in the Praehistorische Staatssammlung in Munich (Zahlhaas 1975: 32–3, 76, no. 22, pl. 21). This better-preserved example helps us to interpret two details that are not clear on the Paphos mirror. First, what survives under the Cupid on the lower right is a tiny remnant of a small altar on

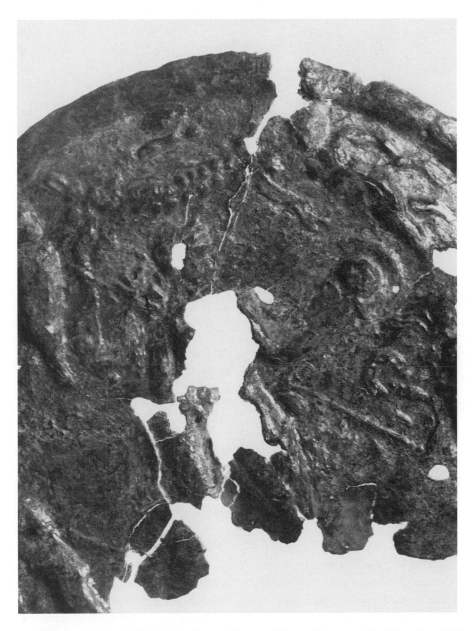

Figure 4. Mirror, P.M. 2536/88. Detail of central figure of Venus. Photograph by Xenophon Michael.

Figure 5. *Mirror, P.M. 2536/88. Detail of two Cupids on the right. Photograph by Xenophon Michael.*

which he stands; and second, the strange object in the top center, above the garland, is a phallus depicted in mid air. The Munich lid also helps fill in the lower part of the scene, which does not survive on the Paphos example. There probably was a shield leaning against the column in the center, while below, under the straight groundline on which the figures stood, several other weapons may have been depicted. It would seem, moreover, that this was the point where lids were normally attached to the

Figure 6. Mirror, P.M. 2536/88. Detail of herm on lower left. Photograph by Xenophon Michael.

mirrors. This is supported by the impression left by the hinge on a couple of examples and by the fact that the lower center of several lids is broken away.

Another example (fig. 8), found in Beirut and now in the Staatliche Antikensammlungen in Berlin, although fairly similar, has some significant differences (Zahlhaas 1975: 77 no. 20, pl. 20; Zimmer 1987: 35, 41, pl. 25). The canopy-like garland above the central figure is unsupported and appears to hang as if from a wall. This leaves all five Cupids represented free to play with the weapons or attend to Venus. The two flying Cupids are now holding the crown and the staff, while on the lower left, instead of the ithyphallic herm, there is a Cupid carrying a cuirass(?) on its shoulders. The Cupid on the lower right is now playing with the helmet, which means that Venus has to content herself with a sword. One completely new element is a fifth Cupid who bends down in order to tie the goddess's sandal.

Zahlhaas has shown that, if one excludes an early group found at Pompeii and Herculaneum, the number of known Roman relief mirrors come to only 35 (1975). Only a handful of new finds have

Figure 7. Mirror in Munich. Zahlhaas (1975: pl. 21).

since been added to this surprisingly small number of examples, among which mention can be made of three mirrors that have entered the collection of the Museum of Fine Arts in Boston (Vermeule and Comstock 1988: 74–82, nos. 94–96, figs. 94–96). The scenes depicted on these mirrors vary, but by far the most common themes derive from mythology and are associated with Dionysos (e.g., Baby Bacchus and the Nymphs of Nyssa [Zahlhaas 1975: no. 9, pl. 9]; Bacchus and Ariadne [Zahlhaas 1975: nos. 12–14, 35, pls. 12–15, 31] etc.) and, above all, with the power that female beauty can exert. Naturally, Venus is frequently represented. Apart from the examples already mentioned, there is Venus in a sea-shell (Zahlhaas 1975: no. 25, pl. 23), Venus and Cupid (Zahlhaas 1975: no. 23), the toilet of Venus (Zahlhaas 1975: no. 24, pl. 22), women at the bath of Venus (Vermeule and Comstock 1988: 78–79, no. 94, fig. 94) and Proserpina, Minerva and Venus (Zahlhaas 1975: nos. 5–8, pls. 5–8). There are also several depictions of the Three Graces (Zahlhaas 1975: nos. 1–4, pls. 1–4), as well as depictions of famous lovers, like Bacchus and Ariadne (see above) and Europa and the Bull (Zahlhaas 1975: no. 18, pl. 16), all of which belong to a type that is normally considered to be appropriate decoration for objects for the private use of women. There is also, however, a very risqué depiction of the eagle making love to Ganymede (Zahlhaas 1975: no. 19, pl. 24), which hardly seems appropriate in this sense.

As for the date of these mirrors, Zahlhaas proposed the period from Hadrian to the late Antonines and more specifically around A.D. 160 for the Venus mirrors (1975). One of the coins found in the Paphos tomb, however, is of Gordian III, who reigned from A.D. 238 to 244, which would indicate either that the production of these objects continued later than Zahlhaas had assumed or that this particular mirror was nearly a century old when it was buried. Of course, there is always the possibility that the burial of the subadult came after that of the owner of the mirror and the coin with it.

The depiction on the Paphos mirror is an interesting version of the theme of Venus bearing arms. The concept of a goddess carrying weapons is a very ancient one, going back to prehistoric *xoana*. This particular type began to enjoy great popularity as from the end of the 1st century B.C., perhaps as a result of the new impulse given to the worship of Venus under Julius Caesar and his successors. As is well-known, Caesar and the whole of the *gens Iulia* claimed Venus as their mythical ancestor. In fact, Dio Cassius (*Hist. Rom.* 43.43.2) mentions that Caesar's signet ring was decorated with this very scene of Venus bearing arms; he also states (*Hist.Rom.* 47.41.2) that it was this ring that Octavian wore at the battle of Philippi and thereafter. The type, known as *Venus Victrix*, was adopted by Octavian, who, in his propaganda policy, used it on some of his *denarii*, while it also appears on gems of other members of the *gens Iulia*. This theme eventually became the most common of all iconographic types of Venus on Roman gems (Flemberg 1991: 110–13 on all these issues; for inscriptions, see Speidel 1984; for other versions of the armed Venus, see Schmidt 1997: 211–12, nos. 192–207). The iconography, which is believed to derive from a sculpted prototype, was standardized from the beginning: Venus is depicted in three-quarter view from the back, leaning on a column, with drapery covering her thighs but leaving her buttocks exposed. In her outstretched right hand she carries a helmet (or sometimes a

Figure 8. Mirror in Berlin. Zimmer (1987: pl. 25).

sword), and in her left hand she holds a spear. A shield rests against the column. In later representations, like those on relief mirrors, she is surrounded by Cupids carrying more weapons and garlands. The meaning of the original Roman version is clear: Venus as ancestor, *Genetrix*, of the Iulii is also *Victrix*, the goddess that makes them victorious. Beneath this meaning, however, must also lie the concept of the goddess that brings peace, since it was she who managed literally to disarm her lover who was none other than Mars, the god of war. Moreover, the fact that Venus' husband was Vulcan, the maker of arms himself, cannot be without significance. Venus disarming Mars is fairly commonly represented in ancient art (Simon 1984: 544–49, 556–58, nos. 346–89), but normally the goddess plays the role of seductress and is quite different from the *Venus Victrix* type. Cupids play an important role in these representations, however, and it would seem that it is from there that they gradually migrated to the iconography of *Venus Victrix*. It is from there, too, that the extra weapons sometimes depicted with the *Venus Victrix* type derived.

Whatever the origins and initial symbolism of the motif, there is no doubt that it gradually came to be associated with women, and many of the rings with depictions of *Venus Victrix* must have belonged to women. We can assume that the general meaning behind many of the later representations is that of the victorious power of love. With regard to decorated mirror lids, we find that this symbolism also emanates from depictions of other themes, such as the Three Graces, where weapons underline the disarming quality of female grace (Zahlhaas 1975: 17–19, with mention of other works with depictions of weapons and Cupids playing with them). At the same time, there is no denying that most of these mirrors have a mildly erotic character that is sometimes made more explicit, as in the case of the Paphos mirror where, apart from the rather excited Priapos herm on the left, there is the phallus above the central figure.

This mirror raises two important points that are relevant to the attempt to engender Aphrodite; both point towards a certain intentional ambiguity. One is the fact that, although Venus is the feminine goddess par excellence, her femininity, that is her genitals and her breasts, are hidden from the spectator. This is fine for the mythical *Victrix* of the Iulii, but why was it transposed to objects of a clearly intimate, feminine character? In a much more general sense, it is interesting to observe that, although it was the feminine charms of Venus that made her all-powerful and victorious, in order to underline this power, it was deemed necessary to give her weapons, a specifically male attribute, and furthermore represent her in the company of an ithyphallic herm and a phallus. A possible explanation for the presence of the last two features is that Venus, being the goddess of fertility, has the power to fertilize as well as be fertilized. After all, it must not be forgotten that, according to Clement of Alexandria (*Protr.* 2.12–13), during the rites in honor of the Cypriot Aphrodite, the initiated gave some money to the goddess as to a prostitute and received in return a ball of salt and phalloi. Arnobius (*Adv. gent.* 5.1) tells a similar but simpler story, omitting the salt but qualifying the phalloi as *propitii numinis signa*.

Furthermore, one must not forget that notions of androgyny (as distinct from homosexuality) were always present in classical mentality and art (Licht 1949, 124–32; Delcourt 1958; Delcourt 1966). As Licht (1949: 124) has rightly observed, "The Greeks possessed a really astonishing notion of the double sexual (hermaphroditic) nature of the human being in the embryonic condition and of the androgynous idea of life generally." One can assume that such notions were inherited by the Romans, and to these can be attributed, for example, the continued popularity of the Hermaphroditos and other such representations. The subject is too vast to be discussed here, but I would like to end by pointing out that a not inconsiderable portion of our knowledge regarding this theme, mainly in relation to Aphrodite, has a Cypriot association. It was Giovacchino De Agostini who, in 1872, first discussed two "bearded Aphrodite" figurines discovered by Cesnola and associated them with information gleaned from literary sources, in particular a passage from Macrobius' *Saturnalia* (see below). In 1985, S. Sophocleous analyzed the passage again, collected further relevant literary information from ancient texts, and discussed several representations of androgynous character dating from the Chalcolithic to the Archaic periods.

The theme of androgyny is, indeed, strong in the information handed down to us by Macrobius (*Saturn.* 3.8.1–3, followed by Servius in *Virg. Aen.* 2.623). Arguing that in certain passages Virgil refers to Aphrodite as a god and not as a goddess, and discussing Aristophanes' calling the goddess Ἀφρόδιτος, he mentions other authors and a statue in Cyprus in support of his argument. The statue depicted a bearded Aphrodite, wearing a woman's dress but holding a man's sceptre and having a man's stature, who was considered both man and woman. It is also worth mentioning another statue of the bearded Aphrodite, despite the fact that it does not seem to have a Cypriot link. In *Suidas*, under the word Ἀφρόδιτος, one reads a story in which Roman women stopped using combs after losing their hair as a result of a contagious skin desease. They regained their hair after praying to Aphrodite, and they honored the goddess with a statue holding a comb and having a beard because, the story continues, the goddess has both male and female organs; it is said that she is the patron of all birth and her upper part is in the shape of a man and her lower part in the shape of a woman.

These statues do not survive, but the terracotta figurines found by Cesnola mentioned above may be a proof for the existence of such an iconographic tradition. These date to the Cypro-Archaic period and depict a bearded figure with the drapery and posture of the Astarte type. Although some doubts have been expressed, mainly because of the somewhat undefined genitals and unpronounced breasts, as to whether this is a bearded female rather than a male figure (Perrot and Chipiez 1885: 560; Karageorghis 2000: 145), there is no denying the generally androgynous nature of these objects. One is in the Metropolitan Museum of Art in New York (inv. no. 74.51.1565; Cesnola 1877: 132; Perrot and Chipiez 1885: 559–60, fig. 383; Cesnola 1894: pl. 28, no. 228; Myres 1914: no. 2159; Sophocleous 1985: 86–87, pl. 15:4; Karageorghis 2000: 145, no. 219 and col. ill.). Another similar figurine, with legs and feet missing, and also from Amathus, was acquired by De Agostini (1872: 7) from Cesnola; while bound in the copy of the De Agostini booklet in the Cyprus Museum, there is a drawing of yet another figurine with the handwritten indication that it comes from a tomb at Pissouri and is 17 cm high (illustrated in Marangou 2000: 219).

No doubt whatsoever can exist about the ambiguous nature of some works of art found on Cyprus dating to the Hellenistic and Roman periods. Although armed Venuses are by no means unique to Cyprus, the island furnishes at least three representations other than that on the Paphian mirror. The earliest is a fragmentary marble statuette from the Temple of Aphrodite at Soloi dated to the Hellenistic period (Westholm 1932, 175; Westholm 1936, 108, no. 466, pl.6:1–2; Westholm 1937, 503–504, 521, 524–25, pl. 155:1–2; Hadjioannou 1981; Flemberg 1991: 87–90, no. 13, figs. 38–39), and there is also the famous statue from the Polish excavations at the Villa of Theseus in Nea Paphos, dated to the 2nd/3rd century A.D. (Daszewski 1976: 220–22, pl. 36:1; Hadjioannou 1981; Daszewski 1982; Flemberg 1991: 67–71, no. 2, figs. 12–15). These two statues derive from different iconographic traditions where, in the first case, Venus holds a sheathed sword by her left side, and, in the second, brandishes a naked sword with her raised right hand. More recently, the Polish excavations in Nea Paphos have brought to light the mosaic floor of a house (very close to where the above-mentioned statue was discovered) depicting another armed Venus, this time holding a spear and represented frontally, revealing all her feminine charms (Christou 1994: 683; Daszewski 1994: 107). It is interesting to observe in this context that the 6th century lexicographer Hesychios (*s.v.* Ἔγχειος) mentions that the Cypriots called Aphrodite Ἔγχειος, that is holding a spear or a sword.

Under the word Ἀφρόδιτος, Hesychios mentions that according to Theophrastus, it means the Hermaphrodite, while according to Paeon, who wrote about Amathus, the goddess Aphrodite took the shape of a man in Cyprus. Also of interest in the context of androgyny is further information attributed to Paeon, preserved by Plutarch (*Theseus* 20.2–4). According to this evidence, Theseus abandoned the pregnant Ariadne on Cyprus where she died before giving birth to their child. Theseus returned to the island and, full of remorse, gave money to the locals in order that they initiate an annual sacrifice in her honor. He also ordained that during these sacrifices a young man should lie in bed shouting and imitating a woman in labor. Also according to Paeon, the Amathusians call the grove, in which Ariadne's tomb is found, the grove of Ariadne Aphrodite.

Returning to Venus, we can conclude that the depiction on the Roman mirror from Nea Paphos, although belonging to a clearly Roman tradition with strong links with official, imperial imagery and propaganda, fits well into the local tradition of the androgynous nature of Aphrodite.

ACKNOWLEDGMENTS

I would like to thank the following for their precious help: Andreas Georghiades, Conservator in the Department of Antiquities, for treating and painstakingly putting together the numerous small and crumbling fragments of the lid; Xenophon Michael, Photographer of the Department of antiquities for figs. 1, 3–6; Stella Demesticha for providing figs. 7 and 8; Glynnis Fawkes for the drawing (fig. 2); and Anna G. Marangou for bringing the De Agostini pamphlet to my attention.

REFERENCES

Cesnola, A. P. di

1877   *Cyprus, Its Ancient Cities, Tombs and Temples.* London: John Murray.

1882   *Salaminia (Cyprus). The History, Treasures, and Antiquities of Salamis in the Island of Cyprus.* London: Trübner and Co.

1894   *A Descriptive Atlas of the Cesnola Collection of Cypriote Antiquities in the Metropolitan Museum of Art, New York.* Vol. 2. New York: The Metropolitan Museum of Art.

Chavane, M. -J.

1990   *La Nécropole d'Amathonte. Tombes 110–385.* Vol. 4: *Les petits objets.* 'Etudes Chypriotes XII. Nicosia: Service des Antiquités de Chypre, École Française d'Athènes, et Fondation A. G. Leventis.

Christou, D.

1994   Chronique des fouilles et découvertes archéologiques à Chypre en 1993. *Bulletin de correspondance hellénique* 118: 647–93.

Daszewski, W. A.

1976   Les fouilles polonaises à Nea Paphos 1972–1975. *Report of the Department of Antiquities of Cyprus*: 185–225.

1982   Aphrodite Hoplismene from Nea Paphos. *Report of the Department of Antiquities of Cyprus*: 195–201.

1994   Nea Paphos 1993. *Polish Archaeology in the Mediterranean 1993*: 101–110.

De Agostini, G.

1872   *Lettera di Giovacchino De-Agostini al Conte Luigi Palma di Cesnola.* Vercelli: Tipografia Fratelli Gugliemini.

Delcourt, M.

1958   *Hermaphrodite. Mythes et rites de la bisexualité dans l'Antiquité classique.* Paris: Universitaires de France.

1966   *Hermaphroditea. Recherches sur l'Ltre double promoteur de la fertilité dans le monde classique.* Collection Latomus 86. Brussels.

Flemberg, J.

1991   *Venus Armata. Studien zur bewaffneten Aphrodite in der griechisch-römischen Kunst.* Stockholm: Svenska Institutet i Athen.

Hadjioannou, K.

1980   ʿΗάρχαία Κύπρος εἰς τάς ἑλληνικάς πηγάς. Vol. 4. Nicosia: Publications of the Holy Archbishopric of Cyprus.

1981   Aphrodite in Arms. *Report of the Department of Antiquities of Cyprus*: 184–86.

Karageorghis, V.

1983   Chronique des fouilles et découvertes archéologiques à Chypre en 1982. *Bulletin de correspondance hellénique* 107: 905–53.

1984   Chronique des fouilles et découvertes archéologiques à Chypre en 1983. *Bulletin de correspondance hellénique* 108: 893–966.

Karageorghis, V. et al.

2000   *Ancient Art from Cyprus. The Cesnola Collection in The Metropolitan Museum of Art.* New York: The Metropolitan Museum of Art.

Licht, H.

1949   *Sexual life in Ancient Greece.* 5th ed. London: Routledge and Kegan Paul.

Marangou, A. G.

2000   *Life and Deeds. The Consul Luigi Palma di Cesnola 1832–1904.* Nicosia: The Cultural Centre of the Popular Bank.

Myres, J. L.

1914   *Handbook of the Cesnola Collection of Antiquities from Cyprus.* New York: Arno.

Perrot, G., and Chipiez, C.

1885   *Histoire de l'Art dans l'antiquité.* Tome 3: *Phénicie-Chypre.* Paris: Librairie Hachette.

Richardson, E. H.
1964   *The Etruscans: Their Art and Civilization.* Chicago: University of Chicago.
Schmidt, E.
1997   Venus. Pp. 192–230 in *Lexicon Iconographicum Mythologiae Classicae* 8. Zurich: Artemis.
Schwarzmaier, A.
1997   *Griechische Klappspiegel. Untersuchungen zur Typologie und Stil. Athenische Mitteilungen* 18. Beiheft. Berlin: Mann.
Simon, E.
1984   Ares/Mars. Pp. 505–59 in *Lexicon Iconographicum Mythologiae Classicae* 2. Zurich and Munich: Artemis.
Sophocleous, S.
1985   L'Aphrodite en tant qu'androgyne. *Archaeologia Cypria* 1: 79–96.
Speidel, M.
1984   Venus Victrix. Roman and Oriental. Pp. 2225–38 in *Aufstieg und Niedergang der römischen Welt* 2. Berlin and New York: Walter de Gruyter.
Thomson de Grummond, N., and Lambert, L.
1982   The Usage of Etruscan Mirrors. Pp. 166–86 in N. Thomson de Grummond, *A Guide to Etruscan Mirrors.* Tallahassee, FL: Archaeological News, Inc.
Van der Meer, L. B.
1995   *Interpretatio Etrusca. Greek Myths on Etruscan Mirrors.* Amsterdam: J. C. Gieben.
Vermeule, C. C., III, and Comstock, M. B.
1988   *Sculpture in Stone and Bronze in the Museum of Fine Arts, Boston. Additions to the Collections of Greek, Etruscan, and Roman Art.* Boston: Museum of Fine Arts.
Vessberg, O., and Westholm, A.
1956   *The Swedish Cyprus Expedition.* Vol. 4, 3: *The Hellenistic and Roman Periods in Cyprus.* Stockholm: The Swedish Cyprus Expedition.
Westholm, A.
1932   Sculptures from the Temple-Site of Soloi-Holades. Pp. 173–88 in *Corolla archaeologica … Gustavo Adolph dedicata. ActaRom-4°,* 2. Lund: C. W. K. Gleerup.
1936   *The Temples of Soli. Studies in Cypriote Art during the Hellenistic and Roman Periods.* Stockholm: The Swedish Cyprus Expedition.
1937   Soli: The Temples at Cholades. Pp. 416–547 in *The Swedish Cyprus Expedition* Vol. 3: *Finds and Results of the excavations in Cyprus 1927–1931.* Stockholm: Pettersons.
Zahlhaas, G.
1975   *Römische Reliefspiegel.* Munich: Michael Lassleben Kallmünz Opf.
Zimmer, G.
1987   *Spiegel im Antikenmuseum.* Berlin: Mann.
Züchner, W.
1942   *Griechische Klappspiegel. Jahrbuch der Deutschen Archäologischen Instituts,* Ergänzungheft 14. Berlin: Walter de Gruyter.

THE UNGENDERING OF APHRODITE

BONNIE MACLACHLAN

Department of Classical Studies
University of Western Ontario
London, Ontario, Canada N6A 3K7
bmacl@uwo.ca

Greek historians have attributed to the dark side of the worship of Cypriot Aphrodite indications that she was considered to be bisexual. Not only were statues made of her in which she wore a beard, but her votaries engaged in transvestite and trans-gendered rituals. This paper attempts to make sense of an "ungendered" Aphrodite by exploring the textual and archaeological evidence and by making some suggestions for the motivation behind this striking feature of her cult.

At the beginning of this century, two of the principal historians of Greek religion, L. R. Farnell and Martin Nilsson, looked at the cult of Aphrodite on Cyprus and found certain features disturbing. Belonging to the dark side of her worship, in their view, were hints of bisexuality, a confusion of male and female elements. Farnell attributed these to a "mysterious Oriental fancy" (1895: 628), and Nilsson considered that it was among *"den dunkelsten Problemen"* (1906: 370). This paper attempts to shed some light on this darkness by exploring the extent of a dual-gendered divinity on Cyprus who eventually went by the name of Aphrodite and to propose some explanation for this phenomenon, looking at textual and archaeological evidence that establishes, beyond a doubt, that bisexuality was an important feature of her cult.

TEXTUAL EVIDENCE[1]

Farnell and Nilsson were drawing upon a body of texts from antiquity that attest to a bisexual representation of Cyprian Aphrodite, and to transvestite or transgendered rituals carried out in her honor. Virgil's account of Aeneas' departure from Troy, for example, describes the presence of the hero's mother as *deo ducente* (*Aen.* 2.632, Appendix, no. 1). Aphrodite/Venus was guiding him as a god, not a goddess. This prompted confusion among early commentators, as is clear from the discussion of the text by both Servius and Macrobius toward the end of the 4th century C.E. Servius (*ad Aeneid* 2: 632, Appendix, no. 2) explains Virgil's *deo* on two accounts: first, that some people believe that divinities can participate in both male and female aspects, and second, that in Cyprus there was a statue of Venus whose body was female in form and dress, but that was bearded, possessed male genitalia, and carried a scepter. This divinity they call by the masculine name *Aphroditos*, Servius continues, and the cross-gendering is reflected in ritual, for in sacrificing to her/him, men dress as women and women as men.

Macrobius, defending the reading *deo* in *Aeneid* 2.632 in the face of those who would emend the text to preserve a feminine Venus, offers the same description of a bisexual statue as we find in Servius, adding that people believe Aphrodite to be both male and female (*Sat.* 8.1–3, Appendix, no. 3). He points out that *Aphroditos* was a name assigned to this divinity as early as the Classical period, by Aristophanes. Macrobius quotes the Hellenistic historian Philochorus who, in his history of Attica, referred to the bisexuality of Aphrodite as comparable to that of the moon;[2] the belief that she was male and female accounted for the transvestism of her votaries during sacrifice, the ritual activity reported by Servius.

The picture of a dual-gendered Aphrodite on Cyprus is further supported by a quotation in Hesychios from Paeon, a Cypriot historian of the Hellenistic period (Appendix, no. 4). In his account of Amathus, Paeon said that on Cyprus the goddess took the form of a man. This feature may explain Catullus' reference to the goddess as *duplex Amathusia* (C. 68. 51). From Plutarch we get another striking detail of the cult as it was preserved in Paeon's account. This involved a transgendered ritual commemorating the arrival of Theseus and Ariadne on Cyprus after they left Crete. Driven off course by a storm, the pair put ashore long enough for the pregnant Ariadne to disembark, but Theseus was driven back out to sea. The local women tend Ariadne, but she dies in childbirth. In memory of that event, Paeon says, there is an annual sacrifice for Ariadne-Aphrodite in which a young man lies down and imitates the cries of a woman in labor (*Theseus* 20. 3, Appendix, no. 5).

The Cypriot cult of Aphrodite had ties to human fertility: it was introduced to Attica by King Aegeus in the hope of curing his sterility (Pausanias 1.14.7). The goddess complied and Theseus was born. References to a bisexual Aphrodite with links to human fertility continued through the Roman period until later antiquity. The *Suda*, for example, describes a statue of Aphrodite erected by the Romans which had a beard and both male and female genitalia; its upper torso was male and its lower was female (Appendix, no. 6). This entry in the *Suda* makes explicit a connection between Aphrodite's bisexual features and her powers over birth and generation.

The textual evidence is clear: on Cyprus there was a bisexual goddess whom Greeks and Romans identified with Aphrodite/Venus, a goddess connected with fertility in whose honor people engaged in transvestite and transgendered rituals.[3] The material evidence supports this figure in dramatic ways.

ARCHAEOLOGICAL EVIDENCE

As early as the 6th millenium B.C.E., anthropomorphic figures from the Neolithic settlement at Sotira combine an erect phallus with enlarged female thighs/buttocks, an impressive statement of reproductive power. The best-known dual-sexual representation is the limestone figure of uncertain date and provenance that surfaced during ploughing operations at the locality Arkolies near the Sotira settlement in 1981 (Swiny and Swiny 1983: 56–59). It is of exceptional quality and multi-representational in form: a view from one side gives the impression of a seated female figure with an elongated neck, long legs bent at the knees and a deep incision representing the vaginal cleft; from the other side, it presents an equally clear an image of a phallus and scrotum; the lateral view resembles a free-standing animal. The purpose of this and other similar figurines from Sotira is unclear: the variety in the representation argues against their being icons of a single divinity; their durability argues against their being ornaments or playthings, and the suggestion has been made that they served as images of family ancestors in a Neolithic cult of the dead (J. Karageorghis 1977: 17). The striking feature, so marked in the Arkolies figure, is the explicit representation of bisexuality.

A larger limestone figure from the Chalcolithic period (ca. 3900–2900 B.C.E.) may also represent a female figure with a phallus-head (Peltenberg 1977: 140–43). She was found in the debris of Building 1 at Lemba-*Lakkous* near Paphos. She has enlarged hips, pendulous breasts and a prominent pubic triangle. Her truncated arms are outspread, horizontal in relation to her body. The size of the figure, together with the special nature of the building in which she was found, suggest to Peltenburg that this figure was iconic, a cult figure.

Also dating to the Chalcolithic period and resembling in broad outline the "Lemba Lady," as she is popularly called, are smaller figurines (height 10–12 cm) with outstretched arms whose length and position render them cruciform. Many were pierced in order to be worn as pendants, as is demonstrated by the recovery of one at Yialia which itself wears a smaller cruciform pendant around its neck (Vagnetti 1974: pl. 5.1). These figurines have legs which are tightly bent in a squatting position, and they possess an elongated neck and an elliptical, tilted head. Most have been found in the Paphos region and are made of local picrolite, suggesting to some that these are iconic precursors of Aphrodite (J. Karageorghis 1977: 30). However, a recent discovery of Chalcolithic figurines at Kissonerga-*Mosphilia* near Paphos has shifted the emphasis in the study of the cruciform figurines in the direction of their birthing symbolism. In a ritual deposit at Kissonerga, stone and terracotta figures were uncovered that depicted the act of giving birth. Found with them were replicas of birthing stools. The fact that these figurines show signs of wear in places has prompted the suggestion that women rubbed or clutched them during labor (Bolger 1993: 34–36). The similarity in the overall shape of these Kissonerga figurines to the cruciform ones, along with the squatting position of the latter, links the cruciform figures to childbirth, a high-risk experience during the 3rd millennium (Bolger 1993: 36–37). If there was a goddess behind the rituals associated with these figurines, her role must have included the protection of women, not just the promotion of fertility.

The question of the sexual identity of the cruciform figurines is a complex one. Facial details and sexual markers are frequently absent; only on some are breasts indicated in relief, along or just under the intersection of the arms and body (Vagnetti 1974: 28). One type, classified by Vagnetti as the *Salamiou* variety (1974: 29), consists of double figurines in which a second figure replaces the arms. This second figure is usually identical to the first, but in at least one case the vertical figure possesses breasts while the transverse figure does not. It is possible to argue for a bisexual representation here but only with caution since there are no masculine sex markers and the transverse figure is also shown with knees drawn up in a squatting position. The elongated neck with the ovoid head can be seen as a variation of the (more explicit) phallic form of the "Lemba Lady" and this, when combined with the birthing position of the lower torso, has led to the suggestion that the figurines represent a bisexual divinity. While this view is currently regarded with some skepticism (Vagnetti 1974: 31), it is once again striking that the conventional distinction between male and female has been deliberately overridden. In the case of the cruciform figurines, this is (as far as is known to date) a uniquely Cypriot mode of representation, for no parallels have yet been found either in the Near East or in the Aegean.

About one thousand years later, during the Early–Middle Cypriot periods (ca. 2000–1800 B.C.E.), Cypriot artisans began to produce a very different type of anthropomorphic figure that also displays an indifference to, or deliberate transgression of, traditional sexual markers. These ceramic artifacts, of Red Polished ware with incised decoration, are known as "Plank Figures," because of their flat form. Of the approximately 80 representations uncovered to date, most have come from burial contexts, at least half from the cemetery of Lapithos in the north of the island. Most are highly stylized, with incised facial features and geometric decoration indicating multi-stranded necklaces and perhaps clothing. Many, but not all, have breasts, and a few cradle infants, in some cases two. Other sexual markers are rare: in one case the figure possesses breasts and a penis and holds a child. More than one quarter of these figures are double-headed (J. Karageorghis 1977: 55–56, e and f); one of the latter represents a couple in bed (J. Karageorghis 1977: 56 h). Another figure has three necks and one head (J. Karageorghis 1977: 56 g). A dramatic variation is found in some figures that are single-headed in front but double when seen from the back.

The meaning and function of the plank figures are not easy to determine (see Talalay and Cullen, this volume). Many of the figurines were found in multiple burials; some show signs of wear and deliberate breakage before being placed in a tomb. The duplication or multiplicity in the representation of these images, whether they were functional in life or after death, has been read as symbolic of a familial or group identity: The nuclear family could be represented by the single bisexual figure with child; the open-endedness of the single/double figure could be symbolic of an individual conscious of his/her place in a group setting. The duality of the double figures or the kourotrophic ones cradling twins can be read as generic duality: child-rearing may have been regarded as a communal function in these cultural groups. The activities represented by the plank figures—child-rearing, marriage (the couple in bed)—reflect daily life, and this seems to be a feature of other artifacts of the period (J. Karageorghis 1977: 57). Given the predominance of female markers (where markers are present), the figures could demonstrate the multi-faceted tasks of women in these communities. This seems to be the case on contemporary artifacts where the female figures dominate, and males when represented are smaller in size and appear to be engaged in secondary roles (J. Karageorghis 1977: 58).

The 3rd millennium in Cyprus witnessed the arrival of immigrants from Anatolia and a change in the economic base for communities like Lapithos. Agricultural techniques had developed to the point where farming produced a surplus instead of maintaining subsistence, and the beginning of copper-mining was producing wealth, with the social stratification which would be a natural consequence (V. Karageorghis 1982: 40–43; Tatton-Brown 1997: 13). The complexity of the symbolic representation of the plank figures may reflect the tensions produced by this social evolution in which individuals sought to redefine their place in a changing world. The bisexuality/dual sexuality represented by some of these images is but one way in which traditional binary divisions were ignored in the interests of projecting something more important. Once again, the ingenuity behind the design of the plank figures appears to have been essentially Cypriot. Direct parallels elsewhere have not been found.

We cannot assume, in any study of antiquity, that daily life was "secular" and distinct from ritual occasions or other events that invited the presence of divinities. In the ancient world, particularly as early as the Bronze Age, it is safer to assume that all aspects of life were permeated by divine forces.[4] The distinction sacred/secular is a modern gloss on a very different world-view (cf. Bremmer 1994: 1). The dimorphic plank figures could represent a divine couple or a divinity with two aspects as well as a human couple or a multivalent portrait of an individual.

With the mining of copper and metal production in the Bronze Age, wealth and prosperity came to Cyprus and fell, naturally enough, under the patronage of the gods. In the 14th century an important cult and bronze-working complex was constructed at Athienou (Lubsen-Admiraal and Crouwel 1989: 120). In the next century, twin temples were erected at Kition in close proximity to one another, resembling Near Eastern prototypes that were dedicated to twin deities, male and female (V. Karageorghis 1976: 57; J. Karageorghis 1977: 93). Near the temples were two sources of wealth: a sacred garden and quantities of copper slag, the latter indicating smelting-workshops in the vicinity. One of the two temples was substantially remodeled in the 12th century and another added, coinciding with the arrival of Achaean Greeks and the consequent improvement in metalworking techniques. The garden was remodeled and retained, and direct access was provided from the sacred precinct to the adjacent cop-per-smelting workshops (V. Karageorghis 1971: 388, 1976: 64–67, 72–74). This, together with the fact that votive-sized miniature ingots have been found at Enkomi from this period, confirms the link between metallurgy and religion in Cyprus' Bronze Age.[5] Roughly contemporary with the second temple-building at Kition was a sanctuary at Enkomi in which a bronze statue of a smiting god was found (V. Karageorghis 1976: 128, fig. 55). He stands on a base shaped like an ox-hide ingot, as does a companion-piece, a bronze statuette of a female deity, acquired recently in Oxford (V. Karageorghis 1976: 128, fig. 56). She was originally thought to have come from Syria, but the fact that she too stands on an ingot-shaped base links her closely to the so-called Ingot God of Enkomi.

The evidence from Kition and Enkomi suggests that the flourishing metal industry on Cyprus in the 13th and 12th centuries B.C.E. was under the patronage of twin male/female divinities. Could this cult have been a precursor to the later worship of a bisexual Aphrodite? The gardens connected with the temples at Kition recall the later association of Aphrodite with gardens: Strabo reports (14.683–684) that in the Classical period Aphrodite was worshipped on Cyprus in a place called *Hierokepis* or *Hierokepia* ("sacred garden"). In the Greek world, Aphrodite's connection with metalworking was expressed in myth through her marriage to the smithy-god, Hephaistos. In the Athenian Agora, the temple of Hephaistos was close to the place where Aegeus built the shrine of Paphian Aphrodite (Pausanias 1.14.7). Remains of metalworking operations dating to the sixth century B.C.E. have been uncovered in the vicinity (V. Karageorghis 1976: 75).

The more infamous sexual partner of Aphrodite was Ares, the warrior god. The Cypriot forebear of these two Greek mythical partners of Aphrodite may have been the smiting god standing on the ingot. A consort or spouse can represent the externalized qualities of a single divinity; internalized, the different qualities can be expressed by bisexual features or other attributes.[6] The bearded, bisexual statue of Aphrodite described by Macrobius carried a sceptre; Pausanias mentions armed statues of the goddess at Sparta and Kythera (2.5.1; 3.15.10; and 3.23.1) and Hesychios refers to a Cypriot tradition of "Aphrodite with a spear" (Ἔγχειος Ἀφροδίτη).[7] At Nea Paphos, two statues of Aphrodite-in-arms have been found dating to the Hellenistic period. Neither of these is explicitly bisexual, however; apparently a more limited message was intended.

At Ayia Irini, on the northwest coast of Cyprus, a sanctuary was excavated in the 1930s by the Swedish Cyprus Expedition which yielded over two thousand votive figurines from the Cypro-Archaic I period (750–600 B.C.E.). Among the many warrior images are theriomophic figures, centaurs, and bull-men, several of which have bisexual features. One has a bovine body with a woman's breasts, long tresses and male sexual organs. It carries a cup (Sophocleous 1985: pl. 16, fig. 10). The director of the Swedish Cyprus Expedition, E. Gjerstad, suggested in 1963 that the sanctuary in its earliest phase (Late Bronze Age) was dedicated to a goddess who was tauromorphic (Sophocleous 1985: 92, n. 100), and while there were other figures in the Archaic collection whom Gjerstad identified as representatives of the goddess, this bisexual tauromorph could be vestigial of the earlier form. A second, strikingly bisexual image in the Archaic collection is a human figure with arms uplifted, in the pose common to Near Eastern votive objects identified as goddesses, priestesses or votaries "with upraised arms" (V. Karageorghis 1977: 5, 7, n. 12, 13).[8] A serpent crawls up her back and rests its head on her left shoulder. This figure has breasts but also a beard outlined in black paint (Sophocleous 1985: pl. 16, fig. 9). A second example of this type was found in the collection, and others have been found on Cyprus (V. Karageorghis 1973: 47, fig. 1).

At Larnaca in the 19th century, L. P. di Cesnola found a large statue of a bearded figure holding a cup in one hand and a dove in the other. Although the objects carried by the statue suggested to Cesnola that this represented a priest of Aphrodite, he noted the enlarged breasts on the figure and its female features (1878: 132), details which have led other archaeologists to identify the figure with Macrobius' bisexual statue. Cesnola also uncovered two terracotta small statues of a bearded figure in a necropolis at Amathus, which have been dated to the 6th century B.C.E. (Perrot and Chipiez 1970: 560; Cesnola 1878: 132). Traces of paint remained on the lips, beards, eyes and eyebrows, and pubic area. The breasts are only slightly contoured and the upper half of the body looks masculine; the pelvic area and pubic triangle suggest that the lower half was intended to be female. This recalls the testimony of the *Suda*, that the statue of Aphrodite was masculine above the groin and feminine below, and the figurine has been linked directly with the descriptions of Macrobius and Servius. The image is almost certainly connected with a ritual of the goddess: the clothing resembles that of other exclusively female figures connected with the cult of Astarte, nude or dressed in a transparent robe, whose arms extend the length of the body and whose legs are pressed against one another. One of these female figures was found in the collection at Ayia Irini (Sophocleous 1985: 87, n. 66; Perrot and Chipiez 1970: 560). Other small hermaphroditic figures have been unearthed from Amathus. The fact that they are without beards and wear masculine clothing associated elsewhere with priest-figures suggests that they may represent priest-servants of the goddess rather than the goddess herself. The sexual crossing-over would be consistent with the rites of Ariadne-Aphrodite at Amathus.

Although bisexual statues have been found throughout the island, it was with Paphos that Aphrodite was associated in antiquity.[9] She was called *Aphrodite* by Homer, but Paphian syllabic inscriptions refer to her only as *Wanassa* ("Ruling Lady") until the end of the Classical period. This is a title found in Mycenean texts and may reflect the survival of Greek traditions introduced by immigrants from mainland Greece. Votive figurines from the sanctuary in the Archaic and Classical periods consist of female figures, representing either the goddess herself or votaries elaborately dressed. There appears to have been no cult statue of the goddess: the conical meteorite stone that represented the goddess from the time of the founding of the sanctuary (ca. 1200 B.C.E.) was still symbolic of Paphian Aphrodite on coins of the Roman period. A Phoenician inscription of the 3rd century B.C.E. attests to the fact that Astarte was worshipped in the sanctuary, and at the same time we find the first inscriptions to the named goddess, *Aphrodite Paphia* (Maier and Karageorghis 1984: 183, with n. 23).

THE DIVINE ANDROGYNE: POSSIBLE EXPLANATIONS

Although no bisexual statue or votive figurine has been found at Palaepaphos, it is clear that the traditional boundaries between male and female were not always observed in the iconography connected with Cypriot cults of the goddess who ultimately took the name of Aphrodite. What does this transgression of boundaries suggest? Mircea Eliade, in a survey of myths and ritual practices around the world, has explored the motif of duality-in-unity and studies the way in which androgyny is implied by this (Eliade 1965). Marie Delcourt has built upon Eliade's analysis, applying it to the Greek world in two important works studying the figure of the hermaphrodite (Delcourt 1961, 1966). It is clear that the archetype of the divine androgyne is a widespread one, appearing in cosmogonic myths, philosophic-religious constructs, alchemy, mystical techniques, and the aesthetic imagination. From Eliade's discussion emerge four different impulses that can account for androgynous divine figures: cosmogonic narratives, the image of divine perfection, the concept of sexual union, and the desire for eschatological completeness. In what follows I will attempt to connect these impulses to the bisexual figures on Cyprus whose features are also found in Macrobius' statue of Aphrodite.

Cosmogonic Narratives

In the excavation of the sanctuary at Ayia Irini, terracotta votaries of the 7th century B.C.E. were found encircling a spherical/ovoid stone that bore traces of fire and oil. The Swedish excavators identified this stone with the object of the cult, although they believed that the veneration of the stone itself might have begun much earlier (in the Late Bronze Age) with the founding of the sanctuary. It may, in some respects, have embodied the powers of the male and female deities who were patrons of the sanctuary (cf. Sophocleous 1985: 92–93, where this stone is compared with similar shapes elsewhere which had divine status because they were seen to embody creation). In Egypt, the solar disk was associated with the bisexual creator-god Atum, or the scarab's ball (its *khepri*), containing the eggs for the next generation. The sphere and the egg were regarded as two representative forms of creation, the sphere symbolizing perfection and totality (in some mythical constructs the sun-creator) and the egg its biological counterpart.

In myth, a bisexual creator is frequently found with the cosmic egg. Eliade finds this mythical construct diffused throughout the Mediterranean Near East but also in other archaic cultures, and attributes its widespread appearance to the fact that the image offered a satisfactory picture of the ultimate reality as an indivisible totality (Eliade 1965: 109). A primordial androgyne embodies the whole. The act of creation is frequently envisioned as initiated by the splitting of an egg or the partition of a sphere that separates into the primary divisions characterizing the temporal world, including that of male and female. Through various rituals, mortals engage in symbolic androgynization in order to experience symbolically a return to the plenitude of the pre-creation phase represented by the primordial androgyne and the sphere/egg.

In the Greek world, this myth was most clearly presented by the Orphic cosmogonies in which a cosmic egg splits. The two fragments of its shell become heaven and earth, and the bisexual figure Phanes/Protogonos emerges to begin the process of creation.[10] Zeus becomes the supreme god and finishes the act of creation by swallowing Phanes and becoming *pantogenethlon*, "progenitor of all," (*Orphic Hymn* XV) or "Zeus the male, Zeus the immortal bride" (Orphic fr. 21a Kern). Aristophanes (*Birds* 695–96) preserves some Orphic cosmogony in his description of creation occurring when an egg is produced by Night. Out of the egg comes a winged Eros who produces the human race. Eros in Greek iconography was regularly represented as bisexual.[11] As a god, Eros embodied the totality necessary for a creator-god, as we learn from Athenaeus, quoting the comic poet Alexis: "Eros is neither male nor female, god nor human, thoughtless nor reflective, but made up of elements of all parts in one form, a multiplicity of characters" (*Deipn.* 13.13.562B). The Orphic Hymn LVIII describes Eros as *diphues*, "dual-natured." The myth preserved in Hesiod of the castration of the Sky-God Ouranos, which resulted in the birth of Aphrodite from the sea foam at Cyprus, may revert to an older version in which a primordial being (analogous to the egg) is cut in two, forming Heaven and Earth (Delcourt 1966: 43). If we assume a parallel deep structure between these myths, we can explain the androgynous nature of Aphrodite and of her counterpart Eros as a requirement in accordance with their powers over human and animal generation, with the need both to embody male and female qualities, and with the physical processes necessary to generate new life.[12]

At 7th century Perachora (near Corinth), in the sanctuary of Hera Limenaia, was found a terracotta figure of Aphrodite emerging from a genital sac: the black paint and the dots running down her cheeks and across her skin are unmistakable evidence for the fact that she is bearded. Parallel figures were found in Sparta (Payne et al. 1940: 232), attesting to the fact that the goddess, as she emerged from the primordial severing of the whole, embodied the dual features necessary for her to assume creative powers.

Near the sphere/egg at Ayia Irini stood a bearded female votive figure with a serpent crawling up her back. A creation myth attributed to the Pelasgians described the creator-goddess Eurynome rising naked from Chaos, dividing the sea from the sky and dancing upon the waves. Rubbing the North Wind between her hands, she produces the serpent Ophion who couples with her. She then turns herself into a dove; she broods upon the waves and lays the Universal Egg. Eurynome instructs Ophion to coil about the egg, which splits in two for all creation to emerge.[13] It is tempting to see here a strong parallel with Cypriot Aphrodite rising from the waves to become a goddess of generation, Aphrodite for whom the dove became an attribute.[14] The figure with the serpent at Ayia Irini may have received the same legacy.

The Concept of Sexual Union

Aphrodite was celebrated in Greek literature as the goddess of sexual activity. Her very presence ensured that lovemaking was a necessity. The poet of the fifth *Homeric Hymn* describes her leaving the temple at Paphos for Troy, to the bed of her mortal lover Anchises, and placing passionate longing in the breasts of the wild animals who accompany her so that they couple in the thickets (lines 58–73). Greek and Roman writers looked upon Cyprus as a center of sexual activity connected with the cult of Aphrodite.[15] Clement of Alexandria and Arnobius, writing in the Christian period, described a festival at Paphos as the celebration of a mystery cult in which initiates were given a lump of salt (as token of Aphrodite's birth) and a phallus as a sign of the goddess' blessing (Appendix, no. 7, 8). The participants offered Aphrodite a coin, the Church Fathers said, as lovers would a courtesan.

The act of heterosexual lovemaking is an experience of momentary androgyny that, in the sense of wholeness it confers, resembles the type of completeness associated with divinity. Eliade quotes Jacob Boehme, one of the German Romantics whose view of lovemaking may be similar to that of the votaries at Paphos:

> sexual love should not be confused with the instinct for reproduction. Its true function is to help men and women to integrate internally the complete human image, that is to say the divine and original image. (Eliade 1965: 101)

This sexual duality-in-unity could account for the rich nexus of Cyprus-based myths of incest:[16] mating with one's own progeny preserves two-in-one. This is frequently the case with cosmogonic myth; divine creators are all-in-one but initiate the process of sexual procreation by mating with an offspring, as Gaia does with Ouranos. Ovid transmits the sequence of Cypriot incest myths (*Met.* 10. 238–420). Pygmalion, an early king of Cyprus, sculpted a marble statue of the perfect woman and promptly fell in love with it at the instigation of Aphrodite. During a festival of the goddess he laid a gift-offering on the altar of the goddess and asked her for a wife like his statue. The goddess complied and fired Galatea with life. In an act of (artistic) incest, Pygmalion mated with his own creation. In the next generation, Kinyras became king by marrying the daughter of Pygmalion (Apollodorus, *Lib.* 3.14.3–4). Kinyras was a priest-favorite of Aphrodite (Pindar, *Pyth.* 2. 17) and was associated with the wealth of Cyprus. Indeed, Pindar speaks of Cyprus as being "weighed down" with the prosperity loaded on the island by Kinyras (*Nem.* 8. 18). Kinyras was seduced by his own daughter Myrrha, who gave birth to Adonis, consort of Aphrodite. Through his association with Aphrodite in cult and myth, Adonis brought fertility and prosperity to Cyprus. These myths likely took their basic shape during the Late Bronze Age when, with the arrival of Aegean Greeks, copper-production on Cyprus was developed to a degree that ensured wealth for the island. The archaeological record suggests that this wealth was under the patronage of twin divinities, male and female, and was accumulated in a cultural context in which male/female duality was frequently combined in a single image, whether expressed in stories of incest or in bisexual statues.

The All-Perfect God

The figure of a divine androgyne is found frequently in cosmogonic myths and can be accounted for by the need to embody all characteristics required in creation. It also occurs when a god's supremacy is represented by bisexual features. A Carian terracotta relief from the 4th century B.C.E. depicts Zeus with female features, a triangle of six breasts on his chest (Eliade 1965: 109). He is flanked by two dedicatees of the plaque, the king of Caria and his wife, who was also his sister. This royal pair, Idreus and Ada, were preceded in Caria by another, more famous pair of royal siblings, Mausolus and his queen Artemisia. There could be a connection between the portrait of a bisexual Zeus and of the royal siblings. Royal marriages between brother and sister could give the impression of divine-like perfection, particularly in cases where kings were also the chief priests. The close connection between Cypriot kings and the goddess is made clear by a Phoenician inscription found at Paphos to "King Astarte" (Maier and Karageorghis 1984: 183).

Like the Carian couples, closely tied heterosexual pairs informed mythical narratives of incest connected with Cypriot Aphrodite. The bisexual images found in Cypiot cult contexts could represent the same aspiration to imitate divine perfection through sexual complementarity. Carian Zeus with female breasts recalls the Hesiodic Zeus ensuring his supremacy by swallowing Metis. It also recalls the Orphic Zeus father-bride.

In Cyprus, the perfection of bisexual Aphrodite would entail, above all, powers of sexual activity and procreation and could celebrate the human experience of momentary androgyny in the sexual act.

Plato's memorable account of the origin of erotic desire, given mythical form in his *Symposium* (190B–193B), expresses this well: in the beginning, before the fall from divine favor, men and women were whole, integrated pairs of men/men, women/women and men/women; with the fall from the perfect state the pairs were separated into discrete singles, in which form we remain, constantly desiring our former state of wholeness.[17] Aphrodite as Eros stimulates this erotic desire, in essence our longing to return to the state of perfection. The Greek myth that assigned Aphrodite's place in cosmogonic succession placed her, as it did Eros, at the moment when creative forces were released by the splitting of the whole. For Aphrodite this entailed castration, the separation of Heaven and Earth. Male and female began as one, and with the energy of generation released by their separation, the power of Aphrodite obliges them to seek a return to oneness, to the momentary experience of androgyny in an act that is necessary to ensure new life.

Eschatological Completeness

Akin to the desire for perfection or cosmological wholeness is the wish to anticipate the completeness that will be experienced at "the end of time"—eschatological fulfillment. The Gnostic Gospel of Thomas quotes Jesus as saying, "When you make the man and woman into a single one, so that the man shall not be man and the woman shall not be woman, then you shall enter the Kingdom" (*Logion* 21). Eliade, in his survey of rituals and mystical experiences of androgyny, found that transcending the category male/female was one of the main characteristics of the notion of spiritual perfection (1965: 106). Just as the divine creator embodies all contraries, so all creatures possess this totality in embryonic form, permitting this to be experienced for discrete periods of time through ritual or mystical techniques of integration.

One of the rituals of integration found elsewhere in Greece and Rome, particularly in adolescent or nuptial initiation rites, was transvestism. Plutarch describes brides dressing as men in Sparta (*Lyc.* 15) or Argos (*de Virt. Mul.* 245 D) and bridegrooms dressing as women at Cos (*Qu. Gr.* 58, *Mor.* 304C). Transvestism was also practiced at the Athenian Oschophoria, a grape-harvest festival, and at the Hybristika in Argos, on a day honoring Hermes and Aphrodite. Servius and Philochorus record the practice of men and women on Cyprus exchanging clothing in honor of Aphrodite. These various contexts have in common occasions recognizing the importance of fertility.[18] Eliade considers the purpose of these intersexual disguises and concludes that it embodies the desire to transcend the historically controlled situation in order to recover the initial completeness that existed prior to creation, an "intact source of holiness and power" (1965: 113). Tapping into this power releases the regenerative force required for fertility. The desire to gain access to this power could lie behind the rituals of cross-dressing on Cyprus, the bisexual cruciform figures and other sexually ambiguous images found on the island from earlier periods. By reaching beyond the normal categories imposed by the post-creation era one could, like shamans who symbolically assume both sexes, gain access to a reserve of sacred power, primordial plenitude.

Boundary-crossing in image-making evokes liminality and mutability, both of which can be agents of empowerment (Green 1997: 898). Carl Jung invited us to enter this psychic and metaphysical space to obtain power through the wholeness that comes from recognizing the *animus* as well as the *anima* in each of us. Bearded Aphrodite from Cyprus may reside in this space: from here arose one of *den dunkelsten Problemen* for scholars of religion who saw only one side of her. By acknowledging her beard as a sign of wholeness, we bring light to this darkness.

NOTES

1. The principal texts discussed below are cited and translated in full in the Appendix.
2. On the bisexuality of the moon, compare Plato's *Symposium* 190B and Plutarch's *Amator* 19.746D.

3. For an example of the legacy left by transvestism in rites of Aphrodite taking the form of transgendered Christian saints, see Cook 1914: 175–76, with n. 2.

4. Thales: πάντα πλήρη θεῶν εἶναι ("all things are full of gods") fr. 91*KRS*.

5. For other examples of this connection found in the Near East, see V. Karageorghis 1976: 75–76.

6. For the idea that divine pairs can be a later elaboration of a primordial androgynous divinity, see Eliade 1965: 111.

7. A statue of a nude Aphrodite holding a sword in her right hand, probably of a Hellenistic date, was found at Nea Paphos (Hadjioannou and Daszewski 1983: 281).

8. The initial study of this type was done by St. Alexiou in 1958 (Κρητικά Χρονικά 12 [1958] 179–299). The Cretan type finds a striking parallel in the famous "Lady" from the Bronze Age Sanctuary at Phylakopi (Renfrew 1985: frontispiece). Noteworthy is the fact that she, like the Cypriot "goddesses with upraised arms" has a protruding chin suggestive of a beard. For a discussion of this type of figure, see V. Karageorghis 1977.

9. The direct association begins with the song of Demodocus in *Odyssey* 8.362, where Aphrodite, after the exposure of her adultery with Ares, "returns to Paphos on Cyprus, where stands her sacred precinct and smoky altar."

10. For Orphic hymns that refer to other bisexual creator-figures that emerge from an egg, see Delcourt 1961: 69.

11. Images of a bisexual Eros are shown in Delcourt 1966: pls. 2, 5, 6.

12. On the legacy of sea-born, bisexual Aphrodite taking the form of bisexual saints, see Cook 1914: 175–76, n. 2.

13. For sources, see Graves 1960: 27–28.

14. It is also tempting to recall here Genesis 1:2, in which the spirit of God, like an incubating bird, "broods" (*rahap*) upon the waters and creation begins.

15. On evidence for ritual prostitution practiced in the Cypriot cult of Aphrodite, see MacLachlan 1992: 145–62.

16. There may be a similar connection between hermaphrodism and pederasty; see Delcourt 1966: 65–66.

17. A Gnostic Jewish text gives a variant of the creation story in Genesis 1:26–27, which is strikingly similar to Plato's account. In this account, Adam possesses two faces, two sets of genitals, and four arms and legs; the double being is back-to-back until split in two by God (Pagels 1976: 298).

18. It is preferable, I believe, to see the focus on fertility in nuptial rites of cross-dressing rather than to attribute it to the intent to deceive an evil spirit who accompanied the danger of defloration (Nilsson 1906: 372).

APPENDIX
PRINCIPAL TEXTS CITED

1. Vergil, *Aeneid* 2.632–33:

Descendo, ac ducente deo flammam inter et hostes
expedior: dant tela locum flammaeque recedunt.

I descend and, guided by a god, move quickly among the foes
and fire: weapons give way and the flames draw back.

2. Servius, *ad Aeneid* 2. 632 (*ac ducente deo*)

secundum eos qui dicunt, utriusque sexus participationem habere numina … est etiam in Cypro simulacrum barbatae Veneris, corpore et veste muliebri, cum sceptro et natura virili, quod Ἀφρόδιτον *vocant, cui viri in veste muliebri, mulieres in virili veste sacrificant.*

ac ducente deo following those who say that divinities partake of both sexes. For there is on Cyprus a statue of bearded Venus, in a woman's body and clothing, with a sceptre and man's genitals, whom they call *Aphroditos*, to whom men make sacrifice in women's clothing and women in men's.

3. Macrobius, *Saturnalia* III. viii.1–3
Nonnullorum quae scientissime prolata sunt male enuntiando corrumpimus dignitatem, ut quidam legunt: "discedo ac ducente dea flammam inter et hostes expedior" *cum ille doctissime dixerit:* "ducente deo" *non* "deá." ... *Signum etiam eius est Cypri barbatum corpore sed veste muliebri, cum sceptro ac natura virili, et putant eamdem marem ac feminam esse. Aristophanes eam* Ἀφρόδιτον *appellat.* ... *Philochorus quoque in* Atthide *eamdem affirmat esse lunam et ei sacrificium facere viros cum veste muliebri, mulieres cum virili, quod eadem et mas aestimatur et femina.*

By an incorrect reading we ruin the importance of several texts which have been composed with considerable learning. So several read "I descend and, with the goddess guiding, hasten through the flame and the foes" when the poet said, with superior knowledge, "with the god guiding," not "the goddess." ... There is a statue of her on Cyprus, bearded in body but in women's dress, with a scepter and male genitalia, and they think that the same figure is both male and female. Aristophanes calls her *Aphroditos*. Philochorus also, in *Atthis*, says that the moon is the same and that men make sacrifice to her in women's dress and women with men's, because she is considered both male and female.

4. Hesychios, s.v. Ἀφρόδιτος · Θεόφραστος μὲν τὸν Ἑρμαφρόδιτόν φησιν, ὁ δὲ τὰ περὶ Ἀμαθοῦντα γεγραφὼς Παίων εἰς ἄνδρα τὴν θεὸν ἐσχηματίσθαι ἐν Κύπρῳ λέγει.

Aphroditos: Theophrastus says that it refers to Hermaphroditos, but Paeon, writing the book about Amathus, says that on Cyprus the goddess is depicted as a man.

5. Plutarch, *Theseus* 20. 4 ἐν δὲ τῇ θυσίᾳ τοῦ Γορπιαίου μηνὸς ἱσταμένου δευτέρᾳ κατακλινόμενόν τινα τῶν νεανίσκων φθέγγεσθαι καὶ ποιεῖν ἅπερ ὠδίνουσαι γυναῖκες· καλεῖν δὲ τὸ ἄλσος Ἀμαθουσίους, ἐν ᾧ τὸν τάφον δεικνύουσιν, Ἀριάδνης Ἀφροδίτης.

(Paeon says that) at the sacrifice on the second day of the month of Gorpiaeus one of the young men lies down and cries out and behaves just as women do in labor. The people of Amathus call the grove in which they show her tomb that of Ariadne Aphrodite.

6. *Suda* (s.v. Ἀφροδίτη). ... εὐξαμένας δὲ τῇ Ἀφροδίτῃ ἀνατριχωθῆναι, τιμῆσαί τε αὐτὴν ἀγάλματι, κτένα φέρουσαν καὶ γένειον ἔχουσαν, διότι καὶ ἄρρενα καὶ θήλεα ἔχει ὄργανα. ταύτην γὰρ λέγουσιν ἔφορον γενέσεως πάσης, καὶ ἀπὸ τῆς ὀσφύος καὶ ἄνω λέγουσιν αὐτὴν ἄρρενα, τὰ δὲ κάτω θήλειαν.

Praying to Aphrodite to be given hair again, they honor her with a statue that carries a comb and wears a beard, wherefore it has male and female genitals. For they say that she is the overseer of all generation; from her loins and upwards they say she is male while below she is female.

7. Clement of Alexandria, *Protrepticus* 13P ἡ Κινύρᾳ φίλη ... ὡς ἀσελγῶν ὑμῖν μορίων ἄξιος γίνεται καρπός, ἐν ταῖς τελεταῖς ταύτης τῆς πελαγίας ἡδονῆς τεκμήριον τῆς γονῆς ἁλῶν χόνδρος καὶ φαλλὸς τοῖς μυουμένοις τὴν τέχνην τὴν μοιχικὴν ἐπιδίδοται· νόμισμα δὲ εἰσφέρουσιν αὐτῇ οἱ μυούμενοι ὡς ἑταίρᾳ ἐρασταί.

She (Aphrodite) is dear to Cinyras … a worthy fruit of wanton genitals in your view. In the mysteries celebrating this pleasure of the sea a lump of salt is given as a witness of her birth, and a phallus to those being initiated into the art of lechery. The initiates bring to her a coin as lovers do to a courtesan.

8. Arnobius, *Adv. nat.* 5. 19 *nec non et Cypriae Veneris abstrusa illa initia praeteribimus, quorum conditor indicatur Cinyras rex fuisse, in quibus sumentes ea certas stipes inferunt ut meretrici et referunt phallos propitii numinis signa donatos.*

Nor will we pass over those secret mysteries of Cyprian Venus, whose founder Cinyras proved to have been king, (mysteries) in which, as they enter them, they bring particular gifts as they would to a courtesan, and they bring back phalluses given as a sign of the favoring divinity.

REFERENCES

Bolger, D.
1993   The Feminine Mystique: Gender and Society in Prehistoric Cypriot Studies. *Report of the Department of Antiquities of Cyprus:* 29–41.

Bremmer, J.
1994   *Greek Religion: Greece & Rome.* New Surveys in the Classics no. 24. Oxford: Oxford University.

Cesnola, L.
1878   *Cyprus: Its Ancient Cities, Tombs and Temples.* New York: Harper.

Cook, A. B.
1914   *Zeus: A Study in Ancient Religion.* Vol. 1. Cambridge: Cambridge University.

Delcourt, M.
1961   *Hermaphrodite: Myths and Rites of the Bisexual Figure in Classical Antiquity.* Trans. J. Nicholson, from French. London: Studio Books.

1966   *Hermaphroditea: Recherches sur l' être double promoteur de la fertilitè dans le monde classique.* Brussels: Latomus.

Eliade, M.
1965   *The Two and the One.* Trans. J. M. Cohen, from French (originally published as *Méphistophélès et l'Androgyne*). London: Harvill; New York: Harper and Row.

Farnell, L. R.
1895   *The Cults of the Greek States.* Vol. 2. Reprint ed. New Rochelle, NY: Caratzas.

Graves, R.
1960   *The Greek Myths.* Vol. 1. Revised edition. New York: Penguin.

Green, M. J.
1997   Images in Opposition: Polarity, Ambivalence and Liminality in Cult Representation. *Antiquity* 71: 898–911.

Hadjioannou, K., and Daszewski, W.A.
1983   The Ἔγχειος Ἀφροδίτη Again. *Report of the Department of Antiquities of Cyprus*: 281–82.

Karageorghis, J.
1977   *La grande déesse de Chypre et son culte. A travers l' iconographie, de l' époque néolithique au Vième s. a. C.* Lyon: Maison de l'Orient.

Karageorghis, V.
1971   Chronique des fouilles à Chypre en 1970. *Bulletin de correspondance hellénique* 95: 335–432.

1973   Figurines de terre cuite chypriotes aux jambes articulées. *Bulletin de correspondance hellénique* 97: 47–57.

1976   *View from the Bronze Age: Mycenean and Phoenician Discoveries at Kition.* New York: E. P. Dutton.

1977   The Goddess With Uplifted Arms in Cyprus. Pp. 5–45 in *Scripta Minora 1977–1998 In Honorem Einari Gjerstad*, ed. B. Stjernquist. Lund: Royal Society of Letters.

1982   *Cyprus: From the Stone Age to the Romans.* London: Thames and Hudson.

Lubsen-Admiraal, S., and Crouwel, J.
1989   *Cyprus and Aphrodite.* 's-Gravenhage: SDU uitgeverij.

MacLachlan, B.
1992   Sacred Prostitution and Aphrodite. *Studies in Religion/Sciences Religieuses* 21: 145–62.

Maier, F.G., and Karageorghis, V.
1984   *Paphos: History and Archaeology.* Nicosia: A. G. Leventis Foundation.

Nilsson, M.
1906   *Griechische Feste von religiöser Bedeutung.* Leipzig: Teubner.

Pagels, E.
1976   What Became of God the Mother? Conflicting Images of God in Early Christianity. *Signs* 2: 293–303.

Payne, H., et al.
1940   *Perachora: The Sanctuaries of Hera Akraia and Limenia. Excavations of the British School of Archaeology at Athens 1930–1933. Architecture, Bronzes, Terracottas.* Oxford: Clarendon.

Peltenburg, E. J.
   1977   Chalcolithic Figurine from Lemba, Cyprus. *Antiquity* 51: 140–43.
Perrot, G., and Chipiez, C.
   1970   *Histoire de l'art dans l'Antiquité*. Vol. 3. Graz: Akademische Druck-u. Verlansanstalt.
Renfrew, C.
   1985   *The Archaeology of Cult: The Sanctuary at Phylakopi*. London: Thames and Hudson.
Sophocleous, S.
   1985   L'Aphrodite en tant qu'androgyne. Pp. 49–86 in *Archaeologia Cypria* 1. *In Honour of Professor Einar Gjerstad*, ed. S. Sophocleous et al. Nicosia: Association of Cypriot Archaeologists.
Swiny, H. W., and Swiny, S.
   1983   An Anthropomorphic Figurine from the Sotira Area. *Report of the Department of Antiquities of Cyprus*: 56–59.
Tatton-Brown, V.
   1997   *Ancient Cyprus*. Revised ed. London: British Museum.
Vagnetti, L.
   1974   Preliminary Remarks on Cypriote Chalcolithic Figurines. *Report of the Department of Antiquities of Cyprus*: 24–34.

PART SEVEN

GENDER AND CYPRIOT ARCHAEOLOGY: CRITICAL VIEWS

WOMEN IN CYPRIOT PREHISTORY:
THE STORY SO FAR

NAOMI HAMILTON

Department of Archaeology
University of Edinburgh
Infirmary Street, Edinburgh EH1 , Scotland
nhamilto@hsy1.ssc.ed.ac.uk

Until recently, neither women nor gender were regarded as legitimate topics for archaeological research. This is now widely recognized, but only because a considerable number of women both within and without the profession have spoken out. Although matters have improved, they have not changed much. Those who work in the field of gender are well aware of the fringe status it retains. The fact that a general reading list was included in the call for papers for this conference suggests both that participants were not expected to be involved already with gender research and that gender is still so marginal to archaeology that practitioners are not likely to be conversant with the basic literature or with the theoretical and methodological models in use.

Women and gender were not excluded as topics of research by a male-dominated profession merely because they were considered to be uninteresting but also because they were believed to be inaccessible through the archaeological record (see also Wylie 1992). Of course, this did not stop archaeologists from finding men, as it is well-known that all interesting features of society, be they technological innovation, political organization, economic control or bringing home the bacon, are male preserves. Although this attitude has also changed to some extent, it lingers on—and with reason. Much work that professes to be about gender is actually about women, and of the "add women and stir" variety, rather than an investigation of gender as a system and a querying of received knowledge about men as well as women. Both types of research are needed, but the methodologies and implications for theory and interpretation differ. Small-scale revisions of the picture, minor studies of female technologies on the sidelines of the "real thing," can make little impression on the overall vision of the past.

Gender is not just about women, and it is perhaps unfortunate that the subtitle of this conference appears to exclude men from study. Gender is a culturally constructed binary social system that allocates roles, abilities and aspirations according to physiological sex (which may itself be a socially constructed category) and defines the interaction between the genders as well as the activities and behavior appropriate to each. It is well-known among social scientists that gender is neither natural nor universal in its construction. However, gender is one of the most basic concepts of Western culture, so completely naturalized that many of us have difficulty envisaging social systems in which gender differs from our own model, unable even to recognize that we have just one model among many. Understanding the complex social system described in the word "gender" requires an integrated approach to the data. It also requires clear analytical and theoretical models that, on the whole, are still lacking (see Scott 1986; Wylie 1992). It is my contention that because of the centrality of gender to how we all, including archaeologists, view the world, gender must be central to all archaeological work and ever-present in our theories, interpretations and practice if we are ever to gain a real and rounded understanding of past societies. To do this we need to rethink all our premises, and this involves recognizing the bias of the past.

Little work has been carried out specifically on gender or women in Cyprus, and most relevant work has been based on four topics: burials, anthropomorphic figurines, scenic compositions and Aphrodite/Astarte (or goddesses, in general). The first three data groups are very tempting because they seem to link archaeologists more closely to the real people of the past than abstract areas such as technology, the economy, or buildings. However, it may be that this perceived closeness has obscured the difficulties of using the data and, in particular, the influence of cultural stereotypes on our interpretations. Aphrodite and Astarte lie beyond the scope of this paper, arriving on the scene too late, but their powerful influence is seen in the attitude of many archaeologists to prehistoric figurines.

Despite the paucity of research focusing on gender, comments and interpretations relevant to gender have been reasonably common in archaeological work on Cyprus, and it is these that I wish to examine briefly and critically as part of the rethinking of premises and recognition of bias recommended above. I shall also be considering the implications of that work for an understanding of prehistoric Cypriot society as well as examining the theoretical basis for past research. For reasons of space I can only select a few examples in this paper and do not pretend that this is a comprehensive review. I shall cover the period from the 1930s, when archaeology proper began in Cyprus, to the present. I shall finish by considering recent work on gender and the possibilities for future research.

COMMENTS/INTERPRETATIONS IN NON-GENDER ORIENTED RESEARCH

Burials

My examination of non gender-oriented work starts with a look at the treatment of burials. When reporting on the skeletal remains from Khirokitia, Angel bemoaned the quality of the material: "Out of a sample of 123 people only 38 provided measurable skulls, and of these less than half were relatively undeformed adult males" (1953: 416). The implication of this comment is that adult males, rather than adult skulls, are the standard from which to work, suggesting that females are somehow deviant. In the next paragraph he discussed the frequency of cranial deformation, including the greater number of female than male deformed skulls. Beyond commenting that it is possible that all babies were subjected to artificial skull-shaping to some degree, perhaps by being tied to cradle boards, he does not suggest a social or ideological context for this behavior or for the preference for changing the shape of female babies' heads. Instead he offers an essentialist biological explanation (Angel 1953: 416): "There is room for speculation on physiological versus social sex distinctions here: boy infants may have resisted head-flattening more actively than girls or just possibly may have recovered more fully." This speculation reflects recent Western views about behavior appropriate to the sexes, particularly the belief that males should be active and females passive. Numerous sociological studies have demonstrated that these attitudes cause different treatment of male and female babies, leading to different levels of activity among boys and girls, and, therefore, researchers have difficulty in studying how children would behave without such social controls (see for instance Fausto-Stirling 1994, chap. 5 for a discussion and references). Whether similar social attitudes prevailed in the Neolithic period in Cyprus is entirely unknown, so to argue from the present to the past in an attempt to understand archaeological data is dangerous and liable to lead to circular arguments. In her recent discussion of the material, Niklasson added a further twist to Angel's comments, noting that according to his 1961 data table there were, in fact, more male than female deformed skulls (1991: 60)! It is tempting to speculate on how Angel might have interpreted this result in either social or biological terms.

The widespread habit of sexing skeletons according to grave goods also betrays cultural bias as to the belongings and activities appropriate to each sex and ignores the fact that, quite apart from the strong chance that social attitudes were very different in the distant past, we cannot even know whether grave goods were personal possessions, gifts, or work-related items. Dikaios generally avoided such methods, and although he noted that at Khirokitia needles were buried with men and a child, not with women, he made no gender inferences. However, when discussing artifacts found in a domestic context, he commented that,

> A bone needle (no.1340) was found on the lowest level of the rectangular platform on floor VII of tholos X (II), from which the smaller hearth-platform projected. As already explained, the larger platforms were used for sitting or sleeping near the hearth, and the discovery of a needle on one of them allows us to imagine a homely scene by the fire, with the housewife busy with her needle. On the same floor, a fragment of mother-of-pearl (no. 1339), a woman's ornament, was also found. (Dikaios 1953: 213)

While this is certainly a change from extrapolating gender information from grave goods in the case of needles, no explanation was offered for rejecting an association of needles with men in life, while accepting an association of necklaces with women in life based on the mortuary record.

Although Stewart and Stewart noted the unreliability of grave goods for sexing skeletons, he used them repeatedly at Vounous. Regarding tomb 90, for instance, he commented that, "If it is safe to judge by the criteria of personal possessions, body A may have been male (knife and whetstone) and B female (whorl)," and regarding tomb 120 he noted "the possibility that the A corpse was female," and explained in the footnote that, "On the principle that spindle-whorls denote the female sex, perhaps not a very reliable criterion (Stewart and Stewart 1950: 94)." Stewart was in a position to know that these criteria were not very reliable because tomb 110 contained a single skeleton in chamber B that was accompanied by grave goods including a spindle-whorl, a knife and a whetstone. Why he should have persisted in sexing skeletons female if they had spindle-whorls and male if they had a knife and/or whetstone is, therefore, puzzling. The skull in tomb 110 was sexed tentatively as female. Only 16 skeletons were sexed, and sexing was based only on the skulls. Unfortunately, the reasons guiding the selection of these skulls is nowhere explained, and only two in addition to those from tomb 110 were from single burials, which also contained materials commonly regarded as sex/gender related. These were a sexed male from tomb 154, with grave goods including two bronze knives and a whetstone; and an individual sexed as possibly male from tomb 160, with grave goods including a bronze knife. This is hardly conclusive evidence for sex/gender-typing of grave goods or the usefulness of grave goods in assigning sex/gender to skeletons. Neither spindle whorls nor knives were very common, and other metal tools such as axes and daggers invariably occurred alongside knives rather than alone, suggesting perhaps a tool-kit rather than sex-linked objects.

Stewart's treatment of the data may be explained by a further entry, that shows that he was convinced that metal was both a sign of wealth and power and a male prerogative. Tomb 131 contained three skeletons—the primary one (A), which had been pushed aside, and two more (B and C), lying parallel to each other, one on its front, the other on its back. According to Stewart (Stewart and Stewart 1950: 276), "The left arm of C was in contact with the left arm of B. Two pins were found on each skeleton, one upon each shoulder…The sex of the bodies B and C could not be determined, but the presence of a whorl in association with B may indicate that it was a female." In a footnote he adds,

> Miss Grace considers that pins are never found with male burials. There is no anthropological evidence on the point from Vounous, but the writer is disinclined to accept Miss Grace's thesis without further confirmatory evidence. On her assumption, both bodies in this grave would be female. Such a rich interment of two women in a primitive society seems extravagant, unless a form of matriarchy existed. (Stewart and Stewart 1950: 278, note 4)

Two pins each hardly seems an extravagance of wealth when one considers what other tombs contained, the greatest quantities being two knives, two axes and one dagger with one skeleton (tomb 161); and five knives, two axes, one chisel and one awl with two skeletons (tomb 105). It seems that cultural bias was at work. Unfortunately, Miss Grace's work, referred to by Stewart, appears to be based similarly on assumptions of sex/gender-appropriate grave goods and a system of elimination, rather than on anthropological research (see Grace 1940).

There is a serious shortage of sexed and aged skeletal material from prehistoric sites in Cyprus, despite the vast numbers of tombs that have been excavated—or at least opened in the name of research—in the last century and a half. In her comprehensive study of prehistoric burials, Niklasson did not attempt to deal with gender in any structured way, and until better data is available it will be difficult to do so (Niklasson 1991). However, her work is important in that she both collected the data in a very useful and useable form and highlighted its problems—not only the lack of information but also the failure to publish the basic data and the contradictory results produced by different scholars ageing and sexing the Khirokitia skeletons.

Figurines

The study of figurines has been the most prominent area in which the role of women in prehistory has been discussed, and judgments such as Stewart's concerning the value and role of women in the past have been commonplace even recently. Thus Orphanides, discussing figurines from tombs, suggested in 1983 (and, indeed, at this conference) that "The female figures may represent the wife (wives) or female servant(s) of the dead. It seems reasonable that, in the Near Eastern society of those times, their companionship or service to their husbands or masters, among other daily chores, was primarily sexual (1983: 46)." The view that dead men need female company, and preferably sex, in the afterworld, while dead women do not, is culturally based and linked to the historical denial in Western culture that women have any sexual needs at all, while male sexuality is viewed as barely controllable. In the context of Cypriot prehistory, however, when many Chalcolithic and Bronze Age figurines are interpreted as birthing charms or related to childbirth and motherhood, it is particularly peculiar that figurines in tombs are thought to accompany men for sex rather than women for rebirthing. In mentioning servants, Orphanides is also implying a stratified society, which he explicitly sees as patriarchal or at least male-dominated. There is no evidence for these statements, and, as I have mentioned previously (Hamilton 2000), there is some evidence that figurines may have been placed with female skeletons. If that is correct, following Orphanides' general principles of interpretation, one would have to see a female-dominated lesbian society.

Desmond Morris, who has interpreted figurines as fertility charms (Morris 1985: 162), was, nonetheless, forced to make an exception in the case of the plank idols: "There is something so un-sexual about these stocky little figures that one is left with nagging doubts. Could they after all be substitute figures—effigies of widows placed in their husbands' graves to accompany them in death, thereby avoiding the unhappy entombment of the real widows?" This comment brings up several issues relevant to gender: in addition to the suggestion that women could be, or had been, disposable upon the death of a man, he echoes the view that dead men need female company in the afterworld. Marital terminology such as "husband" and "widow" carries a host of modern connotations, including culture-specific aspects relating to the expected roles of spouses—roles which may have had no meaning in prehistory and which, in my view, should be avoided. Finally, the idea that fertility charms should be sexy is linked to a common confusion in figurine studies between "sexual characteristics" as physiological sex indicators, and "sexual activity," reflecting a modern attitude connected to taboos about the naked body and sexuality generally. Breasts and pubic triangles may be the simplest symbolic way to convey information concerning sex, gender or age-status, and the modern association of nakedness with sexuality and fertility may be completely inappropriate. A similar attitude is rarely shown towards male figures, as though archaeologists regard male nakedness as normal and female nakedness as naughty.

A Campo's recent thesis covers Chalcolithic and Early Bronze Age figures in both stone and clay (a Campo 1994). I can only look briefly at this detailed formal and symbolic analysis, touching on a few points. Unlike those who believe figurines were placed in graves to provide future services, a Campo states that only a minority of plank idols occur in graves, with a small minority of individual burials, and suggests that this makes universalist interpretations such as "symbols of human rebirth" or "servants and concubines" less likely. Moreover, she comments that "a function in sympathetic fertility magic seems somehow unlikely, in view of the fact that the main concern of the artists was the detailed representation of decoration rather than that of the female body" (1994: 167). She then suggests that the decorations could indicate a woman's marital status, or, following Talalay, that the idols could be marriage contracts, but from an idea with interesting possibilities she moves rapidly, with no evidence, to decision: "In short, the primary meaning of plank figures seems to be the representation of individual, human women in role as wife and mother, with their 'lineage'," adding later on the same page that, "Whatever their function, the plank figures certainly seem to reflect a concern with female status based on marriage and lineage, less so on motherhood (a Campo 1994: 169)." I have commented above on the danger of using marriage terminology for prehistoric cultures. There are other difficulties with a Campo's statements. For a start, despite the unresolved debate on sexing these figurines, she believes all plank idols are female with no substantial justification:

The sex of a "sexless" figurine belonging to a series which includes figurines with indication of sex, may be determined by analogy and therefore all plank idols can be regarded as female whether or not they have breasts. (a Campo 1994: 172)

This highly contentious statement appears to be linked to her interpretation that assumes that women were traded between lineages. This idea suggests that women were viewed as commodities, exchangeable wives and mothers, which I find culturally biased and narrow. Nowhere does she discuss why only *female* figurines should be used as marriage contracts, and I find this a serious limitation.

A Campo suggests that both Chalcolithic cruciform figures and Early Cypriot plank figures—both of which she believes represent women—probably played their prime role during the life of the owner:

In the case of the Chalcolithic cruciforms the woman is impersonal and the formal emphasis lies on her *posture* expressing childbirth. In the normative plank-figure, on the other hand, the emphasis lies on her apparel and identity: she is *personalised*. [my emphasis] (a Campo 1994: 170)

She goes on to draw the conclusion that the attitude towards the function of women in society differed considerably between the two periods:

In the Chalcolithic (women's) function was primarily based on motherhood, since the prime concern of Chalcolithic symbolism … was female fertility. This concern was obviously less pronounced in the Early Cypriot period. Consequently, a woman's status was not primarily defined by her role as a mother, but rather by her marriage *and family connections*. [my emphasis] (a Campo 1994: 171)

While it is refreshing to see a lifetime use hypothesis put forward for plank idols, the heavy burden of interpretation on such slim evidence, the passive nature of women's suggested role, and the lack of interest in how any parallel male status might have been defined, is disappointing. I get the impression that male status and/or function is regarded as assured and given, while female status must be developed.

Not all scholars have interpreted figurines from patriarchal perspectives. Some, such as J. Karageorghis (1977), have seen figurines as manifestations of a goddess-worshipping matriarchy, while Christou (1989: 90) has commented that, "all the Paphian picrolite cruciform figurines have been correctly interpreted as cult images of a female or a mixed female and male divinity connected with fertility." However, this approach has run into a number of difficulties. To begin with, the lack of theorization of matriarchy makes it difficult, if not impossible, to recognize such a social form archaeologically. Indeed, there is no agreement on whether such a social system has ever existed, which in turn is linked to the lack of theory and clear models. There is also no consensus regarding the sex of many figurines, despite a long-standing habit of regarding all prehistoric human images as female (see for instance Ucko 1968; Hamilton 1996a; 2000). The lack of provenance for large numbers of figurines leads to serious problems regarding context, and the common practice of lumping all figurines together regardless of context, date or material has added to the growing disenchantment with such interpretations. Moreover, there are broad questions concerning how to recognize representations of deities as well as religious or ritual places. There is also some urgency in determining whether religion and deities, as we presently conceive them, existed before the Bronze Age. These are major issues which require integrated and interdisciplinary work before the idea of a mother goddess can be accepted, and it remains a matter for debate. It should also been noted that historical mother goddesses, such as Kybele and Artemis, were not depicted giving birth or with babies.

Lately, Chalcolithic figurines have been widely interpreted as birth charms, following Morris (1985: 122). He notes the frequency of the bent leg posture and its similarity to parturition posture in many cultures and links it to more explicitly birth-giving figurines from Kissonerga-*Mosphilia*, an idea which Peltenburg elaborates (1992: 32). While the fact that women gave birth in the past is neither novel nor unexpected (see Frankel 1993a), this approach to figurines does treat them in terms of what they can tell us about real lives. Goring, on the other hand, has suggested that the terracotta figurines in the Kissonerga-*Mosphilia* hoard should be regarded as teaching devices, possibly used by a midwife, while the stone ones could have been held by women in labor (Goring 1991: 52, 54). This innovative approach, involving detailed study of wear on figurines and consideration of their tactile qualities, weight, and context of deposition, is an example of what can be achieved through a data-led rather than purely ideologically-based study of figurines and again relates them directly to real lives and real women (and perhaps men, too?). These ideas are unusual in carrying no sub-text regarding women's position in society and in having no religious overtones.

Debates over the sex of figurines have played an important role in a number of studies (e.g., Merrillees 1980; Morris 1985) but have become less prominent recently. It is noticeable that a Campo's discussion assumed that figurines are female unless proven otherwise, rather than getting involved in the issue, and Mogelonsky's attribute typology does not include indications of sex (Mogelonsky 1991). Although both these scholars used large data sets and attempted to understand figurines through an examination of form and function, neither sets out to examine sex or gender. While in some ways this may be a step forward, in other ways it may ignore important elements of the data.

Scenic Compositions

In the past, scenic compositions have often been regarded as ritual objects. The most famous of these, the Vounous bowl, was interpreted by Dikaios as a sacred enclosure in which all but one person was male, the single female carrying a baby which was a sacrificial victim (Dikaios 1953: 118–125). While other interpretations have been offered, no one has so far questioned the basic premise that the scene represents male power. However, Morris has argued strongly for the Vounous bowl and all scenic compositions to be understood as scenes of everyday life (1985: 264–90). It may come as no surprise that his view of everyday life in the Bronze Age is not far from that of the present: women grind grain, make bread and wash clothes, while men do the high status things like leach copper, milk deer for possible ritual purposes, and sit around doing nothing. In studying the Oxford Bowl, Morris originally thought both men and women were shown baking, although he imagined men baking "sacred pyramid loaves" and women baking "ordinary day-to-day flat loaves." However, he felt this did not explain certain elements on the pot such as the presence on the "male side" of a deer and a small unidentifiable quadruped. His decision to abandon male bakers in favor of copper leachers made him more comfortable, despite the fact that it explains fewer of the elements, which led him to seek an alternative explanation of the male tasks in the first place. It does not explain the animals, and now the "baker's stick" also has no purpose (Morris 1985: 273–74). Moreover, the pit or trough for collecting sludge is not shown outside the enclosures, a strange omission among such detail, but Morris does not comment on this. While noting that the figures on one side of the bowl are shown with genitals (male) and those on the other side have none, he does not speculate on why this should be. Why, for instance, are the males shown full-frontal, while the supposed females are mainly back-views, with the few shown from the side encumbered by such items as a large pestle? Perhaps it was simply not feasible to show sex on all the figures; perhaps it was enough to show sex on those which could be modeled with ease, to be extrapolated to the rest of the series as a Campo suggests; or perhaps Morris is right and the absence of penises is used on this scene to denote female, as an absence of breasts is often thought to denote male. All these possibilities should at least be considered and discussed before interpretations involving a sexual division of labor are offered.

Following Morris, the everyday nature of the majority of scenic compositions has been accepted by a number of scholars such as Frankel, Swiny and Merrillees. Swiny disagrees with the identification of the scene as one of copper leaching on technical grounds but notes that where the coroplast deemed it necessary to specify sex, there is an impression of segregated activities (1989: 24), a point made also by Frankel (1993a: 140). In fact, we simply do not know why some potters showed the sex of figures, and figures apparently carrying out the same activities may be shown as male, female or sexless, although not always in the same scene. Karageorghis interprets the so-called bread-making and copper-leaching scenes as pot-making, which, as the scenes appear on pots, seems eminently reasonable. However, his reason for disagreeing with the copper-leaching interpretation is a cultural judgement, namely that, "It is far more natural for such a potter, most probably a woman, to be inspired from her own everyday life, her own craft of which she knew all the details, than from metallurgical activity, which was carried out near the woods, was highly specialized and must have been exclusively confined to men" (1991: 37; quoted in Webb and Frankel 1995: 107). It is relatively recently that pottery was transferred conceptually to the female sphere in archaeological interpretation, following ethnoarchaeological studies (e.g., Hill 1970; Longacre 1972). It was reasoned that women might accidentally have discovered pottery while cooking (a job always in the female sphere in archaeological interpretation). Metallurgy is also likely to have been discovered accidentally at the hearth. Why, then, has metallurgy not followed the same conceptual transfer route? It is worth noting that an x-ray study of Bronze Age pottery from Italy showed a piece of metal in a pottery sherd (Loney 1995: 393–96).

The conceptual switch of pottery manufacture to women has been accompanied by theories of female exogamy to account for overall similarity but regional variation in ceramics. Frankel, for example, has stated, "One may suggest that some movement of people, rather than pottery, was taking place, and that women might be exchanged between villages, not in direct exchange for metal, but rather to establish kinship links which could serve as a framework for some forms of trade" (1974: 205–6). This view sees women as passive pawns in political and economic systems controlled by men. It does not even grant them the status of innovative potters; rather, they passively copy and repeat styles learned at home. Although numerous studies have questioned the soundness of the work on which such conclusions have been based (e.g., Crossland and Posnansky 1978; Plog 1978; Stanislawski and Stanislawski 1978, to name but a few), the idea of female exogamous potters persists in Cypriot archaeology (e.g., Frankel 1993a: 141–42). Female exogamy generally offers less social power for women than male exogamy on account of the absence of friends and relatives for support and networking, so this has broad social implications for gender that have rarely, if ever, been discussed. Stewart viewed the Early Bronze Age pottery industry as specialized and workshop-based, "too large to have been delegated to the women of the household" (1962: 290). Note not just the content of this suggestion but the terminology employed, the word "delegated" suggesting male power over female choice of work. If the scenic compositions do show women making pots, this would support the idea of female potters, while the fact that they work in groups suggests workshop-type production. This, in turn, could, though need not, suggest kin-based work-groups of women with female residence patterns. Stylistic variation could perhaps be accounted for by movement of pots or motifs in other contexts (see, e.g., Crossland and Posnansky 1978; Hodder 1978: 58; Stanislawski and Stanislawski 1978). Female residence groups would have implications for social structure, gender relations, and power. On the other hand, if scenic compositions such as the Oxford Bowl show men firing pots made by women, perhaps we should be thinking about household production, which could, but need not, have involved sex-linked tasks. We must remember, however, that household production, generally viewed as female work, need not only be undertaken for household consumption but can also be carried out for purposes of exchange and trade (e.g., Arnold 1978; Crossland and Posnansky 1978).

RECENT RESEARCH ON SOCIETY AND GENDER

The late 1980s and 1990s have seen an upsurge of interest in social archaeology. Gender, however, has been notably absent from the scene. No paper on gender can be found in the proceedings of the conference on Early Society in Cyprus, held in Edinburgh in 1988 (Peltenburg 1989), although a number of papers contained pertinent comments. This seems a strange omission from a conference dealing with society. Social complexity has become something of a buzz word in recent years, but gender has not featured in the debates. The important American Schools of Oriental Research consultation on the topic (published in issue 292 of the *Bulletin*) contained scant references to gender and no discussion of it. The (invited) male contributors appear to have conceived of social complexity as merely a macro-political scenario and—notwithstanding Knapp's discussion of complexity terminology (Knapp 1993: 86–88)—to have conceived of the consultation as an opportunity to pinpoint that now elusive point in Cypriot prehistory at which men took control of society (and its metal wealth), a problem that had not troubled earlier scholars. The only female archaeologist involved was dealing with a later period. In examining complexity, the hunt was on for high status groups, the manipulation of exchange systems (Peltenburg 1993: 14), and "the development of lineages, and the diachronic possession of rights and status" (Manning 1993: 43), although Frankel noted that "nothing in the ceramic inventory shows significant regional, status, or gender-based differences" (1993b: 61). It was left to the (female) anthropologist to mention the range of social organizations known in comparable cultures, including gender-based lodges and dormitories for unmarrieds (Kingsnorth 1993: 108), but as her role was to comment on what the participants had said, she had little scope for involving a broader gender perspective.

The 1991 Congress in Göteborg, which had no specific theme, did rather better. It included a session on women, but only one paper materialized. This paper, by Åström (1992: 5–8), offered a useful review of recent work of interest, commenting on earlier scholarship and on topics worth pursuing: for example, the different average life expectancy allocated to each sex by various researchers (an area with social implications in terms of authority and the transmission of culture), and the presence of both metal weapons with females and elaborate jewelry with males in burials. Other comments of Åström's are more in line with old thinking, such as, "Did (women) perform other duties than the traditional ones of spinning and weaving?" (1992: 5). At the same Congress, Vassos Karageorghis gave a paper on toys that contained a number of controversial ideas concerning the identification of toys versus figurines with ritual significance. In discussing a figure with beard and breasts, a plumed helmet and a sword sheath, he commented that "this suggests that he is a soldier and the indication of breasts should not be taken seriously. He hardly looks like a 'hermaphrodite': breasts are often represented on male figures in ancient iconography without any particular significance" (V. Karageorghis 1992: 173). Merrillees had said much the same when he suggested that breasts on plank idols need not indicate femaleness as males have breasts too (Merrillees 1980: 174). Neither they nor others discussing "hermaphrodite" figures have attempted to move beyond binary sex/gender models (see also Hamilton 2000).

Nevertheless, there has been some change recently with research by a handful of scholars, in particular Bolger, Webb, Frankel and the present author, which has examined the theoretical bases of interpretations and offered new ways of looking at the data. Bolger has produced a series of important articles attempting to put gender on the agenda in Cypriot archaeology. She has examined the misunderstandings about gender, including the assumptions that past society can be modeled on the present and the lack of attention to gender in recent discussions of prehistoric society (Bolger 1993). She has also attempted to work with data sets from an explicitly gendered viewpoint, looking at the production of pottery and picrolite figurines (Bolger 1994), the uses of figurines, and interpretation of skeletal data (Bolger 1993, 1996). Webb and Frankel's discussion of gender inequity in archaeology started from a different perspective, examining the inbuilt bias against gendered work and against certain research topics by undertaking a survey of the involvement of men and women in different aspects of archaeology in Cyprus and their levels of power to influence the discipline. In the paper outlining their results, they comment on the need to change the whole approach of the discipline, the gender differential in career structure and opportunities, and the male control of research aims and broad theory. They conclude with a discussion of theory and explanation in Cypriot prehistory, especially the use of presentist gender ideologies. They note how neatly the assumed gender division of labor in the past complies with the one they have just described in the profession (Webb and Frankel 1995). In a paper examining the discipline in America, Gero has commented on male control of "high-status" areas of research and the marginalization of female research with rather similar results to Webb and Frankel (Gero 1994). These two papers highlight serious problems within archaeology that need to be tackled by the profession as a whole if a rounded vision of the past is to be achieved. My own work has centered on understanding and unmasking the gender bias in archaeological research, its political roots and the conceptual difficulties archaeologists have with issues of sex and gender that are foreign to our own cultures (Hamilton 1996a, 2000). I have also attempted to use new approaches to traditional data, such as figurines and burials, to obtain more rewarding and sound information about social structure. This has involved looking more carefully at both localized and broad contexts of figurines (Hamilton 1994), investigating change over time that may relate to changes in gender ideology (Hamilton 1996b), and considering non-binary options of sex and gender when dealing with figurines of ambiguous sex (Hamilton 2000) or burials that appear to cross sex/gender demarcation lines (Hamilton 1996b).

Overall, archaeologists in the 1990s have arrived at a general consensus that pre-Bronze Age society in Cyprus was basically egalitarian, but the debate as to when that changed has paid little attention to gender issues, simply assuming that power and prestige will be controlled by men.

FUTURE PROSPECTS

Gender is neither natural nor universal but a social construction, and this must be the guiding principle of social research into prehistory. Webb and Frankel's (1995) research is pertinent to the future prospects of gender in Cypriot archaeology. They have pointed to the role of sex/gender in controlling the types of research being carried out—that in general, male archaeologists have set the agenda. Gero's work demonstrates the sexual division of research interest and method (Gero 1994). It is hard to escape the conclusion that in our world what men do is interesting while what women do is boring stuff at home, so that conversely, in interpreting the past, if it is interesting, men did it; if it is boring stuff at home, women did it. In this regard, it is worth considering that once upon a time, the domestic sphere may well have been the main, if not sole, sphere of activity. Who had high status then?

As I stated in the introduction, I believe that the centrality of gender to our own lives means that we must put gender at the center of archaeology. We need to see gender as an aspect of interpretation, embedded in all thinking about society, rather than being hived off into a separate area on the sidelines, and we need to develop a methodology for this task. Any broad theory must look at the bases of social behavior, not just at the "interesting bits" concerning power and politics in external relations. Knowing as we do that other social, economic and political systems existed in the recent past until European imperialism destroyed them (and still exist in some places today), it is not just foolish but culpable to continue to interpret past societies through modern paradigms. Gender is one of these systems, and it is no more static than any other social system. I suspect that it is through changes in the gender system that we are most likely to understand how it operated at any one time. I have been attempting to do this by using a broad range of data and looking across time periods, but that is not necessarily the only way.

It is widely believed that a focus on gender and women is a modern idea and that scholars of the past should be excused for their narrow approaches to society. However, as I have mentioned elsewhere (Hamilton 1996a), the formative period of archaeology and related academic disciplines, in the mid to late 19th century, was something of a melting pot of ideas and a time when a far more massive women's movement than that of the 1960s and 1970s was challenging male laws, science and social norms (for example, see Jackson 1994 with references; Poovey 1988). No academics could have been unaware of the debates transforming Victorian Britain, and the version of the past which was presented by these academics for public consumption must, therefore, be seen as reactionary and political, not as naïve.

Changing our old ways involves more than changing our thinking about gender and society; it involves re-thinking the academic enterprise, which may also involve taking note of gender differences in the use of data. Men are expected to be incisive, and male dominated academia requires clear interpretation and results, solid knowledge of a kind that is rarely approachable in dealing with prehistory. A list of possibilities and areas for consideration is regarded as a cop-out, a failure to achieve results, yet I believe that such an approach is more likely to lead to an approximate understanding of the past. This treatment of the data is more commonly found among female scholars and, being inconclusive, is rarely recognized as having the status of being major work.

CONCLUSION

Work on gender in Cypriot archaeology is long overdue and is still marginal in the extreme. Despite the widespread changes in associated disciplines such as anthropology and geography, a recognition of gender as a social structure and social force has barely been recognized in the mainstream. Even in the late 1990s, after a number of articles bringing the issues of gender and women to the attention of archaeologists working in Cyprus, there has been barely any change, and reactionary, unsupported, presentist attitudes to women, gender and the division of labor in the past are common. Archaeologists appear largely to be still working with views from the first half of the century and, with depressingly few exceptions, those who have attempted to update approaches to early society have failed to address gender at all.

Where work on burials is concerned, I have illustrated above the way ideas from the present have influenced the interpretation of the past, whether it relates to social alteration of the skull shape, sexing of skeletons according to grave goods, or interpreting the use in life of artifacts found in graves. As most excavations of prehistoric tombs took place in the 19ᵗʰ century and the first half of this century, my examples have been drawn from early work. However, very little recent work exists, and the dearth of good skeletal data makes it extremely difficult for modern scholars to rework the material with more open minds. On the other hand, there is also a range of other work that could be done that could help us to understand sex and gender but appears, so far, not to have been applied to prehistoric Cypriot material. For example, stable isotope studies of bones could examine whether men and women had similar diets and had equal access to animal protein; studies of teeth can furnish other types of dietary information; an investigation of work-related bone damage could explore age- and sex-based task differentiation; and DNA analysis could be used to consider lineages and relationships, in particular the issue of female exogamy (although place of burial need not follow the same pattern as place of residence). If a number of studies were used in concert, we might get nearer to real people than through generalized assumptions about sex/gender roles based on grave goods. Proper and extensive sexing of skeletons could certainly establish whether some grave goods are sex-related, but an integration of this data with information concerning work-related bone damage and artifact use-wear analysis might lead us closer to an understanding of whether grave goods were personal belongings of the dead. Reliably-sexed skeletons and DNA derived lineage data could be linked to studies of cemetery layout to produce a better understanding of various social relationships. Because of the range of new scientific techniques now available, the future is bright for burial studies.

The study of figurines is the most common area in which gender roles have been discussed, but this is not because of anything intrinsic to the artifacts. Rather, it is because of the edifice built by scholars, past and present, concerning the assumed roles of men and women and the influence on these roles of the sex of deities. Figurines have usually been studied alone rather than as part of a wider data set, and often figurines from a number of periods have been regarded as essentially the same, although there is good reason to suggest that not all figurines from a single period had the same uses, let alone those from multiple periods. They have either been seen as goddesses, in which case they are not human and have little or no relevance to the position of women in society (e.g., Ehrenberg 1989: 23); they are often associated with matriarchy; or they are regarded as sex toys for men. The argument about the existence of a goddess, be she mother, earth or fertility goddess, relates to political and social attitudes to women in the present. Those involved often have their own, perhaps unrecognized, perspective. Thus, in the late 1960s and 1970s, a number of women began to offer different interpretations of gender roles in the past, using an interpretation of figurines as goddesses to bolster their case (although they often used the same arguments of "nature" and "biology" that have been used against the suggestion that women have ever been other than wives and mothers). It is scarcely surprising, therefore, that studies of figurines carried out by men in the 1980s tended to stress the sexual or maternal rather than the political or economic role of women in the past (see Hamilton 1996a). The wider implications of comments, such as those by Orphanides and Morris quoted above, were not explored, as only the narrow topic of figurines was being examined, and these interpretations represented almost throw-away remarks rather than strongly argued and supported positions. There are few in the 1990s who would be so confident that women in prehistory were purely expendable sexual playthings under the control of men.

Although many figures on scenic compositions do not have sex indicated (and those that do seem often to be carrying out the same tasks), archaeologists frequently offer different interpretations according to the sex or assumed sex of the figure. The suggestion that prehistoric women spent their time at the wash-tub comes straight from modern attitudes to cleanliness and cultural bias regarding appropriate female activities. The assumption of high-status work for men is similarly biased. It is noticeable that while suggested daily activities for women are varied and typically domestic—washing, baking, brewing, grinding grain—few daily activities are suggested for men and none before the Bronze Age, when those on offer include public and prestige roles.

Morris's insistence on the everyday rather than ritual nature of scenic compositions ensures that women are kept in a domestic role, while his determination to see a sexual division of labor permits men to move into a public role as controllers of copper wealth. If we look instead at the communal aspect of many work scenes and reject ideas about women washing clothes all day, perhaps these are ritual activities after all. This would have implications for gender and for women's public roles. Peltenburg has recently attempted to link the Vounous bowl to changes both in social complexity and in gender structures, with a new male hierarchy being validated by usurpation of established legitimation imagery (1994), but his is an isolated paper and deals only with a single scenic composition. My own contribution on the subject of the Vounous bowl shall be made in a separate paper for reasons of space.

Until now, prospects for incorporating into mainstream Cypriot archaeology an understanding of gender and an interest in those aspects of life associated in the present with women have been bleak. This conference is an important step forward. It shows that a growing number of people are taking gender seriously, and it is encouraging that although the usual "women" topics are well represented, other areas of research also feature. This suggests that many researchers, particularly female researchers, have been awaiting the opportunity to pose legitimately some unusual questions. Nevertheless, there is still an almost total absence of broad theory. This is a serious problem, as the general picture painted of the past still reflects the modern public world of men. That is not the whole world, and it certainly was not the whole of the ancient world.

ACKNOWLEDGMENTS

Many thanks are due to Nancy Serwint and Diane Bolger for organizing the conference at CAARI, which brought the topic of gender to the notice of many archaeologists working on Cyprus and for their commitment to seeing the papers through to publication.

REFERENCES

a Campo, A. L.
1994   *Anthropomorphic Representations in Prehistoric Cyprus: A Formal and Symbolic Analysis of Figurines, c. 3,500–1,800 B.C.* Jonsered: Åströms.

Angel, J. L.
1953   The Human Remains from Khirokitia. Appendix II, pp. 416–30 in P. Dikaios, *Khirokitia.* Oxford: Oxford University.

Arnold, D.
1978   Ceramic Variability, Environment and Culture History among the Pokom in the Valley of Guatemala. Pp. 39–59 in *The Spatial Organisation of Culture*, ed. I. Hodder. New Approaches in Archaeology. Cambridge: Cambridge University.

Åström, P
1992   Approaches to the Study of Women in Ancient Cyprus. Pp. 5–8 *in Acta Cypria.* Acts of an International Congress on Cypriote Archaeology Held in Göteborg on *22–24 August 1991* Part 2, ed. P. Åström. Jonsered: Åströms.

Bolger, D. L.
1993   The Feminine Mystique: Gender and Society in Prehistoric Cypriot Studies. *Report of the Department of Antiquities of Cyprus*: 29–41.
1994   Engendering Cypriot Archaeology: Female Roles and Statuses before the Bronze Age. *Opuscula Atheniensia* 20: 9–17.
1996   Figurines, Fertility, and the Emergence of Complex Society in Prehistoric Cyprus. *Current Anthropology* 37, 2: 365–73.

Christou, D.
1989   The Chalcolithic Cemetery 1 at Souskiou-Vathyrkakas. Pp. 82–94 in *Early Society in Cyprus*, ed. E. Peltenburg. Edinburgh: Edinburgh University.

Crossland L. B., and Posnansky, M.
1978   Pottery, People and Trade at Begho, Ghana. Pp. 77–89 *in The Spatial Organisation of Culture*, ed. I. Hodder. New Approaches in Archaeology. Cambridge: Cambridge University.

Dikaios P.
1953   *Khirokitia.* Oxford: Oxford University.

Ehrenberg, M.
1989   *Women in Prehistory.* London: British Museum.

Fausto-Sterling, A.
1994   *Myths of Gender: Biological Theories about Women and Men.* 2nd ed. New York: Basic Books (Harper Collins).

Frankel, D.
1974   Inter-site Relationships in the Middle Bronze Age of Cyprus. *World Archaeology* 6: 190–208.
1993a   Is This a Trivial Observation? Gender in Prehistoric Bronze Age Cyprus. Pp138–42 in *Women in Archaeology: A Feminist Critique*, eds. H. du Cros and L. Smith. Canberra: Australian National University.
1993b   Inter- and Intrasite Variability and Social Interaction in Prehistoric Bronze Age Cyprus: Types, Ranges and Trends. *Bulletin of the American Schools of Oriental Research* 292: 59–72.

Gero, J. M.
1994   Gendered Division of Labor in the Construction of Archaeological Knowledge in the United States. Pp. 144–153 in *Social Construction of the Past: Representation as Power*, eds. G. Bond and A. Gilliam. One World Archaeology Series no. 24. London: Routledge.

Goring, E.
1991   The Anthropomorphic Figurines. Pp. 39–60 in *Lemba Archaeological Project* 3, 2: *A Ceremonial Area at Kissonerga*, ed. E. Peltenburg. Studies in Mediterranean Archaeology 70:3. Göteborg: Åströms.

Grace, V.
1940   A Cypriote Tomb and Evidence for its Data. *American Journal of Archaeology* 44: 10–50.

Hamilton, N.
1994   A Fresh Look at the "Seated Gentleman" in the Pierides Foundation Museum, Republic of Cyprus. *Cambridge Archaeological Journal* 4, 2: 302–312.

1996a   The Personal is Political. [In Viewpoint: Can We Interpret Figurines? Hamilton et al.] *Cambridge Archaeological Journal* 6, 2: 282–85.

1996b   Figurines, Clay Balls, Small Finds and Burials. Pp. 215–64 in *On the Surface: Çatalhöyük 1993–95*, ed. I. Hodder. Cambridge: McDonald Institute for Archaeological Research/London: British Institute of Archaeology at Ankara.

2000   Ungendering Archaeology: Concepts of Sex and Gender in Figurine Studies in Prehistory. Pp. 17–30 in *Representations of Gender from Prehistory to the Present. Proceedings of the Conference on Gender and Material Culture Held at Exeter University, July 1994*, eds. M. Donald and L. Hurcombe. Studies in Gender and Material Culture Series. London: Macmillan.

Hill, J. A.

1970   *Broken K Pueblo: Prehistoric Social Organisation in the American Southwest.* Anthropological Papers no. 18. Tucson: University of Arizona.

Hodder. I.

1978   The Maintenance of Group Identities in the Baringo District, Western Kenya. Pp. 47–74 in *Social Organisation and Settlement: Contributions from Anthropology, Archaeology and Geography*, Part 1, eds. D. Green, C. Haselgrove, and M. Spriggs. BAR. International Series (Supplementary) 47. Oxford: British Archaeological Reports.

Jackson, M.

1994   *The Real Facts of Life: Feminism and the Politics of Sexuality c.1850–1940.* London: Taylor & Francis.

Karageorghis, J.

1977   *La grande déesse de Chypre et son culte.* Lyon: Maison de l'Orient.

Karageorghis, V.

1991   A Middle Bronze Age Scenic Composition: Copper Leaching or Pot-making? Pp. 33–37 in *Cypriote Terracottas. Proceedings of the 1st International Conference of Cypriote Studies, Brussels-Liège-Amsterdam, 29 May–1 June 1989*, eds. F. Vandenabeele and R. Laffineur. Brussels-Liège: A. G. Leventis Foundation, Vrije Universiteit Brussel, Université de Liège.

1992   Soldiers and Other Toys in the Coroplastic Art of Cyprus. Pp.171–83 in *Acta Cypria. Acts of an International Congress on Cypriote Archaeology Held in Göteborg on 22–24 August 1991*, Part 2, ed. P. Åström. Jonsered: Åströms.

Kingsnorth, A.

1993   Complexities of Complexity: An Anthropological Concern. *Bulletin of the American Schools of Oriental Research* 292: 109–120.

Knapp, A. B.

1993   Social Complexity: Incipience, Emergence and Development on Prehistoric Cyprus. *Bulletin of the American Schools of Oriental Research* 292: 85–108.

Loney, H. L.

1995   The Development of Apennine Ceramic Manufacture: Xeroradiographic Analysis. Unpublished Ph.D. Dissertation, University of Pennsylvania.

Longacre. W. A.

1972   Archaeology as Anthropology. Pp. 316–19 in *Contemporary Archaeology*, ed. M. Leone. Carbondale: Southern Illinois University.

Manning, S. W.

1993   Prestige, Distinction and Competition: The Anatomy of Socioeconomic Complexity in Fourth to Second Millenium B.C.E. Cyprus. *Bulletin of the American Schools of Oriental Research* 292: 35–58.

Merrillees, R. S.

1980   Representation of the Human Form in Prehistoric Cyprus. *Opuscula Atheniensia* 12: 171–84.

Mogelonsky, M. K.

1991   A Typological System for Early and Middle Cypriot Anthropomorphic Terracotta Figurines. *Report of the Department of Antiquities of Cyprus*: 19–36.

Morris, D.

1985   *The Art of Ancient Cyprus.* London: Phaidon.

Niklasson, K.

1991   *Early Prehistoric Burials in Cyprus.* Studies in Mediterranean Archaeology 96. Jonsered: Åströms.

Orphanides, A. G.
  1983   *Bronze Age Anthropomorphic Figurines in the Cesnola Collection at the Metropolitan Museum of Art*. Göteborg: Åströms.
Peltenburg, E.
  1992   Birth Pendants in Life and Death: Evidence from Kissonerga Grave 563. Pp. 27–36 in *Studies in Honour of Vassos Karageorghis*, ed. G. C. Ioannides. Nicosia: Society of Cypriot Studies.
  1993   Settlement Discontinuity and Resistance to Complexity in Cyprus, ca. 4500–2500 B.C.E. *Bulletin of the American Schools of Oriental Research* 292: 9–24.
  1994   Constructing Authority: The Vounous Enclosure Model. *Opuscula Atheniensia* 20: 157–62.
Peltenburg, E., ed.
  1989   *Early Society in Cyprus*. Edinburgh: Edinburgh University.
Plog, S.
  1978   Social Interaction and Stylistic Similarity: A Re-analysis. Pp. 143–82 in *Advances in Archaeological Method and Theory* 1, ed. M. Schiffer. Orlando: Academic.
Poovey, M.
  1988   *Uneven Developments: The Ideological Work of Gender in Mid-Victorian England*. Chicago: University of Chicago.
Scott, J.
  1986   Gender: A Useful Category of Historical Analysis. *American Historical Review* 91: 1053–75.
Stanislawski, M. B., and Stanislawski, B. B.
  1978   Hopi and Hopi-Tewa Ceramic Tradition Networks. Pp. 61–76 in *The Spatial Organisation of Culture*, ed. I. Hodder. New Approaches in Archaeology. Cambridge: Cambridge University.
Stewart, E., and Stewart, J.
  1950   *Vounous 1937–1938*. Skrifter utgivna av Svenska institutet i Rom 14. Lund: Gleerup.
Stewart, J.
  1962   The Early Cypriot Bronze Age. Pp. 205–391 in *The Stone Age and Early Bronze Age in Cyprus*, by P. Dikaios and J. Stewart. *The Swedish Cyprus Expedition* Vol. 4, 1A. Lund: Swedish Cyprus Expedition.
Swiny, S.
  1989   From Round House to Duplex: A Re-assessment of Prehistoric Cypriot Bronze Age Society. Pp. 14–31 in *Early Society in Cyprus*, ed. E. Peltenburg. Edinburgh: Edinburgh University.
Ucko, P. J.
  1968   *Anthropomorphic Figurines of Predynastic Egypt and Neolithic Crete with Comparative Material from the Prehistoric Near East and Mainland Greece*. Royal Anthropological Institute Occasional Paper 24. London: Szmidla.
Webb, J. M., and Frankel, D.
  1995   Gender Inequity and Archaeological Practice: A Cypriot Case Study. *Journal of Mediterranean Archaeology* 8, 2: 93–112.
Wylie, A.
  1992   The Interplay of Evidential Constraints and Political Interests: Recent Archaeological Research on Gender. *American Antiquity* 57, 1: 15–35.

GENDER, SEX AND THE CYPRIOT SYLLABIC INSCRIPTIONS: FEMALES IN THE WRITTEN RECORD OF ANCIENT CYPRUS

GEORGIA BONNY BAZEMORE

P. O. Box 1982
Sylvania, GA 30467
bazemore_cyprus@hotmail.com

The syllabic inscriptions constitute the primary source of textual material for ancient Cyprus. Only the corpus of syllabic inscriptions from a single city kingdom, that of Marion (modern Polis), provides adequate information to document the participation of females in the written record. Females are identified through the grammatical gender of personal names and the form of their concorded satellites and through their grammatical association with words whose lexical meaning is limited to women. Such a study depends on the accurate reading of the inscribed signs and a transcription into the Greek alphabet, which is considered linguistically probable or certain. The linguistic arguments for disputed or uncertain interpretations are discussed. I argue that the methodology used by many scholars to achieve Greek transcriptions is flawed and based on unproven assumptions. These flawed transcriptions have obscured the evidence for non-Greek speaking (EteoCypriot) and female Cypriots. Conclusions about the assured role of women among the Greek-speaking population of Cyprus are presented.

The written record gives the historian unique insight into the lives of people in antiquity. It is only through the written record, either in preserved literary sources or in the ancient inscriptions themselves, that individual personalities can be discerned. The written texts reveal the personal names, family relations, and in a few lucky instances, individual exploits of those people whose remains are so closely studied by the archaeologist. None of the Cypriot literary works created in antiquity has been preserved.[1] Literary sources for this island in the 1st millennium B.C. are primarily confined to mention in the mainland Greek sources.[2] Cyprus, however, has produced a large body of inscriptions from this time period.

The primary writing system on Cyprus throughout the first millennium B.C. was the Cypriot syllabary, a rectilinear script of about 60 individual signs, each representing a single open syllable.[3] Other writing systems were also found on the island during this period, primarily Phoenician, and, after the end of the 4th century B.C., the Greek alphabet.[4] The use of the Greek and Phoenician writing systems in Cyprus appears to have been confined to distinct groups of immigrants.[5]

The Cypriot syllabary was used to write inscriptions in two languages: an archaic dialect of Greek and a non-Hellenic language, still undeciphered, believed to be that indigenous to the island; this language is known as EteoCypriot. Scylax Geographicus (103), dated probably to the 4th century B.C., identifies cities in Cyprus as Greek, Phoenician, and autochthonous. While Salamis and Marion are specifically named as Greek cities, Amathus is referred to as autochthonous. Other cities in the interior, he says, were barbarian. This information correlates well with the evidence of the syllabic inscriptions. In syllabic texts, the EteoCypriot language is found primarily in Amathus (Masson 1983: nos. 190–96) and, presumably one of Scylax's barbarian cities of the interior, Golgoi (Masson 1983: nos. 283, 286, 291, 293, 295, 298, 299). These examples include many of the longest and most easily readable of all syllabic inscriptions. Shorter EteoCypriot inscriptions are found all over the island. This linguistic group is well documented in the epigraphic record down to the Hellenistic period.

This paper will discuss the inscriptional evidence for the role of women in ancient Cyprus. As the EteoCypriot language remains undeciphered, the evidence discussed in this paper is taken exclusively from inscriptions using the linguistically and grammatically complex dialect of Greek peculiar to Cyprus. It must, therefore, be recognized that evidence from autochthonous language texts cannot be included in this study. As a result, the conclusions drawn from the evidence of a single linguistic group in an attested multi-linguistic environment may have only limited applicability within the island as a whole.

Few syllabic inscriptions in the Greek language are of the length and clarity to indicate unambiguously the presence of proper names of the feminine gender. An exception is found in the city-kingdom of Marion, which had a tradition, unique within the island, of inscribing gravestones with the names of two, and sometimes even three, generations of the family of the deceased. The detail of familial relationships given in these inscriptions allows female names to be identified with certainty. Furthermore, Marion has produced more syllabic inscriptions than any city-kingdom in Cyprus with the exception of Paphos (Bazemore 1998: 237–38), and the majority of these are written in easily readable Greek. Marion thus provides the best opportunity in the syllabic repertoire for the examination of the role of females in the written record. This information can then, at some later time, be compared with the less plentiful evidence of females in the inscriptions found in the remainder of the island and abroad.

METHODOLOGY: SYNTACTIC GENDER AND BIOLOGICAL SEX

A language may have any (reasonable) number of genders, say from two to a dozen or a score.[6] Ancient Greek grammar is limited to three genders, masculine, feminine and neuter. Gender is a property of syntax, which places a given noun in a particular sub-class of the class of nouns in the grammar of that language. Gender may often be found marked by an affixed morphological segment; this is what frequently results in rhyme through the operation of concord or agreement. Gender, however, is not always overtly signaled on the surface of every noun. Grammatical gender (like number) requires concord, or agreement, i.e., the matching of satellites with their syntactic heads. Thus, all adjectives, demonstrative pronouns, and articles must agree in grammatical form with the gender (and number) of the nouns they modify or replace (Aronoff 1994; Finegan and Besnier 1989: 90–91; *Random House Dictionary of the English Language* 1987, *s.v.* gender).

For anthroponyms, or personal names, Greek recognizes two genders only, masculine and feminine. Personal names that have a grammatically masculine gender are limited to persons of male sex, and those of a grammatically feminine gender to persons of female sex. Sex here refers to the anatomical structure of the person named. Sex also can refer to the cultural or sexual orientation of a person, although it is not known to be so used in the ancient Greek inscriptions of Cyprus.

In discussing gender, there are three distinct notions, often regrettably conflated, that must be carefully and consistently distinguished: semantic or biological sex, syntactic gender, and the written signs or pronounced indicators in the language that betray or call attention to gender. As applied in this paper, these notions are the identification of persons of the female biological sex by the syntactic gender of their personal names and/or the pronounced indicators of that syntactic gender, specifically the definite article, the demonstrative, and terminology limited to the female sex (mother, wife).

It is important to recognize the ambiguities inherent in such a study: that syntactic gender is not overtly signaled on the surface of every noun, e.g., ὁ, ἡ βοῦς, ἡ νῆσος, τό κράτος; that the sign or indicator of the gender, the definite or demonstrative article, does not always accompany a proper noun; and that lexical terminology limited to the female sex frequently is not included. Complicating matters, the orthographic rules of the Cypriot syllabary[7] result in a lack of phonetic specificity when recording the Greek language that can make recognition of precise gender, number and case of nouns, and hence of proper names, difficult, i.e., ambiguous. Furthermore, the language recorded represents an archaic dialect of Greek that preserved both medial and initial digamma and displayed a peculiar set of intervocalic glides; its content presents numerous *hapax legomena*.[8]

SYLLABIC INSCRIPTIONS FROM THE
KINGDOM OF ANCIENT MARION, MODERN POLIS

All inscriptions naming females discussed in this paper are incised on local limestone and derive, when documentation exists, from funerary contexts (Masson 1983: 150–88). These inscribed monuments come from the necropoleis surrounding the ancient city of Marion as well as from outlying settlements in this city-kingdom. When datable, they can be assigned to the 6th to the 4th centuries B.C. (Masson 1983: 152).

The inscriptions are presented below in groups according to content; unusual vocabulary and grammar are addressed. The majority of these inscriptions have been the object of scholarly discussion for more than a century. Here, however, citations are given only for the mid-20th century compilation of Masson (1983). A complete bibliography for the syllabic inscriptions of Marion can be found in Bazemore (1998: 364–98). Within the Greek texts, the device of a vertical stroke I is used to represent puncts, i.e., marks placed by syllabic writers to divide words and phrases or to indicate sentence or document end.

Monuments Commemorating Females Identified as Wives

Six inscribed tombstones have been found in the city-kingdom of Marion that bear dedications to a wife. They are Masson (1983):

no. 84   ΚυπροκρατίϜος Ι ἠμὶ Ι ὀ λᾶο(ς) ὄδε Ι ὄ μοι πόσις Ι᾿Ονασίτιμος ΔιϜισωνίδας Ι δίπας Ι ἠμί

no. 154   ᾿Ισαζά(?)θας τᾶς ᾿Ονάσα(ν)τος γυναικός ᾿επέστασε ὀ παῖς Παρμένων Ι

no. 100   Φιλοκύπρας ἀ Τιμόρμω γυνά ἠμι

no. 154B[9]   Τιμοκύπρα ἐμὶ γυνὰ ΜανέϜος τὸ Στασάνορος

no. 144   ΤιμοϜανάσ(σ)ας τᾶς ᾿Ονασαγόραυ γυναικός ἠμι

no. 154A[10]   Ζόχαρις κατέστασε τᾶι γυναῖκι Τιμίλαι

Cypriot syllabic inscriptions are highly formulaic in content. The maximal formulaic expression consists of two verbal sequences, the first containing ἠμι (often not expressed) and the second containing a form of ῐστημι (infrequently not expressed). The verbal sequence, or sentence, containing ἠμι reports the person for whom the monument was made, while the sentence containing ῐστημι reports the person who caused the inscribed monument to be created and placed. An example of this maximal expression can be seen in no. 154. Each sentence can appear independently,, with the verbal sequence with ἠμι found far more often than that with ῐστημι. The subject of the sentence with ἠμι can be the person for whom the monument was created, and thus their name would appear in the nominative case; this locution is seen in no. 154B. More commonly, however, the subject of ἠμι is the stone or inscribed object itself, with the name of the person for whom the monument was created expressed in the genitive case. Such an expression is known as a *titulus loquens* and can be seen in nos. 84 and 144. In no. 100, the genitive case of Philokypra does not stand, as one might expect, in concord with the nominative case of the article and the word "wife." The only grammatical explanation for this form is to posit that this inscription contains two independent clausal phrases, both with the verb ἠμι, in which the subject of one is the wife and the subject of the other is the stone. The two speakers, the inscribed object and the person for whom the monument was created, are presented in the inscription as equal and discourse-equivalent. In this respect, the grammar of no. 100 is paralleled by no. 84. The grammar of no. 154A presents an alternative locution where the two formulaic expressions are collapsed into a single sentence. Here the information given in the first formulaic verbal sequence with ἠμι is found in a dative phrase in a sentence using ἵστημι.

Although following the conventions of Cypriot formulaic expressions, inscription no. 84 is unusual in its length and the information that it contains. In syllabic inscriptions, *tituli loquentes* rarely contain nouns in the nominative specifying the inscribed object. Here the subject of the first verbal sequence, λᾶο(ς), stone, is seen in the Cypriot dialectal form for λᾶας. This inscription presents the only known example of this word in the syllabic repertoire (Egetmeyer 1992: 79, *s.v.* la-o¹). Also unique in this inscription is the use of the word πόσις, husband (Egetmeyer 1992: 145, *s.v.* po-si-se). The identification of Onasitimos as husband implies both that Kyprokratis is female and that she is his wife. This information about Kyprokratis is not otherwise imparted by the grammar, as the surface form of the noun gives no indication of gender, no satellites occur with this noun, and the noun itself finds no parallel in the syllabic repertoire. The occurrence of digamma in an apparent i-stem noun is peculiar to the Cypriot dialect. In no other syllabic inscription does a female give the number of her children, but here Kyprokratis is described as two-childed. There are several possible explanations to this seemingly small number of offspring. Kyprokratis could have died young, before being able to give birth to a number of children; a small number of surviving children could imply a high infant mortality rate or this number could refer only to a select group of her children, such as her sons.

In these funeral stelai commemorating wives, the females are always named, with the name of the husband recorded as well. Females carry no second name in these inscriptions, but husbands could be identified more fully with the addition of a patronym (no. 154B) or patronymic adjective (no. 84). The use of the second Cypriot formulaic phrase indicating the person who had the monument created and placed, with a form of ἵστημι stated or implied, is found only twice in this group of inscriptions in no. 154 and no. 154A. In no. 154, Isazatha is identified in her role as wife, but her monument specifically states that it was set up by her son. In no. 154A, Timila is identified as a wife, but her relationship to Zocharis is not clear. It is important to note that, among inscriptions commemorating wives, in no case is it stated unambiguously that the monument was created by the husband. That Zocharis of no. 154A was the husband of Timila is a logical possibility, however, the evidence of no. 154 in this group and nos. 167 and 167N discussed below presents strong parallels for the alternative interpretation that he is her son. The second formulaic phrase naming the person who caused the monument to be created is missing in most of the inscriptions commemorating wives. This lack could indicate that either this information is not important or that this information has already been imparted in the phrase with the verb ἠμι, when the name of the husband is given. If it should be understood in any of these inscriptions that it is the husbands who have caused these monuments to be created and placed, it must logically follow that their wives have then predeceased them.

These inscriptions can be studied because they are written in the Greek language. The proper names given in these inscriptions, although exhibiting unique compound forms and peculiar dialectal variations, are easily recognizable as Greek. However, two names require further attention: Isazatha and Manes. This feminine form Isazatha is found only in no. 154, with a single example of a masculine counterpart, Isazathos, seen in a syllabic inscription from nearby Kato Arodhes (Masson 1983: no. 79). There are several difficulties presented in the reading of this name. First, the standard epigraphic form and the phonetic value of ‹za› are uncertain (Egetmeyer 1993: 145–55). Further, the repetition of the a-grade vowel in the second and third syllables suggests that one may be a "dummy" vowel, the unpronounced vocalic attachment to a single consonant in a cluster, repeating the vowel grade of the cluster, and demanded by syllabic writing. Finally, the aspiration of the dental in the syllable ‹ta› is not dictated by the text but rather is the result of modern editorial decision. Such ambiguity prevents a convincing reconstruction of this name and thus precludes any attempt at its interpretation in the Greek language.[11]

The name Manes, or perhaps better Maneus, is represented in the repertoire of syllabic inscriptions by this single example in inscription no. 154B. Mitford interprets this as a Semitic name (1960: 186 and n. 2). If Mitford's interpretation is correct, it would be a clear indication that intermarriage took place between seemingly Hellenic and non-Hellenic elements in Marion. Responding to Mitford's suggestion that Manes was a non-Greek name, Masson says, "on aurait ici une preuve de l'influence phénicienne à Marion au milieu du Vᵉ s(iecle)" (1983: 173, s.v. no. 154B). Masson, however, goes on to deny this possibility and implies that Mitford's proposal was groundless: "Mais il paraît clair qu'il s'agit d'un example du nom asianique et spécialement phrygien, fréquent dans l'onomastique grecque." Masson seems to argue, then, that Manes is a foreign loan name used among native Greeks, and its presence among the epitaphs of Marion implies no foreign or non-Hellenic influence. Egetmeyer (1992: 87, s.v. ma-ne-wǫ-se) cites Masson's interpretation only, omitting mention of Mitford's alternate suggestion. Masson's rejection of Phoenician influence in Marion in the middle of the 5ᵗʰ century B.C. is surprising in light of historical fact: from ca. 470 to 450, this city-kingdom was ruled by a Phoenician, King Sasmas, son of Doxandros (Masson and Sznycer 1972: 79–81; Masson 1983: no. 168). With an undeniable Phoenician presence in Marion during this period, the idea that the name Manes is Phoenician cannot be ruled out.

In understanding the nature of the relations between Phoenician-speaking and Greek-speaking elements in Marion at this time, it is important to note that the father of the Phoenician King Sasmas carries a Greek name, Doxandros. So, too, does the father of the Manes of our inscription, whose name is Stasanor. Furthermore, the wife of Manes carries a Greek name, Timokypra. Both Manes and Sasmas chose to communicate in writing in the Greek language through the medium of the syllabary. If proper names carry any indication of linguistic and, perhaps, ethnic identity, the evidence of Manes and Sasmas suggests that Phoenicians and Greeks shared the closest of familial bonds. Timokypra's marriage to Manes may not have been unique, and the Phoenician names given to sons of fathers with Greek names might indicate that the mother or other close relative was of non-Greek heritage. Anthroponyms, however, may not be indicative either of language or of ethnicity. If it is to be argued that Cypriot anthroponyms are not indicative of language or ethnicity, then the frequent occurrence of Greek onomastica in the readable syllabic inscriptions, as well as the use of an archaic dialect of the Greek language, seems to have been a preferred or selected action by at least certain groups within the society.

The husband of Kyprokratis in inscription no. 84 identifies himself using a patronymic adjective. The suggestion of patronymic adjectives in syllabic inscriptions is rare (Masson 1983: nos. 15, 18B, 74W, 84, 167). This grammatical form indicates membership in a group claiming descent from a common ancestor who could be either an historical personage or a mythological character (Smyth 1956: 233–34, §§ 845, 848). The linguistic composition of this patronymic, Diwisonidas, is not clear. Masson (1983: 140–41) would see it as a compound created from the name of Zeus and the verb σεύω, meaning "to drive out," "to drive before," or "to drive onwards." Neumann (1992: 51–52) rejects the interpretation of diwi- as a form of the name of the god Zeus and instead reads this as *δFɩ-, "two;" he suggests that this word be translated as "doppelt stark, doppelt groß." Neumann's interpretation is followed by Egetmeyer (1992: 193 s.v. ti-wi-so-ni-ta-se). There are problems with both reconstructions. Neumann's interpretation of diwi- as "two" rather than a form of the name of Zeus seems unfounded. The dative form δι(F)ι- for Zeus is widely attested in Greek (Liddel, Scott and Jones: 1996, s.v. Ζεύς). More crucially, Neumann fails to account for the fact that the word "two" appears in its expected form, di-, in another word in the very same inscription, δίπας. It is important to note that the form diwi-, meaning "two," is not securely attested in the syllabic repertoire. Rather than attempting to interpret this patronymic adjective by means of unique forms, it is better to see the first element of this compound as what it apparently seems to be, the name of Zeus. The second element of this compound, -σων-, is less apparent. If created from or cognate with the verb σεύ(F)ω, neither the loss of digamma in the Cypriot dialect nor the form -σων- can easily be explained; the same remarks can be made for the proposed verb base σά(F)ω, meaning "to save" or "to deliver" (Hamp, personal communication). Whatever the exact etymology, the patronymic adjective Diwisonidas identifies the family of Onasitimos as godly or having privileged relations or communication with a deity, seemingly that one formally known on the Greek mainland as Zeus.

Kyprokratis was not the only wife commemorated in these inscriptions whose husband defined himself by his membership in a specified group or clan. In a rare instance of syllabic inscriptions demonstrably appertaining to two related individuals, the epitaph of Onasagoras, the husband of Timowanassa in no. 144, was found in the same tomb as her own (Masson 1983: no. 143). Her husband's inscription, following Cypriot formulaic convention, reads simply, Ὀνασαγόραυ τῶ Στασαγόραυ τῶ διφθεραλοιφῶν ἠμί. Onasagoras, son of Stasagoras, describes himself as a διφθεράλοιφος (*diphtheraloiphos*), an arcane term that literally means "leather painter," "leather oiler," or possibly even "leather anointer." Hesychius, writing in the 5th century A.D., defines this term as γραμματοδιδάσκαλος παρὰ Κυπρίοις, a teacher of letters/writing according to the Cypriots. This inscription provides valuable insight into ancient Cypriot literate practices, in which the levels of literacy of those creating inscriptions are not known and cannot be assumed. First, it presents incontrovertible evidence that syllabic writing was systematically taught on Cyprus. This term also carries information about the process of writing itself in Cyprus. If "oiler" is meant by this term, it could refer to the preparation of the leather as a medium for writing by rubbing it with oil. If "painter" is meant, however, the term may refer to the act of writing itself by painting signs upon leather using ink or colored liquid. The meaning "anointer," on the other hand, would imply a social, as well as physical role in the act of writing, as anointing is a religious ritual in which a person or object is infused with some degree of sacredness. The epitaph of Onasagoras shows that literate practices in Cyprus were not confined to inscriptions upon stone but at least one other medium was employed, that of leather. Given the climate of Cyprus, the acts of literacy implicit in this term would not be reflected by the evidence of the archaeological record.

Masson, interpreting διφθεραλοιφῶν as a masculine, genitive, singular noun identifies this inscription as the "Épitaphe de maître d'école, Onasagoras." However, syllabic orthographic convention creates ambiguities in the exact reading of this term: τῶ διφθεραλοιφῶν could represent a genitive singular, with the addition of -ν to the usual Cypriot second declension ending of ō (Buck 1955: 146, no. 198. 1), but it could equally well represent a genitive plural, where the -ν is absent from the article (Egetmeyer 1992: 195, *s.v.* to[4]). A perfectly plausible alternative reading then emerges in which Onasagoras belongs to or is a member of the Diphtheraloiphoi. Such a locution would imply a group of writing teachers, possibly in the form of a social caste, recognized professional group, or even familial clan. The idea that the *diphtheroloiphoi* were a caste or professional group finds support in the fact that, almost a millennium later, Hesychios still knew them by their arcane name.

Thus we have seen that two of the six females of Marion commemorated in their epitaph as wife, Kyprokratis and Timowanassa, had husbands who are identified as belonging to a defined clan and/or professional group. Such nomenclature strongly suggests then that both men and their wives were members of distinguished religious and social groups. They were, then, among the elites of their society.

In determining the social standing of the women named in these inscriptions as wives, it is important to note that the monument to Timila, upon which inscription no. 154A is written, provides a rare exception to the plain, undecorated stones common to the inscriptions of Marion. The upper part of this stele has been molded in low relief to represent pediment and acroteria, which then was decorated in paint now red in color (Mitford 1960: 182–84, no. 3). Further indication of the special care taken in the preparation of this group of inscriptions to wives is no. 84, where the lapidary has created signs of high epigraphic quality. Similarly, the fine tool marks evident on both nos. 143 and 144 indicate a greater than normal attention to the aesthetic quality of an object carrying a syllabic inscription. The epigraphic forms seen in inscription no. 154B are far less consistent in form and design[12] than those found in no. 84, but they were adorned in antiquity, as remaining traces indicate, with bitumen.

Finally, it is interesting to note that fully half of the women commemorated by these inscriptions have names that contain, either as first or second element, -kypr-: Kyprokratis, Philokypra, and Timokypra. Although Homer knew the island by its modern name (*Od.* 8.359–66), it was not until the beginning of the 4th century B.C. that Kypros is identified in the Cypriot epigraphic record as the native name for the island (Masson 1981: 254–55 and no. 31). This naming pattern reflected in these inscriptions may be a simple coincidence or even the result of a limited number of acceptable choices of feminine names. If, however, anthroponyms were socially meaningful in ancient Cyprus, an etymological interpretation of these names surely presents a powerful and exciting array of female attributes: Kyprokratis, the female ruler of Cyprus, Philokypra, the lady friend or lover of Cyprus, and Timokypra, the lady who honors Cyprus. In this respect the name of Timowanassa is especially interesting. For Wanassa, and not Aphrodite, was the name used by the ancient Paphians to refer to the Great Goddess of their city (Masson 1983: nos. 4, 6, 7, 10, 16, 17, 90, 91). Timowanassa then is a lady who honors or brings honor to the Great Goddess.

Monuments Commemorating Females Identified as Mothers

Only two inscriptions from Marion document the dedication of a funeral monument to a female identified as mother. These are Masson (1983):

no. 167 Masson reads: Ὀνασίας .... τᾶ ματρὶ κὰ(ς) τῷ πατρὶ ....
Mitford[13] reads: Ὀνασίας Φιλαγίδες τᾶ ματρὶ κὰ τῶ πατρὶ τὸ(ν) φαλ(λ)ᾶν
no. 167N Τηλαγόρας ὀ Ἀπάμιϝος τᾶι ματρί

Both examples display the same grammatical structure. The two parts of the dedicatory formula are collapsed into a single sentence with the verb ἵστημι, here in both cases understood; the information which in other inscriptions is provided in the sentence with the verb ἠμι is found in a phrase in the dative case. This grammatical structure has been seen in no. 154A above.

The focus of these inscriptions is far different from that of inscriptions where females are identified as wives. With the exception of no. 154A, the emphasis of each inscription commemorating a wife is the wife herself. Each inscription has as the first word in the text, i.e., the focus position, the name of the deceased wife. Furthermore, the text of the inscription consists primarily of only one part of the available formulaic expressions, the sentence with the verb ἠμι, a locution in which the deceased wife and the inscribed monument are presented as interchangeable speakers.

In the inscriptions on monuments created for mothers, however, the part of the dedicatory formula using ἠμι is absent. The subject in both inscriptions is the son who caused the monument to be created and placed. Reflecting the increased importance of the dedicator, the first word in these texts is not the name of the deceased but the name of the child who caused the monument to be set up. Furthermore, while these children are identified with both their personal name and a patronym or patronymic adjective, the mothers in both instances remain nameless. The language of these inscriptions is clear: the deceased person commemorated by the inscribed monument is not the focus of the inscription but rather the living son responsible for the creation of the monument. The inscription no. 154A commemorating the wife Timila displays a grammatical structure nearly identical to these inscriptions commemorating mothers. The possibility exists that no. 154A is a more compact version of no. 154, where a son sets up a monument to a woman, by implication his mother, specifically named as wife. Zocharis could then be the son rather than the husband of Timila.

Mitford's interpretation of Philagides in no. 167 as a patronymic adjective (1961a: 5–6, no. 4) has not been generally accepted (Masson 1983: 396 *s.v.* p. 180; Egetmeyer 1992: 136, *s.v.* pi-la-ki-te-se). His arguments on the meaning of the locution τὸ(ν) φαλ(λ)ᾶν, however, have faired better. He interprets this word as a *hapax legomenon* and adds, "I take it that the term was current in the dialect to denote these tall and erect monuments, regarded as phallic in appearance." Egetmeyer (1992: 125, *s.v.* pa-la-ne) says, "Dieses Wort dürfte etwa '(Grab)mal, -stele' … bedeuten, seine sprachliche Erklärung steht jedoch noch aus." Syllabic orthography permits this word to be reconstructed in three ways, p/b/ph(a?)l(l)(a?)n, with the a-grade of either the first two syllables a possible "dummy" vowel; that this term may be a non-Greek loan word should be considered. If Mitford's interpretation of phallan as referring to the inscribed object itself is correct, then we see in these inscriptions a distinction between the deceased and the inscribed monument not seen in the inscriptions created for wives. The name of Telagoras' father in no. 167N, Ἀπ/β/φά(?)μιϜος, is not easily recognizable as a Greek proper name. It is suggested that this person carries a name, supplied with a Greek ending, taken from the Phoenician, EteoCypriot, or perhaps another, linguistic group.

Monuments Created by a Female

A single inscription has been found at Marion that a female caused to be created. This is Masson (1983):

no. 167L   [Ὀνα]σίτιμος [κὰς Ἀρι]στοκύπρα Ὀ[νασι]τίμωι[14]

The grammar of this inscription contains the same formulaic structure as seen in the inscriptions created for mothers seen above. Once again, the sentence containing the verb ἠμι is omitted, while the verb form of ἵστημι is to be supplied by the understanding of the reader. If the text is reconstructed correctly, the person commemorated by the monument carries the same name as one of the persons who caused the monument to be created. This inscription is unusual in that two persons, a male and a female, are credited with the creation of this inscription. This content caused Masson to remark, "Les parents ont élevé une stèle pour leur fils." If correct, Masson's interpretation would indicate that, unlike modern Greek cultures where names traditionally skip a generation, in ancient Cyprus a father and son could share the same name, in effect a "Jr.," as it were. The content of this inscription is spare, however, and open to interpretation. It is, indeed, probable that the two Onasitimoi were father and son, but the deceased need not have been the child. The son could well have set up this monument for his deceased father in conjunction with either his mother or wife.

Monuments Commemorating Females Identified as Daughters

Three inscriptions have been found in ancient Marion that commemorate females identified as daughters. They are Masson (1983):

no. 124   Πνυτίλας ἠμὶ τᾶς Πνυταγόραυ παιδός
no. 135   ΦιλόπαϜος ἠμι τᾶς Ὀνασίλω παιδός
no. 167A   Στασιτίμας τᾶ Πυρ(ρ)ιτίο παιδός[15]

In sharp contrast to the grammar seen in inscriptions created by or for a mother, inscriptions created to commemorate daughters are limited to that part of the Cypriot formulaic expression containing the verb ἦμι. As with those inscriptions commemorating wives, the focus of the inscription is once again upon the deceased female. The lack of the formulaic phrase containing ἵστημι seems here also, as with the inscriptions commemorating wives, to be an indication either that this information was unimportant or, rather more likely, a reflection of the fact that this information has already been imparted to the contemporary reader in the naming of the father.

Inscription no. 124 shows that daughters, as well as sons, could carry one or more elements of the father's name in their own. The other two inscriptions commemorating daughters, however, show that this practice was not universal. With such a limited pool of evidence, it cannot be determined how widespread the practice was within the Greek-speaking community of Marion of assigning part or all of the father's names to daughters.

The etymology of these daughters' names is interesting. The name Pnutila in no. 124 appears to be apocopated, or a shortened form of a longer name, and with an hypocoristic suffix, denoting "little" or "small." Thus Pnutila seems to be a nickname, literally "little Pnuta," where Pnut- is a shortened form of a longer name, perhaps even that of the father Pnutagoras. The linguistic underpinning of ΦιλόπαϜος in no. 135 is disputed. The element -παϜος would seem to be the genitive of the base of the word παῖς, child. However, in this same inscription, the genitive of παῖς is also expressed in the form παιδός. This difference has led Neumann to reject the reading of -παϜος as παῖς (1970: 76–79). However, personal names can be quite conservative, and it is not unusual to see archaic forms preserved in names while otherwise lost in the general language (Hamp 1975). Considering that this is a monument to a daughter, it is interesting to note that the name Philopais means something like "beloved child."

In these inscriptions to daughters, the name of the father only is given. In no instance is the mother's name cited. In this regard, it is interesting to note that Aristokypra of no. 167L, the sole female inscriber of Marion, commemorates a male relative and not a female; the possibility that she was the mother of the deceased has been discussed above. A daughter's relationship to her female parent is not recognized in the part of the burial ceremony represented by the syllabic inscriptions. The paternal relationship, at least for the purposes of the social and religious preparation for the afterlife, is the primary identification for the female. This lack of information about the naming patterns of mothers and daughters prevents us from knowing whether daughters could carry elements of the maternal as well as the paternal name.

Monuments Commemorating a Female Identified as Sister

Only two syllabic inscriptions have been found in Marion that commemorate a female identified as sister. They are Masson (1983):

no. 153 Ὀνάϊγος κὰς Φαλα ... Ι ἐπέστασαν τᾶι κασινήται Ι Ὀνασιτίμαι
no. 164 Cypriot syllabic κασιγνήτα
Greek alphabetic κασιγνήτας

Inscriptions to sisters employ both types of Cypriot formulaic expressions. In no. 153, the name of the sister is stated but placed at the very end of the formulaic phrase or sentence with ἵστημι. At the very head of the phrase or sentence are the names of the two dedicators who caused the monument to be made and placed. The final syllables of the second name have been lost in the break on the stone, and from the extant epigraph evidence it cannot be discerned whether this person is a male or female. Thus it cannot be assumed, as Masson does (1983: 171), that only her brothers created this dedication to her.

The monument carrying inscription no. 164 has been inscribed in the Greek alphabetic as well as the Cypriot syllabic script. The use of the Greek alphabet is rare in Cyprus at this time, and this inscription is one of only four syllabic/alphabetic digraphs found in Cyprus before the end of the 5th century B.C. (Bazemore 1998: 13–33). The alphabetic forms in this inscription derive from the archaic Ionic script, with a three-stroke sigma and a box-shaped eta, and the inscription is written sinistrograde, from right to left, with each letter form inversed (backwards). This inscription does not imply a native Cypriot alphabetic tradition but rather reflects the script of Naucratis, its parent city Miletus (Mitford 1960: 179, and n. 3), or perhaps even Knidos (Masson 1983: 177, s.v. no. 164, and n. 3). The alphabetic forms suggest a 6th century or earlier date for this inscription. The syllabic inscription, carved on the long, thin side of the stone, reads from top to bottom. While the alphabetic part clearly shows a feminine genitive noun of the first declension, the grammatical form of the syllabic part of this inscription is debated. This syllabic form has been interpreted both as a variant Cypriot dialectal form of the genitive of a first declension feminine noun where the final sigma is not noted (Egetmeyer 1992: 62 s.v. ka-si-ke-ne-ta) or as a straightforward nominative of the same gender and declension (Mitford 1960: 180). Cypriot orthographic or dialectal conventions allowed the final ‹se› to be omitted in certain positions in a continuous text, however, systematic study has yet to be made on the notation of final ‹se› in non-continuous syllabic texts. This lack of information makes it difficult to identify with confidence the grammatical form intended by the writer of this syllabic inscription. The fact that the deceased is not named led Mitford to suggest that this monument commemorated a sister who died very young and, therefore, nameless. However, we have seen above that women commemorated as mothers also were not named, women who, by definition, had to be of some age and physical maturity. The lack of a name for this sister then need not necessarily be related to age.

Monuments Created for Females with No Specified Familial Relationship

When appearing in the syllabic inscriptions of Marion, females are frequently identified by the role they play in the family structure, i.e., as wife, mother, or daughter. There are seven inscriptions, however, in which the female named is given no explicit familial role, and her relationship with the male named in the same inscription is not clear. These inscriptions are Masson (1983):

no. 96	Τιμοκύπρας ἠμὶ Τιμοδάμω
no. 97	Ὀνασικύπρα ἀ Ὀνασιδάμω
no. 118	Ἀριστοκύπρας ἠμί ἔστασε ῎Αριστος
no. 175	Τιμοκύπρας τᾶ(ς) Ὀνασικύπρω
no. 163	Ἀριστίλας ἠμί ἔστασε ὈνασιϜάναξ
no. 166	Ἀριστίλα ἀ Σελαμινίγα ὈνάσιϜος
no. 167M	Κυπροτίμα ἀ Μινοδάμω

Each inscription is framed firmly in the Cypriot formulaic tradition. As with the inscriptions commemorating wives and those commemorating daughters, these are constructed using the locution with ἠμι, with the deceased standing in either the nominative or the genitive case in relation to the verb. As is common in this locution, the name of the deceased stands at the head of the text, in focus position, and she is the subject of the inscription. Only nos. 118 and 163 overtly name the person who caused the monument to be created, but the idea that this action is implicitly assigned to the named male has been considered above.

Lacking information concerning the role of the female, the relationship between the male and the female named in each of these inscriptions is ambiguous and must be inferred. In four of these seven examples, the name of the female and the name of the male share a common element. The epigraphic evidence for such onomastic repetition is limited to the naming patterns between fathers and their children, both female and male. As noted above, lack of information prevents the naming patterns between mothers and their children from being discerned. On the other hand, such naming patterns are not found in the Cypriot epigraphic record between husband and wife. Indeed, such naming patterns between husband and wife would result only if one of the (potential) partners underwent a name change at the time of betrothal or marriage. Based on the available evidence, then, it would seem that the inscriptions nos. 96, 97, 118, and 175 were all created by fathers for their deceased daughters. The repeated element in the names of no. 175 is unique in this study in that in both cases they stand as the second element of the compound name rather than the first. If these four inscriptions were, indeed, created by fathers for their daughters, they, too, like those which are assuredly dedicated to daughters, make no mention of the mother.

Three of these seven inscriptions, however, display no such onomastic repetition. Daughters' names in Cyprus, as has been seen, need not necessarily share a common element with their patronym. Thus, all seven of these inscriptions could indicate the commemoration of daughters by their fathers. On the other hand, there is nothing overt to negate the possibility that these monuments were created by husbands commemorating their deceased wives. Due to the ambiguity of the evidence, it is not known whether males commemorated the deaths of female relatives in their roles as sons and brothers without the special terminology seen in nos. 154, 167, and 167N. The idea that at least one of these monuments was created by a husband for a wife is suggested by a close study of the monument and decoration upon which inscription no. 166 is written.

The stone bearing inscription no. 166 is among the finest inscribed monuments found in Cyprus. It is a tall stele whose relief decoration shows a female, with hair bound up in a winding cloth, sitting on a backless stool and holding a fluttering dove in her left hand. A plain bracelet is seen on her left wrist, and her right hand, beside her on the stool, holds a flower. Above the seated figure is a pediment decorated by a palmette anthemion. Traces of the original painted decoration remain. The iconography of this stele displays foreign influence as the relief decoration is based on a 5th century model from mainland Greece (Wilson 1969: 62; Childs, 1994: 108–9). The monument of Aristila indicates that she is of a wealthy and, perhaps, powerful family, which held her in such esteem as to have created in memorial to her an artwork of unusual quality, incorporating the latest fashions from abroad. Aristila is further distinguished by the use of a demotic to specify her identity. Demotics are rare in syllabic inscriptions, found only in texts created by persons far away from their native city (Masson 1983: nos. 385, 392, 393, etc.). Here, Aristila is identified as coming from the city of Salamis, located on the east coast, on the opposite side of the island from Marion. It is held, widely and without question, that Aristila is the daughter of Onasis (Masson 1983: 179; Tatton-Brown 1990: 94–96; Nicolaou 1971: 15). But if the deceased female bears any resemblance in age to the figure on the stone, she is not a child. In fact, this figure has been described as a "woman" by Tatton-Brown (1990: 96), who has argued that the iconography found in this relief indicates the preparations for a wedding (Wilson 1969: 61). If it is Aristila's father who is commemorating her death, it would seem that these preparations came to naught.

In attempting to define the relationship between Aristila and Onasis, one must note that Aristila is specifically named a Salaminian, while Onasis is defined no further than his own personal name. It is suggested that this locution is an accurate reflection of the facts, that it was, indeed, only Aristila who was not native to Marion. Onasis then, by implication, would not be her father, but rather must have been her husband. This interpretation finds support both in the age of the female depicted in the relief as well as the iconography suggesting preparations for a wedding. This stele seems to record the marriage between a member of a wealthy and, perhaps, powerful family of Marion with a woman from far-away Salamis. This union was cut short by Aristila's death. It is to be expected that Aristila was of a social status comparable to her bridegroom, and the information given by this monument gives all indication of a dynastic marriage.

Without further information, it cannot be determined whether the Aristila of no. 163 and the Kyprotima of no. 167M are commemorated as daughters or wives.

Monuments Commemorating Females Whose Inscriptions are Partially Illegible

Two inscriptions have been found at Marion that contain a feminine name with the remaining content unreadable. These are Masson (1983):

no. 101   Ὀνα[σι]κύπρας …
no. 125   Θεμιστοκύπρας …

Although both inscriptions are complete, only the first word of each can be read. Gender is overtly signaled in the suffix and the interpretation of these names as feminine is secure. Both inscriptions consist of only short texts. The grammar and position of the feminine name indicates that both inscriptions consist of the formulaic expression with ἠμι. The length of the text suggests that the illegible part of the inscription was limited to the male name and possibly a verb.

The Monument of Diwina: A Female with No Male Association?

The Cypriot dialect of Greek frequently displays grammatical forms unattested elsewhere in that language as well as *hapax legomena*, vocabulary items peculiar to this island alone. Further unknown or ambiguous vocabulary is found in the form of EteoCypriot and Phoenician names and loan words. Only one inscription made by or for a female at Marion displays such ambiguity of content. Certain interpretations of this inscription imply that she stands alone with no stated male association. If correct, then, of all the secure attestations for females in Marion, Diwina is unique.

Mitford (1960: 184–86, no. 4) reads: ΔιϜίν(ν)ας τᾶς Ἀψύχō
Masson (1983: no. 154C) reads: ΔιϜίνας τᾶς ἀψύχω

In grammatical structure, this inscription does not differ from the standard formulaic expression with ἠμι. If the standard wording is used, a male name in the genitive is expected to follow the definite article or demonstrative. Indeed, a name displaying the Cypriot masculine second declension ō is seen. A Greek language reading of a proper name, however, has not been achieved. Mitford (1960: 186–87) interprets this name as Phoenician. Masson (1983: 173 and n. 1) once again rejects the possibility of a non-Greek personal name appearing in these inscriptions. He says, "On verrait plutôt ici le grec ἀψύχω … plutôt que d'un patronym … il doit s'agir de l'épithète ἄψυχος «privée de vie, défunte»." According to Masson, then, rather than stating her familial connection or the name of her kinsman, Diwina tells us that she is dead. This information does, indeed, seem tautologous on a gravestone, and it is not surprising that the locution suggested by Masson finds no parallel in epitaphs from other parts of the Greek world (Peek 1988). Equally puzzling is Neumann's[16] interpretation of this word as a form of ἀπ–ήσυχος, meaning "ruhelos," or restless, as one wonders what implications a "restless Diwina" might have.

The interpretation of Ap/ph/b(a?)suk/ch/go as an epithet rather than a male personal name results in an inscription in which a female stands alone, without any male association given. If this interpretation is correct, this inscription would provide an important variant to the observed formulaic expressions and could serve as a comparandum for other inscriptions in which females, with or without epithets, seem to stand alone without male affiliation. The ambiguity surrounding the reading of the last element of the inscription prevents a confident interpretation of its content. This unusual word should be examined in light of the name of Diwina herself. For this name appears to consist of two elements: ΔιϜ(ι)-, a deity identified as Zeus and ἰνα, daughter, feminine of ἰνος, son (Hamp, personal communication). The name Diwina then means "the daughter of the deity," or "the daughter of Zeus." It is tempting to suggest that clan or professional membership might be indicated by such a name.

Diwina then would have been born into a clan that claimed descent from the deity or alternatively held a position in the religious worship of this deity in which she has assumed the title of daughter. This name is reminiscent of the patronymic adjective Diwisonidas seen in no. 84 above. If her name indicates that Diwina stood in a special relationship with a deity, then epithets such as "deathless" or "restless" might be considered more appropriate. However, such an explanation must account for the grammatical stem ending whereby a feminine would not appear to differ from a masculine.

On the other hand, there is really no compelling reason to place the inscription of Diwina outside established Cypriot formulaic tradition. The final word of the inscription displays the correct grammatical form for the expected male name. The occurrence of Phoenician names in these inscriptions has been discussed above, and we have seen that Phoenician presence is documented in this city in no less a personage than the king himself. Whether Apsuchos was the father or husband of Diwina, this inscription seems to illustrate, once again, close familial ties between persons with names drawn from different linguistic and, perhaps, cultural groups.

Obscuring the Historical Record: The Emendation of Syllabic Texts

Emendation of syllabic texts by modern editors is, unfortunately, not rare. This emendation can take the form of changing the phonetic values within an existing text. Far more often, however, the phonetic equivalent of one to three syllabic signs is attached to a complete inscription in order to render either grammatical forms or entire Greek names not found in the text. The emendation of two inscriptions from Marion is important to the discussion of females in this city-kingdom. These are:

Masson (1983: no. 112)   Ἀριστίγα[υ]
Mitford (1958: 59)[17]   Τιμαγόρα[υ]

By the addition of one sign, the grammatical reading of these texts is changed from a first declension feminine nominative to a first declension masculine genitive in the Cypriot dialect. In the first example, the name Aristiya stands alone. There exists no convincing epigraphic reason to change this form. The reading of Timagora(s) as a genitive, however, seems to find support in the presence of the syllable ‹to› following the name. Construed as a masculine article or demonstrative in the genitive case, τῶ, agreement by concord would require that the name Timagora(s) be a masculine noun in the genitive case. However the syllable ‹to› is the first of a group of five signs for which no transcription into Greek is offered. It is not uncommon in syllabic inscriptions to omit the definite article (demonstrative) with proper names, and this has been seen in inscription nos. 84, 96, 118, 154B, 163 and 164 examined in this study. The possibility, therefore, that ‹to› is the first syllable of a second personal name cannot be dismissed. These emendations seem to result from a general reluctance by the editors of these inscriptions to acknowledge, in cases of ambiguous grammar, possible nominative forms. The interpretation of one inscription (Masson 1983: no. 138) clearly illustrates this. The text consists of a single word, Ἀρίστας, with no concording satellite to indicate gender and case. Masson (1983: 166), without discussion, reads this as a feminine genitive singular form, an interpretation followed by Egetmeyer (1992: 19, *s.v.* a-ri-si-ta-se[2]). This reading is by no means assured, however, for this exact sign sequence is also used to represent the nominative singular masculine form (Egetmeyer 1992: 18–19, *s.v.* a-ri-si-ta-se[1]).

The interpretation of no. 112, Ἀριστίγα[υ], no. 137, Τιμαγόρα[υ], no. 138, Ἀρίστας, as well as no. 164, κασιγνήτα, all provide good illustrations of an unfortunately widespread, unstated, and thus hitherto critically unexamined editorial tradition for the syllabic inscriptions based, I believe, upon an unstated recognition of the formulaic tradition, which has silently dictated that the name of the person commemorated by the monument should appear only in the genitive case. Texts have been systematically emended to reflect this view. But it can clearly be seen, even within the limited scope of this paper alone, that the texts of a number of inscriptions, such as nos. 100, 154B, 97, 166, and 167M examined above, express the name of the person commemorated by the monument in the nominative case. No convincing epigraphical or grammatical evidence exists to discourage the reading of inscriptions nos. 112 and 164 as nominative feminine nouns, no. 137 as a possible nominative feminine noun, and no. 138, based on attested forms, as a probable masculine nominative noun. Such interpretation would allow for inscriptions in which the name of a female stands alone, without identification with a male relation.

Editorial assumptions not only mask the identification of males and females in syllabic inscriptions but often obscure the very language in which an inscription has been written. The following examples are from Marion, but such textual emendation is found in inscriptions throughout the island. Emended inscriptions from Marion include Masson (1983):

no. 110	o-na-sa-ko	Ὀνασαγό[ραυ]
no. 113	to-mo-ke-re	Τιμοκρέ[τεος]
no. 115	a-ri-si-ta-ko	Ἀρισταγό[ραυ]
no. 122	pi-la-ko	Φιλαγό[ραυ]

All four of these inscriptions are complete and present texts that are easily legible and unambiguous. None, as they stand complete by the original writer, presents a proper name in the Greek language. Emendation by the addition of syllables not written in the original text can, indeed, achieve recognized Greek names. Here, once again, the emendations have produced masculine nouns in the genitive case. Indeed, by the efforts of the editors, Greek readings have been produced, but no arguments have been put forth to justify or assure the scholar that such emendations represent, or even bear relation to, the message intended by the writer.

Critical epigraphic analysis cannot proceed without recognizing the systematic nature of these emendations and the unstated assumptions upon which they are based. It is surely folly to accept without question that most or all short, obscure inscriptions in the Cypriot syllabary can be filled out into masculine genitive anthroponyms limited to the Greek language. With a bit of active invention, the same number of added syllables could produce not only the feminine form of these names in Greek, but a host of other possible noun and verb combinations within the Greek lexicon. These options are neither chosen nor mentioned.

The most fundamental assumption of these editors, however, is, of course, the act of emendation itself. Among the lexical possibilities inherent within the ancient Cypriot population, Greek is but simply one choice. Other distinct language groups are well attested in both the literary and archaeological record. In the act of emendation, the very possibility of these non-Greek-speaking inhabitants inscribing in the native syllabic script is denied.

Such denial obscures important evidence for the ancient society of Cyprus. These short texts, emended to the Greek language, find parallel in sign sequences of acknowledged EteoCypriot inscriptions. The phonetic sequence of the text in no. 110, o-na-sa-ko, is found twice in a long inscription from Amathus (Masson 1983: no. 195). In fact the suffix or ending -ako is well-attested among identifiable EteoCypriot vocabulary (Egetmeyer 1992: 307 *s.v.* KO). Using this attested criteria, the texts of no. 115, a-ri-si-ta-ko, and no. 122, pi-la-ko, could also well be examples of words with the same EteoCypriot grammatical form. The sequence ke-re, seen in no. 113, to-mo-ke-re, is also attested in EteoCypriot (Egetmeyer 1992: 314, *s.v.* RE), and, likewise, could have represented a grammatical suffix.

Emendation of texts is based upon, and self-generates, the denial of females and non-Greek populations in the inscribing record of the syllabic script. Faced with complete texts which do not resolve themselves into recognizable words, editorial capacity has been (ab)used in order simply to make them masculine Greek proper names. That the addition of extraneous and arbitrary phonetic elements does violence to the original information imparted by the ancient Cypriot writer seems, generally, to have been ignored. The depth of the manipulation of the textual record is often difficult for the non-specialist to recognize. One thorny example of this practice is an inscription from ancient Paphos (Masson and Mitford 1986: 25–27, no. 3). With the deliberate misreading of the sign ‹ya› as ‹mo›, Masson can, indeed, produce a Greek proper name. Only those familiar with Paphian epigraphic forms are aware that, in the most prolific deposit of syllabic inscriptions yet found, these two signs are carefully distinguished and exhibit no indication of confusion or interchangeability.

Olivier Masson's editorial opinions concerning the Cypriot syllabic inscriptions, few of which have escaped his attention,[18] have received wide and, for the most part, uncritical acceptance. I argue that the emendations produced by this unstated interpretive stance have led to the distortion of the general scholarly understanding of the extant evidence. In turn, distorted scholarly understanding of the material record opens the path for inaccurate arguments which then are used to support erroneous conclusions. This process is taken to an unfortunate extreme in Given's examination of the EteoCypriots (1998: 3, 20–24). In addressing the epigraphic evidence on this topic, Given states that "The main problem is that there are so few inscriptions that definitely belong to this language." Indeed, relying on the editorial opinions of Masson, Given can identify only ten inscriptions as EteoCypriot. Of the number of syllabic inscriptions that cannot be read but that are not identified by Masson as EteoCypriot, Given states that some may be "nonsense" inscriptions "purely for visual effect." The paucity of epigraphic evidence leads Given to conclude that "Ten short inscriptions do not make an ethnolinguistic group." In a rejection of all literary and epigraphic evidence on the topic, Given claims that "there is no secure archaeological or historical evidence for [the EteoCypriots'] existence." His examination of the topic, he tells us, has "achieved 'the end of the Eteocypriots'."

Given's arguments contain serious drawbacks.[19] However, it must be acknowledged that the reliance of a non-specialist upon generally accepted editorial authority has placed his study in a conundrum. Given is searching for evidence of non-Greek populations in a source that consistently obscures their existence. Masson (Mitford and Masson 1983: 27) complained that "Mitford … was often inclined to find Eteo-Cypriote anthroponyms." Building on Mitford's work, critical studies concerning the evidence for both the EteoCypriots and females in the more problematic examples of the epigraphic record have yet to be done.

CONCLUSIONS

There are 1,378 syllabic inscriptions published, to date, of which 149, or 10.81 percent, have been found in the region of Polis (Bazemore 1998: 238, 364–97). Of these 149 inscriptions, 24, or 16.11 percent, can be identified with adequate probability as containing proper names of the feminine gender in the overwhelming majority of Greek language inscriptions. The first thing to be noted about females in the written record of ancient Marion is their relative under-representation. Females were six times less likely to receive an inscribed funerary monument than their male counterparts. There is no secure evidence that females could act alone in the creation of such a monument, and documented participation of women dedicating in conjunction with men is limited to a single example. Those persons named in the inscriptions as having been responsible for the creation and placement of these inscribed monuments were exclusively male. In funerary inscriptions from Marion commemorating women, it has been suggested that locutions that do not overtly name the creator of the monument may contain this information in the male name that accompanied each female one.

The evidence on the females of Marion, then, shows that in the creation of funerary monuments it was always a male relative who was responsible for their creation and placement in commemoration of female kin. Indeed, extant evidence strongly suggests that the creation of inscribed monuments at

Marion was a specifically male domain. Men in ancient Marion had the authority to create these written funerary monuments and the control to monopolize this activity. Male control of the commemorative process actively excluded females: creating fewer monuments for members of the female sex; allowing females to remain nameless in their own monuments; and systematically failing to mention females, specifically mothers, in texts where their male counterpart is mentioned.

The syllabic inscriptions of Marion present a view of society in which the role of the female as mother is denied or obscured. This is seen both in those monuments created for mothers, where the mother's name is absent but the male dedicators are carefully identified, and especially in those inscriptions commemorating a child, where, within the commemorative expression of the named father, the parental status of the mother is ignored. Such naming practices may well indicate a social reality in which the father was the focus of the familial identity and the role of the mother reduced or ignored. The commemorative process itself, coupled with the language used in the extant texts, indicates that family units were under male authority and proves that among these families, descent was reckoned patrilineally. It is noteworthy that patrilineal descent was considered important enough to imprint the father's name in the form of a shared element in a compound upon that of his daughter. The consequence of such naming patterns is that the daughter, even after marriage and the assumption of her husband's name, still exhibited her patrilineal identity.

The obscured role of mother in the syllabic inscriptions of Marion stands in significant contrast with other female roles represented. These inscriptions commemorated females in their roles of wife and mother, mother, daughter, and sister. In most inscriptions, the female is named; her name is placed at the head of the text in focus position, and she is the speaker. The inscription created for mothers, then, forms a distinctly separate group. Moreover, it is interesting to note that Isazatha is commemorated by her son, not in the role of mother, but in her role as wife. As other females so commemorated as wife, Isazatha is named. The same observation can be made for two-childed Kyprokratis, who is identified by her husband. It is not certain what role Aristokypra of no. 167L plays. In Marion, for social reasons not known, mothers do not receive the individual attention received by females commemorated in other roles. Rather, commemoration of the deceased has taken a secondary position with the focus being placed on the creators of the monument. It is acknowledged that these observations are based on a small sample, but the consistency of the epigraphic evidence does lend them strength.

The lack of emphasis on the role of mother as well as the female-restricted nature of the syllabic inscribing process is reinforced by the almost complete absence of women in the creation of these monuments. Females did not—because it seems that they were not socially allowed—participate in the commemoration of their parents, children, siblings, and marriage partner.

The role in which females are most often commemorated is that of wives and those with no stated affiliation. If the interpretation of nos. 96, 97, 118 and 175 as monuments commemorating daughters and no. 166 as commemorating a wife are correct, then the females most often commemorated would be wives and daughters. Wives are defined by the locutions "I am the wife of" or "my husband is." Analogous locutions, such as "I am the husband of" or "my wife is," are not found for men. These texts define women through their husbands in a way that husbands are not defined by their wives. In these inscriptions, at least, all social reference for women, either familial or marital, was through a male figure. Patrilineal association in Marion seems especially important for children, and local anthroponyms display marked patterns of name element sharing. Such name element sharing may have had social significance beyond the figure of the father, as they may have represented family markers indicative of clan affiliation. While female roles were restricted, affection for the female child seems to have been displayed in the grammatical form and etymology of Pnutila, "little Pnuta-," and Philopais, "beloved child."

Those creating the syllabic inscriptions at Marion seem to have been a socially cohesive group following a quite rigid pattern of inscribing practice, limited to specified media and formulae, reflecting only certain actors in their familial and communal roles. The rigidity of syllabic inscriptions at Marion is clearly illustrated by the example of Onasagoras of the Diphtheroloiphoi. A man noted for his literate practices, a teacher of writing, Onasagoras could have framed any sentiment he chose to be copied in writing on his funeral monument. However, he chose not to do so and the language for both himself and his wife does not vary from the accepted formulae. The rigidity of the inscribing practice is emphasized by the fact that the inscribing process at Marion, at least that part that has been preserved in the archaeological record, is limited to a single function only—funerary ritual. These rigid patterns of inscribing practices at Marion could reflect either social or religious convention; these conventions could have taken the form of social or religious prohibition. These conventions are not limited to a single linguistic group, for persons with non-Greek names, including those identified as Phoenician, participated in the syllabic inscribing tradition. As these individuals are seen as family members of persons carrying Greek names, the social group here defined by their creation of funerary monuments with syllabic inscriptions cannot be identified on strict linguistic and, perhaps, ethnic criteria.

Concatenated clues gathered from a close examination of the medium and content of inscriptions commemorating females suggest that they were created by and for the elite. The decoration and care of creation seen in certain monuments has been noted. The use of patronymic adjectives indicates clan affiliation of a much larger scope than a single family. The term Diwisonidas seems to indicate a clan involved in some capacity with the worship of a deity, perhaps Zeus. The union of the writing teachers, of which Onasoagoras was a member, has an unexpectedly long life in the culture of Cyprus, an indication of its vigor and strength. This suggests that these inscriptions were created by the leaders of the community. It has been argued that Aristila may have been brought from Salamis to participate in a dynastic marriage between families of two distant city-kingdoms. Such an arrangement would indicate that the society is virilocal, where the husband would require the bride to leave the home of her parents to become part of his family. The virilocal nature of ancient Marion may have prompted the embedding of patrilineal elements in the names of female children so that clan identification for the female could continue after marriage. A further element in the identification of a defined elite group may be seen in the repetition of the element *kypr-*, found in 11 of the 21 names assigned to females.

The family relationships recorded in these syllabic texts show a patrilineal, androcentric, and male controlled society where female familial relationships were denied or ignored. Conventions arose within this group in which the patrilineal descent is encoded directly upon the name of the child. Women are excluded from the ritual act of commemorating their dead in writing. These observations, however, may be applicable only to certain groups in the island.

It is difficult to reconcile the patrilineal nature of the society of Marion presented by these syllabic inscriptions with the participation of women in the sexual rituals of the cult of Aphrodite. Herodotus (1.199) tells us that in certain areas of Cyprus, females were required to engage in sex with a stranger within the temple grounds. He emphasizes that not even the wealthy elite were exempt. The worship of Aphrodite by the Cypriots was far different than that of the Athenian Greeks, for native Cypriots living in Athens in the 4th century B.C. had to petition to be able to worship this goddess under the customs of their homeland (Gjerstad 1948: 501). These Cypriot customs seemed to include the creation of rooftop gardens, public ceremonies of mourning, as well as ritual prostitution and orgiastic activity (Moscati 1968: 108). Orgiastic activity is clearly portrayed in a decorated bowl from Achna, depicting a line of dancing women, several couples in the act of copulation, and an onlooker (Tatton-Brown 1998: fig. 38). The paternity of children born of such unions then would be in doubt. The participation of females in the ritual activity of the cult of Aphrodite is not consistent with the exclusion of women as mothers and the emphasis upon patrilineal descent seen in the inscriptions of Marion.

The cult of the Great Goddess, known to Greeks as Aphrodite, is documented in Cyprus from the Neolithic period onwards (Karageorghis 1977). It seems probable that the orgiastic rituals of the Great Goddess are a continuation of the cult practices followed for millennia by the indigenous peoples of the island, the EteoCypriots. The Greeks, arriving only in the 12th century B.C., may have brought a far different social system with them. Thus the dichotomy between the evidence of the inscriptions and the literary and iconographic evidence here cited may reflect the culture and society of separate groups on the island, apparently those identified in antiquity by language. The study of the syllabic inscriptions from Marion has shown once again that Iron Age Cyprus was a linguistic and cultural mosaic. The complexities of this society can be understood only through an unbiased, critical reading of the extant written texts.

ACKNOWLEDGMENTS

I would like to thank Dr. Nancy Serwint and Dr. Diane Bolger, the organizers of the conference and the editors of this volume. Thanks go also to Dr. Eric P. Hamp, for his patient discussions, suggestions and corrections.

This paper is dedicated to those scholars who research ancient Marion.

NOTES

1. Ancient sources document for Cyprus the same tradition of Greek language oral poetry that was recorded early on in alphabetic writing on the Greek mainland. Τά Κύπρια is the poem of the Epic Cycle that describes the events leading up to the Trojan War. Extant fragments indicate that the *Kypria* differs from the poems of Homer both in mythological detail and in its elaboration upon the visits of well-known Homeric characters to the eastern Mediterranean and their adventures there. Herodotus supplies the earliest reference to the *Kypria*; Pausanias regarded this work as authoritative, and it is documented that it survived into late antiquity in 11 books. (Herodotus 2.116-17; Aristotle *Poetics* 23.5-7 (1459 a, b); Scholiast on Euripides *Andr.* 898; Laurentian Scholiast on Sophocles *Elect.* 157; Pausanius 10.31.2; Proclus *Chrestomathy* i; see also Coldstream 1990: 59; Hill 1940: 90–93, with detailed references). Pindar (*Pyth.* 2.13.18) documents a Cypriot oral tradition concerning Kinyras, whom Homer (*Il.* 11.15–46) identifies as the founder-king of Paphos and guest-friend of Agamemnon. Both the epic poem the *Kypria* as well as the lays of Kinyras might well have been recorded and preserved in the native syllabic script. Zeno of Kition, founder of the Stoic movement, is renowned for his works on philosophy and ancient Greek grammar (*Dio Chrysostom Or.* 53.4–5). Although Zeno's interest in the Greek language may have sprung from the differences he recognized between Greek and his own native Semitic tongue (Robins 1967: 16), there is no reason to attribute his literacy to Greek influence alone. Although no literary works written in the native syllabary have survived, it is recorded that one of the largest libraries of the pre-Alexandrian world was located in Cyprus (Athenaeus 1.3a); it would be difficult to argue that native literature, in the native writing system, would have been completely absent from such a collection. Indeed, Cypriot syllabic inscriptions record teachers of syllabic writing, perhaps even a scribal class (Masson 1983: no. 143; see discussion below).

2. The ancient Greek sources for the history of Cyprus have been gathered by Hadjioannou (1992) in a monumental, multi-volume work. An abridged version of English translations, primarily taken from the Loeb Classical Library, has been made by Wallace and Orphanides (1990).

3. Several charts of the syllabic sign system have been made. The sign forms and their variants found in the eastern part of the island are best displayed in the chart presented by Deecke (1884), while the sign forms and their variants used in the southwestern part of the island is presented in detail by Mitford (1961a). Masson (1983: figs. 1–6) seems to be the most often consulted.

These charts include only signs with established phonetic values. Study of the epigraphy of the syllabic inscriptions themselves, however, reveals a number of sign forms whose phonetic value has not yet been established and that are not represented in these charts. These signs are found both in inscriptions whose content cannot be read as well as in otherwise readable inscriptions. A systematic discussion of these unread signs is yet to appear. Thus, it is observed that the number of signs used by writers of the Cypriot syllabary was larger than the number of signs given, to date, by scholars in their phonetically-based charts.

4. The most complete published collection of the Phoenician inscriptions of Cyprus is Masson and Sznycer (1972); the most complete published collection of alphabetic inscriptions is Nicolaou (1976). Neither collection

is exhaustive, and numerous individual articles document additional inscriptions in both scripts.

5. It is believed that the Cypriot population widely adopted the Greek alphabet in the 4ᵗʰ century B.C. (Masson 1983: 46). I have argued, however, that the explosion of Greek alphabetic inscriptions at that time is a reflection of the inscribing habits not of the indigenous population but rather of members of the newly installed Ptolemaic administration (1998: 12-80, with references). Recent discoveries show that the syllabary continued in use among Cypriots until the end of the 1ˢᵗ millennium B.C. It is argued that the centuries-long gaps in the archaeological attestation for the use of the syllabic script in the Hellenistic and early Roman periods indicates that syllabic writing was placed primarily upon archaeologically non-recoverable media.

6. For example, the Bantu languages show concord-prefix classes, or noun genders, numbering between six and 18, depending on how one chooses to assign analytically the distinction of singular/plural (Guthrie 1967: 1.35-9; 1971: 2.9).

7. Dentals, labials and velars were undifferentiated for aspiration and voicing; vowels were undifferentiated for length; graphic consonants in word-final or syllable-final position or in non-final clusters received "dummy" vowels whose grade was normally rule-governed; medial and final ν as well as final ς and ι often were not noted. Masson's account of the rules governing the syllabic writing system (Masson 1983: 68–78) conflates separate phenomena and does not take into account regional differences. Ancient Cypriot word accent is not known; accents in the Greek transcriptions have been supplied to facilitate recognition by modern scholars.

8. Even in the late 5ᵗʰ century A.D., Cypriot *hapax legomena* required explanation, a task undertaken by Hesychius Lexicographus.

9. Here Masson follows the reading of Mitford (1960: 186–87, no. 5).

10. Again, Masson follows the reading of Mitford (1960: 182–84, no. 3).

11. However, see Masson (1978: 827–28).

12. Only the first two of the inscription's four lines have been placed between horizontal guidelines. Within this restricted space, these lines have been created using appreciably shorter characters than the final two lines. Mitford (1960: 186-87, no. 5) says that the signs appear to have been roughly, if not carelessly incized.

13. Mitford (1961a: 5–6, no. 4).

14. Here Masson (1983: 411, *s.v.* 167l) follows the reading of Mitford.

15. Here Masson follows the reading of Mitford (1961b: 18–19, no. 3).

16. Cited by Egetmeyer (1992: 11, *s.v.* a-pa-su-ko) as personal communication.

17. This inscription is found in Masson (1983) as no. 137.

18. Masson is the single most prolific editor of Cypriot syllabic texts. He produced the only 20ᵗʰ century compilation of syllabic inscriptions (Masson 1983), which has become the standard reference work on the subject. A consistent detractor of the opinions of the syllabic epigrapher Mitford, it was Masson who edited the two great manuscripts that contained newly published syllabic inscriptions in unprecedented numbers and which had been left unfinished at Mitford's death (Mitford and Masson 1983; Masson and Mitford 1986).

19. In eradicating the EteoCypriots from Iron Age Cyprus, Given fails to account for the fate of the indigenous peoples who have been living on Cyprus several millennia before the arrival of the first Greek colonists in the 12ᵗʰ century B.C. (Karageorghis 1990: 39). He rejects the evidence of Scylax, saying that too little is known about his sources, yet he ignores the fact that the majority of his ten recognized EteoCypriot inscriptions come from areas identified by Scylax as autochthonous, thus providing himself the example where the literary record is supported by archaeological findings. Furthermore, Given strains our credulity by asking us to believe that a society, which itself had been literate over a millennium and which was surrounded by literate cultures, would be motivated to both create and gape at false imitations of literacy. Given ignores the fact that his so-called "nonsense" inscriptions are found on items of elite use, such as marble and decorated reliefs (Masson 1983: nos. 196 and 298), and is not aware that these inscriptions do, indeed, contain recognizable words and phrases that are found throughout the island, including, on occasion, identifiable Greek proper names.

APPENDIX: FEMININE NAMES CITED

Ἀριστίλα	Aristila	nos. 163, 166
Ἀριστοκύπρα	Aristokypra	nos. 118, 167L
ΔιϜίν(ν)α	Diwinna	no. 154C
Θεμιστοκύπρα	Themistokypra	no. 125
Ἰσαζά(?)θα	Isazatha	no. 154
Κυπροκράτις	Kyprokratis	no. 84
Κυπροτίμα	Kyprotima	no. 167M
Ὀνασικύπρα	Onasikypra	no. 97, 101
Ὀνασιτίμα	Onasitima	no. 153
Πνυτίλα	Pnytila	no. 124
Στασιτίμα	Stasitima	no. 167A
Τιμίλα	Timila	no. 154A
Τιμοκύπρα	Timokypra	no. 96, 154B, 175
ΤιμοϜανάσ(σ)α	Timowanassa	no. 144
Φιλοκύπρα	Philokypra	no. 100
Φίλοπα(ι?)ς	Philopas	no. 135

REFERENCES

Aronoff, M.
1994   *Morphology by Itself: Stems and Inflectional Classes.* Linguistic Inquiry: Monograph 22. Cambridge, MA: MIT.

Bazemore, G. B.
1998   The Role of Writing in Ancient Society: The Cypriote Syllabic Inscriptions. Vol. 1: A Study in Grammatology; Vols. 2–3: Corpus of Cypriote Syllabic Inscriptions: A Classed Inventory of Cypriote Syllabic Inscribed Objects and their Surviving Texts with a Complete Bibliographic Listing for each Inscription. Unpublished Ph.D. Dissertation, University of Chicago.

Buck, C. D.
1955   *The Greek Dialects.* Chicago: University of Chicago.

Childs, W. A. P.
1994   The Stone Sculpture of Marion: A Preliminary Assessment. Pp. 107–16 in *Cypriote Stone Sculpture. Proceedings of the Second International Conference of Cypriote Studies. Brussels-Liège, 18–19 May, 1993*, eds. F. Vandenabeele and R. Laffineur. Brussels-Liège: A. G. Leventis Foundation and Vrije Universiteit Brussel-Université de Liège.

Coldstream, N.
1990   The Geometric Period. Pp. 47–64 in *Footsteps in Cyprus*, ed. D. Hunt. London: Trigraph.

Deecke, W.
1884   *Die griechisch-kyprischen Inschriften in epichorischer Schrift.* Sammlung der griechischen Dialekt-Inschriften I, eds. H. Collitz, F. Bechtel and B. Bezzenberger. Göttingen: Vanderhoeck and Ruprecht.

Egetmeyer, M.
1992   *Wörterbuch zu den Inschriften im kyprischen Syllabar. Kadmos* Supplement III. Berlin: Walter de Gruyter.
1993   Kyprisch Za: ein lautliches oder ein graphisches Problem? *Kadmos* 32: 145–55.

Finegan, E., and Besnier, N.
1989   *Language: Its Structure and Use.* New York: Harcourt, Brace, Jovanovich.

Given, M.
1998   Inventing the Eteocypriots: Imperialist Archaeology and the Manipulation of Ethnic Identity. *Journal of Mediterranean Archaeology* 11: 3–29.

Gjerstad, E.
1948   *The Cypro-Geometric, Cypro-Archaic, and Cypro-Classical Periods.* Vol. 4, 2: *The Swedish Cyprus Expedition.* Stockholm: The Swedish Cyprus Expedition.

Guthrie, M.
1967–71 *Comparative Bantu.* 4 vols. Farnborough: Gregg.

Hadjioannou, K.
1992   Ἡ Ἀρχαία Κύπρος εἰς τας Ἑλληνικάς Πηγάς. Nicosia: Ekdosis Ieras Archiepiskopes Kyprou.

Hamp, E. P.
1975   *Alauno-,-ā.* Linguistic Change and Proper Names. *Beiträge zur Namenforschung* 10: 173–78.

Hill, G.
1940   *A History of Cyprus.* Vol. 1: *To the Conquest by Richard Lion Heart.* Cambridge: Cambridge University.

Karageorghis, J.
1977   *La grande déesse de chypre et son culte.* Collection de la Maison de l'Orient Méditerranéen Ancien no. 5. Série Archéologique: 4. Paris: Boccard.

Karageorghis, V.
1990   The Late Bronze Age. Pp. 22–46 in *Footprints in Cyprus*, ed. D. Hunt. London: Trigraph.

Liddell, H. G.; Scott, R.; Jones, H. S.
1996   *A Greek-English Lexicon.* Oxford: Clarendon.

Masson, O.
1978   Le syllabaire chypriote classique: Remarques sur les signes des séries en x, y, z. *Annali della Scuola Normale Superiore di Pisa* 3, 8: 817–32.

1981   Les graffites chypriotes alphabétiques et syllabiques. Pp. 253–84 in *La Chapelle d' Achôris à Karnak*, by C. Traunecker, F. le Saout, and O. Masson. Centre Franco-Égyptien d'Études des Temples de Karnak. Recherche sur les grandes civilsations. Paris: Éditions ADPF.

1983   *Les inscriptions chypriotes syllabiques*. École Française d'Athènes. Études Chypriotes, I. Paris: Boccard.

Masson, O., and Mitford, T. B.

1986   *Les Inscriptions Syllabiques de Kouklia-Paphos*. Ausgrabungen in Alt-Paphos auf Cypern, Band 4. Konstanz: Universitätsverlag Konstanz.

Masson, O., and Sznycer, M.

1972   *Recherches sur les phéniciens à Chypre*. Centre de Recherches d'Histoire et de Philologie II. Hautes Études Orientales 3. Paris: Librairie Droz.

Mitford, T. B.

1958   Three Inscriptions of Marion. *Bulletin of the Institute of Classical Studies* 5: 58–60.

1960   Unpublished Syllabic Inscriptions of the Cyprus Museum. *Opuscula Atheniensia* 3: 177–213.

1961a   *Studies in the Signaries of South-Western Cyprus*. Institute of Classical Studies: Bulletin Supplement no. 10. London: Institute of Classical Studies.

1961b   Unpublished Syllabic Inscriptions of the Cyprus Museum. *Minos* 7: 15–46.

Mitford, T. B., and Masson, O.

1983   *The Syllabic Inscriptions of Rantidi-Paphos*. Ausgrabungen in Alt-Paphos auf Cypern, Band 2. Konstanz: Universitätsverlag Konstanz.

Moscati, S.

1968   *The World of the Phoenicians*. Trans. A. Hamilton from Italian. Praeger History of Civilizations. New York: Praeger.

Neumann, G.

1970   Kyprisch *pi-lo-pa-wo-se*. *Zeitschrift für vergleichende Sprachforschung auf dem Gebiete der Indogermanischen Sprachen* 84: 76–80.

1992   Beiträge zum Kyprischen XIII: 36. ICS 84, 3; 37. ICS 88 a. *Kadmos* 31: 51–55.

Nicolaou, I.

1971   *Cypriot Inscribed Stones*. Nicosia: Department of Antiquities of Cyprus.

1976   *Prosopography of Ptolemaic Cyprus*. Studies in Mediterranean Archaeology 44. Göteborg: Åströms.

Peek, W.

1988   *Griechische Vers-Inschriften: I. Grab-Epigramme*. Reprint ed. Chicago: Aries.

Random House

1987   *The Random House Dictionary of the English Language*, ed. S.B. Flexner. New York: Random House.

Robins, R. H.

1967   *A Short History of Linguistics*. Indiana University Studies in the History and Theory of Linguistics. Bloomington: Indiana University.

Smyth, H. W.

1956   *Greek Grammar*. Rev. ed. Cambridge, MA: Harvard University.

Tatton-Brown, V.

1990   The Archaic Period. Pp. 65–83 in *Footsteps in Cyprus*, ed. D. Hunt. London: Trigraph.

1998   *Ancient Cyprus*. Cambridge, MA: Harvard University.

Wallace, P., and Orphanides, A. D.

1990   *Sources for the History of Cyprus*. Vol. 1: *Greek and Latin Texts to the Third Century* A.D. Albany: State University of New York, Institute of Cypriot Studies.

Wilson, V.

1969   A Grave Relief from Marion. *Report of the Department of Antiquities of Cyprus*: 56–63.

CORRUPTING APHRODITE: COLONIALIST INTERPRETATIONS OF THE CYPRIAN GODDESS

MICHAEL GIVEN

Department of Archaeology
University of Glasgow
Glasgow G12 8QQ, Scotland
m.given@archaeology.arts.gla.ac.uk

The works of travelers and archaeologists in Cyprus during the second half of the 19th century abound in prurient descriptions of the supposed cult of Aphrodite or Ashtart in ancient Cyprus. "Abominable lust, bloodshed and depravity" is by no means the strongest. To these are added the stories of classical mythology and a series of ill-informed stereotypes about Oriental sexuality, both ancient and modern.

These 19th century interpretations of the worship of Aphrodite in ancient Cyprus are a consequence of various ideologies prevalent among Europeans who travelled to the eastern Mediterranean. Prurient travelers escaping the moralistic attitudes of western Europe looked eagerly for exotic and Oriental titillation. Imperial officials and ideologues legitimized their rule by tracing a heritage of amorality from antiquity to the present. Missionaries of western religion and culture found ancient vice and modern heresy convenient tools for the justification of their unpopular proselytising. Two forces, in particular, drove British imperialist attitudes: colonial desire, the urge to conquer and master a feminized, exotic, oriental Other; and colonial fear, whether of the unknown, of being vastly outnumbered, or of the "unnatural practices" that they themselves had projected onto the Orient.

Aphrodite, according to these writers, had corrupted the Cypriot people, and her influence was still to be seen. Because of the imperial relationship, however, it was these Europeans who had corrupted Aphrodite.

The posters and brochures proclaim, "Cyprus, Island of Aphrodite," to tourists who travel "Aphrodite Class" on Cyprus Airways and drink "Aphrodite" wine. It takes little contextual study of the surviving remains of the worship of the Cyprian Goddess in the 1st millennium B.C. (Budin, MacLachlan, Serwint, this volume) to realize that Aphrodite-as-holiday-icon is a shadow of her former self and has clearly been appropriated by the tourist industry. This exploitation, however, is a natural continuation of a less innocent appropriation by the British colonial regime that controlled Cyprus from 1878 to 1960. Modern Aphrodite, far from being the focus of people's cultural identity and a meaningful expression of their existence in the world, was molded by successive imperialist visitors, who quarried antiquity for their personal satisfaction, political advantage and ideological legitimization.

There was never, of course, any "pure" or "original" version of the Goddess, which was subsequently adulterated and perverted by outside forces. Being the construct of a dynamic and constantly changing society, she grew, developed, changed, shrunk, but always remained relevant to her people; hence, presumably, her current position as patron goddess of tourism. But when British colonial officials, travel writers and archaeologists appointed her head of "spiritual wickedness in high places" (Lewis 1894: 132), they were abusing their control of the historical and archaeological sources, deliberately or unconsciously, and trying to prove that Cyprus needed to be ruled. Aphrodite and her worship, they declared, had corrupted the Cypriot people, and the consequences could still be seen. Because of the imperial relationship, however, it was these writers who had corrupted Aphrodite.

Aphrodite still has enormous metaphoric power: she can stand for Cyprus, the ancient Greeks, sex, beauty, women. This explains why she became so useful a vehicle for the two great forces that drove British attitudes toward the people under their control: colonial desire and colonial fear. This metaphoric power also suggests that to examine the image of Aphrodite is to study our own attitudes to Cyprus, for example, or to women. This is why, for me, Aphrodite inhabits the center of this volume on women and society in ancient Cyprus.

COLONIAL DESIRE

In one of her many manifestations, Cyprian Aphrodite during the 19th and 20th centuries was an expression of colonial desire, the yearning of British and other visitors for some sort of imaginary or idealized beauty. In this role she took her classical hellenized form, the one created by Apelles and Praxiteles and their Roman copyists. The 1st century B.C. statue from Soloi became the prime example and was endlessly reproduced; it became, in effect, the logo of Cyprus (cf. Anderson 1991: 182). According to the more philhellenic British visitors in the late 19th century, it was this version of the goddess that superseded another western stereotype, the dissolute Oriental Ashtart: "Under the magic touch of Grecian refinement, the goddess of luxury and wantonness, Astarte, became the most beautiful of ideal creations, the mother of the Graces, the charming Aphrodite" (von Löher 1878: 100). It was this version that was favored by the Greek Cypriot intellectual elite (e.g., Lambrou 1878: 6).

A very few British illustrations of Cypriot women reflect this classical ideal of beauty. One such is entitled "A Princess of Cyprus," published in the illustrated magazine *The Graphic* in 1882 (fig. 1; *The Graphic*, 30 December 1882). The title is a curious one in an island that had seen no princesses since the 15th century, and the classical temple or edifice behind is entirely imaginary. The engraving is a product of the artist's desire to create a luscious, Grecian beauty in the western tradition.

When the British turned their distancing gaze on the local population, it was more common for them to create a disjunction between the "natives" and their own imposed standards of beauty. The ugliness of the Cypriot women, in contrast to the ancient mythical inhabitants of Aphrodite's Island, is a constant and tedious theme in the British travel writing of the late 19th and early 20th centuries. "Why she [Venus] is represented by the exceedingly plain women of Cyprus surpasses the imagination," sneered the explorer Samuel Baker (1879: 243). Never is there so much as a hint of the arduous domestic and agricultural work of the average village woman, in contrast to these western visitors, who were upper class women and men of leisure who used local people's physical appearance to fortify their own feelings of superiority. The desire for an idealized beauty even became the search for a reflection of oneself. Helen Gordon, lamenting the lack of pretty women in what she termed "Love's Island" (the title of her 1925 book), describes how a photographer had to use an Englishwoman as a model for a photograph of a Cypriot girl in national dress (1925: 12).

For the British upper classes of the late 19th century, a journey to a magical (and imaginary) Orient was often an escape from the repressive public morality of late Victorian Britain. Colonial desire became a quest for illicit sex or at least some discreet titillation (Said 1978: 180–88). A western mythology was built up of the harem, the houri, the hamam, the hanoum, and, especially, the veil (Melman 1995: 59–61). Cyprus had no Cairo or Istanbul, but much was made of the Turkish women (commonly known as "ghosts"), and with the vivid imagination of the likes of W.H. Mallock or Emile Deschamps, it was easy to extrapolate from the palm trees, minarets and hidden courtyards. Besides, the spectral

Figure 1. *"A Princess of Cyprus."* The Graphic, *30 December 1882.*

form of Aphrodite was always present, encourging fantasy and desire.

The relationship between western patron and Oriental houri became an expression of that between colonizer and colonized. As in the racial philosophy of Count Gobineau, the two races were "sexualized" (Young 1995: 111): whites were males, and blacks or yellows were female. This is a constant them in late 19th century British accounts of Cyprus, in academic writings as well as travel books, and in references to ancient as as well as modern Cyprus. Ancient Cyprus excelled in the "feminine arts" of sewing, embroidering, clay modeling and dyeing (Dixon 1879: 27). The effeminacy and luxury of the ancient Cypriots were proverbial (von Löher 1878: 158, 160), though the only real evidence concerns the lifestyle of a few 4th century B.C. kings. This contrast between the effeminate east and the masculine west was made explicit by Robert Hamilton Lang (1878: 118).

The most common metaphor of the Orient as an object of desire was the veiled woman. The very fact that her face cannot be seen gives rise to fertile speculation on the part of the observer as well as frustration at his inability to see (an important imperialist urge); this merely serves to heighten desire (see texts collected in Mabro 1991: 40–50; cf. Fanon 1965: 44; Alloula 1986: 7; Melman 1995: 120–21). The veil hiding the face produced the same reaction as the inward-turned house hiding the family or the walled, intricate *medina* hiding the society (Mabro 1991: 40–43). To the imperialist, local society with its tight family structure and its dislike of intruders was not just hidden and mysterious but incomprehensible, different, Other. This is the zone where colonial desire begins to overlap with colonial fear.

The colonial reaction to the veil is to rip it away, thus revealing the hidden, understanding the different, suppressing the fear. Even the colonial women participate. Esme Scott-Stevenson, the wife of the District Commissioner of Kyrenia, describes gloatingly how an ex-member of the Sultan's harem used to unveil herself in front of her and "display her charms most ungrudgingly" (Scott-Stevenson 1880: 83). When the Greek ladies did the same, they displayed "their under garments of Cyprus cotton and coats of Manchester stuff" (1880: 82). Even their underclothes had been colonized by the British.

Entering the harem is an action equivalent to removing the veil. Malek Alloula's study of French colonial postcards showing Algerian women analyzes this symbolic penetration of the photographer into the harem (Alloula 1986: 21, 34, 37). In Cyprus the same implied intimacy is produced by many colonial photographs, for example Ohnefalsch-Richter's representation of two Cypriot girls from Ayios Andronikos (Ohnefalsch-Richter and Ohnefalsch-Richter 1994: pl. 70b). The French traveler Emile

Figure 2. *"Bien venu qui apporte!" Sir Garnet Wolseley and Venus.* Punch, *3 August 1878, p. 46.*

Deschamps, whose book is characteristically entitled *Pays d'Aphrodite* and is full of overblown orientalist fantasy, similarly peeps into a hamam and spies women bathing. An old woman accosts him, but he manages to calm her as she is not a Turk, "only a woman" (1898: 46). Like the imperial explorer who wrote in the "monarch-of-all-I-survey" mode (Pratt 1992: 213), his voyeurism is an expression of power, of forcible penetration into what would normally be forbidden.

Figure 3. *"How Tombs are excavated, and with what Tools." di Cesnola (1877: 255).*

The veil is, of course, metaphorical as well as literal: veils were ripped not just from women, homes, and hamams, but from whole societies and countries (Fanon 1965: 42–43). Western conquests of colonies were often portrayed in sexual terms. When the British took Cyprus in 1878, this was illustrated by *Punch* as a courteous but still dominant Sir Garnet Wolseley, the first High Commissioner, kissing the hand of Aphrodite, who stands for Cyprus (fig. 2; *Punch,* 3rd August 1878, p. 46). On this occasion, the goddess of love and Cyprus is given an appropriately British garment, as the caption says: "Lo, Venus, daughter of the foam, draped in the British flag."

According to the sexualization of the races and the western male attitudes to women of the time, this conquest was actually desired by the victim. In 1939 Sir Richmond Palmer, governor of Cyprus and author of the *palmerkratia*, the oppressive regime of the late 1930s, told a meeting of the Royal Central Asian Society in London about his experience and knowledge of Cyprus: "Several thousand years ago a lady called Aphrodite landed in Cyprus, and the island has never quite recovered. The people of Cyprus make a luxury of discontent and always pretend that they do not like being ruled, and yet, like the lady I have mentioned as a prototype, they expect to be ruled, and, in fact, prefer it" (Palmer 1939: 601). This is, of course, the standard male justification for rape.

In Cyprus, where so much imperialist ideology was expressed through the medium of archaeological and historical discourse, this conquest was reenacted in the earth. One thinks of Howard Carter entering Tutankhamun's virgin tomb in 1922 and the huge popularity of "tombing" in Cyprus in the second half of the 19th century. Cesnola's illustration showing "How Tombs are excavated, and with what Tools" (fig. 3; di Cesnola 1877: 255) clearly exaggerates the depth of the tomb; but this very exaggeration shows how important it was for Cesnola to boast about his penetration of the earth. Archaeology was a safe means of lifting the veil, demonstrating control over the interior, the deeply buried, the hidden, secret Other.

Unsurprisingly, amateur and academic archaeologists were drawn to the Temple of Aphrodite in Palaepaphos. In this way they could penetrate the ultimate harem. Like the pornographic postcards of Algerian women that were presented as "ethnographic" and pseudo-scientific (Alloula 1986: 27–29), these excavations, Cesnola's (1877: 204–16) just as much as Gardner's and Hogarth's (Gardner et al. 1888), were concerned with measurements and foundations and chronology. This was partly due to the urge to appear scientific but was also due to the more fundamental reason that little was found at Palaepaphos to titillate the colonial imagination.

But the colonial imagination was never impeded by lack of concrete evidence. Aphrodite was the greatest expression of the overt, naked, unveiled woman, and so of the feminine orient, which did not just need occupation and control but actually wanted it, as Palmer said. Yet Aphrodite had another manifestation, which paradoxically produced equal fascination and repulsion. She was an expression of colonial fear.

COLONIAL FEAR

In every colony, and especially in the districts away from the capital, a handful of westerners ruled thousands or tens of thousands of local people. In Cyprus in the late 19th century, Paphos and Famagusta were notorious among British officials and their families for their isolation and loneliness. Ever since the Indian Mutiny in 1857, this situation had produced fear: fear of attack, fear of being surrounded and overwhelmed, fear of the vast numbers of dark, incomprehensible natives. Any sign or representation of fertility or a large family was a reminder of this uncontrollable, threatening increase in population (Alloula 1986: 40). The "teeming but merciless goddess Astarte" (von Löher 1878: 99) was one expression of that threat.

This fear was heightened by the paranoia of being watched and examined, particularly as it was felt that watching and scrutinizing were uniquely colonial prerogatives. Travelers are full of references to piercing eyes from under the veil or eyes staring out from the lattices of the harem window (Mabro 1991: 43, 45–47). Esme Scott-Stevenson noted "one of my own sex peeping curiously at me through the doorway" in a monastery (1880: 157), and she comments on the veils worn by Turkish women that "left visible only the single eye that peered so curiously at me as I passed" (20). The desire for what lay within was tempered by the fear of being secretly watched.

Added to this was the fear of impropriety, the public and unashamed rupture of upper class Victorian values: any mention of sex was taboo (though this, like the veil, heightened fascination and desire), let alone open discussion of polygamy, promiscuity, homosexuality or any of the other supposed "unnatural practices" of the Orient. Worst of all was the threat of hybridity: that a union of white male and oriental female would visibly demonstrate that East was not always East nor West West (Young 1995).

In Cyprus, where suitably unnatural Oriental harems and houris, apparently, were harder to find than in Cairo or Istanbul, it was Aphrodite/Ashtart who had to bear the brunt of this projection of sexual and racial fear. Thanks to a handful of ancient references, imperfectly understood, she became the icon for whatever was immoral, degenerate, or ugly. Mrs Bateson Joyner's adaptation of Franz von Löher's travel book in 1878 provides a characteristic account:

> It has long been a recognised fact, though dismal enough, that the instincts of sexuality, cruelty, and mystical superstition, are entwined together as if they grew from the same root. In Cyprus this law of nature seems to have asserted itself throughout the land. In presence of the mysteries of Astarte, in which abominable lust, bloodshed, and depravity reigned triumphant, we gladly shut our eyes (von Löher 1878: 104).

Oriental sexuality has somehow become a law of nature, and torn between fascination and repulsion the author examines her subject with eyes tightly closed (with perhaps just a peep from the corner of her veil).

According to the orientalist discourse of British officials, writers and academics in late 19th century Cyprus, the depravity of the ancient worship of Aphrodite combined with the hot, exhausting climate and effeminate luxury to "enervate" the ancient Cypriots, so that they and their successors became an inferior, degenerate race (e.g., Lang 1878: 12; Smith 1887: 257; Munro and Tubbs 1890: 9; Stewart 1908: 230). This, of course, justified British rule. One of the most influential exponents of this theory, in terms of the breadth and strength of its impact on the discourse, was "General" Luigi Palma di Cesnola, in his book *Cyprus: Its Cities, Tombs and Temples* (1877). Seeing how often it was cited and plagiarized in the 20 years following its publication, it is worth quoting the passage at length and examining its factual basis in some detail.

The main statement of the "enervation" theory comes in the introduction to the book, in a passage where he is trying to characterize the ancient Cypriots:

The easily acquired products of nature, the wealth arising from trade, the enervating climate, and not least, perhaps, the intercourse with the East rendered the people of Cyprus proverbial as the happiest beings on earth as far as luxury and pleasure could make them so, and the natural consequence of this was that there was no excess or refinement of indulgence which they did not practise. In this the worship of Aphrodite played an important part. To a great extent it decided the character of public and private morality thoughout the island, and that the result was highly disgraceful may be seen from numerous passages in the ancient writers [four references]. Every one knows the description which Herodotus gives (1.199) of the custom of Babylonian women at the Temple of Mylitta, the Assyrian counterpart of Aphrodite, and he adds that the same thing prevailed in Cyprus. Later writers entirely confirm what he says, and the pictures which they draw of the grand festivals to the goddess at Paphos leave little for the imagination of man to invent, one would think, in the way of gross indulgence. (di Cesnola 1877: 7–8)

The four references that Cesnola gives, by way of academic confirmation of his theory, consist of two passages from Athenaeus, one from Plautus, and one from Terence. Athenaeus 3.100 is a discussion of tripe served with silphium juice from Cyrene; perhaps Cesnola is confusing Cyprus and Cyrene or else considers the eating of tripe to be an unnatural practice. Athenaeus 13.586–94 is the passage about famous courtesans, who, as it happens, come from all over the Greek world, but not from Cyprus. Beyond the fact that they are prostitutes, albeit socially superior ones, there is nothing that fits Cesnola's description of "gross indulgence." The third reference is Plautus, *Poenulus* 1251, the beginning of the speech where the Carthaginian Hanno reveals to two prostitutes (who had been stolen as girls and bought by a pimp) that he is their father. In Terence, *Adelphi* 2.2, Sannio is about to make a trip to Cyprus with a cargo of "women and other goods." It seems that Cesnola has selected a few general references to prostitution and the slave trade and used them as pseudo-academic proof for his lurid picture of sexual indulgence and dissolution.

The cornerstone of his and others' assessment of the worship of Aphrodite in ancient Cyprus is an offhand remark in Herodotus, who, after describing temple prostitution in Babylonia, adds that "there is a custom similar to this in parts of Cyprus" (1.199). Quite apart from the problems of accepting such a brief comment at face value, there are as many problems with Herodotus's interpretations of the Orient as there are with Cesnola's. Many aspects of modern orientalism and western cultural arrogance actually derived from 5th century B.C. Athens. For Herodotus, as for Cesnola, permissive sexuality is one component of the constructed "otherness" of the Orient. Several ancient writers mention temple prostitution in Cyprus and elsewhere, and many of them are clearly aware of the religious power and social importance of the phenomenon (MacLachlan 1992). These few references, however, were used by imperialists to create a picture of an indulgent and permissive Orient that was simultaneously alluring and threatening.

The natural consequence of the degeneracy of the ancient Cypriots was that they should bequeath it to their modern descendants. This causal connection is implied or, more commonly, explicitly stated in nearly all late 19th century imperialist accounts of Cyprus. It explained, for example, the perceived ugliness of contemporary women: the immorality of ancient worship became a curse on them (Baker 1879: 243), or else the rites with which Aphrodite was worshipped were so impure that they debased the character of the women (Smith 1887: 246).

The main logical mechanism for establishing the connection between ancient and modern degeneracy and moral inferiority was that of continuity, one of the most powerful weapons in the imperialist ideological armoury. Ancient Cyprus was primitive; there are many continuities between ancient and modern Cyprus; therefore modern Cyprus is primitive and needs imperialist rule. Aphrodite and religious worship provided a rich quarry of continuities for the imperialists (and also, conversely, nationalists) to exploit.

The best and most frequently cited continuity was that between Aphrodite of Palaepaphos and Panayia Aphroditissa of Kouklia. To a Greek Cypriot intellectual, this was proof of the continuity of Greek civilization in Cyprus (Lambrou 1878: 13), but to the imperialists it was proof of continuing

Figure 4. *"Modern Priest. Stone head from Golgoi." di Cesnola (1877: 180).*

primitiveness and degeneracy. Cesnola described the continuing reverence paid to the stones of the Temple of Aphrodite (1877: 211). Von Löher mentioned the same idea, though without any specific description (1878: 105), and was then quoted by Thomson (1879: 40) and the devout Presbyterian Agnes Smith, who found the idea "ludicrously incongruous" (1887: 206). The theme quickly became a literary and ideological topos (e.g., Luke 1935: 151–53; Storrs 1945: 496).

Much attention was paid to the famous "holy stones." It made no difference whether these were sacred or functional in origin. To Cesnola (1877: 189) and Deschamps (1898: 220), they were ancient temples or monoliths that were still used for worship. To the more hard-nosed Guillemard (1888: 475) and Hogarth (1889: 20) they were olive mills, but even so the modern dedications being made at them showed the continuity of primitive religion in modern Cyprus (Hogarth 1896: 179–80). Cesnola demonstrated that priests wore the same conical caps in the Iron Age and the 19th century (fig. 4; Cesnola 1877: 180) and, as usual, was plagiarized (Dixon 1879: 265). Kataklysmos, the supposed birthday of Aphrodite still celebrated in modern Cyprus, was another popular continuity (Lewis 1894: 138; Deschamps 1898: 100; Stewart 1908: 119). Taken together, these continuities established the primitive and degenerate nature of modern Cyprus. In this manifestation, Aphrodite was a primitive and threatening Other and had to be suppressed.

CONCLUSION

In the British imperialist discourse, Aphrodite became, as so often was the case, a metaphor for her island and for the women who lived there. Like them, she simultaneously attracted and repelled, disgusted and fascinated. She was the key to hidden fantasies of lust and power and the symbol of open perversion and degeneracy. This ideological exploitation of Aphrodite brought her a long way from the Iron Age where she (or her precursor) had been the center of a profound and sophisticated interpretative system based on the principles of motherhood and nourishment.

Psychologically, the colonial appropriation of Aphrodite did more than provide a convenient ideological legitimization of imperial rule. Lurid fantasies of permissiveness and perversion caused fear and repulsion as well as a certain fascination and attraction. Desire, when linked to power, was easily satisfied. But the only way to conquer fear was by precisely that, conquest. This applied to colonial officials, missionaries, and romantic travel writers alike: by giving expression to the objects of their fear and forcibly accommodating them to their own prejudices, they resolved their own fears and satisfied their desires by means of conquest and control.

REFERENCES

Alloula, M.
1986   *The Colonial Harem*. Trans. M. Godzich and W. Godzich with Intro. by B. Harlow. Theory and History of Literature, Vol. 21. Minneapolis: University of Minnesota.

Anderson, B.
1991   *Imagined Communities: Reflections on the Origins and Spread of Nationalism*. 2nd ed. London: Verso.

Baker, S. W.
1879   *Cyprus as I Saw it in 1879*. London: Macmillan.

Deschamps, E.
1898   *Pays d' Aphrodite: Chypre. Carnet d' un Voyageur*. Paris: Libraire Hachette.

di Cesnola, L. P.
1877   *Cyprus: Its Ancient Cities, Tombs, and Temples. A Narrative of Researches and Excavations During Ten Years' Residence as American Consul in that Island*. London: John Murray.

Dixon, W. H.
1879   *British Cyprus*. London: Chapman and Hall.

Fanon, F.
1965   *Studies in a Dying Colonialism*. Trans. H. Chevalier with new Intro. by A. M. Babu (1989). London: Earthscan Publications.

Gardner, E. A.; Hogarth, D. G.; James, M. R.; and Elsey Smith, R.
1888   Excavations in Cyprus, 1887-1888: Paphos, Leontari, Amargetti. *Journal of Hellenic Studies* 9: 147-271.

Gordon, H. C.
1925   *Love's Island*. Nicosia.

Guillemard, F. H. H.
1888   Monoliths in the Island of Cyprus. *Athenaeum* No. 3155 (April 14): 474–75.

Hogarth, D. G.
1889   *Devia Cypria: Notes of an Archaeological Journey in Cyprus in 1888*. Oxford: Oxford University.
1896   *A Wandering Scholar in the Levant*. London: John Murray.

Lambrou, S. P.
1878   *Peri Kyprou*. Bibliotheke tes Estias 8. Athens: Estias.

Lang, R. H.
1878   *Cyprus: Its History, its Present Resources, and Future Prospects*. London: Macmillan.

Lewis, Mrs.
1894   *A Lady's Impressions of Cyprus in 1893*. London: Remington.

Luke, H. C.
1935   *More Moves on an Easter Chequerboard*. London: Lovat Dickson and Thompson.

Mabro, J., ed.
1991   *Veiled Half-truths: Western Travellers' Perceptions of Middle Eastern Women*. London: I. B. Tauris.

MacLachlan, B.
1992   Sacred Prostitution and Aphrodite. *Studies in Religion* 21: 145–62.

Mallock, W. H.
1889   *In an Enchanted Island, or a Winter's Retreat in Cyprus*. 2nd ed. London: Richard Bentley.

Melman, B.
1995   *Women's Orients: English Women and the Middle East, 1718–1918: Sexuality, Religion and Work*. 2nd ed. Basingstoke and London: Macmillan.

Munro, J. A. R., and Tubbs, H. A.
1890   Excavations in Cyprus, 1889: Second Season's Work: Polis tes Chrysochou, Limniti. *Journal of Hellenic Studies* 11: 1-99.

Ohnefalsch-Richter, M. H., and Ohnefalsch-Richter, M.
1994   *Studies in Cyprus*. Nicosia: Cultural Centre, Cyprus Popular Bank.

Palmer, R.
  1939   Cyprus. *Journal of the Royal Central Asian Society* 26: 599–618.
Pratt, M. L.
  1992   *Imperial Eyes: Travel Writing and Transculturation*. London: Routledge.
Said, E.
  1978   *Orientalism*. Harmondsworth: Penguin Books.
Scott-Stevenson, E.
  1880   *Our Home in Cyprus*. London: Chapman and Hall.
Smith, A.
  1887   *Through Cyprus*. London.
Stewart, B.
  1908   *My Experiences of Cyprus, Being an Account of the People, Mediaeval Cities and Castles, Antiquities and History of the Island of Cyprus; to which is Added a Chapter on the Present Economic and Political Problems which Affect the Island as a Dependency of the British Empire*. 1st rev. ed. London: George Routledge.
Storrs, R. H. A.
  1945   *Orientations*. 2nd def. ed. London: Ivor Nicholson and Watson.
Thomson, J.
  1879   *Through Cyprus with the Camera, in the Autumn of 1878*. 2 vols. London: Sampson Low, Marston, Searle, and Rivington. Reprint: Collectors' Centre, Nicosia, 1978.
von Löher, F.
  1878   *Cyprus, Historical and Descriptive, Adapted from the German with much Additional Matter*. Trans. Mrs. A. Bateson Joyner. London: W. H. Allen.
Young, R. J. C.
  1995   *Colonial Desire: Hybridity in Theory, Culture and Race*. London: Routledge.

PART EIGHT

PANEL DISCUSSION: GENDER EQUITY ISSUES IN ARCHAEOLOGY TODAY

PANEL DISCUSSION: GENDER EQUITY ISSUES IN ARCHAEOLOGY TODAY

The investigation of gender as a focal point of research in Cypriot archaeology would not be complete without an assessment of past and present gender constructs within the academic institutions and professional organizations of archaeology today. Indeed, the belated emergence and slow acceptance of gender as a legitimate scholarly pursuit within the field can be correlated to the differential roles and positions of men and women in fieldwork, teaching, research and publication. Traditionally, the formulation and promotion of theory, methodology and research agendas, as well as the control of funding to develop and legitimize them, has rested largely with males. Although this situation has begun to change over the last decade, there are still marked inequities in the system that need to be overcome if gender parity is to be achieved.

In a recent publication of the American Anthropological Association (Nelson et al. 1994), the position and status of women in archaeology was presented from a broad range of geographical and thematic perspectives, including geographical areas as widely diverse as Asia, the Pacific, Australia, Europe, and North and South America. The book had its roots in a panel discussion at the AAA Annual Meeting in 1991, reflecting a nearly decade long tradition of charting gender inequities within the discipline of anthropology. More recent are the results of surveys conducted in the more traditional fields of classical archaeology (see Cullen's contribution below) and Cypriot archaeology (Webb and Frankel 1995a, 1995b, and see Webb's contribution below). Although these reports seem to indicate increasing levels of participation by women in recent decades, there are still vast inequities in male/female status. Men continue to hold more prestigious positions within the university environment, publish more frequently in "quality" journals, are more likely to become directors of field projects, and are more successful in obtaining funding for research.

One of the main objectives of the discussion that follows, and the decision to include an equity panel as part of the conference structure, was to explore and document specific aspects of gender disparity from the perspectives of women currently active in academic and professional organizations within the Cypriot field. Our starting point was the report by Jenny Webb and David Frankel referred to above, which outlined some of the overall trends in research, teaching, publication and field direction in Cyprus from 1920 to the present. Webb's contribution in the conference panel discussion summarizes this report and identifies some of the changes that appeared to be taking shape as the 20th century drew to a close.

Other panelists were asked to report on areas of the field in which they have a direct involvement and expertise. Tracey Cullen, who at the time was Associate Editor of the *American Journal of Archaeology*, was asked to contribute her views on the differential roles of men and women in archaeological publication in the United States. Frosso Egoumenidou, a member of the faculty of History and Archaeology at the University of Cyprus, and Lone Wriedt Sørensen, a professor at the University of Copenhagen, were asked to share their views and experiences of the differential access of men and women to academic posts within their respective countries. Finally, Despo Pilides, an archaeological officer in the Department of Antiquities, Cyprus, and Jo Clarke, who was then Acting Director of the British School of Archaeology in Jersualem, were asked to examine the role of women in archaeological administration.

We would like to thank all of the panelists for their thought-provoking contributions, which served as the basis for a very lively general discussion. We hope their efforts will be rewarded by changes in the male-dominated academic and administrative structures currently in place and by the greater participation of women in directing fieldwork and establishing new research agendas during the next millennium.

DISCUSSION

Moderator: Diane Bolger (Research Fellow, University of Edinburgh)

Diane Bolger: I'd like to welcome you to our more informal session, "Equity Issues in Archaeology Today." This morning we want to talk about issues that concern women's participation in archaeology, in general, and Cypriot archaeology, in particular. This involves a wide range of issues that can be divided into four areas: excavation, research, publication and employment. The panelists that we have assembled here today represent a broad spectrum of these four aspects of the archaeological process and also represent a range of nationalities (Cypriot, Danish, Australian, British and American):

> Jo Clarke: Doctoral Candidate at Edinburgh University and currently Acting Director of the British School of Archaeology in Jerusalem.*
>
> Dr. Tracey Cullen: Associate Editor of the *American Journal of Archaeology.**
>
> Dr. Frosso Egoumenidou: Assistant Professor, Department of History and Archaeology, University of Cyprus, and formerly a member of the Department of Antiquities of Cyprus.
>
> Dr. Despo Pilides: Archaeological Officer at the Department of Antiquities of Cyprus.
>
> Dr. Lone Sørensen: Professor at the Institute of Archaeology and Ethnology, University of Copenhagen, Denmark.
>
> Dr. Jenny Webb: Australian Research Council Fellow at La Trobe University, Australia and Co-Director of the excavations at Marki-*Alonia.*

We'll begin the discussion with panelists Jenny Webb and Tracey Cullen, who will share information and views on differential participation of men and women in archaeological excavation, publication and research. We shall then turn to the topic of women in university teaching and academia, with presentations by Frosso Egoumenidou and Lone Sørensen. Finally, Despo Pilides and Jo Clarke will offer their views on the participation of women in archaeological administration. Time for general discussion has been allotted after each of the three segments of the panel presentations.

ISSUE 1: EQUITY ISSUES IN FIELDWORK, PUBLICATION AND RESEARCH

Jenny Webb: Gender Inequity in Cypriot Archaeology, Past and Present

My talk this morning is based on research that David Frankel and I presented initially at the Second Australian Women in Archaeology Conference held at the University of New England in Armidale in 1993 (Webb and Frankel 1995a). We expanded this and published it in the *Journal of Mediterranean Archaeology* in 1995 (Webb and Frankel 1995b). We also handed out a questionnaire at the CAARI Workshop in 1994. The main body of the paper examined the proportional representation of men and women in publications and research in Cypriot archaeology. In the second part of the paper, we looked at the interface between the structure of the discipline and the construction of the archaeological record and made suggestions for a more "equitable" practice of archaeology.

---

*Since the time of the conference, Jo Clarke has received her Ph.D. from Edinburgh University and currently is Lecturer in Material Culture Studies in the School of World Art Studies and Museology at the University of East Anglia in Norwich, United Kingdom. Tracey Cullen has moved from her position at *AJA* to become editor of the journal *Hesperia*.

The first source that we looked at was *Who's Who in Cypriote Archaeology*, published by Paul Åström in 1971 (Åström 1971), a compilation of biographies and bibliographies of all Cypriot archaeologists living in 1970. We looked through all of that information and focused on gender and nationality as well as the numbers and types of publications by scholars over the five previous decades (i.e., 1920–1970). We found that there had been a steady growth in the number of publications by both men and women over time and that the male to female ratio had remained roughly constant over the five decades, with publications by women running between 10% and 17% of the total in each decade. We also looked at the relative incidence of male/female contributors by nationality. We found that the contribution by women was less than 20% of the total for all countries involved, except for the United States where female contributions stood at 29%.

We then examined the proceedings from 16 major international conferences in seven different countries between 1969 and 1991, with a view to calculating the relative participation of males and females. Here we found a clear trend toward greater female participation, from less than 15% in the early years to more than 50% at conferences held between 1989 and 1991. In terms of the relative incidence by nationality, we found a general increase in female participation from most countries and a massive increase in the number of American women participating in conferences. American women accounted for the highest number of papers by any single group in the second decade (i.e., the 1980s). In fact, there were more publications by American women than by any other male or female nationality group in that decade.

The third area that we looked at were journal articles, particularly, articles published in the major Cypriot journal, *Report of the Department of Antiquities of Cyprus* (*RDAC*), from 1970 to 1992. We found that women represented 36% of the total number of contributions over those two decades, but that during this period their rate of contribution had barely increased. So, while the overall rate of publication by women in this journal was significantly greater than it had been in the previous five decades, it was still nowhere near as strong or as consistent as in the conference sector, where participation by women has doubled in the last decade.

Next we looked at the differential participation of men and women in the direction of fieldwork by assessing data taken from the 1969–1992 issues of "Chronique des fouilles et decouverts archeologiques a Chypre," published annually in the *Bulletin de correspondance hellénique*. We felt this was particularly important because directing field projects is considered the elite sector of the field where raw data is produced, analyzed and interpreted. The proportion of excavation and survey projects directed by men and women remained relatively constant throughout the two decades from 1969 to 1988. In both decades, women consistently represented less than 20% of the total number of directors and co-directors. Only about 11% of all fieldwork over this period was directed or co-directed by women.

Since the late 1980s, however, the situation has improved significantly. In 1989, 26.5% of all projects were directed or co-directed by women. In 1990, 33% of all projects were directed or co-directed by women. In 1991, female direction or co-direction of projects dropped to 30%, but it rose again in 1992, when 40% of all projects were directed or co-directed by women. Women were also increasingly represented in proportion to the total number of directors: 39.5% in 1992 compared to 21.5% in 1989. This appears to be the result of an increase in the number of projects directed solely by women as well as a rise in the number of projects directed jointly by women. There was significant change here, and we felt there was some cause for optimism.

The 1994 CAARI Workshop questionnaire raised a number of different issues relating to the contemporary work place. The publications we looked at had given us an idea of the structure of the discipline in the recent past. The questionnaire allowed us to look at people's expectations for the future. Most of those who responded were young, primarily students who had been working on excavations in Cyprus that year. Of about 100 people in attendance at the workshop, 49 completed the questionnaire.

One of the questions asked was, "What is your current level of employment in archaeology and what is ultimately your expected level of employment in archaeology?" Generally both men and women were confident. Of the women, 50% expected to become tenured academics or full professors, while 64% of men expected to become tenured academics or full professors. Of 14% who felt they had no prospects, all were women who were more advanced in their careers, i.e., the more qualified they were, the more they realized they weren't going to get anywhere.

Another question posed was, "Do you feel a successful career in archaeology is very much, significantly, a little or no more difficult for women than for men?" Answers to this question were particularly interesting. Whereas almost 30% of men responded that a career in archaeology wasn't any more difficult for women than men, 59% of women responded that a career in archaeology was either significantly or very much more difficult for women than men. There was a clear difference in experience, expectations or perceptions of career difficulties.

We also asked, "What is your current excavation status and what is your expected excavation status or role in the field?" The response was that 33% of women had no expectation of a career in field archaeology, whereas only 9% of men fell into this category. Among the men, 52% expected to become excavation directors, while only 32% of women expected to do so. More women than men said that they would be content to become an assistant director, 14% as opposed to 4%.

It seems, then, that fieldwork is particularly attractive to men, who have a significantly higher expectation of reaching the top in this sector of the discipline. Fieldwork is still largely men's business. Women are more likely to be content with museum based studies and laboratory analyses, the sort of archaeological housekeeping that Joan Gero (1994) has written about. This has significant implications for discussions of gender and other interpersonal relations. If the search for gender relations in the past requires a different sort of archaeology, the continuing under-representation of women in positions of authority in the field is likely to hinder rather than help elucidate this area of human behavior. Increased involvement by women at all levels of the discipline should bring about a broadening of the inquiry base and allow a fuller understanding of the past through the incorporation of alternative perspectives and methodologies.

Tracey Cullen: Research and Publication in Classical Archaeology in the United States

We are only beginning to look into the structure of classical archaeology in the United States. Other disciplines, such as classics and anthropology, have routinely conducted surveys for years to see how men and, particularly, women are faring in the field. The first census of classical archaeologists was only sent out in 1996 and the first history of the discipline is now in press (Dyson 1998; the publication appeared subsequent to the conference). This relative lack of introspection on the part of classical archaeologists is itself of interest, but I mention it now to account for the preliminary nature of my remarks today.

I will be talking mainly about publishing in classical archaeology. I am currently the Associate Editor of the *American Journal of Archaeology* (*AJA*), based at the Archaeological Institute of America (AIA), the largest professional organization of classical archaeologists in the United States. As such, I have access to various kinds of records that illuminate the relative positions of men and women in archaeology. What I have found for classical archaeology, in general, correlates very well with information that Jenny Webb has presented for Cypriot archaeology.

To evaluate men and women's relative rates of publishing, we need to know the numbers of men and women in the field. It is unrealistic to expect that half of the articles and books written in archaeology should be by women, if women do not make up half of the population. It is surprisingly difficult, however, to find out the ratio of men to women in classical archaeology: one cannot simply send out surveys to departments of classical archaeology in the U.S. because there are very few such departments. Programs of classical archaeology are commonly embedded in departments of classics or art history. I used three sources to estimate gender ratios in the discipline: the *AIA Directory of Professionals in Archaeology*; the subscriber list to *AJA* from 1996; and the results of the AIA Survey of Professionals in Archaeology, conducted in 1996 by the AIA Subcommittee on Women in Archaeology.

The *Directory* lists 928 individuals, 43% of whom are women. Although not all classical archaeologists subscribe to *AJA*, it is still one measure of professionalism. Of the roughly 2,600 individual subscribers in 1996, 44% are women. The survey sent out by AIA was similar to the CAARI survey that Webb has described, with questions posed about a wide variety of issues, including publishing activities. Of approximately 1,000 professionals and graduate students who returned the survey, 52% are women. I suspect that this figure is somewhat inflated by the inclusion of graduate students in the sample (two-thirds of whom are women) and by the fact that women appeared to have more to say than men on issues relating to job satisfaction, and thus may have been more diligent in returning their survey forms! I think it is reasonable, on the basis of the above measures, to estimate that approximately 45% of classical archaeologists are women.

Against this admittedly rough baseline, we can look at men and women's relative participation and productivity in publishing in archaeology. Let me give you a rundown of a few tallies I made using *AJA* records. For articles published in *AJA* from 1986 to 1995, 38% of the manuscripts sent in were written by women compared to 62% by men. The acceptance rate was identical: 38% of the articles published in *AJA* for this period were written by women. This is below the expected proportion of 45% but it is very comparable to Webb's estimate for *RDAC* (36%), and it is quite a bit better than some journals in anthropological archaeology: for example, only 11% of the articles published in *American Antiquity* from 1967 to 1990 were written by women, and a third of the articles appearing in the *Journal of Mediterranean Archaeology* over the last seven years were written by women. Both *AJA* and *RDAC* often publish artifact-based or art historical studies, areas in which women have traditionally concentrated, which may explain the higher percentage of female authors represented in those journals.

In 1996 and 1997, the submission and acceptance rates of articles by women in *AJA* increased from 38% to 50%. But before we celebrate, I hasten to add that over the past ten years male reviewers of books in *AJA* have outnumbered female reviewers by nearly two to one. Book reviews, unlike articles, are invited. This discrepancy in the numbers of men and women writing articles and book reviews made me suspect that a difference in status between male and female archaeologists may account for women being less well represented in invited activities. With this possibility in mind, I looked at the relative participation of men and women at the annual AIA conferences. From 1995 to 1997, women gave half or more than half of the papers (papers for presentation are chosen by a committee that reviews anonymous abstracts). On the other hand, for the AIA *invited* lecture series, including the AIA society lecturers and the prestigious endowed lecture tours, only 26% of those invited in 1995 were women. Although this figure rose to 29% in 1996 and 1997, it is still well below the percentage of women who give papers at conferences. In the AIA survey we also asked respondents how often they had been called upon to referee manuscripts for publication, another invited activity. Whereas 48% of men had been asked to serve as referees in the last five years, only 31% of women had been asked to do so. Apparently, when a referee or reviewer is needed, male names come to mind more readily than female.

There appears to be a discrepancy between women's high visibility in giving papers at conferences and their lower publication rate. The AIA survey indicates, for example, that for every publication category (books, journal articles, articles in collections, book reviews, etc.), women publish less often than men. Among doctorates who responded to the survey, men on average had published four articles in collections between 1991 and 1995, while women averaged only three. For journal articles, men averaged five and women only three. To ensure more comparable figures, I also looked at a smaller sub-sample of the survey data: 184 individuals (92 men and 92 women) who had received their doctorate in archaeology and are currently pursuing a career in the field. I then calculated the number of books, articles in collected volumes, and articles in journals that the smaller group had published. Although the average numbers of publications by men and women were closer, men again displayed higher averages in every category, particularly in journal articles (women averaged two articles and men five). Of the 462 journal articles published by this group, 69% had been written by 61 men and only 31% by 59 women. Though roughly the same proportions of men and women were writing articles, men clearly were publishing more frequently.

What are the reasons for this discrepancy in publishing rates, especially in journal articles, between men and women? It has reasonably been suggested that familial responsibilities interfere more with women's ability to publish frequently than with men's. Interestingly, however, only half of the female Ph.D. respondents to the AIA survey had children (cf. 70% of the men), and no marked difference in publishing rates was found between those with children and those without—so it is clearly a more complex issue. Women hold the majority of part-time and temporary positions in the discipline, and these positions do not generally provide adequate resources or incentives for high productivity in publishing. Moreover, many fewer women than men have the security of tenure. Although it is subjective, my impression is that women at universities devote considerably more time to committee work and to mentoring students than do men. Issues of self-confidence and ambition, no doubt, also play a role. Field projects in the Mediterranean provide a ready source of material for publishing, and are usually organized and directed by men. In short, many factors, few of which are specific to archaeology, contribute to the different publication rates between men and women.

Overall, a pattern emerges that is not unlike those described elsewhere for related disciplines. While women hold their own in giving talks at professional meetings, they tend to publish fewer books and articles than men. Nearly half of our field is comprised of women yet, to the extent that I can generalize from the AIA survey, only about a third of the archaeological literature is published by women. It would be interesting to carry out a citation study for classical archaeology, to evaluate the relative impact of work published by men and women. The greater visibility of men in invited activities, such as refereeing manuscripts or reviewing books suggests that men have more influence in the field, presumably backed up by their publication record. More research into the structure and sociopolitics of classical archaeology is clearly essential if we are to understand fully current trends in publication.*

General Discussion

Naomi Hamilton: I'm not sure if you pulled it out, Tracey, but the lower publication rate can be correlated with the fact that men have control of the field; they have it all there and women have to get it unless they are running their own projects. Men will have their names on the front of books and they may not really have done any of the work originally for which they have a permit.

Tracey Cullen: That's a good point. Actually in terms of excavation, the percentage of women directing field projects in Cyprus is only about 27%, so in that sense I'm sure you're right.

Attendee: With regard to the number of people who subscribe to *AJA*, quite a lot of that percentage might be librarians, I would have thought.

Tracey Cullen: We kept them out.

Maro Theodossiadou: I was greatly impressed with the information and data given to us by Jenny Webb, but I feel that in order to test them we must compare them with information coming from other

*Editors' note: Two recent reports by Tracey Cullen (the second co-authored with Donald Keller) on the results of the AIA Survey of Professionals in Archaeology appear in the Winter and Fall 1999 issues of the *AIA Newsletter* (vols. 14.2 and 15.1). The second report, in particular, is concerned with issues of research and publication in archaeology.

fields. Are these percentages referring only to women in archaeology over the five decades or are they pertaining to the role of women working in Cyprus, in general? If we interpret this information only with regard to archaeology, I think we put very tight borders on our stream of thought. From the point of view of Cyprus, I think a wider perspective is very much needed.

Jenny Webb: We were just looking at international contributions by men and women to Cypriot archaeology through that time as reflected in that one source. We certainly haven't done any comparative work on how those figures compare to contributions by international women to other areas of Cypriot research. I don't know how you'd do that.

Maro Theodossiadou: I'm anxious to hear from Despo, or perhaps Frosso will tell us complimentary information. If there are certain actions or activities going on in Cypriot archaeology with regard to women, are the same things going on in the medical services or in philological circles?

Jenny Webb: I would like to point out here that most of the women we looked at were actually foreign women not Cypriot women.

Despo Pilides: With regard to Cypriot women, however, what I have collected recently are some statistics on women archaeologists working in Cyprus, but I would say that by looking at decision-making centers which I will concentrate on, the situation is very similar in most other professions.

Pitsa Kenti: I would like to ask something in relation to other subject areas. Maro Theodossiadou was asking about philologists. I know from the area of education that 90% of students enrolled in the university in the School of Philosophy are women, but that in the higher positions of education there are only men, for example, inspectors in schools.

Diane Bolger: We're getting ahead of ourselves. Frosso Egoumenidou will be dealing with this topic.

Pitsa Kenti: How many women finish in archaeology? I think it's very important to see what they are doing after that.

Demetra Papaconstantinou: In my experience from Greece, women in archaeology are the majority, but very few of them are professors or excavation directors. I have no statistics, but it is certain that the majority of Greek archaeologists are women in all periods.

Mary Grace Weir: Tracey, you gave women about 43% representation in the professional roster, but the survey you had returned consisted of 51% women, which you said included graduate students and I wondered if that didn't have something to do with it, rather than that women were more conscientious. Perhaps there is a higher percentage of women. Certainly in both graduate programs in archaeology that I've been in for my Ph.D., there have been more women graduate students than men in archaeology and I think probably women simply end up going off and doing other things.

Tracey Cullen: That's a very good point because our results show that male and female Ph.D.s in classical archaeology are very evenly divided.

Jenny Webb: That's also the case in the field. We always have three-fourths who are women, but that's not translated through.

Naomi Hamilton: I'd like to pick up on Jenny's conclusion that fieldwork is more attractive to men than women. We certainly talked about this last night as well. It's not so much that women don't find fieldwork attractive—it's very difficult for women. I've been a professional figure in Britain and was repeatedly offered non-fieldwork roles. Although I was being offered a position of field supervisor, I was always asked if I wouldn't like to go and do another kind of job. The fact is that a lot of fieldwork is acquired by men from men, and it doesn't seem to happen with women.

Linda Hulin: In terms of fieldwork, I'm sure my own and I know Jenny's experience is that it's a nightmare trying to combine children and fieldwork. Most people I know simply gave up completely during ten years of their life because they couldn't combine the two. By the time you've been out of the field for that long you really have to know somebody to be able to get back in. On a field level, you're either going to go back to being a supervisor or you have to become an expert in something and you get shunted into dealing with the finds. It's very, very difficult to get back and to continue writing.

Tracey Cullen: This is clear in the survey from the AIA. Women are angry that they've had to drop out of the field and make huge sacrifices in order to have their families and their careers. It's quite striking that men, who have lots more kids, apparently make no sacrifice whatsoever.

Linda Hulin: On the excavation I work on in Egypt, the director's children are exactly the same age as my children, but he can leave them for two months; I have to negotiate for two weeks.

Jenny Webb: It's also true that to become a director of a field project you need to be very senior in your institution in order to get funding and to have access to students, the technology and the systems that you need. It's a circle. Once you are directing your own excavation, you have access to the material, you can publish much more frequently, and your publications are likely to have more impact because it's primary data. You can become a patron and hand that data out to people if you want to.

Jo Clarke: I'd like to pick up on what Jenny was saying about a vicious circle. In Britain, to get a post in a university, you need the whole package—you have to have the teaching experience and you must have the project that you can contribute to the research assessment exercise so that you've got students you can take out on fieldwork and train. Without that field experience it's very unlikely you'll get the job that will give you the position to get more field experience, so it's a complete vicious circle.

ISSUE 2: GENDER AND EQUITY ISSUES IN HIGHER EDUCATION

Lone Wriedt Sørensen: Gender and Employment Inequities in Denmark

In 1994 the Danish Parliament proclaimed that all state institutions with more than 50 employees should make an agenda concerning equality in job situations. Last year, less than half of institutions of higher education had actually replied.

The job situation: In 1979, 14.6% of academic personnel in Danish universities were women, and in 1996 female scientists counted for 17.5%. In 1995, 77 men and 18 women got employed in scientific positions in the universities, and the figures for 1996 are 76 men and 26 women. This is an improvement from a female point of view. A total of 46% of female applicants got the job they wanted, while only 33% of the men succeeded.

Last fall little more than half of all university students were female; one-third of Ph.D. students were female, while 20% of the assistant and associate professors and 6% of professors were women. Even today, 20% of institutions and centers at universities do not have any women employed in scientific positions.

In 1995, academia was asked to look into inequity problems at universities. Last year the following suggestions for improvements were announced: 1) a special advantage must be given to women in science until they represent 40% of the scientific staff; 2) an effort must be made within the next two years to employ an equal number of female and male scientists; if this is not achieved females should have priority; and 3) 30% of professorship positions should be earmarked for women. Last November this proposal was rejected, and the responsible committee was sent back to prepare a new proposal.

A few years ago a female Minister of Science was appointed, and last fall she announced a series of suggestions for improvement. Among these are 1) equality as a management responsibility, 2) an increase in the number of female professors, 3) more focus on job announcements, and 4) presence of both women and men on selection committees. The political future of these suggestions was considered very uncertain. Since the female minister who made the suggestions has been replaced by a man, the future is very uncertain, indeed.

The funding situation: Last November it appeared that only 9% of available funds from research councils is given to women. This is due to several factors: 1) fewer women than men apply for research funding; 2) women's success rate in achieving funding is lower than that for men; and 3) women generally apply for smaller sums of money than men do. A year earlier, in 1996, 23% of the total number of applications to research councils had come from women and they received 18% of total funds given.

The male reaction to the discussion of increasing the number of female scientists in universities: Some male scientists have argued that many young men are not entering the universities because of the growing number of female teachers. Another reaction that has been voiced is that women harm science because they do not bother to do scientific research that really results in progress. So that's where it stands now—a typical male reaction against attempts to improve the situation.

Frosso Egoumenidou: Gender Inequities in Higher Education in Cyprus

Archaeology has always been considered a field of knowledge that requires a long term of study, difficult fieldwork and lifelong devotion, but as a profession it was not so profitable. So, to achieve all this, one needed time and money. Archaeologists were people who could afford to study for several years and then continue research work. Archaeology also involved traveling for extended periods of time, which presupposes a great deal of independence, a fact that was not compatible with the image of an ideal woman. This is true for old times and the first half of the 20th century, at least. Consequently, archaeology did not appear to be an ideal woman's profession.

There used to be more men in archaeology both in Cyprus and abroad. In the *Who's Who in Cypriote Archaeology*, published in 1971 (Åström 1971), mostly men and especially foreigners are listed and very few women. There are five Cypriot women listed: Angeliki Pieridou, Ino Nicolaou, Elli Pitsillidou, Elsie Mathiopoulou, and Katia Dikaios. Also included is Jacqueline Karageorghis, who is half Cypriot! Women had much to gain in terms of rights and also had to sacrifice a great deal in personal and family life in order to cope with the demands of the job. Women who excelled in archaeology had to build strong personalities and go against the tide. They had to be both exceptions and exceptional. This is the old view of women in archaeology; how much is true today?

Today more and more women study archaeology both in Cyprus and abroad; they continue with postgraduate studies and participate in excavations. The Association of Cypriot Archaeologists currently has 47 members; 29 are women and 18 are men.

The job situation for an archaeologist in Cyprus is extremely bleak as it is in many other countries, so many graduates have to enter secondary education as teachers in the humanities (modern and ancient Greek, history, Latin). Here are some statistics:
*   During the academic year 1995/6, of 1,071 teachers in the humanities, 392 were men and 779 women.
*   During the academic year 1996/7, of 1,300 teachers in the humanities, 422 were men and 878 women.

We should not forget that it is primarily in elementary education posts where the majority of positions are filled by women, that women have excelled, and that this has been the case since the 19th century. According to the census of 1891, 61 women were then working as teachers in elementary schools.

In 1989, the University of Cyprus was founded, and in 1992, the Archaeological Research Unit (ARU) was instituted. Since 1996, the ARU has functioned within the Department of History and Archaeology. The Unit covers all the archaeological activities of the Department that concern Cyprus. It offers a full study program for undergraduates of the Department as well as elective courses for students of other departments. The Department gives a joint degree in history and archaeology. This degree qualifies graduates to seek employment in a large number of entities and institutions, such as secondary education, the archaeological service which is in the Department of Antiquities, the diplomatic service, research centers, archives, cultural foundations, museums and galleries, universities, etc. In 1995/6 16 women and two men received undergraduate degrees from the department; in 1996/7 there were no women and two men.

The staff figures for 1997 for the Department of History and Archaeology are as follows:

Academic staff:	Men	Women
Professors	1	0
Associate Professors	2	1
Assistant Professors	2	1
Lecturers	2	1

There are seven men and three women, but if we take only archaeology, there are more women than men. If we look at rank, we find there are fewer women as we approach the highest rank.

I have also compiled figures for the academic staff of the other departments for 1997. In all departments, Professors and Associate Professors are the only permanent members of staff. There is currently only one woman who holds the post of Professor at the University of Cyprus; this is in the Department of Computer Science.

Department of Education:

Academic staff:	Men	Women
Professors	1	0
Associate Professors	7	0
Assistant Professors	4	2
Lecturers	2	3

Department of Foreign Languages and Literatures:

Academic staff:	Men	Women
Professors	1	0
Associate Professors	3	2
Assistant Professors	0	1
Lecturers	2	1

Department of Social and Political Science:

Academic staff:	Men	Women
Professors	0	0
Associate Professors	1	0
Assistant Professors	3	1
Lecturers	0	0

Department of Turkish Studies:

Academic staff:	Men	Women
Professors	1	0
Associate Professors	0	0
Assistant Professors	3	0
Lecturers	1	1

Department of Computer Science:

Academic staff:	Men	Women
Professors	0	1
Associate Professors	6	0
Assistant Professors	2	0
Lecturers	0	0

Department of Mathematics and Statistics:

Academic staff:	Men	Women
Professors	2	0
Associate Professors	4	0
Assistant Professors	9	0
Lecturers	1	1

Department of Natural Sciences:

Academic staff:	Men	Women
Professors	0	0
Associate Professors	6	1
Assistant Professors	5	0
Lecturers	2	1

Department of Economics:

Academic staff:	Men	Women
Professors	3	0
Associate Professors	2	0
Assistant Professors	3	0
Lecturers	1	1

Department of Public and Business Administration:

Academic staff:	Men	Women
Professors	3	0
Associate Professors	4	0
Assistant Professors	4	1
Lecturers	2	0

Department of Byzantine and Modern Greek Studies:

Academic staff:	Men	Women
Professors	1	0
Associate Professors	2	0
Assistant Professors	2	0
Lecturers	1	4

Department of Classics and Philosophy:

Academic staff:	Men	Women
Professors	0	0
Associate Professors	2	1
Assistant Professors	0	0
Lecturers	1	3

In conclusion, the overall picture shows that there is a tendency for the situation to change, but if we consider how many women are graduates in the Department of History and Archaeology, men still have an advantage. It seems that they started earlier and they have gained ground. Despite the optimistic prospect for women, we might add there is still some vestige of discrimination which is perhaps due to a preconception because of the past history, but certainly it is a matter of time for women to gain what they have lost in previous centuries and become equal to men.

General Discussion

Olga Demetriades: I'm not surprised this is the picture. It's sad that a new university which started functioning in 1992, with a strong tradition of women in education, is still monopolized by men. Now, why is this so? I think it has a lot to do with what was called an "Agency for Women;" with another government it was called "A Machinery for the Rights of Women." It has only a consultative or even no role. This is monopolized by all the women representatives of the parties because they have women's sections in the parties and women don't belong to the main body of the party so that they can claim position in the hierarchy, and I think this is greatly our fault as women. I was a pioneer in 1956, coming from a class which was not financially badly off. I went to study in England. I'm ashamed to say that not much has been done. I'm retiring from the Higher Technical Institute in one and a half year's time and I don't see anything being done. We're watchers, standing by and giving figures every now and then. The day for change will come, however, because the Institute has been occupied by the students. I'm very happy that drastic measures are being taken. I feel, since this very important seminar with women from all over the world has been held, you will have some results and some resolutions. Why don't we all take up these issues and try to do something and not keep them simply as another set of figures in a pile for years to come?

Demetrios Michaelides: Since the university is being discussed, I have to clarify some things. I agree with Olga, but I wouldn't use the word "monopolize" by men because the women do not apply. If you look at all the applications for the high jobs in the University, there are hardly any women and this is not a bias of anybody. The second thing I would like to clarify is that there is a higher percentage of women in the lower grades of academia, not because they are considered lower than the professors but because they are mostly younger women so they are at the beginning of their careers, which is, in fact, an indication that things are changing—that they are entering at this level.

Olga Demetriades: May I say something to Demetrios on this point? I've been at the Higher Technical Institute ever since its beginning in 1968. We have four departments: in all of them, department heads and senior lecturers are men. Women are kept low, with no promotion. Why? They say they have reasons, e.g., that I lack public relations experience. That's the argument. We never get excellence. We've never risen higher and the net result is what I'm telling you, although I'm never pessimistic but I've been living through this for all these years. I'm sad that nothing is being done. You know how things are, how people are. I hope you'll be the instigator; if you have any influence in ten years, we can talk and find ways to give women rights.

Attendee: I do think you have to bear in mind that some women want it, but sometimes they don't want it. I'd say you might have to apply, so you can give yourself excuses, but I don't know if you would want it if it was offered to you on a plate. Maybe you would get it, but I think you do sometimes feel responsible for your children.

Attendee: Since I come from the University of Athens, the oldest university, and I've been Professor there for more than twenty years, I can say a few things about how women and men work together there. The situation, of course, is not ideal; an ideal world—impossible! … I happen to be a mathematician interested in archaeology. Since 1982 I've turned my interest towards mathematical archaeology in a way that I understand it. Believe me, I can cooperate with women students much better than men students. My wife is an ex-student of mine. I have written 15 research papers on my own, 15 with my students and 15 with my wife. I am in favor of cooperation. Cooperation, not confrontation, is the only way out.

Maro Theodossiadou: I would like to refer to a firm stand taken by UNESCO. About 40 years ago it was very fashionable in the mass media to have programs for women on TV or radio. UNESCO came out with a very firm point that we must demolish barriers. Whatever problems could be discussed in women's programs should go into general programs, e.g., if you have economic problems or career problems let them be discussed in an overall kind of program for men and women. I think that our conference, and I am sorry I was not here from the beginning, fails a little in this respect because it didn't attract as many men as it should have—only two or three speakers I think. This should give food for further thought. Perhaps it would have been better if it had been more equally represented.

Diane Bolger: You're very right. We actually had six male speakers at the conference, but that's still a minority; we publicized the conference widely and simply considered the abstracts that were sent to us. I think it's a sign that even among archaeologists in Cyprus who have been talking about issues of social complexity and development, gender is not considered to be an important issue.

Attendee: I have a question for Lone Sørensen. I was interested in how you spoke about how people talked in corridors about the "action for women" package. I was wondering how women feel, in the sense that there must be some ambiguous feeling about whether you want a job that's being given to you on a plate that you don't have to compete for, and I wondered how that might relate to your experience in inviting women to write papers.

Lone Sørensen: It's been discussed and some people say this is not the way we want to go, but we may actually have to take it up eventually in order to make things better. Then I read a note from one of my senior colleagues and she said, "Well, I'd rather be inside because I'm a woman than be outside because I'm a woman." So you can take that side, too, and say, "Well, it's correct because I got it—I'm here." It's up to you.

Cecilia Beer: We have some positive results in Sweden, which is a neighboring country. Now there are four professors of classical archaeology and two of them are women. Two of the Swedish classical institutes abroad—in Athens and Rome—are currently being run by women, so in Sweden we can't complain too much.

Lone Sørensen: That situation is more than good, but if we consider all the universities together, the situation is quite different.

Claire Balandier: At the French Archaeological School in Athens twenty years ago, there were three women and seven men. Ten years ago there were half men and half women. Now there are two or three men for seven women. The paradox is that even if six of the seven women are working on an excavation, the direction of the excavation is given to the only man working there, even if he is younger than the women, because of the lack of men.

Olga Demetriades: Answering the gentleman who spoke earlier, there is perfect harmonious "co-operation" between men and women, and, in fact, most often we do the donkey-work; then they appear and get the promotions.

ISSUE 3: WOMEN IN THE ADMINISTRATION OF ARCHAEOLOGY

Despo Pilides: Gender and Administration in the Department of Antiquities, Cyprus

I would like to remind everyone that I'm new at the Department of Antiquities—I've only been there two and a half years. My short time there may absolve me of most of the responsibility, but I do feel responsible for how women will progress and how decisive our impact on the management of archaeology will be in the Department of Antiquities in future years.

I will start with a little reminder of what is happening in the United States. An article in *Museum News* reported that women played an important role in American museums since the beginning of the century. Early on, they helped establish many institutions which have become part of the national fabric. More often than not, however, it was men who held the positions of curator and director. Following the women's movement of the 1960s and 1970s, women flooded the workplaces and graduate schools, finally vying for the museum jobs traditionally held by men. However, it is reported in the *Museum Directory* that the leadership of the largest and best known museums in the United States is still predominantly male.

With regard to the role of the woman archaeologist in the Department of Antiquities of Cyprus, it is obvious that at present there is a concentration of women in less influential and authoritative areas. There has never been a female Director or a female Curator of Museums or Ancient Monuments in the history of the Department of Antiquities.

Starting from the first Annual Reports of the Curator of Antiquities, it is particularly noticeable that women had no role to play, as the list of names of the Museum Committee was exclusively male. The first occurrence of a female name in the Report of the Curator was that of Joan du Plat Taylor in 1933 when she was appointed Honorary Assistant Curator. From 1951 to 1954, only one woman and four men were officially mentioned in the records. One female archaeologist, Angeliki Pieridou, was employed as a clerical assistant from 1947 until 1958 when she was appointed Assistant Records Curator, but she was dismissed in the same year when she became pregnant. The male members increased to five in 1955 and then to six in 1957, when Mrs. Pieridou returned as a Museum Assistant on a provisional basis from month to month. In 1958 her name was mentioned for the first time in the staff records, being the only female archaeologist among six men. She remained the only female archaeologist until 1965. Between 1965 and 1973, there were two women archaeologists and five men, while in 1974, five men and one woman archaeologist are in the staff records.

The situation remained very much the same until relatively recently. In 1986, the number of women archaeologists increased to four in comparison to seven men. In 1990, there were six men and three women. In 1993–1994, there were an equal number of men and women. In 1995, there were six women and four men, with three of the men holding the positions of Director and Curators. Today women are exactly double in number, with six female and three male archaeologists. The situation, however, has not essentially changed as yet, since men are still holding the decision-making positions even though implementation of policy is almost entirely in the hands of women. Given some time, the impact of women will be obvious. Moreover, it is only a matter of time, and possibly not a very long period of time, before the first woman or women curators will be a fact, constituting a substantial change in the role women will play in the more authoritative areas in the future. [Editors' note: Several months after this presentation, Dr. Maria Hadjicosti was appointed Curator of Sites and National Monuments, the first woman to hold this position].

As far as excavation, publication and research are concerned, hierarchy played and continues to play a more significant role as the main criteria for such opportunities rather than specialization. However, in spite of the conservatism prevailing, there is, I believe, some progress, and some hope is emerging for the future of female archaeologists in the Department of Antiquities and the role they will be playing in the management of the archaeology of Cyprus.

I have also done a little research on the position of women outside the decision-making process and how it influences their participation in general archaeological research, publication, etc. It shows that participation in conferences depends primarily on the subject of the conference, the identity of the organizers, and the criteria on which invitations for papers are sent out. In the most recent state-organized conference in Cyprus, where directors of current excavations and university and museum facilities from Greece were invited, there was a clear preponderance of males among the participants, reflecting the corresponding social organization in management positions with regard to archaeology. The symposium referred to earlier by Jenny Webb as having a 50% participation by women was the 1991 conference in Philadelphia. That symposium was concerned with pottery as its main theme, supporting Jenny and David's conclusion that there are gender-based differences in subject selection and that conferences, for example, on harbor archaeology and trade, also recently organized, tend to be male dominated. Female participation in conferences is, therefore, intricately linked with subject selection, another aspect of the above study that still essentially holds true.

Looking at the visitors' book in the storerooms of the Cyprus Museum overwhelmingly confirms that the majority of researchers have been women: in 1995, there were 27 women and eight men; and in 1996, 21 women and five men. Paradoxically, in 1997 there were 16 women and 14 men.

With regard to research topics represented, women concentrated on the study of pottery, spindle whorls, terracottas, sculpture, jewelry, chipped stone, pot marks, ivories and faience, while the male researchers in 1996 studied old or rescue excavation material from a specific site and in 1997 studied metalwork, inscriptions, coins and sculpture.

The conclusion that male research focuses mainly on theory, methodology, problem solving and setting new strategies with more controversial results and results that have a much higher impact has not changed significantly. I want to conclude with a point from my earlier statistical references that social organization, in other words, the fact that men are in possession of the decision-making positions, is also reflected in research and conference contribution, as well as in publication.

Jo Clarke: Gender and the Structure of Administration in the British School of Archaeology, Jerusalem.

I decided to be anecdotal today and tell you of my personal experience in being involved in a foreign school. I could have come up with facts and figures for foreign schools over the last two years, but I felt that it's often the personal experience and the way women get into positions or don't get into positions that we need to hear about. This is very difficult to quantify. So, I thought that in something as informal as this I might just give you an idea of my position. I've worked for the British School of Archaeology in Jerusalem for four years. I started working as the Assistant Secretary. Now, I think that in the history of the Assistant Secretary's post for the British School of Archaeology, there's been one man who lasted only a short time because his accounting was absolutely hopeless and he was removed. Otherwise, it's always been a female job within the school.

For all foreign British institutes, there is usually a director and an assistant director, usually a secretary, often a librarian, and now very often a computing officer in the school structure in the country that the school is based. It depends obviously on the size of the school or institute because some facilities are larger and some smaller. The British School of Archaeology has traditionally had a director, assistant director, a secretary, sometimes a librarian but most recently not. But that was often how the job responsibilities have been split up between the different staff members.

The Director of the British School of Archaeology is currently on sabbatical for the year, from September to September. The British School was looking for a replacement. The Assistant Director had handed in his resignation, so they had no person to actually take over the post for the time of the sabbatical. There was a lot of discussion in meetings about who this person might be, who would be best for the post. It obviously had to be an archaeologist and someone who understood the system and had been working in the area, but it was just for one year because the school is amalgamating with the Amman institute. So they decided that an internal appointment would be best for that year and then the job would be advertised. A number of people were considered for this temporary post, but I wasn't one of them. In fact, I wrote a letter putting myself forward. I think this was rather an aggressive thing to do. I think most women would not do that, and in fact most people, I think, would not do that. I just brought it to their attention that I was sitting there and I was already employed by them; it would save them quite a lot of money and rather than finding someone else, perhaps they would consider me. Of the people who were considered, there were, I think, five men and one woman; the one woman was not available to take the post, so as it was, I offered my services and I was very lucky, I think, to have been given the post for the year. However, what is quite interesting about this situation is that although I hold the post of Acting Director, I am also still Assistant Secretary. So I still carry out the duties of organizing the meetings back in Britain, sending out the agendas, writing the minutes, and doing all the administrative work for the School, as well as making the coffee! It is a very atypical situation, but I think it does reflect quite well a situation that women sometimes find themselves in. But, if women want to get somewhere in higher management, they often find themselves in a position of having started from a bottom post, a secretarial post, and then, through effort on their own part, they manage to come in through what I would call the back door. This is often, I think, the way women manage to get into managerial posts. In the university structures in Britain, there is a great discrepancy between the secretarial role and the management role, so making that great leap from secretary to manager/ administrator within any structure, and I think this also applies to the British schools abroad, is almost impossible. If you start off as a secretary, it's very difficult to get a managerial post unless you manage to find your way in through another route.

Someone interjected: Are you going to get the Amman job?

Jo: No, I mean that is a completely different issue. The post was advertised and the interviews are in two days' time, on the 25th March. I have applied. It's actually based in the Jerusalem office. I hear there's a very good field. I've no idea who has applied.

(There was another question relating to women doing two jobs.)

Jo: What I wanted to point out was that I was actually doing these two jobs, whereas it would be very odd, in the same situation, to find a man, I think, doing two jobs. But, I agree, it's not that I didn't know the situation I was going to be in, so I did say I would do the two jobs.

Attendee: If they'd hired someone who was on sabbatical, they wouldn't have expected him to do both jobs.

Jo: It's an atypical situation because it's an internal appointment; it's a year's post and they were looking for someone within the internal system. When they advertise the new post, whoever gets it, whether woman or man, will have a more equitable position.

Pitsa Kenti: I'm sorry to ask this question, but why did you accept to make the coffee?

Jo: I've actually stood up in those meetings and said "I've taken the minutes. How can I actually make the coffee while I'm taking the minutes and I have to make input into the meeting now I'm Acting Director." Yes, I do wince about making the coffee. This is all I really wanted to point out; women often play these dual roles.

Despo Pilides: This thing about making coffee, it happens everywhere.

Attendee: If I could make a comment on that. I'm interested if other people want to respond because I don't know if it is that atypical that a woman does that kind of thing. I find that I'm in the position where I'm doing two people's jobs at the moment. I'm doing it by choice, but I know that the man who was in the job before me would never ever, ever have thought of doing it. I do it because I think it's simpler if I can do it rather than fight. You just go and do it. Lots of women do that and to say it's atypical is actually not the case.

(At this point there was a great deal of audience interaction, but one of the comments heard was "you lose your job if you don't.")

Attendee continued: In my experience, women who are flexible and who don't actually work in a strict hierarchy, who don't have anything to lose by not working in that strict hierarchy, may have something to gain and, therefore, are prepared to do it.

Demetrios Michaelides: I know you're going to hate me for this, but I have to say this is not a phenomenon exclusive to women. I worked for ten years as Archaeological Officer at Paphos and I had no secretary, no draftsperson, no photographer, no one to make my coffee!

Olga Demetriades: That brings me conveniently to my point. The hierarchy is that men are always exploiting this eagerness of women to be everywhere for service like a master key, you know, that opens all the doors. But when it comes to really assessing the candidate for the hierarchy, this versatility of the woman to do every job, this eagerness, this double role that the woman is playing, this is conveniently forgotten.

Diane Bolger: I'd like to ask both Jo and Despo to elaborate a bit more. We've heard a lot about statistics, who holds the positions, how you got the position, and the interview process. Could you comment a little bit about the day-to-day administration of your job and having to deal with men and getting your decisions accepted or not?

Despo Pilides: Well, as I said, implementation of policy rests entirely upon women. I think that explains most of it. Decisions are being taken, sometimes collaboratively, sometimes collectively, but the actual implementation of what a decision entails is carried out by the archaeological officers, who are mainly women. Then, sometimes, we have an idea about how our work fares, sometimes we don't; it depends on the person who's dealing with it. That is essentially very frustrating, as you were saying, because after we give a lot of our effort and a lot of our body and soul is put into these projects, we're not immediately involved in what happens afterwards. But the picture is not altogether negative. There are persons who will accept consultation, or rather who will seek consultation and who will take into account an archaeological officer's views. However, hierarchy is predominant in policy-making and decisions.

Jo Clarke: There are two aspects of running a British institute abroad. There is dealing with the committee structure in Britain and there is dealing on a day-to-day basis with officials and academics in the country in which you happen to be based. Now I'm based in Israel, so I have two aspects to that as well. I deal with the Palestinians and I deal with the Israelis. I also got in touch with the Director of the Amman Institute, because she's also a woman. In fact, she's the only officially appointed director of one of the British foreign institutes at the moment who is a woman. I asked her about her experiences running an institute in a Muslim country, as I was doing that as well. Her comments were very close to mine. It's very easy for a woman to run a foreign British institute in the Near East, and there are two reasons for that. One is that there is a long history of very strong British females in archaeology in the Levant, and the Jordanians and Palestinians remember women such as Kathleen Kenyon, Crystal Bennett, Diana Kirkbride—all these people had strong personalities. The second is, as we were talking about yesterday, the third gender issue of working within a Muslim country. If you're in a position of power as a female you're no longer seen as a female. You actually lose your gender stance as a female and gain a stance as a senior representative of your country, and that actually makes it very easy to work. On a personal level, it's a lot more difficult as a woman. There are a lot of things you are excluded from and a lot you can't take part in. On a professional level in a Muslim country, it is very easy to work. With the Israelis, I've found it very easy to work as a female. They seem to have a very good representation of women in archaeology, often with husband and wife teams in Israeli academic institutions.

The other side is working with the British management structure. The Council for the British School of Archaeology in Jerusalem is made up, I think, of thirteen men and two women, so it is very much male dominated. (I should have gotten figures for the Councils, or Boards of Trustees as they are called, in the States—I suspect the picture is the same.) There are problems dealing with the structure, but as the Director of the Institute the difficulties are less. Where I find it very difficult, indeed, is that sometimes letters go out from me as Assistant Secretary to the members of my council and sometimes as Acting Director. It is probably very confusing for people to receive these letters and it really depends on the member of the council as to how they perceive me. This situation doesn't exist if you are the officially appointed director.

Frosso Egoumenidou: I'd like to add something. It was not only those British women archaeologists who had very strong personalities, but also those ladies, British travelers, like those who came to Cyprus. They were acting like men and they were seen as men. One of them, I heard the other day, was addressed as Madam Sir, at the same time. May I also add something from my personal experience? When I was appointed as an archaeologist and assistant to the Director General of the Archaeological Service in Athens for the excavations of the Apollo temple at Daphni and Phigalia, I was the only woman archaeologist and there were seven men around me—architects, typographers, conservators. One day, I was asked by the oldest, "Why did you play this male role? You play the man here; why don't you cook for us?" I said, "You can cook for me, you can do everything for me because you are seven and I am only one." So I played Snow White with the seven dwarves.

Linda Hulin: I think, in terms of traditionally strong women, all the great scholars, there has been a tendency not quite to demonize them but to characterize them in a way that their successful male counterparts aren't. Because many of these women were not married, they were not treated as normal women, when, in fact, often the reason they weren't married was that they devoted themselves to scholarship. There have been male archaeologists who were difficult to work with, but they have not been characterized as atypical as an aggressive female would.

Tracey Cullen: The mention of the strong women and the tradition of many strong women in classical archaeology has led to them being held up constantly to show that we have no problems in classical archaeology. I think that has something to do with the delay even in collecting statistics about our discipline. We have these women that we can point to.

Mrs. Nir: I'm from Israel and I'm an archaeologist. I took ten years off because I had my children. So I know the situation very well. I was the only woman surveyor in Israel, riding in jeeps and dealing with men and everything. But when I had to get a job, a high position, the Manager of the Israel Authority told me, "Well, you're all wet around with having children," so I decided if that's the attitude, I'm leaving. (To Jo) I have some remarks for you. With Muslims, it's nothing to do with if you're a woman or not, it's only your position that will create you. In Israel, women in the old generation were much stronger and had good positions. The younger generation is not letting the women get into the archaeological life. Most of this is because there is too much competition, so if you're not strong enough and if you don't have enough publications and if you're busy with everyday life, you can't get into archaeological positions—there are very few of them.

Bonny Bazemore: I think, and I'm speaking from my own personal experience, that when a woman argues very strongly for something, it's considered not feminine. My male counterparts will argue very strongly about something and the response is, "Oh, he's a good scholar." But then I'll come in and present my arguments and the response is, "Oh well, you shouldn't state that so forcefully." So, I think that women get these signals that we can't really do groundbreaking work because we don't get the emotional support throughout our entire scholarship.

REFERENCES

Åström, P.
1971   *Who's Who in Cypriote Archaeology. Biographical and Bibliographical Notes.* Studies in Mediterranean Archaeology 23. Göteborg: Åströms.

Dyson, S. L.
1998   *Ancient Marbles to American Shores: Classical Archaeology in the United States.* Philadelphia: University of Pennsylvania.

Gero, J. M.
1994   Excavation Bias and the Woman-at-Home Ideology. Pp. 37–42 in *Equity Issues for Women in Archeology*, eds. M. C. Nelson, S. M. Nelson, and A. Wylie. Archeological Papers of the American Anthropological Association Number 5. Arlington, VA: American Anthropological Association.

Nelson, M. C.; Nelson, S. M.; and Wylie, A., eds.
1994   *Equity Issues for Women in Archeology.* Archeological Papers of the American Anthropological Association Number 5. Arlington, VA: American Anthropological Association.

Webb, J. M., and Frankel, D.
1995a   "This Fair Paper, This Most Goodly Book." Gender and International Scholarship in Cypriot Archaeology 1920–1991. Pp. 34–42 in *Gendered Archaeology. The Second Australian Women in Archaeology Conference*, eds. J. Balme and W. Beck. Canberra: ANH Publications, Research School of Pacific and Asian Studies, The Australian National University.
1995b   Gender Inequity and Archaeological Practice. A Cypriot Case Study. *Journal of Mediterranean Archaeology* 8: 93–112.

Index

W

Wanassa 343, 370, 403
Writing 397, 401–2, 413–15, 420–21

X

Xenophanes 227

Z

Zeno of Kition 290, 414
Zeus 110, 123, 151–52, 321, 344, 371–72, 401–2, 408, 413